Praise for the First Edition o Programming

"This amazing, thorough book takes an interesting approach by working through the design and development of a simple, yet realistic, iPad app from start to finish. It is refreshing to see a technical book that explains how and why without inundating you with endless toy examples or throwing you into a sea of mind-numbing details. Particularly amazing is that it does this without assuming a large amount of experience at first. Yet it covers advanced topics at sufficient depth and in a logical order for all developers to get plenty of valuable information and insight. Kirby and Tom know this material and have done a great job of introducing the various frameworks and the reasoning behind how, why, and when you would use them. I highly recommend *Learning iPad Programming* to anyone interested in developing for this amazing platform."

—Julio Barros
   E-String.com

"This is a great introduction to iPad programming with a well-done sample project built throughout. It's great for beginners as well as those familiar with iPhone development looking to learn the differences in developing for the larger screen."

—Patrick Burleson
   Owner, BitBQ LLC (http://bitbq.com)

"Kirby Turner and Tom Harrington's *Learning iPad Programming* provides a comprehensive introduction to one of today's hottest topics. It's a great read for the aspiring iPad programmer."

—Robert Clair
   Author, *Learning Objective-C 2.0*

"*Learning iPad Programming* is now my go-to reference when developing apps for the iPad. This book is an absolute treasure trove of useful information and tips for developing on the iPad. While it's easy to think of the iPad as just a bigger iPhone, there are specific topics that need to be treated differently on the iPad, such as making best use of the larger display. *Learning iPad Programming* provides an incredible amount of depth on all areas of iPad programming and takes you from design to fully functioning application—which for me is a killer feature of the book. This should be in everyone's reference library."

—Mike Daley
   Author, *Learning iOS Game Programming*
   Cofounder, 71Squared.com

"A truly well-rounded book with something for every iOS developer, be they aspirant or veteran. If you are new to iOS, there is a solid foundation provided in Part I that will walk you through Objective-C, the core Apple frameworks, provisioning profiles, and making the best of Xcode. If you've been around the block but want solid insight into iPad programming, Part II has you covered: Rather than just providing canned example code, Kirby and Tom give you real code that incrementally builds and improves a real app. And if you've been working with iOS for a while, but would benefit from a walk-through of the plethora of new features that have come our way with iOS 5 and Xcode 4, dive into the chapters on Storyboards, iCloud, and Core Image. Best of all, the book is well-written and conversational, making it a joy to read. This book is stellar."
—Alexis Goldstein
  Coauthor, *HTML5 & CSS3 for the Real World*

"*Learning iPad Programming* is one of the most comprehensive resources on the planet for those developing for Apple's iPad platform. In addition to coverage of the language, frameworks, and tools, it dives into features new in iOS 5, like Automatic Reference Counting, Storyboarding, and connecting your applications with iCloud. But where this book really shines is in the tutorials and the application you will build as you read through this book. Rather than being a toy that employs only off-the-shelf iOS user interface components from Interface Builder, the PhotoWheel app demonstrates custom view programming and view controller containment, nonstandard gesture/user input handling, and provides insight into how a complex iOS project comprised of multiple subsystems is assembled into a shipping application. In other words, *Learning iPad Programming* shows how to deal with the challenges you'll face in real iPad development."
—Erik Price
  Senior Software Engineer, Brightcove

"A thoroughly crafted guide for learning and writing iOS applications, from the humble beginnings in Xcode and Interface Builder to creating a full-featured iPad application. There are many books that try to cover the gamut of knowledge required to take a reader from zero to app; Kirby and Tom have actually done it in this book. It is a fun and comprehensive guide to the world of developing apps for Apple's magical device."
—Rod Strougo
  Founder, Prop Group

"The iPad is changing the way we think about and use technology. *Learning iPad Programming* is one of the most in-depth and well-executed guides to get both new and seasoned developers up to speed on Apple's exciting new platform."
—Justin Williams
  Crew Chief, Second Gear

Learning iPad Programming

Second Edition

Learning iPad Programming

A Hands-On Guide to Building iPad Apps

Second Edition

Kirby Turner

Tom Harrington

✦Addison-Wesley

Upper Saddle River, NJ • Boston • Indianapolis • San Francisco
New York • Toronto • Montreal • London • Munich • Paris • Madrid
Capetown • Sydney • Tokyo • Singapore • Mexico City

Many of the designations used by manufacturers and sellers to distinguish their products are claimed as trademarks. Where those designations appear in this book, and the publisher was aware of a trademark claim, the designations have been printed with initial capital letters or in all capitals.

The authors and publisher have taken care in the preparation of this book, but make no expressed or implied warranty of any kind and assume no responsibility for errors or omissions. No liability is assumed for incidental or consequential damages in connection with or arising out of the use of the information or programs contained herein.

The publisher offers excellent discounts on this book when ordered in quantity for bulk purchases or special sales, which may include electronic versions and/or custom covers and content particular to your business, training goals, marketing focus, and branding interests. For more information, please contact:

U.S. Corporate and Government Sales
(800) 382-3419
corpsales@pearsontechgroup.com

For sales outside the United States, please contact:

International Sales
international@pearson.com

Visit us on the Web: informit.com/aw

Library of Congress Cataloging-in-Publication Data

Turner, Kirby, 1966–
  Learning iPad programming : a hands-on guide to building iPad
apps / Kirby Turner, Tom Harrington. — Second edition.
        pages   cm
  Includes index.
  ISBN 978-0-321-88571-5 (pbk. : alk. paper)
1. iPad (Computer)—Programming. 2. Application software—
Development. 3. Mobile computing. 4. iOS (Electronic resource)
I. Harrington, Tom. II. Title.
  QA76.8.I863T87 2013
  005.258—dc23
                                2013004508

ISBN-13: 978-0-321-88571-5
ISBN-10:   0-321-88571-6
Text printed in the United States on recycled paper at RR Donnelley in Crawfordsville, Indiana.
First printing, May 2013

Editor-in-Chief
Mark L. Taub

Senior Acquisitions Editor
Trina MacDonald

Senior Development Editor
Chris Zahn

Managing Editor
John Fuller

Full-Service Production Manager
Julie B. Nahil

Production Project Manager
Vicki Rowland

Copy Editor
Jill E. Hobbs

Indexer
Ted Laux

Proofreader
Janice R. Norris

Technical Reviewers
Patrick Burleson
Michael Haberman
Andrew Moore

Editorial Assistant
Olivia Basegio

Compositor
Vicki Rowland

❖

To Steve Jobs, who saw further than most.
— Kirby Turner and Tom Harrington

To Melanie and Rowan, for their continuous love and support.
And to my mom, my personal hero.
—Kirby Turner

To Carey, who gave me the courage to pursue my dreams.
—Tom Harrington

❖

Contents at a Glance

Contents

Foreword

I love books. I really love books. Anyone who's known me for any amount of time knows I'm a total bookworm. Well-written books are one of the cheapest and fastest self-education tools. I can remember a number of books that were hugely significant in my personal and professional development—books like *Object Oriented Software Construction* by Bertrand Meyer, Scott Knaster and Stephen Chernicoff's early Mac programming books, Dave Mark's C programming books, Robert C. Martin's horribly titled (but full of wonderful a-ha! moments) *Designing Object Oriented C++ Applications Using the Booch Method*, and, of course, the late W. Richard Stevens' UNIX and Network programming books. I remember lessons learned from these tomes, even those I read many years ago.

Unfortunately, not all books are created equal. I've seen some real stinkers in my time. When I was making the transition from Mac programming to iOS programming, I got some really great books, but also some books that were terrible. Really, really terrible. In some of these volumes, it was almost as if someone had filed the serial numbers off of *Instant Visual Basic Programming Guide for Complete Dummies in 24 Hours*, sprinkled around some square brackets, and pasted in pictures of iPhones. I thumbed through one early iPad programming book that literally had an error on every page. Some were just typos. Some were subtle errors, understandable if you haven't already lived in the Cocoa universe for a couple of years. Some of it was downright bad advice, obviously from someone who did not know what he was doing. There is a certain expectation of trust when you drop your hard-earned currency on a book, and violating that trust is unforgivable.

So, this book—*Learning iPad Programming*. Is it worth the price? Does it fall in my first category of books (awesome), or the second (unequivocally lame)? Good question. Glad you asked!

First, a good book needs to cover its topic, and cover it well. *Learning iPad Programming, Second Edition*, judging just by its heft, contains a lot of material. Well, that's true, assuming you've got the printed version in hand; *War and Peace* weighs the same as *The Little Prince* in ebook form, so it's hard to tell them apart. Just skim through the table of contents—you can see the text covers a lot of stuff. A metric freakload of stuff. And this stuff is all relevant. It covers such basics as installing the development tools. Model-View-Controller. Master-Detail. Storyboards. Segues. Table views. `UIViewController`. Navigation views. Handling device rotation. There are also more advanced topics such as consuming Web services, the media library, touch gestures, data persistence, and the raw unpleasantness that is Apple's device provisioning. And there's some cutting-edge stuff, such as AirPrint, AirPlay, iCloud, and Core Image. Kirby and Tom have suffered the arrows in their backs dealing with months of flaky underdocumented prerelease software so you don't have to.

Very good books are timely, but not exploitative. I saw my first iPad programming book about three months after the device was announced. There was no way this book could convey the iPad gestalt to the reader, simply because the device hadn't been available to any author for a long enough period of time. The book was pumped out as fast as possible to hit the market, and it showed. *Learning iPad Programming* is a mature project, with years of work having gone into it. Good books take time to achieve high levels of awesomeness.

Great books transcend their subject matter. This book is called *Learning iPad Programming*. It'd be easy to assume that it just covers introductory iPad programming in a simplistic manner. "Views are cool!" "Yay! Tapping a button!" But it's more. Not many books have a single project that lives and evolves through the entire narrative. The reason not many books do this is because it is difficult to do well. Important toolkit features get shoehorned into weird places because the author didn't do enough upfront design time. This book, though, takes you from design to prototype to the Real Deal.

And then it goes further. Not many books talk about the inner game of design. This one does. Even fewer books talk about the inner game of debugging. Debugging is a fundamental part (if not *the* fundamental part) of the day-to-day life of a programmer, and few books devote more than a paragraph or two to it. *Learning iPad Programming* has an entire chapter on the topic, and it deals with much more than how to single-step with the debugger. As I was reading a preproduction version of this book, I emitted an audible "SQUEE" when I hit Chapter 26. I love debugging, and I love seeing such an important topic covered in detail in what is ostensibly a beginner's book. And as you can tell, I love learning stuff. I learned some stuff from Chapter 26, even after 23 years of programming professionally.

Finally, those who **create** the great books transcend the ordinary. The Mac and iPhone community is pretty small and well connected. You tend to learn quickly who the trusted players are. Many of the lame books I alluded to earlier were written by individuals I had never heard of before, and never heard from again. No blogs, no appearances at conferences, no footprint on the community. Get in, crank out something, exploit the community, and get out.

Kirby and Tom are different. They're known entities. They have blogs. Tom has his name on other books. They've shipped products. They've shipped the first edition of this book. They have happy customers. They answer questions online. They organize and speak at conferences. They're involved with CocoaHeads. They have invested a great deal of their time into the betterment of the community. It is why I am honored and humbled that they asked me to write this foreword.

As you can probably tell, I'm pretty excited about this book. There are many excellent introductory iOS programming books. I recommend reading all of them (at least the good ones) because iOS is such a huge topic that even Kirby and Tom can't cover everything you need to know in one volume. But if you're specifically targeting the iPad, this one is the one to get.

—Mark Dalrymple
  Cofounder of CocoaHeads, the international Mac and iPhone programmer community
  Author of *Advanced Mac OS X Programming: The Big Nerd Ranch Guide*
  February 14, 2013

Preface

In October 2011, Apple CEO Tim Cook shared some interesting facts about the iPad:

- Ninety-two percent of Fortune 500 companies are testing or deploying iPads.
- More than 80 percent of U.S.-based hospitals are testing or piloting the iPad.
- Every state in the United States has some type of iPad deployment program in place or in pilot.

Just a year later, in October 2012, Tim Cook announced that 100 million iPads had been sold. Think about that for a moment: 100 million iPads sold in just two and a half years! That is an amazing feat.

And the news about the iPad doesn't stop there. The FAA has approved the use of the iPad instead of paper charts for on-duty airline pilots. Without a doubt, the iPad is changing the way people think about (and use) computers today. And it continues to get better with the release of iOS 6, the latest operating system for iPad and iPhone devices.

Make no mistake, the iPad packs a punch. With its patented multi-touch interface, an onboard graphics chip, the powerful A6X processor, and 4G and Wi-Fi networking, the iPad is the benchmark in a post-PC world. More important, though, is how the iPad fits into the Mac/iOS ecosystem. Mac OS X and iOS users can use FaceTime for video chat from desktop to device. What's more, iOS iMessage enables users to text from their iPad to reach other iPad, iPhone, and Mac users. The iPad represents a unique marriage of hardware and technology, and it is the Gold Standard for tablets.

This book was written with iOS 6 in mind and is aimed at new developers who want to build apps for the iPad. The book will also appeal to iPhone developers who want to learn more about how to make their apps sing on the iPad. While some people look at the iPad as just a bigger iPhone, it really isn't. There is a lot more that you as a developer can do with the iPad from a user interface perspective that you just can't do on the iPhone.

While this book includes brief discussions of iPhone programming where appropriate, its primary focus is the iPad. *Learning iPad Programming* highlights those areas of the iOS SDK that are unique to the iPad, and it isn't a rehash of similar books targeting the iPhone. Additionally, the book covers new features in iOS, such as embedded segues, container view controllers, iCloud, and Core Image, as well as some of the great new features in Xcode 4, such as storyboarding. Apple has gone to great lengths to make it easier for you to develop for iOS and OS X, and the plan for this book is to make it even easier for you to get there.

What Will I Learn?

This book will teach you how to build apps specifically for the iPad, taking you step by step through the process of making a real app that is freely available in the App Store right now! The app you'll build in this book is called PhotoWheel.

> **Download the App!**
>
> You can download the PhotoWheel app from the App Store.[1] The app is freely available, so go ahead—download PhotoWheel, and start playing around with it.

PhotoWheel is a spin on the Photos app that comes on every iPad (pun intended). With PhotoWheel, you can organize your favorite photos into albums, share photos with family and friends via email, and view photos on your TV wirelessly using AirPlay.

Even more important than the app itself is what you will learn as you build it.

You will learn how to take advantage of the latest features in iOS and Xcode, including storyboarding, Automatic Reference Counting, iCloud, and Core Image. You will learn how to leverage other iOS features such as the Activity View Controller, AirPrint, AirPlay, and Grand Central Dispatch (GCD). And you will learn how to extend the boundaries of your app by communicating with Web services hosted on the Internet.

Think of this book as an epic-length tutorial, showing you how you can create a real iPad app from start to finish. You'll be coding along with the book, and we'll explain things step by step. By the time you have finished reading and working through this book, you'll have a fully functional version of PhotoWheel that you can proudly show off to friends and family (you can even share it with them, too). Best of all, you'll have confidence and the knowledge of what it takes to design, program, and distribute iPad apps of your own.

What Makes the iPad So Different?

While the iPad runs the same version of iOS that runs on the iPhone, iPod touch, and Apple TV, the iPad is significantly different from those other iOS-based devices. Each device is used differently, and iOS brings certain things to the table for each of them. For example, the version of iOS that runs in your Apple TV doesn't yet offer the same touch interface; in fact, the interface is totally different. Apple TV's user interface (UI) runs as a layer on top of iOS, providing a completely different user experience.

But the iPad is so different. It is not something you can hold in the palm of your hand—unless you have an iPad mini. The iPad is something you use with both hands. You swipe. You touch. You interact with it more than with most iPhone apps. It's easy to dismiss the iPad as "just a large iPhone," but it really isn't.

---

1. PhotoWheel: https://itunes.apple.com/app/photowheel/id424927196&mt=8

While the physical size is the obvious difference between the iPad and iPhone, the real difference—the difference that sets the iPad apart from the iPhone—is conceptual. The conceptual differences stem from how an iPad application is designed and how the user interacts with the application. And the conceptual differences start with the bigger display.

Bigger Display

The iPad's bigger screen provides more than double the screen real estate found on the iPhone. In turn, your application can display more information, giving you more space to work with for your user interface. A good example of this is WeatherBug.

WeatherBug HD has been designed to take full advantage of the iPad's larger screen. As you can see in Figure P.1, the iPad version of WeatherBug displays much

Figure P.1   On the left is the WeatherBug app displayed on the iPad. The screen shot on the right is the same WeatherBug app running on the iPhone. (Used with permission of Earth Networks.)

more weather-related information on a single screen than you can get on the iPhone version. Instead of your having to touch and swipe (and sometimes pray) to find additional weather information, WeatherBug HD on the iPad gives you everything you need to know right on the main screen—no additional touching or swiping needed. Of course, additional detail is still available at a touch.

Less Hierarchical

Because of the smaller screen, many iPhone applications tend to sport a hierarchical navigation system. You see this throughout many iPhone apps. The user taps an item and a new screen slides into view. Tap another item and another view slides in. To navigate back, you tap a back button, usually found in the upper-left corner of the screen.

The Dropbox app illustrates the hierarchical navigation system quite well. Dropbox, for those who may not know, is an online service that allows you to store your data files, documents, and images in the cloud. Stored files are then synced across all of your computers and devices that run the Dropbox client software. Suppose you are working on a text document from your laptop. You save the text document to your Dropbox folder. Later you need to review the text document, so you open the same text document on your iPhone. Dropbox makes this possible.

When you use the Dropbox app on your iPhone, you see a list of files and folders sorted alphabetically. Tapping a file or folder will open it, causing the new screen to slide into view. If you open a file, you see the contents of the file. If you open a folder, you see a new list of files and folders. Continue tapping folders to navigate farther down the hierarchy.

To move back up the hierarchy, tap the back button in the upper-left corner of the screen. The text label for this button can vary. Usually it displays the name of the previous item on the stack, but sometimes it displays the word *Back*. While the text label may vary, the style of the back button does not. The back button has a pointy left side. This almost arrow-like style conveys a sense of moving backward through the screens.

The forward and backward navigation through the hierarchy is illustrated in Figure P.2.

Dropbox is also available for the iPad. So how did the developers redesign an app that obviously requires hierarchical navigation to make it feel flatter, less hierarchical? They took advantage of an iOS object available only to the iPad called `UISplitViewController`, shown in Figure P.3.

The split view controller is a nonvisual object that controls the display of two side-by-side views. When you hold your iPad in landscape mode, the two views are displayed side by side. Rotate your iPad to portrait orientation, and the left-side view disappears. This allows the user to focus his attention on the main content displayed on the right side.

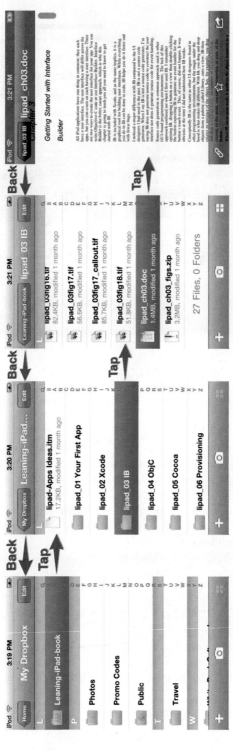

Figure P.2   Example of navigating the hierarchy of folders and files using the Dropbox app on the iPhone. You tap to move forward, or drill down, to more content, and you tap the back button to move backward.

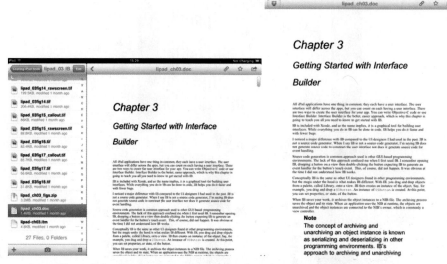

Figure P.3   Screen shots of Dropbox running on the iPad. Notice how the navigation is displayed in the left-side view when the device is held in a landscape orientation, but is hidden when the iPad is rotated to portrait.

> **Note**
>
> You get hands-on experience writing a split-view-based application in Chapter 8, "Creating a Master-Detail App."

This view pattern, in which the master view is displayed on the left side and the detail view is displayed on the right side, is often called "master-detail." The master view is used to navigate the hierarchy of data, or in the case of Dropbox, the master view is used to navigate the list of files and folders. When you find the file you want to view, tap it in the master view and the file contents are displayed on the right in the detail view. Rotate your iPad to a portrait position to focus your attention on the file's content, hiding the master view.

Orientation Matters

Most iPhone applications support only a single orientation. Many iPhone games are played in landscape mode, while many other iPhone apps are displayed in portrait mode. Like the iPad, the iPhone does support rotation and changes in orientation, but the small size of the device makes supporting different orientations unnecessary. Most users hold their iPhones in portrait mode with the Home button at the bottom when using applications, rotating to landscape orientation only to play a game.

The iPad is different. With the iPad, users grab the device and turn it on without regard to a certain orientation. This is even truer when the iPad is not in a case. Try this little experiment . . .

Place your iPhone, or iPod touch, on your desk or table with the Home button pointing at 10 o'clock. Walk away or turn around. Come back to the device and pick it up. Take a look at the device as you hold it in your hand. There's a good chance that as you picked up the device, you rotated it so that the Home button is at the bottom. You did this rotation even before turning on the device. It is an almost natural instinct to hold your iPhone with the Home button at the bottom.

Now try the same experiment, but this time use your iPad. Place it on your desk or table. Make sure the Home button is positioned away from you—say, at 10 o'clock— and then walk away. Come back and pick up your iPad. Chances are good you did not rotate the device. Instead, you are likely holding your iPad in the same orientation it was in before you picked it up.

Multi-Touch Amped Up

Did you know that the iPad and the iPhone support the same multi-touch interface? They do. As a matter of fact, the iOS multi-touch interface supports up to 11 simultaneous touches. This means that you can use all your fingers—and maybe one or two more if you have a friend nearby—to interact with an application.

The iPad, with its larger screen, makes multi-touch use more feasible. While two-handed gestures have limited use on the iPhone, they can become a natural part of interacting with an iPad application. Take, for example, Apple's own Keynote app for the iPad. It takes advantage of the multi-touch interface to provide features once reserved for the point-and-click world of the desktop. Selecting multiple slides and moving them is just one example of how Keynote on the iPad maximizes the user experience with multi-touch.

So you already know that the multi-touch interface supports up to 11 simultaneous touches, but how can you confirm this? Write an iPad app that counts the number of simultaneous touches. That is exactly what Matt Legend Gemmell did. He wrote a really neat iPad app, shown in Figure P.4, that shows the number of simultaneous touches. But Matt went beyond just showing the touch count. He made the app sci-fi-looking, which also makes it fun to play with.

You can read more about Matt's iPad multi-touch sample and download the source code from his blog posting.[2]

Another way to explore the iPad multi-touch interface is to play with Uzu for iPad, only $1.99 in the App Store.[3] Uzu is a "kinetic multi-touch particle visualizer" and it's highly addictive. (Figure P.5 doesn't do the app justice; you should really download and play around with Uzu if you want to see some clever use of multi-touch.)

---

2. Multi-touch sample: http://mattgemmell.com/2010/05/09/ipad-multi-touch/

3. Uzu: https://itunes.apple.com/app/uzu/id376551723?mt=8

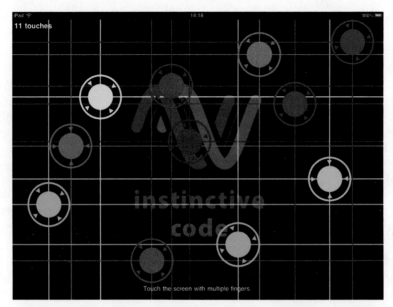

Figure P.4   Matt Legend Gemmell's multi-touch sample app for the iPad illustrating 11 touches

Figure P.5   Uzu, the particle visualizer for the iPad

The iPad Bridges the Gap between the Phone and the Computer

So, everyone agrees that the iPad is not an oversize iPhone. Great, glad to have you on the same page here. Now on to the larger question: Is the iPad a replacement for a laptop or desktop? No, not yet, but it's pretty darn close.

For many users, the iPad represents a mobile device bridging the gap between the smartphone and a full-fledged computer, whether a laptop or desktop computer. While many individuals use the iPad for content consumption, the iPad is also used to perform a good number of tasks previously left to the desktop or laptop computer. This causes iOS developers to rethink how to implement software concepts that have been around for eons. Word-processing software is one such concept that is seeing new life on the iPad.

The iPad opens the door to a wide range of applications not feasible on the small form factor of the iPhone. Word processing, again, is one such application that comes to mind.

While the iPhone is great for capturing quick notes, it is not ideal for writing lengthy documents. And while it is technically possible to implement a full-featured word processor on the iPhone, why would you? The screen is too small, and even in landscape mode, typing two-thumbed on a tiny screen would be less than productive. The iPhone is ideal for performing simple, quick tasks—writing a note, scheduling an event, marking a to-do item as complete—but it is less than ideal for lengthier tasks such as writing a book.

Enter the iPad

The iPad provides an experience similar to a small laptop. And when combined with a wireless keyboard, your iPad becomes a nice setup for writing long documents. I'm speaking from experience. A lot of the text in this book was originally written on an iPad. I can't imagine what writing a book on an iPhone would be like, but I know what it is like on the iPad, and it is a joy. Best of all, the iPad allows you to concentrate on a single task. This eliminates distractions and gives you better focus on the task at hand.

Organization of This Book

This book provides you with a hands-on guide for, as the book's title states, learning iPad programming. It walks you through every stage of the process—from downloading and installing the iOS SDK to submitting the first application to Apple for review.

There are 28 chapters and one appendix in the book, as follows:

- Part I, "Getting Started"

  Part I introduces you to the tools of the trade. Here you learn about developer tools such as Xcode and Interface Builder. You learn how to write code using

Objective-C and the Cocoa framework. And you learn what it takes to provision your iPad as a development device.

- Chapter 1, "Your First App"

  This chapter immediately immerses you in creating your first application. It provides a step-by-step guide to creating a simple, but functional, iPad application that runs in the iPad Simulator. You'll use Xcode to create the application, which means there is also some light coding to be done, but knowledge of Objective-C is not required at this point in the book. The goal of this chapter is for you to immediately get your hands on the tools and the code you'll use to create iPad apps.

- Chapter 2, "Getting Started with Xcode"

  Xcode is the developer's integrated development environment (IDE) used to write Objective-C code for iPad applications. This chapter highlights key features of Xcode, including recommended preference settings, commonly used shortcut keys, and descriptions of the various windows you will see when using Xcode.

- Chapter 3, "Getting Started with Interface Builder"

  In this chapter, you explore Interface Builder (IB). Interface Builder is the tool used to create an application UI with no programming required. This chapter explains how to use IB and many of its useful features. In addition, the chapter warns you about common mistakes made when using IB, such as forgetting to associate an event with an IBAction.

- Chapter 4, "Getting Started with Objective-C"

  This chapter introduces Objective-C by providing a brief overview of the programming language of choice for iPad programming. It is not intended to be a comprehensive review of the programming language, but instead to provide enough information to get you started in writing your first real iPad app.

- Chapter 5, "Getting Started with Cocoa"

  A programming language is only as powerful as the frameworks that support it, and Cocoa provides an impressive stack of frameworks and a library that make it possible for you to build your iPad app in less time.

- Chapter 6, "Provisioning Your iPad"

  Walking down the yellow brick road to the wonderful world of iPad development can have its own set of scary moments. One of the scariest is dealing with provisioning profiles, certificates, and registering a device for testing. Xcode 4 provides improvements in this area, but it is still far from perfect. This chapter guides you through the ominous forest of provisioning profiles, certificates, and device registration.

- Chapter 7, "App Design"

    You can't build an app if you don't know what you're building. This chapter shares tips on designing an application before the first line of code is ever written.

- Part II, "Building PhotoWheel"

    Part II is the heart of the book—where you get hands-on practice with building a real iPad app. The app you build is no simple "Hello, World" app. Rather, it is PhotoWheel, a full-featured photo app. In Part II, you learn about everything from creating custom animations for view transitions to iCloud syncing to viewing your photos on TV.

    - Chapter 8, "Creating a Master-Detail App"

        You start building PhotoWheel by first building a prototype of it. While building the prototype, you have a chance to learn about the splitview controller used in master-detail apps.

    - Chapter 9, "Using Table Views"

        In this chapter, you learn the basics of displaying data using table views. You also learn how to reorder, delete, and even edit data displayed in a table view.

    - Chapter 10, "Using Collection and Custom Views"

        In this chapter, you dive into the world of views. Here you learn how to use the collection view introduced in iOS 6, and create a custom wheel view for displaying photos.

    - Chapter 11, "Using Touch Gestures"

        This chapter teaches you how to take advantage of the iPad's multi-touch screen. You learn to use touch gestures so that users can interact with your app.

    - Chapter 12, "Adding Photos"

        PhotoWheel deals with photos, so it is only natural that you need to learn how to add photos to the app. In this chapter, you discover how to retrieve photos from the Photos app library and how to take new photos using the device's built-in camera.

    - Chapter 13, "Data Persistence"

        PhotoWheel won't be very useful if people can't save their work. In this chapter, you explore Core Data, and you learn how to use it to persist data in your application.

    - Chapter 14, "Storyboarding in Xcode"

        A storyboard is an exciting new way to design an app's user interface. In this chapter, you get hands-on practice with storyboarding, and you learn how you can do more with less code by using Interface Builder.

- Chapter 15, "View Controllers and Segues"

A storyboard can take you only so far. At some point in time, you must write code to make your app really shine. In this chapter, you learn how to take advantage of view controllers to do more, and you learn how to create segues that transition between view controllers.

- Chapter 16, "Building the Main Screen"

In this chapter, you dive into PhotoWheel. Prototyping is over and you have the basic UI in place with a storyboard. Now it's time to build the main screen, and that's exactly what you do in this chapter. You also learn how to use container view controllers, and you build a custom grid view that can be used in other projects.

- Chapter 17, "Creating a Photo Browser"

In this chapter, you learn how to use a scroll view to create a full-screen photo browser. You also learn how to use a pinch gesture to zoom in and out on a photo.

- Chapter 18, "Supporting Device Rotation"

Users expect iPad apps to display properly regardless of how the device is being held. A user may hold his iPad with the Home button on the left or right, or maybe on the top or bottom. As a developer, it is your job to ensure that your app displays properly regardless of the device's orientation. That is what you learn in this chapter: how to support device rotation. You also learn how to leverage Cocoa Auto Layout for supporting rotation of your user interface.

- Chapter 19, "Printing with AirPrint"

This chapter gets straight to the point and teaches you how to print from your app using AirPrint.

- Chapter 20, "Sharing with Others"

Virtually everyone has an email account these days, and everyone loves looking at photos. So it only makes sense that PhotoWheel users will want to share photos with family and friends using email. In this chapter, you learn how to send email from your app. But the chapter doesn't stop there—you also learn how to use the Activity View Controller for sharing photos through social networks such as Facebook and Twitter.

- Chapter 21, "Web Services"

Adding photos already found on your iPad to PhotoWheel is a nice exercise, but many people keep their photos stored elsewhere. In this chapter, you learn how to make an iPad app communicate with a Web server so that you can search for and download photos from Flickr.

- Chapter 22, "Syncing with iCloud"

  Many people have multiple iOS devices, and it would be great if they could use PhotoWheel with the same data on all of them. Syncing can be a challenge, but with iCloud it becomes a lot easier. In this chapter, we add online syncing of photos and albums.

- Chapter 23, "Producing a Slideshow with AirPlay"

  The iPad has a great screen, but you might want to show photos to a group, and it's awkward to gather everyone around a hand-held device. In this chapter, you see how to make use of external wireless displays—a large TV set, maybe—from an iPad app. You'll use AirPlay for this purpose, so you don't need to run cables across the room.

- Chapter 24, "Visual Effects with Core Image"

  Core Image is an amazingly cool framework for analyzing and changing images. As if color effects and automatic photo enhancement weren't enough, you can also use Core Data Image to locate the faces of any people in the picture. You add all of these capabilities to PhotoWheel in a convenient user interface that allows people to preview effects before committing to them.

- Chapter 25, "Going Universal"

  Part II wraps up with a discussion of turning your iPad app into a universal app. A universal app takes full advantage of the device it's running on, and it extends the target audience for your iPad app to include iPhone users.

- Part III, "The Finishing Touches"

In the final part of the book, you learn tips on debugging your app. Even more important, you learn how to distribute your app to others.

- Chapter 26, "Debugging"

  At this point you know how to create an iPad application, but what happens when a problem occurs? This chapter is devoted to application debugging. It explores the LLDB. and shows you how to turn breakpoints on and off, and how to use sounds to debug your app. The chapter also introduces you to more advanced debugging techniques such as using Instruments to track down memory leaks.

- Chapter 27, "Distributing Your App"

  At this point, the application has been written, debugged, and tested. The next step is to get the application into the hands of users. This chapter explores the options for distributing iPad applications, focusing on the two most commonly used distribution methods: Ad Hoc and App Store.

- Chapter 28, "The Final Word"

  The book ends with some final words of encouragement for the new iPad programmer.

- Appendix A, "Installing the Developer Tools"

  This appendix walks you through the steps needed to start programming for the iPad. These measures include setting up an iOS developer account, downloading the iOS SDK, and installing the developer tools on your Mac.

Learning iPad Programming takes you from app design to the App Store. Along the way, you learn about the developer tools, the programming language, and the frameworks. But more important, you learn how to build a full-featured iPad app that you can show off to family and friends.

Audience for This Book

This book is intended for programmers who are new to the iOS platform and want to learn how to write applications that target the iPad. The book assumes that you are new to iPad programming and have little to no experience with Xcode and the Objective-C programming language. At the same time, it assumes that you have some prior programming experience with other tools and programming languages. *Learning iPad Programming* is not intended for individuals with absolutely no prior programming experience.

This book is targeted to programmers who want to learn how to develop sophisticated applications for the iPad using iOS 6. You are expected to have a Mac on which you can create programs using Xcode and Interface Builder, as well as an iOS developer account and an iPad. Some programming experience is helpful, particularly knowledge of the C programming language, although there is a chapter on object-oriented programming with Objective-C to give you a head start in this area.

Learning iPad Programming will also appeal to experienced iOS developers—people who have programmed and submitted apps to the App Store for the iPhone and iPod touch. If you are an experienced reader, you can skip over the basics, if you so choose, and quickly get to work on the example projects used throughout the book.

Getting the Source Code for PhotoWheel

The source code from each chapter as well as the source code for PhotoWheel as presented in this book is available from the book's Web site.[4] Work on PhotoWheel doesn't stop at the end of this book, either. There is so much more to do with the app and so much more to learn. The most up-to-date source code is available on github.[5]

---

4. PhotoWheel source code: http://www.learningipadprogramming.com/source-code/

5. PhotoWheel on github: https://github.com/kirbyt/PhotoWheel

You will also find more how-to articles and tips for improving PhotoWheel at the book's blog site.[6]

Should you have additional questions, or want to report a bug or contribute a new feature to PhotoWheel, feel free to send email to **kirby@whitepeaksoftware.com** or **tph@atomicbird.com**, or send a message to **@kirbyt** or **@atomicbird** on Twitter and App.net.

There is plenty of code to review throughout the book, along with exercises for you to try, so it is assumed that you have access to the Apple developer tools such as Xcode and the iOS SDK. Both of these toolkits can be downloaded from the Mac App Store as part of the Xcode download.[7]

Artwork Provided by

Matt McCray is the swell guy who provided the artwork in PhotoWheel. Reach out to Matt if you're looking for a designer for your next app. He can be reached at matt@elucidata.net and his Web site is at **www.elucidata.net**.

---

6. Book's blog site: http://www.learningipadprogramming.com/blog/
7. Xcode download: https://itunes.apple.com/us/app/xcode/id497799835?mt=12

Acknowledgments

As for any book that gets written, there's an entire cast and crew who remain hidden from the limelight; please take a moment to hear us out as we thank the supporting cast. . . .

Acknowledgments from Kirby Turner

I want to first thank my wife, Melanie, and my son, Rowan, for their support and patience while I focused on completing this book, and their understanding when I said I want to write a second edition. I want to thank Tom for agreeing to co-author this book. I want to give a huge THANKS to Chuck Toporek for convincing me to write, and Trina MacDonald for being an outstanding and patient editor. I also want to thank the production team for their hard work making this book look good. And, of course, I want to say thanks to the technical reviewers, Andrew, Michael, and Patrick. Your feedback is invaluable.

Lastly, I want to thank the amazing team of engineers at Apple for bringing the fun back to programming for me. And I want to thank the Mac and iOS developer community. None of this would be possible if not for the passion and spirit of this unique community.

Acknowledgments from Tom Harrington

I'd like to thank Kirby for inviting me to be part of this book. I'd also like to thank our technical reviewers and the rest of the production team for all their hard work making me look good in print. Apple continues to advance its software and tools at a breakneck pace, which makes it a challenge to write a book and get it into print while it's still current. Everyone involved has done a great job dealing with the challenges of writing a book on a topic that's constantly in flux.

On a closely related note, thanks to everyone at Apple for their hard work on iOS and the iPad. Without them we wouldn't have such a cool topic to write about.

About the Authors

This book is brought to you by. . . .

Kirby Turner is an independent software developer and Chief Code Monkey at White Peak Software Inc., where he focuses on iOS and Mac programming. When Kirby is not sitting behind the keyboard, he can be found hanging out with his wife and son, hiking the mountains of New England, kayaking the waters in and around Salem, Massachusetts, and snowboarding down mountains in search of magic powder. Follow Kirby on Twitter and App.net: @kirbyt.

Tom Harrington is an independent iOS and Mac software developer and is available for contract work, technical conferences, and parties. He also organizes iOS developer events in Colorado. Follow Tom on Twitter and App.net: @atomicbird.

We Want to Hear from You!

As the reader of this book, you are our most important critic and commentator. We value your opinion and want to know what we're doing right, what we could do better, what areas you'd like to see us publish in, and any other words of wisdom you're willing to pass our way.

You can email or write me directly to let use know what you did or didn't like about this book—as well as what we can do to make our books stronger.

Please note that we cannot help you with technical problems related to the topic of this book, and that due to the high volume of mail we receive, we might not be able to reply to every message.

When you write, please be sure to include this book's title and author as well as your name and phone or email address.

Email: trina.macdonald@pearson.com

Mail: Reader Feedback
Addison-Wesley Learning Series
800 East 96th Street
Indianapolis, IN 46240 USA

Reader Services

Visit our website and register this book **informit.com/register** for convenient access to any updates, downloads, or errata that might be available for this book.

Part I

Getting Started

1

Your First App

There is no better way to learn than by actually doing something, so let's dive in by writing a really simple iPad app. The first application you will write is a Hello World app. Yes, the Hello World sample application is overdone, but don't worry—you will be building more sophisticated applications later in this book. For now, it's important to get your hands dirty with some code and the tools.

The goal for this chapter is to give you a sneak peek at the tools you will be using to build your iPad applications. If you are already familiar with Xcode, you may wish to skip ahead to Chapter 4, "Getting Started with Objective-C," or Chapter 6, "Provisioning Your iPad." If you are new to Xcode, please continue reading.

The rest of this chapter will guide you through the steps needed to create your first iPad application. The chapter does not go into detail about Xcode. Instead, those details are covered in the following chapters: Chapter 2, "Getting Started with Xcode," and Chapter 3, "Getting Started with Interface Builder."

> **Note**
>
> Before you begin, you must have Xcode and the iOS SDK installed on your Mac computer. If you do not have these installed, jump to Appendix A, "Installing the Developer Tools," for instructions on how to set up your Mac for iPad programming. This book assumes you are using Xcode 4.5 or newer. And yes, a Mac computer is required.

Creating the Hello World Project

Let's begin by launching Xcode. If you are running Mountain Lion (Mac OS X 10.8) and you downloaded Xcode from the Mac App Store, it is available in Launchpad, shown in Figure 1.1; otherwise, you can find it in your Applications folder. Click the Xcode icon to launch it.

> **Note**
>
> You may find having Xcode on the Dock more convenient than using Launchpad. Adding Xcode to the Dock is simple. First, launch Xcode from Launchpad. While Xcode is running, right-click (or **Control-click**) on the Xcode icon that appears in the Dock and select **Options > Keep in Dock.** This will keep the Xcode icon in the Dock even when the program is not running, making it easier to launch Xcode the next time you need it.

Figure 1.1   The Xcode icon as seen in Launchpad

The first window you see after launching Xcode is the Welcome to Xcode screen, shown in Figure 1.2. You can do a number of things from this window, including creating a new project, connecting to a source code repository, going to the *Xcode 4 User Guide* (a tutorial on using Xcode), or visiting Apple's Developer site.[1] If you have created or opened Xcode projects in the past, you will also see a list of recent projects on the right side of this screen. You can open a recent project by selecting it from the list and clicking **Open**.

Tucked away in the lower-left corner is the **Open Other...** button. You can click this button to open an existing Xcode project found on the file system. Next to this button is a check box indicating whether the Welcome to Xcode window is displayed when Xcode launches.

> **Note**
>
> If you are new to Xcode, you should take the time to read through the *Xcode 4 User Guide*, which provides complete coverage of the entire Xcode tool set. You will learn about Xcode in this book; however, reading the official guides from Apple is always a good thing.

You want to create a new iPad application, so click the **Create a new Xcode project** button. This opens the new project window, as shown in Figure 1.3. Let's

---

1. Apple Developer site: http://developer.apple.com

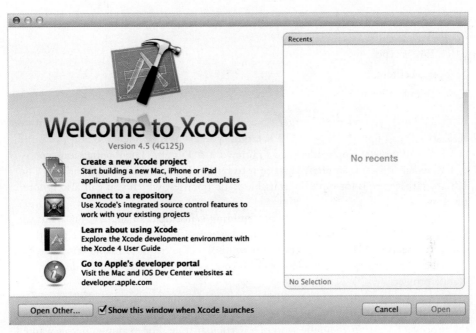

Figure 1.2   Welcome to Xcode window

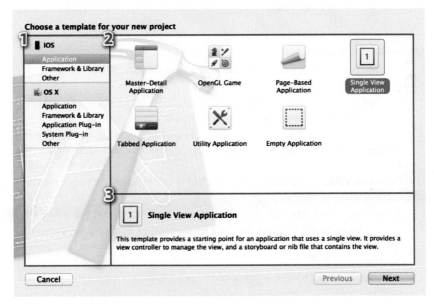

Figure 1.3   The new project window in Xcode, with
callouts on sections of Xcode's user interface
(1: target type; 2: project template; 3: template detail)

explore this window for a moment before continuing. As you can see in the figure, the new project has three main sections:

1. Target type
2. Project template
3. Template detail

In section 1, you select the target type: iOS or Mac OS X. iPad applications run on iOS, so you can ignore the Mac OS X target type for now. Under iOS you can build two types of targets: Application and Framework & Library. The Application type is exactly what the name implies; you use it to build iPhone and iPad applications. The Library target type is for building reusable static libraries, which you can also ignore for now.

The Hello World application you are building is just that, an application. Thus, in section 1 under iOS, you select Application. When you do so, you'll notice that the content in section 2 changes. Section 2 now displays the list of available templates for the selected target type. A template is used to generate the initial files needed for an Xcode project.

If you have spent time playing with your iPad, you may have noticed that there are some common application types, or styles. The templates listed in section 2 help speed the process of creating an application of a particular style. For example, if you wanted to create an application that looks similar to the Mail app on the iPad, you would select Master–Detail Application.

Application Templates

The application templates you'll encounter in Xcode after selecting iOS as your target include the following types:

- **Master-Detail Application:** Select this template when you have a master-detail style of application and wish to leverage the split view controller for display.
- **OpenGL Game:** Select this template when you want to create a game using OpenGL ES. This template provides a view with an OpenGL scene and timer to animate the view.
- **Page-Based Application:** Select this template to create a book- or magazine-style app that uses the page view controller.
- **Single View Application:** Select this template for applications that use a single view.
- **Tabbed Application:** Select this template for applications that have separate areas defined by tabs. This template provides a tab bar controller and view controllers for two tabs.
- **Utility Application:** Select this template for applications that have a main view and an alternate view.
- **Empty Application:** This template provides a starting point for any type of application. Select this template when you want to start with a bare-bones project shell.

The Hello World application will consist of a single view, so select Single View Application from the list of templates. When you do so, notice that the content of the template detail section changes. This section shows a brief description of the template selected in the project template section.

Clicking the **Next** button takes you to the project options screen, shown in Figure 1.4. Project options vary slightly based on the template. Each template has options for the Product Name, Organization Name, Company Identifier, Bundler Identifier (which is completed for you based on the Company Identifier and Product Name), Class Prefix, and Device Family. Additional options that may be found on an application template include Use Storyboard, Use Automatic Reference Counting, Use Core Data, and Include Unit Tests. The application template you select determines which additional options are made available.

For the Hello World app you are building, enter "Hello World" for the Product Name. The Organization Name can be any value you like, as it is used only in the copyright message included in the comment section that is added to the top of each *.h* and *.m* file created by Xcode for the project.

For the Company Identifier, enter your name or company name using the reverse domain name format. (For example, com.kirbyturner is my individual name and com.whitepeaksoftware is my company name.) Chapter 6, "Provisioning Your iPad," explains the relationship between the company and bundle identifiers and describes how they are used to form the App ID.

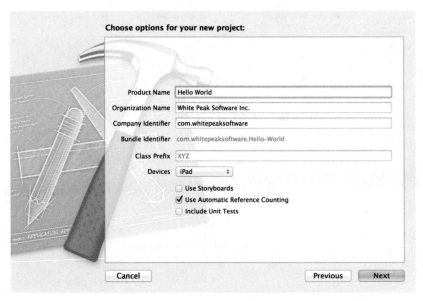

Figure 1.4   Project options for the Single View Application template

The Class Prefix can be used to append a string value to the beginning of each class generated by the application template. For the purpose of simplicity, you can leave the Class Prefix blank for this app.

Next, select iPad as the Device Family. There are three device family types in iOS: iPad, iPhone, and Universal. The device family iPad indicates that the app is designed for and runs on the iPad only. The iPhone device family indicates that the app is designed for the iPhone, and Universal says that the app is designed for and runs on both the iPad and the iPhone.

You do not need storyboard and unit tests in this Hello World app, so leave those options unselected. (Storyboarding is covered in Chapter 14, "Storyboarding in Xcode.") But do select the Use Automatic Reference Counting option—it determines how memory of an object is managed, and is explained in the Memory Management section of Chapter 4, "Getting Started with Objective-C." Click the **Next** button, choose a storage location for the Xcode project, and then click the **Create** button (shown in Figure 1.5).

> **Note**
>
> I like to keep all my source code together in a single location, so I created a *Source* directory within my home directory. I place all my Xcode projects under *Source* so I can easily locate them in the future.

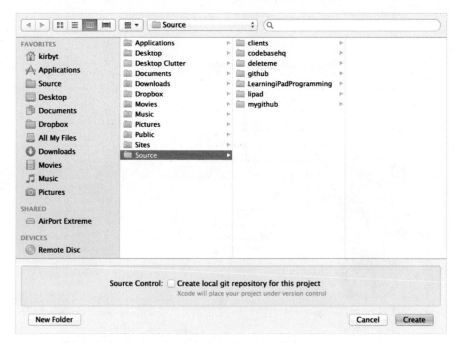

Figure 1.5   Choose the location where your Xcode project is stored.

Figure 1.6 Xcode project window for the Hello World app

Congratulations! You just created your first iPad application. You don't believe it? Click the **Run** button (shown in Figure 1.6), or press **Command-R**. Be sure the active schema is set to the iPad Simulator. If it is not, click it and change it to the simulator.

Universal App

iPhone apps can run on the iPad, but they run in an iPhone emulator. Because they do not take advantage of the iPad's full screen, this behavior leads to a less than ideal user experience. A universal app, in contrast, is designed to take full advantage of the screen real estate provided by both the iPhone and the iPad. When a universal app is run on an iPhone, it looks as if it was designed for the iPhone. Conversely, when a universal app is run on an iPad, it looks like an iPad app, not an iPhone app.

A universal app gives the user the best of both worlds—a single app that looks great on both devices. However, this comes at a cost to you, the developer. Developing a universal app, in many ways, is like developing two separate apps, one for the iPad and one for the iPhone, and packaging them into a single app binary.

Universal apps are designed to target both the iPad and the iPhone. The focus of this book, however, is on writing iPad applications. To keep you focused, and to avoid the additional complexities of writing universal apps as you start your journey toward becoming an iOS developer, universal apps are not covered until the end of Part II in this book.

Figure 1.7   A "blank" single view app running in the iPad Simulator

When you click **Run**, Xcode compiles the project, builds an application package, installs the application on the iPad Simulator, and finally launches the application inside the simulator. As you can see in Figure 1.7, the application is nothing more than a white screen. Guess what? You just built your first flashlight app for the iPad!

> **Note**
>
> Sometimes you will notice a delay between the time the simulator is launched and the time your app launches within the simulator. When this delay happens, you see nothing but a black screen within the simulator. This is normal, and it usually happens only the first time you launch your app in the simulator.

You can take your newly created flashlight application and submit it to Apple for review. However, there is a high level of certainty that Apple will reject your masterpiece because of its lack of functionality. Besides, you are not done with this app. You want to build a Hello World application, and, as you can see, "Hello World" does not appear when this application is run. So let's continue working on it.

First, stop the app, which is running in the simulator. You can do so by clicking the **Stop** button at the upper-left side of Xcode or by pressing **Command-.** in Xcode (not in the simulator). Now you're ready to start modifying the app.

> **Note**
>
> When you use a project template, Xcode gives you a valid, runnable iPad application without your having to write a single line of code. Perhaps it is because I still have memories of being a teenager building apps 30 years ago, but I always get a little warm, fuzzy feeling when I see a new application run for the first time. As a matter of fact, the first thing I do when I create a new Xcode project is to build and run it. Seeing the application run for the first time gives me a little jolt of excitement.

Getting Text on the Screen

This is a Hello World app, so it should display "Hello World" somewhere on the screen. This can be accomplished by writing some code, but the easiest approach is to use Interface Builder. Interface Builder, or IB as it is often called, is the visual user interface designer built into Xcode. You'll learn more about IB in Chapter 3, "Getting Started with Interface Builder," but for now steps are provided to guide you through turning this blank application into a not-so-useful Hello World app.

To add "Hello World" to the display, you'll edit the file *ViewController.xib*. A *.xib* file, pronounced "zib," is an XML representation of a NIB file. A NIB file, or *.nib*, is the binary predecessor of the *.xib* file. Being text based, a *.xib* file has the benefit of working better with version-control systems when compared to the earlier binary *.nib* version. That said, *.xib* files are still compiled down to *.nib* files when you build the application.

What is a NIB file? It is a file created by Interface Builder to archive interface objects and their relationships. Put another way, a NIB represents the objects that make up the visual display of a screen. You create and edit NIB files using IB, and your application uses the NIB files at run time to display the user interface of the app.

Note

iOS developers often refer to a *.xib* file as a NIB file because it is, after all, just a text-based representation of a NIB file.

History

The *N* in NIB is a carryover from the NeXTSTEP days when it was used to indicate the NeXT-style property list file. The *IB* indicates that the file is an Interface Builder file.

Begin by opening the file *ViewController.xib*, available in the Project navigator. This changes the contents of the Editor area. It displays the NIB file using the IB designer, as shown in Figure 1.8.

Note

Chapter 3, "Getting Started with Interface Builder," covers all the utilities available with IB.

IB has a set of available utilities for working with a NIB file. Press **Control-Option-Command-3** to display the Object library. The Object library contains a list of visual and nonvisual components that are used to construct the user interface. In the filter bar at the bottom, type "Label" without the quotes. This will filter the object list, displaying only label-type objects.

Drag and drop the label object onto the view's canvas area. This creates a new UILabel instance, which is the type of object representing a label. Next, open the Attributes inspector (**Option-Command-4**). At the top of the Attributes inspector is a property named Text. Change the default value "Label" to "Hello World." Xcode should now look similar to Figure 1.8.

You may need to resize the label to view the entire "Hello World" content. To resize it, move the mouse cursor to the right edge of the label object. The cursor will change to the resize indicator. Click and drag the mouse to the right to increase the width of the label.

Build and run the app in the iPad Simulator. Congratulations! You have written your first Hello World app for the iPad.

Note

Don't worry if none of this is making sense yet. Remember—the goal of this chapter is to give you a sneak peek into iPad programming by way of a step-by-step guide. This discussion is intended to give you a sense of what it is like to program for the iPad. Later chapters will explain all you need to know in detail, and before you know it, the steps for creating iPad applications will be second nature to you.

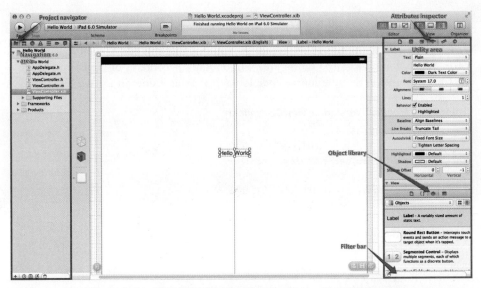

Figure 1.8   Adding "Hello World" to the main view of the app

Say Hello

Now that the excitement of creating your first application for the iPad has worn off, let's extend the application by adding some functionality to it. Instead of having it always display "Hello World," let's change the app to first ask for a name, then display a "Hello" message in response to the name entered. This exercise is more involved and requires you to write some Objective-C code. Do not worry if you have never seen Objective-C code before. You will be told exactly what to type, and you will explore Objective-C in more detail in Chapter 4, "Getting Started with Objective-C."

In life there is often more than one way to accomplish a task. The beauty of iPad programming is that there are many different ways to do something. It is this flexibility in the development tools that makes many programmers prefer Xcode to other development tools. But it does take time to learn all the ins and outs, which can be frustrating for programmers new to Xcode.

One of the goals of this book is to show you the different ways a task can be accomplished. Armed with this knowledge, you can decide which approaches work best for you. For example, it is possible to use IB to generate Objective-C code that declares objects and actions defined in a *.xib* file. However, this discussion is saved for a later chapter. Instead, you're going to write the Objective-C code yourself to extend functionality in the Hello World app.

Two screen elements are needed: one that accepts user input for the name and the other to display "Hello." A third element, a button, is also needed to tell the app when to display the "Hello" message. The NIB file defines the objects that make up the user interface, but there is no automatic connection between the objects and the source code. Instead, you must make the connection.

Start by opening the file *ViewController.h*. You can find this file in the Project navigator. When you click it, the Editor area will display the contents of the file. Modify the file's contents so that the source code looks exactly as it does in Listing 1.1.

Listing 1.1 Modified Version of *ViewController.h*

```
#import <UIKit/UIKit.h>

@interface ViewController : UIViewController

@property (nonatomic, weak) IBOutlet UILabel *helloLabel;
@property (nonatomic, weak) IBOutlet UITextField *nameField;

- (IBAction)displayHelloName:(id)sender;

@end
```

Next, open the file *ViewController.m*. Replace the generated source code found in the file with the source code in Listing 1.2.

Listing 1.2 Modified Version of *ViewController.m*

```
#import "ViewController.h"

@implementation ViewController

@synthesize helloLabel;
@synthesize nameField;

- (IBAction)displayHelloName:(id)sender
{
    NSString *hello = [NSString stringWithFormat:@"Hello %@", [nameField text]];
    [helloLabel setText:hello];
}

@end
```

The code in Listing 1.1 does a number of things. First, two properties are added to the class ViewController. These properties are marked with IBOutlet, which is a hint to IB that the class contains a reference to an object. Next, the method -displayHelloName: is declared. It is marked with IBAction, another hint to IB, this time telling IB that an action exists in the class definition. At this point, the interface for the class ViewController has been defined.

What Are `IBOutlet` and `IBAction`?

`IBOutlet` and `IBAction` are special indicators for Interface Builder—hence the IB prefix. Interface Builder uses these indicators to connect objects and actions to elements in the user interface.

An `IBOutlet` is used to connect an object reference defined in Objective-C code to the object instance used in Interface Builder. For example, earlier in this chapter you placed a label on the view. That label is actually a `UILabel`. (`UILabel` is the class name for the label.) To access the label in code, you must have a reference to the instance of the `UILabel`. You will see later in this chapter how you connect the reference declared in code to the instance displayed in IB.

An `IBAction` is used to connect an event sent by an object to a method defined in code. For example, a button has an event that is fired when a user lifts her finger. This action can be connected to the `IBAction` defined in the Objective-C class.

The code in Listing 1.2 represents the implementation for the class `ViewController`. This implementation begins by synthesizing the two properties declared in the class interface, `helloLabel` and `nameField`. Property synthesis is an Objective-C compiler feature that generates the accessor methods for these properties at compile time. You'll learn more about this feature in Chapter 4, "Getting Started with Objective-C."

The property synthesis is followed by the implementation for the method `-displayHelloName:`. This method is the action that is called when the user interacts with the app—specifically, when the user taps a button—which you will provide momentarily. The implementation of this method creates a local string variable containing the name entered by the user with the prefix "Hello." This string is then displayed on the screen as the text value for the `helloLabel`.

If you were to run the app at this point, you would see no difference from the earlier version. While the code has been updated to do what you want it to do, the user interface has not been updated and the connections for the outlets and actions have not been made.

Note

This decoupling of the source code—in this particular case, the controller—and the user interface (also known as the view) is representative of the Model-View-Controller design pattern, which is discussed in Chapter 5, "Getting Started with Cocoa."

To complete the app, you need to update the user interface and connect the UI objects to the properties defined in the controller class. Once again, open the file *ViewController.xib*. Double-click the "Hello World" label and change its text value to "What is your name?" Resize the label as needed to display the entire text.

Search through the Object library in the Utilities area for the Text Field object. Alternatively, you can filter the object list by typing "text field" in the filter bar. Drag and drop a text field to the right of the "What is your name?" label.

Now search through the Object library for the Round Rect Button. Drag and drop an instance of this button to the right of the text field. In the Attributes inspector, change the Title property to "Say Hello."

Finally, search the Object library for Label, and drag and drop a new label onto the canvas, placing it under the other objects. Be sure to increase the width of the label to accommodate the string value created in the method -displayHelloName:. The view should look similar to Figure 1.9.

Now it's time to connect the objects and events defined in the NIB with the outlets and actions defined in the view controller source code. One way to connect objects to outlets and actions is to **Control-click** an object, and then drag the mouse cursor to another object. When the mouse button is released, IB will display a Heads-Up Display (HUD) of the connection options. For example, when you **Control-click** the *File's Owner* object (the translucent cube displayed in the left sidebar in the Editor area) and drag it to the text field (shown in Figure 1.10), a HUD is displayed, allowing you to connect the text field to the properties `nameField` and `view`. Select `nameField` to connect the text field to the property defined in *ViewController.h*.

Do the same thing to connect the label to the property `helloLabel`. **Control-click** the *File's Owner* cube and drag to the label where the output of the `-display HelloName:` will be displayed.

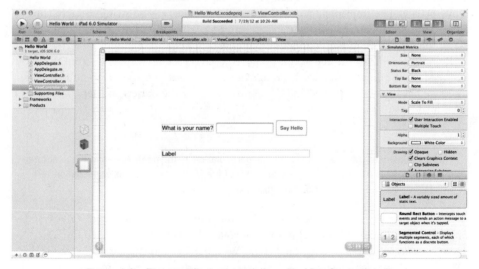

Figure 1.9   The modified user interface file *ViewController.xib*

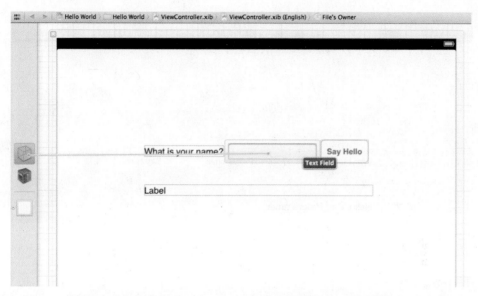

Figure 1.10   Connect the `nameField` property to the text field
defined in the NIB file.

To connect the action to the **Say Hello** button, you **Control-click** the button and drag to the *File's Owner* cube. This will assign the action `-displayHelloName:` to the button event *Touch Up Inside*.

With the connections in place, the Hello World app is now functional. Build and run the app in the simulator. Tap the name field in the simulator to enter a value, and then tap the **Say Hello** button to dissplay the "Hello" message. The final app should look similar to Figure 1.11.

You might be wondering how IB is able to identify the correct Objective-C header file. It's simple: The file's owner is defined as being of type `ViewController`. This tells IB which source file to look at for outlets and actions. You can see this by clicking the *File's Owner* cube, and then typing **Option-Command-3**. The class name is set to `ViewController`. This is how an object defined in IB knows its type.

> ### Note
>
> A common mistake made in Interface Builder is forgetting to associate your outlets and actions. If you run the application and notice that the display does not update after the **Say Hello** button is touched, chances are good that the *Touch Up Inside* event for the `UIButton` is not associated with the `-displayHelloName:` action.

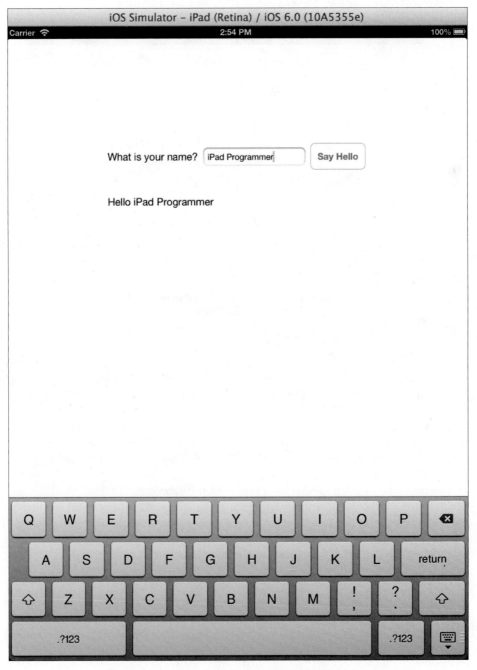

Figure 1.11   The new and improved Hello World app

Summary

Congratulations! You have completed your first iPad application—and you just got a sneak peek into iPad programming. This chapter should leave you itching to learn more. Before you dive into the meat of iPad programming, however, you need to learn more about the tools and programming language you will use. Let's begin by taking a closer look at Xcode in the next chapter.

Getting Started with Xcode

In Chapter 1, "Your First App," you used Xcode to create your first iPad application—but what is Xcode exactly?

Xcode is the combination of an Integrated Development Environment (IDE) and a collection of stand-alone development tools forming a complete developer tool set for Mac and iOS software development.

Xcode is the world you live in as you create and build your iPad apps. As you work on your apps, Xcode will become your friend. There will be times when the two of you get along nicely, but there will also be times when you disagree. You may even become annoyed with your new friend from time to time, but there's good news. As you spend more time together, you will get to know each other much better, and your friendship will grow. Who knows? You may even become BFFs (metaphorically speaking, of course).

Over more years than I care to count, I have used many different IDEs. When I first encountered Xcode—version 3 at the time—I thought I was stepping back in time. I thought, "It's a glorified text editor with some handy menu items and shortcuts for compiling projects." My opinion changed over time as I grew more accustomed to using Xcode day in and day out (and sometimes all night long). And with Xcode 4, things have only gotten better.

Xcode is simple, fast, and powerful, just like the applications you create with it for the Mac, iPhone, and iPad. An app appears simple on the surface, but its true power is exposed as you become better acquainted with the software. Xcode is no different. As you become more familiar with Xcode, you'll start seeing its real power and realize how it is more than just a glorified text editor.

This chapter helps jump-start your friendship with Xcode and helps you become better acquainted with this tool. Let's get started.

The IDE

Xcode is the developer tool most often used to create and build applications for the iPad. You use this complete IDE to write Objective-C code, manage project files and settings, and make builds of your iPad applications. You also debug your apps using Xcode, and you can even unit test your code with it. Xcode does all this and more.

Disclaimer

Obviously there is no way to talk about all things Xcode in a single chapter. Some topics are covered in later chapters (such as debugging in Chapter 26, "Debugging"), while other, more advanced topics (such as refactoring) are left out completely. This chapter is not intended to be a complete guide to Xcode but rather a starting point for becoming familiar with it.

The programming language of choice for most iPad applications is Objective-C, so it is only natural that Xcode provides outstanding support for Objective-C. But Xcode also supports other programming languages. After all, Xcode is used for programming duties other than writing iPad apps.

Xcode supports the C, C++, Objective-C, Objective-C++, Python, Ruby, Apple-Script, and Java programming languages. Xcode also supports, with the help of third parties, GNU Pascal, Free Pascal, Ada, C#, Perl, and a host of other languages. In addition, it does a reasonable job of supporting HTML and JavaScript.

Note

Despite Xcode's support for a number of programming languages, you are limited to C, C++, and (most commonly) Objective-C for writing iPad applications in Xcode. You cannot use the other languages, such as Java or Perl, for writing iPad applications. That doesn't mean you will not have a need for these other programming languages in Xcode. Many iPad developers use programming languages such as Python or Ruby to write scripts that aid in producing iPad applications. For example, I use Python scripts to make Ad Hoc and App Store distribution builds of my applications.

Workspace Window

Xcode can open a project or workspace. A workspace is an Xcode file type that stores references to one or more projects that are typically related to one another, although such a relationship is not required. When you open a project or workspace in Xcode, it is displayed in a workspace window.

The workspace window has five distinct areas, shown in Figure 2.1:

1. Toolbar area

2. Navigation area

3. Editor area

4. Utility area

5. Debug area

Toolbar Area

The toolbar is displayed at the top of the workspace window (Figure 2.2). It provides quick access to run and stop the app defined by the active scheme, change the active scheme and set the run destination (a device or the simulator), turn breakpoints on and off, change editors, show and hide the other areas (Navigation, Utility, and Debug),

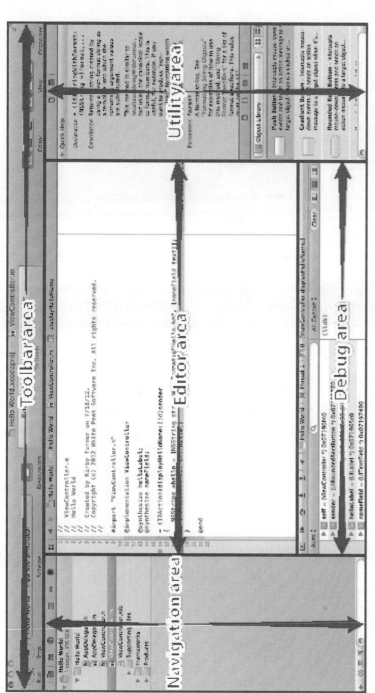

Figure 2.1   The workspace window and its areas

Figure 2.2   The workspace window toolbar

and display Organizer. The center of the toolbar displays the current status of the project (e.g., is running, finished running, build succeeded).

Navigation Area

The Navigation area is where you navigate through a project. A mini-toolbar at the top of this area gives you access to seven different navigators (Figure 2.3):

1. **Project navigator**: Displays the project files in a hierarchical tree. Use this navigator to open files within the project.

2. **Symbol navigator**: Provides a way to quickly navigate a project using local symbols such as classes and protocols that make up the application.

3. **Search navigator**: Performs project-wide find-and-replace queries.

4. **Issue navigator**: Shows compiler warnings and errors as well as live issues found as you edit code.

5. **Debug navigator**: Shows debug information by thread and by queue—a helpful feature when you are writing a multithreaded application.

6. **Breakpoint navigator**: Shows the breakpoints defined within the project. You can also manage (edit, enable/disable, delete, and so on) breakpoints from here.

7. **Log navigator**: Shows logs from current and past debug and build sessions.

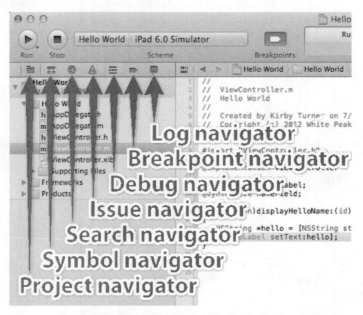

Figure 2.3   The workspace window's Navigation area

To switch between the navigators, you can use either the mini-toolbar found at the top of the Navigation area or **View > Navigators** from the menu. Shortcut keys are also available. Use **Command-1** for the Project navigator, **Command-2** for the Symbol, **Command-3** for the Search, and so forth through **Command-7**, which shows the Log navigator. You can also show and hide the Navigation area with **Command-0**.

At the bottom of the Navigation area is the filter bar. Use it to limit the scope of the items displayed within the navigator.

Editor Area

The Editor area, which is always visible, is where file editing occurs (Figure 2.4). The editor changes based on the file type. When you select, for example, a source code file (a *.h* or *.m*), the standard text editor is displayed. Select the project file, and the project editor appears. Select a NIB, and the UI designer Interface Builder becomes active.

At the top of the Editor area is a mini-toolbar. Its first button displays a popup menu of recently opened files and unsaved files. The next two buttons, go back (**Control-Command-Left**) and go forward (**Control-Command-Right**), enable you to navigate through your browsing history. The jump bar follows; it provides a quick way to jump between files and locations within the current file. Just click any part of the jump bar to display files and locations within files that you can jump to.

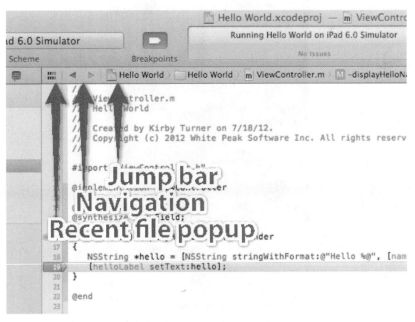

Figure 2.4   The workspace window's Editor area

Utility Area

The Utility area, which you can show and hide using **Option–Command–0**, displays different inspectors and libraries (Figure 2.5). The inspectors made available will vary based on the file type, but every file type has at least two inspectors—the File and

Figure 2.5   The workspace window's Utilities area split into
two subareas, Inspector area and Library area

Quick Help inspectors. To switch between inspectors, either click the icons in the mini-toolbar displayed at the top of the Utilities area or use the shortcut keys **Option-Command-1**, **Option-Command-2**, **Option-Command-3**, and so on for each mini-toolbar item.

Below the Inspector area is the Library area. It contains four libraries:

1. File Template library

2. Code Snippet library

3. Object library

4. Media library

You use the File Template library to create and add new files to the project. Drag and drop a file template into the project to create a new file based on the template.

The Code Snippet library contains a set of code snippets that can help speed up development. To use a code snippet, drag and drop it into the text editor. You can also create your own code snippets by dragging and dropping a block of code from the text editor into the Code Snippet library. To view the contents of a code snippet, click the snippet and wait a second or two. A popover will appear that shows the snippet's content. You can also edit snippets that you create from the popover.

Note

To learn more about Xcode code snippets and ways to create your own code snippets, read the article "Be More Productive in Xcode Using Code Snippets"[1] found on the informIT.com Web site.

The Object library is used by Interface Builder. It contains objects used to construct the user interface of your app. Depending on the object, you will drag and drop the object to the designer canvas, to the canvas of another object such as a view, or to the IB dock. (Using IB to create user interfaces is discussed in Chapter 3, "Getting Started with Interface Builder.")

The Media library displays the list of media (images and sounds) available in the project. Like the Object library, it is used by Interface Builder. In IB, you can drag and drop an image into your user interface. This will create a view to display the image. In addition, you can drag and drop an image on an object that can contain an image, such as a UIButton, to have that object display the image. Sounds work the same way: Drop a sound on a UIButton to assign the sound to the button.

A filter bar appears at the bottom of the Utilities area. It limits the number of items displayed in the selected library.

---

1. Be More Productive in Xcode Using Code Snippets: http://www.informit.com/articles/article.aspx?p=1914191

Figure 2.6   The workspace window's Debug area

Debug Area

You use the Debug area (**Shift-Command-Y** to show and hide it) debugging your app (Figure 2.6). Like the other areas discussed so far, it has a mini-toolbar at the top, which allows you to control the debugging session. From here you can pause the running app, step over a line of code, step into a line of code, and step out from a call. Below the mini-toolbar is the watch area for variables, and next to that is the console window.

> **Note**
>
> More information on the Debug area, as well as tips and how-to instructions for debugging, is provided in Chapter 26, "Debugging."

The Design of the Workspace Window

It might not be obvious, but the workspace window reflects a well-thought-out design. Understanding this design makes using the workspace window a bit easier.

The workspace window is designed to flow from left to right. Navigation begins on the left and drills down toward the right. This flow is seen most easily by clicking a file in the Project navigator, which comprises the leftmost area of the workspace window. When you click the file, its contents are displayed on the right in the editor.

This left-to-right flow goes deeper than just displaying the contents of a file. Take the project settings, for example. When you click the project file in the navigator, the project editor is displayed on the right. On the left side of the project editor is another navigator with which you can choose project or target settings. Click the project to see project-specific settings, or click a target to see the settings for the selected target.

This left-to-right design flow doesn't stop here. In some cases detail flows farther to the right through its display in the Utility area. With the project selected in the Project navigator, open the Utility area and then the File inspector (**Option-Command-1**) to see additional project settings not found in the project settings editor.

The same can be done for other project files. For instance, select a .h file in the Project navigator (on the left) and then look at the File inspector (on the right) for additional settings related to the file.

As you can now see, from a conceptual standpoint, navigating the workspace window starts on the left and moves to the right. Knowing this can be helpful when working within the workspace window. As a general rule, when looking for a certain piece of information, just continue looking toward the right while navigating from the left.

This left–right design applies, to some extent, to certain shortcut keys as well. Toggle the display of the Navigation area, which is displayed on the left, by pressing **Command-0**. Access the subareas within the Navigation area by pressing **Command-1**, **Command-2**, **Command-3**, and so on for each toolbar item.

The Utility area, which is displayed on the right, uses a similar pattern. Toggle the Utility area display by pressing **Option-Command-0**, and quickly access the Utility area toolbar items by pressing **Option-Command-1**, **Option-Command-2**, **Option-Command-3**, and so on.

You can think of this organization in terms of left versus right. Use **Command–[*some number*]** for quick access to the Project navigator and its items, which appear on the left side of the workspace window. Use **Option-Command–[*some number*]** to do the same with the Utility area, which appears on the right side of the workspace window. In other words, **Command-#** for the left side and **Option-Command-#** for the right side.

Preferences

Xcode can be customized to your liking. The Xcode Preferences (**Xcode > Preferences** or **Command-,**) has a long list of options that you can set to fine-tune the appearance and behavior of Xcode. Developers new to Xcode will find the default preference settings suitable for day-to-day work. The exception, however, might be the display of the text editor. Programmers are a picky bunch who tend to prefer a certain look and feel in the text editors they use, so it should come as no surprise that you can customize the look of the text editor used in Xcode.

Fonts and Colors

For starters, you can change the fonts and colors used by the text editor (Figure 2.7). Xcode provides a list of predefined themes that you can select from, or you can add your own theme by duplicating an existing theme or creating a new theme from one of the available templates.

> **Note**
>
> Xcode includes the Presentation theme in Fonts & Colors. This theme uses a larger font size that is ideal for display on a projector. If you ever find yourself giving a presentation at a meeting or a conference and you need to show off some code, you will definitely want to use the Presentation theme. It will help ensure that everyone in the room—including the people sitting in the back—can see your source code.

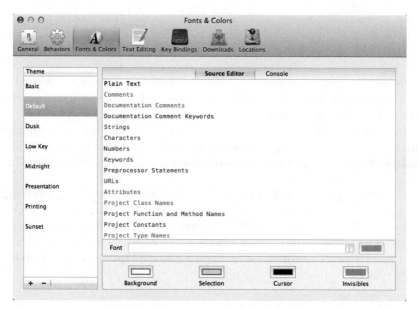

Figure 2.7   Fonts & Colors preferences

Text Editing

Fonts and colors are not the only changes you can make to the text editor. Other customizations for the text editor are available under Text Editing. Select Editing in the Text Editing preferences (shown in Figure 2.8) to show or hide line numbers, set the page guide column position, and turn the code folding ribbon (also known as the focus ribbon) on and off. Figure 2.9 provides an example of what the text editor looks like with these settings turned on. You can also change code completion behavior and configure how the text editor will handle things such as end of line and file encoding.

The fun with text editor changes doesn't end here. An Indentation preferences option is also available for the Text Editing preferences, as seen in Figure 2.10. Here you can control behaviors such as using spaces in place of tabs, enabling line wrapping, and using syntax-aware indenting.

What Is Code Folding?

Code folding is a feature that allows you to selectively show and hide blocks of code. It's a handy way to manage large source code files. You can think of code folding as a way to expand and collapse blocks of code in much the same way you expand and collapse an outline.

The introduction of code folding into Xcode allowed the Xcode development team to include other useful features built around the code folding feature. One such useful feature is code focus, which shows the scope depth of a particular block of code. A high-level view of the scope depth can be seen in the code folding ribbon (also known as the focus ribbon) displayed in the gutter. To view the scope depth within the text editor, simply mouse over the code folding ribbon.

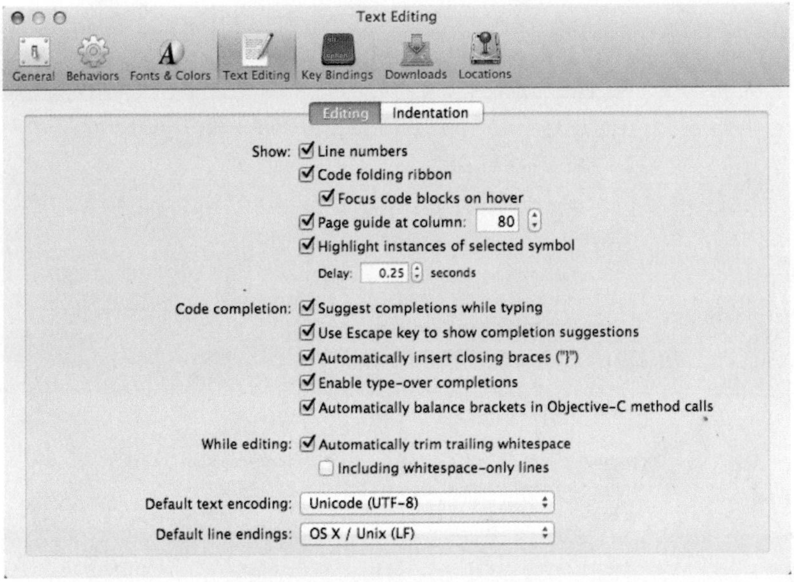

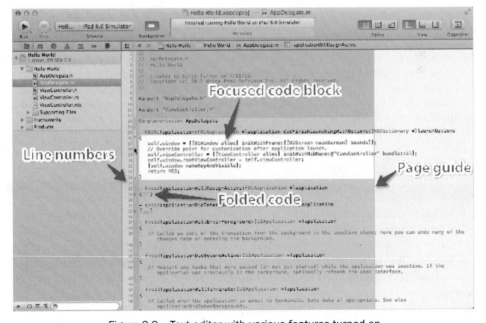

Figure 2.8   Text Editing preferences

Figure 2.9   Text editor with various features turned on

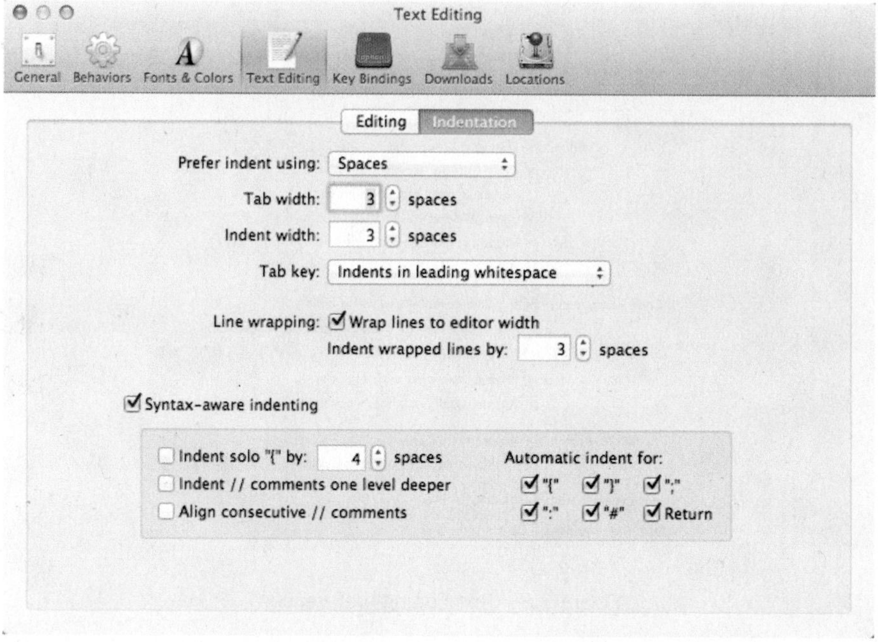

Figure 2.10   Text Editing Indentation preferences

> **Note**
>
> Having the tab key insert spaces is one of the first settings I make with any text editor, so it's no surprise that I do the same with Xcode. I prefer spaces over tabs for the simple reason that with spaces you know how indented code looks regardless of the program used to display it. Although Xcode allows you to specify the tab width, not all applications do, and in many applications the tab width defaults to eight spaces. This can make your code look ugly when a tab character is used instead of spaces and the source code is displayed in another application, such as a Web browser or an email message.

Line Wrapping

Line wrapping is an interesting setting. I originally did not use this setting, which is turned off by default, because I assumed it worked the same way as word wrapping in other text editors. A friend encouraged me to turn it on, and I haven't turned it off since.

Xcode's wrapping doesn't wrap the line to the first column of the next line. Instead, the wrapped line is indented under the starting line, as seen in Figure 2.11. Also, you can use the Text Editing preferences to configure the number of spaces for wrapped line indention. Using line wrapping with indentions keeps the structure and readability of your code intact, which is something I like.

```
13   @implementation AppDelegate
14
15   - (BOOL)application:(UIApplication *)application didFinishLaunchingWithOptions:
         (NSDictionary *)launchOptions
16   {
17       self.window = [[UIWindow alloc] initWithFrame:[[UIScreen mainScreen] bounds]];
18       // Override point for customization after application launch.
19       self.viewController = [[ViewController alloc] initWithNibName:@"ViewController"
            bundle:nil];
20       self.window.rootViewController = self.viewController;
21       [self.window makeKeyAndVisible];
22       return YES;
23   }
24
25   - (void)applicationWillResignActive:(UIApplication *)application
26   {
27       // Sent when the application is about to move from active to inactive state. This can
            occur for certain types of temporary interruptions (such as an incoming phone call
            or SMS message) or when the user quits the application and it begins the
            transition to the background state.
28       // Use this method to pause ongoing tasks, disable timers, and throttle down OpenGL
            ES frame rates. Games should use this method to pause the game.
29   }
30
31   - (void)applicationDidEnterBackground:(UIApplication *)application
32   {
```

Figure 2.11   Example of line wrapping. Lines 15, 19, 27, and 28 are wrapped.

Coding Styles

When you start changing the behavior of a text editor with settings such as spaces instead of tabs, indentions of three characters instead of four, and so on, you start forming your own coding style. Sticking to a coding style can be important, especially if you work on a team with other developers. There is nothing more annoying than seeing multiple coding styles within a project. A standard, consistent coding style within a project makes the code easier to read and maintain.

Selecting a coding style is often a matter of personal preference. A developer who works alone will typically have his or her own style. Convincing that developer to change styles can be a tough battle—and there may be times when *you* are the developer who must change to conform to the coding style of the team.

If you are reading this book, you are likely new to iPad and Objective-C programming; if so, now is a good time to learn a coding style. You can start by bringing over elements of style from past experience, or you can learn from the coding styles of others. Here are three guidelines for coding styles that you may find helpful:

- *Google Objective-C Style Guide*[2]
- *Zarra Studios Coding Style Guide*[3]
- *WebKit Coding Style Guidelines*[4]

2. Google Objective-C Style Guide: http://google-styleguide.googlecode.com/svn/trunk/objcguide.xml
3. Zarra Studios Coding Style Guide: http://www.cimgf.com/zds-code-style-guide/
4. WebKit Coding Style Guidelines: http://www.webkit.org/coding/coding-style.html

Key Bindings Preferences

Now that you have configured Xcode to your liking, it's time to get more productive with Xcode by using shortcut keys. Shortcut keys save you time by allowing you to execute some action by simply pressing a combination of keys. For instance, pressing **Command-S** to save changes to a file is faster than moving your hand to the mouse, moving the mouse cursor to the menu bar, clicking the File menu item, and finally clicking the Save menu item.

Xcode comes with a long list of shortcut keys, which Xcode calls *key bindings*. As you might expect, Xcode allows you to select from a list of predefined key bindings, change existing key bindings, and create new key bindings of your own. These options are found in the Key Bindings preferences, shown in Figure 2.12.

The hardest part about becoming more productive using shortcut keys is remembering the long list of key combinations. One recommended technique is to learn at least one new shortcut key per week. If you find yourself repeating the same action, review the Key Bindings preferences to see if a shortcut key exists. If no shortcut key exists, add one. Make a point to use the shortcut key throughout the week until it is ingrained in your brain. It's not a perfect process, and you will find yourself relearning and re-remembering the same helpful but less-frequently-used shortcut keys all the time. Even so, the more shortcut keys you can learn, the more productive you will be using Xcode.

Table 2.1 shows some of the commonly used shortcut keys.

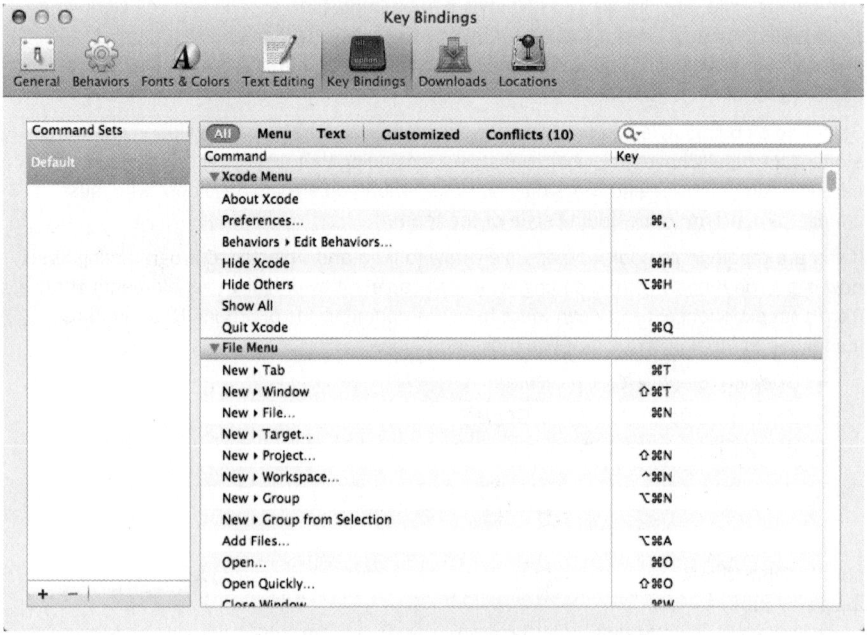

Figure 2.12   Key Bindings preferences

Table 2.1   Essential Keyboard Shortcuts for Xcode

Shortcut	Description
Control-Command-Up and Control-Command-Down	Switches between the *.h* and *.m* files
Control-Command-Left	Moves to the previous file in the File History
Control-Command-Right	Moves to the next file in the File History
Escape	Displays the list of available code completions
Command-/	Inserts comments and comment/uncomment blocks of selected lines
Command-0	Shows and hides the Navigation area
Option-Command-0	Shows and hides the Utilities area
Shift-Command-Y	Shows and hides the Debug area
Command-[	Indents the current line or selected lines
Command-]	Unindents the current line or selected lines
Control-I	Formats the selected block of code
Option-Command-Left	Folds code
Option-Command-Right	Unfolds code
Command-S	Saves the current file
Option-Command-S	Saves all modified files
Command-B	Builds the project
Shift-Command-K	Cleans the project
Command-R	Runs the app (and builds it if needed)
Command-`	Switches between different Xcode windows

Colin Wheeler's Xcode Shortcut List

Colin Wheeler, also known as Cocoa Samurai,[5] has compiled a list of Xcode shortcut keys and published it in a free PDF document.[6] Sure, you can view the same list in Xcode's Key Bindings preferences, but it's a pain compared to Colin's outstanding list.

Colin publishes two versions: one in color and the other in black and white. I highly recommend downloading his shortcut list. Then print it out and tape it somewhere near your monitor for use as a quick-and-easy reference. I keep a copy taped on the wall between my MacBook Pro and my external monitor.

---

5. Cocoa Samurai: http://www.cocoasamurai.com
6. Xcode keyboard shortcut: http://cocoasamurai.blogspot.com/2011/03/xcode-4-keyboard -shortcuts-now.html

Code Completion

Code completion is a standard feature in any modern-day IDE. It helps speed development by displaying a popup list of possible code fragments to insert into your source code. Xcode's code completion determines the possible code bits after you type only a couple of characters and wait briefly. You can also display the popup list by pressing **Escape** or **Control-.**. Press the **Enter** key to select the appropriate completion code from the list.

> **Note**
> Preference settings for code completion are found under the Editing section of the Text Editing preferences.

A really cool feature of code completion is *placeholders*. A placeholder is inserted as a parameter on a method call, as shown in Figure 2.13. The placeholder displays the data type and parameter name, making it easier to determine what is needed to satisfy the call. To speed up the development process even further, press **Control-/** to move from one placeholder to another or press **Tab** to move to the next placeholder and **Shift-Tab** to move to the previous one.

More Ways to Be Really Productive

Shortcut keys and code completion are just two options that make you more productive in Xcode. A variety of third-party add-ons can also extend and enhance your productivity. Here are two very popular tools:

Code Pilot[7] is a favorite of many Xcoders. Code Pilot makes project navigation easier. If you are a keyboard junkie like me, you owe it to yourself to try out Code Pilot.

Accessorizer[8] is my personal favorite. It saves time during app development by generating boilerplate code for you. For instance, you can use Accessorizer to generate the @synthesize code for declared properties and to generate accessor methods using a number of different design approaches. Accessorizer can do a lot more for you as well. If you want to save time while writing code in Xcode, there is no better add-on tool than Accessorizer.

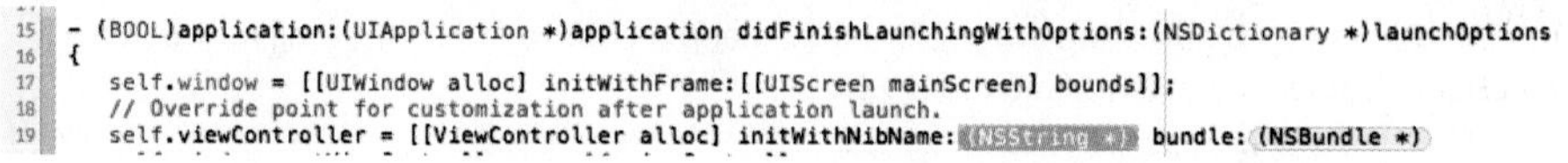

```
15  - (BOOL)application:(UIApplication *)application didFinishLaunchingWithOptions:(NSDictionary *)launchOptions
16  {
17      self.window = [[UIWindow alloc] initWithFrame:[[UIScreen mainScreen] bounds]];
18      // Override point for customization after application launch.
19      self.viewController = [[ViewController alloc] initWithNibName:(NSString *) bundle:(NSBundle *)
```

Figure 2.13   Placeholders for the -initWithNibName:bundle: method on line 19

7. Code Pilot: http://codepilot.cc
8. Accessorizer: http://www.kevincallahan.org/software/accessorizer.html

Developer Documentation

Apple provides a great deal of really useful documentation with Xcode. The developer documentation, which is available from the menu bar by selecting **Help > Documentation and API Reference**, includes all the information you need to do iPad programming, from well-written programming guides, to API documentation, to sample source code. The only negative mark on the documentation is its size. The amount of documentation is enormous, consisting of tens of thousands of pages. For instance, the UIKit Framework document has nearly 1,100 pages devoted to it, and it is just one of the many frameworks used for application development. Combine the documentation for various frameworks, how-to guides, code samples, and other general and overview documentation included in the developer documentation, and you can easily become overwhelmed. Given the sheer size of the documentation, you might imagine that it can sometimes be a challenge to find precisely the information you need. That's where books like this one help, by consolidating the wealth of knowledge from Apple into a condensed guide.

Even so, referring to the official Apple developer documentation is sometimes essential, and Xcode does a great job of helping you find the documentation you need. For instance, you can **Option-click** a class or method name to display a Quick Help popup, as seen in Figure 2.14. You can also view the Help by opening the Quick Help inspector (**Option-Command-2**). The Quick Help inspector shows context-aware help based on position of the text cursor within the editor.

Figure 2.14   Example of the Quick Help popup and Quick Help inspector

Figure 2.15   The Standard editor displaying the text editor

Editors

Xcode provides three different editors:

1. Standard editor

2. Assistant editor

3. Version editor

They are not really editors per se, but rather modes of an editor.

Standard Editor

The Standard editor is your main editor (Figure 2.15). You use this editor to edit source code, design a user interface, or create a data model. The editor changes based on the file type of the selected file. For instance, when you are editing source code, the Standard editor displays the text editor. When you are editing a user interface file (NIB or storyboard), Interface Builder is displayed. If you select the project file in the Project navigator, the Standard editor displays the project editor.

Assistant Editor

The Assistant editor provides a split view editor (Figure 2.16), which allows you to view and edit different parts of the same file or different files at the same time. The Assistant editor is a handy way to view the *.h* and *.m* files of a class side by side. In fact, the Assistant editor will automatically display the counterpart file for you. When you have

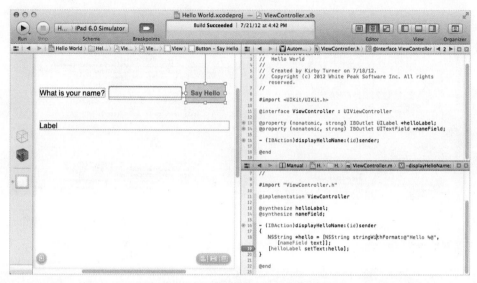

Figure 2.16   The Assistant editor displaying IB in one window and a text editor
in another two windows

the Assistant editor open and you select a *.h* file, the Assistant automatically displays the
corresponding *.m* file in the second editor window. You can also manually open another
file in the Assistant editor by using the jump bar at the top of the editor window. In
addition, you can open more than one Assistant editor to view more than two files at the
same time—just click the **+** button on the Assistant editor's mini-toolbar.

The Assistant editor not only displays the counterpart of a file or another file that
you have manually selected, but it can display other very useful information as well,
such as the callers and callees of a method. To tell the Assistant editor to display other
related files, you click the first segment of the Assistant editor's jump bar and then
select the related file you wish to view. Figure 2.17 provides an example.

Figure 2.17   Use the Assistant editor's jump bar to select and
display the related file to view

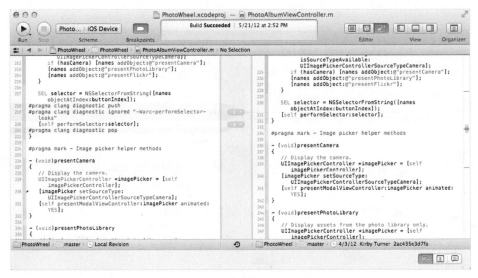

Figure 2.18   The Version editor

Version Editor

The third editor mode is the Version editor (Figure 2.18), which lets you compare a revision to another version of the same file. You can use Xcode's snapshot feature to keep a history of changes, but a better approach is to use a source code repository. Xcode supports Git and Subversion. Using a source code repository makes the Version editor even more useful, allowing you not only to compare revisions, but also to view the blame and log for the file. Use the icon bar found in the lower-right corner of the Version editor to switch between the revisions, blame, and log views.

Project Settings

When you select a project file in the Project navigator, the project settings editor becomes active (Figure 2.19). Here you can set various options for the project and targets belonging to the project.

Two types of settings for a project are available: Info and Build Settings. Info lets you set basic preferences for the project, including the iOS deployment target, base configuration files for the build types (debug, release, and so on), and the default build configuration for command-line builds. Build Settings enables you to fine-tune the build process. The number of Build Settings options is too large to cover in this chapter, or even in this book. Luckily, the default settings work for most iOS projects, so covering them here is not necessary.

Project settings represent the base settings for each target created by the project. A target is the artifact created by a build process. For example, the iPad app created when you build a project is a target. A project has one or more targets, and each target has its own set of settings. The target settings are derived from the project settings. In other

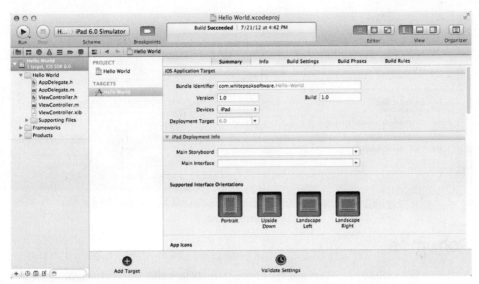

Figure 2.19   The project settings editor

words, the project settings represent the base, or default, settings across all targets, and the target settings contain nondefault settings that are unique to the particular target.

As someone new to Xcode and iPad programming, you do not need to worry about project and target settings yet. The default settings are fine for the sample apps presented in this book and most apps that you initially create. You'll start making changes to the settings only when you want to do more advanced work, such as supporting earlier versions of iOS or using a different compiler.

Setting the Organization Name

One particular project setting does not appear in the project settings: the organization name. The organization name constitutes part of the copyright notice generated in the top comment block when you create a new source file, as shown in Figure 2.20. If you find you are working on different projects for different companies (as a freelancer, contractor, or consultant), you may want to use a different organization name for each project.

Perform these steps to change the organization name for a project:

1. Select the project file in the Project navigator.

2. Open the File inspector in the Utilities area (**Option-Command-1**).

3. Type in the name in the Organization field found in the Project Document section (Figure 2.20).

That's it. The new organization name will be used when you create new source files. Changing the organization name does not change the name used in the commented copyright notice found in previously created source files. You must either manually change those names or use Find and Replace to substitute another name.

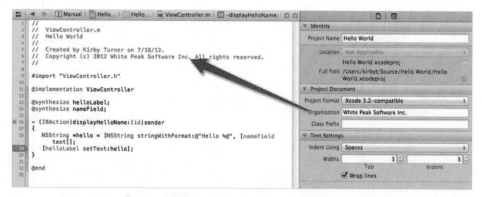

Figure 2.20   Set the organization name in the File inspector for
the project file

Schemes

A scheme is a collection of settings specifying targets to build, build configurations to use, unit tests to execute, and run destinations to use when a target is launched. Xcode creates a default scheme for you when a new project is created. For iOS projects, the default scheme has two run destinations: devices and simulator.

You can create as many schemes as you want, or edit and delete existing schemes from the manage schemes screen (**Product > Manage Schemes...**), shown in Figure 2.21. Note that when a scheme is created, it is intended for personal use only. If you are working on a project as part of a team, other team members will not see the schemes you create. Only shared schemes can be used by all team members. To share a scheme, mark the Shared check box for the scheme in the manage schemes window.

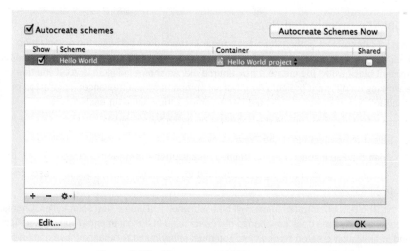

Figure 2.21   The manage schemes window

Figure 2.22   The Scheme popup menu found in the workspace window toolbar

You can change the active scheme and run destination by using the Scheme popup found in the upper-left corner of the project window (see Figure 2.22). You can also edit the scheme, create a new one, and manage all the schemes from the popup menu.

Organizer

Organizer, shown in Figure 2.23, is a project-independent window available in Xcode (**Shift-Command-2** or **Window > Organizer**). You use it to manage your devices, add and remove source code repositories, view project cache areas and snapshots, access product archives, and view developer documentation.

One of the really nice things about Organizer is its device management. Here you can view and add developer and distribution provisioning profiles. You can manage copies of earlier iOS software releases. The feature that many developers find most useful, however, is the ability to view the crash logs found on devices.

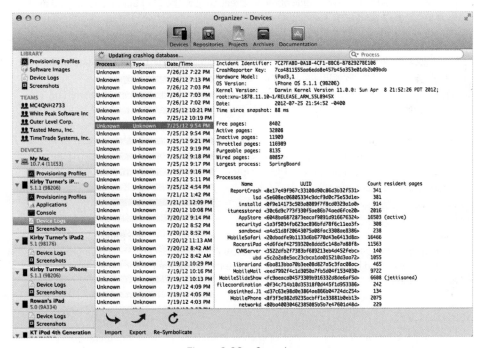

Figure 2.23   Organizer

If you connect a device to your computer, Organizer will detect it. Once the device is connected, you can view the crash logs stored on your device (found under Device Logs). Not only can you see the crash logs for your app, but you can view the logs from any app on the device. This capability can be helpful if you want to report a crash to a fellow iOS developer. You can also view, using Organizer, the console for an attached device—a helpful step when you are troubleshooting an app that is running on the device.

Other Xcode Tools

As mentioned earlier, Xcode is much more than just an IDE; it is also a collection of developer tools provided by Apple. So far we have talked about only Xcode the IDE, but what are some of the other developer tools included in Xcode?

The iPad Simulator, which you used in Chapter 1, "Your First App," is one of the Xcode tools that you will use most frequently. The iPad Simulator allows you to test your iPad application from your computer without using a physical iPad device. While there is no substitute for running your application on a real device, there is no faster way to debug your app than with the iPad Simulator.

Note

The iPad Simulator does an incredible job of simulating the iPad device, but at the end of the day you still need to test your application on a real device. The iPad Simulator, as good as it is, is just that—a *simulator*. Consequently, it may sometimes behave differently from a real device. There are also limitations on what you can test using the simulator. For example, you cannot test the accelerometer in the iPad Simulator; for that, you need a real device. The same goes for testing OpenGL ES code, which tends to run faster on your desktop or laptop (thanks to a faster processor and loads more RAM) than on an iOS device.

A general rule of thumb: Always test your application on a iOS device before submitting it to Apple or distributing it to users.

Instruments is another invaluable tool included with Xcode. With Instruments, you can create a profile of your application to find memory leaks, determine memory usage, monitor activity, and take CPU samples. You will learn more about Instruments in Chapter 26, "Debugging."

Note

A great way to learn more about profiling and performance-tuning your application is to read the *Instruments User Guide*,[9] available in the iOS Developer Library. This guide provides everything you need to know to trace and analyze the performance and behavior of your iOS and Mac apps.

---

9. Instruments User Guide: https://developer.apple.com/library/ios/#documentation/ DeveloperTools/Conceptual/InstrumentsUserGuide/Introduction/Introduction.html#// apple_ref/doc/uid/TP40004652

Summary

Clearly, Xcode is more than a fancy text editor; it encompasses a collection of developer tools that you use to build applications for the Mac, the iPhone, and, of course, the iPad. Some of the tools are built into Xcode's IDE (i.e., text editing, Interface Builder, project file management, build, and debugging), while other tools are separate, stand-alone applications (i.e., iOS Simulator and Instruments). This combination of developer tools gives Xcode its remarkable power.

This chapter highlighted the areas of Xcode that new iPad programmers are likely to find most useful. A lot of details are missing, as are advanced features, such as refactoring. To cover everything provided by Xcode would take an entire book. That's why it is strongly recommended that you read through the *Xcode User Guide* (**Help > Xcode User Guide** from the Xcode menu bar), which covers Xcode in more detail.

Meanwhile, do not worry if you do use all of the features of Xcode on day one. Learning a new development environment takes time.

That said, one particular tool of Xcode deserves more attention: Interface Builder, the built-in user interface design tool. It is the subject of its own chapter, Chapter 3, "Getting Started with Interface Builder."

3

Get Started with Interface Builder

All iPad applications have one thing in common: Each has a user interface. The user interface will differ across the apps, but you can count on each app having one. You can create the user interface for your app in either of two ways: You can write Objective-C code or use Interface Builder. Interface Builder (IB) is the better, easier approach, which is why this chapter teaches you all you need to know to get started with IB.

Interface Builder

IB is built into Xcode. As its name implies, IB is a graphical tool for building user interfaces. While everything you do in IB can be done in code, IB helps you do it faster and with fewer bugs.

You may find IB different from the user interface (UI) designers you have used in the past, with the biggest difference being that IB is not a source code generator. That is, it does not generate source code to construct the user interface, nor does it generate source code for event handling.

Source code generation is a common approach used in other graphical user interface (GUI)-based programming environments. This omission can be confusing when you first encounter Xcode. For instance, suppose you want to display a button on a screen and have that button perform some action. With other UI designers, you drop a button into a design canvas and then double-click the button to jump to the event handler for the button. The designer generates the event handler shell code when you double-click the button. This, of course, does not happen with IB.

> **Note**
>
> I say, "IB doesn't generate code," but that's not exactly true. You will learn later in this chapter that you can force Xcode to generate code by using IB with the Assistant editor.

Conceptually, IB is the same as other UI designers found in other programming environments, but the magic under the hood is what makes IB different. With IB, you drag and drop objects from a palette, called Library, onto a canvas, such as a view. IB then creates an instance of the object. For example, suppose you drag and drop a `UIButton`. An instance of `UIButton` is created. At this point, you can set the properties, or state, of the button.

When IB saves your work, it archives the object instances to a NIB file. The archiving process saves the object and its state. When an application uses the NIB at run time, the object is unarchived and the object instances are connected to the NIB's owner, which is commonly a view controller.

> **Note**
>
> The concept of archiving and unarchiving an object instance is known as serializing and deserializing in other programming environments. IB's approach to archiving and unarchiving UI objects might seem familiar to those developers coming from Delphi and C++ Builder, as those programming environments use a similar approach. Think of a *.xib* file as being the same as a *.dfm* file.

How Does IB Work?

Understanding how IB works is one of the biggest challenges faced by new iOS developers. I know this because I spent countless frustrating hours trying to design user interfaces that behaved the way I wanted, only to abandon IB in favor of doing it all in code. What I didn't realize at the time was how much harder I was making it for myself. I also ended up writing more code than necessary, which I had to support. Simple changes to the UI were no longer simple because I had to dig through lines of Objective-C code instead of applying the changes in IB.

How does IB work? For starters, it stores information about the user interface and its supporting objects in a NIB file. The name NIB is a carryover from the NeXT days. Older versions of IB stored the user interface data in a binary-formatted file with the *.nib* extension, but this has since changed. Today IB stores the data in an XML-formatted file. Because the data format has changed, Apple decided to change the file extension for NIB files; the new extension is *.xib*.

When IB saves a NIB file, it archives the objects contained in the NIB. All state information for the objects is saved when they are archived. When an application loads the NIB file, the objects are unarchived and object instances are connected to your code. In Objective-C code, you give IB hints—in the form of `IBOutlet` and `IBAction`—about how to connect the object instance to your code. `IBOutlet` connects an ivar or declared property defined in your code to an object instance in the NIB, and `IBAction` connects a method defined in your class code to events called by objects in the NIB.

Note

Ivar is short for "instance variable." An instance variable is a variable defined as part of an Objective-C class that is available to instances of the class. See Chapter 4, "Getting Started with Objective-C," for more details on ivars.

Admittedly, this can become confusing. You define a property in your class—say, a UILabel, to display some text message. You create an instance of UILabel in IB, and then set its position, font, text color, and other state. You then connect the UILabel to the declared property using IB. This seems counterproductive, even error prone, but it is faster in practice than it sounds. Also, Apple is constantly improving Xcode and IB, and the process is getting better all the time.

Note

Interface Builder has been around since 1988, and it was one of the first applications of its kind to allow the developer to draw interface objects such as buttons, labels, menus, and windows directly in an interface using a mouse. Check out the Interface Builder page at Wikipedia to learn more about the history of IB.[1]

Getting Hands-On Practice with IB

IB has many useful features. The best way to explore these features is with hands-on practice. Let's begin by creating a new iPad project in Xcode. This time around the steps are provided for creating a new project but not as many screen shots. Revisit Chapter 1, "Your First App," if you want to see screen shots of each step.

Okay, let's get started.

1. Launch Xcode.
2. Create a new project (**File > New Project** or **Shift-Command-N**).
3. Select the Single View Application template (Figure 3.1).
4. Click the **Next** button.
5. Enter "IBPlayground" as the product name and class prefix.
6. Select iPad for the device family.
7. Uncheck Use Storyboards.
8. Leave the other options as is and click the **Next** button.
9. Save the project to the source directory of your choosing.
10. Build and run (**Command-R**) the app. You will see a blank application running in the iPad Simulator.
11. Exit the app and return to Xcode.

---

1. Brief history of Interface Builder: http://en.wikipedia.org/wiki/Interface_Builder

Now have some fun playing with IB. In the Project navigator, find and select the file *IBPlaygroundViewController.xib*. Doing so will open and display the file in IB, which is displayed in the Standard editor (Figure 3.2).

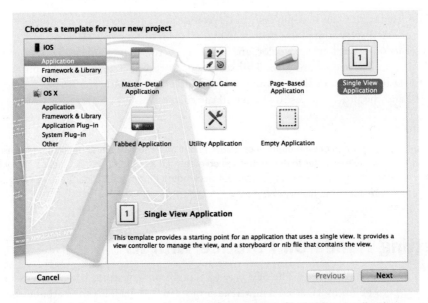

Figure 3.1   Create a new Xcode project using the Single View Application template for the iPad.

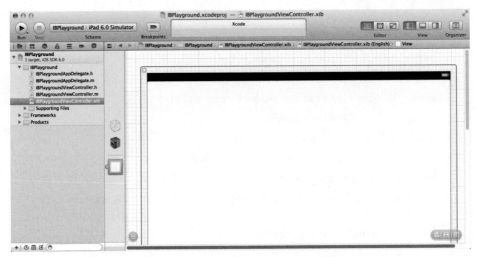

Figure 3.2   Select the file *IBPlaygroundViewController.xib* to display it in IB under the Standard editor.

To help you focus on IB, press **Command-0** to hide the Navigation area and press **Option-Command-0** to show the Utilities area. Finally, press **Control-Option-Command-3** to show the Object library. The workspace window should look like Figure 3.3. You already know about the Utilities area, which was covered in Chapter 2, "Getting Started with Xcode," but you may not be as familiar with IB as it is displayed in the Standard editor.

To the far left is the IB dock. The dock shows icons for the objects that make up the user interface. The main content area is the design canvas. Grid lines decorate the designer canvas. The canvas has one visible object in it, a view, which is of type UIView. Toward the lower-left corner is a round disclosure indicator. Click it to switch between the IB dock and the Document Outline area (Figure 3.4). You can also switch between the two by selecting the **Editor > Show (Hide) Document Outline** menu item.

The NIB should now be open in IB. Add two labels to the view so that you have something to play with. To accomplish this, scroll through the list of objects in the Object library and look for the label object. If scrolling isn't your thing, you can use the filter box to find the label for you. The filter box is at the bottom of the Library area. Keyboard junkies can press **Option-Command-L** to jump to the filter box.

Type the word "label" to filter the list of available objects. You can also filter the list by entering the class name, UILabel. Now drag and drop a label object from the Library window to the view window. While you are at it, drag a second label object to the view window so that the view looks similar to Figure 3.5.

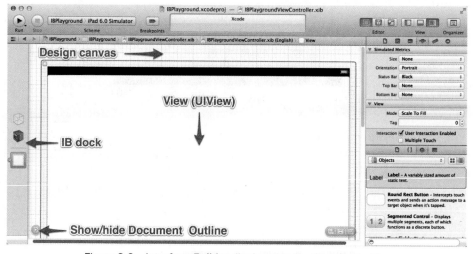

Figure 3.3   Interface Builder displayed in the Standard editor

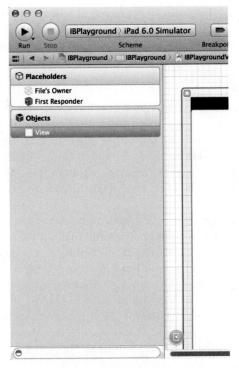

Figure 3.4   The workspace window with the document outline showing
instead of the IB dock

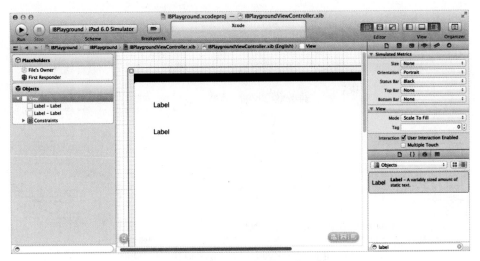

Figure 3.5   Add two labels to the view.

Selecting and Copying Objects

Dragging and dropping two labels from the Library window isn't the only way to place these two items on the view. You can copy an object in the view by clicking and dragging the object while holding down the **Option** key. This creates a copy of the selected object.

> **Note**
> To delete an object from a view, select the object and press the **Delete** key.

You can use this trick to copy more than one object as well. Simply select multiple objects within the view, **Option-click**, and drag—and now you have copies of the selected objects. To select multiple objects, use your mouse, click and drag on the view (which draws a box on the screen), and then box off the objects to select. Alternatively, you can mouse-click an object to select it, and then mouse-click the additional objects while holding down **Command** key.

Neat trick, eh? And it gets even better.

Aligning Objects

Click and drag a label, moving it to the right of another label. IB displays alignment guides for you, and you can use these vertical and horizontal guides to achieve the desired alignment. You can also align two or more objects by selecting **Editor > Align** and choosing from the list of available alignment options (Figure 3.6).

For additional help with aligning and positioning objects, add one or more vertical (**Editor > Add Vertical Guide**, or **Command-|**) and horizontal (**Editor > Add Horizontal Guide**, or **Command-_**) guides, seen in Figure 3.7. You place these guides at specific locations within the view by sliding the guide up and down or left and right using the mouse. To do so, position the mouse cursor over the guide. When

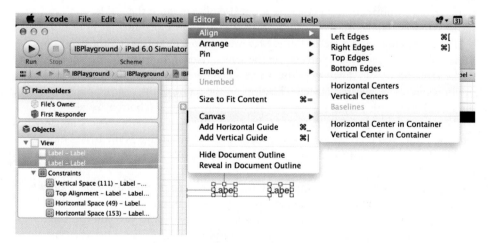

Figure 3.6   **Editor > Align** lists additional alignment options.

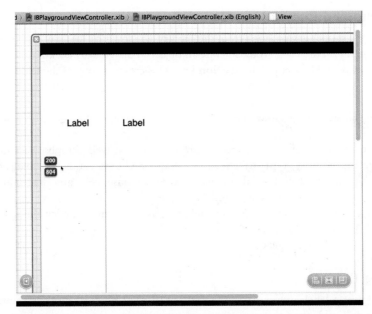

Figure 3.7   Example of the horizontal and vertical guides. Note the point
location of the horizontal guide. This is displayed as you move the guide.

the mouse cursor changes to the resize cursor, mouse-click the guide and move the
mouse up and down for horizontal guides and left and right for vertical guides.

As you move a guide, you will notice two numbers displayed. These numbers
represent the distance between the guide and the edge of the view. For instance, a
horizontal guide displays the distance between the guide and the top edge of the view
as the top number. The distance to the bottom of the view is displayed as the bottom
number. This information supports more precise placement of the guide.

To remove a guide, drag the guide off the view. Poof! Gone in a puff of smoke!

The positioning guides are one of my favorite alignment features. They help you
achieve precise positioning of objects on the screen. Here's how to do it. Select an object
in the view. Now hold down the **Option** key, making sure the mouse cursor is not
positioned over the selected object. This displays the frame of the selected object and the
distances between the object's frame and the top, left, right, and bottom edges of the
container view, as seen in Figure 3.8. Use the arrow keys to move the object up, down,
left, and right. You'll notice that the distances to the edge change as the object moves.

This, however, is not the only reason positioning guides are a favorite alignment
feature.

Continue to hold down the **Option** key and move the mouse cursor over another
object in the view. The guide changes to show you the distance between the selected
object and the object under the mouse cursor (Figure 3.9). And yes, you can use the
arrow keys to move the selected object while displaying the distance between the two
objects. How awesome is that!

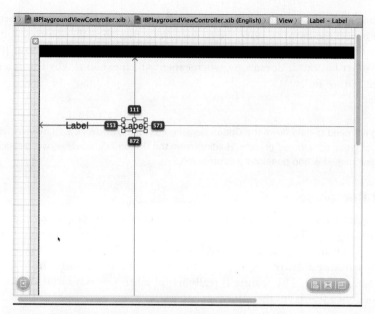

Figure 3.8   Select an object and then hold down the **Option** key to get position information about the object.

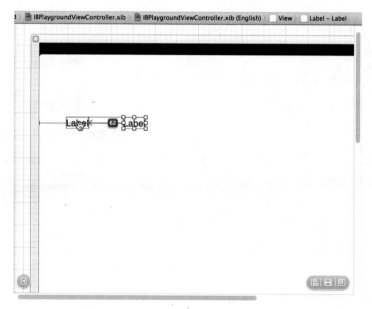

Figure 3.9   Select an object and then mouse over another object. Hold down the **Option** key to see the distance between the two objects.

Ever had a request to place two buttons on the screen exactly 10 pixels apart? To do so, select one of the buttons, place the mouse cursor over the other button, and hold down the **Option** key. Now use the arrow keys to move the selected button 10 pixels from the other button. It doesn't get much easier, which explains why this is a favorite alignment feature in IB.

> **Note**
>
> You do not need to hold down the **Option** key when using the arrow keys to move a selected object or group of selected objects. Holding down the **Option** key, however, will display the really useful guides and positioning information.

Layout Rectangle

While playing with the position guides, did you notice the rectangle that surrounded the selected object? This rectangle is handy for seeing the layout of an object, especially for objects that do not have visual borders. You can turn on this feature for all objects by selecting **Editor > Canvas > Show Layout Rectangles** from the menu, as seen in Figure 3.10. This feature is really useful when you want to make sure one object does not overlap another object.

> **Note**
>
> You can also show the bounds rectangle (**Editor > Canvas > Show Bounds Rectangles**) if the size of an object is all that interests you.

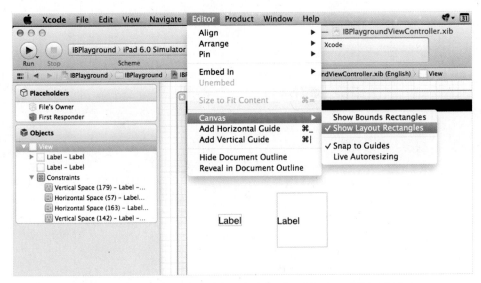

Figure 3.10   Layout Rectangles enabled. Notice that one of the labels has a larger frame than the others. You would not be able to see this with Layout Rectangles turned off.

Inspectors

You can view and edit an object's state information by using one of the inspectors found in the Inspector area within the Utilities area. From setting the font size for text to explicitly stating the object's position, these inspectors give you fine-grained control over the object's state.

Recall from Chapter 2, "Getting Started with Xcode," that the Inspector area comes equipped with the File and Quick Help inspectors. Four additional inspectors are available when you're using IB: Identity (**Option-Command-3**), Attributes (**Option-Command-4**), Size (**Option-Command-5**), and Connection (**Option-Command-6**).

Identity Inspector

The Identity inspector (Figure 3.11) is where you specify the class name for the object. The class name is one of the classes from the Cocoa Touch Framework or a custom class created within your Xcode project. You also set the accessibility settings for the object in the Identity inspector. Enabling Accessibility makes it possible for visually impaired individuals to use your application.

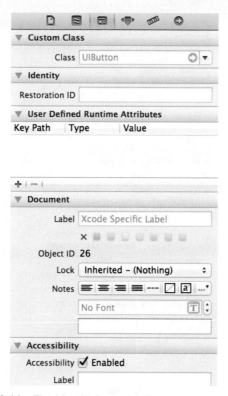

Figure 3.11   The Identity inspector for a `UIButton` object

Attributes Inspector

The Attributes inspector is where you set the property values, or attribute values, for the selected object (Figure 3.12). The list of attributes will vary based on the object type. Examples of attributes include content mode, alpha setting, background color, tag value, and drawing settings. Setting an attribute value is a simple matter of entering a new value, selecting from a list of possible values, or ticking or unticking a check box.

Size Inspector

The Size inspector (Figure 3.13) enables you to set the size and position of the selected object without having to size and move the object with the mouse. It represents a faster way to size and position an object when you know its exact dimensions and position. Also within this inspector, you can view and set Cocoa Auto Layout constraints and priorities for the object.

 With Cocoa Auto Layout, you define rules that control the layout of the visual elements that make up your user interface. These rules comprise a combination of constraints and priorities that represent the relationship between an object, its parent, and other surrounding objects. For example, you might want a text label that is anchored slightly right from the leftmost side of its parent view while also being adjacent to a text field.

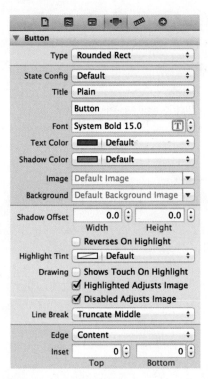

Figure 3.12   The list of attributes, or properties, for a `UIButton` as seen in the Attributes inspector

While this type of complicated layout is possible with the old springs-and-struts autosizing approach used prior to iOS 6, Cocoa Auto Layout makes it easier while at the same time being more powerful. For instance, suppose you localize your app for languages that are read from right to left, such as Hebrew and Arabic. Cocoa Auto Layout will automatically reverse the left-to-right layout for proper display when your app is localized for right-to-left language.

More Information

To learn more about Cocoa Auto Layout, including how you can programmatically define constraints using an ASCII-art inspired format string called the Visual Format Language, read the *Cocoa Auto Layout Guide*[2] available in the iOS Developer Library.

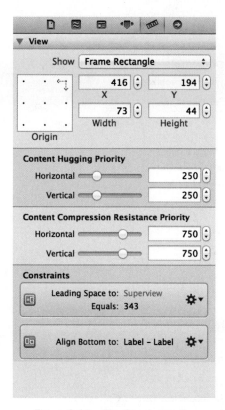

Figure 3.13   The Size inspector

---

2. *Cocoa Auto Layout Guide*: https://developer.apple.com/library/ios/#documentation/
   UserExperience/Conceptual/AutolayoutPG/Articles/Introduction.html

Connections Inspector

The Connections inspector shows the connections between the selected object and some other object. You can also make new connections within this area. Take a look at Figure 3.14, noticing the small circles to the right of the events and outlets references. If you were to move the mouse cursor over one of the empty circles, it would change to a circle with a plus sign in it. Clicking and dragging the plus sign draws a line on the screen. As you move the mouse around while dragging the end of the line, objects supporting the connection become highlighted. Objects that do not support the connection are not highlighted. When you find the desired object, drop the plus sign on the object to connect it. A list of actions or outlets that can be used for the connection then pops up, and you can select the appropriate action or outlet to make the connection.

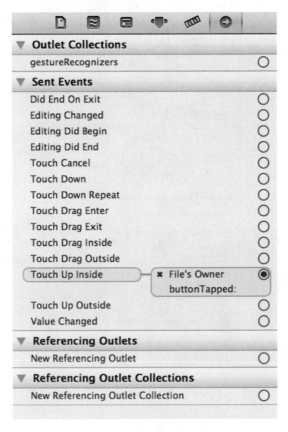

Figure 3.14   List of events and outlets references for a `UIButton` as seen in the Connections inspector

What Is the File's Owner?

When looking at the IB dock or Document Outline area, you might notice an object named File's Owner. File's Owner identifies the object that owns the NIB when it is loaded at run time. A placeholder object represents the File's Owner. A placeholder object is a reference to an object that is not created by the NIB. Other names for this placeholder include "proxy" and "external object," as it is called in the Object library.

The File's Owner placeholder object is used to indicate the type of object that owns the NIB once loaded. The object type, or class name, is displayed in the Identity inspector, and it can be changed in the same inspector, as shown in Figure 3.15.

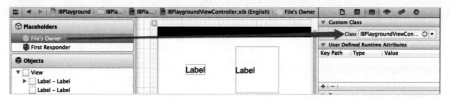

Figure 3.15   The File's Owner is a placeholder object. Its type is the class
name set in the Identity inspector.

The File's Owner type is the name of the class that is responsible for managing objects at run time that are defined in the NIB. It is typically the view controller class, though it does not have to be a view controller. Likewise, you can have other placeholder objects defined in the NIB that are not the File's Owner.

IB uses the class type to determine which header file to read when it's looking for outlets and actions. You'll see this capability in action momentarily.

Connecting Your NIB to Your Code

The objects created in a NIB are connected to classes defined in source code by way of two IB hints, IBOutlet and IBAction. These special macros resolve to nothing and void, respectively, but Interface Builder uses them as a way to identify references for outlets and actions defined in source code. From the point of view of the source code as well as the compiled application, these macros do nothing—they are useless. IB, however, uses them as hints for finding and connecting outlets and actions to objects defined in the NIB.

So what are outlets and action? An outlet is a reference to an object, and an action is a reference to a method implemented by a class.

For the moment, you can think of a view as a representation of the screen the user sees in your application. The view displays a label object with some text and a button object. A controller class manages interaction with this view. The controller contains a reference to the label defined in the view. The label reference is the outlet because it is a reference to an object. If the controller needs a reference to the button, another outlet can be defined referencing the button object.

Now assume that when the user taps the button, text in the label changes. In this case, the button has a touch event that calls a method. The method is implemented in the controller class and is responsible for changing the label's text. This method represents the action.

An object reference defined in a class interface is decorated with `IBOutlet`, and a method declaration is decorated with `IBAction`. Each of these macros is connected to objects and events defined in a NIB. IB looks for these macros to find the available outlets and actions defined within a class. In this way, objects created in a NIB are connected to the source code that powers your application.

> **Note**
>
> If you are familiar with the design pattern Model-View-Controller (MVC), some of what was just said should make sense. iOS applications use MVC throughout. The MVC pattern is covered in Chapter 5, "Getting Started with Cocoa."

To connect an object created in the NIB to an object reference or an object's event to a method, your code must define the outlet and the action. Two approaches can be used to accomplish this: You can add the code manually to the class interface, or you can use IB with the Assistant editor.

Defining an Outlet in Code

For many iOS programmers, adding an outlet or action declaration manually to a class interface is a more natural workflow. Manually adding outlets and actions gives you the opportunity to focus on the class interface and implementation without concerning yourself with the look of the user interface.

To see how this works, go back to the previous scenario where you have a view containing a label and a button. When the user taps the button, the label's text changes to display "Hello from iOS." To implement this feature, your source code needs a reference to the `UILabel`, which is the outlet, and a reference to a method, which is the action that executes the code needed to update the label text.

To make this so . . .

Show the Project navigator (**Command-0**) and select the file *IBPlaygroundViewControl ler.h*. Update the class interface to include the code in Listing 3.1.

Listing 3.1   **Code to Be Added to *IBPlaygroundViewController.h***

```
@interface IBPlaygroundViewController : UIViewController

// Add the following code:

@property (nonatomic, weak) IBOutlet UILabel *label;
```

```
- (IBAction)buttonTapped:(id)sender;

// End of code to add.

@end
```

What's going on here? First, a declared property is added. `@property` is special Objective-C sauce instructing the compiler to define an instance variable name `label` that stores a reference to an instance of `UILabel`. IBOutlet is the hint given to IB to create a connection from the instance of `UILabel` defined in the NIB to the declared property found in the class interface. Second, a forward declaration for the method `-buttonTapped:` is defined. Note that the return type is set to `IBAction`; it tells IB that this method represents an action.

If you try compiling the project, you will receive a build warning. This warning arises because the implementations for the `IBAction` method have not been provided. So open the file *IBPlaygroundViewController.m* (**Control-Command-Up** or **Control-Command-Down** while in the counterpart *.h* file) and add the implementation code shown in Listing 3.2.

Listing 3.2   Updated *IBPlaygroundViewController.m*

```
#import "IBPlaygroundViewController.h"

@implementation IBPlaygroundViewController

// ----
// Add the following code:

@synthesize label;

- (IBAction)buttonTapped:(id)sender
{
    NSLog(@"button was tapped.");
    [label setText:@"Hello from iOS."];
}

// End of new code.

// Other code provided by the template is not presented here.

@end
```

For the moment, we'll assume that you have little to no Objective-C experience. In that case, this code may seem strange, especially the `@synthesize` statement. `@synthesize` is more special sauce from Objective-C that tells the compiler to create getter and setter methods for the declared property. In the case of this code, @synthesize creates the getter and setter methods for the declared property label. You can write the getter and setter methods, but why bother when the compiler can do it for you?

> **Note**
>
> For the moment, do not worry about the details of @property and @synthesize. All will be revealed, including how @synthesize is no longer required, in Chapter 4, "Getting Started with Objective-C."

Following the synthesizing of the declared property is the implementation for the method -buttonTapped:. This method accepts a single parameter named sender. sender is a reference to the object calling the method. In our current scenario, sender is the button found in the view.

The method itself contains two lines of code. The first statement calls NSLog(). NSLog() is a C function that sends output to the console. The output, of course, is the string parameter to the NSLog() call. The second line of code sets the text property for the object reference label. This is where the source code actually uses the IBOutlet.

What's Really Going On?

As mentioned earlier, IB looks at IBOutlet and IBAction for hints about the available outlets and actions. But how does IB know which files to look at? The File's Owner! The File's Owner is of type IBPlaygroundViewController, and it tells IB to read and parse the header file *IBPlaygroundViewController.h* for any IBOutlet and IBAction hints.

With IBOutlet and IBAction defined in the class interface, it's time to update the user interface. Select the file *IBPlaygroundViewController.xib* in the Project navigator to open the NIB in IB. Add a new button (UIButton) to the view defined in the NIB. We'll assume the view contains at least one label from the earlier playtime. If not, add a label to the view as well.

Right-click the button found in the view to bring up a list of events triggered by the object. Click and drag the circle for the *Touch Up Inside* event and drop it on the File's Owner (Figure 3.16). IB displays the list of available actions; -buttonTapped: should be the only action available at this time. Click the -buttonTapped: action to connect the button's *Touch Up Inside* event to the -buttonTapped: action method.

> **Note**
>
> Another way to connect the button to the action is to **Control-click** the button and drag the mouse cursor to the File's Owner. This will connect the -buttonTapped: action to the *Touch Up Inside* event of the button.

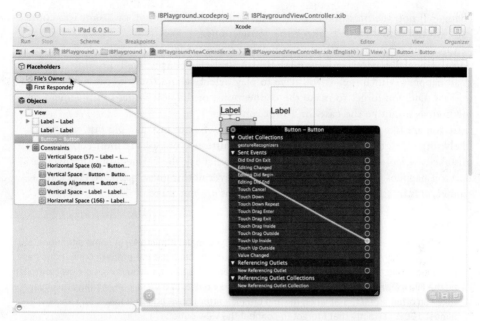

Figure 3.16   Right-click the button to see the list of events. Click and drag an
event to connect it to an action defined in another object.

The label should be connected as well; otherwise, the app will not behave the way
you want. In the Document Outline area, right-click the File's Owner, and then drag
and drop the circled plus sign onto a UILabel instance found in the view. This connects the label to the declared property outlet label.

> **Note**
>
> Here again you can **Control-click** the File's Owner and drag the mouse cursor to the label to
> make the connection.

Think about what is happening for a moment. The header file includes an outlet
referencing a UILabel and a method declaration representing an action. Nowhere in
the code do you find the instantiation of the label object, nor do you see a reference
of any sort identifying the button that calls the method -buttonTapped:. Instead,
the objects for the label and button are defined in the NIB, as are the connections to
IBOutlet label and IBAction -buttonTapped:. The Cocoa Framework performs
the magic for you, creating the object instances and making the connections. The real
beauty here is that you did not have to write code, and IB did not generate source code,
to create the object instances and connect the event callbacks.

At this point, you should be able to build and run (**Command-R**) the app without
errors. Run it and see what happens. When you tap the button, does the label's text

change? If not, the most likely cause is that either the IBOutlet or IBAction connection was not made. Double-check the connections.

One note of caution: When a connection is not made, the compiler does not warn you and typically your app will not crash. All that happens is, well, nothing. Nothing at all happens, which means you have to play detective and find the cause of the nothingness. Did you forget to make the connections, or did you forget to implement the method, as might be the case for IBAction?

If you are like many other iOS programmers who are just starting out, you will likely forget to make the connections. This omission is one of the most common mistakes, which explains why you should always check the connections first when nothing happens. This bears repeating: Whenever nothingness happens, check the connections in IB. Chances are the connections are not there.

Note

While nothingness is the common behavior when you make a mistake, in some situations exceptions may be thrown that cause your app to crash because the proper connections have not been made. The most notable of these occasions arises when you define a view controller as the File's Owner and you do not connect the view outlet to a view. I often make this mistake—so often, in fact, that when my app crashes after I have added a new NIB, I know with almost 100% certainty that I forgot to connect the view outlet.

Checking Outlet and Action Connections

Forgetting to connect outlets and actions is a common mistake that we all make from time to time. If something isn't working as expected, then chances are good that you have forgotten to make a connection to an outlet or action.

Here are some ways to check connections:

1. Look at the connection indicator found in the gutter of the text editor (Figure 3.17). An empty circle indicates there is no connection for the outlet or action. In contrast, a circle containing a dot indicates that a connection exists. Clicking the dotted circle shows the connection, and clicking the connection jumps you to the NIB or storyboard scene where the connected object is defined.

```
10
11    @interface IBPlaygroundViewController : UIViewController
12
⊙ 13    @property (nonatomic, strong) IBOutlet UILabel *label;
⊙ 14    @property (strong, nonatomic) IBOutlet UILabel *label2;
○ 15    @property (weak, nonatomic) IBOutlet UILabel *label3;
16
⊙ 17    - (IBAction)buttonTapped:(id)sender;
⊙ 18    - (IBAction)buttonTapped2:(id)sender;
19
20    @end
21
```

Figure 3.17   Connection indicators displayed in the text editor's gutter

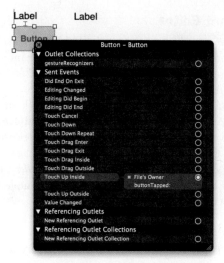

Figure 3.18   HUD displaying the list of connections

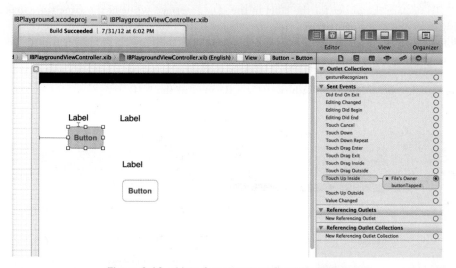

Figure 3.19   List of connections for `UIButton`

2. Control-clicking the object in IB pops up the list of connections in a HUD (Figure 3.18). You can also create and remove connections from the HUD.

3. Select the object in IB and then switch to the Connections inspector (**Option-Command-6**) to see the list of connections (Figure 3.19). Connections can be created and removed from the Connections inspector as well.

Using the Assistant Editor

The other way to connect outlets and actions is to use the Assistant editor. With the Assistant editor, you can drag objects from IB into the class interface and have Xcode create the necessary source code for you.

To see this feature in action, add another label and button to the view. Now you have new objects to connect, and you didn't have to go back and delete the other code. Next, show the Assistant editor (**Option–Command–Return**). The screen might be a little crowded, so you may want to hide the Navigation (**Command-0**) and Utilities (**Option-Command-0**) areas. Notice that when you show the Assistant editor, it automatically displays the *IBPlaygroundViewController.h* file. Xcode knows it is the counterpart file for the NIB. Figure 3.20 shows an example of the workspace window with IB and the Assistant editor open.

> **Note**
>
> If for some reason *IBPlaygroundViewController.h* is not open in the Assistant, use the jump bar to open it.

To declare the outlet for the label in the class interface while at the same time making the connection, **Control-click** the label and drag the mouse cursor to the class interface in the Assistant window. When you release the mouse, a popover is displayed, prompting you for the name of the outlet (Figure 3.21). Call it "label2" and click the **Connect** button. This step creates the declared property decorated with IBOutlet and makes the connection with the object defined in the NIB.

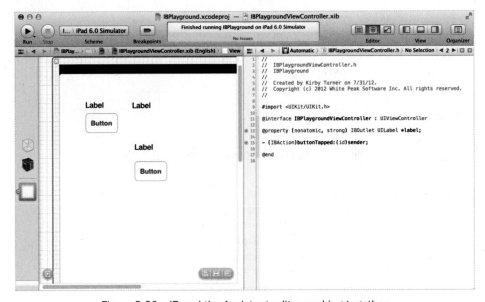

Figure 3.20   IB and the Assistant editor working together

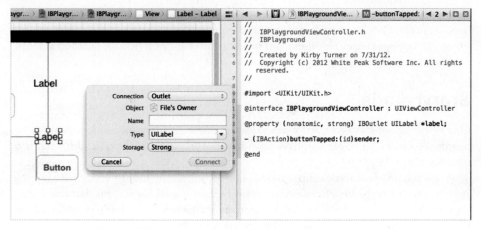

Figure 3.21   Popover displayed when connecting an outlet
using the Assistant editor

Note

You can place the outlet declaration anywhere you like, so long as it appears between the `@interface` and `@end` statements for the class.

You do the same thing to declare the action and connect the button. **Control-click** the button and drag the mouse cursor to the class interface. When the popover appears this time, change the connection from Outlet to Action and name the action "button2Tapped." The popover should look like Figure 3.22. Finally, click the **Connect** button to create the action.

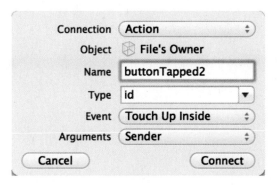

Figure 3.22   Popover displayed when connecting an action
using the Assistant editor

When you add an action using the Assistant, this editor not only creates the declaration in the class interface but also adds the method stub to the implementation. Open *IBPlaygroundViewController.m* and scroll to the bottom to see the method stub for `-button2Tapped:`.

Storyboards

One of the options you may see when creating a new Xcode project is Use Storyboards. So far in this book, you have been told not to check this option. But what is a storyboard?

A storyboard, or storyboarding, is a way of designing the user interface for your application. It has the benefit of simultaneously showing all the screens that make up the app. This feature is built on top of Interface Builder, so everything you learned in this chapter about using IB with a NIB applies to storyboards. The primary difference, however, is that a storyboard can display multiple screens, or NIBs if you will, at the same time. This gives you a complete, single picture of the application's user interface and the relationships between the screens.

You begin using storyboards in Chapter 14, "Storyboarding in Xcode."

Summary

This concludes our brief tour of Interface Builder. We hope you enjoyed your flight and will consider using IB for future UI designs.

All kidding aside, you now have the basic knowledge needed to use Interface Builder. This feature might seem daunting in the beginning, but its use becomes easier over time. The key point to remember is to always make the connections for outlets and actions. If you created a super-nice UI but it is not displaying content or actions are not invoked on touch, chances are good the connections are missing.

4

Getting Started with Objective-C

Objective-C is the programming language used in this book, so it makes perfect sense to include a chapter on this mighty fine programming language. Besides, Objective-C is the programming language you will use as you learn iPad programming. It is not the only programming language used for iPad programming, but it is by far the most popular. In addition, Apple recommends Objective-C for iOS programming. That's why all of the source code provided in this book is written in Objective-C.

All things Objective-C is simply too large a topic to be covered in a single chapter, and it is beyond the scope of this book. There are, however, some excellent books devoted to Objective-C:

- *Learning Objective-C 2.0: A Hands-on Guide to Objective-C for Mac and iOS Developers, Second Edition, by Robert Clair (Addison-Wesley, 2013)*
- *Programming in Objective-C 2.0, Fifth Edition, by Stephen G. Kochan (Addison-Wesley, 2012)*
- *Objective-C Programming: The Big Nerd Ranch Guide by Aaron Hillegass (Big Nerd Ranch, Inc., 2011)*

These outstanding books dive deep into the Objective-C programming language.

Meanwhile, this chapter covers the basics of Objective-C, giving you the jump start needed to write your first iPad app. Once you finish this book, you can read one of the recommended Objective-C books to gain a deeper understanding of the language.

What Is Objective-C?

Objective-C is an extension to the C programming language that turns C into an object-oriented programming language. But unlike C++, which is derived from C, Objective-C is a set of extensions added to the C programming language.

To make this happen, a small set of new syntax is added to the language. The compiler converts the Objective-C syntax to C as part of the compile process. Objective-C also relies on a runtime environment, which gives Objective-C its dynamic nature.

Objective-C is modeled after Smalltalk, one of the first object-oriented programming languages to come onto the scene. Like Smalltalk, Objective-C sends a message to a receiver. The receiver, which is an object, then invokes a method based on the message it receives. This allows apps written in Objective-C to construct a message at run time that is sent to an object, which in turn invokes a method. This is different from other programming languages such as C++, which bind method calls at compile time.

The dynamic behavior of Objective-C makes it an ideal programming language for frameworks and software development kits (SDKs), which is likely one of the reasons Apple uses it in its own frameworks, SDKs, and operating systems.

> **Note**
>
> Objective-C extends the C programming language, turning it into an object-oriented programming language. If you already know C, learning Objective-C will be a snap. But don't worry if you have never written a line of C code. You can learn Objective-C without any prior C knowledge.

Hands-On Practice with Objective-C

The best way to learn Objective-C is to use it, and that's what you will do now. You are going to create a simple coin toss application that runs in the Terminal window. Writing this app will help you gain insight into Objective-C.

Begin by launching Xcode. Next, create a new Command Line Tool app. You can either select the "Create a new Xcode project" option on the Welcome to Xcode screen (Figure 4.1), or you can select **File > New > New Project** (**Shift-Command-N**) from the menu bar.

Figure 4.1   Welcome to Xcode window

You want to create a console app. A console app runs from the command line in the Terminal window. iOS does not support command-line applications, so you want to select the Command Line Tool project template found under the Mac OS X group, shown in Figure 4.2. Select this template and then click the **Next** button.

Name the project "CoinToss." Select **Foundation** as the Type (Figure 4.3). This creates a console application that links to the Foundation framework. You will learn

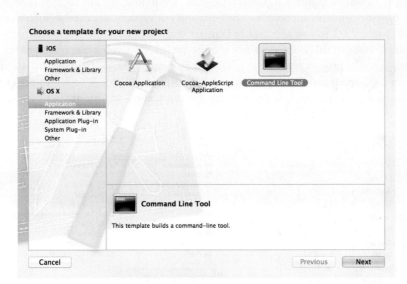

Figure 4.2   Select the Command Line Tool template.

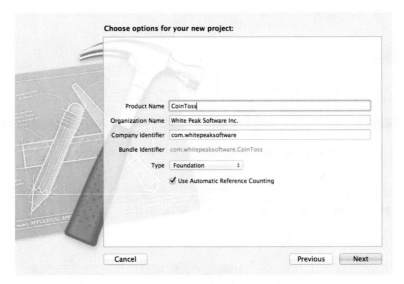

Figure 4.3   Project options

more about Foundation and other frameworks in Chapter 5, "Getting Started with Cocoa." Be sure to turn on the Use Automatic Reference Counting option. This option is described later in this chapter. Click **Next** to continue.

Save the project to your source directory. If you do not have a source directory yet, create one.

You may have noticed the option to create a local Git repository at the bottom of the screen shown in Figure 4.4. Git is a popular distributed version control system. Xcode provides built-in support for both Git and Subversion, another popular version control system. Unless you are already familiar with Git, leave this option unmarked. The sample code in this book does not require the use of a version control system.

Make sure the project was properly created by doing a build (**Command-B**) and then run it (**Command-R**). The resulting app displays "Hello, World!" to the console window, as seen in Figure 4.5. Because the app is a command-line application, you

Figure 4.4   Save the project to your source directory.

Figure 4.5   Output window displaying "Hello, World!" from the console app

will not see the output unless you have the output window open in the Debug area. You can open the output window by pressing **Shift-Command-C**.

Let's Write Some Code

With the project in place, it's time to write some code. In the Project navigator, open the file *main.m*. C programs always start with a `main()` function, which is found in the *main.m* file. The *main.m* file is your first hint that you are using Objective-C: C-language source files have *.c* as the file extension, whereas Objective-C source files use *.m* as the file extension.

Find and delete the line of code that reads `NSLog(@"Hello world!")` and insert the following code in its place:

```
// Get random integer between 1 and 10.
int randomValue = (arc4random()%10) + 1;
if (randomValue % 2) {
    NSLog(@"Heads");
} else {
    NSLog(@"Tails");
}
```

The source code for *main.m* should now look like Listing 4.1.

Listing 4.1   **Simple Coin Toss Algorithm in** *main.m*

```
#import <Foundation/Foundation.h>

int main(int argc, const char * argv[])
{
    @autoreleasepool {

        // Get random integer between 1 and 10.
        int randomValue = (arc4random()%10) + 1;
        if (randomValue % 2) {
            NSLog(@"Heads");
        } else {
            NSLog(@"Tails");
        }

    }
    return 0;
}
```

This code retrieves a random integer value from the function `arc4random()`. The C modulo operation (`%`) is used to limit the return value to a whole number between 0 and 9. The modulo operator finds the remainder of a division of two numbers. In this particular line of code, the modulo operator divides the `arc4random()` return value by 10 and returns the remainder value, which is then added to 1.

Next, the code determines whether the random value is an even or odd number, again using the `%` operator. An odd number logs "Heads" to the console, and an even number logs "Tails."

> **Note**
>
> NSLog is a C function that displays output to the standard console. It is the Objective-C equivalent of the `printf` function found in the C programming language. NSLog is commonly used to send output to the console when debugging an application. You will find out more about using NSLog in Chapter 5, "Getting Started with Cocoa."

Build and run (**Command-R**) the application. As you can see in the output window (**Shift-Command-C**), this is not a very exciting app. It just performs a single coin toss. To do more coin tosses, you must run the app again and again. Let's make the app a bit more interesting by changing the source code to loop through 10 times to see how random the coin tosses actually are. To accomplish this, add the following code (new lines of code are bold):

```
for (int index=0; index < 10; index++) {
    // Get random integer between 1 and 10.
    int randomValue = (arc4random()%10) + 1;
    if (randomValue % 2) {
        NSLog(@"Heads");
    } else {
        NSLog(@"Tails");
    }
}
```

The app is slightly more interesting now—but what's even more interesting is that so far you haven't written any Objective-C code. Let's change that by creating a `CoinTosser` object.

Object

What is an object? In the software world, an object is a programming unit that contains attributes and behavior. That is, the object contains data and code, where data represents the attributes (also known as properties) and code represents the behavior of the object (methods performed by the object). The object's data and code are related in that the code performs some action using the data contained within the object.

An object encapsulates related data and code into a single unit, making it easier to reuse the unit in other parts of the application. Many times an object models a real-world concept. If, for example, you were writing a payroll application, *Employee* would likely be one of the objects found within the application.

CoinToss is not a complex or large application, but it can still benefit from using objects. Instead of including the coin toss logic in the for loop of the main function, the app can use a CoinTosser object. CoinTosser becomes responsible for flipping the coin. This means that as the app grows and becomes more complex, the logic for flipping the coin does not have to be copied throughout the app. Instead, the app can use the CoinTosser object when it wants to flip a coin.

The new CoinTosser object can have some intelligence, too. It doesn't have to be just a dull worker bee flipping coins all day: It can keep track of the number of times a coin has been flipped, and it can track the number of times the coin lands on heads and tails. This "intelligence" can be used for reporting the statistics of a set of coin tosses.

Class

An object is used by an application when it is running, but before the object can be used, it must be defined. A class defines an object; that is, it describes the attributes and behaviors supported by the object. In more practical terms, the class is what you create in source code that defines the object. The object is an instance of the class created at run time.

To use a CoinTosser object in the CoinToss app, you must first define the class for the object. To do so, you need to create a new file (**File > New > File** or **Command-N**). Select the Objective-C class template found under **Mac OS X > Cocoa** (Figure 4.6).

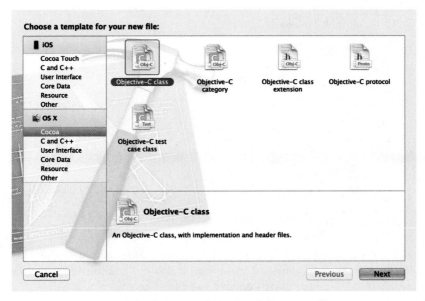

Figure 4.6   Select the Objective-C class template.

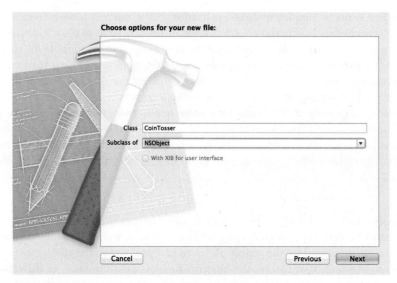

Figure 4.7   Create the new class `CoinTosser`, a subclass of `NSObject`.

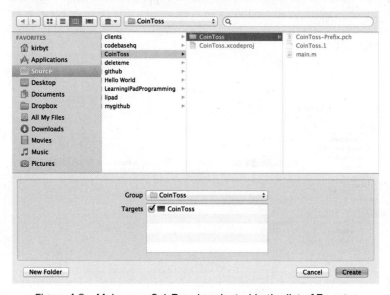

Figure 4.8   Make sure CoinToss is selected in the list of Targets.

Click the **Next** button. Xcode asks you for the class name and the subclass. Enter "CoinTosser" for the class name, and make it a subclass of `NSObject` (Figure 4.7). Don't worry if the idea of a subclass doesn't make sense to you now; it will be explained later in the chapter.

Click the **Next** button, and then click the **Create** button to create and add the new class file to the project. A tick should appear next to the target CoinToss (Figure 4.8). It tells Xcode to not only add the class to the project, but also add it to the list of source code that is compiled to make the CoinToss app.

Let's talk for a moment about what just happened.

When you created the new `CoinTosser` class, two files were added to the project: *CoinTosser.h* and *CoinTosser.m*. Objective-C, like C, uses two files to represent a source module. This is different from other programming languages such as C# and Java in which one file is used as a source module.

The *.h* file is the header file. The header file defines the interface for the class. The interface tells you which properties and methods (attributes and behaviors, respectively) are supported by the class. The header file simply describes the interface for the class; it does not provide the implementation for the class.

The implementation for the class is found in the *.m* file. This implementation file contains the source code that instructs the computer to do something.

At the moment, the `CoinTosser` class does nothing. It has no attributes (properties) and no behavior (methods). It's time to change that. Start with the interface for the class. Open the file *CoinTosser.h*, which is the interface file for the class `CoinTosser`. Now add the code in Listing 4.2 (new code to add is highlighted in bold).

Listing 4.2 *CoinTosser.h*

```
#import <Foundation/Foundation.h>

@interface CoinTosser : NSObject

@property (nonatomic, assign) int headsCount;
@property (nonatomic, assign) int tailsCount;
@property (nonatomic, strong) NSString *lastResult;


- (void) flip;

@end
```

The first line is `#import <Foundation/Foundation.h>`. *Foundation.h* is another header file that defines the references for all functions and classes found in the Foundation framework. For the C programmers reading this chapter, `#import` is similar to `#include`. However, `#import` ensures that the file is included only once, avoiding the problem of recursive includes.

The angled brackets surrounding `Foundation/Foundation.h` indicate that the header file is a system header file. System header files are stored outside of the project and are provided by the development environment and SDK. The system header files needed for iPad programming are added to your computer when you install Xcode and the iOS SDK.

If you want to import a header file that is part of the project, you enclose the header file name with quote characters—for example, #import "CoinTosser.h". An example can be found in the *CoinTosser.m* implementation file.

Foundation is imported into the CoinTosser class so that it can reference other classes defined within the Foundation framework. The next line of code, for example, includes a reference to NSObject. NSObject is a Foundation object. In other words, it is defined in the Foundation framework.

NSObject

NSObject is the root object for all Objective-C objects (with only a few exceptions). NSObject provides the foundation for the class CoinTosser to be an object; that is, it provides the base properties and methods for all objects so that other objects do not have to reimplement the same code. This is a key advantage of using objects. An object can inherit properties and methods from another object. When a class inherits from another, it is called a subclass. CoinTosser is a subclass of NSObject; NSObject is the superclass to CoinTosser.

Because CoinTosser inherits from NSObject, it is able to do anything NSObject can do. The same is not true for the superclass. NSObject cannot do the same things CoinTosser can, because NSObject does not inherit properties and methods from CoinTosser. Conversely, CoinTosser does inherit properties and methods from NSObject.

Objective-C, like Java, C#, and Object Pascal, supports single class inheritance. Other programming languages, such as C++, Perl, and Python, support multiple class inheritance. Ambiguities can occur with multiple inheritance, which is why languages such as Objective-C follow the single inheritance model.

Interface

To define a class you use @interface. In Listing 4.2, the CoinTosser class definition starts with the line @interface CoinTosser : NSObject. The @interface is Objective-C syntax that tells the compiler that what follows is a class definition. CoinTosser is the name of the class. The colon character separates the class name from the name of its superclass. The new class inherits properties and methods from the superclass.

The class definition starts with @interface and ends at the first occurrence of @end. This compiler directive tells the compiler it has reached the end of the class definition.

A class interface has three distinct sections. Class variables called instance variables —ivars, for short—are declared between the curly braces. Declared properties and methods are defined after the curly braces. The order of the declared properties and methods does not matter, but Objective-C convention is to declare properties after ivars and to declare methods after properties.

Now you might notice that Listing 4.2 does not include any curly braces. There are no curly braces because there are no ivars defined for this class. Back in the day, ivars were required to store data within the class instance (i.e., the object). Today, however, the convention is to use a so-called declared property to store data in the object. There was a time when Objective-C required each declared property to have an explicitly declared ivar, but that is no longer the case. The compiler implicitly declares the ivar for a declared property for you.

What does all this mean? Let's take a closer look, starting with instance variables.

Instance Variables

An instance variable is created by and made available to the class instance, which is an object. Instance variables are used to store data needed within the object. Ivars can be C data types, such as `int`, `float`, or `double`, or Objective-C classes, such as `NSString`, `NSArray`, or `NSDictionary`.

When you define an ivar of an Objective-C class type, you are actually defining a pointer to the object. Pointers are denoted in C and Objective-C with the asterisk character (`*`).

Take a look at the ivars defined for the old-style version of the `CoinTosser` class shown in Listing 4.3. This code defines three ivars. Two are defined as C `int` types; the `int` data type is a primitive C data type. Primitive data types are not pointers—hence the lack of the asterisk. The third ivar is of type `NSString`; `NSString` is an Objective-C object defined in Foundation. Because it is an object, the ivar is declared as a pointer. So `NSString *lastResult` says that the ivar `lastResult` is a pointer to an instance of class `NSString`.

Listing 4.3   **Old-Style Version of the `CoinTosser` Interface**

```
#import <Foundation/Foundation.h>

@interface CoinTosser : NSObject
{
@private
    int headsCount;
    int tailsCount;
    NSString *lastResult;
}

@property (nonatomic, assign) int headsCount;
@property (nonatomic, assign) int tailsCount;
@property (nonatomic, strong) NSString *lastResult;

- (void)flip;

@end
```

Listing 4.3 shows the old style for defining a class, in which ivars provide a storage location for declared properties. The declared properties are those items in the listing that start with @property. This style of coding is no longer common in Objective-C thanks to improvements in the compiler and Objective-C runtime. Today's programmers typically do not explicitly declare the ivars, but instead let the compiler take care of this task. But even though explicitly declaring ivars is becoming a thing of the past, understanding the role ivars play is important, especially when you are talking about declared properties.

Declared Properties

The general convention followed in most object-oriented programming languages is to never directly get or set an ivar from outside the object that defines it. The standard convention, instead, is to use getter and setter accessor methods for this purpose. These methods hide the details of the data storage from the outside world, where the "outside world" is defined as any code using the object. Information hiding—termed encapsulation—is a key concept in object orientation.

An object encapsulates the data to protect the rest of the application from changes that might occur within the object. When accessor methods are used, changes can be made to the data inside that object without affecting the rest of the application. For example, suppose you have a Person object, and this object has an ivar called name. The application using this object gets and sets a person's name as needed. Sometime later, you decide that you need to have firstName and lastName. name becomes the concatenation of first and last name. If you are using getter and setter accessor methods for name instead of accessing the ivar directly, the implementation details for the accessor methods can change without affecting the rest of the application.

The problem with getter and setter access methods is that you have to declare each as part of the interface. Thus, for every ivar value that is exposed to the outside world, you need to declare two methods. The code for the Person interface looks like this:

```
@interface Person : NSObject {
@private
    NSString *_name;
}
- (NSString *)name;
- (void)setName:(NSString *)newName;
@end
```

> **Note**
>
> The Objective-C convention for getter methods is to use only the name. Other object-oriented programming languages prefix the method with get (e.g., getName).

In addition to the getter and setter accessor methods being declared in the interface, each method must be implemented in the implementation file. This means you must write a lot of boilerplate code just to get and set a property value. Luckily, Objective-C 2.0 introduced the concept of declared properties to eliminate this drudgery.

A declared property is a compiler directive that generates the accessor methods for you. As a consequence, you do not need to declare the accessor methods in the interface. Thus the `Person` class interface becomes this:

```
@interface Person : NSObject {
@private
    NSString *_name;
}
@property (strong) NSString *name;
@end
```

To make things even easier, with the release of the iOS 4.0 SDK, explicit declarations for ivars are no longer required. Now the `Person` class interface becomes this:

```
@interface Person : NSObject
@property (strong) NSString *name;
@end
```

Using declared properties is more convenient when ivars are no longer required. Before you use a declared property, however, you need to understand how to define one.

A declared property is defined with the compiler directive `@property`. This tells the compiler that what follows is a declared property. The declared property definition ends at the first semicolon (`;`) character following the `@property` directive.

A number of attributes are available to the `@property` directive, including `nonatomic`, `assign`, `copy`, `retain`, `readwrite`, and `readonly`. These attributes are enclosed with parentheses found after `@property`. You can use a combination of the settings, but not all settings can be combined. Combining `readwrite` with `readonly`, for example, makes no sense.

> **Note**
>
> Two additional declared property attributes, `strong` and `weak`, are available when Automatic Reference Counting is enabled. These attributes are covered later in this chapter.

Declared properties are, by default, considered atomic. There is no attribute keyword to denote atomic. The omission of `nonatomic` indicates that the property is atomic.

An atomic property is thread safe. The property value retrieved by the getter or set by the setter can be performed safely in a multithreaded application regardless of other concurrently executing threads. This thread safety does introduce a slight overhead in the accessor methods, but it is well worth the cost if multiple threads access the object at the same time.

The `nonatomic` property is not thread safe. Thus, if two threads running concurrently attempt to get and set the property value at the same time, unexpected results can occur.

The assign, copy, and retain properties control how memory is managed within the setter method for the declared property. assign simply assigns the new value to the ivar. (Remember, an ivar is still used even when you do not explicitly declare it.) You always want to use assign when declaring a property of a primitive data type such as int, float, double, and BOOL. copy and retain are used for Objective-C objects; these two attributes extend the lifetime of the object. assign is also used with objects, but it does not extend the object's lifetime.

In addition to assign, copy, and retain, two other attributes are available for use when Automatic Reference Counting is turned on. These two attributes—strong and weak—also control how memory is managed. Details on memory management of objects are covered in the Memory Management section found later in this chapter. For now, just know that these attributes control how memory is managed.

The readonly and readwrite attributes do exactly as their names imply. readonly makes the declared property read only. This means that the property does not have a setter method and users of the object cannot change its value. readwrite tells the compiler to generate both the getter and setter methods. The default is readwrite when neither attribute is explicitly declared.

Two additional attributes come in handy from time to time: getter and setter. These attributes allow you to rename the getter and setter accessor methods. The getter attribute is commonly used with property values of Boolean (BOOL) type. The Objective-C convention for naming Booleans is to leave off the is prefix. For instance, instead of having a property named isVisible, the convention is to name the property visible. However, to make the code more readable, the getter accessor method is renamed isVisible. You define this property like this:

```
@property (assign, getter = isVisible) BOOL visible;
```

> ### Note
>
> BOOL is the Objective-C type equivalent of bool found in C. While you can use bool in Objective-C code, it is recommended that you stick with BOOL because all of Apple's Objective-C frameworks use it. This keeps your code compatible with Apple should the company ever decide to change the BOOL type. Also, YES and NO, not true and false, are the preferred Objective-C values for setting and testing BOOL values.

Methods

Take another look at the CoinTosser class interface. Following the declared properties is the declaration for a method named -flip. The method declaration looks like this:

```
- (void)flip;
```

A method performs an action on behalf of the object. The action typically involves using data that is associated with the object. The method -flip, for example, executes the code needed to flip a coin. It then stores the results in the declared properties for the object.

A method can have a return value and zero, one, or more parameters. The data type for the return value is specified in parentheses before the method name. A method with no return value uses void as the data type. Parameters are included as part of the method name. Objective-C does not use named parameters. Instead, the colon character is used to indicate the presence of a parameter. This tends to make Objective-C more verbose but more readable, compared to other programming languages. Here is an example of a method declaration with parameters:

```
-(int)incrementValue:(int)value bySomeValue:(int)someValue;
```

Methods come in two flavors: class methods and instance methods. A class method is denoted with a + character at the beginning. A class method is executed from the class, not an object (which is an instance of the class). Class methods are commonly provided by a class as a matter of convenience. For instance, many of the Foundation classes provide class methods that return an instance of the class. Using [NSArray array] is much more convenient than using [[[NSArray alloc] init] autorelease].

In contrast to a class method, an instance method is a method available only to an instance of the class (i.e., the object). Instance methods are denoted with a - character at the beginning. The -flip method defined for the CoinTosser class is an instance method.

Implementation

A class is made up of two pieces: an interface and an implementation. The interface defines what the class looks like—its properties and methods. The implementation is where code that is executed at run time lives. In Objective-C, the implementation file uses the *.m* file extension. Why *.m*? Well, according to a thread on StackOverflow, the creator of Objective-C, Brad Cox, said that m is used "because *.o* and *.c* were taken. Simple as that."[1] Others believe *.m* stands for "messages" or "methods." Regardless, the implementation of an Objective-C class is in the *.m* file.

Let's take a look at the implementation file for the CoinTosser class, which is shown in Listing 4.4. Be sure to open the file *CoinTosser.m* and add this code to your CoinTosser class (new code is in bold).

Listing 4.4 **CoinTosser Class Implementation**

```
#import "CoinTosser.h"

@implementation CoinTosser

@synthesize headsCount = _headsCount;
@synthesize tailsCount = _tailsCount;
```

---

1. Why .m?: http://stackoverflow.com/questions/652186/why-do-objective-c-files-use-the-m
   -extension/652266#652266

```
@synthesize lastResult = _lastResult;

- (id)init
{
    self = [super init];
    if (self) {
        [self setLastResult:@""];
    }

    return self;
}

- (void)flip
{
    // Get random integer between 1 and 10.
    int randomValue = (arc4random()%10) + 1;
    if (randomValue % 2) {
        [self setLastResult:@"Heads"];
        [self setHeadsCount:[self headsCount] + 1];
    } else {
        [self setLastResult:@"Tails"];
        [self setTailsCount:[self tailsCount] + 1];
    }
}

@end
```

The implementation of a class starts with the compiler directive @implementation. The @implementation section ends with the first occurrence of the @end compiler directive. The implementation is the code or actions performed by the class. It consists of methods that are defined as part of the class interface as well as methods not defined by the interface. Methods not defined by the class interface are private and can be used only within the class itself.

Synthesize

The first block of code found in the implementation is the @synthesize statement for each declared property. The @synthesize statement is responsible for telling the compiler that it needs to provide the accessor methods for the declared properties. The @synthesize directive is followed by the name of the property to synthesize. For instance, `@synthesize headsCount` will generate the required accessor methods for the declared property `headsCount`.

By default, a synthesized property uses an ivar that has the exact same name as the property. For example, the statement `@synthesize headsCount` implicitly declares an ivar named `headsCount`. You can change the ivar name by setting the synthesized property name equal to another name, as follows:

```
@synthesize headsCount = _headsCount;
```

This line of code synthesizes the declared property `headsCount`. It generates the accessor methods for the property, and it implicitly declares the ivar `_headsCount`. The underscore is just a naming convention; it does not have any special meaning. The ivar could be called `headsCount_` or even `bob`.

Why would you want to rename the ivar to something other than the property name? One of the best reasons to rename the ivar is to avoid conflicts with parameter names used in method declarations. If the parameter name for a method matches the ivar name, the compiler will produce a warning that the local variable hides the ivar.

As a real-world example, consider a view controller that contains a table view. The declared property for the table view is named `tableView`. In the implementation, the `tableView` property is synthesized and the ivar is not renamed—that is, it remains `tableView`. You declare the delegate methods for the table view delegate object, and each of these methods has a parameter named `tableView`. These parameters now hide the ivar from the method's implementation, producing a warning message from the compiler.

The example just described likely sounds foreign to you, but it will make sense later after you spend time writing your first iPad app. For now, just know that renaming the ivar for a declared property is usually a good thing. In fact, starting with Xcode 4.4, it became easier to rename the ivar with the underscore prefix—just don't use the `@synthesize` statement.

Wait. What?

Yes, you read that correctly. The easiest way to rename the ivar is to not use the `@synthesize` statement. Just as you no longer need to explicitly declare ivars, so you no longer need to explicitly declare `@synthesize` statements for your declared properties. Instead, the compiler will implicitly create the ivar for you with the underscore prefix.

This is a very welcome change to Objective-C. Whereas you once had to explicitly declare the ivar for a declared project and synthesize the property, which resulted in three lines of code for a single property, you now simply need to define the declared property. Three lines of code reduced to a single line of code thanks to the compiler.

> **Note**
>
> Feel free to delete the `@synthesize` statements found in the implementation file *CoinTosser.m* if you like, as those statements are optional.

init

Following the @synthesize statements is the method named -init. This method is defined in the NSObject class, which is why you do not see it in the CoinTosser interface. The method -init is called when an object is created. In Objective-C, you commonly see the following pattern:

```
MyClass *myObject = [[MyClass alloc] init];
```

The method +alloc is a class method. It is responsible for allocating a new object as an instance of the class. The instance method -init is called to initialize the object. It typically contains the code responsible for initializing the object. For instance, the -init method for CoinTosser sets the lastResult property to a zero-length string.

The -init method for the CoinTosser class makes references to the variable self. The self variable is a special variable that references the current instance of the class. It is used within the methods of a class to access properties and methods defined by the class. The line of code [self setLastResult:@""] is saying to call the -setLastResult: method (which is the setter method for the declared property lastResult) on this instance of the class.

> **Note**
>
> Other object-oriented programming languages use self, this, and me to reference the current instance of a class.

super

The first line of code in the -init method from Listing 4.4 is self = [super init]. The keyword super instructs the code to call the method from the superclass. You often call super when you override a method defined in the superclass. This ensures that behavior from the superclass is executed as part of the implementation for the overridden method.

> **Designated Initializer**
>
> A class can have more than one initialize method. When implementing such a class, it's important that one of the initialize methods drives the initialization. In other words, generally speaking, only one method should call the superclass initializer. This primary initializer method is referred to as the "designated initializer."

flip

The final method defined in the CoinTosser implementation is -flip. This method is an instance method, which means it can be called only on an instance of the CoinTosser class. The -flip method uses the same algorithm used earlier in the C version of the app. It generates a random number and determines whether the number is even or odd. The difference, however, is that the results of the flip are no longer reported via the `NSLog` function. Instead, the declared property `lastResult` is set to either "Heads" or "Tails," and the heads and tails counts are incremented.

This code may look a bit odd at first. You might be curious about the brackets enclosing some of the lines of code, and the string literal that has an @ symbol at the beginning. In fact, what you see here is Objective-C code. More specifically, when you look at the implementation for the `-flip` method, you see a mixture of C and Objective-C code. `int randomValue = (arc4random()%10) + 1` and `if (randomValue % 2)` are C statements. The statements enclosed with brackets are Objective-C statements.

A quick way to identify Objective-C statements is to look for the brackets, though this is not always true, as you will see in a moment.

The string literals `@"Heads"` and `@"Tails"` are Unicode strings used by Objective-C. The @ symbol signals to the compiler that the string literal is part of the Objective-C code. An Objective-C string literal is actually shorthand syntax to define a pointer to an Objective-C string object. If the @ symbol is missing, the compiler assumes that the string literal is a C string literal, which is generally not used in Objective-C. A C string literal is a pointer to a char data type and not an object.

Objective-C Literals

An Objective-C literal is special syntax providing a shorthand way to create certain Objective-C object types. Objective-C literals can be used to create an instance of `NSString`, `NSNumber`, `NSArray`, and `NSDictionary`. Using literals makes your code more concise, which in turn makes your code more readable.

A string literal begins with the @ symbol, which is followed by a string value enclosed with quotes. Here's an example:

```
NSString *s = @"string value";
```

A number literal begins with the @ symbol, which is followed by the scalar value: signed and unsigned integers (`char`, `short`, `int`, `long`, `long long`), floating-point numbers (`float`, `double`), and Boolean values (`BOOL`, `bool`). Here are some examples:

```
NSNumber *one = @1;
NSNumber *two = @2;
NSNumber *pi = @3.14159;
NSNumber *yesNumber = @YES;
NSNumber *noNumber = @NO;
```

Collection literals are used to create arrays and dictionaries. An array literal begins with the @ symbol, which is followed by square brackets. A dictionary literal begins with the @ symbol, which is followed by braces. The braces contain the key value pair separated by a colon. Here are examples:

```
NSArray *weekendDays = @[ @"Saturday", @"Sunday"];
NSArray *mixedArray = @[@"hi", @42, @YES];
NSDictionary *values = @{@"city" : @"Salem", @"state" : @"MA"};
```

```
NSDictionary *collection = @{@"weekendDays":weekendDays,
                             @"mixedArray":mixedArray, @"values":values};
```

To learn more about Objective-C Literal, read the Objective-C Literals clang documentation[2] and Mark Dalrymple's blog post Objective-C Literals, Part 1.[3]

Let's take another look at a snippet of the Objective-C code from the -flip method:

```
[self setLastResult:@"Heads"];
[self setHeadsCount:[self headsCount] + 1];
```

What exactly is going on here? The first line of code is, of course, Objective-C code. The brackets tell you (and the compiler) that self is the object and the receiver of the message -setLastResult:. Message, not method? Yes, message.

The Objective-C runtime environment is a dynamic environment. It is a message-based environment similar to Smalltalk. Thus, while the code might appear to be calling the method -setLastResult:, it is actually sending a message to the object self, which is the receiver, and the message it receives is setLastResult:. This message is then mapped to the method -setLastResult:, implemented in the class that defines the object. Although it looks as if the code is calling the method -setLastResult:, under the Objective-C hood a message is being sent to the receiver self. And this all happens at run time.

Why is this important? This behavior means that the method (or message) is not required to be known at compile time, but rather can be determined at run time.

Selector

A method is the implementation of some functionality within a class. At run time, a message is sent to a receiver (object), which in turn invokes the method. The message is called a selector, and a selector is another data type in Objective-C. The SEL type defines a selector. In code, you can create a reference to a selector by using the @selector compiler directive. For example:

```
SEL selector = @selector(flip);
```

This line of code assigns a selector for the message flip to the variable selector. The selector can then be invoked by calling -performSelector:, which is available on NSObject. Consequently, the Objective-C code you write can determine at run time which selector (or method) to invoke. Chapter 16, "Building the Main Screen," provides an example.

---

2. Objective-C Literals documentation: http://clang.llvm.org/docs/ObjectiveCLiterals.html
3. Objective-C Literals, Part 1: http://weblog.bignerdranch.com/398-objective-c-literals-part-1/

You can do more than just dynamically invoking methods with selectors. For example, you can use selectors to determine whether an object implements a particular method. Thus you can query an object at run time to determine if it supports a particular method. If the method is supported, it is called; otherwise, a different course of action is taken. Examples of this behavior are found throughout this book, starting with Chapter 15, "Doing More with View Controllers."

Let's return to the code snippet:

```
[self setLastResult:@"Heads"];
[self setHeadsCount:[self headsCount] + 1];
```

In this code, self is the object that receives the message. self is also considered the receiver, and the message is the selector. In the first line of code, the message is setLastResult:. This message corresponds to a method defined in the class for self. self is an instance of the class CoinTosser, so the message corresponds to the method -setLastResult: defined in the class CoinTosser. But this method is not defined anywhere in the class. Why?

The method -setLastResult: is a setter method for the declared property lastResult. The @synthesize statement for lastResult generates the -setLastResult: method at compile time, which is why it is not explicitly declared in the class implementation.

The same is true for the line of code that follows. headsCount is a property. It is synthesized, making the setter method -setHeadsCount: available in the object. But the second line of code includes the statement [self headsCount]. This is the getter method for the declared property. What you see here, then, is two lines of Objective-C code accessing declared properties using the accessor methods for the properties.

Now you can, if you want, access the property values directly by using the ivar for each property. The code looks like this:

```
_lastResult = @"Heads";
_headsCount = _headsCount + 1;
```

The problem, however, is that you should never (except under very rare circumstances) directly access the ivar. Accessing the ivar is not good object-oriented programming. A declared property does more than just wrap access to the ivar—it manages the memory associated with the ivar.

In the case of lastResult, directly setting the ivar _lastResult can result in a memory leak. In fact, the line of code _lastResult = @"Heads" can cause a memory leak. The ivar may have been pointing to another NSString object. By directly setting the ivar and bypassing the memory management provided by declared properties, you have orphaned the other NSString object, leaving it in memory until the app quits. Leaking memory from one NSString object will not crash your app, but leaking memory from hundreds, or even thousands, of objects will potentially crash your app and annoy your users.

The general rule of thumb, then, is never to access ivars directly. Always use accessor methods to get and set property values.

But you say, "Okay, I'll use only the accessor methods. But isn't there a way to simplify the code and avoid the brackets?" Why, yes, there is, but . . .

Dot Syntax

Objective-C supports dot syntax. Dot syntax is a shortcut to writing code that accesses properties. Here is the same code snippet as in the previous example, this time using dot syntax:

```
self.lastResult = @"Heads";
self.headsCount = self.headsCount + 1;
```

Each line of code still states the object (or receiver) and the method (or message and selector), but the brackets have been eliminated to make the code easier to read.

While dot syntax simplifies the code, its use in Objective-C has spurred a religious war of sorts. Some Objective-C developers like using dot syntax anywhere and everywhere, while others are completely opposed to its use. Both groups have good arguments favoring their beliefs. You can do a Google search on the phrase "Objective-C use dot syntax or not" to read arguments from both sides.

This book does not take a stance on the use, or lack of use, of dot syntax. However, most of the code in this book uses the messaging-style format instead of dot syntax. Why? For many newcomers to Objective-C, the messaging style is easier to grok.

Using the `CoinTosser` Class

Let's get back to the CoinToss app. You have created the class `CoinTosser` and added it to the project. If you have not, go back to the Class and Implementation sections in this chapter, and copy the code from the listings.

Now open the file *main.m* and update it with the code from Listing 4.5.

Listing 4.5   Updated *main.m* File

```
#import <Foundation/Foundation.h>
#import "CoinTosser.h"                                    // 1

int main(int argc, const char * argv[])
{
    @autoreleasepool {

        CoinTosser *tosser = [[CoinTosser alloc] init];   // 2
        for (int index = 0; index < 10; index++ ) {       // 3
            [tosser flip];                                 // 4
            NSLog(@"%@", [tosser lastResult]);             // 5
        }
```

```
    NSLog(@"Tally: heads %i tails %i",
        [tosser headsCount], [tosser tailsCount]);        // 6


    }
    return 0;
}
```

Now let's walk through the code changes:

1. The first change is the addition of the `#import "CoinTosser.h"` header file. The code in *main.m* uses the `CoinTosser` class, so the header file must be imported.

2. A local variable named `tosser` is created. It is a pointer to an instance of the class `CoinTosser`. The class method `+alloc` is called to create the object, and the instance method `-init` is called to initialize the object.

3. A `for` loop is created that loops 10 times. This `for` loop is standard C code.

4. The instance method `-flip` is called. Under the hood, Objective-C sends the message flip to the receiving object `tosser`, which in turns invokes the method `-flip`. But to keep things simple, let's just say the method `-flip` is called.

5. The function `NSLog` is called. It sends the current string value for the declared `lastResult` to the output window.

6. After the `for` loop completes, an additional `NSLog` is called to show the total number of times the coin lands on heads and lands on tails.

After you make the changes to *main.m*, run the app (**Command-R**) and see how many times the coin lands on heads and tails.

Memory Management

One aspect of programming for iOS that is a pain point for newcomers is memory management. The iOS platform is designed for mobile devices, which have limited available memory. Apple does not publish information about the amount of available RAM on the iPad, but it's believed that the first-generation iPad has only 256MB and the iPad 2 has 512MB of memory. Compare these relatively puny amounts to the MacBook Air, which starts with 2GB of memory and can go up to 4GB, or the MacBook Pro, which starts with 4GB and supports up to 16GB. The iPad, by today's standard, doesn't have much memory.

The iOS platform is finely tuned for these low-memory mobile devices, which means some technology trade-offs were necessary to ensure high performance and great battery life. One such trade-off is the lack of garbage collection, a technology that many of today's programmers take for granted. Without garbage collection, you, the programmer, are responsible for memory management within your application. But what does this mean exactly?

Each time you allocate an object, you are responsible for releasing it. If you fail to release the object, the object leaks. In other worlds, the memory used by the object remains allocated with no way of releasing it. A memory leak is one of the most common errors found in iOS apps today, and it leads to low-memory conditions on the device, which can ultimately crash the app. And no one likes a crasher.

Memory leaks are caused by sloppy programming where a programmer is not following the retain-and-release pattern. When you allocate (or copy) an object, you take ownership of the object. It's like saying, "You retain ownership of this object." As the owner of the object, it is your job to release (or free) the object when it is no longer needed. If the object is not released, it sits in memory until the app quits—hence the retain-and-release behavior. If you retain an object, you must release it. No *ifs*, *ands*, or *buts*.

Garbage collection frees the programmer from having to worry about memory management. The garbage collector monitors the object and memory usage, and it automatically releases the object when it knows the object is no longer needed. Garbage collection, however, is not available on iOS. But fear not, soon-to-be-skilled iOS programmer, because Apple engineers have come up with a way to relieve you from the burden of memory management while at the same time keeping iOS a finely tuned mobile OS without garbage collection.

Automatic Reference Counting

Automatic Reference Counting (ARC) is a compiler-level feature that simplifies the memory management of an object. It resembles garbage collection, but works better for mobile devices.

Objects in Objective-C are reference counted. Thus, each time you retain an object, the reference count for that object is incremented. When you release the object, the reference count for the object is decremented. When the reference count reaches zero, the object is de-allocated. This frees the memory used by the object, giving the memory back to the operating system so that it can be allocated for another purpose at another time.

With ARC, your code is analyzed during compile time, and the appropriate management of the lifetime for an object is injected into the compiled binary. As a consequence, you never need to release an object; that step takes place automatically. Prior to ARC, you had to explicitly call `release` on each object that you retained. This is no longer required. In fact, calling `release` is no longer possible. Attempting to call `release` on an object while using ARC will result in a compile error.

What does ARC mean for you, the newcomer to iPad programming? It means you don't have to worry (as much) about the lifetime (i.e., memory management) of an object. You allocate an object when it is needed, and it is released automatically for you. This behavior translates into less code for you to write, making your code easier to read and less likely to ever cause a memory leak.

ARC also introduces two new property attributes for declared properties: weak and strong. These two keywords control the memory management aspects of the property. The keyword strong is used in place of retain. A strong property claims "ownership," and its object is automatically released when the object is no longer referenced.

A weak property does not extend the lifetime of the object. In other words, it does not assume ownership, so it is possible that the object might be released while the property has a reference to it. However, weak properties are automatically set to nil when the object is released. This behavior, known as "zeroing weak reference," is a huge benefit to the iOS programmer.

Before ARC, when an object was released, the reference to the de-allocated object still pointed to the memory address for the object. If you attempted to call the released object, it would crash your app.

With ARC, when the object pointed to by a weak property is released, the reference is automatically set to nil. In Objective-C, sending a message to a nil object does absolutely nothing. This means that your app will not crash. It does *not* mean that your app will function properly, but at least the crasher has been eliminated.

When you create a new iOS project, one of the project options is "Use Automatic Reference Counting." In general, you should always turn on this feature.

Summary

As stated at the beginning, this chapter is a brief overview of Objective-C. The goal is to arm you with enough knowledge that you can work your way through this book. You will learn more as you read along, but there is so much more to Objective-C than the topics covered here.

If you want to learn more about Objective-C, or you're not yet comfortable with Objective-C, read one of the books mentioned at the beginning of the chapter. Or read the Objective-C Programming Language[4] and Object-Oriented Programming with Objective-C[5] documents published by Apple and available for free online at developer.apple.com and in the iBookstore.

---

4. Objective-C Programming Language: http://developer.apple.com/library/ios/#documentation/Cocoa/Conceptual/ObjectiveC/Introduction/introObjectiveC.html

5. Object-Oriented Programming with Objective-C: http://developer.apple.com/library/ios/#documentation/Cocoa/Conceptual/OOP_ObjC/Introduction/Introduction.html

Getting Started with Cocoa

Objective-C is the preferred programming language for writing iOS applications. The ability to use Objective-C for writing iOS applications would be limited, however, if not for the support of a solid, well-designed application framework called Cocoa. It is the combination of Objective-C with Cocoa that makes it possible for you to write iOS applications.

Cocoa is an application framework—written mostly in Objective-C—that makes it possible to rapidly write robust, full-featured applications for iOS. Cocoa provides frameworks, libraries, and application programming interfaces (APIs) for virtually every conceivable development necessity imaginable. Without Cocoa there would not be hundreds of thousands of iOS applications available in the App Store today.

This chapter introduces you to the Cocoa stack, two of its key frameworks (Foundation and UIKit), and common design patterns found in Cocoa. These frameworks and patterns are fundamental to iOS programming and require a general understanding before you continue beyond this chapter.

This chapter is split into four sections. The first section introduces you to the Cocoa architectural stack. A quick reference to many of the more frequently used classes found in the Foundation framework then follows. UIKit, the framework responsible for providing objects that create and manage the user interface for the applications you will create, is covered after Foundation. Finally, the chapter wraps up with a review of common design patterns found in Cocoa and in the sample code for the book.

Let's get started by talking more about the Cocoa stack.

The Cocoa Stack

Cocoa is the application environment for iOS. Its collection of frameworks, libraries, and APIs provides the building blocks for creating awesome iOS applications. The breadth and richness of the Cocoa stack are truly amazing.

Cocoa's architectural stack for iOS applications consists of four key layers (Figure 5.1).

- **Cocoa Touch**: Supports iOS applications. This layer includes frameworks such as UIKit, GameKit, iAd, and Map Kit.

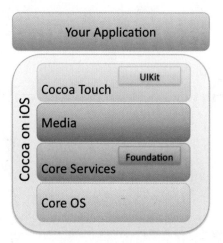

Figure 5.1   Cocoa's architectural stack for iOS. Note the two key frameworks,
UIKit and Foundation.

- **Media**: Provides graphical and multimedia support to the Cocoa Touch layer,
  and depends on Core Services. This layer includes frameworks such as Core
  Animation, Core Audio, AVFoundation, Core Graphics, OpenGL ES, and
  Core Text.
- **Core Services**: Provides core services such as string management, collections
  classes, networking, URL utilities, and preferences. This layer also provides
  frameworks for hardware-based services such as GPS, compass, accelerometer,
  and the gyroscope, as well as services and frameworks for data persistence. Some
  of the key frameworks found in the Core Services layer include Core Data,
  Foundation, Core Foundation, Core Location, and System Configuration.
- **Core OS**: The foundation for Cocoa. This layer abstracts the rest of Cocoa from
  the actual operating system. It provides the kernel, the file system, networking
  infrastructure, security, power management, and device drivers.

Cocoa is also available on Mac OS X, where it is the predominant application environment for building Mac applications. Most, but not all, of the frameworks provided
in Cocoa for iOS are available on Mac OS X. Cocoa Touch, for instance, is not found
on OS X. Because the majority of the frameworks are available on both platforms,
however, you can achieve a certain amount of code reuse when developing applications for both iOS and Mac OS X.

As you read this book, you will get hands-on experience with different Cocoa
frameworks, but you need to be aware of two key frameworks before continuing:

Foundation and UIKit. Much of what you do with Cocoa centers on these two frameworks, so much so that a brief overview is warranted.

> **Note**
>
> When I learn a new programming environment, the first thing I like to do is get an overview of which features are available. I don't need to know the intimate details; I just need a quick reference of what's available so that my mind can start relating features of the new environment to environments I've worked with in the past. That's the purpose of the remainder of this chapter: to give you an overview of Cocoa's two key frameworks.

If you have been reading since Chapter 1, "Your First App"—and you probably have—you have already used both Foundation and UIKit. So what are these two frameworks?

Foundation is a library of Objective-C classes providing the following features:

- A set of useful primitive data classes
- Small utility classes
- Support for Unicode strings
- Support for object persistence

Foundation also provides a level of OS independence. It is this OS independence that allows you to reuse the same code between iOS and Mac OS X.

UIKit is a library of user interface objects for constructing and managing an application's user interface. Unlike Foundation, UIKit is tied directly to iOS. This means you cannot use UIKit-related code for Mac OS X applications.

> **Note**
>
> Mac developers use a similar user interface framework called AppKit.

Let's look at some of the more frequently used classes in these two frameworks, starting with Foundation.

Foundation

Foundation, as the name implies, provides the foundation for many primitive data type classes, utility classes, Unicode string support, and object persistence for iOS applications. Much of Foundation is, just to reiterate, available on iOS and Mac OS X, so code you write using Foundation can be used in applications built for both platforms.

This chapter does not cover every class in Foundation—there are simply too many classes to cover each one—but it does cover the ones you will see most often, especially throughout this book.

Foundation versus Core Foundation

It's not uncommon for developers to think that Foundation and Core Foundation are the same thing, but in truth the two frameworks are different. Core Foundation is a library found further down the Cocoa stack. It provides types and interfaces implemented in C, not Objective-C. Foundation, in contrast, is an object layer that sits on top of Core Foundation, providing Objective-C objects for Foundation types and services.

A quick way to determine whether you are working with a Foundation type versus a Core Foundation type is to look at the prefix in the type's name. Foundation types are prefixed with NS, and Core Foundation types are prefixed with CF. For example, `NSString` resides in the Foundation framework and `CFString` resides in Core Foundation. The same goes for other types such as `NSDate` and `CFDate`, `NSArray` and `CFArray`, `NSDictionary` and `CFDictionary`, and `NSNumber` and `CFNumber`.

Most Core Foundation types have counterparts in the Foundation framework. This close relationship between types means that Foundation types can be used in place of Core Foundation types—a practice called "toll-free bridging."

Toll-free bridging makes it possible to use the types interchangeably with a simple cast. For example, Foundation's `NSDate` is toll-free bridged with `CFDate` found in Core Foundation. This means you can use an `NSDate` instance on API calls that expect `CFDate` as a parameter.

Data Type

As you learned in Chapter 4, "Getting Started with Objective-C," you can use the primitive C data types in your applications. Foundation also provides a set of classes for primitive data types that help simplify your code.

> **Note**
>
> Some of the Foundation types are Objective-C classes and others are structure types defined in C. The only way to tell the difference is to look at the documentation or the header file where the type is defined.

Some Foundation classes come in two flavors: immutable and mutable. An immutable type cannot have its value changed once it has been initialized. Immutable types are, in a sense, static. Their values cannot change. A mutable type, in contrast, can have its value changed over and over during the life of the object.

So why have both immutable and mutable classes? Immutable classes, on the one hand, tend to be more efficient because immutable objects do not have to worry about data changes. Mutable classes, on the other hand, are more flexible in that the data managed by a mutable object can change during the life span of the object. The general rule of thumb is that unless you have a need to change an object's value, you want to use immutable types whenever possible.

> **Note**
>
> A mutable type has the word "mutable" in its name—for example, NSMutableString, NSMutableArray, and NSMutableDictionary. Immutable types do not—for example, NSString, NSArray, and NSDictionary.

NSData and NSMutableData

NSData provides an object interface for a byte buffer. NSData is used to store a stream of bytes in memory. It includes methods for retrieving the bytes, retrieving subsets of bytes, and determining the length of the byte buffer, as well as methods for writing the bytes to a file. NSMutableData is the mutable version of NSData, which means its data can change. Listing 5.1 provides an example of using NSData, and Listing 5.17 shows an example of using NSMutableData.

Listing 5.1 New NSData Instance Loaded with Bytes from the Image File *home.png*

```
NSString *path = [[NSBundle mainBundle] pathForResource:@"home" ofType:@"png"];
NSData *data = [NSData dataWithContentsOfFile:path];
```

NSCalendar

NSCalendar is an object representing a system of time in which beginning, length, and subdivisions of the year are defined. NSCalendar is often used when performing date arithmetic with NSDate. Use the class method currentCalendar to return the logical calendar for the user. This calendar is created from the user's system locale and custom settings from System Preferences. You can also specify the calendar by calling -initWithCalendarIdentifier: and passing in one of the NSLocale calendar keys, as shown in Listing 5.2. Listing 5.3 provides sample code using NSCalendar.

Listing 5.2 NSLocale Calendar Keys

```
NSString * const NSGregorianCalendar;
NSString * const NSBuddhistCalendar;
NSString * const NSChineseCalendar;
NSString * const NSHebrewCalendar;
NSString * const NSIslamicCalendar;
NSString * const NSIslamicCivilCalendar;
NSString * const NSJapaneseCalendar;
NSString * const NSRepublicOfChinaCalendar;
NSString * const NSPersianCalendar;
NSString * const NSIndianCalendar;
NSString * const NSISO8601Calendar;
```

NSDate

NSDate is an object representing a single point in time. It provides methods for creating dates, comparing dates, calculating time intervals, and other date-related functionality. NSDate is toll-free bridged with CFDate. Listing 5.3 provides sample code using NSDate.

NSDateComponents

NSDateComponents is used to create a date object from the parts of a date and time: month, day, year, hour, minute, and second. You can also use NSDateComponents to retrieve the parts of the date and time. Listing 5.3 provides sample code using NSDateComponents.

Listing 5.3   Sample Code Calculating My Son Rowan's Age Based on His Birth Date

```
NSCalendar *calendar = [NSCalendar currentCalendar];
NSDate *now = [NSDate date];

NSDateComponents *components = [[NSDateComponents alloc] init];
[components setDay:29];
[components setMonth:3];
[components setYear:2008];
[components setCalendar:calendar];
NSDate *birthdate = [components date];

// Flag determining which components of the date we want.
NSUInteger unitFlags =
      NSYearCalendarUnit|NSMonthCalendarUnit|NSDayCalendarUnit;

NSDateComponents *age = [calendar components:unitFlags
                            fromDate:birthdate
                              toDate:now
                             options:0];

NSLog(@"Rowan is %li years %li months %li days old.",
      [age year], [age month], [age day]);
```

NSDecimalNumber

NSDecimalNumber is an object wrapper for decimal numbers derived from NSNumber. According to Apple's developer documentation, NSDecimalNumber can represent any number that can be "expressed as mantissa $\times$ 10^exponent where mantissa is a decimal integer up to 38 digits long, and exponent is an integer from −128 through 127."[1] An example of using NSDecimalNumber is provided in Listing 5.4.

---

1. NSDecimalNumber: https://developer.apple.com/library/mac/#documentation/Cocoa/
   Reference/Foundation/Classes/NSDecimalNumber_Class/Reference/Reference.html

> **Note**
>
> NSDecimalNumber isn't the easiest object to work with, but Marcus Zarra makes a darn good argument as to why you should use it, especially if you are dealing with currency. Read his blog posting and don't be lazy with NSDecimalNumber.[2]

Listing 5.4   **Rounding Example Using NSDecimalNumber**

```
NSDecimalNumber *number = [NSDecimalNumber decimalNumberWithMantissa:1445
                                                exponent:-3
                                                isNegative:NO];

NSDecimalNumberHandler *behavior = [NSDecimalNumberHandler
                    decimalNumberHandlerWithRoundingMode:NSRoundPlain
                                                scale:2
                                        raiseOnExactness:NO
                                        raiseOnOverflow:NO
                                        raiseOnUnderflow:NO
                                     raiseOnDivideByZero:NO];

NSDecimalNumber *result = [number
                decimalNumberByRoundingAccordingToBehavior:behavior];

NSLog(@"%@ rounds to %@", number, result);
```

NSInteger and NSUInteger

NSInteger is a C typedef to describe an integer. NSInteger is a 32-bit integer in 32-bit applications and a 64-bit integer in 64-bit applications. NSUInteger is an unsigned NSInteger. Examples of using the integer types are shown in Listing 5.5.

Listing 5.5   **Examples of Initializing NSInteger and NSUInteger**

```
NSInteger x = 5;
NSInteger y = -20;
NSUInteger z = 12;
```

---

2. Don't Be Lazy with NSDecimalNumber (Like Me): http://www.cimgf.com/2008/04/23/cocoa-tutorial-dont-be-lazy-with-nsdecimalnumber-like-me/

> **Note**
>
> NSInteger and NSUInteger provide architecturally safe data types for the corresponding C scalar types. This can be helpful when sharing code between iOS and Mac OS X. Sometimes, however, you may want to use the C scalar type. For instance, the use of NSInteger could cause unnecessary memory bloat to your application. A 4-byte integer uses half as much memory as an 8-byte integer. If your application is storing millions of short integers in memory, using the C scalar type may make more sense. Generally speaking, though, using the Foundation types is fine, and recommended, for most applications where the number of these values stored in memory at one time is relatively small and the lifetime of the value is short-lived—that is, a local function variable.

NSNumber

NSNumber is an immutable object representing any C scalar (numeric) type. It provides methods for getting and setting signed and unsigned C scalar types char, short int, int, long int, long long int, float, double, and bool. NSNumber also includes a -compare: method to compare values from two NSNumber instances. Listing 5.6 shows examples of using the NSNumber object.

Listing 5.6   Examples of Using NSNumber to Initialize and Retrieve Values

```
NSNumber *number;
number = [NSNumber numberWithFloat:1.5];
float aFloat = [number floatValue];
number = [NSNumber numberWithBool:YES];
BOOL aBool = [number boolValue];

// Same as above but with object literals.
NSNumber *number;
number = @1.5f;
float aFloat = [number floatValue];
number = @YES;
BOOL aBool = [number boolValue];
```

NSNull

NSNull is a singleton object used to represent NULL in a collection object, such as NSArray and NSDictionary, where nil is not allowed. An example of using the NSNull object in an NSArray is shown in Listing 5.7.

Listing 5.7   Example of Using NSNull to Add a NULL Placeholder Object to an Array

```
// [NSNull null] places a null object in the array.
// nil ends the array.
NSArray *items = [NSArray
        arrayWithObjects:@"one", @"two", [NSNull null], @"four", nil];
```

```
NSLog(@"items = %@", items);

// Same thing but with object literals.
NSArray *items = @[@"one", @"two", [NSNull null], @"four"];
NSLog(@"items = %@", items);
```

NSObject

NSObject is the root class for most Objective-C classes. Any class you create that does not derive from an existing class higher up the object hierarchy should derive from NSObject. Listing 5.8 shows an example of a class that is a subclass of NSObject.

Listing 5.8   **Example of a Class Derived from NSObject**

```
@interface MyClass : NSObject
// Declared properties and methods go here.
@end
```

NSString and NSMutableString

NSString is an object representation of a text string. It provides methods for determining the length of the string, retrieving characters at a particular position within the string, and performing text string comparisons.

The text string is stored as an array of Unicode characters. Unicode string literals are enclosed with double quotation marks and prefixed with the @ symbol. C string literals are enclosed with only double quotation marks; there is no @ symbol prefix. You will receive a compile error if you try to set an NSString to a C string literal. Listing 5.9 shows an example of creating a new NSString instance with a string literal.

Listing 5.9   **Creating a New NSString Instance from a String Literal**

```
// Create a new NSString instance with a string literal.
NSString *aString = @"This is a string literal";
```

Use NSMutableString when you need to update the string value after it has been initialized, as shown in Listing 5.10.

Listing 5.10   **Simple Sample of Appending New Strings to an NSMutableString**

```
NSMutableString *string = [[NSMutableString alloc] init];
for (int i=0; i < 10; i++) {
    [string appendFormat:@"Item %i\n", i];
}
NSLog(@"%@", string);
```

Collection Classes

Foundation also includes a set of collection classes. Like the classes previously discussed, the collection classes come in two flavors, immutable and mutable. The collection classes provided by the Foundation framework are profiled here.

NSArray and NSMutableArray

NSArray manages an ordered collection of objects. NSArray creates a static array, and NSMutableArray creates a dynamic array. An object added to the array receives a retain message. When the object is removed, which is possible only with NSMutableArray, the object receives a release message. Also, when the array is released, all objects contained by the array receive a release message. An example of using NSArray is shown in Listing 5.11.

Listing 5.11   **Example of Using NSArray and NSMutableArray**

```
NSArray *staticArray = @[@"one", @"two", @"three", @"four"];
NSLog(@"%@", staticArray);


NSMutableArray *dynamicArray = [[NSMutableArray alloc] init];
[dynamicArray addObject:@"one"];
[dynamicArray addObject:@"two"];
[dynamicArray addObject:@"three"];
[dynamicArray addObject:@"four"];
NSLog(@"%@", dynamicArray);
```

NSDictionary and NSMutableDictionary

NSDictionary manages a static collection of unordered objects associated by key-value pairs. NSMutableDictionary manages a dynamic collection of unordered objects. The key identifies the object and the value is the object. As with NSArray and NSMutableArray, an object added to a dictionary receives a retain message. The object receives a release message when removed from the dictionary. In addition, all objects contained in the dictionary receive a release message when the dictionary is released. Listing 5.12 provides examples of using dictionaries.

Listing 5.12   **Examples of NSDictionary and NSMutableDictionary**

```
NSDictionary *dict = @{
    @"name":@"John Doe",
    @"city":@"Seattle",
    @"state":@"WA"};
NSLog(@"dict=%@", dict);


NSMutableDictionary *mutableDict =
    [NSMutableDictionary dictionaryWithDictionary:dict];
```

```
[mutableDict setObject:@"555-1212" forKey:@"phone"];
[mutableDict setObject:@"john.doe@domain.com" forKey:@"email"];
NSLog(@"mutableDict=%@", mutableDict);
```

NSSet, NSMutableSet, and NSCountedSet

NSSet, NSMutableSet, and NSCountedSet manage a collection of unordered objects. You use a set in place of an array when order is not important and you need to check whether the set contains the object.

> **Note**
>
> Checking for the existence of an object in an array is not as fast as checking a set. Thus, if order is not important and you need to determine whether an object already exists in some collection, use one of the set objects.

NSSet creates a static set of distinct objects. Objects cannot be added or removed after the set is initialized. You can, however, change the object contained in a static set. In other words, you can change the properties of an object contained in an NSSet, but you cannot remove the object reference from the static set.

NSMutableSet creates a dynamic set of distinct objects. Objects can be added and removed even after this set has been initialized.

NSCountedSet is a mutable set of indistinct objects. Whereas NSSet and NSMutableSet contain at most one reference to an object, NSCountedSet can contain any number of references to the same object. NSCountedSet keeps track of the number of times an object is added to and removed from the set. To completely remove an object from NSCountedSet, the object must be removed the same number of times as it is added. Examples of using sets are shown in Listing 5.13.

> **Note**
>
> NSCountedSet is also known as a bag.

Listing 5.13   Examples of Using NSSet, NSMutableSet, and NSCountedSet

```
NSString *peter = @"Peter";
NSString *mary = @"Mary";
NSString *paul = @"Paul";

NSSet *set = [NSSet setWithObjects:paul, mary, nil];
NSLog(@"%@", set);

NSMutableSet *mutableSet = [NSMutableSet setWithSet:set];
[mutableSet addObject:peter];
NSLog(@"%@", mutableSet);
```

```
NSCountedSet *countedSet = [NSCountedSet setWithObjects:
                              peter, paul, mary, peter, nil];
NSLog(@"%@", countedSet);
```

Utility Classes and Functions

The Foundation framework also includes a number of utility classes and functions that help simplify coding with Objective-C. Here are some of the more commonly used utility classes and functions.

NSLog

NSLog sends a message to the Apple System Log facility. This message can be viewed in the console. When calling NSLog, you first pass the format string followed by a variable number of arguments displayed as part of the output message. Table 5.1 lists some of the more common format specifiers supported by format strings. For a complete list, read the "String Format Specifiers" article[3] in the developer documentation.

Table 5.1 **Commonly Used String Format Specifiers**

Specifier	Description
%@	Objective-C object; displays the string returned by `descriptionWithLocale:` (if available) or `description`
%%	"%" literal character
%d, %D, %i	Signed integer
%u, %U	Unsigned integer
%f	Floating-point number
%s	Null-terminated char array (8-bit, C language string)
%S	Null-terminated Unicode char array (16-bit)
%p	Pointer address displayed in hex

NSBundle

NSBundle is an object representing a location on the file system containing the code and resources used by the application. In iOS, NSBundle is used to find the path to resources such as images and *plist* files included in your application. An example of using the NSBundle object is shown in Listing 5.14.

---

3. String Format Specifiers: http://developer.apple.com/library/ios/#documentation/Cocoa/Conceptual/Strings/Articles/formatSpecifiers.html

Listing 5.14   **Example of Retrieving the Path to the Application's Icon Image File Using NSBundle**

```
NSString *path = [[NSBundle mainBundle] pathForResource:@"icon" ofType:@"png"];
```

> **Note**
>
> A bundle can be one of three types: Application, Framework, or plug-in. However, under iOS, you can create a bundle only of type Application. iOS third-party developers cannot create Framework and plug-in bundles.

NSFileManager

NSFileManager is a class wrapper for performing generic file system operations such as copying, or moving, a file from one path to another; determining whether a file exists; creating a new directory path; and so on.

> **Note**
>
> NSFileManager provides a singleton reference by calling the class method +defaultManager. However, it is recommended that you use [[NSFileManager alloc] init] instead of the singleton object to ensure thread safety.

NSDateFormatter

NSDateFormatter creates a string representation of an NSDate and can convert string representations of a date to NSDate. You can specify the date and time format or use predefined date and time styles. Using a style is preferred because it takes into account the user's localization settings for the date and time formatting in the System Preferences.

NSNumberFormatter

NSNumberFormatter is used to convert a string representation of a number to an NSNumber and to convert an NSNumber to a string.

NSPredicate

NSPredicate is used to create logical conditions for searching and filtering data. Predicates are created using a format string that looks similar to SQL syntax. Predicates are used to search and filter fetched data, as with Core Data, and for in-memory searching and filtering. An example of using NSPredicate is shown in Listing 5.15.

Listing 5.15   **Example of Filtering an Array of Names Using NSPredicate**

```
NSArray *names = @[@"Peter", @"Paul", @"Mary"];
NSPredicate *predicate = [NSPredicate
                        predicateWithFormat:@"SELF BEGINSWITH[cd] 'P'"];
NSArray *namesBeginningWithP = [names filteredArrayUsingPredicate:predicate];
NSLog(@"%@", namesBeginningWithP);
```

NSRegularExpression

NSRegularExpression is a utility class for creating and applying regular expressions to strings.

NSTimer

NSTimer is used to create a timer object. A timer object waits until some time interval has elapsed, and then calls the desired action on a target. A timer is not a real-time mechanism. Instead, it is fired when the associated run loop determines that the time interval has passed. Timers are good choices for performing actions after a period of time has passed and the time interval does not have to be exact. For instance, timers are useful when you want to update the display after some time interval. An example of using a timer is shown in Listing 5.16.

Listing 5.16 **Example of Setting up a Timer That Fires Every 5 Seconds**

```
NSTimer *timer = [NSTimer scheduledTimerWithTimeInterval:5.0
                                      target:self
                                      selector:@selector(timerFired:)
                                      userInfo:nil
                                       repeats:YES];
```

NSXMLParser

NSXMLParser is a forward-only, event-based SAX parser for XML. The parser notifies your code as it walks through the XML tree. Your code is responsible for maintaining the state and creating objects for data you want to track as the XML is parsed. Your application receives the notifications by implementing methods defined by the NSXMLParserDelegate protocol.

Other XML Parsers

While NSXMLParser is the only XML parser provided by Cocoa, it is not the only parser available to you. A number of open source alternatives are available for consuming and producing XML. Some of the more popular parsers include libxml2, TouchXML, and KissXML.

Ray Wenderlich has an outstanding blog post on choosing the best XML parser for your iOS project.[4] His blog post includes an overview of the most popular XML parsers available to iOS developers, and he has included a sample app for testing XML parser performance. If you plan to consume XML in your application, Ray's blog posting is a must-read for you.

---

4. How to Choose the Best XML Parser for Your iPhone Project: http://www.raywenderlich.com/553/how-to-chose-the-best-xml-parser-for-your-iphone-project [Author note: "chose" in the URL is correct.]

NSJSONSerialization

NSJSONSerialization is used to convert JSON data to Foundation objects and to convert Foundation objects to JSON. You will get hands-on practice with NSJSONSerialization in Chapter 21, "Web Services."

NSURLRequest

NSURLRequest represents a URL load request in a protocol- and URL-schema-independent manner. Listing 5.17 provides an example of using NSURLRequest.

NSURLConnection

NSURLConnecton performs the request as defined by an NSURLRequest instance. Listing 5.17 provides an example of using NSURLConnection.

Listing 5.17   **Example of Downloading Data from the Web Using NSURLRequest, NSURLConnection, and NSMutableData**

```
// ---- SimpleDownloader.h ----
@interface SimpleDownloader : NSObject

- (void)downloadWithURL:(NSURL *)url;

@end



// ---- SimpleDownloader.m ----
#import "SimpleDownloader.h"

@interface SimpleDownloader ()
@property (nonatomic, strong) NSURLConnection *connection;
@property (nonatomic, strong) NSMutableData *receivedData;
@end

@implementation SimpleDownloader

- (id)init
{
    self = [super init];
    if (self) {
        [self setReceivedData:[[NSMutableData alloc] init]];
    }
    return self;
}

- (void)downloadWithURL:(NSURL *)url
{
    NSURLRequest *request = [[NSURLRequest alloc] initWithURL:url];
```

```
        NSURLConnection *connection = [[NSURLConnection alloc]
                                        initWithRequest:request
                                        delegate:self
                                        startImmediately:NO];
        [connection scheduleInRunLoop:[NSRunLoop currentRunLoop]
                        forMode:NSRunLoopCommonModes];
        [connection start];
        [self setConnection:connection];
}


- (void)connection:(NSURLConnection *)connection
didReceiveResponse:(NSURLResponse *)response
{
    [[self receivedData] setLength:0];
}


- (void)connection:(NSURLConnection *)connection
    didReceiveData:(NSData *)data
{
    [[self receivedData] appendData:data];
}


- (void)connectionDidFinishLoading:(NSURLConnection *)connection
{
    NSLog(@"%@", [self receivedData]);
    if ([self connection] == connection) {
        [self setConnection:nil];
    }
}

@end
```

Now that you have an understanding of commonly used Foundation classes, let's move up the Cocoa stack to UIKit and explore what is available for constructing really useful user interfaces.

UIKit

UIKit provides a set of objects for creating and managing the user interface for your application. These objects display text, accept input from the user, display lists of data, and provide pick lists for the user and touchable buttons to request that your application perform some action. Although UIKit is not *required* for building application user interfaces—plenty of apps available in the App Store, mostly games, use other frameworks, such as OpenGL ES, for UI creation and management—it is the most common way to create user interfaces for iOS applications.

> **Note**
> Unlike Foundation, UIKit is available only on iOS. As a consequence, you cannot use UIKit-related code for Mac applications.

UIApplication

UIApplication is a singleton object providing control for applications running on iOS. Each application has only one UIApplication, or subclass of UIApplication, instance. You can access this application object by calling the class method [UIApplication sharedApplication].

UIWindow

The UIWindow object manages the window of your application. A window is the root view in a view hierarchy. It is responsible for sending events to the views contained within the window. iOS applications typically have only one window. There are, however, good reasons for having multiple windows. For instance, if your application supports video sent to a secondary display, your app will need at least two windows: a primary window for display on the device and a secondary window for display on the external monitor or device.

UIScreen

The UIScreen object contains information about a device's entire screen. This information is typically used when setting up a window in your application.

UIView

UIView defines a display area on the screen. It manages the content in that area and is responsible for rendering any content contained within the view.

UIViewController

UIViewController is the controller for a UIView. It coordinates interactions between the model and the view.

UIWebView

UIWebView is a view for displaying HTML content. It supports rendering of HTML and execution of JavaScript. You can track and change behavior as the Web content is loaded by setting the delegate property to an object conforming to the UIWebViewDelegate protocol.

UILabel

UILabel displays read-only text. You can exert control over the visual aspects of this object by setting properties such as the font family type, size, color, justification, shadow effects, and more. UILabel can display single or multiple lines of text.

UITextField

`UITextField` displays a single line of editable text (Figure 5.2). You can set the various visual aspects such as the font type, size, and color. `UITextField` includes a placeholder property for display of default text when the text field value is empty. `UITextField` is ideal when your application needs to capture a small amount of text from the user.

UITextView

`UITextView` displays multiple lines of editable text in a scrollable view. You would typically use this object to display large amounts of text or to allow the user to enter and edit multiple lines of text.

> **Note**
>
> A property missing from `UITextView` is `placeholder`. `UITextField` has a `placeholder` property, which is used to display default text to the user, but this property is not available on a text view. The default text is typically used to give the user an indication of how to use the `UITextField`, which type of input the object expects, or what the purpose of the field is. It is unfortunate that `UITextView` doesn't have the same property.
>
> To get around this problem, I wrote a subclass to `UITextView` that provides a `placeholder` property. You can read more about this property and download the source code from my blog site.[5]

UIButton

`UIButton` is the base class for button display (Figure 5.3). You use it to provide an area on the screen that, when touched, will tell your application to perform an action. `UIButton` supports a number of touch events, but typically your application should respond to the `-touchUpInside:` event. Why? A button should typically tell the app

Placeholder text

Figure 5.2   `UITextField` with the placeholder property
set to "Placeholder text"

Button

Figure 5.3   Round rectangle `UIButton`

---

5. Adding Placeholder Text to UITextView: http://blog.whitepeaksoftware.com/2010/12/08/
adding-placeholder-text-to-uitextview/

to perform the action when the user lifts her finger, which is touching the button, from the device.

UIButton also supports different display styles with rounded rectangle as the default. The custom style is commonly used to display an image as a button. One style sadly missing from UIButton is a gradient button style.

How to Make a Gradient Button

Many developers new to iOS are surprised to learn that UIButton does not include a gradient button style. What makes this omission surprising is the fact that many of Apple's own applications display gradient buttons, and many views managed by the iOS SDK, such as an action sheet, display gradient buttons. Fortunately, the iOS development community has stepped up to fill this void in the iOS SDK.

One way to display a gradient button is to place a gradient image on the button's background. But how do you make the background image look like the gradient buttons displayed by parts of the iOS SDK and other Apple applications? ButtonMaker is one option.

ButtonMaker is an iPhone application designed to run in the simulator only. It uses private APIs to create really nice gradient images for your buttons. ButtonMaker is an open source app and is available on github.[6]

Another option, and the one I tend to prefer, is to use the gradient button class created by Jeff LaMarche. The class makes it possible to display a gradient button without relying on a background image.

Jeff's gradient button class is open source code that is licensed under the MIT License, which means you can use the code in your application even if it's a commercial app. The original source code is hosted in a Google Code project,[7] with improved versions available on github.

UITableView and UITableViewCell

UITableView is used to display a scrollable list of data (Figure 5.4). A table view has only one column, but you can customize the table view cell to give the appearance of multiple columns. Each row of the table view contains a UITableViewCell, which defines the look of the cell within the table view. The table view cell supports a number of predefined cell display styles, or you can customize the cell's look by using a custom view.

UIScrollView

UIScrollView provides a scrollable view. You use a scroll view to display content that is larger than the display area on the screen. The user uses swiping gestures to scroll through the content. The scroll view can also let the user zoom in and out on the content using pinching gestures.

---

6. ButtonMaker: https://github.com/dermdaly/ButtonMaker
7. iPhone Gradient Buttons: http://code.google.com/p/iphonegradientbuttons/

Figure 5.4   The UITableVIew on the left is a plain style, whereas the one on the right supports prototype content.

Figure 5.5   UIPageControl indicating a total of five pages, with the second page as the current page

Figure 5.6   UIPickerView

Figure 5.7   UIDatePicker

UIPageControl

UIPageControl displays a set of dots (Figure 5.5). Each dot represents a page within some context. The page control is often used with a UIScrollView to indicate the number of pages and current page for the scrollable content.

UIPickerView

UIPickerView is a base class for providing a pick list of values (Figure 5.6). The picker displays the list of values using a spinning wheel or slot-machine-style metaphor. The user uses flick gestures to spin the wheel of values up and down.

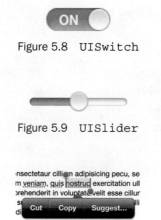

Figure 5.8   `UISwitch`

Figure 5.9   `UISlider`

Figure 5.10   `UIMenuController`

UIDatePicker

`UIDatePicker` is a specialized `UIPickerView` class that provides a pick list of date and time values (Figure 5.7). The date picker can also be used to display time intervals for a countdown timer.

UISwitch

`UISwitch` displays an **On/Off** button (Figure 5.8).

UISlider

`UISlider` displays a horizontal bar representing a continuous set of values (Figure 5.9). An indicator, or thumb, is displayed on the horizontal bar indicating the current value. The user slides the thumb left and right to change the value.

UIMenuController and UIMenuItem

`UIMenuController` is a singleton object that displays a menu for the **Cut**, **Copy**, **Paste**, **Replace**, **Select**, **Select All**, and **Delete** commands (Figure 5.10). You can add your own menu items by adding instances of `UIMenuItem` to the `menuItems` property.

UIImage

`UIImage` is a wrapper class for holding the bytes of an image. Table 5.2 provides a complete list of image types supported by `UIImage`. You can use `UIImage` to convert an image from one type to another, although you most commonly use it to provide an image to `UIImageView`.

Table 5.2   **Image Formats Supported by `UIImage`**

Format	File Name Extension
Tagged Image File Format (TIFF)	*.tiff, .tif*
Joint Photographic Experts Group (JPEG)	*.jpg, .jpeg*
Graphic Interchange Format (GIF)	*.gif*
Portable Network Graphic (PNG)	*.png*
Windows Bitmap Format (DIB)	*.bmp, .BMPf*
Windows Icon Format	*.ico*
Windows Cursor	*.cur*
XWindow bitmap	*.xbm*

UIImageView

`UIImageView` provides a container view for displaying a single image (Figure 5.11) or an animated set of images.

Figure 5.11   `UIImageView` displaying a `UIImage`

UINavigationBar

`UINavigationBar` is a bar used to navigate a hierarchy of data (Figure 5.12). This bar, which is typically displayed at the top of a screen, has buttons for navigating up and down within the data hierarchy. The navigation bar has three primary properties: a left button for moving back (up) through the data, a title displayed in the center of the bar, and an optional right button. You can also use custom views for these properties to provide a customized look.

> **Note**
>
> You will often use a `UINavigationController`, which creates and manages a `UINavigationBar` for you, instead of creating and managing the navigation bar yourself.

UINavigationController

`UINavigationController` is a specialized view controller that manages the navigation of hierarchical data. It creates and manages a `UINavigationBar`, and it manages view controllers using a navigation stack. The bottom item on the navigation stack is the root view controller, and the top stack item is the view controller currently displayed. You add view controllers to the stack by pushing a view controller onto the stack. Pushing the view controller will cause its view to display because it is the top view controller on the stack. When you pop a view controller from the stack, the topmost view controller is removed and the new topmost view controller is displayed. You can programmatically pop view controllers from the stack, or `UINavigationController` will do it for you when the user taps the "back" button on the navigation bar.

UIToolbar

`UIToolbar` displays a bar of buttons (Figure 5.13). Typically this toolbar is displayed at the bottom of the screen in iPhone apps and at the top of the screen in iPad applications. Each button displayed in the toolbar is a `UIBarButtonItem`.

Figure 5.12   `UINavigationBar` created by a
`UINavigationController`

Figure 5.13   `UIToolbar`

Figure 5.14   `UITabBar`

UITabBar

`UITabBar` displays a set of buttons used to navigate to particular areas of your application (Figure 5.14). The buttons act like a set of radio buttons, in that one button is always in a selected state. `UITabBar` can display only a limited number of buttons on the screen at one time. If the tab bar is configured with more buttons than can be displayed on the screen, a **More** button is displayed as the last button.

The **More** button displays a list of all available buttons. The user can select a button from the list to navigate to the particular area of the application. The user can also select which buttons to display in the tab bar from the More screen.

UIBarButtonItem

`UIBarButtonItem` is a specialized button for display on a `UINavigationBar` and `UIToolbar`. The bar button item has a style property that you set to control the display of the item. The *plain* style will make the button glow when tapped. The *border* style gives the item a rounded-corner rectangle look. The *done* style gives the item a highlighted background color. You typically use the *done* style to indicate that the bar button item will complete some action, such as saving data, and then return to the previous view. You can also display a custom view for additional display control.

The iOS SDK provides a set of system-supplied bar button items for common purposes. Some examples include **Done**, **Cancel**, **Edit**, **Save**, **Add**, **Reply**, **Action**, **Camera**, **Trash**, **Play**, **Pause**, **Rewind**, and **Fast Forward**. Using a system-supplied bar button item gives your application a consistent look that users will find familiar.

There are two special-case system-supplied bar button items: flexible space and fixed space. You use these invisible bar button items to control the spacing and positioning of visible bar button items. A flexible space bar button item fills the area between two bar button items, or the edges of the bar, with spaces. Fixed space fills the area between two bar button items, or the edges of the bar, with a fixed amount of space.

UISegmentedControl

`UISegmentedControl` displays a horizontal group of segments, with each segment acting as a button (Figure 5.15). As with the `UITabBar`, only one segment is selected at a time. `UISegmentedControl` is typically used within a screen to display related information.

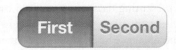

Figure 5.15   `UISegmentedControl`

> **Note**
>
> `UIToolbar`, `UITabBar`, and `UISegmentedControl` are similar yet different. The primary purpose of each is what differentiates these controls. You use `UIToolbar` to display a set of buttons that typically perform some type of action. `UITabBar` displays a set of buttons that, when tapped, navigate the user to new screens, or areas, of the application. `UISegmentedControl` displays a set of buttons that group content displayed on the screen. However, unlike `UITabBar`, `UISegmentedControl` does not navigate the user to a new screen. Instead, it displays a new grouping within the current screen.

That completes our tour of Cocoa on iOS and its two key frameworks, Foundation and UIKit. Now let's turn our attention to design patterns commonly found in Cocoa.

Common Design Patterns in Cocoa

In Cocoa, as with other application environments and programming languages, common design patterns have emerged to become the de facto standard for constructing applications. To cover them all would fill a book, but two patterns are so commonly used in iOS app development (and throughout the sample code in this book) that they deserve special mention: Model-View-Controller and Target-Action.

> **Note**
>
> To learn more about these two design patterns and 26 other commonly used patterns in Cocoa, read the book *Cocoa Design Patterns* by Erik M. Buck and Donald A. Yacktman (Addison-Wesley, 2009).

Model-View-Controller

Model-View-Controller (MVC) is central to iOS development. Its use is not only encouraged, but actually enforced by the development tools. Views created in Interface Builder are expected to have a view controller, and this enforcement is even more obvious when using storyboards. But what is MVC?

> **Note**
>
> Storyboards are discussed in Chapter 14, "Storyboarding in Xcode."

To understand MVC, you must understand each component that makes up the design pattern.

The model is an object representing data and state used by the application. The model responds to requests about the data, and it responds to requests to change the state (or data) managed by the object. The model also defines business rules and relationships between objects.

The view is a visual representation of the model, and it provides user interaction with the visually rendered model data. It comprises the user interface element, such as a text field, or collection of elements (e.g., labels, text fields, selection boxes) that make up the screen presented to the user.

The controller mediates the interactions (requests and responses) between the view and the model. It receives the user input from the view and instructs the model object to perform a particular action or change state based on the user input. It also updates the view based on responses from the model.

The decoupling of the view and the model increases the flexibility and maintainability of the code. As a result, MVC has become a commonly used pattern not only in Objective-C but also in other programming frameworks, including Web frameworks such as Ruby on Rails, Django, and web2py.

> **Note**
>
> For an entertaining lesson on MVC, watch the video of James Dempsey singing his MVC Song at WWDC 2003.[8]

Target-Action

Target-Action is a pattern whereby a dynamic relationship is formed between two objects such that one object holds information needed to send a message to the other object when an event occurs. You can think of Target-Action as a callback mechanism for objects where one object calls a method (the action) on the other object (the target) when an event occurs.

> **Note**
>
> Read more about Target-Action in the "Cocoa Application Competencies for iOS" document provided by Apple.[9]

Target-Action is commonly used with UI elements (such as `UIButton`) where the target and the action are specified for a particular event (such as *Touch Up Inside*). You can set the target and action on an object in code or by using Interface Builder.

---

8. MVC Song: http://www.youtube.com/watch?v=YYvOGPMLVDo
9. Target-Action: http://developer.apple.com/library/ios/#documentation/general/conceptual/ Devpedia-CocoaApp/TargetAction.html

Summary

In this chapter, you took a closer look at Cocoa, the application framework used with Objective-C that makes it possible to rapidly create great iOS applications. You reviewed a list of commonly used classes and objects from Cocoa's two key frameworks, Foundation and UIKit. Finally, you got an overview of common design patterns used throughout Cocoa.

Provisioning Your iPad

Before you ship the next killer app, you must test it on an iPad. Using the iPad Simulator to test and debug your application will get you only so far. That's why it's important to always test your app on the real thing. Before your app will run on a real device, however, you must set up your iPad as a development device. This is where provisioning comes in, and that's exactly what you will do in this chapter: provision your iPad for development purposes.

The steps involved are tedious. Fortunately, you do not have to repeat them often, only a few times a year. Also, Apple is continuously improving the provisioning process. Provisioning a device today using Xcode is easy-peasy compared to what one had to do back in the day . . . the dark days of 2008.

About the iOS Provisioning Portal

The iOS Provisioning Portal is the Web site, shown in Figure 6.1, used to request and download certificates, register device IDs, create App IDs, and create and download provisioning profiles. The Web site and all of its features are not available to everyone. You have access to the portal if you are one of the following:

- An individual registered as a paid member of the iOS Developer Program. You can be registered as an individual or a company.

- An individual registered as a team member for a company that is a paid member of the iOS Developer Program. Depending on your team member role, your access to the Provisioning Portal may be limited. There is no cost to the individual team member, and team members have access to all of the same developer resources that a paid member has, courtesy of the paid company membership.

If you are not a paid member or a team member of a company, you will not have access to the iOS Provisioning Portal. Without access, you will not be able to provision your device.

> **Note**
>
> You can read more about joining the iOS Developer Program in Appendix A, "Installing the Developer Tools."

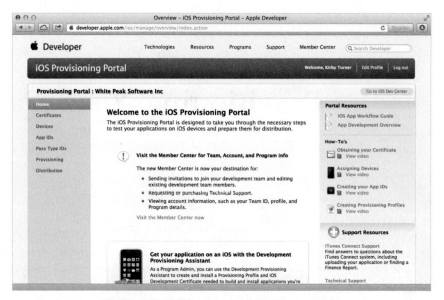

Figure 6.1   iOS Provisioning Portal home page

iOS Developer Program Team Roles

When you join the iOS Developer Program as a paid member, you have the option to join as an individual or a company. The main difference between the two is that a company can include team members and an individual cannot. As a company, you can invite other developers to join your team and assign roles to them. These roles are as follows:

- **Team Agent:** A Team Agent is the individual who originally enrolled in the iOS Developer Program. A Team Agent has full access to the iOS Provisioning Portal—privileges not available to others. A Team Agent can invite others to be Team Admins or Team Members. A Team Agent can also approve certificate requests, register devices, create App IDs, create Push Notification Service SSL certificates, enable In App Purchase, retrieve the distribution certificate, and create development and distribution provisioning profiles.

- **Team Admin:** A Team Admin can invite new Team Admins and Team Members to join the team. The Team Admin can also approve certificate requests, register devices, and create development provisioning profiles.

- **Team Member:** A Team Member can request and download a development certificate and download development provisioning profiles.

- **No Access:** No Access is a role given to developers to prevent them from accessing the iOS Provisioning Portal. This role is used when the company is enrolled in multiple Apple developer programs—that is, the iOS Developer Program and Mac Developer Program.

The Provisioning Process: A Brief Overview

Provisioning a new device is not difficult in and of itself, but a number of steps must be performed first. You must be a paid member of the iOS Developer Program or be a team member of a company that is a paid member. You must request and install a development certificate on your development machine. You must register your device ID. You must create an App ID. You must create and install a development provisioning profile. All of this must be done before you can provision your iPad and run your application on it.

> **Note**
>
> It should go without saying, but you really should have an iPad if you plan to write iPad applications. You can learn iPad programming without an iPad, but you will be limited in what you can test. It's my opinion that having an actual device available is a necessity for anyone who is serious about iPad programming.

Luckily, you do not have to perform each of these steps often. Some of the steps, such as requesting and installing a development certificate, need to be done only once a year, and Xcode performs other steps for you as needed. Even so, knowing about each step helps when a problem does come up, and yes, you will encounter a problem with the process at some point in your iOS career. It's just the nature of writing apps for mobile devices.

> **Note**
>
> A development certificate is valid for one year. You must request a new development certificate when the old one expires.

A number of new terms have been thrown your way, such as "device ID," "App ID," and "provisioning profile," but exactly what are these?

What Is a Device ID?

A device ID, also known as the Unique Device Identifier (UDID), is a 40-character string that uniquely identifies the device. The UDID is tied to a single device; no two devices will ever share the same device ID. The device ID is added to a provisioning profile. Its inclusion restricts applications built with the provisioning profile to run on only the devices associated to the profile.

You register devices in the iOS Provisioning Portal. You can register a maximum of 100 devices per year. The devices you register are for development and testing purposes only. You do not register the devices of your customers who download and install your application through the App Store.

Registering a device counts toward your yearly limit even if you remove the device. Suppose you register your iPad, but later delete it from the list of registered devices. It still counts toward your annual limit of registered devices. After deleting your iPad

UDID from the list, if you decide to add it back, then it will count again toward your yearly limit. Put another way, deleting a registered device does not reduce the number of devices registered for the year.

What Is an App ID?

The App ID is used during the development and provisioning processes to share Keychain data among a suite of applications, and it is used for document sharing, syncing, and configuration of iCloud. The App ID also allows the application to communicate with the Push Notification Service and external hardware accessories.

The App ID is the combination of a Bundle Seed ID and a Bundle Identifier. The Bundle Seed ID is a universally unique, 10-character, alphanumeric string. Its value is generated by Apple within the iOS Provisioning Portal. The Bundle Identifier is a string value you add to your application bundle. The operating system uses this value to identify your application for tasks such as applying application updates.

The naming convention commonly used for the Bundle Identifier is the reverse domain name style. For example, if your company name is Acme and your application name is Awesome App, you would define the Bundle Identifier as com.acme. awesomeApp.

The Bundle Identifier portion of the App ID can contain the wildcard character (*). The wildcard character, if used, must be the last character of the Bundle Identifier—for example, com.acme.*. Using the wildcard character allows the App ID, and its associated provisioning profiles, to be used with multiple applications.

> **Note**
>
> The Bundle Identifier portion of the App ID can be a wildcard only. In other words, the Bundle Identifier value can be a single asterisk character. As you will learn momentarily, the wildcard App ID created by Xcode's Organizer window is a single asterisk character.

A wildcard App ID is convenient because it can be used for multiple applications. Xcode's Organizer window creates a wildcard App ID that can be used by any application. The App ID looks like the last example in Table 6.1.

Table 6.1 App ID Examples

App ID	Remarks
ABCDE12345.com.acme.awesomeApp	An explicit App ID for Acme's Awesome App
ABCDE12345.com.acme.*	A wildcard App ID for Acme applications
ABCDE12345.*	A wildcard App ID for all applications

> **Note**
>
> When creating an App ID in the Provisioning Portal, you add a description of the purpose of the App ID. The App ID created by Organizer has the description "Xcode: Wildcard AppID."

You can also create an explicit App ID. An explicit App ID restricts the provisioning profile to a single application. Certain Apple services such as Game Center, Push Notification, and In App Purchase require an explicit App ID. If you plan to use an Apple service, you must use an explicit App ID.

Changing from a Wildcard to an Explicit App ID

You can change from a wildcard App ID to an explicit ID. You may find that you need to do this if, for example, you decide to add Game Center support to your application after it has been released. While you will be changing the App ID, you must not change the Bundle ID as defined in your application's info.plist. The Bundle ID defined in the app is used to identify your application for new releases—that is, updates to your application. Changing this value breaks the app update process, and Apple will reject your app update submission if the Bundle ID changes.

Changing the Bundle ID suffix in the App ID is not the same thing as changing the Bundle ID in the application. This is why you can safely switch from a wildcard App ID to an explicit App ID. Changing the App ID's Bundle ID suffix does not change the application's real Bundle ID.

To change from a wildcard App ID, you must create a new App ID. You can use the same Bundle Seed ID or generate a new one. For the Bundle ID suffix, enter the bundle ID exactly as it is defined in your application's info.plist.

Because you now have a new App ID, you need to create a new provisioning profile that uses the new App ID.

Note

If your existing application uses the Keychain, select the same Bundle Seed ID for the new App ID. If you use a different Bundle Seed ID, your application will not be able to access any existing Keychain data.

What Is a Development Provisioning Profile?

A development provisioning profile ties developers, devices, and App IDs to a development team. The developer can then install and run the application on a device for the purpose of debugging and testing. To make this possible, the development provisioning profile must be installed on the device. A device, however, can contain more than one development provisioning profile.

Note

A second type of provisioning profile exists: the distribution provisioning profile. A distribution provisioning profile is used for Ad Hoc distribution—distribution to registered devices for the purpose of testing an application—and App Store distribution. More information on the distribution provisioning profile is included in Chapter 27, "Distributing Your App."

Now that you understand the pieces of the provisioning process, let's get your development computer and device ready.

Do I Need a Dedicated Development Device?

A common question asked by new iOS developers is whether a dedicated development device is truly needed. The answer to this question depends entirely on you. Many iOS developers own only one device, but many other developers own multiple devices.

I have eight devices at the time of this writing: three iPads (one from each generation), three iPod touches (first generation, second generation, and fourth generation), one iPhone 3GS, and one iPhone 4 CDMA. I use the older iPod touches to test my applications on older versions of iOS. I use the newer iPod touch to test apps on the latest beta version of iOS. I usually keep one iPad up-to-date with the latest public release of iOS, and I use the newest iPad, which is my primary iPad development device, to run beta versions of iOS. In addition, I run an older version of iOS on my first-generation iPad for testing purposes.

I use my iPhone 3GS, running an older version of iOS, and my iPhone 4, running the current iOS release, for testing on a phone, which can behave differently from an iPod touch—when receiving incoming phone calls and SMS messages, for example.

I write a number of client apps, and my clients have different requirements, which is why I have multiple devices—and that number continues to grow as I buy new devices. It's doubtful that the average iOS developer needs quite so many devices. You can produce your application using only one device. Even so, having a dedicated development device has clear benefits.

During app development, I often find that I need to reset my device to the factory-install state, or I want to test my app on the latest beta release of iOS. You can still do this while working with only one device, but it does mean your device is constantly changing. That game you bought last night and got halfway through will be deleted when you reset your device, or your favorite app might crash on the new iOS beta release. This can be frustrating if your development device is your only device and you use the device for personal reasons.

For this reason, it is helpful—and it saves you time—to own devices dedicated to development purposes. Owning multiple devices, however, can get expensive, especially for the iPad. That's why I typically buy used devices for development. The Apple Refurbish Store is a good place to shop for used devices at an affordable price. Also, ask family and friends what they plan to do with their old devices if they are upgrading to newer hardware. This might be an opportunity to score a development device for free or close to free.

Setting Up Your Development Machine

The first thing you must do is set up your Mac development machine for code signing. Code signing your application serves two purposes: It confirms the app author, and it guarantees that the app has not been altered since it was signed. iOS requires each application to be digitally signed before the app can run on a device. Code signing is never a joy, but it is a necessity, ensuring that the application comes from a trusted source.

To code sign your app, you must have a public and private key pair and a digital certificate. When your application is in development, you use a development certificate to code sign the application. This allows you to run and test your app on your own device. When you are ready to deploy your application to other devices, whether through the App Store or through Ad Hoc and enterprise distribution, you use a distribution certificate to code sign the app.

> **Note**
>
> Chapter 27, "Distributing Your App," covers distribution of your application. Thus this chapter does not discuss the distribution certificate. Steps to request and install the distribution certificate are described in Chapter 27.

Requesting a Development Certificate

To prepare your development Mac for code signing, you must first request a development certificate. To request a development certificate, you need to generate a Certificate Signing Request (CSR). You use the Mac desktop application Keychain Access to generate the CSR. As Keychain Access creates your CSR, it also generates a public and private key pair for you and stores the pair in the login Keychain. The key pair identifies you as an iOS developer and is associated to the development certificate.

The Keychain Access application is available in the **Applications > Utilities** folder. Alternatively, you can launch this app by using Spotlight. Press **Command-Space** and start typing "Keychain," without the quotes, in the Spotlight box. Spotlight will find the Keychain Access application for you. All you need to do then is press the **Enter** key to launch the application.

The first thing you need to do in Keychain Access is to select Preferences from the menu (or press **Command-,**). Click **Certificates** and turn off the Online Certificate Status Protocol (OCSP) and Certificate Revocation List (CRL), as shown in Figure 6.2.

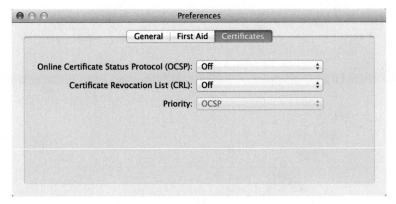

Figure 6.2   Turn off the OCSP and CRL settings in the
Preferences > Certificates screen.

Close the Preferences window, then select **Keychain Access > Certificate Assistant > Request a Certificate from a Certificate Authority** from the menu bar. At this point, you are ready to enter the certificate information, as seen in Figure 6.3. Enter your email address in the User Email Address field. It must be the same email address you submitted when registering as an iOS Developer.

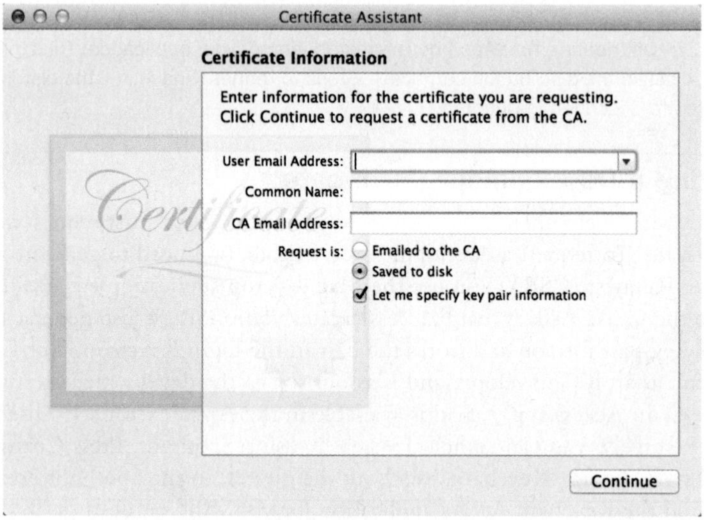

Figure 6.3   Certificate Assistant window in Keychain Access

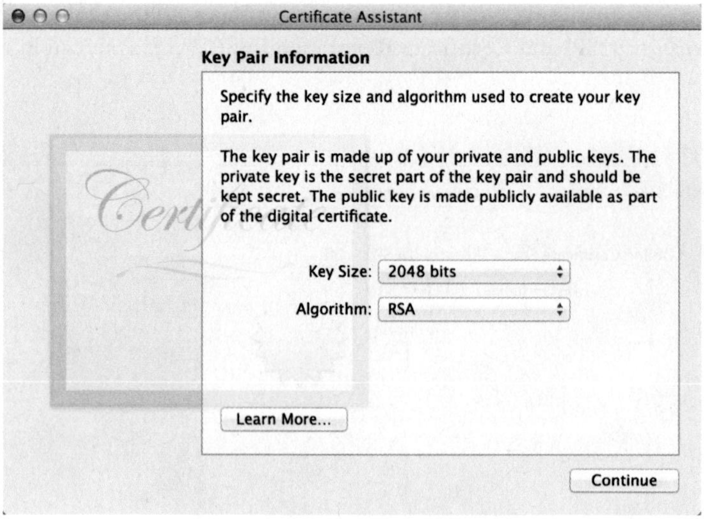

Figure 6.4   Key Pair Information window

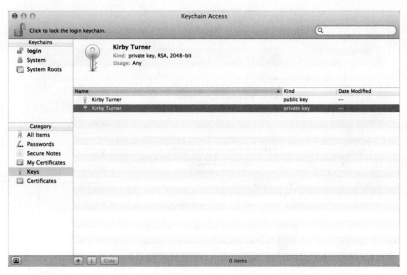

Figure 6.5   Public and private key pairs stored in the login Keychain

Enter your name in the Common Name field. This name must match the name submitted when you registered as an iOS Developer. Leave the CA Email Address field blank. Mark the options "Saved to disk" and "Let me specify key pair information." When you have finished, click the **Continue** button. The Assistant will ask where to save the CSR. Your desktop is as good a place as any, so save the CSR to your desktop.

Make sure you selected the "Let me specify key pair information" option in the Certificate Information window (Figure 6.3). It tells the Certificate Assistant to display the Key Pair Information window, shown in Figure 6.4. Here you set the options for generating the key pair. Select 2048 bits for the Key Size and RSA for the Algorithm. Your certificate request will be rejected if you do not specify the Key Size as 2048 bits and the Algorithm as RSA. Click **Continue**.

The Certificate Assistant will generate the CSR and save it to your desktop. A public and private key pair is also generated for you and stored in the login Keychain. You can view this key pair in the Keychain Access application under the Keys category, as seen in Figure 6.5.

Click **Done** to close the Certificate Assistant. The generated CSR file will appear on your desktop. Your next step is to submit the CSR for approval.

How-to Video

Apple has published a how-to video showing these steps.[1] Watch it if you encounter any problems.

---

1. Obtaining Your Certificate video: https://developer.apple.com/ios/videos/popupcerts.action

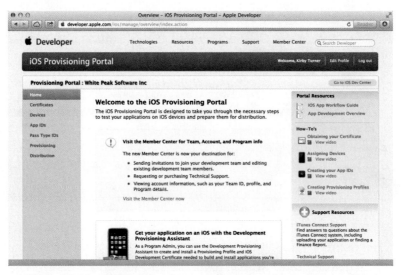

Figure 6.6   Portal Resources containing a user guide and how-to video

Getting More Help

The iOS Provisioning Portal requires you to perform a number of steps before you can test your application on your iPad and prepare your applications for distribution. A set of helpful resources is available in the Portal Resources.

The Portal Resources include a detailed user guide and how-to videos for requesting and installing your development certificate, assigning devices, creating App IDs, and creating provisioning profiles. If you need additional help with the iOS Provisioning Portal or if you prefer seeing the steps performed, you should check out the Portal Resources.

The Portal Resources are available on the iOS Provisioning Portal home page under the section Portal Resources, found on the upper-right side of the page, as seen in Figure 6.6.

Submit Your CSR for Approval

The next step is submitting your CSR for approval, and it is less involved than the previous step. Upon its submission, a Team Agent or Admin will either approve or reject your CSR. You will receive an email notifying you of your certificate status. If your request is approved, you can download your digital certificate from the Provisioning Portal and install it on your development machine.

Note

All certificate requests must be approved through the iOS Provisioning Portal. If you are the Team Agent or Team Admin, you still must approve your own certificate request.

Figure 6.7   iOS Provisioning Portal link available on the
iOS Dev Center home page

To submit your CSR, sign in to the iOS Provisioning Portal. If you have trouble remembering the URL of the iOS Provisioning Portal, sign in to the iOS Dev Center.[2] Toward the upper-right side of the iOS Dev Center home page is a section titled iOS Developer Program, shown in Figure 6.7. This section includes links for the iOS Provisioning Portal, iTunes Connect, Apple Developer Forums, and the Developer Support Center. Click the **iOS Provisioning Portal** link to be transported to the portal Web site.

From the iOS Provisioning Portal home page, click the **Certificates** link found in the left-side menu bar. Next click the **Development** tab, then the **Add Certificate** button. Scroll down to find the **Choose file** button; click it and select the CSR file that you saved to the desktop. Click the **Submit** button to upload your CSR. If you are unable to submit your CSR through the Web site, email the CSR file to the Team Agent.

Download and Install Your Certificate

The Team Admin will be notified by email after your submitted CSR has been received. Once the Admin approves or rejects your request, you will receive a notification email with your certificate status. When it has been approved, you can sign in to the Provisioning Portal again, then click **Certificates > Development**. You'll see your approved certificate listed at the top. Click the **Download** button under the Action column to save the certificate to your development machine.

---

2. iOS Dev Center: http://developer.apple.com/ios

> **Note**
>
> If this is your first time setting up your development machine, you need to download and install the WWDR intermediate certificate. Click the WWDR intermediate certificate download link found on the Development Certificates page, and save the *AppleWWDRCA.cer* file to your development machine. Use Finder to navigate to the saved *AppleWWDRCA.cer* file, and double-click the file to launch Keychain Access; this installs the certificate on your machine.

On your development machine, use Finder to locate the saved *.cer* file, which is most likely in your *Downloads* directory. Double-click the *.cer* file to launch Keychain Access and install your certificate. Save the certificate to your login Keychain. Once it is installed, you can view the certificate by selecting the Certificates category for the login Keychain in Keychain Access (Figure 6.8). Your certificate name will be "iPhone Developer: Your Name."

While still in Keychain Access, click the Keys category for the login Keychain. Here you will see your public and private keys generated by the Certificate Assistant. Expand the private key by clicking the disclosure triangle. You will see that the certificate has been associated to your private key. Apple never receives your private key when you submit the CSR; instead, your private key is available only to you. This is why it is important that you do not lose it.

> **Note**
>
> Make sure you have a backup of your key pair. If you do not have a backup and you lose the private key, you must go through the certificate request process all over again. I use Time Machine to make hourly backups of my primary development machine. I also use SuperDuper! to make complete system backups weekly. This provides a suitable backup of my public–private key pair. You should do something similar.

Figure 6.8   You can view your certificate in the Certificates category.

Your development machine is now set up to code sign builds of your application, but you cannot run your app on your iPad yet. You still have a few more steps to follow. Next up: setting up your device.

Exporting and Importing Your Code Signing Assets

Will you be using multiple development machines for iOS development? If so, then you need to copy your code signing assets to each of the machines. You can accomplish this using the Devices organizer.

To export your code signing assets (Figure 6.9):

1. Open the Organizer window in Xcode, and click **Devices**.
2. Select your team in the Teams section.
3. Click **Export** found at the bottom of the window.
4. Enter a file name and a password, and then click **Save**.

This will generate a password-protected file containing the items you need to code sign your apps. The file contents include the provisioning profiles, certificates, and private keys needed to install apps on your development device. Be sure to remember your password—you will need it to import the file on a separate development machine.

Figure 6.9   Export code signing assets

Figure 6.10   Import code signing assets

To set up a second development machine, begin by copying the code signing assets file to the second machine, and then import the file by following these steps (Figure 6.10):

1. Open the Organizer window in Xcode, and click **Devices**.
2. Select your team in the Teams section.
3. Click **Import** found at the bottom of the window.
4. Select the file containing your code signing assets.
5. Enter the password for the file and then click **Open**.

Setting Up Your Device

Now that your development machine is set up, it's time to set up your iPad for development. Here's what needs to happen:

1. You need to register your device ID.
2. You need to create an App ID.
3. You need to create a development provisioning profile.
4. You need to download and install the development provisioning profile.

These steps can be performed in one of two ways: by using either the Xcode Organizer window or the iOS Provisioning Portal. Using Organizer is by far the easier way to set up your iPad for development. It performs the steps automatically for you. This approach, however, is not without its limits.

Organizer creates a wildcard App ID, and as you may recall, a wildcard App ID cannot be used if you plan to use Apple services such as Game Center, In App Purchase, and Push Notification. That said, you should still let Xcode do its magic. While you may not use a wildcard App ID for your next awesome iPad app, you can use Xcode to build and run sample apps and to test proofs of concept and prototype applications on your iPad.

Use for Development

The steps to set up your iPad for development are quite easy using Xcode. Connect your iPad to your development computer. Launch Xcode and open the Organizer window (**Windows > Organizer** or **Shift-Command-2**). Organizer shows the list of registered and attached iOS devices. Attached devices have a status icon displayed to the right of the device name. A white status icon means the device is not ready for development; a green status icon means the device is ready for development; a yellow status icon means the device is busy.

Click the name of your iPad in the Devices list. You should see a screen similar to the one shown in Figure 6.11. Click the **Use for Development** button. Xcode will prompt you to provide your iOS Provisioning Portal credentials. Enter your Apple ID and password used for your iOS Developer account.

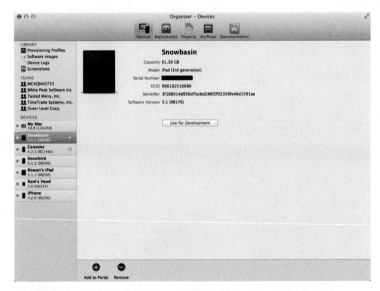

Figure 6.11   Organizer window with a new Apple device
attached to the computer

Xcode automatically sets up your device for development. It registers your device with the iOS Provisioning Portal; creates a wildcard App ID and development provisioning profile, if needed; and downloads and installs the provisioning profile.

This process can take a few minutes. While the process is running, the status icon is yellow. Do not disconnect your iPad from your computer during this time. Once the process is complete, the status icon changes to green and you will see a screen similar to the one in Figure 6.12.

You are now ready to build and run iOS applications on your iPad. To test that everything has been set up correctly, create a new project in Xcode. You can select any iOS application template; it does not matter which one. Make sure you select your iPad as the device for the active scheme (Figure 6.13). Build and run (**Command-R**) the project. Assuming your development machine and iPad are set up correctly, you will see the sample app running on your iPad.

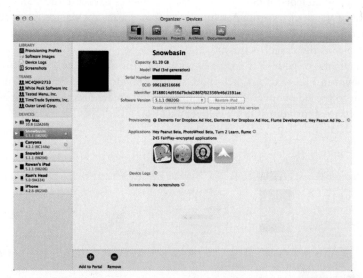

Figure 6.12   Organizer window with an attached Apple device
ready for development

Figure 6.13   Use the **Scheme** popup menu to set the run destination.

> **Note**
>
> Sign in to the iOS Provisioning Portal to see the App ID and development provisioning profile
> created by Xcode. The App ID has the description "Xcode: Wildcard AppID," and the develop-
> ment provisioning profile has the name "Team Provisioning Profile: *." The status for the pro-
> file will also show "Managed by Xcode."

As you just learned, using Xcode is the easiest way to set up a new device. But what happens if there is a problem? And what if you plan to use Apple services such as Push Notification, Game Center, or In App Purchase, which require an explicit App ID? You need to use the iOS Provisioning Portal to manually perform the steps.

Using the iOS Provisioning Portal

As you already know, the iOS Provisioning Portal is used to request and download developer certificates, register devices, create App IDs, and create and download provisioning profiles. You have already gone through the steps for requesting and downloading the developer certificate; the rest of this chapter focuses on the other areas of the Provisioning Portal.

Adding a Device ID

You can add a device ID individually, or you can upload a batch of device IDs in a *.deviceids* file generated by the iOS Configuration Utility. The iOS Configuration Utility is available to enterprise members only, so it is not covered here. Instead, the following discussion walks you through the process of adding an individual device ID.

Start by signing into the iOS Provisioning Portal Web site,[3] then click **Devices** in the left-side menu bar. Click the **Add Devices** button found on the right side of the Devices Web page. Enter a device name followed by the 40-character device ID (Figure 6.14). Click the plus sign (+) button to enter another device. When you have entered all the devices, click the **Submit** button. That's it. The device IDs are now registered.

> **Note**
>
> Only the Team Agent and Team Admin can register a device ID. A Team Member must send his
> device ID to the Team Agent or Team Admin to be registered.

You can edit the name of a registered device, but you cannot change the device ID. If a device ID is no longer valid—for example, if you no longer own the device—you can remove the device from the list by marking the check box next to the device name, then clicking the **Remove Selected** button at the bottom of the registered device list.

---

3. iOS Provisioning Portal: https://developer.apple.com/ios/manage/overview/index.action

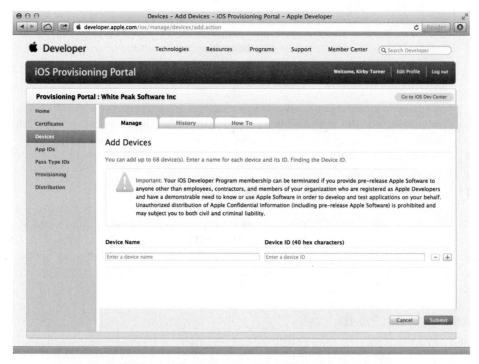

Figure 6.14   Add Devices page in the iOS Provisioning Portal

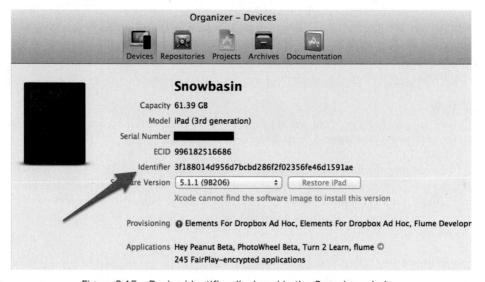

Figure 6.15   Device identifier displayed in the Organizer window

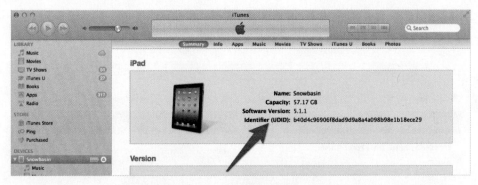

Figure 6.16   Device identifier displayed in iTunes

How to Find the UDID for a Device

Finding the UDID for a device is not hard if you know where to look. There are different ways to find the ID of a device. For developers, the easiest option is to use Xcode's Organizer window. Open the Organizer window (**Shift-Command-2**) and select the device. The device ID is displayed in the Identifier field, as shown in Figure 6.15.

Another way to find the ID, albeit a somewhat more obscure approach, is to use iTunes. Connect your device to your computer and launch iTunes. In iTunes, select the device to see the device information screen (Figure 6.16). Click the serial number. This will display the UDID in place of the serial number. Once the UDID appears, press **Command-C** to copy it to the clipboard. Click the field again to return to the serial number. Note, you can also click the software version to see the build number.

Another commonly used way to retrieve the UDID is to take advantage of one of the many free UDID apps available in the App Store. These apps not only retrieve the UDID from the device but also provide options to copy the ID to the clipboard and to email the device ID to the recipient of your choosing. Using a UDID app is the easiest way for nondevelopers to send you their device IDs.

To download a UDID app, go to the App Store and search on "UDID." Select the app that most appeals to you.

Be aware that Apple has deprecated the API call that apps use to programmatically retrieve a device's UDID. While many of the UDID apps are still available in the App Store today (as of this writing), there is always the possibility these apps will disappear from the App Store sometime in the future.

Adding an App ID

Adding an App ID is almost as easy as registering a device ID. Once again, sign in to the iOS Provisioning Portal. Click the App IDs menu item in the left-side menu bar, and then click the **New App ID** button found on the right side of the page (Figure 6.17). This takes you to the Create App ID page.

Note

The Team Agent is the only team member who can add a new App ID.

Figure 6.17   Click the New App button found on the App IDs page in
the iOS Provisioning Portal.

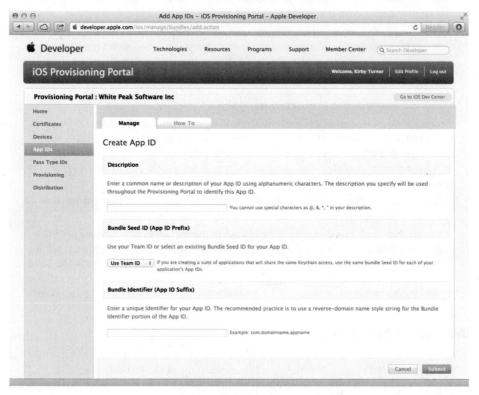

Figure 6.18   The Create App ID page

On the Create App ID page, seen in Figure 6.18, enter the description for the App ID. Use a name or description that makes sense to you. For instance, you might use the name of your application when creating an explicit App ID. The description you enter is used throughout the portal, so choose a name or description that will help you identify the App ID.

Next, set the Bundle Seed ID, also known as the App ID prefix. You can have the portal generate a new seed for you, or you can select from a seed that you previously generated. If you plan to share Keychain data access among multiple applications, you need to use the same Bundle Seed ID for each application's App ID.

Last, enter the Bundle Identifier, also known as the App ID suffix. Remember to use the reverse domain name naming convention. Include an asterisk (*) as the last character if you wish to create a wildcard App ID.

Click the **Submit** button to save the App ID. Clicking this button returns you to the App IDs page. Scroll down the page to see the newly created App ID in the list of App IDs.

In the list of App IDs, you can choose between two actions: Details and Configure. The Details action is available only for wildcard App IDs. Click the action to see the details of the wildcard App ID.

The Configure action is available only for explicit App IDs. Click the action to configure the App ID for Push Notification. You do not need to configure the explicit App ID for In App Purchase and Game Center services, as these services are enabled by default for explicit App IDs.

Note

You cannot delete an App ID once it has been created.

Creating a Development Provisioning Profile

The development provisioning profile brings you (the developer), your device, and your App ID together so that you can run and test your application on your iPad. To create a new development provisioning profile, log in to the iOS Provisioning Portal and click the **Provisioning** link found in the left-side menu bar. Click the **Development** tab at the top of the Provisioning screen, then click the **New Profile** button. This will take you to the Create iOS Development Provisioning Profile page, seen in Figure 6.19.

Note

Only the Team Agent and Team Admin can create development provisioning profiles.

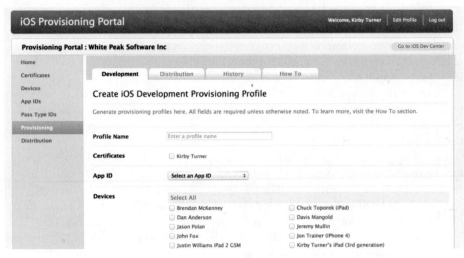

Figure 6.19   Create iOS Development Provisioning Profile page

Enter a name for the provisioning profile. (I like to use descriptive names—for example, "Hey Peanut Dev Profile.")

Select the development certificates that will be associated to the provisioning profile. This step identifies the development certificates used to code sign the application for development. You should select the developer certificate for each team member who will be using the development provisioning profile.

Select the App ID for the profile. Each profile can have only one App ID. You can use a wildcard App ID if you wish to use the same development provisioning profile for more than one application.

Finally, select the devices that the developers can use to run and test the application on a device. Click the **Submit** button to generate the final development provisioning profile.

Downloading a Development Provisioning Profile

Once a development provisioning profile has been generated, team members can download and install the profile. To download the development provisioning profile, log in to the iOS Provisioning Profile, click the **Provisioning** menu item, and then click the **Development** tab on the Provisioning page. You will see a list of development provisioning profiles, as shown in Figure 6.20. Click the **Download** button for the profile you wish to install.

Now you are ready to install the provisioning profile.

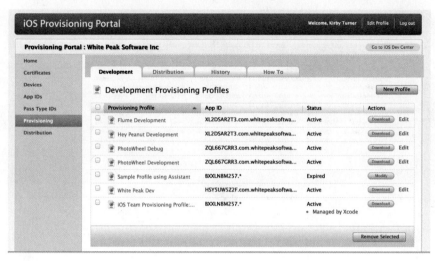

Figure 6.20   List of development provisioning profiles

Installing a Development Provisioning Profile

You can install a development provisioning profile in several different ways. For example, you can copy the profile file to ~/*Library/MobileDevice/Provisioning Profiles*, but the most common way is to use the Organizer window in Xcode. This approach ensures that the profile is stored in the proper directory, and it creates the directory if it does not already exist.

> **Note**
>
> The development provisioning profile you download has the file extension *.mobileprovision.*

To install using Organizer, launch Xcode and open the Organizer window (**Shift-Command-2**). Select **Provisioning Profiles** in the Library section, and then click the **+** button to select the downloaded *.mobileprovision* file. Alternatively, you can drag and drop the *.mobileprovision* file onto the Provisioning Profiles list in the Organizer window (Figure 6.21).

Another way to install a development provisioning profile is to drag and drop the file onto the iTunes icon in the dock. Note, however, that this technique will fail if the provisioning profile directory does not exist.

You can also copy the *.mobileprovision* file directly to the ~/*Library/MobileDevice/ Provisioning Profiles* directory. To make this process easier, add a shortcut for the directory to Finder. When you need to install a new provisioning profile, simply drag and drop the downloaded file onto this shortcut (Figure 6.22).

Figure 6.21   Click the + button or drag and drop the *.mobileprovision*
file to add the development provisioning profile.

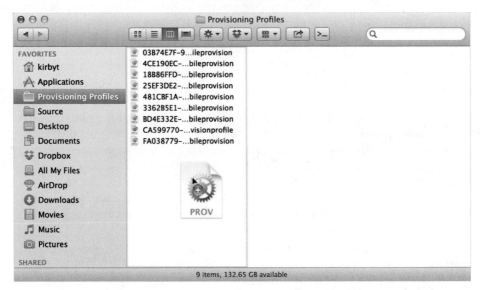

Figure 6.22   Finder window with a shortcut folder to the
provisioning profile directory

Yet another option is to drag and drop the provisioning file onto the Xcode icon in the Dock. This will copy the provisioning profile to the appropriate directory and to your iPad device if connected.

That's it for installing a development provisioning profile.

Summary

At this point, your development machine should be set up for code signing iOS applications and your iPad should be ready for development. You're now ready to write iPad applications that you can run on your own device. Before diving into the app writing process, let's talk a bit about app design as it relates to the iPad.

7

App Design

Before you can write the next killer app, you have to know what it is you are creating. You need to spend time up front coming up with the app design. App design, in the context of this chapter, doesn't mean making your app look pretty, though that is an important part of the process. Rather, it means that you need to know what it is you are building, for whom you are building it, and how it will work.

The app design represents the blueprint for your application. It tells you what, who, and how before you write a single line of code. Without it, you are likely to lose focus, and this confusion will come across in your final product.

Good app designs consist of two main parts: an App Charter and UI mockups. The App Charter defines your app; it tells the "what" and "who" about your app. The UI mockups tell the "how"—that is, how the app will work from the user's point of view.

Let's talk about these two parts in more detail.

Defining Your App

The first thing you need to do when designing your app is to understand what it is you want to create. You need to define your application, what it will do, and who it is for. A good place to start is with the App Charter.

The App Charter describes your app, providing the basis for creating the blueprint for the product you're building. Creating the App Charter forces you to think about your app before you spend time and money writing code. This upfront time will either leave you excited about the app idea or tell you that you have a dud. Either way, you have gained a better understanding of your app idea without spending a ton of time or money.

The App Charter is also a good way to share your idea with others. You may think that keeping your app concept a secret is a good idea, but it isn't. You need to share the idea with others to get their feedback. Often the feedback you receive will help you improve on what you believe is already an awesome concept, but other times the feedback will tell you it's time to jump ship and focus on another app idea. Either way, feedback from others at the early stage is invaluable.

What goes into the App Charter? The list of items included in the App Charter is short. In fact, you really only need the following:

- **App name**: The actual app name or a tentative name
- **App summary**: A short description of your application and its differentiator
- **Feature list**: A list of features that will someday be included in the app
- **Target audience**: The ideal user of your application
- **Competing products**: A list of other apps competing against yours

Let's take a closer look at each of these items.

App Name

Every app has a name, but coming up with a great name can sometimes be more challenging than building the app itself. In fact, there are Madison Avenue-type agencies that specialize in coming up with *über*-cool names. Of course, these companies charge thousands of dollars, which is something most iOS developers don't have, so it's up to you to name your app.

You don't need to spend a lot of time thinking of the app name. Often a good name comes to you later as you are developing the app, so it's okay to use a tentative app name in the beginning.

Using a tentative app name is common practice in the software development world—so common, in fact, that many software shops always use code names when referring to apps that are in development. A code name is nothing more than a tentative name you give your app while it is in development.

Using a theme for code names is also common practice. For instance, Apple uses cat names for major releases of OS X and names of ski resorts for iOS,[1] and Microsoft uses names of mountains and cities for different flavors of Windows OS. You can use whatever code name you like, but following a theme can be fun. (I'm a snowboarder, so I like to use the names of ski trails from my favorite resorts as code names.)

Of course, you don't have to use a code name. Maybe you already have the perfect name, which is great. But if you don't have that perfect name yet, use a code name for now and move on with your app design. Who knows? You might decide to use the code name as the app name. The point is to give your app a name while it is in development. You can always change it later.

App Summary

The app summary is a brief description of your application. It should be about a paragraph long, no more than three or four sentences. It should give the reader a general understanding of your application, and it should include what makes your application unique. This is called the differentiator or "unique value proposition." The unique

---

1. iOS code names: http://www.imore.com/ios-version-codenames

value proposition is what makes your application stand out from all the rest. It's the added value your app provides its users that other similar apps do not provide.

Let's look at an example. Here is the app summary for a fictitious app called Ovation:

> Ovation is a Twitter client for the iPad that focuses on finding conversations about your company and products. It searches Twitter's public timeline and streamlines the processing of responses to comments made about your organization.

Many Twitter clients are available for the iPad. Ovation is different in that its primary function is to find mentions of your company and products within the public timeline on Twitter. Ovation's primary function is its unique value proposition, its differentiator. It's what makes this application different from the rest.

The app summary not only describes your app but also helps you decide which features to include in the app. When deciding which features to include, you should ask, "Does this feature fit within the app summary?" If it's not a fit, chances are good that the feature does not belong in the app.

This brings us to the next piece of the App Charter, the feature list.

Feature List

An app is nothing without features. Features are the tasks the application performs. A feature list tells what your application can and will do. You need to come up with the feature list for your app—but how do you get started? Brainstorming feature ideas is a wonderful way to begin this process.

What Is Brainstorming?

Brainstorming is a technique by which you capture all ideas, suggestions, and creative solutions to a problem or topic. There are no bad ideas when you're brainstorming. Every idea is welcome, even if it seems unrealistic or far-fetched. The goal of brainstorming is to capture as many ideas as possible.

Brainstorming works best when at least one other person participates, but it is still an outstanding approach for the one-person team.

To brainstorm, put yourself in front of a whiteboard, grab some paper or a stack of Post-It Notes, and then start capturing every idea that comes to mind. Mind mapping on the iPad works well when you're brainstorming on a solo basis (Figure 7.1). The medium that you use to capture the ideas doesn't matter; all that matters is that you capture each and every idea.

> **Note**
>
> Post-It Notes and index cards are useful in brainstorming sessions because you can move them around, group them by release schedule or priority, and so on. Try different ways of capturing ideas during brainstorming sessions. Eventually you will find what works best for you and your team.

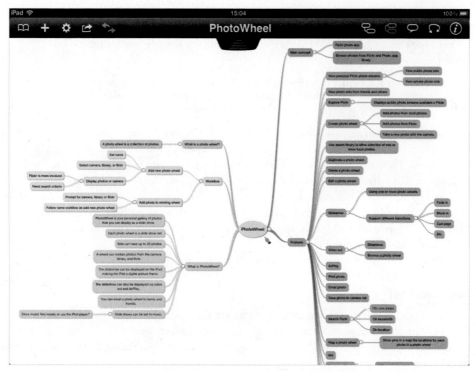

Figure 7.1   Representation of a mind map, using iThoughts, of
concepts and features for PhotoWheel

My Big Fat Feature List

Have a brainstorming session to create your feature list. Capture every conceivable feature that comes to mind, even the far-fetched ones. Remember, you are brainstorming
here, so there are no wacky or unrealistic features. It's doesn't matter how outlandish a
feature might seem; it belongs on the list.

You may be thinking to yourself, "I will end up with a big list of features," and you
are right: You will end up with a big list of features. That is the goal, to produce a big
fat feature list. Not to worry—you'll trim the list soon enough.

The big list gives you something to work with when it's time to decide exactly
what goes into the application. It also gives you insight into the potential of your
application. For instance, that wacky feature you imagined might turn into the differentiator for your application.

Target Audience

With your big feature list complete, start thinking about the target audience for your
app. Think about every possible user—from the individual who will see your app once

for only 30 seconds to the power user who will do things with your app you never dreamed possible. Within this range is your ideal user.

Start thinking about the ideal user for your app and list the characteristics of this user. Is the user male or female, a teenager or a retired senior? Is the user someone who travels often? A soccer mom? Does she love snowboarding but doesn't get to the slopes as often as she would like? Capture every conceivable characteristic of the ideal user.

As you think about your ideal user, imagine the conditions the user might face when she is using your app. Add this information to your list of characteristics. Will the user be under a lot of stress at the moment she is using your application? Is the user likely to be in a rush? Is it likely the user will be hiking the backcountry with no network access while using your app? These types of characteristics should be captured as well, as they can have a direct impact on the features and usability of your application.

Once you determine the characteristics of your ideal user, you know who your target audience is. Armed with this knowledge, you can start trimming your feature list until it includes only those features that complement the characteristics of your target audience.

Note

Often you will think of new features as you think about the target audience. When this happens, be sure to add the new features to your big feature list.

Revisit Your Feature List

Creating the App Charter is an iterative process. You don't make one pass defining the aspects of your app; you make multiple passes, constantly refining the definition based on new knowledge. As you list the characteristics of the ideal user, for instance, new features will likely come to mind. Those features should be added to the big feature list.

At some point, however, you must decide what actually goes into your application. A good time to start trimming the feature list is after you understand who the target audience is. Then you can whittle the big list of features into the list of features that appeal to the target audience.

As you trim the feature list, make sure you consider the device. A particular feature may or may not make sense on the iPad. If the feature is inappropriate for the device, strike it from the list.

The cut-down version of the feature list is what you include in the App Charter. This list represents all the features that you would like to see in your app over its lifetime. Don't assume this list represents version 1.0 of your app. Version 1.0 will most likely include only a small subset of the feature list.

Competing Products

Knowing your competition is important. It helps you decide what makes your app different. It also tells you if a market exists for your application. If there is zero competition for your app, either your idea goes beyond anything ever conceived before, which is unlikely, or there is no market for your app, which is the more likely scenario.

If you think Google or Yahoo! invented the search engine, think again. Before these search engines existed, there was Archie (see www.searchenginehistory.com for more on search engine history). Google and Yahoo! simply found better ways of indexing and searching . . . and to beat out the competition.

To beat the competition, you must know who the competition is, and this information should be included in the App Charter. Including the competition in the App Charter forces you to acknowledge that competition exists. It also forces you to learn who your competition is and to determine if a market for your app exists.

What you capture about your competition is up to you, but at a minimum you want the name of the app, the vendor's name, the URL to the app's Web site, and any notes or remarks you have about the competing app.

A Sample App Charter

In Part II of this book you will build an iPad app. Before you begin, you need to know what the app is and who it is for—that is, you need its App Charter. Following is the App Charter for the app you will build in the next part of this book.

> **Note**
>
> The app summary section shown here is not that of a top 100 app in the App Store, but it does convey the primary intention of the app—to teach programmers how to write iPad applications. This differentiator will not result in millions of downloads, but it does provide focus as you write the application. The app is not attempting to be the best photo library app in the App Store. It is a means to an end, where the end is you becoming a competent iPad programmer.

Target Audience for PhotoWheel

The target audience in the PhotoWheel App Charter might seem a bit odd. It's not your typical ideal user for an app, but PhotoWheel is not your typical app. When I thought about the target audience for PhotoWheel, four types of users came to mind:

- The individual who downloads all available free apps
- The individual looking for another way to store photos
- The individual looking to store favorite photos from Flickr
- The iOS programmer learning iPad programming

The first user type is not someone whom PhotoWheel cares about. This person will likely download the app, use it for 10 seconds, and then post a 1-star rating saying the free app costs too much.

The second and third user types are good ideal users for PhotoWheel, but they don't fit the application summary.

App Name

PhotoWheel

App Summary

PhotoWheel puts a spin on personal photo libraries. Collect your favorite photos in one or more photo albums. Print and email photos, apply special effects, and display them on your TV using AirPlay.

PhotoWheel is a personal photo library app for the iPad written as the companion app to the book *Learning iPad Programming: A Hands-on Guide to Building Apps for the iPad*, which teaches programmers how to build iPad applications.

Feature List (in no particular order)

- Display photos from one or more photo albums.
- Add, edit, and remove photo albums.
- Rename photo albums.
- Add and remove photos from photo albums.
- Import photos from the Photos app library.
- Import photos from Flickr.
- Print one or more photos.
- Email one or more photos.
- View slideshows of photos.
- Display slideshows over AirPlay.
- Sync photo albums between multiple devices.

Target Audience

The iOS programmer who is reading *Learning iPad Programming*

Competing Products

Flickpad HD

Vendor: Shacked Software LLC

Price: $2.99

Rating: 4.0 stars

Last update: July 2, 2011

Web site: **flickpadapp.com/**

iTunes: **http://itunes.apple.com/us/app/flickpad-hd-for-facebook-flickr/
        id358635466?mt=8**

Photo Stack

Vendor: Seong Hun Lim

Price: Free (pro version $0.99)

Rating: 4.0 stars

Last update: May 27, 2011

Web site: None

iTunes: **http://itunes.apple.com/us/app/photo-stack/id427552502?mt=8**

Why make this distinction? PhotoWheel is intended to help you learn iPad programming. It says so in the app summary. Its goal is not to support photo editing and other photo sites such as SmugMug.com. The second and third user types will expect such full support, which is beyond the scope of the app you are building. This could change over time, but for now these two user types are not PhotoWheel's ideal users.

The fourth user type, the programmer learning iPad programming, is the ideal user. This user is you, and your goal at the moment is not to write a top-100 photo app. Your goal is to learn how to write iPad apps. This user type fits nicely within the app summary, and for these reasons this is PhotoWheel's target audience.

UI Design Considerations

You have completed your App Charter. You know what you want to build and for whom, but you don't know how your app will work. Your next step is to come up with the UI design. But before you start sketching a UI for your app, there are a few things you need to consider and do.

Read the HIG

A must-read for all iOS developers is the *iOS Human Interface Guidelines,*[2] more commonly referred to as just "the HIG." This guideline, published by Apple, provides a general overview of what you should and should not do in an iOS application. Apple publishes updates to the HIG whenever it issues a new build of the iOS SDK, which means you should reread this document from time to time.

> **Note**
>
> The iOS HIG is also available in the iBookstore. Search for "Apple Developer Publications" or "Human Interface Guidelines" to find it.

Much of what is covered in the HIG is based on Apple's usability research for iOS devices and apps, and Apple shares this information with you. You are doing a disservice to yourself, your app, and your users if you don't read the HIG before designing your app's UI.

Make Your App "Tapworthy"

Another invaluable resource for the nondesigner type of programmer is Josh Clark's book *Tapworthy: Designing Great iPhone Apps* (O'Reilly Media, 2010). While

---

2. *iOS Human Interface Guidelines*: https://developer.apple.com/library/ios/#documentation/ UserExperience/Conceptual/MobileHIG/Introduction/Introduction.html#//apple_ref/doc/ uid/TP40006556

Tapworthy's focus is on iPhone app design, many of the principles apply to iPad app design. For example, the ideal hit target for an on-screen object is 44 pixels. Why 44 pixels? Well, that's about the size of an adult fingertip. Make the hit target smaller, and people will have trouble tapping it.

Design for the Device

When designing your iPad app, keep in mind that you are designing for a touch environment, not a point-and-click environment. The rules for the iPad are different from those for the desktop or even a Web site. Touches and mouse clicks, for example, are different, yet sometimes designers, programmers, and even users compare them as if they were the same and required the same amount of effort. But this is not true: A touch is not the same as a mouse click.

Mouse clicks are often considered "expensive." Consequently, designers constantly try to find the best design that requires the fewest number of clicks. This is why you see a lot of Web sites that cram a ton of content onto the home page. While mouse clicks are considered expensive, the same is not necessarily true for touches.

A touch is not as involved as moving a mouse, aligning the mouse cursor to the correct screen location, and then clicking the mouse button. With a touch, you see the object you wish to see; you move your finger and tap the object. That's it.

Touching is so simple that an 18-month-old can do it. There's even a YouTube video[3] of a cat playing with Smule's Magic Piano. The point here is that, by nature, humans are a tactile lot, and that's why the iPad has taken off so quickly. It's much easier to launch an app, touch or swipe something, and get it to quickly do what you want. Compare that to Microsoft Word, with all its toolbars, menus, and palettes. If all you want to do is type a letter to someone, Word is overkill; in fact, it's like a death sentence (no pun intended).

Keep this in mind while designing your application. Don't just assume that because a particular design practice is commonplace in the point-and-click world, it will translate to the touch world. (I can't imagine trying to use a touch-based version of Word, but give me Pages[4] for iPad and I can tear things up.)

People Use iOS Devices Differently from the Web or Desktop

When designing your iPad app, keep in mind that people do not use iOS devices in the same way they use the Web or desktop. This distinction should be reflected in the design of your application. Web site designs, for example, try to display as much information as possible at the top half of the page. This area is dubbed "above the fold," a term that comes from the newspaper world. It indicates the section of a newspaper that is literally above the fold, where the paper is folded in half. It is where newspapers print the biggest headlines and other attention-grabbing information.

---

3. Cat investigates an iPad: http://www.youtube.com/watch?v=Q9NP-AeKX40
4. Pages: http://itunes.apple.com/us/app/pages/id361309726?mt=8

On the Web, the concept of "above the fold" refers to everything you see before scrolling down. Web site designers try to display the most important, eye-catching content at the top half of the Web page to grab the reader's attention. The rationale is that the user is unlikely to scroll down a Web page to view additional content. This is one of the reasons SEO (Search Engine Optimization) experts say you want your Web site to appear above the fold when a user does a search. Those first four or five matches are the ones the user is most likely to click. Matches falling below the fold—those that are hidden until the reader scrolls down—are less likely to be clicked.

This is not true on iOS devices. Scrolling is a natural behavior, whether it's flicking up and down or left and right. As a consequence, you do not need to cram a ton of information on the screen at one time. Instead, you want to provide a balanced amount of information in a visually pleasing manner and allow the user to use touch gestures to scroll and pop over for additional information.

Wear Your Industrial Designer Hat

App design for iPad is a bit more involved than app design for the point-and-click world. With the iPad, the user interacts directly with the objects on the screen by touching them. This leads to a different set of sensations compared to the indirect interaction of using a mouse. It also means your app design must consider user interaction within the app from an industrial design point of view.

Industrial design considers the aesthetics, ergonomics, and usability of a product. The iPad has no physical buttons interacting with your application—even the keyboard is virtual—so it's up to you to include on-screen objects with which the user interacts. The placement of these objects is important to the usability and the ergonomics of your application. Left-handed users, for example, will find certain object placement more ideal than right-handed users. This is more noticeable on the iPhone than on the iPad, but it's still important to consider when designing your iPad app.

Apple has made some recommendations in the iOS HIG that fall into the industrial design realm. Toolbars should be displayed at the top of the screen on the iPad. This is a change from the recommendation for the iPhone, where toolbars are displayed at the bottom of the screen. This difference arises because the user interacts with the devices differently. An iPhone user often interacts with toolbar buttons using a thumb. Placing the toolbar at the bottom of the screen makes it easier for the user to thumb tap the buttons. Meanwhile, an iPad user is likely to hold the device in one hand, freeing the other hand to tap the screen. With the toolbar at the top, the user is made more aware of its presence, and she can easily tap the desired button with her free hand.

Metaphors

iOS has a complete set of UI objects that you can use to construct your app's user interface. These standard controls make it easier for users to use your application because the UI looks familiar, but the standard controls look rather bland. Also, using the standard controls will not make your app stand out. Instead, it will look like all the other apps in the App Store that use the same standard controls.

Figure 7.2   An iBooks library

One way to stand out in the crowded App Store is to provide a real-world-like experience to the user. You accomplish this goal by making use of various metaphors that loosely mimic the real world. The user interacts with the iPad using touch gestures, which mimic behaviors in the real world—for instance, turning a page in a book. This is a much more engaging experience compared to the point-and-click world of the personal computer. Proper use of metaphors will not only give the user a sense of interacting with real objects, but also provides a user interface that is familiar to the user and is easier to learn.

Metaphors should be subtle, not overdone. iBooks[5] is a good example of an iPad application that pushes the limits of real-world metaphors without going overboard. With this app, your books are displayed on a wood-grain bookcase, as shown in Figure 7.2. Tap a book cover to open it. Flick your finger left and right to turn pages. This experience is similar to picking a physical book from a bookshelf and reading it. The trick, however, is not to go too far with metaphors. Metaphors should be subtle.

---

5. iBooks: http://itunes.apple.com/us/app/ibooks/id364709193?mt=8

How could iBooks take the real-world metaphor too far? For starters, if the iBooks bookcase looked anything like many real-world bookcases, the books would be two or three levels deep. Books would be crammed into every possible space, sitting on top of one another, turned so the book title is hidden, and sitting at different angles. In addition, there would be a slight bend in the shelves caused by the weight of all the books.

Luckily, Apple did not take the bookcase metaphor this far. If it had, iBooks would not be the beautiful, useful app it is today. Instead, it would cause the same frustrations you might experience in the real world when looking for a particular book.

Learn from Apple: Keep the metaphors simple and don't go overboard.

Sound Effects

Another way to give your application that real-world feel is to provide audio feedback with sound effects. But just as with visual metaphors, it's important that you not go over the top with them.

The virtual keyboard provided by iOS is a good example of appropriate audio feedback. As you type on the keyboard, you hear soft clicking sounds. This sound effect resonates with users, taking advantage of hearing to give a sense of typing on a real keyboard.

You should do the same with your users—that is, you should tap into their sense of hearing by providing subtle sound effects within your application. Suppose your app displays a light switch that the user flicks on and off. Adding a soft click as the user flicks the switch will give your app a real-world sensation.

Your goal when using sound effects is to tap into the users' senses, not to annoy them. Don't go overboard with sound effects; keep them subtle. And remember, users can use device controls that affect sounds. They can switch the device to silent mode with the Silent switch, and they can turn the volume up and down with the volume controls. Users can even listen to music from the Music app while they use your app. Be mindful of these possibilities when adding sound effects to your app.

> **Note**
>
> The HIG has a lengthy section on using sounds in apps, but you already know this because you have read the HIG. You have read the HIG, right?

Customize Existing Controls

A common pitfall encountered by programmers new to iOS is reinventing the wheel. Suppose the programmer wants to implement a real-world metaphor—say, a three-way switch. The initial thought is to write this UI control from scratch because there is no three-way switch in the list of standard controls. But that would be a waste of time. A better approach is to reexamine the standard controls and find one that provides the basic behavior you are looking for. When you find the right standard control, customize its look and behavior.

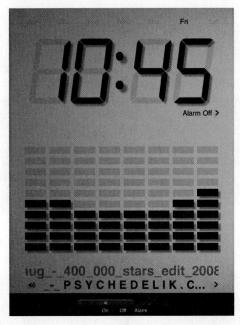

Figure 7.3   Alarm Clock Radio from Raizlabs. Notice the
On/Off/Alarm switch at the bottom of the screen. This is the
standard control `UISlider` with a new look.

This is exactly what the team at Raizlabs did with their app Alarm Clock Radio,[6] shown in Figure 7.3.

At the bottom of Alarm Clock Radio's screen is a three-way switch. You can slide the switch to the On, Off, and Alarm positions. This action of sliding the switch is similar to using `UISlider`.

`UISlider` is a horizontal bar that allows the user to select a value from a continuous range of values. This is the same behavior found in the On/Off/Alarm switch in Alarm Clock Radio. The slider is configured to support three values representing On, Off, and Alarm. The switch slides along a horizontal bar, which again is a behavior found in `UISlider`. Thus, to implement the three-way switch in Alarm Clock Radio, Raizlabs customized the `UISlider` control. They didn't have to reinvent the wheel; they just took an existing wheel and gave it a new look.

Before you start down the path of creating your own custom control, study the standard controls provided by iOS. Chances are very good that the behavior you are looking for has already been implemented in one of the standard controls. All you need to do is give the control a new look.

---

6. Alarm Clock Radio: http://itunes.apple.com/us/app/id320108713?mt=8

Hire a Designer

Unless you are a master of Photoshop and have an eye for design, your best option for creating an awesome-looking application is to hire a designer. If you happen to be one of those rare (and lucky) programmers who possess both programming and design skills, you might be able to avoid hiring a designer. But for the everyday programmer, hiring a designer is the best way to create an amazing-looking app.

A designer can help you in many different areas. Your budget will determine how you can best leverage the skills of a designer. At a minimum, you should have a designer create your app icon. The app icon is the first visual impression potential users will have of your application when deciding whether to download it. If you stick an ugly icon on your app, you run the risk of losing customers before they even load your app's profile page in the App Store. Remember, first impressions can mean a lot, and if you've got some cheap, cheesy graphic as an app icon, chances are your app won't sail to the top of the charts, no matter how great and useful it is.

If you can afford it, get a professional designer involved in the design of your app, specifically the UI design. This step could save you time down the road when you're polishing your app—in other words, making it look pretty.

So far, you have defined your app. You have read the HIG. You are starting to visualize what your app might look like and the metaphors it will use. You may have even hired a designer to help out. Now it's time to start sketching UI designs for your app.

Mockups

One of the fastest ways to validate your app design is with mockups. Mockups make it possible to get a sense of how your app looks and flows between screens. They also help reduce software development costs in that they help identify major flaws within the app design prior to your writing a single line of code.

What Is a Mockup?

A mockup is a static rendering of a visual design—"static" because a mockup is rendered in a format that does not allow user interaction in the same way a real application does. Mockups are used to show a visual design concept and give a basic sense of what the app screen will look like when finished.

> **Note**
>
> Mockups are used for a variety of visual designs. In the software development world, they are used for everything visual from artwork to screen design. For brevity's sake, this section focuses on mockups for screen design.

A mockup can come in many different forms. It can be a hand-drawn sketch, as seen in Figure 7.4, or it can look exactly like the real application. A mockup can even be as basic as a wireframe produced in Keynote or some other drawing app. Regardless of the form, a mockup serves the same purpose: to convey the look and feel of a visual design.

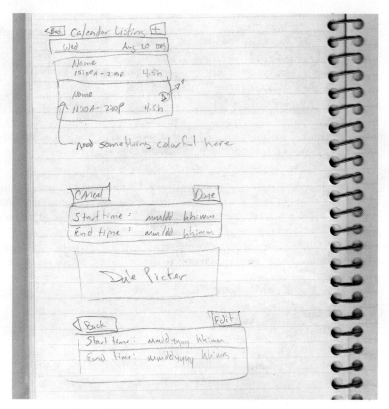

Figure 7.4   A set of wireframes sketched by hand

Wireframes are the easiest kind of mockup to create. A wireframe is nothing more than boxes and simple objects sketched to show the general layout of the application screen. What makes wireframes easy is that you can sketch them with nothing more than pencil and paper, and no artistic skills are required.

A mockup can be made to look like the real application screen. This is a bit more involved and requires more than pencil and paper. A realistic-looking mockup is great when you are pitching an app concept to a potential client because it shows exactly how the application will look. Wireframes, by comparison, require the people reviewing them to use a bit of imagination, but this is not a bad thing.

As awesome-looking and impressive as realistic mockups can be, they are not without their own set of problems. First, creating realistic-looking mockups requires more time. Second, showing realistic mockups can mislead clients and others into thinking the app is nearly complete even though not a single line of code has been written. People who do not understand software development see a realistic-looking screen mockup and think all you now need to do is sprinkle in some code and the app is done. As a programmer, you know better.

Figure 7.5   Example mockups for the Labor Mate app icon, starting with hand-drawn sketches and ending with the final app icon

> **Note**
>
> This has happened to me on more than one occasion. I present a set of mockups to the client, where each mockup looks like a real screen shot. The client knows little about the software development process and, upon seeing the realistic-looking mockups, jumps to the conclusion that the app is nearly finished—this despite my explanation that the material being reviewed is only a mockup, a static rendering of a screen design. I'm now of the opinion that it is best to avoid creating realistic-looking mockups unless you know that the person reviewing them understands that they were drawn and not created from snapshots of a functioning app.

What to Mock Up

What to mock up really depends on the circumstances. You can mock up as little or as much of the application as you feel is necessary. Remember, the goal of mockups is to convey the basic look and feel of the application, including the flow of the app. They need not be perfect or contain every possible detail. They just need to include enough details for everyone to understand the UI design and workflow of the app.

It's not always necessary to create a mockup of each and every screen. If a mockup has done its job in conveying the app design, you can assume that the additional screens not included in the mockups will follow the same look and feel. However, if the app you are building is for a client, the client might expect, and prefer, mockups for every screen. Use your best judgment when deciding how much or how little to mock up.

Using mockups is not just about designing screens for your application. Mockups are also really useful for designing artwork that is included in your application. Figure 7.5 shows some of the mockups for the Labor Mate[7] app icon.

There are no limits to what you can mock up. The more mockups you create, the better the impact on your design. Best of all, creating mockups is a great way to get the creative juices flowing.

Tools to Use

How you create a mockup can vary as much as the details you include in the mockup. You may find that drawing sketches with paper and pencil works best for you. Alternatively, you might decide that a combination of hand-drawn sketches and wireframes created in Keynote is best. Find what works best for you and run with it.

---

7. Labor Mate: http://itunes.apple.com/app/labor-mate-contraction-timer/id293822973?mt=8

> **Note**
>
> My approach varies based on the project. I tend to start with paper sketches. Once I'm comfortable with the design, I may or may not redo the mockups in Keynote or iMockups. If the mockup is for a client, I will typically redo the mockups in an app. The result is a more professional appearance when I present the UI designs to clients.

To find what works best for you, you need to know which tools are available for creating mockups. Let's go over some of the more popular ones.

Paper and Pencil

Paper and pencil is by far the most commonly used mechanism for creating mockups. A paper mockup is quick and simple, and it doesn't require a learning curve. You just start drawing. Best of all, artistic skills are not required. Your sketch doesn't have to look great. It simply needs to convey a sense of how the screen looks and behaves within the app.

Hand-drawn sketches are no longer limited to paper, however. The iPad has become an excellent device for sketching. Apps such as Penultimate[8] make drawing sketches as much fun as finger painting. Unfortunately, using a finger can be somewhat troublesome, especially if you are doing a large number of sketches. To get around this problem, a number of folks use a capacitive stylus for drawing on the iPad. Whether you use your finger or a stylus, the iPad is a good alternative to paper.

Photoshop

Another option for creating mockups is Adobe Photoshop. This software is a popular choice with designers who have designed Web sites for years using Photoshop.

Doing mockups in Photoshop has a few advantages over paper. First, you can create a mockup that looks exactly like the real thing. Photoshop is an excellent choice when you want to create realistic-looking mockups. Second, Photoshop makes it easy to slice out custom artwork that will be included in your app.

The downside to using Photoshop is the time it takes to learn. Many designers already know how to use Photoshop and can produce mockups in a short amount of time. For other folks, using Photoshop to create a good-looking mockup is about as realistic as my mom, who has never programmed before, writing a good iOS application in a short amount of time. It's not that it can't be done; it's just that it is difficult to do in a reasonable amount of time.

All is not lost should you still want to create realistic mockups using Photoshop. A number of templates are available to help you get started. One template that looks particularly good is the iPad GUI PSD.[9] This PSD includes most, if not all, of the standard elements you need to create really useful, realistic-looking mockups using Photoshop.

---

8. Penultimate: http://itunes.apple.com/us/app/penultimate/id354098826?mt=8
9. iPad GUI PSD: http://www.teehanlax.com/blog/ipad-gui-psd/

> **Note**
>
> A trick you can use to suggest a real app using nothing more than mockups is to save each screen mockup as a *.png* or *.jpg* image. Copy the images to your iPad and view the images using the Photos app. Although the screen elements will not be functional, you can still flip through the screens to get a sense of how the application will look and feel on the device.

Keynote

Keynote might seem like an odd choice for creating mockups, but it's a really useful way to create nice-looking mockups for the nondesigner type who struggles with Photoshop. Keynote, and PowerPoint for those who prefer it, make it possible to create realistic-looking iPad screen mockups with very little effort. Keynote also does an outstanding job of drawing boxes, making wireframe mockups a snap to create.

As with Photoshop, starting with a template can save you time. One inexpensive template is MockApp.[10] MockApp is designed for creating realistic-looking iPad mockups using Keynote (and even PowerPoint).

Another Keynote template for creating iPad wireframes is Keynote Kung-Fu,[11] a wireframe toolkit for Keynote. You won't be creating realistic-looking iPad mockups with Keynote Kung-Fu, but they can look darn close to the real thing. The toolkit makes it easy to create good-looking wireframes for iPad applications. It also includes a really nice feature that allows you to link wireframes to one another. For example, a screen element can be made clickable, sending you to another wireframe screen. This is a great way to prototype the application workflow in a low-cost, efficient manner.

Keynote Wireframe Toolkit comes with support for Keynote and PowerPoint, and the cost is only $12.

Icon Sets

Creating realistic-looking screen mockups means including artwork for icons. Creating original artwork will ensure that your application has a unique look, but sometimes you just don't have enough time. In these situations, you can use stock icons within your mockups and the real application.

A number of free and paid icon sets are available on the Internet. One of the most popular is Glyphish,[12] which includes more than 200 stylish icons designed for iPhone and iPad.

One additional note: While stock icon sets are great for in-app displays on buttons, toolbars, and tab bars, they don't make for great app icons. Your app icon should be original artwork. If you are not a designer, hire one to create your app icon. Remember, the app icon creates the first visual impression potential users will have of your app. This impression should be a good one, not a bad one, so spend the extra money to have your app icon professionally designed.

---

10. MockApp: http://mockapp.com/
11. Keynote Kung-Fu: http://keynotekungfu.com/
12. Glyphish: http://glyphish.com/

Mockup Apps

Another option you have for creating screen mockups is to use an app devoted to creating wireframes. Mockup apps have all the features you need for creating screen mockups, but they focus on creating wireframe mockups, not realistic-looking ones. Don't view this as a limitation. Remember, realistic mockups can lead to confusion. Wireframes, in contrast, allow you to focus on the screen layout and screen flow without worrying about pixel-perfect display.

One useful app available on the iPad is iMockups,[13] shown in Figure 7.6. iMockups makes it possible to create UI mockups for iPad, iPhone, and Web apps. It includes page linking so that you can prototype your app's workflow, and it supports VGA output for presenting your mockups on an overhead projector. iMockups includes a library for every screen widget you need, and you can export mockups. iMockups is the perfect iPad app for creating professional-looking wireframe mockups of your app.

OmniGraffle[14] from OmniGroup, shown in Figure 7.7, is another popular application for creating wireframe mockups. OmniGraffle is available for the Mac desktop and iPad. It works by using stencils of different object types and shapes. The wide

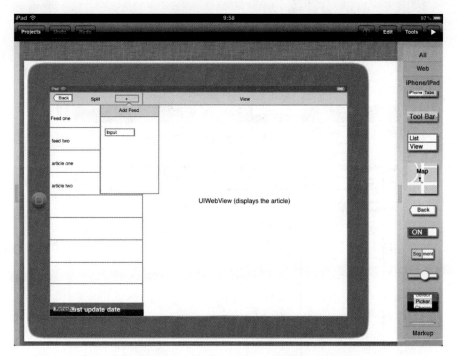

Figure 7.6   iMockups wireframe for an RSS feed reader app

13. iMockups: http://itunes.apple.com/us/app/imockups-for-ipad/id364885913?mt=8
14. OmniGraffle: http://itunes.apple.com/us/app/omnigraffle/id363225984?mt=8

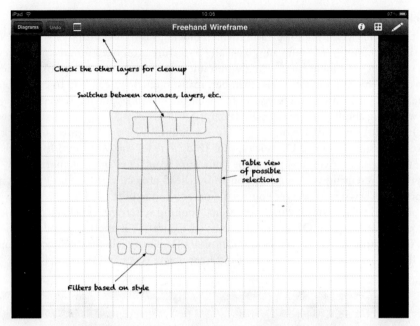

Figure 7.7   Screen shot of OmniGraffle for the iPad

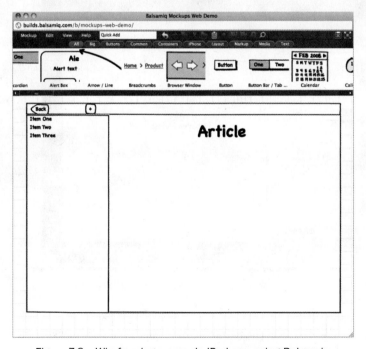

Figure 7.8   Wireframing a sample iPad app using Balsamiq

array of stencils, provided by OmniGroup and the user community, makes it possible to create virtually any type of diagram you need, from flowcharts to wireframes. OmniGraffle on the iPad also has a freehand mode in which you can draw your mockups using your finger or a stylus.

> **Note**
>
> The $50 price tag for OmniGraffle for iPad may give you sticker shock, but OmniGroup does offer a unique 30-day money-back guarantee. If you are unhappy with the iPad version of OmniGraffle for any reason, send OmniGroup a copy of your iTunes receipt and the company will issue you a refund. Now that's customer service.

Another app that is a popular choice for creating wireframes and mockups is Balsamiq Mockups,[15] shown in Figure 7.8. Balsamiq is a cross-platform desktop app for sketching mockups. It is also available as a plug-in for Confluence, JIRA, FogBugz, and XWiki, and a Web version is available. In addition to including all the features you would expect from a mockup and wireframing app, the folks at Balsamiq have released an online collaboration solution called myBalsamiq. myBalsamiq enables remote teams to work together on UI design and mockups.

Prototyping

A mockup is a good way to validate your UI design, and tools such as iMockups, Balsamiq, and Keynote make it possible to create clickable mockups that simulate the workflow of your app. But sometimes this is not enough.

Maybe you need to see the animation between screen transitions, or maybe you want to verify that data can be retrieved from a Web service. These types of validations are not possible in a static mockup. In such a case, you need to prototype the concept in a functional app.

What Is a Prototype?

In the realm of software development, a prototype is a sample application written to validate a design concept or group of concepts. This quick-and-dirty version of a sample application is intended to be a throwaway. As with mockups, the goal of a prototype is to validate a design concept or decision. Unlike a mockup, however, a prototype is a functioning application. This means that you can interact with it, add and retrieve data, perform calculations, and more.

The primary purpose of a prototype is to validate a concept or show how something might be accomplished. This goes a step further than a mockup, in that a prototype is a real application written with source code. However, a prototype is not a

---

15. Balsamiq Mockups: http://www.balsamiq.com/

complete application—it is not an app that someone would use on a regular basis to accomplish a task.

A prototype should be limited to validating a design concept or proving that an approach is feasible. Often a prototype is buggy, contains no error handling (unless you are prototyping how to handle errors), and is ugly. A prototype is quick and dirty—not something you would want to share with the world.

You should not spend a lot of time on developing a prototype. There is no reason a prototype should look and behave like the real application. You should treat a prototype as a throwaway. This last point is very important and deserves repeating: You should treat a prototype as a throwaway.

Often programmers will turn a prototype into the real application. This is a huge mistake. A production app—that is, the real app, the one you share with the world—should be far more robust than a quick-and-dirty prototype.

When writing a prototype, it's likely you will not follow good coding styles and conventions. After all, you're writing something quick and dirty. As a consequence, you will likely take shortcuts that you would never include in a real application. Turning this same code into a real application makes your application less stable, uncaught bugs are more likely, and enhancing and maintaining the app written from prototype code is a nightmare. In the long run, you will end up wasting more time with a prototype app turned into a production app than you would had you thrown out the prototype and written the real app from scratch.

Throwing out the prototype app might seem like a waste, but it is not. Remember, the primary goal of the prototype is to validate one or more concepts. In the course of creating the prototype app, you gain knowledge about which techniques work and which ones do not. Armed with this knowledge, you are able to write better code for the real app in less time.

How to Create a Prototype

Of course, you can use a clickable mockup for creating your prototype. This technique is fast and efficient, but you are limited to prototyping the workflow of your app. To go beyond this, you need to create a prototype app.

A prototype app is like any other app. The only difference is that your prototype app will not be shared with the world, and the world will not use your prototype to solve real-world problems. Instead, your prototype app will be used by you and maybe a small, select group of interested individuals for a short period of time to validate that the concept does, indeed, work. For example, suppose you are writing a streaming radio app. The first thing you might do is write a prototype app that proves you can play back streaming audio from the Internet. The user interface for this app will be ugly, or there may be no UI at all. Also, the URL to the radio station is likely to be hard-coded in the prototype app.

This is not the type of app you share with the world. It's not the type of app Apple approves for the App Store. But this app does serve a purpose: It proves that you know how to stream audio from the Internet, and that is very important knowledge to have if you're planning to write a streaming radio app.

Often the fastest way to write a prototype app is to use one of the application templates provided in Xcode. These templates provide a jump start to a working app. With this template in place, you are free to hack away with your prototype code. It doesn't matter which application template you use. Pick the one that best matches the purpose of your prototype app.

> **Note**
>
> A short description of each application template is available in the "Application Templates" sidebar found in Chapter 1, "Your First App."

Summary

App design is a very important part of creating iPad applications. You need to spend the time upfront thinking about and designing your app before you write a single line of code. Create an App Charter to define the "what" and "who" of your application. Engage in brainstorming sessions to come up with a big list of app features, and then trim that list once you know who your target audience is.

Take advantage of visual and audio metaphors within your application, but don't go overboard. The metaphors should enhance the user experience, not distract from it. Also, look for ways to customize the standard UI controls instead of writing a new control from scratch.

Don't forget to consider the ergonomics and aesthetics of your application. Take a step back and look at your app design with the eyes of an industrial designer.

Hire a professional designer. Enough said. Unless you have design skills, you're better off letting a designer give your application a polished look.

When it's time to figure out the "how" of your app, use mockups and prototypes. Creating mockups and prototypes is a cost-effective way of validating your app design before you begin writing code for the real application. Remember, mockups are great for validating visual designs, and prototypes are great for validating designs that can be tested only in code. Use both throughout your software development process to save time and build better apps.

And last, read the *iOS Human Interface Guidelines,* the HIG. Then read it again in a few months. Then read it again, and again, and again. Apple has spent an extraordinary amount of time researching and performing usability testing for iOS. Your app can only benefit from the advice provided in the HIG.

Part II

Building PhotoWheel

Creating a Master-Detail App

In Part I you learned about the tools, programming language, and frameworks used to build iPad apps. Now it's time to use what you have learned to build a real app. This is no simple app you are building. It's not yet another flashlight app. No, it's a real-world app that uses most, if not all, of the most commonly used elements of iOS. You will be building an app that displays photos, has animation, persists data in a local database, and calls Web services over the Internet.

What's the app? It's PhotoWheel, and its App Charter was presented in Chapter 7, "App Design."

Just to recap: PhotoWheel is a photo app that allows you to store your favorite photos in one or more albums. It gets its name from the spinning wheel, or disc, of photo albums. You use your finger to rotate through the set of photo albums displayed in the wheel.

It's a good idea to read Part II with your computer nearby so that you can work on the app as you read. This hands-on approach will help you learn faster. If you are the type who prefers to know what's going on first, feel free to read the chapter and then return to the beginning to work on the app.

Let's get started building PhotoWheel.

Building a Prototype App

As you learned in Chapter 7, "App Design," a commonly used technique for building a new application is to start with mockups followed by a prototype app. The mockups for PhotoWheel have already been created for you. Figure 8.1 shows the mockup for the prototype app. The prototype app is used to prove core concepts of the app you are building. It is a throwaway, and it will look nothing like the final app. The mockup of the final PhotoWheel app is shown in Figure 8.2.

A quick way to build a prototype app is to use one of the application templates provided by Xcode. PhotoWheel will contain a collection of photo albums, and each photo album will contain one or more photos. This is the classic Master-Detail pattern, where the photo album represents the master data and the photos within the album represent the detail. The Master-Detail Application template is perfect for this type of app, so let's use it for the prototype app. But first . . .

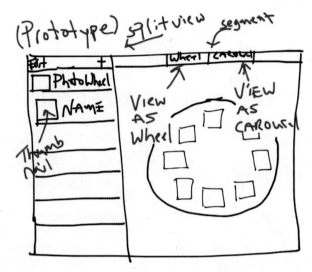

Figure 8.1　Early mockup drawing of the PhotoWheel prototype app

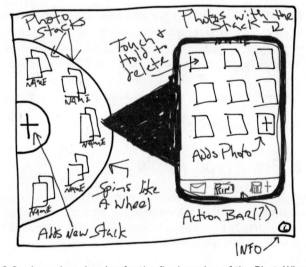

Figure 8.2　A mockup drawing for the final version of the PhotoWheel app

What Is the Split View Controller?

The iPad application created from the Master-Detail Application template uses a split view controller to display master and detail information. The split view controller—or more specifically `UISplitViewController`, which is the class name—is a nonvisual controller that manages the display for two view controllers, a master view controller and a detail view controller.

When the iPad orientation is landscape, the split view controller displays the views for both view controllers at the same time. The master view is displayed on the left side of the screen and the detail view is displayed on the right side.

When the device is rotated to the portrait orientation, only the detail view is displayed. Hiding the master view in this way allows the user to focus on the content presented in the detail view. The master view is still available to the user as a button on the toolbar, but its view is hidden.

The Mail app included on the iPad uses UISplitViewController, as seen in Figure 8.3. When you hold the iPad so that the **Home** button is on the left or right (called landscape orientation), you see the list of inboxes, accounts, and emails on the left side of the screen. Tap an email on the left side to view its contents on the right side. Now rotate the iPad so that the **Home** button is at either the top or the bottom (called the portrait orientation). Only the email's contents are displayed. If you need to navigate the list of emails, inboxes, and accounts while in portrait orientation, tap the button in the upper-left corner. This will reveal the view managed by the master view controller.

Now that you know what the split view controller is and what it does, let's create a new master-detail app to serve as the PhotoWheel prototype.

Figure 8.3   The Mail app in action on the iPad

Create a New Project

To begin, you need to create a new project in Xcode. Start by launching Xcode. Next, select **File > New > Project** (or press **Shift-Command-N**). Choose **Master-Detail Application** from the list of iOS application templates, and then click the **Next** button, shown in Figure 8.4.

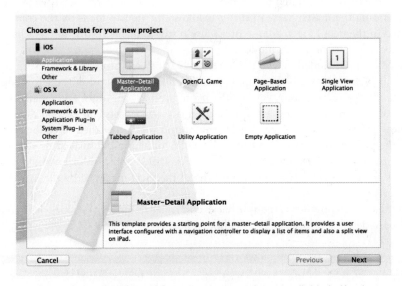

Figure 8.4   List of the iOS application templates available in Xcode

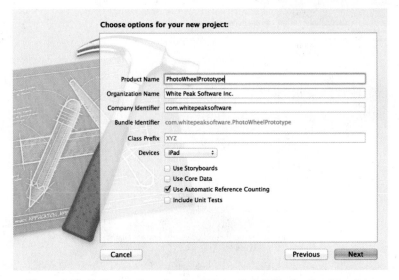

Figure 8.5   Project options for the Master-Detail Application template

Figure 8.6   Select the scheme from the list found near the upper-left corner of the Xcode project window.

Enter "PhotoWheelPrototype" as the product name. Accept the default Company Identifier value or edit it to reflect the identifier you prefer to use. Refer back to Chapter 6, "Provisioning Your iPad," to learn more about the Company Identifier value.

Leave the Class Prefix field blank. Select iPad for the Device Family, and uncheck the options Use Storyboard, Use Core Data, and Include Unit Tests. These options are not needed for the prototype and will be covered in later chapters. Finally, select the option Use Automatic Reference Counting. Your settings for the project should look like those in Figure 8.5.

Click the **Next** button, and then select a folder in which to store the project. Finally, click the **Create** button.

> **Note**
>
> If you are a Git user and you wish to use this resource, select "Create local git repository for this project." For the purpose of this book, Git is not required and will not be discussed.

You now have a master-detail app project. Build and run (**Command-R**) the project to see the generated app in action. Be sure to select the simulator from the scheme list, shown in Figure 8.6, to run the app in the simulator; otherwise, the app will run on your iPad, assuming it is tethered to your computer.

Using the Simulator

Using the iPad Simulator is a fast and easy way to test your app. By default, the simulator launches with the device orientation in portrait mode. To rotate the device, press **Command-Left** and **Command-Right** (or **Hardware > Rotate Left** and **Hardware > Rotate Right** from the menu bar).

Also by default, the device size is displayed at 50%. You can make it larger by selecting **Window > Scale > 100%** (**Command-1**) or **Window > Scale > 75%** (**Command-2**). **Window > Scale > 50%** (**Command-3**) returns the simulator to a 50% scale.

Take a look under the Hardware menu item for more juicy goodness. You can have the simulator simulate the shake gesture, tap the **Home** button, and lock the screen. There are also options to call up the keyboard, simulate low memory warnings, and simulate an external display with TV Out.

PhotoWheelPrototype is a master-detail application, which means it uses the split view controller. To see it completely, you need to rotate the iPad Simulator to the landscape orientation. Press **Command-Left** (or **Command-Right**) to rotate the simulated device. You should now see the app as shown in Figure 8.7.

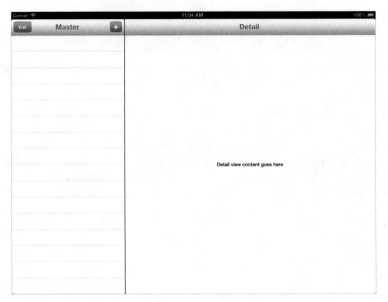

Figure 8.7   Master-detail application using the `UISplitViewController`
running in the iPad Simulator

How to Quit Your App

You may have noticed that when you run your app from Xcode, whether in the simulator or on the iPad, and you touch the **Home** button to exit the app, the app doesn't actually quit. Xcode shows that the app is still running.

What's going on here?

iOS has a service called multitasking. Multitasking allows one or more apps to run at the same time when the active app is in the foreground and all other running apps are in the background. When you launch an app, it becomes the foreground app. When you tap the **Home** button or fast swap to another app, the foreground app transitions to the background. When you return to the app, it transitions from the background to the foreground. Your app receives messages such as `applicationDidBecomeActive:` and `applicationDidEnterBackground:` as it transitions from the foreground and background so that the app can act accordingly based on the new state.

This is an overly simplified explanation of multitasking on iOS. For a more complete explanation, read the "App State and Multitasking" section of the iOS App Programming Guide[1] provided by Apple. But until you do, all you need to know is that when you touch the **Home** button, your app doesn't actually quit; it simply moves to the background. This is why Xcode shows that your app is still running.

---

1. App State and Multitasking: http://developer.apple.com/library/ios/#documentation/
   iPhone/Conceptual/iPhoneOSProgrammingGuide/ManagingYourApplicationsFlow/
   ManagingYourApplicationsFlow.html#//apple_ref/doc/uid/TP40007072-CH4-SW3

There is a logical reason for this behavior. It allows you to debug your app while it runs in the background. If Xcode automatically terminated the app when you touched the **Home** button, there would be no way to debug apps running in the background.

So what do you do when you want to quit or terminate your app? A couple of options are available to you. Every time you finish a debugging session, you can click the **Stop** button or use the shortcut **Command-.** in Xcode. This will terminate your app. The other option is to quit the simulator, which is as simple as pressing **Command-Q.** I tend to use **Command-Q** to quit the simulator most often.

A Closer Look

When you ran the app, you may have noticed that the application template did a number of things for you. First and most important, it created a functional master-detail app. Granted, this app isn't useful, but it does have basic functionality commonly found in master-detail apps.

You can rotate the device to change from the master-detail view to the detail-only view. A toolbar button is added that displays the master view in a popover when the device orientation is portrait. Also, items can be added and removed from the master view. The template has set up a functional project structure that can be used to build a really useful app.

Project Structure

The application template creates the project structure shown in Figure 8.8. The project contains the following files:

Figure 8.8   Project navigator for the PhotoWheelPrototype project

- **AppDelegate.h and AppDelegate.m**: The application delegate. It derives from `UIResponder` and conforms to the `UIApplicationDelegate` protocol.

- **MasterViewController.h and MasterViewController.m**: The view controller for the master view. It derives from the `UITableViewController`.

- **DetailViewController.h and DetailViewController.m**: The view controller for the detail view—the view displayed on the right side of the screen when the iPad orientation is landscape. This class derives from `UIViewController` and conforms to the `UISplitViewControllerDelegate` protocol.

- **MasterViewController.xib**: The user interface NIB file for the master view. It contains a table view and it is controlled by `MasterViewController`.

- **DetailViewController.xib**: The user interface NIB file for the detail view. It contains a label in the center of the view and is controlled by `DetailViewController`.

These files represent the primary source code to your app, and they are the files you will work with most often. Nevertheless, a few more files created by the application template are worth mentioning. Click the disclosure indicator next to the Supporting Files group to open it. You'll see the following files:

- **PhotoWheelPrototype-Info.plist**: The *info.plist* file for your application. It contains additional metadata about the application used by the build process. Settings in the *info.plist* are used to define various characteristics about the app, such as supported interface orientation, main NIB file or storyboard, version number, and icon files.

- **PhotoWheelPrototype-Prefix.pch**: The precompile header file. It is used by the compiler to improve compile-time performance and typically contains references to other frequently used header files.

- **main.m**: A source file containing the `main()` function needed by all programs created in the C programming language. It calls the function `UIApplicationMain()`, which in turn loads the main NIB file if defined in the *info.plist* file, causing the app delegate class to be instantiated.

App Delegate

From the iOS developer's point of view, the app delegate is the launch point of the application. The class `AppDelegate` defines the app delegate for the PhotoWheelPrototype app. Let's examine this class a bit more. Open the *AppDelegate.h* file in Xcode. You accomplish this by clicking the file name in the Project navigator. You will see the code in Xcode's text editor as shown in Listing 8.1.

Listing 8.1 **Source Code from the *AppDelegate.h* File**

```
#import <UIKit/UIKit.h>

@interface AppDelegate : UIResponder <UIApplicationDelegate>
```

```
@property (strong, nonatomic) UIWindow *window;
@property (strong, nonatomic) UISplitViewController *splitViewController;
@end
```

The first line of code is #import <UIKit/UIKit.h>. It tells the compiler to include the UIKit header file, which contains declarations for the objects found in the UIKit framework.

The next line of code begins with the compiler directive @interface. It indicates the start of the interface declaration for the class AppDelegate. This line of code makes it clear that AppDelegate derives from the class UIResponder as indicated by : UIResponder. AppDelegate also conforms to the protocol UIApplicationDelegate as indicated by <UIApplicationDelegate>.

> **Note**
>
> In Objective-C, a class can be derived from one and only one class—a concept called single inheritance. While an Objective-C class can inherit behaviors and features from only one class, it can conform to more than one protocol. To indicate that a class conforms to more than one protocol, separate each protocol listed between the < and > symbols with a comma—for example, <UITableViewDataSource, UITableViewDelegate>.

Next, the code contains a set of property declarations. There are two declared properties in Listing 8.1: window of type UIWindow and splitViewController of type UISplitViewController.

> **Note**
>
> As you learned in Chapter 4, "Getting Started with Objective-C," the @property compiler directive indicates a declared property. Following the @property is the list of settings for each declared property. The asterisk in front of each of the property names tells the compiler that the property is a pointer. A pointer is a reference to an object or data stored in memory. Refer back to Chapter 4 for a refresher on declared properties.

The class definition ends with the @end compiler directive. This concludes the interface declaration for the class AppDelegate.

You now have an idea of what the class AppDelegate looks like, but you still don't know how it is implemented. To see the implementation, open the file *AppDelegate.m*. A portion of the implementation file is shown in Listing 8.2.

> **Note**
>
> A quick way to navigate between the *.h* and *.m* files is to use the **Control-Command-Up** and **Control-Command-Down** shortcut keys.

Let's step through Listing 8.2 so that you have a better understanding of what is happening.

Listing 8.2   ***AppDelegate.m***

```objc
#import "AppDelegate.h"
#import "MasterViewController.h"
#import "DetailViewController.h"

@implementation AppDelegate

- (BOOL)application:(UIApplication *)application
didFinishLaunchingWithOptions:(NSDictionary *)launchOptions
{
    self.window = [[UIWindow alloc]
                    initWithFrame:[[UIScreen mainScreen] bounds]];
    // Override point for customization after application launch.

    MasterViewController *masterViewController =
        [[MasterViewController alloc]
         initWithNibName:@"MasterViewController" bundle:nil];
    UINavigationController *masterNavigationController =
        [[UINavigationController alloc]
         initWithRootViewController:masterViewController];

    DetailViewController *detailViewController =
        [[DetailViewController alloc]
         initWithNibName:@"DetailViewController" bundle:nil];
    UINavigationController *detailNavigationController =
        [[UINavigationController alloc]
         initWithRootViewController:detailViewController];

    masterViewController.detailViewController = detailViewController;

    self.splitViewController = [[UISplitViewController alloc] init];
    self.splitViewController.delegate = detailViewController;
    self.splitViewController.viewControllers =
        @[masterNavigationController,detailNavigationController];
    self.window.rootViewController = self.splitViewController;
    [self.window makeKeyAndVisible];
    return YES;
}

@end
```

> **Note**
>
> If you are looking at the implementation file in Xcode, you'll notice that the application template generates much more code than that shown in Listing 8.2. The additional code is not used at the moment. For the sake of brevity, Listing 8.2 shows only the parts of the implementation file that are of interest now.

The first things you see in Listing 8.2 are three #import statements. The first imports the header file for the AppDelegate class. This is followed by imports of the MasterViewController and DetailViewController header files. The header files for these two classes are imported so that the classes can be used within the code in this file.

Following the #import statements is the @implementation compiler directive. It is the counterpart to the @interface compiler directive found in the *AppDelegate.h* file. @implementation tells the compiler that what follows is the implementation for the class AppDelegate.

> **Note**
>
> If you have programmed with iOS before Xcode 4.5, then you may have noticed the lack of @synthesize statements for the declared properties in Listing 8.2. Starting with Xcode 4.5, @synthesize is no longer required. Instead, the compiler will generate the statement for you, naming the ivar with an underscore prefix followed by the declared property name—for example, _window and _splitViewController.

The @implementation line is followed by the -application:didFinish LaunchingWithOptions:. This method is defined as part of the UIApplication Delegate protocol. It is called after the operating system has launched the app. Under normal circumstances, this is the first opportunity your code has to do something useful such as initial the app and its delegate for use.

For the master-detail app shown in Listing 8.2, a new instance of a UIWindow is created. This is the first thing to happen in this method. The window instance created is the main window displayed by the application. Next, an instance of MasterView Controller is created and used to initialize a new UINavigationController instance. An instance of DetailViewController is created next, and it is also used to initialize a new UINavigationController instance. This is followed by the creation of the UISplitViewController.

The DetailViewController instance is made the delegate for the split view controller, and the navigation controllers—one containing the MasterViewController instance and the other containing the DetailViewController instance—are added to the split view controller. The navigation controller masterNavigationController represents the "master," and the other navigation controller, detailNavigation Controller, represents the "detail."

The steps for initialization can and will differ between apps. You just saw, for example, the steps needed to prepare a split view controller with master and detail controllers. However, the final lines of code shown in Listing 8.2 tend to be common among all apps. Those steps include

- Setting the rootViewController property for the window
- Making the window visible by calling makeKeyAndVisible on the window
- Returning YES

Setting the `rootViewController` property for the `window` assigns the view managed by the root view controller as the content view for the window. `makeKeyAnd Visible`, as its name implies, makes the window the key—a key window is the active window—and makes it visible.

The concept of a key window comes from the OS X world, where an application often has more than one window. Unlike the desktop, however, an iPad app has only one window except when the iPad is connected to an external display. At this time the iPad app can create a second window that is used to display content on the secondary screen. But even with a secondary screen the iPad app has only one key window, and that is the window displayed on the device itself.

Lastly, `-application:didFinishLaunchingWithOptions:` returns `YES`. If it were to return `NO`, the app would not finish launching. Therefore, your app will almost always return `YES` for this method. Sometimes, however, `NO` is the appropriate return value—for instance, when the app is unable to handle the launch options. Here's why.

Launch Options

`-application:didFinishLaunchingWithOptions:` has two input parameters: `application` and `launchOptions`. `application` is a reference to the `UIApplication` instance for the running app. `launchOptions` is a key-value pair dictionary indicating the reasons for launching the application.

`launchOptions` are used when your application is launched by some means other than the user tapping the app icon from the Home screen. For instance, suppose your app supports a particular file type and the user received an email attachment of that file type. The user has the option to open the file type in a different app from within the Mail app. When the user does this, your app is launched from the Mail app and the `launchOptions` dictionary contains the URL to the file attachment. Your app can now open the file attachment and process its contents.

If the app is able to process the incoming file attachment successfully, the return value for `-application:didFinishLaunchingWithOptions:` is `YES`. But if the file attachment cannot be processed—say it's a bad file format—then `NO` is the appropriate return value. Returning `NO` tells the operating system that your app will not continue the launch process.

Other UIApplicationDelegate Methods

`-application:didFinishLaunchingWithOptions:` is not the only method implemented by the app delegate. There are others, although they are not as frequently implemented. The other commonly implemented `UIApplicationDelegate` methods are as follows:

- **`-applicationWillResignActive:`** This method is called when the application is about to change from an active state to an inactive state. This can happen for a number of reasons: an incoming phone call, SMS message, or push notification, or when the user has quit the app by tapping the **Home** button. You typically pause your app when this method is called. This could mean disabling timers, pausing long-running operations, or, if your app is a game, pausing game play.

- **-applicationDidBecomeActive:**: This method is called when the app changes from an inactive state to an active one. At this point, your app would restart any tasks previously paused in -applicationWillResignActive:.

- **-applicationDidEnterBackground:**: This method is called when the user leaves your app. It is a good place to save data and release shared resources used by your app. This method is also called if your application supports multitasking, which it does by default; otherwise, -applicationWillTerminate: is called.

- **-applicationWillEnterForeground:**: This method is the opposite of -applicationDidEnterBackground:. It is called when your application becomes active, but only if your app supports multitasking.

- **-applicationWillTerminate:**: This method is called just prior to the operating system terminating your app. It is a good place to save any unsaved data changes within your app. Because termination of your app is controlled by the operating system, your code has only a few seconds to complete any remaining tasks before termination. Given this fact, the code you implement in this method should do its job quickly and efficiently. This is not the place for a long-running task such as updating data to a Web service, as there is no guarantee that the operating system will let the task complete before the app is terminated.

A Tour of `UISplitViewController`

As you have already learned, `UISplitViewController` is a nonvisual controller that manages the display of two view controllers, a master and a detail. `UISplitViewController` has two properties, shown in Listing 8.5.

Listing 8.5 **`UISplitViewController` Interface**

```
@property(nonatomic, copy) NSArray *viewControllers;
@property(nonatomic, assign) id <UISplitViewControllerDelegate> delegate;
```

`viewControllers` is an array consisting of two elements. The first element, `objectAtIndex:0`, is the master view controller and the second element, `objectAtIndex:1`, is the detail view controller.

> **Note**
>
> `-objectAtIndex:` is a method on `NSArray`, which is the data type for the `viewControllers` property. Note that arrays in C and Objective-C are zero based, not one based.

UISplitViewController's other property is delegate. It is a reference to an object that conforms to the UISplitViewControllerDelegate protocol. The methods from this protocol are shown in Listing 8.6, which is taken from the *UISplitViewController.h* header file. Let's take a closer look.

Listing 8.6 **UISplitViewControllerDelegate Definition**

```
@protocol UISplitViewControllerDelegate

@optional

// Called when a button should be added to a toolbar for a hidden view controller.
- (void)splitViewController: (UISplitViewController*)svc
     willHideViewController:(UIViewController *)aViewController
          withBarButtonItem:(UIBarButtonItem*)barButtonItem
       forPopoverController: (UIPopoverController*)pc;

// Called when the view is shown again in the split view, invalidating the
// button and popover controller.
- (void)splitViewController: (UISplitViewController*)svc
     willShowViewController:(UIViewController *)aViewController
  invalidatingBarButtonItem:(UIBarButtonItem *)barButtonItem;

// Called when the view controller is shown in a popover so the delegate can
// take action such as hiding other popovers.
- (void)splitViewController: (UISplitViewController*)svc
          popoverController: (UIPopoverController*)pc
  willPresentViewController:(UIViewController *)aViewController;

@end
```

UISplitViewControllerDelegate has three methods that tell the delegate when the master view controller is about to hide, when it is about to become visible, and when the master view is about to show in a popover as the result of the user tapping the bar button item.

The delegate method -splitViewController:willHideViewController :withBarButtonItem:forPopoverController: is called when the master view controller is about to be hidden. This happens when the device orientation changes from landscape to portrait, which allows the user to focus attention on the detail view. As a convenience, this method also provides the UIBarButtonItem and UIPopoverController.

You should add the bar button item to the toolbar or navigation bar displayed in the detail view. The user can then view the contents of the master view controller without rotating the device back to the landscape orientation.

The `UIPopoverController` passed in this method call is a reference to the popover controller that displays the master view when the bar button item is tapped. You can store the reference within your view controller or ignore it, depending on your needs.

When the user taps the bar button item, the `-splitViewController:popoverCon troller:willPresentViewController:` method is called. It gives your code a chance to perform some action prior to the display of the master view within the popover control. For example, if the app is already displaying a popover, this is a good time to close it before displaying the master view popover.

The third and final method is `-splitViewController:willShowViewControl ler:invalidatingBarButtonItem:`. This method is called when the user rotates the device back to the landscape orientation. The bar button item added to the toolbar during the hide method is no longer needed at this point, because the master view will now be displayed on the left side of the screen. Therefore, you should remove the bar button item from the toolbar.

Viewing Header Files

When implementing a class that conforms to a particular protocol, you will often want to copy and paste the method declarations. This technique saves you the time of typing the sometimes lengthy declaration statements. There are two ways to copy the method declaration:

1. Copy from the SDK documentation.
2. Copy from the header file.

For many programmers new to Xcode, copying a method declaration from the SDK documentation is the popular choice. To do so, you launch the documentation view in Organizer, search for the protocol, and then copy the desired methods from the documentation page.

A quick way to reach the documentation page for a protocol is to **Option-double-click** the protocol name in Xcode's text editor. This will take you to the documentation page displayed in the Organizer.

While new Xcode programmers often choose to copy delegate methods from the documentation, this is not the fastest way to insert these methods into code. Also, you are limited to copying only one method at a time. If you need to implement more than one method, as is the case for many protocols, bouncing back and forth between the documentation and the text editor can be less than efficient. A better approach is to copy the method declarations from the header.

There are two quick ways to open a header file. The first is to select **File > Open Quickly...** (**Shift-Command-O**) from the menu bar. This approach works well when you know the name of the header file you wish to open. An even better, faster way is to use the Xcode feature *Jump to Definition*, which works from within the text editor and doesn't require knowing the name of the header file.

To open the header file for a protocol in the text editor, **Command-click** the protocol name. This action jumps you to the header file containing the protocol definition. You can also place the text editor cursor on the protocol name and press **Control-Command-D** (or select

Navigate > Jump to Definition from the menu bar) to jump to the header file containing the protocol definition.

From the header file, you can see all the methods defined for the protocol and copy one or more to include in your app. I tend to copy all the methods, paste them into my app, and then remove the ones I don't need.

The best part of this trick is that Jump to Definition is not limited to protocols defined in the SDK. You can jump to definitions found in your own code. Also, the item doesn't have to be a protocol. It can be a class name, a variable, a declared property, and more.

In fact, a common pattern you see in Objective-C code is to separate blocks of code with a `#pragma mark` - statement. `#pragma mark` - allows you to include a brief remark following the dash character that describes the block of code. This technique is often used to denote a block of delegate methods. A common practice is to include the name of the protocol for the delegate methods in the `#pragma mark` - statement, as seen in Figure 8.9. Doing so makes it easy for you (and other developers who might have to support your code down the road) to jump to the protocol definition.

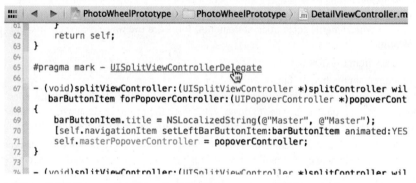

Figure 8.9   You can **Command-click** the name even if it is part of a comment or `#pragma mark` -.

Assigning the Split View Controller Delegate

As you saw in Listing 8.2, the split view controller delegate is set to an instance of the `DetailViewController`. If you take a look at the source file *DetailViewController.h*, you will see that the interface declaration shows that the class conforms to the `UISplitViewControllerDelegate` protocol. And if you look at *DetailViewController.m*, you will see the implementation for the `UISplitViewControllerDelegate` methods used by `DetailViewController`, courtesy of the application template. The template-generated code is also shown in Listing 8.7.

Listing 8.7   **Implementation of `UISplitViewControllerDelegate` Methods in**
DetailViewController.m

```
#pragma mark - Split view

- (void) splitViewController: (UISplitViewController *) splitController
     willHideViewController: (UIViewController *) viewController
          withBarButtonItem: (UIBarButtonItem *) barButtonItem
       forPopoverController: (UIPopoverController *) popoverController
{
    barButtonItem.title = NSLocalizedString(@"Master", @"Master");
    [self.navigationItem setLeftBarButtonItem:barButtonItem animated:YES];
    self.masterPopoverController = popoverController;
}

- (void) splitViewController: (UISplitViewController *) splitController
      willShowViewController: (UIViewController *) viewController
  invalidatingBarButtonItem: (UIBarButtonItem *) barButtonItem
{
    // Called when the view is shown again in the split view,
    // invalidating the button and popover controller.
    [self.navigationItem setLeftBarButtonItem:nil animated:YES];
    self.masterPopoverController = nil;
}
```

As you can see, the application template provides implementations for both the hide and show delegate methods. In the hide method, the button title is set to the string literal `"Master"` and the button is added to the navigation bar. In the show method, the button is removed from the navigation bar. You can see this code in action by running the project (**Command-R**) and rotating the device (or simulator) between the landscape and portrait orientations.

NSLocalizedString

You may have noticed the C function `NSLocalizedString()` in Listing 8.7. This function is used to retrieve the localized version of a string. The first parameter is the key, and the second parameter is the comment string. The key is used to look up the localized string resource, which is then returned by the `NSLocalizedString` call. The key value is returned if the string resource does not exist.

The comment string is just that—a comment. Its value can be anything you like, such as the context of the string or additional instructions for the language translator. The comment is never displayed within your app.

I'm of the opinion that developers should always use `NSLocalizedString()` even if there are no initial plans to support other languages. By preparing your code for this possibility at the outset, you save time down the road should your original plans change. That said, for brevity's sake, `NSLocalizedString()` is not used in the sample code from this book.

More information on internationalizing your app is available in the Introduction to Internationalization Programming Topics[2] provided by Apple.

Detail View Controller

The `DetailViewController` is not only the delegate for the `UISplitViewController`; it is also the controller for the detail view displayed on the right side of the screen when the device orientation is landscape or in full-screen view when the orientation is portrait. The view for the controller is defined in the *DetailViewController.xib* file.

The view in this NIB contains only a label (`UILabel`), which is displayed in the center of the screen. The view and label are connected to outlets defined as declared properties in the `DetailViewController` class. What you don't see in the *DetailViewController.xib* file is the toolbar displayed across the top of the view. That's because a toolbar is not actually used.

Navigation Controller

When you run the app, you see what looks like a toolbar across the detail view. However, it is not actually a toolbar (`UIToolbar`). Instead, what you see is a navigation bar (`UINavigationBar`).

The navigation bar is provided by the navigation controller (`UINavigationController`) created in the `AppDelegate` (see Listing 8.2). The navigation bar works like a toolbar in that it can contain buttons and other subviews. However, unlike a toolbar, the navigation bar is created and managed by a navigation controller.

`UINavigationController` is a specialized controller that manages a stack of view controllers. It provides methods for pushing and popping view controllers on and off the stack, and it can display a navigation bar with a back button, making it possible for the user to return to a previous view with the tap of a finger.

When you create an instance of a `UINavigationController`, you assign a view controller as the root view controller. The root view controller is the first view controller on the stack managed by the navigation controller, and its view is displayed as the default content view for the navigation controller.

In the case of the master-detail app, both the `MasterViewController` and the `DetailViewController` are root view controllers for two separate navigation controllers. One navigation controller represents the master view controller used by the split view controller, and the other navigation controller is the detail view controller

---

2. Introduction to Internationalization Programming Topics: http://developer.apple.com/library/ios/#documentation/MacOSX/Conceptual/BPInternational/BPInternational.html

for the split view controller. Thus, while `MasterViewController` is, conceptually, the master view for the split view, the actual master view controller instance for the split view is the navigation controller object containing the `MasterViewController` instance as its root view controller. In other words, `objectAtIndex:0` of the split view controller's `viewControllers` property is the `UINavigationController` containing the `MasterViewController` instance.

The same is true for the detail view controller. `objectAtIndex:1` of the split view controller's `viewControllers` property is the `UINavigationController` containing the `DetailViewController` instance as its root view controller.

Why use a navigation controller? As you will see in the next chapter, additional view controllers will be displayed within the master area of the split view controller. Using a navigation controller gives the user a way to navigate back through the stack of view controllers.

Note

Revisit Listing 8.2 to see the code that sets up the split view controller with the two navigation controllers, one containing the master view controller and the other containing the detail view controller.

So what does the `MasterViewController` look like?

Master View Controller

`MasterViewController` is a class that derives from the `UITableViewController`. `UITableViewController` is a specialized view controller that simplifies the display and management of a `UITableView`. The `UITableView` is one of the most frequently used views in UIKit. Many apps, especially on the iPhone, use table views to display data.

Like the detail view controller, the master view controller defines its user interface in a NIB file. Open *MasterViewController.xib* to see the view for the master view controller. Notice that the NIB contains one table view—the table view managed by the master view controller.

You'll learn how to use a table view and see how the controller interacts with the table view in the next chapter, so no further details are given here.

Summary

This chapter covered the Xcode project and project files generated by the Master-Detail Application template. While the focus has been on one particular application template, most of the discussion in this chapter applies to the other iOS application templates.

Each template has its own unique characteristics. The Master-Detail Application template creates a shell project that uses the split view controller for the iPad; the

Single View Application template creates a shell app that uses a single view; and so on. The key takeaway, however, is that other than their unique characteristics, each application template performs pretty much the same duties.

Each template creates an Xcode project with an app delegate, an *info.plist* for the project, and so on. Thus, while the walk-through in this chapter focused on the Master-Detail Application template, most of what you learned applies to the other application templates as well.

> **Note**
>
> Refer back to Chapter 1, "Your First App," for a detailed list of iOS application templates.

Exercises

1. Change the title for the bar button item to display "Photo Album" instead of "Master."

2. Change the font for the "Detail view content goes here" label displayed in the detail view controller to bold.

3. Change the font color for the same label to red.

4. Create a project for each iOS application template. Build and run the projects and compare the app types. Identify which templates are for the iPad, the iPhone, and both (called universal).

Using Table Views

In the last chapter you created a master-detail app using the application template provided by Xcode. While the app is functional, it is not very useful. In this chapter you will start making the app more useful by adding the ability to add, edit, and remove photo albums. You'll learn how to work with a table view and its data source and delegate protocols, create a new view with a controller, and communicate between view controllers.

First Things First

When the app runs and the device orientation is landscape, the word *Master* is displayed at the top of the master view. The table view represents a list of photo albums, so naming this list "Master" doesn't really make sense. Changing the text is simple: You set the title for the `MasterViewController`. That's it. The `UINavigationController` does the work of actually displaying the title for you.

A good place to set the title is in the `-initWithNibName:bundle:` or `-viewDidLoad` method. The template-generated code sets the title in the former, but the latter is preferable. Setting the title in the `-initWithNibName:bundle:` method will work only when that method is called. If, for example, the `MasterViewControl ler` is loaded without a NIB file, the title will not be set. However, `-viewDidLoad` is always called, regardless of whether the controller is created with a NIB file.

Update the code in *MasterViewController.m* to set the title in `-viewDidLoad` by moving the line of code that sets the title in `-initWithNibName:bundle:` to the `-viewDidLoad` method, then change "Master" to "Albums." Listing 9.1 on the next page shows the changes that need to be made.

Listing 9.1 **Set the Title for `MasterViewController`**

```
- (id)initWithNibName:(NSString *)nibNameOrNil
              bundle:(NSBundle *)nibBundleOrNil
{
    self = [super initWithNibName:nibNameOrNil bundle:nibBundleOrNil];
    if (self) {
        self.clearsSelectionOnViewWillAppear = NO;
        self.contentSizeForViewInPopover = CGSizeMake(320.0, 600.0);
    }
    return self;
}

- (void)viewDidLoad
{
    [super viewDidLoad];
    // Do any additional setup after loading the view, typically from a
    // NIB file.
    self.navigationItem.leftBarButtonItem = self.editButtonItem;

    UIBarButtonItem *addButton =
        [[UIBarButtonItem alloc]
            initWithBarButtonSystemItem:UIBarButtonSystemItemAdd
            target:self
            action:@selector(insertNewObject:)];
    self.navigationItem.rightBarButtonItem = addButton;

    self.title = NSLocalizedString(@"Albums", @"Albums");
}
```

The `-initWithNibName:bundle:` method contains a couple of lines of code worth discussing. The first, `self.clearsSelectionOnViewWillAppear = NO`, sets the property found on `UITableViewController`, the superclass for `MasterView Controller`. This property determines whether the object should clear the selection within the table view just before the view appears to the user.

Following that line is

```
self.contentSizeForViewInPopover = CGSizeMake(320.0, 600.0);
```

`contentSizeForViewInPopover` is a property of `UIViewController`, which is the superclass to `UITableViewController`. This property tells the popover control, if any, the preferred content size for the view. This property doesn't guarantee that the popover will be resized. It does, however, state that the popover should be at least this size.

Run the app and test your change. With the device orientation in landscape, the title for the master view now reads "Albums," as shown in Figure 9.1. Now rotate the device to portrait orientation. The button added to the navigation bar reads "Master." Not exactly what we're going for—it should read "Albums" to be consistent with the `MasterViewController` title. But how do you change the text to read "Albums"?

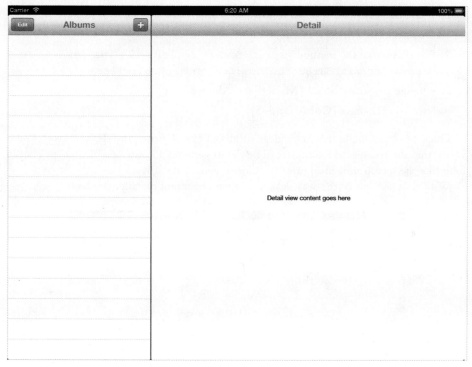

Figure 9.1   The PhotoWheelPrototype app in landscape orientation

> **Note**
>
> `contentSizeForViewInPopover` is used when a view managed by the view control-ler is displayed within a popover, such as when the `MasterViewController` view is displayed after the navigation bar button is tapped when the iPad is in portrait orientation. This property provides a hint to the popover controller of the initial size for the popover's content area. It doesn't actually control the size of the popover. Say, for example, you have two views displayed within a popover controller. The controller for the first view sets the `contentSizeForViewInPopover` to 320 × 600. The controller for the second view sets the property to 320 × 400. You might think that the content area for the popover will resize itself to the smaller size when the second view is displayed, but that will not happen. The pop-over's content area only grows larger, not smaller.
>
> To force the content size to be smaller, you must explicitly set the size in the `UIPopoverController`. This is accomplished by setting the `popoverContentSize` property of `UIPopoverController`.

The split view controller's delegate adds the button to the navigation bar, and the delegate is the `DetailViewController`. Thus the `DetailViewController` is responsible for displaying the button on the navigation bar, not the `MasterViewController`. Therefore, to change the button text from "Master" to "Albums" you need to make a change in *DetailViewController.m*.

Here are the steps you want to follow:

1. Open the file *DetailViewController.m*.

2. Scroll down to the method `-splitViewController:willHideView Controller:withBarButtonItem:forPopoverController:`.

3. Change the string literal "Master" to "Albums."

4. Save your changes (**Command-S**).

Once you have made these changes, build and run (**Command-R**) the project and verify that the changes are complete. The detail view for PhotoWheelPrototype should look like the screen shot in Figure 9.2. Check your work if it does not.

With that task out of the way, let's now turn our attention to table views.

Figure 9.2   The PhotoWheelPrototype app in portrait orientation

A Closer Look

The table view is a visual control for displaying a list of information. It is widely used on iPhone and has its place on iPad as well. The table view implements common features needed when displaying a list of data, including scrolling up and down, item selection, and highlighting. It has two styles, grouped and plain, and has different built-in layouts for data display. It also allows you to completely customize the look.

UITableView

A table view is an instance of the class `UITableView`. `UITableView` derives from `UIScrollView`, which gives the table view its scrolling behavior. But unlike `UIScrollView`, which supports scrolling horizontally and vertically, `UITableView` supports only vertical scrolling.

One of the more surprising aspects of `UITableView` is that it supports only a single column of data. This design choice was made to support the small screen of iPhone and iPod touch devices. While `UITableView` supports only one column, it is possible to customize the look of the table view to give it the appearance of multiple columns.

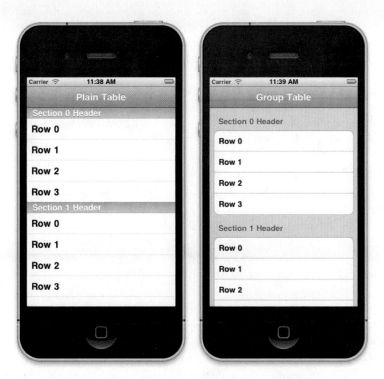

Figure 9.3   On the left is a sample of a plain table;
a grouped table is shown on the right.

UITableView supports two styles, which must be specified when creating the instance of the table: plain and grouped. The style cannot be changed after the table instance is created. A plain table displays a single list of data. A grouped table allows rows to be visually separated into individual sections. UITableView can also display a header and footer, and it can display section headers and footers. Figure 9.3 shows examples of each table style.

UITableViewCell

Each row of the UITableView is called a cell. The cell is an instance of UITableView Cell or a subclass of the same. A cell's position within the table view is determined by the NSIndexPath. The NSIndexPath has two properties that are used to determine the cell's location within the table view: section and row. The section is the section index within the table, and the row is the row index within the section.

UITableView has methods for accessing cells using an index path, and there are also methods for scrolling to a particular row based on the index path.

UITableViewDelegate

In addition to configuring a UITableView through its properties, a delegate object conforming to the UITableViewDelegate protocol is used to provide additional settings, such as those pertaining to the height of rows and the views returned for section headers and footers. Also included in the UITableViewDelegate protocol are methods that manage row selections, editing, and reordering.

UITableView interacts with your application by way of the UITableView Delegate to configure and manage rows of the table, but a different protocol is used to populate the table view with data. This protocol is UITableViewDataSource, and as the name implies, it defines methods for providing data to the table view.

UITableViewDataSource

The UITableView property dataSource references an object that conforms to the UITableViewDataSource protocol. The dataSource provides information about the data needed to construct and maintain the table view. It tells the table view how many sections are in the table and how many rows are in each section. It provides the title for each section's header and footer, and the cell object used to display the content for each row. The dataSource also has methods to determine if rows can be added, removed, and reordered.

UITableViewController

One other class that is useful when working with a table view is UITableView Controller. This specialized controller handles common management tasks when you are working with a table view, reducing the amount of code you must write to display and work with a table view.

With the introductions out of the way, it's time for some hands-on work with table views.

Working with a Table View

To use a table view, a few things must happen first. First and foremost, an instance of `UITableView` must be created. This task is handled for you in `MasterViewController`'s NIB file. `MasterViewController` is a subclass of `UITableViewController`, and as previously mentioned, `UITableViewController` is a specialized controller for displaying a `UITableView`.

Also needed are the table view's `delegate` and `dataSource`. The `MasterView Controller` will play the role of both by conforming to the protocols `UITableView Delegate` and `UITableViewDataSource`.

A Simple Model

Before the table view can display data, the data must be defined and stored in a model. The data needed for the table view in the PhotoWheelPrototype app is the photo album. At the moment, the only attribute needed from a photo album is name. You could create a custom class called `PhotoAlbum` that has a single property called `name`, but that's overkill. After all, you're still in the prototyping stage of the app.

So which data structure should be used as the model for the photo albums? An array of strings works nicely, where each string in the array is the name of a different photo album. iOS also has an `NSOrderedSet` collection type, which was introduced in iOS 5.

`NSOrderedSet` manages a collection of objects that are stored in sequential order, just like `NSArray`. Unlike `NSArray`, however, `NSOrderedSet` stores a particular object once and only once. In contrast, `NSArray` allows the same object to be added to the array at multiple indexes. For the PhotoWheelPrototype, you want only one instance of each photo album to exist in the collection, so `NSOrderedSet` is the better data structure for the prototype app.

To create the model data, you need to create an ordered set. The user should be able to add photo albums to the app, so the set needs to be mutable. Thus the data type needed is `NSMutableOrderedSet`. Also, the `MasterViewController` is the only controller interested in the list of photo albums, so you'll add the mutable set to `MasterViewController`.

Start by opening *MasterViewController.h*. Add a declared property called `data` of type `NSMutableOrderedSet`. The modified interface for `MasterViewController` should now look like the code in Listing 9.2. The necessary code change is highlighted in bold.

Listing 9.2 **`MasterViewController` Interface Modified to Include the data Property**

```
#import <UIKit/UIKit.h>

@class DetailViewController;
```

```
@interface MasterViewController : UITableViewController

@property (strong, nonatomic) DetailViewController *detailViewController;
@property (strong, nonatomic) NSMutableOrderedSet *data;

@end
```

> **Note**
>
> The property detailViewController was added by the Xcode application template
> when the master-detail project was created.

Before the declared property data can be used, the accessor methods—the getter and setter methods—must be created. Prior to Xcode 4.5, you needed to add the compiler directive @synthesize data to the MasterViewController's @implementation section. This step is no longer required. Instead, the compiler will create the getter and setter methods, along with the _data ivar, automatically. It is still up to you, however, to create the instance of NSMutableOrderedSet that data points to.

A good place to create this instance is in the -viewDidLoad event. This method is called after the content view managed by the view controller has been loaded. While you are at it, go ahead and add a couple of entries to the order set.

To accomplish this, follow these steps:

1. Open the file *MasterViewController.m.*

2. Scroll to the -viewDidLoad method.

3. At the bottom of -viewDidLoad add the following code:

   ```
   NSMutableOrderedSet *data = [NSMutableOrderedSet orderedSet];
   [data addObject:@"A Sample Photo Album"];
   [data addObject:@"Another Photo Album"];
   [self setData:data];
   ```

4. Save your changes.

The -viewDidLoad method should now look like the code in Listing 9.3, with the code changes in Step 3 highlighted in bold.

Listing 9.3　Instantiate data and Add Two Sample Photo Albums

```
- (void)viewDidLoad
{
    [super viewDidLoad];
    // Do any additional setup after loading the view, typically from a
    // NIB file.
    self.navigationItem.leftBarButtonItem = self.editButtonItem;

    UIBarButtonItem *addButton =
```

```
    [[UIBarButtonItem alloc]
        initWithBarButtonSystemItem:UIBarButtonSystemItemAdd
        target:self
        action:@selector(insertNewObject:)];
    self.navigationItem.rightBarButtonItem = addButton;

    self.title = NSLocalizedString(@"Albums", @"Albums");

    NSMutableOrderedSet *data = [NSMutableOrderedSet orderedSet];
    [data addObject:@"A Sample Photo Album"];
    [data addObject:@"Another Photo Album"];
    [self setData:data];
}
```

Note

The source code in Listing 9.3 mixes the use of dot syntax with the messaging style. The Xcode template generated the dot syntax code in the listing. In a real-world project, you would clean up this code so that it uses one style consistently throughout the project.

You may have noticed that -viewDidLoad already had code in it before you made your changes. The first line, [super viewDidLoad], tells the object instance to invoke the -viewDidLoad method implemented in the superclass. The implementation in MasterViewController overrides the method in the superclass UITableViewController. It is unknown whether the superclass's implementation performs any important tasks. Calling the super's implementation ensures that important tasks, if any, are executed prior to executing the code in the local implementation.

The [super viewDidLoad] call is followed by code that adds an **Edit** button to the left side of the navigation bar and an Add button to the right side. The **Edit** button is provided by the view controller. The view controller creates this button for you and provides a default implementation that is executed when the user taps the button. This default implementation puts the view controller into edit mode. In the case of the MasterViewController, edit mode changes the mode for the table view, making it possible for the user to delete and reorder rows. This default table behavior is provided courtesy of UITableViewController, which is the superclass for MasterViewController.

The **Add** button, added to the right side of the navigation bar, is a new instance of UIBarButtonItem. This instance is created from the system-provided button UIBarButtonSystemItemAdd. You should use a system button whenever possible, as this practice ensures a consistent look across multiple apps.

The **Add** button is connected to the target self, which is the instance of MasterViewController. The action is the selector insertNewObject:. Thus, when the user taps the **Add** button, the -insertNewObject: method implemented in the MasterViewController class is called.

The last line of existing code sets the title for the view controller. You added this line of code earlier in this chapter.

Display Data

`MasterViewController` now has model data to display, and the collection set representing the model data has two items in it representing photo albums: "A Sample Photo Album" and "Another Photo Album." However, when you run the app, these album names do not appear in the table view, because you haven't told the table view what to display.

To tell a `UITableView` about data, your code must provide a data source object that conforms to—that is, implements—the methods of the protocol `UITableView DataSource`. `MasterViewController` is a subclass of `UITableViewController`, so by default the `dataSource` property for the `UITableView` is set to the `Master ViewController` instance. This can be done explicitly in the code by saying `[[self tableView] setDataSource:self]`, although this step is not necessary when using an instance of `UITableViewController` unless the data source is an object instance other than the controller itself.

That's right: A data source does not have to be the view controller. However, it is usually convenient to have the view controller serve as the data source for a `UITableView`. In fact, the application template used to create the PhotoWheelPrototype project has already generated method stubs for responding to `UITableViewDataSource` calls. These calls do not know about the ordered set `data`, so it is up to you to tell the `UITableView` about the data by way of the `UITableViewDataSource` methods. Listing 9.4 shows the changes, in bold, you need to make before the table view can display data.

Listing 9.4 **UITableViewDataSource Method Implementations in**
          MasterViewController.m

```
#pragma mark - Table View

- (NSInteger)numberOfSectionsInTableView:(UITableView *)tableView
{
    return 1;
}

- (NSInteger)tableView:(UITableView *)tableView
 numberOfRowsInSection:(NSInteger)section
{
    NSInteger count = [[self data] count];
    return count;
}

// Customize the appearance of table view cells.
```

```objectivec
- (UITableViewCell *)tableView:(UITableView *)tableView
        cellForRowAtIndexPath:(NSIndexPath *)indexPath
{
   static NSString *CellIdentifier = @"Cell";

   UITableViewCell *cell =
      [tableView dequeueReusableCellWithIdentifier:CellIdentifier];
   if (cell == nil) {
      cell = [[UITableViewCell alloc]
              initWithStyle:UITableViewCellStyleDefault
              reuseIdentifier:CellIdentifier];
   }

   NSString *albumName = [[self data] objectAtIndex:[indexPath row]];
   [[cell textLabel] setText:albumName];
   return cell;
}
```

Let's walk through the code in Listing 9.4.

The first method is -numberOfSectionsInTableView:. This method returns the number of sections within a table view. Sections are a way to group related data within the table view. The table view for this app has only one section, so the return value is always 1.

The next method implemented is -tableView:numberOfRowsInSection:. This method is called for each section, where the number of sections is determined by -numberOfSectionsInTableView:. PhotoWheel has only one section, so -tableView:numberOfRowsInSection: is called only once to load the table. The number of rows is determined by the number of elements in the data set. This means the return value is the count of data.

Note

You may be wondering why I chose to implement -tableView:numberOfRowsInSection: as two lines of code, setting the count to a local variable and then returning the count stored in the local variable. I use this pattern to make the code easier to debug. The method could have been implemented with a single line of code, return [[self data] count]. While this is perfectly valid, it makes it harder to see the count when debugging the app. By setting a local variable to the count, I'm able to see the value during a debug session, which lists the local variables in scope at the point where the program is stopped. You'll learn more about debugging an app in Chapter 26, "Debugging."

The last method implemented from the UITableViewDataSource protocol is -tableView:cellForRowAtIndexPath:. The indexPath is of type NSIndexPath, and it consists of two properties of interest, section and row. The section property returns the index of the current section. Because this app has only one section, the section value will always be 0. `row` is the index of the current row within the section. For this app, `row` is equal to the index identifying the element from `data` to be displayed. Plainly put, the parameter variable `indexPath` tells the code which element in `data` to retrieve. But before the app can display the name of the photo album, it needs a `UITableViewCell` instance.

Recall that `UITableViewCell` is used to display content within a `UITableView`. The method `-tableView:cellForRowAtIndexPath:` is called by the table view to request the cell for display. `UITableViewCell` is a subclass of `UIView`, meaning that the cell is really nothing more than a view. `UITableViewCell`, however, comes with a set of standard display styles:

- **UITableViewCellStyleDefault**: Displays a basic cell with a text label and an optional image view.

- **UITableViewCellStyleValue1**: Displays a left-aligned label on the left side of the cell and a right-aligned label with blue text on the right side.

- **UITableViewCellStyleValue2**: Displays a right-aligned label with blue text on the left side and a left-aligned label on the right side.

- **UITableViewCellStyleSubtitle**: Displays a left-aligned label at the top of the cell and a left-aligned label with gray text at the bottom.

More complex views can be displayed by customizing the cell. This can be accomplished by adding subviews to the cell's `contentView` hierarchy. PhotoWheel's needs are simple at the moment, so the default style `UITableViewCellStyleDefault` will work nicely.

To return a `UITableViewCell` in the method `-tableView:cellForRowAtIndexPath:` the code must create an instance of `UITableViewCell`. Creating a new cell for each row, especially when the table has many rows, can hurt the scroll performance of the table view. A better approach is to create a new instance of `UITableViewCell` only when absolutely necessary. Luckily for you, the Apple engineers already recognized this problem and have provided a solution.

A table view may contain more rows than are visible at a given point in time. Keeping cells reserved for nonvisible rows needlessly consumes system resources. To reduce memory overhead, nonvisible cells can be disposed of. This is wasteful, too, given that once a nonvisible row becomes visible, a new cell instance must be created. But, as already been mentioned, creating a new cell instance each time hurts performance as the user scrolls through the list of rows.

The solution the Apple engineers came up with is to cache, or queue, unneeded table view cells. As a cell goes from a visible state to a nonvisible state, it is placed in a queue to be reused. When the table view requests a cell for a particular `indexPath`, a call is made to the table view asking to dequeue a previously used table cell. If no queued cells are available, your code must create a new instance, but if a queued cell is available, it is recycled and used as the return value for -tableView:cellForRowAt IndexPath:. This means that at any given time, the total number of table view cells in memory is equal to the number of visible rows plus a small number of additional, queued cells. This approach reduces memory overhead and improves performance.

That explains how to create and return a UITableViewCell. Let's now see how this strategy is translated into code. Refer back to Listing 9.4 and look at the implementation for the UITableViewDataSource delegate method -tableView:cell ForRowAtIndexPath:.

The first line sets a local variable to the string literal "Cell." This value is used to identify the cell within the queue. If, for example, the table view consists of cells with different formats, a different identifier is used. This allows the table view to queue cells of different formats, or styles. Your code uses the identifier to dequeue the cell of the appropriate format. The next line of code demonstrates this strategy: A local variable called cell is created and is set to a dequeued, reusable cell with the specified identifier.

When the -dequeueReusableCellWithIdentifier: method is called, the table view returns a reference to an instance of a cell with the specified identifier. If there is no available cell, nil is returned. The nil return value means it's up to your code to create a new cell instance as seen in the if (cell == nil) statement.

Within the if block is the code needed to create an instance of UITableViewCell. The standard alloc init pattern is used here.

Once a cell instance is retrieved, either by dequeuing or with alloc init, it is configured with the data to display. Following the if block is NSString *album Name = [[self data] objectAtIndex:[indexPath row]]; this statement retrieves the object for the current row from the data set. NSMutableOrderedSet can contain objects of any type, but we know our set contains only strings, so it is safe to set a local string variable to the object.

The table cell was initialized with the style UITableViewCellStyleDefault. The default style has a text label; the property name of this text label is textLabel. textLabel is of type UILabel, which has a text property. Thus, to set the display text, you set the text property of the textLabel of the cell as shown in the statement [[cell textLabel] setText:albumName].

Note

Other cell styles display secondary text. The property for the secondary text is called detailTextLabel.

At this point the table view has the information it needs to display photo album names contained in the data set. Now you should build and run the app to make sure the changed code works. Two photo albums are listed in the master view (Figure 9.4).

Figure 9.4   The PhotoWheelPrototype app with sample photo albums

Add Data

At this point, the table view displays the list of photo albums in data, but the user cannot add a new album. Let's change that right now.

What we need is a way for the user to tell the app she wishes to add a new photo album. The **Add** button, added by the Xcode template, in the navigation bar on the master view side of the split view controller is perfect for this task. Let's take a closer look at the code used to create the **Add** button.

```
UIBarButtonItem *addButton =
   [[UIBarButtonItem alloc]
      initWithBarButtonSystemItem:UIBarButtonSystemItemAdd
      target:self
      action:@selector(insertNewObject:)];
self.navigationItem.rightBarButtonItem = addButton;
```

The **Add** button is an instance of UIBarButtonItem. This button is initialized with the system button UIBarButtonSystemItemAdd. The target is set to self, and the action is set to the selector insertNewObject:.

The compiler directive @selector is used to create a reference to insertNewObject:. It's important that the colon character follow the selector name "insertNewObject"; otherwise, the method -insertNewObject: is not called when the **Add** button is tapped. The colon character is part of the message signature, and leaving it off changes the signature. In other words, the methods -insertNewObject and -insertNewObject: have different signatures and are, therefore, different methods. When specifying a selector, then, you must be sure to use the correct message signature for the desired method.

After the **Add** button instance is created, it is added to the navigation bar. You do not add it directly to the UINavigationBar instance, however. Instead, UIView Controller has a property called navigationItem. A navigationItem, or, as it is defined in UIKit, UINavigationItem, represents the navigational items available within the scope of the current view controller. In other words, it manages the display of navigation items for the view controller.

> **Note**
>
> You use the navigationItem property only when your view controller is part of a navigation stack managed by a UINavigationController.

To display a button on the left side of the navigation bar, you set the leftBarButton Item property of the navigation item. To place a button on the right side, you set the rightBarButtonItem. That's exactly what self.navigationItem.rightBar ButtonItem = addButton does—it places the addButton on the right side of the navigation bar.

With the **Add** button added to the right side of the navigation bar, it's time now to implement the action for the **Add** button. The method -insertNewObject: already exists in the template-generated code found in *MasterViewController.m*. However, this code does not know how to work with the data ordered set. Also, the user will want to enter a name for the photo album, so the app needs a way to prompt the user for a photo album name.

Let's tackle the second requirement first. We'll modify the app so the user can enter a photo album name. Start by creating a new view controller named NameEditor ViewController. This view controller will let the user enter the name of a new photo album. Here are the steps to follow:

1. Select **File > New > File** or press **Command-N**.

2. Under **iOS > Cocoa Touch**, select the Objective-C **class** file template (shown in Figure 9.5).

3. Click the **Next** button.

4. Type NameEditorViewController for the class name.

5. Set the "Subclass of" to UIViewController.

6. Do not select the "Targeted for iPad" check box. The name editor will be smaller than a normal iPad view.

7. Select the "With XIB for user interface" check box. This will create a companion *.xib* file for the view controller.

8. Click the **Next** button.

9. Click the **Create** button. This will save the class files to the project directory.

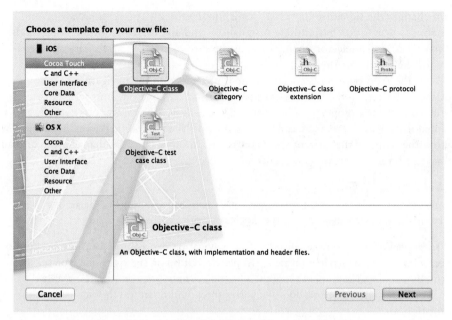

Figure 9.5   Select the Objective-C class file template.

These steps create three new files and add them to the Xcode project, as seen in Figure 9.6. The class `NameEditorViewController` is defined in the *NameEditor ViewController.h* interface file, and its implementation is in the *NameEditorViewControl ler.m* file. The view for this controller is defined in the NIB file *NameEditorViewCon- troller.xib*. These three files contain the basic setup of a view controller and its view. Your next step will be to modify these files to display the name editor for a new photo album.

The name editor is really simple. All it needs to do is allow the user to type in a name that is used as the photo album name. Xcode created the shell view controller and NIB file needed for the name editor, but it is up to you to complete the imple- mentation. To do so, however, you need to know the requirements.

The name editor will allow the user to edit a name, which is nothing more than free-form text (i.e., a string). To do so, the controller needs to expose a name property of type `NSString`. However, the user interface also needs a text field into which the user can type data. `UITextField` is perfect for this purpose, and because it stores the current text, it can be used to retrieve the photo album name.

You also want to make the user interface as friendly as possible. If the user acciden- tally taps the **Add** button, the name editor should provide a way for the user to cancel that action. Also, the user interface should include a way for the user to indicate he is finished editing the name of the new photo album. The cancel and done features can be provided as buttons displayed at the top of the name editor.

Figure 9.6 `NameEditorViewController` added to the project

All that is left with regard to defining the requirements for the name editor is a mechanism for communicating back to the calling view controller. This communication is needed to inform the calling view controller of the user's desire to cancel or save the photo album. For this purpose, you'll define a protocol that allows callbacks to the calling view controller.

Now that you understand the requirements, let's make the needed changes.

Open the interface file *NameEditorViewController.h* and add a declared property of type `UITextField` with the name `nameTextField`. Note that this property will be connected to an instance of `UITextField` defined in the NIB file, so make sure that the text field is also defined as an `IBOutlet`. Take a look at Listing 9.5 to see an example.

The requirements also call for two actions, cancel and done, so add two methods for these actions to `NameEditorViewController`'s interface. These methods will be connected to buttons defined in the NIB file, so set the return type for each action to `IBAction`. This helps IB find the action methods. Also, as you saw earlier with the `UIBarButtonItem`, include the `(id) sender` parameter to the actions. Although the sender is not required, it's a good idea to explicitly state it because you never know when you will need it.

One last piece is needed for the `NameEditorViewController` interface: a delegate that is told when the user cancels or is done with the name editor. The delegate is an instance of an object—also called a receiver in this context—that receives one or more messages based on some action or condition. A protocol is defined to ensure that the delegate implements the appropriate methods. The delegate must then conform to the protocol if it wishes to receive the messages.

> **Note**
>
> If you're coming from another programming language such as Java or C#, you can think of the protocol as an interface that is implemented by some other object. Read Chapter 4, "Getting Started with Objective-C," if you need a refresher on protocols.

As a convention, the delegate protocol name for a view controller is often the name of the view controller followed by the suffix "Delegate." You have already seen this convention used with the protocol `UITableViewDelegate`. Following the same convention, the protocol for `NameEditorViewController` will be called `NameEditorViewControllerDelegate`. Because this protocol is always used in conjunction with the `NameEditorViewController`, it is perfectly acceptable to include the protocol declaration in the same *.h* interface file as the view controller. In our example, the declaration for `NameEditorViewControllerDelegate` is added to *NameEditorViewController.h*.

Defining the protocol is only part of the step. The `NameEditorViewController` must have a declared property that references the delegate object. To meet this criterion, you need to add another property to `NameEditorViewController` called `delegate`. Because the object can be of any type, the `delegate` property is declared as type `id`. To assist the compiler, the protocol name is included with the type `id`. This tells the compiler to verify that the delegate conforms to the protocol. The declared property looks like this:

```
@property (nonatomic, weak) id<NameEditorViewControllerDelegate> delegate;
```

Weak, Not Strong

The `delegate` declared property is a weak reference, not `strong`. The `NameEditor ViewController` does not assume ownership of the `delegate`. If it did—that is, if a `strong` reference were used—then it would be possible to create a retain cycle, which can cause a memory leak.

A retain cycle occurs when one object, Object A, creates a second object, Object B, and Object A stores a `strong` reference to the newly created Object B. Object B, in turn, stores a `strong` reference back to Object A. When the creator of Object A releases the object, it's not actually removed from memory because Object B still has a `strong` reference to it. Objects A and B are now orphaned in memory, causing the memory leak.

A misconception is that ARC will handle this scenario for you—but it doesn't. ARC will not release two objects that store `strong` references to each other. Therefore, it's up to you, the programmer, to ensure that retain cycles do not occur even when you are using ARC.

The `NameEditorViewControllerDelegate` protocol introduces an interesting problem in the *NameEditorViewController.h* file. The interface `NameEditorViewCon troller` has a property that refers to the `NameEditorViewControllerDelegate` protocol, but the protocol has not been defined. As you will see shortly, the protocol also refers to the class name `NameEditorViewController` for the data type of one of the method parameters. In turn, either the class or the protocol must have a forward declaration in the *NameEditorViewController.h* file. A common convention is to forward declare the protocol with an `@protocol` statement, then define the protocol after the class definition. This is the approach used in Listing 9.5.

The protocol `NameEditorViewControllerDelegate` supports two optional methods: `-nameEditorViewControllerDidFinish:` and `-nameEditorViewControllerDidCancel:`. The delegate object is not required to implement these methods because they are declared as optional. To make the methods required, use the compiler directive `@required`.

You might be thinking that the names of these two methods are a bit wordy, and you would be right. The method names could be `-didFinish:` and `-didCancel:`, but those method names are not very descriptive. Imagine if you had another view controller delegate protocol that had the same message names as `-didFinish:` and `-didCancel:`; it would be difficult to distinguish the protocol implementations. By prefixing the protocol method name with the name of the primary sender—in this case, the view controller name—you make your code much more readable while avoiding the confusion caused by having two protocols with the same method name.

This raises another point, or rather points, about another convention. Similar to action methods, which include a `sender` parameter, it is common practice for delegate protocol methods to include a parameter referencing the object that is sending the message. However, this parameter is not called `sender`; instead, a more meaningful parameter name is used. For example, only an instance of `NameEditorViewController` will ever send a `NameEditorViewControllerDelegate` message, so the parameter name representing the sender is called `controller`.

This is a lot to chew on for someone new to iOS programming. Don't worry. The changes needed to *NameEditorViewController.h* are shown in Listing 9.5. Go ahead and make these changes to your project.

Listing 9.5 *NameEditorViewController.h* after Making the Needed Code Changes

```
#import <UIKit/UIKit.h>

@protocol NameEditorViewControllerDelegate;

@interface NameEditorViewController : UIViewController

@property (nonatomic, weak) IBOutlet UITextField *nameTextField;
@property (nonatomic, weak) id<NameEditorViewControllerDelegate> delegate;

- (IBAction)cancel:(id)sender;
- (IBAction)done:(id)sender;

- (id)initWithDefaultNib;
```

```
@end


@protocol NameEditorViewControllerDelegate <NSObject>
@optional
- (void)nameEditorViewControllerDidFinish:(NameEditorViewController *)controller;
- (void)nameEditorViewControllerDidCancel:(NameEditorViewController *)controller;
@end
```

With the interface defined, it's now time to update the implementation. Implementation for `NameEditorViewController` is fairly straightforward. You need to implement methods for the two actions, `-cancel:` and `-done:`, and for the custom initializer, `initWithDefaultNib`. More on the initializer in a moment.

The code for these changes is given in Listing 9.6.

Listing 9.6 *NameEditorViewController.m* **after Making the Needed Code Changes**

```
#import "NameEditorViewController.h"

@interface NameEditorViewController ()

@end

@implementation NameEditorViewController

- (id)initWithDefaultNib
{
  self = [super initWithNibName:@"NameEditorViewController" bundle:nil];
  if (self) {
      // Custom initialization.
  }
  return self;
}

- (id)initWithNibName:(NSString *)nibNameOrNil bundle:(NSBundle *)nibBundleOrNil
{
    self = [super initWithNibName:nibNameOrNil bundle:nibBundleOrNil];
    if (self) {
        // Custom initialization
    }
    return self;
}

- (void)viewDidLoad
{
    [super viewDidLoad];
```

```
    // Do any additional setup after loading the view from its NIB file.
}


- (void)didReceiveMemoryWarning
{
    [super didReceiveMemoryWarning];
    // Dispose of any resources that can be recreated.
}


#pragma mark - Actions methods

- (IBAction)cancel:(id)sender
{
    id<NameEditorViewControllerDelegate> delegate = [self delegate];
    if (delegate &&
        [delegate respondsToSelector:@selector(nameEditorViewControllerDidCancel:)])
    {
        [delegate nameEditorViewControllerDidCancel:self];
    }
    [self dismissViewControllerAnimated:YES completion:nil];
}


- (IBAction)done:(id)sender
{
    id<NameEditorViewControllerDelegate> delegate = [self delegate];
    if (delegate &&
        [delegate respondsToSelector:@selector(nameEditorViewControllerDidFinish:)])
    {
        [delegate nameEditorViewControllerDidFinish:self];
    }
    [self dismissViewControllerAnimated:YES completion:nil];
}


@end
```

The first thing you may notice in *NameEditorViewController.m* is the `@interface` `NameEditorViewController ()` code block. It is called a class extension. The class extension makes it possible to define additional ivars, declared properties, and method declarations that are private to the class—that is, used internally to the class. `NameEditorViewController` does not need the class extension, but it is shown in Listing 9.6 because it was generated by the Xcode file template.

Next, let's talk about `-initWithDefaultNib`. This is jumping ahead, but. . . . A new view controller that has a companion NIB file is instantiated in code with the `-initWithNibName:bundle:` method. This init method makes it possible for different NIB files to be used with the same controller. However, in most iOS applications, a view controller works with one and only one NIB file. Therefore, it is handy to include the custom init method -initWithDefaultNib that loads the NIB file for you. Its implementation knows which NIB file to load, which means the NIB file name does not have to be scattered throughout your application if the view controller is used in multiple places.

> **Note**
>
> Because -initWithDefaultNib is used outside NameEditorViewController, it must be included in the controller's interface, as shown in Listing 9.5.

-initWithDefaultNib is followed by three methods generated by the Xcode file template:

1. -initWithNibName:bundle:
2. -viewDidLoad
3. -didReceiveMemoryWarning

The first of these methods, -initWithNibName:bundle:, is used to initialize the view controller instance with a particular NIB file. The custom init method -init WithDefaultNib calls this method to initial the controller with the NameEditor ViewController NIB file.

The second method, -viewDidLoad, is called after the content view for the controller has been loaded. You typically add code to the method when additional initialization is needed after the NIB file has been loaded.

The third method, -didReceiveMemoryWarning, is called when the operating system detects a low memory condition on the device. This gives the view controller an opportunity to release objects from memory that are no longer needed—for example, a cache of objects. NameEditorViewController is not holding onto additional objects, so there is nothing to release within this call.

These three methods are followed by the two action methods, which implement the functionality needed for the **Cancel** and **Done** buttons. Both implementations are similar with only slight differences. -cancel: calls the -nameEditorViewCon trollerDidCancel: method on the delegate object, and -done: calls the -nameEditorViewControllerDidFinish: method.

The first line in each of these methods sets a local variable to the delegate. This is done so that [self delegate] does not have to be used throughout the method. Having [self delegate] all over the place can make the code look messy and be more difficult to read. The ivar _delegate could also have been used, but direct access to ivars is not good object-oriented programming; this is why a local variable is used instead.

The if statement performs two checks. It first checks whether delegate points to an object. If delegate is nil, the if statement short-circuits and the method returns control to the caller. If delegate is not nil, a check is made to ensure that delegate

has an implementation for the particular selector: -nameEditorViewControllerDid
Cancel: for the -cancel: method and -nameEditorViewControllerDidFinish:
for the -done: method. This is one of Objective-C's strengths—that is, the ability to
query an object to determine what it does and does not implement. If the delegate
does not implement the method, the program flow control does not enter the if block;
otherwise, the if block is entered and the delegate method is called.

It is always a good idea to check that an object implements a particular method when
a protocol method is defined as @optional. Calling a missing optional method is a
surefire way to crash your app. The check is not needed if the method is @required.
Even so, it can still be a good idea to perform the -respondsToSelector: check on
required methods. This step protects your code should you (or someone else) change the
method from required to optional in the future.

> **Note**
>
> In Objective-C, sending a message to a nil object does nothing. Thus the if statement
> could have been written as follows:
>
> ```
> if ([delegate respondsToSelector:@selector(nameEditorViewControllerDidFinish:)])
> ```
>
> The first check to test whether delegate is nil is not needed. However, after years of pro-
> gramming in various other programming languages, this old dog finds that eliminating tests for
> nil in Objective-C is a hard habit to break.

The view controller NameEditorViewController is ready to go. Its interface has
been defined, a protocol has been created to call back to a delegate object, and the
NameEditorViewController implementation is complete. All that remains before
the app can use this view controller is to complete the user interface (i.e., the view).

The view will display a toolbar at the top. The toolbar will have two buttons: a **Cancel** button displayed on the left and a **Done** button displayed on the
right. Below the toolbar in the view area will be a UITextField—that is, the
text input box that the user uses to enter a new name. The UITextField will be
connected to the IBOutlet nameTextField. The **Cancel** button will connect
to the -cancel: IBAction method, and the **Done** button will connect to the
-done: IBAction method. Here are the steps to follow:

> **Note**
>
> Read Chapter 3, "Getting Started with Interface Builder," if you have problems with these
> steps.

1. Open the file *NameEditorViewController.xib*.
2. Drag and drop a toolbar (UIToolbar) from the Library to the view. Place the
   toolbar at the top of the view.
3. Drag and drop a flexible space bar button item (UIBarButtonItem) on the
   toolbar, placed to the right of the **Item** button already displayed in the toolbar.

4. Drag and drop a bar button item (`UIBarButtonItem`) on the toolbar, placed to the right of the flexible space bar button item.

5. Change the bar button item on the left to "Cancel" by opening the Attributes inspector (**Option–Command–4**) and selecting **Cancel** in the Identifier list.

6. Do the same for the button on the right, but select **Done** in the Identifier list.

7. Drag and drop a text field (`UITextField`) on the view and place it just below the toolbar. Size the text field to fill most of the width of the view.

8. In the Attributes inspector for the text field, set the Placeholder property to "Enter the photo album name."

At this point your view should look like Figure 9.7. Make any needed adjustments if it does not. Once that step is complete, move on to connecting the `IBActions` and `IBOutlets`.

Freeform Views

The main view for the NIB file is set at a fixed size by default. Because the iPhone was selected as the device family when creating the `NameEditorViewController` NIB file (i.e., the "Target for iPad" check box option was not selected), the view size defaults to the size for an iPhone. You can leave the view at this default size, as it will be resized automatically at run time. However, if you wish to manually size the view, select the view, go to the Attributes inspector, and select **Freeform** from the Size drop-down list found in the Simulated Metrics section. This allows you to size the view to any size you like. However, this view will still be resized automatically at run time due to the presentation style used when presenting the view controller.

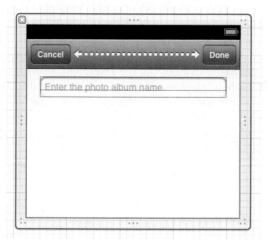

Figure 9.7   The NameEditorView NIB file

Follow these steps to connect the actions and outlets to your view:

1. **Control-click** (or right-click) the File's Owner placeholder object. Note that the Xcode file template already assigned File's Owner to the class `NameEditor ViewController` as seen in the Class field of the Identity inspector.

2. Connect the `nameTextField` outlet to the text field in the view.

3. Connect the `-cancel:` action to the **Cancel** button.

4. Connect the `-done:` action to the **Done** button.

5. Save your changes (**Command-S**).

That's it. The view is now ready. All that remains is to modify `MasterViewCon troller` so that it can use the new `NameEditorViewController`. Start by adding `#import "NameEditorViewController.h"` to the top of *MasterViewController.h*. Next, add `<NameEditorViewControllerDelegate>` to the `@interface` declaration for `MasterViewController`. The interface file should look like the code in Listing 9.7.

Listing 9.7   **Updated *MasterViewController.h***

```
#import <UIKit/UIKit.h>
#import "NameEditorViewController.h"

@class DetailViewController;

@interface MasterViewController : UITableViewController
<NameEditorViewControllerDelegate>

@property (strong, nonatomic) DetailViewController *detailViewController;
@property (strong, nonatomic) NSMutableOrderedSet *data;

@end
```

Now for the implementation. At the bottom of *MasterViewController.m*, add the implementations for the `NameEditorViewControllerDelegate` methods. You also need to modify the `-insertNewObject:` method in *MasterViewController.m* to create an instance of `NameEditorViewController`, set the `delegate`, and display the view. The code changes are given in Listing 9.8. For brevity's sake, only the changes are included in the listing, not the complete code source.

Listing 9.8   **Modifications Needed in *MasterViewController.m***

```
@implementation MasterViewController

/* Other code purposely left out for brevity's sake. */
```

```objc
- (void)insertNewObject:(id)sender
{
    NameEditorViewController *newController =
        [[NameEditorViewController alloc] initWithDefaultNib];
    [newController setDelegate:self];
    [newController setModalPresentationStyle:UIModalPresentationFormSheet];
    [self presentViewController:newController animated:YES completion:nil];
}

#pragma mark - NameEditorViewControllerDelegate

- (void)nameEditorViewControllerDidFinish:(NameEditorViewController *)controller
{
    NSLog(@"%s", __PRETTY_FUNCTION__);
}

- (void)nameEditorViewControllerDidCancel:(NameEditorViewController *)controller
{
    NSLog(@"%s", __PRETTY_FUNCTION__);
}

@end
```

What is `__PRETTY_FUNCTION__`?

`__PRETTY_FUNCTION__` is a macro that returns the name of the current class and method as a C string. Because the return value is a C string and not an Objective-C string, the `%s` format specified is used instead of `%@`, which is used for Objective-C strings and objects. `__PRETTY_FUNCTION__` comes in handy when you are debugging your app and you want to see when a method is called.

Take a look at the modified version of the `-insertNewObject:` method. Earlier it contained code generated by the Xcode template, but now it contains functionality to display the name editor. It creates an instance of the `NameEditorViewController` using the custom init method `-initWithDefaultNib`. It sets the `delegate` to `self`, which is the current instance of `MasterViewController`, which conforms to the `NameEditorViewControllerDelegate`.

The name editor will display modally. To ensure a good look, the controller's `modalPresentationStyle` is set to `UIModalPresentationFormSheet`. This will resize the view for the view controller and center it on the screen, graying out the background view. It will also adjust the name editor's position when the virtual keyboard is displayed. After the presentation style is set, the code then displays the new controller modally using `-presentViewController:animated:completion:`. This causes the new controller to slide up from the bottom and display in the screen's center.

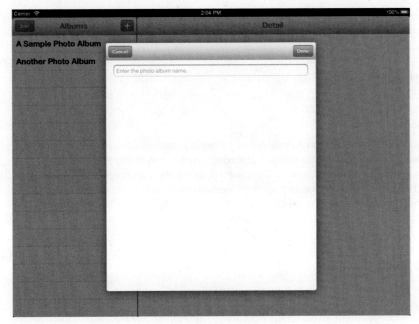

Figure 9.8   The name editor

You can now build and run the app. When you tap the **+** button, the new Name
EditorViewController is displayed. Tapping the **Cancel** button displays [Master
ViewController nameEditorViewControllerDidCancel:] in the debug output
window, and tapping the **Done** button displays [MasterViewController nameEdi
torViewControllerDidFinish:]. The finished version should look like Figure 9.8.

Before returning focus to the UITableView, a few loose ends remain to be tied up.
The **Done** button should add a new entry into the data array, so replace the Master
ViewController's implementation for -nameEditorViewControllerDidFinish:
with the code in Listing 9.9.

Listing 9.9   Updated **-nameEditorViewControllerDidFinish:** in
            MasterViewController.m

```
- (void)nameEditorViewControllerDidFinish:(NameEditorViewController *)controller
{
    NSString *newName = [[controller nameTextField] text];
    if (newName && [newName length] > 0) {
        [[self data] addObject:newName];
        [[self tableView] reloadData];
    }
}
```

Let's walk through this code. In -nameEditorViewControllerDidFinish: a local variable, newName, is set to the string returned by the text field displayed in NameEditorViewController. If the newName is not nil and the string length is greater than zero, the new name is added to the data set as a new photo album and tableView is told to reload the data.

That's it. The user can now add a new photo album to the table view.

> **Note**
>
> Calling reloadData on a table view is a quick and easy way to update the display. However, the table view will go through the process of rebuilding and displaying the cells for the table. If you want to avoid this extra processing, use the UITableViewDataSource protocol methods for inserting and deleting table rows (-tableView:commitEditingStyle:forRowAtIndexPath: and -tableView:canEditRowAtIndexPath:).

Edit Data

What good is adding data if the user can't edit it? Let's add an edit feature that enables the user to change the name of an existing photo album. To save time, you'll reuse the name editor, this time to edit an existing name.

You need a way for the user to tell the app to edit an existing item. Luckily, UITableView already supports the concept of editing. When a UITableView is in edit mode, the table cells are indented, a red circle is added to allow deleting a row, and rows in the table can be reordered. To put the table in edit mode, we need an **Edit** button. A good place for the **Edit** button is on the left side of the navigation bar for the MasterViewController, our master view. Thanks to the Xcode application template, the **Edit** button already exists in the navigation bar for the master view controller.

In the -viewDidLoad method of the MasterViewController, you'll find this line of code:

```
self.navigationItem.leftBarButtonItem = self.editButtonItem;
```

editButtonItem is provided by the superclass UIViewController. It toggles the button title and state between "Edit" and "Done." This button also toggles the table view between the edit and display modes when using the UITableViewController, which happens to be the superclass for MasterViewController.

Even though the **Edit** button is available, the user is still not able to edit an album name. You need to add some code to make this happen. To do so, you must modify the NameEditorViewController to support edit mode. UIViewController already has an editing property that can be used to tell the controller it is in edit mode. But the controller needs to know more, such as the index path to the row that is being edited.

Let's start by updating `MasterViewController`. The code changes are shown in Listing 9.10. The first change sets the accessory type for the table cell when the table is in edit mode. The next change adds an implementation for the `UITableViewDelegate` method `-tableView:accessoryButtonTappedForRowWithIndexPath:`. This method is called when the user taps the detail disclosure button on a cell. The implementation creates an instance of the name editor, prepares it for editing, and then displays it. Last, the `-nameEditorViewControllerDidFinish:` method is changed to support editing. Add the changes in Listing 9.10 to your project.

Listing 9.10   Modifications to *MasterViewController.m* to Support Editing a Photo Album Name

```
- (UITableViewCell *)tableView:(UITableView *)tableView
        cellForRowAtIndexPath:(NSIndexPath *)indexPath
{
    static NSString *CellIdentifier = @"Cell";

    UITableViewCell *cell = [tableView dequeueReusableCellWithIdentifier:CellIdenti
fier];
    if (cell == nil) {
        cell = [[UITableViewCell alloc] initWithStyle:UITableViewCellStyleDefault
                                      reuseIdentifier:CellIdentifier];
        [cell setEditingAccessoryType:UITableViewCellAccessoryDetailDisclosureButton];
    }

    // Configure the cell.
    NSString *text = [[self data] objectAtIndex:[indexPath row]];
    [[cell textLabel] setText:text];

    return cell;
}


- (void)tableView:(UITableView *)tableView
accessoryButtonTappedForRowWithIndexPath:(NSIndexPath *)indexPath
{
    NameEditorViewController *newController =
        [[NameEditorViewController alloc] initWithDefaultNib];
    [newController setDelegate:self];
    [newController setEditing:YES];
    [newController setIndexPath:indexPath];
    NSString *name = [[self data] objectAtIndex:[indexPath row]];
    [[newController nameTextField] setText:name];
    [newController setModalPresentationStyle:UIModalPresentationFormSheet];
    [self presentViewController:newController animated:YES completion:nil];
}


- (void)nameEditorViewControllerDidFinish:(NameEditorViewController *)controller
```

```
{
    NSString *newName = [[controller nameTextField] text];
    if (newName && [newName length] > 0) {
        NSInteger index = [[controller indexPath] row];
        NSMutableOrderedSet *data = [self data];
        if ([controller isEditing]) {
            [data replaceObjectAtIndex:index withObject:newName];
        } else {
            [data addObject:newName];
        }
        [[self tableView] reloadData];
    }
}
```

> **Note**
>
> As before, only the changes are shown in Listing 9.10. The full version of *MasterView Controller.m* is not displayed to save the trees.

For the moment, the project will not compile. A change to `NameEditorViewController` is needed before it will do so—namely, a new declared property called `index Path` of type `NSIndexPath` must be added. This change is shown in Listing 9.11.

Listing 9.11 Changes to *NameEditorViewController.h*

```
@interface NameEditorViewController : UIViewController

/* Other code purposely left out for brevity's sake. */

@property (nonatomic, strong) NSIndexPath *indexPath;

@end
```

Once the change is complete, run the project and see what happens. Be sure to test the new edit feature. Did you notice anything funny going on? The name editor does not display the original photo album name when in edit mode, despite setting the `nameTextField`'s `text` property prior to displaying the view. What's going on?

`nameTextField` is a `UITextField` that is instantiated by the NIB file when the NIB is loaded. The `MasterViewController` calls `[[newController nameText Field] setText:name]` to set the text value, but the text field has not been created and initialized yet. When it is finally initialized, it uses an empty string for the text value, which explains why the photo album name is not displayed. How do you get around this problem?

The solution involves two steps:

1. Add a declared property to `NameEditorViewController` called `defaultName Text` of type `NSString`.

2. During the `-viewDidLoad` method, set the `text` property of the `nameText Field`.

This works because `-viewDidLoad` is not called until the view has been loaded and its subviews have been initialized.

The code changes to `NameEditorViewController` are shown in Listing 9.12.

Listing 9.12 **Changes Needed to *NameEditorViewController.h* and**
           NameEditorViewController.m

```
//////////////
// NameEditorViewController.h

@interface NameEditorViewController : UIViewController

/* Other code purposely left out for brevity's sake. */

@property (nonatomic, copy) NSString *defaultNameText;

@end

//////////////
// NameEditorViewController.m

@implementation NameEditorViewController

- (void)viewDidLoad
{
    [super viewDidLoad];
    if ([self isEditing]) {
        [[self nameTextField] setText:[self defaultNameText]];
    }
}

/* Other code purposely left out for brevity's sake. */

@end
```

Now the final change: replace the `[[newController nameTextField] setText :name]` call in *MasterViewController.m* with `[newController setDefaultName Text:name]` as shown in Listing 9.13.

Listing 9.13   Change to *MasterViewController.m* Needed to Set the Default Name Text

```
- (void)tableView:(UITableView *)tableView
accessoryButtonTappedForRowWithIndexPath:(NSIndexPath *)indexPath
{
    NameEditorViewController *newController =
        [[NameEditorViewController alloc] initWithDefaultNib];
    [newController setDelegate:self];
    [newController setEditing:YES];
    [newController setIndexPath:indexPath];
    NSString *name = [[self data] objectAtIndex:[indexPath row]];
    [newController setDefaultNameText:name];
    [newController setModalPresentationStyle:UIModalPresentationFormSheet];
    [self presentViewController:newController animated:YES completion:nil];
}
```

Delete Data

Let's not stop with adding and editing data. Let's makes it possible for the user to delete data.

The user interface is already in place to support deleting a row. The user can tap the **Edit** button and then tap the red circle, which causes the table view to display a **Delete** button for the cell. Also, the user can swipe his finger across the row, when the table is not in edit mode, to call up the **Delete** button. But before a row can be deleted, a bit more plumbing is needed in `MasterViewController`.

To allow for row deletion, you need to implement two additional methods from the `UITableViewDataSource` protocol: `-tableView:canEditRowAtIndexPath:` and `-tableView:commitEditingStyle:forRowAtIndexPath:`. The first method allows the app to control whether a particular row in the table is editable. For the purposes of this project, the method always returns `YES`, but you may have apps in the future that return `YES` for some rows and `NO` for others.

The next method is `-tableView:commitEditingStyle:forRowAtIndexPath:`. In previous code, when a new row was added or an existing one was edited, the code called `[tableView reloadData]`. Here a different approach is used. Instead of reloading the data (a strategy that does work), the existing row is removed from the table view. This provides a better user experience in that the removal of the row is animated and the table view is not completely redrawn. In this particular case, `UITableViewRowAnimationFade` is used to fade out the row being deleted.

The implementation for these two methods is shown in Listing 9.14. Be sure to add this code to your project. Note that the Xcode application template may generate code for these two methods. If it does, replace the generated implementation with the code in Listing 9.14.

Listing 9.14   **Add Data Deletion Support to *MasterViewController.m***

```
- (BOOL)tableView:(UITableView *)tableView
canEditRowAtIndexPath:(NSIndexPath *)indexPath
{
    return YES;
}

- (void)tableView:(UITableView *)tableView
commitEditingStyle:(UITableViewCellEditingStyle)editingStyle
forRowAtIndexPath:(NSIndexPath *)indexPath
{
    if (editingStyle == UITableViewCellEditingStyleDelete) {
        [[self data] removeObjectAtIndex:[indexPath row]];
        [tableView deleteRowsAtIndexPaths:@[indexPath]
                        withRowAnimation:UITableViewRowAnimationFade];
    }
}
```

> **Note**
>
> @[indexPath] is shortcut syntax for creating an NSArray. It is the equivalent of
> [NSArray arrayWithObject:indexPath]. This shortcut syntax is called an
> Objective-C literal. Take a look at the sidebar on Objective-C literals in Chapter 4, "Getting
> Started with Objective-C," for more information on using this syntax.

Reorder Data

There is another nifty feature of UITableView, reordering data. UITableView makes it possible for the user to move rows up or down to change the sequence. Adding support for reordering is a simple two-step process:

1. Configure the cell to display the reorder control.

2. Implement the UITableViewDataSource protocol method -tableView:move RowAtIndexPath:toIndexPath:.

The code changes for *MasterViewController.m* are shown in Listing 9.15. Make and save these changes to your project, and then run the app to test reordering.

Listing 9.15   **Changes in *MasterViewController.m* Needed to Support Reordering of Table Rows**

```
- (UITableViewCell *)tableView:(UITableView *)tableView
cellForRowAtIndexPath:(NSIndexPath *)indexPath
{
    static NSString *CellIdentifier = @"Cell";
```

```
    UITableViewCell *cell =
        [tableView dequeueReusableCellWithIdentifier:CellIdentifier];
    if (cell == nil) {
        cell =
            [[UITableViewCell alloc] initWithStyle:UITableViewCellStyleDefault
                                 reuseIdentifier:CellIdentifier];
        [cell
setEditingAccessoryType:UITableViewCellAccessoryDetailDisclosureButton];
        [cell setShowsReorderControl:YES];
    }

    NSString *albumName = [[self data] objectAtIndex:[indexPath row]];
    [[cell textLabel] setText:albumName];
    return cell;
}

- (void)tableView:(UITableView *)tableView
moveRowAtIndexPath:(NSIndexPath *)fromIndexPath
       toIndexPath:(NSIndexPath *)toIndexPath
{
    [[self data] exchangeObjectAtIndex:[fromIndexPath row]
                    withObjectAtIndex:[toIndexPath row]];
}
```

As with editing a row, the UITableViewDataSource protocol includes a method named -tableView:canMoveRowAtIndexPath: that allows your code to determine if a row can be moved. Return YES to allow the row to be moved, and return NO to prevent moving the row. The superclass implementation for this method returns YES, so the method is not needed in MasterViewController.

Select Data

There is one last feature you need to implement before we close this chapter on table views. When a user taps a row in the table view, the detail view controller—Remember that fella? It's been a while since we spoke of him—needs to be told which item was selected. This process works similarly to editing a row. UITableViewDelegate includes the method -tableView:didSelectRowAtIndexPath:, which is called when the user taps the row.

Before the MasterViewController can tell the DetailViewController about the selected item, the MasterViewController needs to know about the Detail ViewController instance. The master view controller must have a declared property of type DetailViewController that points to the instance of DetailViewControl ler created in the AppDelegate, and this property must be set after the detail view controller instance is created. Fortunately, the Xcode application template has already done the work for you. Let's take a look at the code.

Open the file *AppDelegate.m* (Listing 9.16) and scroll to the `-application:did`
`FinishLaunchingWithOptions:` method. In this method, you'll see the following
line of code:

```
masterViewController.detailViewController = detailViewController;
```

It tells `masterViewController` which `DetailViewController` instance to use.
As you can see in Listing 9.16, this happens after the new instance of `DetailView`
`Controller` is created.

**Listing 9.16   `-application:didFinishLaunchingWithOptions:` in
*AppDelegate.m***

```
- (BOOL)application:(UIApplication *)application
didFinishLaunchingWithOptions:(NSDictionary *)launchOptions
{
    self.window = [[UIWindow alloc]
                    initWithFrame:[[UIScreen mainScreen] bounds]];
    // Override point for customization after application launch.

    MasterViewController *masterViewController =
        [[MasterViewController alloc]
         initWithNibName:@"MasterViewController" bundle:nil];
    UINavigationController *masterNavigationController =
        [[UINavigationController alloc]
         initWithRootViewController:masterViewController];

    DetailViewController *detailViewController =
        [[DetailViewController alloc]
         initWithNibName:@"DetailViewController" bundle:nil];
    UINavigationController *detailNavigationController =
        [[UINavigationController alloc]
         initWithRootViewController:detailViewController];

    masterViewController.detailViewController = detailViewController;

    self.splitViewController = [[UISplitViewController alloc] init];
    self.splitViewController.delegate = detailViewController;
    self.splitViewController.viewControllers =
        @[masterNavigationController,detailNavigationController];
    self.window.rootViewController = self.splitViewController;
    [self.window makeKeyAndVisible];
    return YES;
}
```

Now open the file *MasterViewController.h* (Listing 9.17). Here you see the declaration for the `detailViewController` property. Once this property is set, the

MasterViewController instance will be able to communicate with the Detail
ViewController instance.

Listing 9.17   ***MasterViewController.h***

```
#import <UIKit/UIKit.h>
#import "NameEditorViewController.h"

@class DetailViewController;

@interface MasterViewController : UITableViewController
<NameEditorViewControllerDelegate>

@property (strong, nonatomic) DetailViewController *detailViewController;
@property (strong, nonatomic) NSMutableOrderedSet *data;

@end
```

Did you notice the `@class` directive toward the top of *MasterViewController.h*? This
directive is used to inform the compiler that the class name `DetailViewController`
is available. This approach is used instead of importing the *DetailViewController.h*
header file.

The compiler does not need to know the interface for the class until the class is
actually used—for example, when creating a new instance of the class or sending a
message to a class instance. Only when the class is used must its interface be imported.
Plainly put, if you use the class in your implementation, you must include the
`#import` for the class header in your *.m* file. However, the `DetailViewController`
class is not used in *MasterViewController.h*; it is only referenced. Thus the `@class`
directive is used instead of importing *DetailViewController.h*.

In general, when you need to reference a class in a *.h* file, you forwardly declare
the class using the `@class` compiler directive. But, if the header file declares an
interface that extends another class or conforms to a protocol, you need to include
the `#import`. For instance, the interface for `MasterViewController` shows that it
conforms to the `NameEditorViewControllerDelegate` protocol. This protocol is
defined in *NameEditorViewController.h*, which means *NameEditorViewController.h* must
be imported. In this case, the protocol is being *used* by the `MasterViewController`
interface.

> **Note**
>
> The approach of telling the compiler that something exists without providing the details
> is called a forward declaration. Forward declarations are common in the C programming
> language and, therefore, are common in Objective-C. The compiler directive `@class` is a
> forward declaration of a class name, but forward declarations are not limited to class names.
> Forward declarations are used throughout C and Objective-C to inform the compiler about
> protocols, methods, and functions that are yet to be defined.

Now that you understand how the master view controller knows about the detail view controller, let's make a code change to display the selected photo album's name in the detail view. To do so, you implement the method -tableView:didSelectRowAt IndexPath:.

The implementation of this method should look familiar to you. You use the index Path to retrieve the photo album name from the data set, and then you pass the value to the detail view controller. This is similar to the approach used to edit a row. The biggest difference is that the detail view controller has already been created, so there is no need to create a new instance. Let's take a look at the code shown in Listing 9.18, which replaces the code generated by the Xcode template.

Listing 9.18   Code Added to *MasterViewController.m* to Display the Photo Album Name in the Detail View Controller

```
- (void)tableView:(UITableView *)tableView
didSelectRowAtIndexPath:(NSIndexPath *)indexPath
{
    NSString *name = [[self data] objectAtIndex:[indexPath row]];
    [[self detailViewController] setDetailItem:name];
}
```

As you can see, the name of the photo album is retrieved from the data set. The name is then passed to the detail view controller, which in turn displays the album name on the screen.

That's it. Build and run the app. When you tap a photo album in the table view, its name should appear in the detail view. Check your work if you see different behavior.

> **Note**
>
> Some versions of Xcode have a bug in the Master-Detail Application template in which the detailDescriptionLabel outlet is not connected to the UILabel in the NIB file *DetailViewController.xib*. If the album name does not display in the detail view, open *DetailViewController.xib* and connect the detailDescriptionLabel outlet in the File's Owner to the UILabel displayed in the center of the content view.

Summary

This chapter focused on UITableView and its supporting protocols and classes. In addition, it introduced several other essential concepts, including creating and displaying view controllers, communicating between view controllers using delegates, and using the Target-Action pattern. It's a lot of information to take in at once. Don't worry, though. You'll be repeating the essential concepts again and again as you progress through the book.

Exercises

1. Open the header file for `UITableViewDelegate` and `UITableViewData
   Source`. Review the list of delegate methods provided by these protocols. (Refer
   back to Chapter 8, "Creating a Master–Detail App," for tips on opening header
   files.)

2. Move the **Edit** button to the right side and the **+** button to the left. When you
   are done, move the buttons back.

3. Change the bar button item style for the **+** button to other styles and note the
   visual difference.

4. Modify the app to prevent the first table view row from being edited.

5. Modify the app to prevent the user from moving the last row.

10

Using Collection and Custom Views

In the last chapter you learned about using view controllers and communicating between them. In this chapter you learn how to create interesting layouts using collection views as well as how to create your own custom view. To keep things interesting, you'll move on from the photo album concept, focusing instead on displaying photos within the prototype app.

Let's get started with collection views.

Collection Views

A collection view provides a way to display a set of data in a flexible layout. It is similar to a table view in that it manages the presentation and scrolling of the data for you, it uses a data source object to retrieve data, and a delegate object is used for additional configuration. Unlike the table view, however, the collection view is not restricted to a single-column layout.

The layout for a collection view can be virtually any layout that you can imagine—a grid of items displayed with multiple rows and columns, items laid out in a circle or stacked on top of one another, items displayed randomly on the screen or in an orderly fashion on a single line. The layout is entirely up to you and your imagination.

Not only is a collection view's layout flexible, but it's changeable as well. You can have a collection view change between layouts at run time. Best of all, the collection view animates the transition between two layouts for you, providing for a pleasant user experience. This saves you a lot of extra work. Imagine, for example, you want to display a stack of photos. The user should be able to use a pinch gesture to zoom out on the stack causing the stack of photos to transition into a grid layout. You can accomplish this using a collection view with two layouts, and with far less code than you would need if you were to write the same feature without a collection view.

The Collection View Family of Objects

A collection view is made up of multiple objects. UICollectionView defines the visible area for the collection view. UICollectionViewController provides a view controller for managing the collection view. Just as with UITableViewController, you can choose to use this view controller (or not) when working with a collection view.

The content of a collection view is managed by an object conforming to the UICollectionViewDataSource protocol. Additional configuration can be performed on a collection view by implementing methods from the UICollectionViewDelegate protocol.

A cell is used to present each item in a collection view. It must be of type UICollectionReusableView, which supports the dequeuing and reuse of a cell to improve scroll performance. UICollectionViewCell is a specific type of UICollectionReusableView, and it is the type you generally subclass from when defining your own custom cell.

These objects should look familiar to you. The collection view follows a similar pattern found with the table view. However, unlike with a table view, a collection view relies on additional objects that define the layout of each item.

UICollectionViewLayout is the base class used to define a layout object. A layout object is responsible for defining the size and location of the item as well as other visual attributes for the cell. During the layout process, the layout object creates a UICollectionViewLayoutAttributes object that stores the attributes (e.g., size, location) for each cell.

The layout object also receives instances of UICollectionViewUpdateItem. These objects are used when new cells are inserted, deleted, or moved within the collection view.

Flow Layout

The most commonly used layout for a collection view is the flow layout, which is used to display items in a grid of columns and rows. The flow layout can also be used to display items in a single line and to create visual effects such as cover flow.

To use a flow layout, you create an instance of UICollectionViewFlowLayout. This class is provided by the iOS SDK, and it's a welcome addition for those programmers who have had to implement their own grid layout class in the past.

UICollectionViewFlowLayout also supports headers, footers, and sections. In addition, you interact with the flow layout object by way of the UICollectionViewDelegateFlowLayout protocol; it lets you define item sizes and spacing between items.

The PhotoWheel app will display a grid of photos. Because you're still in the prototyping stage, let's use this opportunity to obtain some hands-on practice with collection view and flow layout objects, using them to display a grid of items. This will make things easier when the time comes to build the main screen for PhotoWheel, which you will do in Chapter 16, "Building the Main Screen."

You can use the `UICollectionViewController` as the view controller for the collection view. Given that you already have a view controller for the detail view, however, we'll start by adding a `UICollectionView` to the detail view.

1. Open the file *DetailViewController.xib*.

2. Delete the label in the center of the view.

3. Open the Object library (**Control-Option-Command-3**).

4. Drag and drop a collection view object (`UICollectionView`) onto the view. Center it within the view, and let it fill the entire view area.

5. **Control-click** and drag the collection view to the File's Owner, and connect the `dataSource` outlet.

6. **Control-click** and drag the collection view to the File's Owner, and connect the `delegate` outlet.

7. Open the Assistant editor (**Option-Command-Return**).

8. **Control-click** and drag the collection view to the `@interface` section in the *DetailViewController.h* file displayed in the Assistant editor.

9. Name the outlet `collectionView` and set the storage type to weak.

The view is ready. Next up is the implementation of the `UICollectionView DataSource` and `UICollectionViewDelegate` protocol methods. Start by adding these two protocols to the `DetailViewController` interface. Open the file *DetailViewController.h* and make the changes shown in Listing 10.1.

Note

You can return to the Standard editor by pressing Command-Return.

Listing 10.1 Changes to *DetailViewController.h*

```
#import <UIKit/UIKit.h>

@interface DetailViewController : UIViewController <UISplitViewControllerDelegate,
UICollectionViewDataSource, UICollectionViewDelegate>
```

1. Collection View Programming Guide for iOS: https://developer.apple.com/library/ios/#documentation/WindowsViews/Conceptual/CollectionViewPGforIOS/Introduction/Introduction.html#//apple_ref/doc/uid/TP40012334-CH1-SW1

```
@property (strong, nonatomic) id detailItem;

@property (weak, nonatomic) IBOutlet UICollectionView *collectionView;
@property (weak, nonatomic) IBOutlet UILabel *detailDescriptionLabel;
@end
```

Now open the file *DetailViewController.m*, and add the changes shown in Listing 10.2.

Listing 10.2   **Changes to *DetailViewController.m***

```
@implementation DetailViewController

/* Other code purposely left out for brevity's sake. */

- (void)viewDidLoad
{
    [super viewDidLoad];
    // Do any additional setup after loading the view, typically from a NIB file.
    [self configureView];

    [[self collectionView] registerClass:[UICollectionViewCell class]
            forCellWithReuseIdentifier:@"cellID"];
}

#pragma mark - UICollectionViewDataSource and UICollectionViewDelegate

- (NSInteger)collectionView:(UICollectionView *)collectionView
    numberOfItemsInSection:(NSInteger)section
{
    return 1000;
}

- (UICollectionViewCell *)collectionView:(UICollectionView *)collectionView
                cellForItemAtIndexPath:(NSIndexPath *)indexPath
{
    UICollectionViewCell *cell =
        [collectionView dequeueReusableCellWithReuseIdentifier:@"cellID"
                                            forIndexPath:indexPath];
    [[cell contentView] setBackgroundColor:[UIColor blueColor]];
    return cell;
}

- (void)collectionView:(UICollectionView *)collectionView
didSelectItemAtIndexPath:(NSIndexPath *)indexPath
{
    UICollectionViewCell *cell =
```

```
      [collectionView cellForItemAtIndexPath:indexPath];
    [[cell contentView] setBackgroundColor:[UIColor yellowColor]];
}

- (void)collectionView:(UICollectionView *)collectionView
didDeselectItemAtIndexPath:(NSIndexPath *)indexPath
{
    UICollectionViewCell *cell =
        [collectionView cellForItemAtIndexPath:indexPath];
    [[cell contentView] setBackgroundColor:[UIColor blueColor]];
}

@end
```

So what exactly did you change? For starters, you registered UICollectionView
Cell as the class used for the collection view cell when dequeueing a cell with the
identifier cellID. Each item displayed in a collection view is a cell. Before the collection view can display the cell, however, it must dequeue the cell. Because a collection
view can display more than one type of cell at a time, each cell type must have its own
string identifier.

You may recall from Chapter 9, "Using Table Views," dequeuing a table view cell
with code that looks like this:

```
static NSString *CellIdentifier = @"Cell";
UITableViewCell *cell =
[tableView dequeueReusableCellWithIdentifier:CellIdentifier];
if (cell == nil) {
    cell = [[UITableViewCell alloc]
            initWithStyle:UITableViewCellStyleDefault
            reuseIdentifier:CellIdentifier];
}
```

Here the table view is asked to dequeue a cell with the string identifier "Cell." A
check is then performed to see whether the table view returned a cell. If it did not,
then a new instance of the cell is created.

With a collection view, you do not need to create an instance of the cell. The collection view will always return a cell to you. For this approach to work, the collection
view needs to know which type of cell to create for a given identifier. That's why
you must register the cell class and identifier, which you accomplished by using the
-registerClass:forCellWithReuseIdentifier: method. This method tells the
collection view to create an instance of the given class when dequeuing a cell with a
given identifier. In Listing 10.2, the registered class is UICollectionViewCell and
the reuse identifier is cellID.

If you had created a custom cell class (i.e., a class derived from UICollection
ViewCell), then you would need to register it with the collection view. Also, you

can register a NIB file instead of a class if you created a custom cell using IB, which you will do in a few moments. But first, let's continue reviewing the code changes in *DetailViewController.m*.

> **Note**
>
> As of iOS 6, you can register a class and a NIB file with a `UITableView` just as you do with `UICollectionView`. In turn, the table view will create an instance of the cell if one is not available, eliminating the `if (cell == nil)` check you saw earlier.

The `UICollectionViewDataSource` and `UICollectionViewDelegate` protocol methods follow a pattern similar to `UITableViewDataSource` and `UITableViewDelegate`. The method `-collectionView:numberOfItemsInSection:` returns the number of items within a section. The implementation of this method in Listing 10.2 always returns `1000`, which tells the collection view to display 1,000 items. In a real-world app, you would not hard code this value. Instead, the return value would be based on the number of data items you need to display within the given section.

The method `-collectionView:cellForItemAtIndexPath:` returns the cell to be displayed. The implementation in Listing 10.2 gets an instance of the cell by dequeuing it from the collection view. If there are no available cells in the queue, the collection view will create one for you. Once an instance of the cell has been returned, the background color of the cell's content view is set to blue. This is not very exciting, but it does get something on the screen quickly, which is precisely the point of a prototype—to try something quickly. Lastly, this method returns the cell to the caller.

The last two methods in Listing 10.2 are `-collectionView:didSelectItemAtIndexPath:` and `-collectionView:didDeselectItemAtIndexPath:`. The first method is called the first time the user taps a cell within the collection view. The second method is called when a previously selected cell is tapped again. The implementation here changes the background color of the selected cell to yellow. The background color is changes back to blue when the cell is deselected.

The collection view is currently configured to allow only one cell to be selected. However, the collection view does support multi-cell selection. Run the app as is and tap different cells in the detail view. Only one cell is ever yellow—the selected cell. Now add the following line of code to the bottom of `-viewDidLoad` in the file *DetailViewController.m*, and run the app again:

```
[[self collectionView] setAllowsMultipleSelection:YES];
```

This time when you tap a cell, its background turns yellow and stays yellow until you tap it again. Tapping other cells will turn their backgrounds yellow as well, and tapping those same cells again will turn the background back to blue (Figure 10.1).

Fine-tuning the Flow Layout

The steps you just followed were fairly straightforward. You added an instance of `UICollectionView` to the content view defined in the *DetailViewController.xib* file. You connected the collection view's `dataSource` and `delegate` outlets to the File's

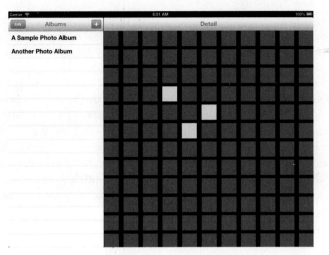

Figure 10.1   The collection view displayed in the detail view

Owner, which is the instance of the `DetailViewController` class. You added a new outlet, named `collectionView`, to the `DetailViewController` interface, and you connected that outlet to the collection view instance. Then you registered the cell class and reuse identifier with the collection view. Next, you implemented the `UICollectionViewDataSource` and `UICollectionViewDelegate` methods, which tell the collection what to display. But nowhere during these steps did you tell the collection view which layout to use.

The collection view you created in IB uses the flow layout by default. This is why the collection view works with the steps you performed. You can use IB to change the layout from flow to a custom layout as well as make other changes to fine-tune the layout. These changes can also be made in code—but why write code when you can let IB do the work for you?

Let's take a look at what you can do with the collection view from within IB.

Open the file *DetailViewController.xib* and then open the Attributes inspector (**Option-Command-4**). Under the Collection View section (Figure 10.2), you can specify the layout. The flow layout is the default. If you implement your own custom layout, change this setting to Custom and enter the class name for your custom layout.

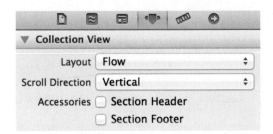

Figure 10.2   The Collection View section in the Attributes inspector

> **Note**
>
> This book does not cover custom layouts. To learn more about custom layouts, watch the WWDC 2012 video *Advanced Collection Views and Building Custom Layouts*.[2]

The flow layout supports both vertical and horizontal scrolling, but not both at the same time. The default scroll setting is vertical. Change this setting to horizontal and then run the app to see how the layout automatically adjusts to a horizontal flow layout.

Now open the Size inspector (**Option–Command–5**). Here you see the Collection View Size section. This section allows you to adjust the size of the cell displayed in the collection view. You can also set the minimum spacing between cells and lines, and you can change the section inset to indent cells within a section.

Go ahead and make the cell size larger or smaller, and play with the other size settings. Run the app to see your changes in action.

Custom Cells

Up to this point, the collection view created in the prototype app does nothing more than display blue and yellow squares. A real-world app, of course, will display a custom cell. You can create a custom cell using a number of different approaches. One approach is to add subviews to the content view of the `UICollectionViewCell`, but this requires writing code that creates and adds the subviews. A much easier way to create a custom cell is to use Interface Builder.

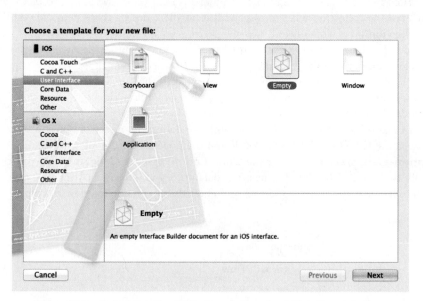

Figure 10.3   Select the Empty file template under **iOS > User Interface**

---

2. Advanced Collection Views and Building Custom Layouts video: https://developer.apple.com/videos/wwdc/2012/?id=219

Let's create a custom cell for the prototype app. Start by adding a new file to the project (**Command-N**). Select **User Interface** under the iOS section, and then select **Empty** as the file template (Figure 10.3). Click the **Next** button to continue.

Select **iPhone** as the device family. You're creating an empty NIB file, so the device family doesn't really matter. Then click the **Next** button.

Finally, save the file as "CustomCell" and click the **Create** button. You now have an empty NIB file to work with.

In the Object library, find the collection view cell object (UICollectionView Cell) and drop it onto the design canvas. Resize it to have a width and height of 100 (Figure 10.4).

Now drag a label (UILabel) from the Object library and drop it on the collection view cell. Stretch the label's width to fill the cell view, and center it vertically within the cell view. Change the color to white so the text is visible on a blue background.

Next, specify the reuse identifier for the cell. Remember, this identifier is used when registering the cell with the collection view, and it is used to dequeue the cell from the collection view. To set the reuse identifier, click the cell in the document outline, open the Attributes inspector, and enter "CustomCell" in the Identifier field (Figure 10.5).

Note

The reuse identifier can be any string value you choose. I find it helpful to use the class name as the reuse identifier when using a custom cell class.

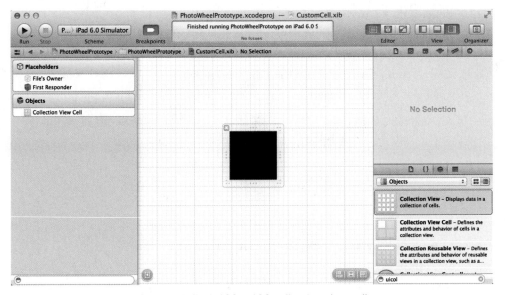

Figure 10.4   A 100 x 100 collection view cell

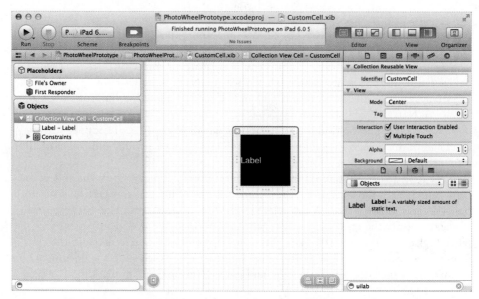

Figure 10.5   Specifying the reuse identifier for the custom cell

Next, you need to create a new Objective-C class for the custom cell. This class will define an outlet for the label, so its text can be set programmatically. Here are the steps to follow:

1. Create a new file (**Command-N**).

2. Select **iOS > Cocoa Touch**.

3. Select the Objective-C class file template and then click the **Next** button.

4. Name the class CustomCell.

5. Enter UICollectionViewCell as the subclass name.

6. Click the **Next** and **Create** buttons to create the file and add it to the project.

Now open the file *CustomCell.h*, and define an outlet for the UILabel displayed in your custom cell. The code is shown in Listing 10.3.

Listing 10.3   *CustomCell.h*

```
#import <UIKit/UIKit.h>

@interface CustomCell : UICollectionViewCell

@property (nonatomic, weak) IBOutlet UILabel *labelText;

@end
```

Before we can use the custom cell, you need to tell the CustomCell NIB file about the `CustomCell` class, and you need to connect the label to the `labelText` outlet. Open the file *CustomCell.xib*. Click the Custom View Cell in the document outline, and then open the Identity inspector (**Option-Command-3**). Enter "CustomCell" in the Class field.

Now connect the `labelText` outlet to the `UILabel` displayed in the cell. To do so, **Control-click** and drag the Custom Cell in the document outline to the label displayed in the cell view.

All that remains is updating the `DetailViewController` to register and use the new custom cell. The code changes are shown in Listing 10.4.

Listing 10.4   **Changes to *DetailViewController.m***

```objc
#import "DetailViewController.h"
#import "CustomCell.h"

@implementation DetailViewController

/* Other code purposely left out for brevity's sake. */

- (void)viewDidLoad
{
    [super viewDidLoad];
    // Do any additional setup after loading the view, typically from a NIB file.
    [self configureView];

    UINib *nib = [UINib nibWithNibName:@"CustomCell" bundle:nil];
    [[self collectionView] registerNib:nib forCellWithReuseIdentifier:@"CustomCell"];
}

- (UICollectionViewCell *)collectionView:(UICollectionView *)collectionView
              cellForItemAtIndexPath:(NSIndexPath *)indexPath
{
    CustomCell *cell =
        [collectionView dequeueReusableCellWithReuseIdentifier:@"CustomCell"
                                          forIndexPath:indexPath];
    [[cell contentView] setBackgroundColor:[UIColor blueColor]];

    NSString *text = [NSString stringWithFormat:@"%i", [indexPath item]];
    [[cell labelText] setText:text];

    return cell;
}

@end
```

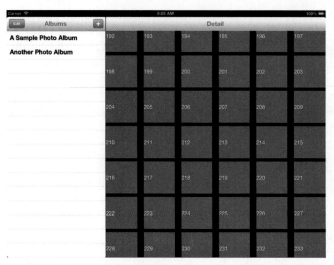

Figure 10.6   Custom cells displayed in the collection view

Save your changes and run the app. What happened? The label text doesn't display correctly. Why not?

The dimensions for the custom cell you created are 100 × 100, but cell size defined in the collection view is 50 × 50. To fix this discrepancy, open the file *DetailViewController.xib*, click the Collection View, open the Size inspector, and set the cell size to 100 for both the width and height. Save your changes and run the app again. It should now look like Figure 10.6.

Custom Views

Collection views make it easy to present data with interesting layouts, and UIKit, in general, provides an outstanding set of views that make it easier and faster to create iOS apps. Sometimes, however, your app's UI needs more than what is provided by the SDK. This is where custom views come in. Creating a custom view is not difficult; in fact, it's as easy as creating a new `UIView` subclass.

> **Note**
>
> You have already created a type of custom view using a combination of a NIB file and a custom class when you created the custom collection view cell. Now you will learn how to create a custom view that manages its own layout.

Why would you ever need to create a custom view? There are many reasons. Typically, you will take this road because you want to present something visually that is not possible out of the box using the iOS SDK. You might also create a custom view because you want to reuse a particular layout in other parts of your app.

Suppose, for example, that the app must present the same set of visual controls—for instance, a `UILabel` and `UITextField`—to display a prompt label followed by a text input box. Now suppose the display of these controls is repeated over and over throughout the app. The constant repetition of UI elements and code violates the DRY ("Don't repeat yourself") principle, making your code more difficult to maintain. You can simplify the app's code base by creating a new view that is responsible for displaying the label and text field. Then, instead of repeating the label and text field combination throughout the app, only the custom view containing the label and text field is repeated. Also, should you need to make a change to the custom view, such as reversing the order of the two controls, the change can be made in one place and propagated throughout the app.

What Is DRY?

DRY, short for "Don't repeat yourself," is a fundamental software engineering principle whose goal is to reduce redundancy. When it is applied, blocks of code, logic, sets of UI elements, and so forth exist only once and are reused instead of being copied and pasted throughout an application. To learn more about DRY and other useful principles of programming, read *The Pragmatic Programmer: From Journeyman to Master* (Addison-Wesley, 1999).

View Controller... Not

Creating a custom view is simple. The challenge comes when deciding whether a user interface element is better implemented as a custom view or as part of a view controller. It's not uncommon to implement a view controller to display some part of the UI, only to discover later that the code can be made more reusable if implemented as a view. And not only is the view easier to reuse as opposed to the view controller, but you can also create specializations of the custom view, extending its appearance and behavior.

Take, for example, a set of photos displayed in a circular formation. An initial solution for implementing the UI is to write a view controller that manages the layout of the photos. But once you do so, you'll realize that a good amount of controller code is devoted to the layout of the photos. It's the implementation of the layout code that is ideal for a custom view, not a view controller.

Let the view controller mediate data between the view and the model, and let the view manage the visual layout of the data provided by the view controller.

A good example of this approach can be seen with a wheel view. Looking at the sketch of the prototype app, shown in Figure 10.7, you see a wheel of photos. The photo wheel is nothing more than a set of photos laid out to form a circle. While this can be implemented within the `DetailViewController`, a better approach is to create a new custom view that manages the layout of photos. Let's take a look at how a wheel view can be implemented as a custom view.

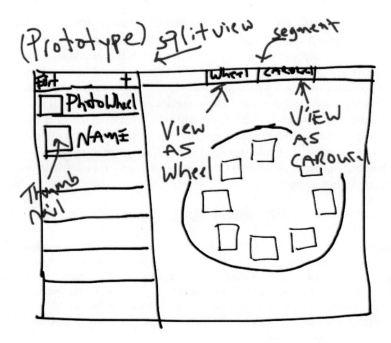

Figure 10.7   Sketch of the PhotoWheelPrototype app

Note

A collection view with a custom circle layout object can be used to create a wheel view of items. In fact, Apple provides sample code for displaying a circular layout. However, as you will see in Chapter 16, "Building the Main Screen," PhotoWheel has some specific needs in its `WheelView` class that cannot easily be satisfied with a custom collection view layout object.

The circle layout sample is part of the WWDC 2012 sample code,[3] and it is presented in the WWDC 2012 video *Advanced Collection Views and Building Custom Layouts*.[4]

A Wheel View

The wheel view displays a set of subviews laid out in a circle. Why a set of subviews and not a set of photos? There's no good reason to limit the wheel view to photos only. A `UIView`, or some subclass of it such as a `UIImageView`, is all that is needed to display a photo. The wheel view doesn't care which type of subview it is given, so long as it receives at least a view of some sort. In turn, the wheel view doesn't have to be limited to the display of photos, but rather can be used to display any view you see fit.

---

3. WWDC 2012 sample code: https://developer.apple.com/devcenter/download.action?path=/ wwdc_2012/wwdc_2012_sample_code/wwdc_2012_session_code.dmg

4. *Advanced Collection Views and Building Custom Layouts* WWDC video: https://developer.apple. com/videos/wwdc/2012/?id=219

How does the wheel view know about the subviews to display? One option is to pass in an array or set of views, but this means the views must be created in memory before they are referenced by the wheel view. This can waste valuable system resources (i.e., memory) on a mobile device. Instead, a better approach is to have the wheel view ask some source for each subview as it needs it.

This pattern should sound familiar to you, because it's the same pattern used by `UITableView` and `UICollectionView`. These two objects have no intimate knowledge of the cell displayed in each row. Instead, they rely on a `dataSource` object to provide each cell when needed. The wheel view you create will do the same.

To begin, you need to create a new class, which we'll call `WheelView`. Follow these steps to accomplish this:

1. Press **Command-N**.

2. Select **iOS > Cocoa Touch >** Objective-C **class**.

3. Click the **Next** button.

4. Name the class `WheelView`.

5. Make it a subclass of `UIView`.

6. Click the **Next** button.

7. Click the **Create** button.

Open the interface file *WheelView.h* and add the code in Listing 10.5.

Listing 10.5   **Source Code for *WheelView.h***

```
#import <UIKit/UIKit.h>

@protocol WheelViewDataSource;
@class WheelViewCell;

@interface WheelView : UIView

@property (nonatomic, weak) IBOutlet id<WheelViewDataSource> dataSource;

@end


@protocol WheelViewDataSource <NSObject>
@required
- (NSInteger)wheelViewNumberOfCells:(WheelView *)wheelView;
- (WheelViewCell *)wheelView:(WheelView *)wheelView cellAtIndex:(NSInteger)index;
@end


@interface WheelViewCell : UIView
@end
```

Walking through this code, you first see the #import statement for *UIKit.h*. Importing this header file allows the WheelView class to reference classes within UIKit. Following this are two forward declarations, one for the protocol WheelViewDataSource and one for the class WheelViewCell. The forward declarations tell the compiler about the types when it encounters a reference to the protocol or class prior to the actual declaration of each.

Next up is the interface declaration for WheelView. The class derives from UI View, and it has one declared property called dataSource. dataSource can be any Objective-C object regardless of the kind of class, so the id data type is used as the property's data type. To assist the compiler with sy ntax checking, the protocol Wheel ViewDataSource is added to the id data type. It tells the compiler that the object referenced by dataSource must conform to the WheelViewDataSource protocol.

Note that dataSource is also marked as an outlet. This designation allows you to set the property reference within IB, which you will see momentarily.

Following the interface declaration for WheelView is the protocol declaration for WheelViewDataSource. WheelView needs to know two things about the data it will be displaying:

1. The number of cells to display

2. The cell for a particular index

In turn, the two required methods are added to the WheelViewDataSource protocol. Any object that conforms to this protocol must provide implementations for these methods.

Last, in the source code you see the declaration for WheelViewCell, which is a subclass of UIView. We have said that WheelView does not care about the type of view displayed in the wheel, but this could change down the road. There might come a time when WheelView needs to store internal information on the object. By declaring a generalized class now, you prepare the code for possible changes down the road. Also, because this class type is used in the methods for the WheelViewDataSource protocol, you reduce the magnitude of changes to the app should WheelView need to store internal data within the view cell.

> **Note**
>
> You may be wondering why WheelView, WheelViewDataSource, and WheelView Cell are all defined in the same interface file. Each could have been defined in its own interface file, but I elected to keep them together because each is tightly coupled with the others. In addition, it's easier to reuse WheelView in other projects by copying *WheelView.h* and *.m* files instead of copying *WheelView.h* and *WheelView.m*, *WheelViewDataSource.h*, and *WheelViewCell.h* and *WheelViewCell.m*.

Now open *WheelView.m* and replace the template-generated code with the code presented in Listing 10.6.

Listing 10.6 **WheelView's Implementation**

```objc
#import "WheelView.h"

@implementation WheelView

- (void)setAngle:(CGFloat)angle
{
    // The following code is inspired by the carousel example at
    // http://stackoverflow.com/questions/5243614/3d-carousel-effect-on-the-ipad

    CGPoint center = CGPointMake(CGRectGetMidX([self bounds]),
                                 CGRectGetMidY([self bounds]));
    CGFloat radiusX = MIN([self bounds].size.width,
                          [self bounds].size.height) * 0.35;
    CGFloat radiusY = radiusX;

    NSInteger cellCount = [[self dataSource] wheelViewNumberOfCells:self];
    float angleToAdd = 360.0f / cellCount;

    for (NSInteger index = 0; index < cellCount; index++)
    {
        WheelViewCell *cell = [[self dataSource] wheelView:self
                                               cellAtIndex:index];
        if ([cell superview] == nil) {
            [self addSubview:cell];
        }

        float angleInRadians = (angle + 180.0) * M_PI / 180.0f;

        // Get a position based on the angle
        float xPosition = center.x + (radiusX * sinf(angleInRadians))
            - (CGRectGetWidth([cell frame]) / 2);
        float yPosition = center.y + (radiusY * cosf(angleInRadians))
            - (CGRectGetHeight([cell frame]) / 2);

        [cell setTransform:CGAffineTransformMakeTranslation(xPosition, yPosition)];

        // Work out what the next angle is going to be
        angle += angleToAdd;
    }
}

- (void)layoutSubviews
{
    [self setAngle:0];
}
```

```
@end
```

```
@implementation WheelViewCell
@end
```

Online Help

Did you notice the comment in Listing 10.6 that mentions the origin of the algorithm used to lay out the subviews? This algorithm comes from a posting on stackoverflow.com, and kudos to "Tommy" for providing a nice solution.

Programming today is far different from what it was like 30 years ago. Back in the 1980s, I needed to implement the YMODEM file transport protocol for a system I was working on. I found out that sample code was available in a past issue of *Dr. Dobb's Journal*, so I went to the library at the local university to look at a copy of the magazine.

Unfortunately, the issue wasn't available. I had to request the microfilm of the magazine, which took a few days to arrive. When it did, I had to return to the university's library to view the microfilm on its reader. I found the article I needed, read through it multiple times until I was confident I understood it, and I wrote, by hand on paper, the sample source code. If I remember correctly, the entire process, from research to implementation, took almost two weeks before I had a working version of the transfer protocol.

Today, many programming problems can be solved in minutes, not days or weeks. Thanks to the Internet, Google.com, and online developer communities and forums such as stackoverflow.com and Apple's own devforums.apple.com, programming today can be much easier. You should definitely make a habit of checking online resources, such as these Web sites, when faced with a programming challenge or when you just want to see how others might implement solutions to the same problems. In turn, you should be a good developer community citizen by giving back with postings of your answers and solutions to questions from others.

`WheelView` is now ready to be used within the app. The wheel view will be displayed in the `DetailViewController`. IB doesn't know about `WheelView`, so you must tell IB about it. This is accomplished by changing the class name in the Identity inspector from `UIView` to `WheelView`. Once IB knows that the view is of type `WheelView`, the File's Owner can be set as the data source to the wheel view. Here are the steps to follow:

1. Open *DetailViewController.xib*.

2. Add a new `UIView` instance to the main content view. (Yes, the view will be on top of the collection view added earlier.)

3. Open the Size inspector (**Option-Command-5**) and set the width and height to 768.

4. Center the `UIView` within the screen. You can do this in the Size inspector by setting X to 0 and Y to 118.

5. Open the Identity inspector (**Option-Command-3**).

6. Change the class name from `UIView` to `WheelView`.

7. **Control-click** the `WheelView` and connect the `dataSource` outlet to the File's Owner (Figure 10.8).

> **Note**
>
> Seeing a `UIView` within a `UIView` can be difficult if both views have the same background color. To get around this problem, turn on Layout Rectangles by selecting **Editor > Canvas > Show Layout Rectangles** from the menu bar.

Finally, the `DetailViewController` must be updated with implementations for the `WheelViewDataSource` protocol methods. This is necessary because `Detail ViewController` is the File's Owner, and the File's Owner has been set as the data source for the wheel view.

To accomplish this, start by opening *DetailViewController.h* and add `WheelView DataSource` to the list of protocols implemented by the class. Note that you will also need to import *WheelView.h*, which contains the declaration for `WheelView DataSource`. Once modified, the header file should contain the code found in Listing 10.7.

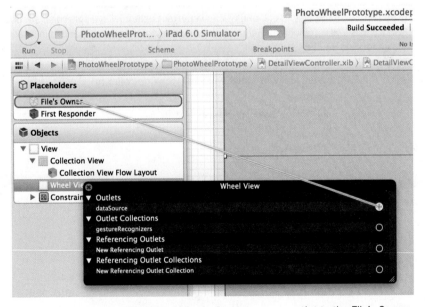

Figure 10.8   Connect the Wheel View's `dataSource` outlet to the File's Owner

Listing 10.7   **Modified Version of *DetailViewController.h***

```
#import <UIKit/UIKit.h>
#import "WheelView.h"

@interface DetailViewController : UIViewController
  <UISplitViewControllerDelegate, UICollectionViewDataSource,
  UICollectionViewDelegate, WheelViewDataSource>

@property (strong, nonatomic) id detailItem;

@property (weak, nonatomic) IBOutlet UICollectionView *collectionView;
@property (weak, nonatomic) IBOutlet UILabel *detailDescriptionLabel;
@end
```

Before you can implement the `WheelViewDataSource` methods within `Detail`
`ViewController`, the app needs a collection of views to display. A good place to create this data is in the `-viewDidLoad` event of the `DetailViewController`. A private
data property is needed to store the collection of views. The code changes are shown
in Listing 10.8.

> **Note**
>
> Caching the cell views for the `WheelView` inside the `DetailViewController` is a
> bad design. The better approach is to let `WheelView` manage its own cache and provide a
> dequeuing mechanism like that found with `UITableView` and `UICollectionView`. But
> you're still at the prototyping stage, and what's important right now is displaying a set of sub-
> views in a circle. You'll implement the internal cache and dequeuing mechanism in Chapter 16,
> "Building the Main Screen."

Listing 10.8   **Initializing an Array of Views in *DetailViewController.m***

```
@interface DetailViewController ()
@property (strong, nonatomic) NSArray *data;
// Other code left out for brevity's sake.
@end

@implementation DetailViewController

// Other code left out for brevity's sake.

- (void)viewDidLoad
{
    [super viewDidLoad];
// Do any additional setup after loading the view, typically from a NIB file.
    [self configureView];

    UINib *nib = [UINib nibWithNibName:@"CustomCell" bundle:nil];
    [[self collectionView] registerNib:nib
```

```
                forCellWithReuseIdentifier:@"CustomCell"];
    [[self collectionView] setHidden:YES];

    CGRect cellFrame = CGRectMake(0, 0, 75, 75);
    NSInteger count = 10;
    NSMutableArray *newArray = [[NSMutableArray alloc] initWithCapacity:count];
    for (NSInteger index = 0; index < count; index++) {
        WheelViewCell *cell = [[WheelViewCell alloc] initWithFrame:cellFrame];
        [cell setBackgroundColor:[UIColor blueColor]];
        [newArray addObject:cell];
    }
    [self setData:[newArray copy]];
}

// Other code left out for brevity's sake.


@end
```

Note

The line of code `[[self collectionView] setHidden:YES];` in Listing 10.8 hides the collection view from the user. This line is included so you can test the `WheelView` without the collection view getting in your way. If you prefer, you can mark the view as hidden in IB instead of hiding the view via code.

`DetailViewController` is the data source for the wheel view, and it contains the private property `data`, which in turn contains the array of views to display in the `WheelView`. All that remains is to implement the `WheelViewDataSource` protocol methods. Add the code in Listing 10.9 to the bottom of the `DetailViewController`'s implementation (but before the @end statement).

Listing 10.9   **Updated *DetailViewController.m***

```
#pragma mark - WheelViewDataSource methods

- (NSInteger)wheelViewNumberOfCells:(WheelView *)wheelView
{
    NSInteger count = [[self data] count];
    return count;
}


- (WheelViewCell *)wheelView:(WheelView *)wheelView
                 cellAtIndex:(NSInteger)index
{
    WheelViewCell *cell = [[self data] objectAtIndex:index];
    return cell;
}
```

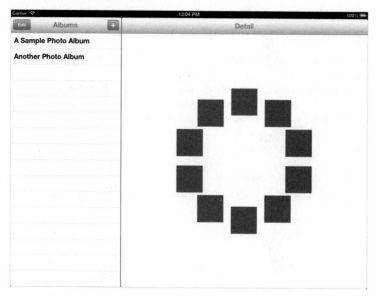

Figure 10.9   The prototype app with a wheel of squares

Build and run the app. The detail view within the app now displays a circle of blue square views, as shown in Figure 10.9.

A Carousel View

A benefit of using a custom view is that the layout of the view can change with little or no impact on the app. How might `WheelView` change? It looks nice as is, but a carousel view might look better. You won't know until you try it.

The wheel can be turned into a carousel with some minor tweaking of the algorithm used to lay out the wheel view cells. This is a perfect time to experiment. After all, this is a prototype app, and there is no better place to experiment with concepts than in a prototype app.

Making the carousel is as simple as turning the wheel on its side, but which way looks better? A good way to compare the options is to add a feature to the prototype app that enables the user to switch between the two display styles.

To make it so, open *WheelView.h* and add a new declared property called `style`. To make the code more readable, use an enumeration type to define the list of display styles. Your code should look like the code in Listing 10.10.

Listing 10.10   **Modified Version of *WheelView.h***

```
#import <UIKit/UIKit.h>

@protocol WheelViewDataSource;
```

```
@class WheelViewCell;

typedef enum  {
    WheelViewStyleWheel,
    WheelViewStyleCarousel,
} WheelViewStyle;

@interface WheelView : UIView

@property (nonatomic, weak) IBOutlet id<WheelViewDataSource> dataSource;
@property (nonatomic, assign) WheelViewStyle style;

@end


@protocol WheelViewDataSource <NSObject>
@required
- (NSInteger)wheelViewNumberOfCells:(WheelView *)wheelView;
- (WheelViewCell *)wheelView:(WheelView *)wheelView cellAtIndex:(NSInteger)index;
@end


@interface WheelViewCell : UIView
@end
```

> **Note**
>
> The declared property `style` uses the property setting `assign`. This is used instead of `strong` because `style`'s data type is an enumeration, which is a C type, not an Objective-C object. C scalar types and enumerations always use `assign` when defined as a declared property.

Now it's time to add carousel support to the `WheelView` class. Open *WheelView.m*. When the `style` property is set, the layout of the view must change. Therefore, you need to add a custom implementation for the `style`'s setter method. The code changes are given in Listing 10.11.

Listing 10.11   Implementing a Custom Setter Method in *WheelView.m*

```
@implementation WheelView

// Other source code not shown for brevity's sake.

// Add to the bottom of the WheelView implementation.
- (void)setStyle:(WheelViewStyle)newStyle
{
    if (_style != newStyle) {
```

```
    _style = newStyle;

    [UIView animateWithDuration:0.3 animations:^{
        [self setAngle:0];
    }];
}
}

@end
```

Let's take a closer look at the setter method `-setStyle:`.

This method determines whether the new style is different from the current style. If it is, the current style is set to the new style. This part of the code should be obvious to you, but not so obvious is the rest of the code in the `if` block.

A call is made to `-setAngle:` to force `WheelView` to redraw. At the moment, the app always passes in `0` for the angle. In Chapter 11, "Using Touch Gestures," you'll change the app to use different angle values, but `0` works for the current needs of the app.

More odd than always passing `0` is the code before and after `[self setAngle:0]`. This is your first look at using Core Animation. This bit of code wraps the drawing of the wheel as it changes from one style to another in an animation block. The `+animateWithDuration:animations:` method on `UIView` tells Core Animation to animate the UI changes contained in the code block. The method `-setAngle:` will draw the view based on the new style, and Core Animation calculates and renders the visual aspects needed to animate the transition from one style to another.

> **Note**
>
> Core Animation is an extremely powerful framework for producing animations within iOS applications, and it is used throughout iOS. The bounce effect you see when scrolling through the app icons on the Home screen, the animation effect you see when launching and quitting apps, the pushing and popping of view controllers from a navigation controller—these are all examples of where Core Animation is used.
>
> To learn more about Core Animation, read Marcus Zarra and Matt Long's book *Core Animation: Simplified Animation Techniques for Mac and iPhone Development* (Addison-Wesley, 2009), and Bill Dudney's *Core Animation for Mac OS X and the iPhone: Creating Compelling Dynamic User Interfaces* (Pragmatic Programmers, 2008).

Now you need to tweak the display algorithm in the `-setAngle:` method. To give the wheel a carousel look, the circle needs to look more like an oval. Also, the views displayed in the back of the carousel should be smaller than those in the front and slightly faded. This gives an effect of visual depth to the carousel. The updated code is shown in Listing 10.12.

Listing 10.12   Updated `-setAngle:` Method Supporting the Carousel as a Display Style

```objc
#import "WheelView.h"
#import <QuartzCore/QuartzCore.h>

@implementation WheelView

// Other source code not shown for brevity's sake.

- (void)setAngle:(CGFloat)angle
{
    // The following code is inspired by the carousel example at
    // http://stackoverflow.com/questions/5243614/3d-carousel-effect-on-the-ipad

    CGPoint center = CGPointMake(CGRectGetMidX([self bounds]),
                                 CGRectGetMidY([self bounds]));
    CGFloat radiusX = MIN([self bounds].size.width,
                          [self bounds].size.height) * 0.35;
    CGFloat radiusY = radiusX;
    if ([self style] == WheelViewStyleCarousel) {
        radiusY = radiusX * 0.30;
    }

    NSInteger cellCount = [[self dataSource] wheelViewNumberOfCells:self];
    float angleToAdd = 360.0f / cellCount;

    for (NSInteger index = 0; index < cellCount; index++)
    {
        WheelViewCell *cell = [[self dataSource] wheelView:self
                                               cellAtIndex:index];
        if ([cell superview] == nil) {
            [self addSubview:cell];
        }

        float angleInRadians = (angle + 180.0) * M_PI / 180.0f;

        // Get a position based on the angle
        float xPosition = center.x + (radiusX * sinf(angleInRadians))
            - (CGRectGetWidth([cell frame]) / 2);
        float yPosition = center.y + (radiusY * cosf(angleInRadians))
            - (CGRectGetHeight([cell frame]) / 2);

        float scale = 0.75f + 0.25f * (cosf(angleInRadians) + 1.0);

        // Apply location and scale
        if ([self style] == WheelViewStyleCarousel) {
            [cell setTransform:CGAffineTransformScale(
```

```
                        CGAffineTransformMakeTranslation(xPosition, yPosition),
                                  scale,
                                  scale)];
        // Tweak alpha using the same system as applied for scale,
        // this time with 0.3 as the minimum and a semicircle range
        // of 0.5
        [cell setAlpha:(0.3f + 0.5f * (cosf(angleInRadians) + 1.0))];

    } else {
        [cell setTransform:CGAffineTransformMakeTranslation(xPosition,
                                              yPosition)];

        [cell setAlpha:1.0];
    }

    [[cell layer] setZPosition:scale];

    // Work out what the next angle is going to be
    angle += angleToAdd;
    }
}

// Other source code not shown for brevity's sake.

@end
```

The code has now been modified to support two different display styles: wheel and carousel. To produce the carousel effect, the Y-axis is adjusted to be 30% of the X-axis. Also, the scale and alpha values for each cell are set based on the position within the circle. The last change is the setting of the Z-position for the layer. This effectively mimics setting the draw order of the views without having to actually reorder the list views.

> **Note**
>
> If Xcode reports a warning message on the line of code `[[cell layer] setZPosition:scale]`, you likely forgot to include the `#import <QuartzCore/QuartzCore.h>` statement at the top of the *WheelView.m* file. Add the import statement and the warning will go away.

Now that `WheelView` is ready, it's time to update the app so that the user can switch between the two display styles. A segmented control in the `DetailView`'s navigation bar is a good way for the user to do this. But first, the `DetailViewController` needs a new outlet that references the wheel view so that the style can be changed programmatically. Open *DetailViewController.h* and add the new outlet for the `WheelView`. The source code is shown in Listing 10.13.

Listing 10.13   **New Outlet Added to `DetailViewController`**

```
#import <UIKit/UIKit.h>
#import "WheelView.h"

@interface DetailViewController : UIViewController
    <UISplitViewControllerDelegate, UICollectionViewDataSource,
    UICollectionViewDelegate, WheelViewDataSource>

@property (strong, nonatomic) id detailItem;

@property (weak, nonatomic) IBOutlet UICollectionView *collectionView;
@property (weak, nonatomic) IBOutlet UILabel *detailDescriptionLabel;
@property (weak, nonatomic) IBOutlet WheelView *wheelView;
@end
```

Now open *DetailViewController.xib* and connect the `WheelView` instance to the `wheelView` outlet by **Control-clicking** and dragging the File's Owner to the `Wheel View` instance.

Next you need to add a segmented control to the navigation bar. The navigation bar is managed by the `UINavigationController` containing the `DetailViewController` instance. The navigation controller displays a label that contains the view controller's title in the middle of the navigation bar. In the prototype app you are working on, the view controller's title is set to "Detail" in the `-initWithNibName:bundle:` method found in the *DetailViewController.m* file.

The navigation controller can also display a custom view in place of the title label in the middle of the navigation bar. To do this, set the `titleView` property of the view controller's navigation item.

You want to display a `UISegmentedControl` instead of the default title view in the navigation bar. To do this, you must create a new instance of `UISegmentedControl` and set the `titleView` property on the navigation item for the `DetailViewController` instance. You also need to define a new action that is called when the user taps a segment. The action's implementation will set the `wheelView` style based on the selected segment index. And while you're at it, let's make the segment control provide an option to show the collection view created earlier.

The code to accomplish these tasks is shown in Listing 10.14. Add the same code to your project.

Listing 10.14   **Update to *DetailViewController.m***

```
- (void)viewDidLoad
{
    // Other source code not shown for brevity's sake.

    // Add to the bottom of viewDidLoad.
    NSArray *segmentedItems = @[@"Wheel", @"Carousel", @"Flow"];
    UISegmentedControl *segmentedControl = [[UISegmentedControl alloc]
```

```
                                                 initWithItems:segmentedItems];
   [segmentedControl addTarget:self
                     action:@selector(segmentedControlValueChanged:)
           forControlEvents:UIControlEventValueChanged];
   [segmentedControl setSegmentedControlStyle:UISegmentedControlStyleBar];
   [segmentedControl setSelectedSegmentIndex:0];
   [[self navigationItem] setTitleView:segmentedControl];
}


- (void)segmentedControlValueChanged:(id)sender
{
   NSInteger index = [sender selectedSegmentIndex];
   if (index == 0) {
     [[self collectionView] setHidden:YES];
     [[self wheelView] setHidden:NO];
     [[self wheelView] setStyle:WheelViewStyleWheel];
   } else if (index == 1) {
     [[self collectionView] setHidden:YES];
     [[self wheelView] setHidden:NO];
     [[self wheelView] setStyle:WheelViewStyleCarousel];
   } else {
     [[self collectionView] setHidden:NO];
     [[self wheelView] setHidden:YES];
   }
}
```

That's it. Save the changes, and then build and run the app. Test the new feature by tapping Wheel and Carousel in the navigation bar. The carousel should look like Figure 10.10.

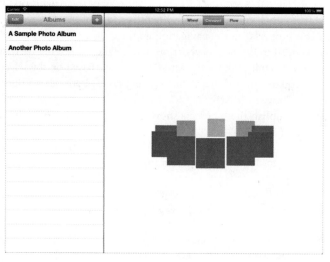

Figure 10.10   The new carousel display style

A Photo Wheel View Cell

You now have a generic, reusable view that displays a wheel or carousel of subviews, but the specific needs of the app call for the display of photos. What is needed now is a specialized type of `WheelViewCell`. This subclass of `WheelViewCell` will display an image.

The easiest way to display an image is to use `UIImageView`. To do so, simply create an instance of `UIImageView` and add it to the view hierarchy. Next, set the image view's `image` property to an image.

This is not the only way to display an image. You can also set content for the layer that backs the view. (It sounds complicated but it's not.)

In iOS, each `UIView` is backed by a `CALayer`, which means that each `UIView` has a `CALayer` instance making it possible to take advantage of Core Animation effects on the `UIView`. You can think of a layer as something that sits behind or within the view that stores additional information for drawing and animating views.

> **Note**
>
> Views on Mac OS X are not backed by a `CALayer` by default. Instead, you must explicitly turn on backing if you need a `CALayer`-backed view.

Placing an image on a `CALayer` is a common practice when you need to display a large number of images. Its use is overkill for the prototype app, but let's use it anyway so you can see how it's done. Also, while you're at it, draw a border and shadow around the image to enhance the visual display.

Here are the steps to follow. Note that the steps are purposely brief, as you should now be familiar with creating new classes.

1. Create a new Objective-C class.

2. Name the new class `PhotoWheelViewCell`.

3. Specify `WheelViewCell` as the superclass for the new class.

`PhotoWheelViewCell` needs a way to set the current image. This can be implemented as a declared property, but the cell view has no need to hang on to the image. The image will, instead, be added to the contents of the view's layer. Thus, instead of adding a new property to the class, all that is needed is a single method, `-setImage:`, that will add an image to the layer's contents. The header and implementation files for `PhotoWheelViewCell` are shown in Listing 10.15.

Listing 10.15   Interface and Implementation for `PhotoWheelViewCell`

```
////////////
// PhotoWheelViewCell.h

#import "WheelView.h"
```

```
@interface PhotoWheelViewCell : WheelViewCell

- (void)setImage:(UIImage *)newImage;

@end


/////////////
// PhotoWheelViewCell.m

#import "PhotoWheelViewCell.h"
#import <QuartzCore/QuartzCore.h>

@implementation PhotoWheelViewCell

- (void)setImage:(UIImage *)newImage
{
    // Add the image to the layer's contents.
    CALayer *layer = [self layer];
    id imageRef = (__bridge id)[newImage CGImage];
    [layer setContents:imageRef];

    // Add border and shadow.
    [layer setBorderColor:[UIColor colorWithWhite:1.0 alpha:1.0].CGColor];
    [layer setBorderWidth:5.0];
    [layer setShadowOffset:CGSizeMake(0, 3)];
    [layer setShadowOpacity:0.7];
    [layer setShouldRasterize:YES];
}

@end
```

The implementation starts by importing *PhotoWheelViewCell.h* and *QuartzCore.h*. The QuartzCore header is needed because the code uses an object of type `CALayer`.

The implementation of `-setImage:` is straightforward. It grabs a local reference to `[self layer]` to make the code more readable. Next, the `CGImageRef` from the given image is stored in a local variable.

Okay, so maybe the code here is not that straightforward. Here's what is going on. To display an image in the contents of a layer, you must set the contents to a `CGImageRef`. `CGImageRef` is a C structure that contains bitmap information about the image. It is a Core Foundation-style object, and its lifetime is not automatically managed by ARC.

> **Note**
>
> Revisit Chapter 4, "Getting Started with Objective-C," if you need a refresher on ARC.

In contrast, `contents` is an Objective-C object of type `id`. `id` is a general object type for any kind of Objective-C object regardless of the class. To set `contents` to a `CGImageRef`, the image ref must be cast to `id`. This is true anytime you need to cast between an Objective-C type and a Core Foundation–style object.

To cast between the types, you must use the `__bridge` syntax. (`__bridge type`) performs a noop cast. (`__bridge_transfer type`) releases the reference being cast. (`__bridge_retain type`) adds a count to the retain count. For `PhotoWheelViewCell`, only a noop cast is needed. The `CGImageRef` returned by `[newImage CGImage]` is cast to `id`; it can then be passed to the layer's `contents`. Also, because `__bridge` syntax is used, ARC will not attempt to manage the memory for `id`, nor will the compiler complain about not knowing the memory ownership for the local reference.

The rest of the code is used to draw the border and shadow effect around the image. Feel free to play with these settings to see which other effects you can create.

Using PhotoWheelViewCell

Now that `PhotoWheelViewCell` has been implemented, it's time to put it to good use. The prototype app doesn't yet have the ability to add new photos to a photo wheel, so let's add a default photo to the app that will be displayed until the user adds a photo.

Included with the sample source code for this chapter are two image files: *defaultPhoto.png* and *defaultPhoto@2x.png*. The *@2x* version is the same image but at twice the size. This is the image used on retina versions of the iPad (third- and later-generation iPads). For normal display, *@defaultPhoto.png* is used. As the programmer, you don't need to worry about which image to use. As long as both images are included in the project, iOS will pick the correct image based on the device's display capabilities.

Add these files to your project by dragging and dropping them from Finder to the Xcode Project navigator for your project. Be sure to select the option "Copy items into destination group's folder (if needed)," as shown in Figure 10.11. This will ensure that the files are copied to the project directory.

As you may recall, `DetailViewController` is responsible for creating the array of wheel view cells. It does this in its `-viewDidLoad` method. The code must be changed to create instances of `PhotoWheelViewCell` and to set the image to *defaultPhoto.png*. The code changes are given in Listing 10.16.

Listing 10.16   **Modification of `DetailViewController` to Use `PhotoWheelViewCell`**

```
#import "DetailViewController.h"
#import "CustomCell.h"
#import "PhotoWheelViewCell.h"

// Other source code not shown for brevity's sake.

@implementation DetailViewController
```

```
// Other source code not shown for brevity's sake.

- (void)viewDidLoad
{
    [super viewDidLoad];
    // Do any additional setup after loading the view, typically from a NIB file.
    [self configureView];

    UINib *nib = [UINib nibWithNibName:@"CustomCell" bundle:nil];
    [[self collectionView] registerNib:nib
            forCellWithReuseIdentifier:@"CustomCell"];
    [[self collectionView] setHidden:YES];

    UIImage *defaultPhoto = [UIImage imageNamed:@"defaultPhoto.png"];
    CGRect cellFrame = CGRectMake(0, 0, 75, 75);
    NSInteger count = 10;
    NSMutableArray *newArray = [[NSMutableArray alloc] initWithCapacity:count];
    for (NSInteger index = 0; index < count; index++) {
        PhotoWheelViewCell *cell =
        [[PhotoWheelViewCell alloc] initWithFrame:cellFrame];
        [cell setImage:defaultPhoto];
        [newArray addObject:cell];
    }
    [self setData:[newArray copy]];

    NSArray *segmentedItems = @[@"Wheel", @"Carousel", @"Flow"];
    UISegmentedControl *segmentedControl = [[UISegmentedControl alloc]
                                    initWithItems:segmentedItems];
    [segmentedControl addTarget:self
                    action:@selector(segmentedControlValueChanged:)
            forControlEvents:UIControlEventValueChanged];
    [segmentedControl setSegmentedControlStyle:UISegmentedControlStyleBar];
    [segmentedControl setSelectedSegmentIndex:0];
    [[self navigationItem] setTitleView:segmentedControl];
}

// Other source code not shown for brevity's sake.

@end
```

The default photo image is loaded into memory by calling [UIImage image
Named:]. This method returns a reference to the image that is passed to the Photo
WheelViewCell. Within the for loop, the code that created instances of WheelView
Cell and set the background color to blue is replaced with PhotoWheelViewCell
and the image is set to defaultPhoto.

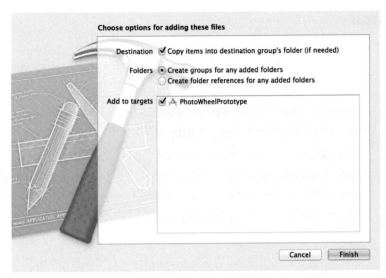

Figure 10.11   Select "Copy items into destination group's folder" when adding the image to the project.

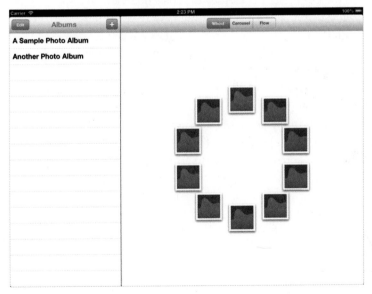

Figure 10.12   A photo wheel with stylish cells

With these changes, your `PhotoWheelViewCell` class can now be used to display an image as the wheel cell instead of the boring blue box. Build and run the app, and you will see the new display as shown in Figure 10.12.

Summary

In the chapter you learned how to create and use a collection view. You learned about layouts and got hands-on practice with the flow layout object. In addition, you learned how to write your own custom cell view for a collection view.

You also learned how to create a custom view that manages its own layout. You learned how to make use of a delegate protocol to decouple a view from the data it displays. Finally, you learned how to create a specialized class for a view to extend the visual display even further.

You may have already noticed a recurring theme over the last couple of chapters. The collection view, as well as the wheel view you created, loosely follows the same design pattern used by `UITableView`. The patterns of reusable views, delegates and data sources, and custom views to extend the appearance of apps are common in iOS.

Exercises

1. Adjust the settings to the flow layout object, such as the scroll direct, cell sizes, and inset settings, to see how they affect the collection view.

2. Update the `CustomCell` used by the collection view to display the default photo image.

3. Play with the math used in the wheel and carousel algorithm to change the display effects. Some modifications to try include changing the Y-axis percentage and changing the scale size of the background views.

4. Change the border color and size of the photo wheel view cell. Change the shadow effect of the cell.

5. Add more cells to the photo wheel. Display fewer photos in the wheel.

6. Comment out the animation used in the `WheelView -setStyle:` setter method. Make note of how it differs from the animated version of the code.

11

Using Touch Gestures

The wheel view you built in the last chapter looks nice, especially when you use the photo wheel view cell. And the transitions between wheel and carousel are smooth thanks to Core Animation. But there's still something missing. The user cannot interact with the photo wheel. That changes in this chapter, as you learn about touch handling and gesture recognizers.

Touch Gestures Explained

Prior to iOS, most touch interfaces on mobile devices simply replaced the mouse with a finger. Users used a finger to move the mouse cursor around the screen, tapped to simulate a mouse click, and double-tapped to simulate a double click. Needless to say, this was a less than ideal user experience. Mouse-driven operating systems expect the mouse cursor to be much more precise than what can be achieved with a normal-size human finger (remember the rule of 44 mentioned in Chapter 7, "App Design"). iOS changed all of this.

iOS was built from the start with multi-touch as the central feature of the platform. It was not an attempt to implement a multi-touch interface on top of a desktop OS. Instead, iOS has introduced a whole new way for users to interact with software using nothing more than a finger.

There are two ways your application can handle and respond to touch events. One is to respond to touch events sent by the operating system. These touch events are forwarded to your app by way of the `UIResponder` class.

The Apple documentation says, "The `UIResponder` class defines an interface for objects that respond to and handle events." `UIView` is a subclass of `UIResponder`, so any `UIView` can respond to and handle events. But which events?

Two types of events pass through `UIResponder`: touch and motion. The primary touch events are `-touchesBegan:withEvent:`, `-touchesMoved:withEvent:`, `-touchesEnded:withEvent:`, and `-touchesCancelled:withEvent:`. The primary motion events include `-motionBegan:withEvent:`, `-motionEnded:withEvent:`, and `-motionCancelled:withEvent:`. All a view must do to respond to and handle any of these events is to override one or more of these methods. If, for example, you want `PhotoWheelViewCell` to respond to a single or double tap, you would override the `-touchesBegan:withEvent:` and `-touchesEnded:withEvent:` methods in the `PhotoWheelViewCell` class.

The problem with this approach is that code for commonly used touch gestures is copied throughout your view classes, and you must subclass `UIView` to override the touch handling events. If two different view classes must respond to a double tap, each class must implement the same logic needed to detect the double-tap gesture. This violates the DRY principle discussed in Chapter 10, "Using Collection and Custom Views." To get around this problem, Apple engineers created the `UIGestureRecognizer` class.

The `UIGestureRecognizer` class was introduced in iOS 3.2, the first iOS version for the iPad. The class is an abstract base class used to create concrete gesture recognizers. Concrete gesture recognizers are added to views that need to respond to and handle specific touch gestures. This approach to handling gestures means that logic for a touch gesture is implemented only once, as opposed to the "old way" that required the logic to be reimplemented in each view that needed to respond to a particular gesture.

Predefined Touch Gestures

When Apple introduced gesture recognizers to the SDK, it also provided implementation, or concrete, classes for a number of common touch gestures. Here is the list of gestures provided by the SDK:

- **`UITapGestureRecognizer`**: Detects one or more taps from one or more fingers.
- **`UIPinchGestureRecognizer`**: Detects the two-finger pinch gesture.
- **`UIRotationGestureRecognizer`**: Detects the two-finger rotation gesture.
- **`UISwipeGestureRecognizer`**: Detects a swipe gesture in one or more directions.
- **`UIPanGestureRecognizer`**: Detects the panning, or dragging, gesture.
- **`UILongPressGestureRecognizer`**: Detects long presses of one or more fingers touching a view for a minimum amount of time.

Gesture Types

Gestures are broken down into two types: discrete and continuous. A discrete gesture calls the action once for the touch sequence. `UITapGestureRecognizer` and `UISwipeGestureRecognizer` are examples of discrete gesture recognizers. The action is called once each time the gesture is detected.

A continuous recognizer calls the action message at each incremental change until the sequence has completed. `UIPinchGestureRecognizer`, `UIRotationGesture`

Recognizer, `UIPanGestureRecognizer`, and `UILongPressGestureRecognizer` are all continuous gesture recognizers.

How to Use Gesture Recognizers

Using a gesture recognizer is as easy as creating an instance of the recognizer and adding it to the view that will receive the touch events. Each recognizer has its own set of properties that enable you to fine-tune the behavior of the gesture recognizer. For instance, `UITapGestureRecognizer` has two tap-specific properties: `numberOfTapsRequired` and `numberOfTouchesRequired`.

The property `numberOfTapsRequired` specifies the number of times the user must tap the screen. The default is 1. If you wish to detect a double tap, you would change this value to 2. A triple tap would be 3, and so on.

The property `numberOfTouchesRequired` tells the recognizer how many fingers are required to detect the gesture. Again, the default value is 1. If you want to detect a tap with two fingers, you would set the property to 2. Here is an example of using a tap gesture recognizer to detect a double tap with two fingers:

```
UITapGestureRecognizer *twoFingerDoubleTap =
    [[UITapGestureRecognizer alloc] initWithTarget:self
    action:@selector(twoFingerDoubleTapped:)];
[twoFingerDoubleTap setNumberOfTapsRequired:2];
[twoFingerDoubleTap setNumberOfTouchesRequired:2];
```

You can also extend the behavior of a recognizer by setting the delegate property and implementing the methods defined in the `UIGestureRecognizerDelegate` protocol. The app can then extend the behaviors of the recognizer without having to subclass `UIGestureRecognizer`.

To get a better understanding of how to use gesture recognizers, let's modify the PhotoWheel prototype app to use a gesture recognizer or two. First, you'll add a single-tap recognizer to each cell of the photo wheel and have the action implementation do nothing more than log the class and method name. (Hint: Use `NSLog(@"%s", __PRETTY_FUNCTION__)` to output the class and method name to the Debug Console window.) Next, you'll add a double-tap recognizer to each cell and log the class and method name in the action implementation. Let's get started.

> **Note**
>
> The real implementation for the tap action comes in Chapter 12, "Adding Photos," where a single tap is used to add a photo to a cell. For now, the app will report the class and method name as a way to verify that the gesture is properly detected and wired to the correct action method.

To add the tap gesture recognizer to the cell, open *DetailViewController.m* and add a new instance of `UITapGestureRecognizer` to each cell. The recognizer could be added to the `PhotoWheelViewCell` class, but that would reduce the reusability of the cell class. The tap action is specific to this app, which means the view controller is the more appropriate place for the action.

The code change is shown in Listing 11.1.

Listing 11.1   Tap Gesture Recognizer Added to Each Photo Wheel View Cell

```
@implementation DetailViewController

// Other code left out for brevity's sake.

- (void)viewDidLoad
{
    [super viewDidLoad];
    // Do any additional setup after loading the view, typically from a NIB file.
    [self configureView];

    UINib *nib = [UINib nibWithNibName:@"CustomCell" bundle:nil];
    [[self collectionView] registerNib:nib
            forCellWithReuseIdentifier:@"CustomCell"];
    [[self collectionView] setHidden:YES];

    UIImage *defaultPhoto = [UIImage imageNamed:@"defaultPhoto.png"];
    CGRect cellFrame = CGRectMake(0, 0, 75, 75);
    NSInteger count = 10;
    NSMutableArray *newArray = [[NSMutableArray alloc] initWithCapacity:count];
    for (NSInteger index = 0; index < count; index++) {
        PhotoWheelViewCell *cell =
        [[PhotoWheelViewCell alloc] initWithFrame:cellFrame];
        [cell setImage:defaultPhoto];

        // Add a single-tap gesture to the cell.
        UITapGestureRecognizer *tap = [[UITapGestureRecognizer alloc]
                                       initWithTarget:self
                                       action:@selector(cellTapped:)];
        [cell addGestureRecognizer:tap];

        [newArray addObject:cell];
    }
    [self setData:[newArray copy]];

    NSArray *segmentedItems = @[@"Wheel", @"Carousel", @"Flow"];
    UISegmentedControl *segmentedControl = [[UISegmentedControl alloc]
                                            initWithItems:segmentedItems];
    [segmentedControl addTarget:self
                    action:@selector(segmentedControlValueChanged:)
            forControlEvents:UIControlEventValueChanged];
    [segmentedControl setSegmentedControlStyle:UISegmentedControlStyleBar];
```

```
    [segmentedControl setSelectedSegmentIndex:0];
    [[self navigationItem] setTitleView:segmentedControl];
}


// Other code left out for brevity's sake.

- (void)cellTapped:(UIGestureRecognizer *)recognizer
{
    NSLog(@"%s", __PRETTY_FUNCTION__);
}


@end
```

That's it. Two lines of code, and now the app can detect taps on each photo wheel view cell. The -cellTapped: method outputs the class and method name to the console window. Obviously, a real application will do more than this.

Next, let's add a double-tap gesture to each cell. This gets slightly more complicated because the cell already has the tap recognizer. Trying to decide when the user is performing single taps versus double taps can be a challenge. Luckily, gesture recognizers make it easy to handle this scenario with the -requireGestureRecognizer ToFail: method. This method says that a gesture is not recognized unless another gesture recognizer fails. In the case of tap and double tap, we want a tap to be recognized only after it has been determined that the user isn't attempting a double tap.

Listing 11.2 shows the updated code that adds the double tap.

Listing 11.2   Adding a Double Tap to the Cell

```
- (void)viewDidLoad
{
    [super viewDidLoad];
    // Do any additional setup after loading the view, typically from a NIB file.
    [self configureView];

    UINib *nib = [UINib nibWithNibName:@"CustomCell" bundle:nil];
    [[self collectionView] registerNib:nib
            forCellWithReuseIdentifier:@"CustomCell"];
    [[self collectionView] setHidden:YES];

    UIImage *defaultPhoto = [UIImage imageNamed:@"defaultPhoto.png"];
    CGRect cellFrame = CGRectMake(0, 0, 75, 75);
    NSInteger count = 10;
    NSMutableArray *newArray = [[NSMutableArray alloc] initWithCapacity:count];
    for (NSInteger index = 0; index < count; index++) {
        PhotoWheelViewCell *cell =
        [[PhotoWheelViewCell alloc] initWithFrame:cellFrame];
        [cell setImage:defaultPhoto];
```

```objc
    // Add a double-tap gesture to the cell.
    UITapGestureRecognizer *doubleTap;
    doubleTap = [[UITapGestureRecognizer alloc]
                 initWithTarget:self
                 action:@selector(cellDoubleTapped:)];

    [doubleTap setNumberOfTapsRequired:2];
    [cell addGestureRecognizer:doubleTap];

    // Add a single-tap gesture to the cell.
    UITapGestureRecognizer *tap = [[UITapGestureRecognizer alloc]
                                   initWithTarget:self
                                   action:@selector(cellTapped:)];
    [tap requireGestureRecognizerToFail:doubleTap];
    [cell addGestureRecognizer:tap];

    [newArray addObject:cell];
  }
  [self setData:[newArray copy]];

  NSArray *segmentedItems = @[@"Wheel", @"Carousel", @"Flow"];
  UISegmentedControl *segmentedControl = [[UISegmentedControl alloc]
                                          initWithItems:segmentedItems];
  [segmentedControl addTarget:self
                    action:@selector(segmentedControlValueChanged:)
           forControlEvents:UIControlEventValueChanged];
  [segmentedControl setSegmentedControlStyle:UISegmentedControlStyleBar];
  [segmentedControl setSelectedSegmentIndex:0];
  [[self navigationItem] setTitleView:segmentedControl];
}

- (void)cellDoubleTapped:(UIGestureRecognizer *)recognizer
{
  NSLog(@"%s", __PRETTY_FUNCTION__);
}
```

Notice that even though the doubleTap gesture recognizer was added to the cell first, the order in which the recognizers are added doesn't matter. The order does not determine whether the tap or double tap is detected first. Instead, the -requireGestureRecognizerToFail: call on the tap gesture determines when a single tap is detected versus when a double tap is detected.

> **Note**
>
> To learn more about gesture recognizers, including how to use them and how they work, watch the WWDC 2010 video *Session 120: Simplifying Touch Event Handling with Gesture Recognizers.*[1]

Custom Touch Gestures

Most iPad apps will only ever need to use the predefined gesture recognizers. If, however, you find that you need to track a gesture that is not provided by the SDK, you can create your own subclass of `UIGestureRecognizer`.

A subclass of `UIGestureRecognizer` will respond to one or more touch handling events: `-touchesBegan:withEvent:`, `-touchesMoved:withEvent:`, `-touchesEnded:withEvent:`, and `-touchesCancelled:withEvent:`. Gesture recognizers operate on a state machine. As incoming touch events are received, the gesture recognizer transitions between states.

All recognizers start in the possible state (`UIGestureRecognizerStatePossible`). Discrete recognizers transition to either a recognized state (`UIGestureRecognizerStateRecognized`) or a failed state (`UIGestureRecognizerStateFailed`). The action message associated with the recognizer is sent to the target when the recognizer enters the recognized state.

Continuous recognizers transition from the possible state to a began state (`UIGestureRecognizerStateBegan`), then to the changed state (`UIGestureRecognizerStateChanged`) as touch events occur, and finally to either the end state (`UIGestureRecognizerStateEnded`) or the cancelled state (`UIGestureRecognizerStateCancelled`). The changed state is optional, and it may occur multiple times during a touch sequence. The action message is sent to the target each time there is a state transition.

When you subclass `UIGestureRecognizer`, you must import *UIGestureRecognizerSubclass.h*. This header file declares the methods and properties that a subclass must override or set. For example, the property `state` is read-only on the abstract base class `UIGestureRecognizer`, but including *UIGestureRecognizerSubclass.h* in your concrete class makes the `state` property a read-write property for use within the subclass implementation only. Users of your concrete gesture recognizer class will still have read-only access to the state property.

That's a brief overview of what you need to know when subclassing `UIGestureRecognizer`. Now let's create one.

---

1. Simplifying Touch Event Handling with Gesture Recognizers: https://developer.apple.com/videos/wwdc/2010/

Creating a Spin Gesture Recognizer

The prototype app has a nice-looking wheel view. How cool would it be if users could spin the wheel? Very cool, that's how cool.

Spinning the wheel view is as easy as rotating the wheel view as the user touches it. And it just so happens that iOS provides the gesture recognizer `UIRotationGesture Recognizer`. The problem with this recognizer is that it requires two fingers to perform the rotation. A spinning gesture is more natural using only one finger, so `UIRotationGestureRecognizer` does not satisfy the app's particular need for spinning. Instead, you need to create a new concrete gesture recognizer to spin a view.

Start by creating a new Objective-C class named `SpinGestureRecognizer` that is a subclass of `UIGestureRecognizer`. This class will have one declared property named `rotation` that is of type `CGFloat`. It will report the rotation of the gesture in radians since its last change. The source code *SpinGestureRecognizer.h* is shown in Listing 11.3.

Listing 11.3   *SpinGestureRecognizer.h*

```
#import <UIKit/UIKit.h>


@interface SpinGestureRecognizer : UIGestureRecognizer


/**
 The rotation of the gesture in radians since its last change.
 */
@property (nonatomic, assign) CGFloat rotation;


@end
```

The implementation for `SpinGestureRecognizer` must import *UIGestureRecog nizerSubclass.h*. This header file is needed so that the subclass can change the `state` property value and override the touch handling events.

The recognizer should work with only one finger. Two or more simultaneous touches will not be allowed, so `-touchesBegan:withEvent:` will check the touch count. With anything greater than 1, the gesture recognizer will fail.

The touch handling events `-touchesEnd:withEvent:` and `-touchesCancel led:withEvent:` will transition the recognizer's state machine to the end state and the cancelled state, respectively. This leaves `-touchesMoved:withEvent:`. The bulk of the work is performed in this event, as will be explained momentarily. The implementation source code is shown in Listing 11.4.

Listing 11.4   *SpinGestureRecognizer.m*

```
#import "SpinGestureRecognizer.h"
#import <UIKit/UIGestureRecognizerSubclass.h>
```

```objc
@implementation SpinGestureRecognizer

- (void)touchesBegan:(NSSet *)touches withEvent:(UIEvent *)event
{
    // Fail when more than 1 finger detected.
    if ([[event touchesForGestureRecognizer:self] count] > 1) {
        [self setState:UIGestureRecognizerStateFailed];
    }
}

- (void)touchesEnded:(NSSet *)touches withEvent:(UIEvent *)event
{
    // Perform final check to make sure a tap was not misinterpreted.
    if ([self state] == UIGestureRecognizerStateChanged) {
        [self setState:UIGestureRecognizerStateEnded];
    } else {
        [self setState:UIGestureRecognizerStateFailed];
    }
}

- (void)touchesCancelled:(NSSet *)touches withEvent:(UIEvent *)event
{
    [self setState:UIGestureRecognizerStateFailed];
}

- (void)touchesMoved:(NSSet *)touches withEvent:(UIEvent *)event
{
    if ([self state] == UIGestureRecognizerStatePossible) {
        [self setState:UIGestureRecognizerStateBegan];
    } else {
        [self setState:UIGestureRecognizerStateChanged];
    }

    // We can look at any touch object since we know we
    // have only 1. If there were more than 1,
    // touchesBegan:withEvent: would have failed the recognizer.
    UITouch *touch = [touches anyObject];

    // To rotate with one finger, we simulate a second finger.
    // The second finger is on the opposite side of the virtual
    // circle that represents the rotation gesture.

    UIView *view = [self view];
    CGPoint center = CGPointMake(CGRectGetMidX([view bounds]),
                                 CGRectGetMidY([view bounds]));
    CGPoint currentTouchPoint = [touch locationInView:view];
    CGPoint previousTouchPoint = [touch previousLocationInView:view];
```

```
CGFloat angleInRadians = atan2f(currentTouchPoint.y - center.y, currentTouchPoint.x -
        center.x) - atan2f(previousTouchPoint.y - center.y, previousTouchPoint.x -
        center.x);

    [self setRotation:angleInRadians];
}

@end
```

Let's walk through the code for `-touchesMoved:withEvent:` to see what is going on.

The moment the recognizer detects movement, the state transitions from the "possible" state to the "began" state. Any additional movement will trigger the transition to the "changed" state. The recognizer does not immediately go from the "possible" state to the "changed" state because a tap could have caused the movement. A tap can have slight movement, so the recognizer transitions first to the "began" state. If it turns out that the touch gesture is a tap, the event will immediately end with a call to `-touchesEnded:withEvent:`. If the touch is not a tap and additional movement is detected, the state transitions to "changed" and the action message is sent to the target.

Once the state transition has been set, the work of calculating the rotation of the spin is performed. The calculation uses the current and previous touch points within the view associated to the gesture recognizer to calculate the current angle of the rotation. It uses an artificial second finger to perform the calculation as if two fingers were rotating around a single center point. This, in essence, causes the spin gesture recognizer to track finger movement around a central point where the central point is the center of the view.

Using the Spin Gesture Recognizer

To see your work in action, you must add the spin gesture recognizer to the wheel view. The recognizer is added to the wheel view instead of the detail view controller to make the spinning wheel a feature of the view. `WheelView` must also be updated to support the new spinning behavior. The updated *WheelView.m* is shown in Listing 11.5.

Listing 11.5   Updated *WheelView.m* with Spinning View Support

```
#import "WheelView.h"
#import <QuartzCore/QuartzCore.h>
#import "SpinGestureRecognizer.h"

@interface WheelView ()
@property (nonatomic, assign) CGFloat currentAngle;
@end
```

```
@implementation WheelView

- (void)commonInit
{
    [self setCurrentAngle:0.0];

    SpinGestureRecognizer *spin = [[SpinGestureRecognizer alloc]
                                   initWithTarget:self
                                   action:@selector(spin:)];
    [self addGestureRecognizer:spin];
}

- (id)init
{
    self = [super init];
    if (self) {
        [self commonInit];
    }
    return self;
}

- (id)initWithCoder:(NSCoder *)aDecoder
{
    self = [super initWithCoder:aDecoder];
    if (self) {
        [self commonInit];
    }
    return self;
}

- (id)initWithFrame:(CGRect)frame
{
    self = [super initWithFrame:frame];
    if (self) {
        [self commonInit];
    }
    return self;
}

- (void)setAngle:(CGFloat)angle
{
    // The following code is inspired by the carousel example at
    // http://stackoverflow.com/questions/5243614/3d-carousel-effect-on-the-ipad

    CGPoint center = CGPointMake(CGRectGetMidX([self bounds]),
                                 CGRectGetMidY([self bounds]));
```

```
CGFloat radiusX = MIN([self bounds].size.width,
                      [self bounds].size.height) * 0.35;
CGFloat radiusY = radiusX;
if ([self style] == WheelViewStyleCarousel) {
   radiusY = radiusX * 0.30;
}

NSInteger cellCount = [[self dataSource] wheelViewNumberOfCells:self];
float angleToAdd = 360.0f / cellCount;

for (NSInteger index = 0; index < cellCount; index++)
{
   WheelViewCell *cell = [[self dataSource] wheelView:self cellAtIndex:index];
   if ([cell superview] == nil) {
      [self addSubview:cell];
   }

   float angleInRadians = (angle + 180.0) * M_PI / 180.0f;

   // Get a position based on the angle
   float xPosition = center.x + (radiusX * sinf(angleInRadians))
   - (CGRectGetWidth([cell frame]) / 2);
   float yPosition = center.y + (radiusY * cosf(angleInRadians))
   - (CGRectGetHeight([cell frame]) / 2);

   float scale = 0.75f + 0.25f * (cosf(angleInRadians) + 1.0);

   // Apply location and scale
   if ([self style] == WheelViewStyleCarousel) {
      [cell setTransform:CGAffineTransformScale(
               CGAffineTransformMakeTranslation(xPosition, yPosition),
               scale, scale)];
      // Tweak alpha using the same system as applied for scale, this time
      // with 0.3 as the minimum and a semicircle range of 0.5
      [cell setAlpha:(0.3f + 0.5f * (cosf(angleInRadians) + 1.0))];

   } else {
      [cell setTransform:CGAffineTransformMakeTranslation(xPosition,
                                                   yPosition)];
      [cell setAlpha:1.0];
   }

   [[cell layer] setZPosition:scale];

   // Work out what the next angle is going to be
   angle += angleToAdd;
}
```

```
}

- (void)layoutSubviews
{
    [self setAngle:[self currentAngle]];
}

- (void)setStyle:(WheelViewStyle)newStyle
{
    if (_style != newStyle) {
        _style = newStyle;

        [UIView animateWithDuration:0.3 animations:^{
            [self setAngle:[self currentAngle]];
        }];
    }
}

- (void)spin:(SpinGestureRecognizer *)recognizer
{
    CGFloat angleInRadians = -[recognizer rotation];
    CGFloat degrees = 180.0 * angleInRadians / M_PI;    // radians to degrees
    [self setCurrentAngle:[self currentAngle] + degrees];
    [self setAngle:[self currentAngle]];
}

@end


@implementation WheelViewCell

@end
```

What exactly changed? Let's take a look.

First, the *SpinGestureRecognizer.h* header file is imported. This file, of course, is needed because the wheel view class now uses a SpinGestureRecognizer object.

Following the import, a new private declared property, currentAngle, is added. This property is made private by using an Objective-C feature called class extensions. A class extension is similar to a category, albeit with a few exceptions:

- A class extension is declared just like a category, but without a name.
- A class extension's properties and methods must be implemented in the main @implementation block for the class.
- A class extension allows you to declare required methods and properties for the class in a location other than the main @interface block for the class.

Class extensions are a handy way to declare private methods and properties on the class that are used within the class. As you can see in Listing 11.5, a class extension is created for `WheelView` that declares the private property `currentAngle`. This tells the compiler that the property exists on the class, but it is intended for internal use only.

Class Extensions Explained

To learn more about class extensions, read the outstanding post from Bill Bumgarner entitled "Class Extensions Explained."[2]

Continuing the walk-through of code changes in Listing 11.5, you see a set of init methods in the `@implementation` section: `-commonInit`, `-init`, `-initWithCoder:`, and `-initWithFrame:`. The three init methods are needed to allow the view class to be instantiated by conventions common to iOS. `-init` and `-initWithFrame:` are commonly used when programmatically creating the class instance. The `-initWithCoder:` init method is called when the class instance is created as the result of unarchiving the object. Put simply, this method is called when the class instance is created during the load of a NIB file.

Each init method calls `-commonInit`. This follows the DRY principle and eliminates the need to copy and paste the same initialization code to each init method. `-commonInit` performs the steps needed to initialize the class instance. It sets `currentAngle` to `0.0`, but more important, it creates an instance of `SpinGestureRecognizer` and adds it to the wheel view. This enables the wheel view to detect the spin gesture.

Following the init methods is `-setAngle:`. Nothing has changed in this method; its implementation remains the same as it was before the changes in Listing 11.5.

`-layoutSubviews` and `-setStyle:` have one change each. Instead of calling `[self setAngle:0.0]`, both methods were modified to call `[self setAngle:[self currentAngle]]`. This tells `-setAngle:` to use the most recent angle when drawing the wheel view.

Last but not least is `-spin:`. It is the action method assigned to the `SpinGesture Recognizer` instance created in `-commonInit`. This method is called each time the gesture recognizer's state changes. When this method is called, it grabs the rotation angle in radians from the provided `SpinGestureRecognizer`. Note that the rotation value is negated. The math in `-setAngle:` assumes that degree 0 of the wheel is at the bottom, but the spin gesture recognizer assumes that degree 0 is at the top. By negating the rotation value, the code makes the adjustment for the location of degree 0 within the wheel.

Next, `-spin:` converts the rotation angle from radians to degrees. This conversion could have been avoided by not converting the degrees to radians within `SpinGesture Recognizer`. However, `UIRotationGestureRecognizer` uses

2. Class Extensions Explained: http://www.friday.com/bbum/2009/09/11/
   class-extensions-explained/

radians for its `rotation` property value. `SpinGestureRecognizer` does the same to remain consistent with `UIRotationGestureRecognizer`.

Last, `-spin:` increments the `currentAngle` with the current change in degrees and tells the class to draw the wheel with the new angle setting by calling `-setAngle:`. And with that, you now have a wheel that you can spin with a finger. Build and run the app, and test the new touch gesture.

Summary

This chapter was all about touch. As explained here, gesture recognizers make it much easier to detect different multi-touch gestures without copying and pasting touch handling code throughout your app. Most of the time, your apps will likely use the predefined touch gestures, but you now also know how to create your own concrete gesture recognizer should your app need to support some other touch gesture.

Exercises

1. Remove the negation of the rotation value in `-spin:` and observe the effect it has on spinning the wheel.

2. Remove the need to convert degrees to radians in `SpinGestureRecognizer` and make the needed change to `-spin:` to ensure that spinning still works as expected.

3. In addition to the `rotation` property, `UIRotationGestureRecognizer` has the `velocity` property. Add `velocity` to `SpinGestureRecognizer` and implement the appropriate math needed so that the property returns the correct velocity for the rotation.

Adding Photos

The photo wheel view you created in Chapter 10, "Using Collection and Custom Views," is ready to display photos, but the prototype app does not yet have a way to add photos. It's time to change that situation. In this chapter, you will learn how to access photos managed by the Photos app, which is available on all iPads and iPhones. You will also add support for adding photos to the prototype app you have been building since Chapter 8, "Creating a Master-Detail App."

Two Approaches

The iOS SDK provides two different approaches for third-party apps to retrieve photos and videos from the Photos app. The first is to use the Assets Library framework. The second is to use the image picker controller (`UIImagePickerController`). Which approach an app uses depends largely on the needs of the app.

Assets Library

The Assets Library framework provides classes used to access photos and videos managed by the Photos app. Not only does it give third-party apps access to photos and videos, but it also provides access to metadata associated with each asset. The metadata includes information such as the type of asset, duration if the asset is a video, orientation, creation date, representation (e.g., RAW and JPEG), and location information, which is available only if Location Services has been turned on for the app. Third-party applications can also store and retrieve application-specific metadata for an asset.

To access photos and videos using the Assets Library framework, you create an instance of `ALAssetsLibrary`. You can retrieve a specific asset using the method `-assetForURL:resultBlock:failureBlock:`, and you can retrieve a group of assets using `-enumerateGroupsWithTypes:usingBlock:failureBlock:`.

> **Note**
>
> Prior to iOS 6, users had to turn on Location Services for the app before it could use the Assets Library framework. This changed starting with iOS 6. Now iOS includes a Photos privacy setting that allows users to grant and revoke access to the Photos library on an app-by-app basis.

An asset—that is, a photo or video from the Photos app—is represented by an instance of the class ALAsset. This class has methods and properties for accessing the asset's metadata, making changes to the asset, retrieving the representation (of which there could be more than one), and retrieving the thumbnail of the asset.

Using the Assets Library framework is ideal when your application needs direct access to assets managed by the Photos application. But it does have one limitation: It does not provide a user interface for displaying and selecting photos from the library. There is, however, another option available to third-party developers.

Image Picker Controller

The image picker controller (UIImagePickerController) is a specialized navigation controller that provides a user interface for displaying photos and videos managed by the Photos app. The controller makes it possible for the user to select a photo or video that will be returned to the calling app. In addition, the user can take a photo or record a video, using the image picker controller, that will be returned to the calling app.

Note

As with the Assets Library, apps using the image picker controller must have the user's permission to access the Photos library.

The image picker controller is ideal for apps that want to use the iOS-supplied user interface for taking photos and videos and choosing saved photos and videos for use within the app. The downside to this approach is that the user can take only one photo or video, or select only one photo or video, at a time. This constraint is usually not an issue for most apps. If necessary, you can get around this limitation by leaving the image picker controller open and visible to the user. If, however, you have a need to import more than one photo or video at a time, your best option is to use the Assets Library framework, although you will be required to create your own UI.

For the PhotoWheel prototype, selecting one photo at a time is perfectly acceptable. UIImagePickerController will work nicely in meeting this need. Its use also means that you do not have to create your own user interface for selecting photos. With the image picker controller, the UI is provided for you.

Using the Image Picker Controller

As is true with so many other objects in Cocoa Touch, using the image picker controller is simple and straightforward. You create an instance of UIImagePickerController and present it to the user. User interaction with the views presented by the image picker is managed by the controller, and the results of those interactions are reported back to your app courtesy of a delegate object that conforms to the UIImagePickerControllerDelegate protocol.

In Chapter 11, "Using Touch Gestures," you added a tap gesture to each photo wheel cell. Let's modify that code so that a tap on the cell will display the image picker or camera. When the user selects a photo or takes a new photo, the cell's image will be updated to display the returned photo.

While the image picker controller is simple to use, a number of changes are still needed in the `DetailViewController` class. For starters, when a photo wheel cell is tapped, the cell must be saved as the selected photo wheel cell. Other methods in the view controller need to know which cell is the selected one. Also, if the device has a camera, the app should ask the user the source from which to retrieve the photo. Does the user want to add an existing photo managed by the Photos app, or does she want to take a new photo using the camera? Once the user has selected the photo to add, the app adds it to the selected cell. That should be it for the needed changes.

To start making changes, open *DetailViewController.m* and add a new private declared property named `selectedPhotoWheelViewCell`. Its data type is a pointer to `PhotoWheelViewCell`. Next, modify the `-cellTapped:` method to save the selected cell to the `selectedPhotoWheelViewCell` property. The code changes are given in Listing 12.1.

Listing 12.1 **Adding the `selectedPhotoWheelViewCell` Property to**
DetailViewController.m

```objc
@interface DetailViewController ()

// Other code left out for brevity's sake.

@property (strong, nonatomic) PhotoWheelViewCell *selectedPhotoWheelViewCell;

// Other code left out for brevity's sake.

@end

@implementation DetailViewController

// Other code left out for brevity's sake.

- (void)cellTapped:(UIGestureRecognizer *)recognizer
{
    [self setSelectedPhotoWheelViewCell:(PhotoWheelViewCell *)[recognizer view]];
}

// Other code left out for brevity's sake.

@end
```

`DetailViewController` now knows which photo wheel cell has been selected. Next, the app should check to whether the device supports a camera. `UIImagePicker Controller` can help. It has the method `+isSourceTypeAvailable:` that can determine whether a particular photo or video source is available.

> **Note**
>
> `UIImagePickerController` also has the method `+isCameraDeviceAvail able:`, which one might think is the correct method to call when determining if the device supports a camera. In reality, `+isCameraDeviceAvailable:` is used to determine if a camera is available on the front or rear of the device. This method can be used to determine if a camera device, regardless of location, is available, but it involves performing two checks—one for the presence of the rear camera and one for the front camera. `+isSourceTypeAvailable:` performs this task for us with a single call, which is why it's used here.

If the device has a camera, the app needs to give the user the option of taking a photo or choosing from the library managed by the Photos app. Modify the `-cell Tapped:` method again, this time to perform this check. If the camera is available, the app will display a popup menu of choices (or actions); otherwise, the app should display the image picker. For now, write stub methods for presenting the menu and image picker. The code changes are given in Listing 12.2.

Listing 12.2 **Checking for a Camera on the Device**

```
- (void) cellTapped: (UIGestureRecognizer *) recognizer
{
    [self setSelectedPhotoWheelViewCell: (PhotoWheelViewCell *) [recognizer view]];

    BOOL hasCamera = [UIImagePickerController isSourceTypeAvailable:
        UIImagePickerControllerSourceTypeCamera];
    if (hasCamera) {
        [self presentPhotoPickerMenu];
    } else {
        [self presentPhotoLibrary];
    }
}


- (void) presentPhotoLibrary
{
    NSLog(@"%s", __PRETTY_FUNCTION__);
}


- (void) presentPhotoPickerMenu
{
    NSLog(@"%s", __PRETTY_FUNCTION__);
}
```

Figure 12.1   Logged output to the output window

Build and run the app, first from the iPad Simulator. Tap a photo wheel cell and take a look at the output window. You should see that -presentPhotoLibrary is called, as shown in Figure 12.1. Now run the app on an iPad. You will see that -presentPhotoPickerMenu is called.

Using Action Sheets

Next, you need to provide the real implementation for the stubbed methods. Let's start with -presentPhotoPickerMenu. It will display a popup menu giving the user the choice of taking a photo or choosing an existing one from the Photos library. To do so, the app needs to present a list of actions for the user to choose from, and UIActionSheet is the perfect object for the task.

UIActionSheet is used to display a list of options or actions to a user. An action sheet has an optional title and one or more buttons, where each button represents an action. An action sheet is often used to allow the user to request a specific action such as "send email" or "print." It can also be used to ask the user for confirmation of some action, such as deleting data.

On the iPhone, an action sheet typically slides up from the bottom of the screen. The action sheet is dismissed when the user taps a button, and a cancel button is usually provided so that the user can dismiss the action sheet without requesting an action.

The display of an action sheet on the iPad is different. An action sheet is displayed in a popover that appears in the center of the screen or is anchored to the view with which the user interacted to request the action sheet (for example, a button on a tool-bar). A cancel button is not provided on the iPad. Instead, the user taps outside of the popover to dismiss the action sheet without performing any action.

Let's change the implementation in -presentPhotoPickerMenu to display an action sheet. The action sheet will display two options: "Take Photo" and "Choose from Library." DetailViewController must also be made the delegate to the action sheet. This will inform the view controller which button (or action) the user selected. The code changes are given in Listing 12.3.

Listing 12.3   **Adding an Action Sheet to the `DetailViewController`**

```
////////////
// DetailViewController.h

#import <UIKit/UIKit.h>
#import "WheelView.h"
```

```
@interface DetailViewController : UIViewController
    <UISplitViewControllerDelegate, UICollectionViewDataSource,
    UICollectionViewDelegate, WheelViewDataSource, UIActionSheetDelegate>

// Other code left out for brevity's sake.

@end



/////////////
// DetailViewController.m

#import "DetailViewController.h"
#import "PhotoWheelViewCell.h"

@interface DetailViewController ()

// Other code left out for brevity's sake.

@property (strong, nonatomic) UIActionSheet *actionSheet;

// Other code left out for brevity's sake.
@end

@implementation DetailViewController

// Other code left out for brevity's sake.

- (void)willRotateToInterfaceOrientation:(UIInterfaceOrientation)
toInterfaceOrientation duration:(NSTimeInterval)duration
{
    if ([self actionSheet]) {
        [[self actionSheet] dismissWithClickedButtonIndex:-1 animated:YES];
    }
}

// Other code left out for brevity's sake.

- (void)presentCamera
{
    NSLog(@"%s", __PRETTY_FUNCTION__);
}

- (void)presentPhotoPickerMenu
{
    UIActionSheet *actionSheet = [[UIActionSheet alloc] init];
    [actionSheet setDelegate:self];
```

```objc
    [actionSheet addButtonWithTitle:@"Take Photo"];
    [actionSheet addButtonWithTitle:@"Choose from Library"];

    UIView *view = [self selectedPhotoWheelViewCell];
    CGRect rect = [view bounds];
    [actionSheet showFromRect:rect inView:view animated:YES];

    [self setActionSheet:actionSheet];
}

#pragma mark - UIActionSheetDelegate methods

- (void)actionSheet:(UIActionSheet *)actionSheet
clickedButtonAtIndex:(NSInteger)buttonIndex
{
    switch (buttonIndex) {
        case 0:
            [self presentCamera];
            break;
        case 1:
            [self presentPhotoLibrary];
            break;
    }
}

- (void)actionSheet:(UIActionSheet *)actionSheet
didDismissWithButtonIndex:(NSInteger)buttonIndex
{
    [self setActionSheet:nil];
}

@end
```

As you can see in Listing 12.3, `UIActionSheetDelegate` is added to the list of conforming protocols for `DetailViewController`. The implementations for the `UIActionSheetDelegate` protocol methods `-actionSheet:clickedButtonAt Index:` and `-actionSheet:didDismissWithButtonIndex:` are found in the *Detail ViewController.m* implementation file. The first method, `-actionSheet:clickedBut tonAtIndex:`, checks the `buttonIndex` value. If it is 0, the user has requested to take a photo. If it is 1, the user has requested to pick a photo from the library. This method is called each time the user taps a button in the action sheet.

Note

The `buttonIndex` value is determined based on the order in which the buttons are added to the action sheet. The first button is index 0, the second button is index 1, and so on.

The second method, -actionSheet:didDismissWithButtonIndex:, is called every time the action sheet is dismissed regardless of how it is dismissed (e.g., the user taps a button, the user taps outside the popover, or the action sheet is dismissed programmatically). Here the private declared property for the action sheet is set to nil as the reference is no longer needed.

At the top of the implementation section in Listing 12.3, you can see the declaration for the private property actionSheet. It is followed by a method that has not been discussed yet, -willRotateToInterfaceOrientation:duration:. This method is called when the device is rotated. The HIG recommends dismissing popovers when the device is rotated, and that is what the implementation for this method does. It checks whether the view controller has a reference to the action sheet; if so, it programmatically dismisses the action sheet.

> **Note**
>
> Rotation support is covered in detail in Chapter 18, "Supporting Device Rotation."

The meat of the code change in Listing 12.3 is the implementation for the method -presentPhotoPickerMenu. This is where the action sheet is created and displayed. The method first creates a new instance of UIActionSheet. It sets the delegate to self, which is the DetailViewController instance. Next, two buttons are added: "Take Photo" and "Choose from Library." Then the action sheet is displayed, and finally the actionSheet property is set to the newly created action sheet.

UIActionSheet has a number of methods for displaying the action sheet. The methods, as defined in *UIActionSheet.h*, are as follows:

```
- (void)showFromToolbar:(UIToolbar *)view;
- (void)showFromTabBar:(UITabBar *)view;
- (void)showFromBarButtonItem:(UIBarButtonItem *)item
animated:(BOOL)animated __OSX_AVAILABLE_STARTING(__MAC_NA, __IPHONE_3_2);
- (void)showFromRect:(CGRect)rect inView:(UIView *)view
animated:(BOOL)animated __OSX_AVAILABLE_STARTING(__MAC_NA, __IPHONE_3_2);
- (void)showInView:(UIView *)view;
```

These methods allow the app to anchor the action sheet to specific views within the view hierarchy. To anchor the action sheet to the selected photo wheel cell, -showFromRect:inView:animated: is used. The rect comprises the bounds of the selected photo wheel cell, the view consists of the cell itself, and the animated flag is set to YES to animate the display of the action sheet.

Build and run the app, making sure to **run it on your iPad**; otherwise, you will not see the action sheet. The action sheet, as you know, is displayed only when a camera is available, and the iPad Simulator does not have a camera. Your app should look similar to Figure 12.2.

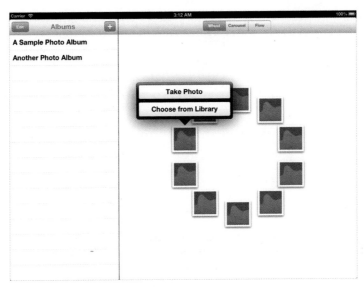

Figure 12.2   The prototype app displaying an action sheet

Using `UIImagePickerController`

Finally, the app needs to use `UIImagePickerController` so that the user can add a photo to the photo wheel. Stub methods already exist to display the photo library and camera: `-presentPhotoLibrary` and `-presentCamera`, respectively.

Let's start by adding a private property to the `DetailViewController` named `imagePickerController` that is a pointer to type `UIImagePickerController`. The image picker will be displayed in a popover controller, so we also add a declared property named `imagePickerPopoverController` as a pointer to type `UIPopoverController`. Lastly, we instantiate the image picker in the `-initWithNibName:bundle:` method; it gives the detail view controller an image picker controller to work with. The code changes are shown in Listing 12.4

Note that the `UIImagePickerController` delegate property expects the object to conform to two protocols: `UINavigationControllerDelegate` and `UIImagePickerControllerDelegate`. `DetailViewController` is derived from `UIViewController`. Therefore, you must add both of these protocols to the list of protocols to which `DetailViewController` conforms, as shown in Listing 12.4.

Listing 12.4   **Adding `imagePickerController` to `DetailViewController`**

```
/////////////
// DetailViewController.h

@interface DetailViewController : UIViewController
  <UISplitViewControllerDelegate, UICollectionViewDataSource,
```

```
        UICollectionViewDelegate, WheelViewDataSource, UIActionSheetDelegate,
        UINavigationControllerDelegate, UIImagePickerControllerDelegate>

// Other code left out for brevity's sake.

@end



////////////
// DetailViewController.m

@interface DetailViewController ()

// Other code left out for brevity's sake.

@property (strong, nonatomic) UIImagePickerController *imagePickerController;
@property (strong, nonatomic) UIPopoverController *imagePickerPopoverController;

// Other code left out for brevity's sake.

@end

@implementation DetailViewController

// Other code left out for brevity's sake.

- (id)initWithNibName:(NSString *)nibNameOrNil bundle:(NSBundle *)nibBundleOrNil
{
    self = [super initWithNibName:nibNameOrNil bundle:nibBundleOrNil];
    if (self) {
        self.title = NSLocalizedString(@"Detail", @"Detail");

        [self setImagePickerController:[[UIImagePickerController alloc] init]];
        [[self imagePickerController] setDelegate:self];
    }
    return self;
}

// Other code left out for brevity's sake.

@end
```

Next, we update the implementation for the stub methods -presentCamera and -presentPhotoLibrary. The first method displays a full-screen camera, and the second method displays the image picker in a popover controller. The new implementations for -presentCamera and -presentPhotoLibrary are shown in Listing 12.5.

Listing 12.5   **-presentCamera** and **-presentPhotoLibrary** Implementations in
DetailViewController.m

```
- (void) presentCamera
{
    // Display the camera.
    UIImagePickerController *imagePicker = [self imagePickerController];
    [imagePicker setSourceType:UIImagePickerControllerSourceTypeCamera];
    [imagePicker setModalPresentationStyle:UIModalPresentationFullScreen];
    [self presentViewController:imagePicker animated:YES completion:nil];
}


- (void) presentPhotoLibrary
{

    // Display assets from the Photos library only.
    UIImagePickerController *imagePicker = [self imagePickerController];
    [imagePicker setSourceType:UIImagePickerControllerSourceTypePhotoLibrary];

    UIView *view = [self selectedPhotoWheelViewCell];
    CGRect rect = [view bounds];

    UIPopoverController *popover = [[UIPopoverController alloc]
        initWithContentViewController:imagePicker];
    [popover presentPopoverFromRect:rect inView:view
        permittedArrowDirections:UIPopoverArrowDirectionAny animated:YES];
    [self setImagePickerPopoverController:popover];

}
```

To display the camera, the image picker controller's source type is set to `UIImage PickerControllerSourceTypeCamera`. Apple recommends using the full screen when displaying the camera, so the modal presentation style for the image picker controller is set to `UIModalPresentationFullScreen`. This choice will present the camera as a full-screen modal view.

The code for displaying the Photos library isn't much different from other code you have seen. The image picker controller's source type is set to `UIImagePickerControl lerSourceTypePhotoLibrary`. Local variable references to the selected photo wheel view cell and its bounds `rect` are created and are used to anchor the popover to the cell, much in the same way that the action sheet was anchored earlier in the code. A new popover controller instance is created and presented to the user. Finally, the popover controller reference is stored in the `imagePickerPopoverController` property on the `DetailViewController` in case it is needed later.

Note

If you specify the source type `UIImagePickerControllerSourceTypePhoto Library` or `UIImagePickerControllerSourceTypeSavedPhotosAlbum`, then you must display the image picker in a popover when running on an iPad. Attempting to display the image picker in full-screen mode using these source types will result in a runtime exception.

The detail view controller needs to do one last thing: It must respond to the UIImagePickerControllerDelegate method -imagePickerController:did FinishPickingMediaWithInfo:, as shown in Listing 12.6. This method is called after the user selects a new photo from the camera or from the Photos library. It receives an NSDictionary object named info, which contains the selected image, among other things. The image reference is retrieved from the dictionary and sent to the selected photo wheel view cell for display.

> **Note**
>
> To see the entire contents of the NSDictionary info, set a breakpoint in the -imagePickerController:didFinishPickingMediaWithInfo: method and type "po info" in the output console window. For more debugging tricks, read Chapter 26, "Debugging."

Listing 12.6 Responding to the UIImagePickerController Delegate Method

```
#pragma mark - UIImagePickerControllerDelegate methods

- (void)imagePickerController:(UIImagePickerController *)picker
didFinishPickingMediaWithInfo:(NSDictionary *)info
{
    // Dismiss the popover controller if available;
    // otherwise, dismiss the camera view.
    if ([self imagePickerPopoverController]) {
        [[self imagePickerPopoverController] dismissPopoverAnimated:YES];
        [self setImagePickerPopoverController:nil];
    } else {
        [self dismissViewControllerAnimated:YES completion:nil];
    }

    // Retrieve and display the image.
    UIImage *image = [info objectForKey:UIImagePickerControllerOriginalImage];
    [[self selectedPhotoWheelViewCell] setImage:image];
}
```

Build and run the app to see the image picker in action, as shown in Figure 12.3. You should run it on both an iPad and in the iPad Simulator. Remember that the action sheet is not displayed when the app is run on the simulator because the simulator does not have a camera device. You can choose the camera or Photos library only when the app is run on a real iPad.

Congratulations! Your prototype app now supports adding photos.

Figure 12.3   The PhotoWheelPrototype app with the image picker controller

> **Note**
>
> You might notice that some photos look a little funny when scaled down to thumbnail size in the photo wheel. A better approach for scaling images is covered in Chapter 13, "Data Persistence."
>
> Also, a quick and easy way to save photos to the Photos app used in the iPad Simulator is to drag and drop images from your desktop environment onto Mobile Safari running in the simulator. Then touch and hold (click and hold, given that you are using the simulator) the image displayed in Safari until the popup menu is displayed. This menu has an option to Save Image. Select this option to save the photo to the Photos app library.

Saving to the Camera Roll

When the camera is used to take a photo, the photo is not automatically saved to the Photos app's camera roll. It's up to the app to save the photo. Your app can save a photo to the camera roll by calling the function `UIImageWriteToSavedPhotosAlbum()`.

```
void UIImageWriteToSavedPhotosAlbum (
    UIImage   *image,
    id        completionTarget,
    SEL       completionSelector,
    void      *contextInfo
);
```

This function has four parameters:

- **image**: The image to save to the camera roll.

- **completionTarget** (optional): The object whose selector is called after the image has been saved to the camera roll.

- **completionSelector** (optional): The selector called on the completionTarget after the image has been saved to the camera roll.

- **contextInfo** (optional): A pointer to any context data you wish to pass to the completion selector.

Note

UIImageWriteToSavedPhotosAlbum() will save the photo to the Photo Stream if Photo Streaming has been enabled on the device.

Go ahead and modify
-imagePickerController:didFinishPickingMediaWithInfo: to use the
UIImageWriteToSavedPhotosAlbum function and save new photos captured with
the camera to the camera roll. The updated source code is given in Listing 12.7.

Listing 12.7 Modification to Save the Photo to the Camera Roll

```
- (void)imagePickerController:(UIImagePickerController *)picker
didFinishPickingMediaWithInfo:(NSDictionary *)info
{
   // If the popover controller is available,
   // assume the photo is selected from the library
   // and not from the camera.
   BOOL takenWithCamera = ([self imagePickerPopoverController] == nil);

   // Dismiss the popover controller if available;
   // otherwise, dismiss the camera view.
   if ([self imagePickerPopoverController]) {
      [[self imagePickerPopoverController] dismissPopoverAnimated:YES];
      [self setImagePickerPopoverController:nil];
   } else {
      [self dismissViewControllerAnimated:YES completion:nil];
   }

   // Retrieve and display the image.
   UIImage *image = [info objectForKey:UIImagePickerControllerOriginalImage];
   [[self selectedPhotoWheelViewCell] setImage:image];

   if (takenWithCamera) {
      UIImageWriteToSavedPhotosAlbum(image, nil, nil, nil);
   }
}
```

Build and run the app. Test the change and make sure that photos captured with the camera are saved to the camera roll.

Summary

The prototype app now supports adding photos to a photo wheel, and you have hands-on experience with the image picker controller. You also learned about action sheets, including how to use them. In addition, you got a glimpse of rotation handling.

The prototype app has proved quite useful, allowing you to explore different iOS concepts that will be used in the final PhotoWheel app. But there is one last concept that must be explored before you are ready to write the "real" app. That concept is data persistence, which is covered in the next chapter.

Exercises

1. Add more action items to the action sheet. Create stub methods that call NSLog() to handle each new action you add.

2. Dismiss the imagePickerPopoverController when the device is rotated. Hint: Call the method -dismissPopoverAnimated: on imagePickerPopoverController to programmatically dismiss the popover controller.

3. Remove the rotation handling code. Observe the side effects when the action sheet is displayed and the device is rotated.

Data Persistence

In the preceding chapter we added the capability for the prototype app to take photos with the device cameras. Now that photos are coming into the app, it's time to develop a system for saving and managing them. In this chapter we'll discuss which kind of data the app will deal with and how to manage and save it effectively. This chapter will implement the Model part of the Model-View-Controller design pattern.

The Data Model

To effectively build the data model, you need to have a clear idea of which kind of data you'll be working with and how the various types of data relate to one another. For this app there are two types of data: photos and photo albums.

Photos

Because this app arranges photos in albums, the most obvious data item is the original photo itself, straight from the device camera. You'll save and display the original photo, so the photo will be part of the data model.

Now think about how the photos will actually be used in the app. When the user is viewing an album, many photos could be on the screen at the same time. Original photos on iPad can be fairly large data objects, even when compressed as JPEG files. To avoid running out of memory, you'll probably want to use thumbnail-size versions of the photo in album views. You might need to have other sizes in other situations. When planning the model, plan for multiple photo sizes, including the original and one or more scaled versions. PhotoWheel will use three sizes, which will be used in various ways in later chapters.

You probably want to store some metadata with each photo, too—the date the photo was taken, for example, or the location.

Finally, each photo will belong to a photo album. The photo data in the model needs to include a reference or relationship of some kind to the album that contains the photo, so that when you are working with a photo you can find other photos in the album. This will be a "to-one" relationship, as each photo will belong to just one album.

Photo Albums

The primary requirement for the photo album is that it must track the photos that the album contains. This is the reverse of the relationship described for photos. Each photo album has a relationship to some number of photos that are the contents of the album. The photo album should also have a thumbnail property or relationship to a separate photo thumbnail object that can be used when displaying a collection of albums.

Albums will have metadata of their own, such as the album name and the date the album was created.

Thinking Ahead

PhotoWheelPrototype has a simple data model. Apps, however, have a tendency to grow in unexpected ways, both before the initial release and in features added in later updates. When planning your data model, it's important to plan ahead, by designing a model that can be adapted and improved as new requirements develop. Initially it's tempting to design the simplest possible model that works. Unfortunately, taking this route can constrain future development if the model isn't flexible or robust enough to be adapted to new requirements. This chapter will cover implementing the data model using Apple's Core Data framework.

Building the Model with Core Data

It can be tempting to push forward and use familiar classes such as `NSArray` and `NSDictionary` to implement the model. That approach is certainly convenient, but as an application's data gets larger or more complex, it can become awkward. Tasks such as keeping memory use under control and managing relationships become increasingly difficult as the data set grows. There are many ways of dealing with this greater complexity, and many developers have devised their own schemes. Apple provides a framework called Core Data that is designed to handle these tasks and many others. Core Data can seem daunting at first, but its principles and the techniques for using it are easy to learn and well worth the effort of doing so.

> **Note**
>
> This chapter provides a basic introduction to Core Data. For more detailed information, see *Core Data for iOS* by Tim Isted and Tom Harrington (Addison-Wesley, 2011).

What Is Core Data?

Core Data is designed to be an object store for your model object. Using Core Data, you read and write model objects directly, without needing to translate between your model objects and the file format. The purpose of Core Data is to provide a persistent data store that can handle whatever type of objects your app uses.

Details of how the objects are stored are mostly irrelevant, leaving you to focus on using those objects in your app. You may have heard that Core Data can use

SQLite to store data, but that is an implementation detail. Core Data is not simply an Objective-C wrapper on SQLite, and although it scales to very large data sets, it is not designed to be used as a database. Core Data can also use other, non-database formats to store data. This is why the term *data store* is intentionally vague. It refers to the means used to store data in a persistent manner, but Core Data isn't tied to a specific means. You can even create your own technique if you need to.

Core Data has the following advantages:

- It helps control memory usage. Core Data loads only the objects you request. If your data set contains millions of objects but you need to work with only a few, only those few objects will be loaded into memory. This makes it possible to deal with data sets that are larger than available memory.

- Relationships are managed automatically. If two objects have a relationship, you assign the relationship using the same syntax as you would to set a property value.

- Core Data provides a rich system of predicates that can be used to search your data set for objects of interest.

- Objects can be automatically sorted when you look them up.

- Core Data provides optional data validation, to enforce rules defining acceptable values for properties.

- Core Data has automatic undo management.

Core Data: A Different Approach

This chapter describes Core Data as using Apple's Core Data framework directly. This is the most direct approach, but it's not the only option. A popular open source framework called Magical Record,[1] created by Saul Mora, implements an Active Record style approach to working with Core Data. If you're familiar with Active Record—especially if you have experience using Ruby on Rails—you might find Magical Record to be easier to understand. Even if you ultimately follow this path, it's worth going through the "official" Apple-supported approach at least once so that you understand the system you're working with.

Managed Objects and Entity Descriptions

When using Core Data, you'll be using managed objects as your model objects. A managed object is an instance of `NSManagedObject` or of a custom subclass of `NSManagedObject`. It contains your model data. Core Data manages it, which means that Core Data handles creating it, maintaining relationships with other objects, saving changed property values, and other important tasks. Managed objects are read from

---

1. Magical Record: https://github.com/magicalpanda/MagicalRecord/

and saved to data stores. Normally your model objects would subclass NSObject or some other Foundation class such as NSDictionary, but with Core Data you must use NSManagedObject.

A managed object makes use of a related object called its entity description object. An entity description is an instance of NSEntityDescription. Entity descriptions contain definitions of all of the properties and relationships of a managed object, as well as optional extra details such as default values and validation rules. An entity description is roughly comparable to a table definition in a database schema, whereas a managed object is roughly comparable to a single entry in a table. Entity descriptions are configured in the managed object model, which defines all the entities available in the data store. You rarely use entity description objects directly in code; instead, you create them in Xcode.

Entity descriptions are defined in the app's data model, which is represented in code as an instance of NSManagedObjectModel. You create the model object in Xcode and then load it when the app runs.

When using Core Data, you start by creating entity descriptions for any model objects you need. Xcode provides a handy graph-based utility for doing this creation work. Once you have an entity description, you can start creating managed objects defined by it.

Although you can work with instances of NSManagedObject, it is usually more convenient to use custom subclasses that correspond to your model objects. The advantage with this approach is that your subclasses can add methods to implement any model-specific behaviors you might need and can provide accessor methods for your model properties. A plain NSManagedObject won't have custom accessor methods, so instead you must use key-value coding (KVC) to access property values. For example, if you have an Employee entity with a name property, you would set and retrieve the employee name on an NSManagedObject instance like this:

```
NSManagedObject *newEmployee = // Defined elsewhere
[newEmployee setValue:@"John Smith" forKey:@"name"];
NSString *employeeName = [newEmployee valueForKey:@"name"];
```

That's fine and it works, but the compiler doesn't perform any type checking to make sure that you are actually assigning a string value for the name property. It also can't verify that you spelled name correctly. What's more, because newEmployee is declared as an instance of a generic class, it may not be immediately obvious which entity description it is intended to use.

If you instead had an Employee class that subclassed NSManagedObject and provided custom accessor methods, the preceding code could be replaced with this:

```
Employee *newEmployee = // Defined elsewhere
[newEmployee setName:@"John Smith"];
NSString *employeeName = [newEmployee name];
```

That's a lot clearer and less error prone.

Xcode can automatically generate `NSManagedObject` subclasses with property-specific accessor methods based on entity definitions. When you load an `NSManaged Object` from a data store, it is normally created as a *fault* object. Fault objects are placeholders, which have the identity of a specific managed object but none of its data. The properties are loaded—or, in Core Data terminology, the fault fires—automatically when you access a property. As a consequence, they use hardly any memory at all until you directly access their properties.

New developers sometimes find the term *fault* confusing in this context. It doesn't indicate that an error has occurred; it's a normal situation. This term is conceptually similar to the term *page fault* used in virtual memory systems to indicate memory pages not yet loaded into memory.

Managed Object Contexts

Your main access point for obtaining and saving managed objects is the managed object context, an instance of `NSManagedObjectContext`. When you need to get your model objects, you'll ask the managed object context. When you need to save changes to model objects, you'll ask the managed object context to save them. The managed object context does most of the actual managing of managed objects.

You get managed objects from the data store by requesting them from the managed object context with a fetch request. Fetch requests specify, at a minimum, which kind of entity you want. They can also include a predicate that determines which instances of that entity are returned and a set of sort descriptors that determine how the resulting objects are sorted. Continuing the previous `Employee` example, the following code would find all employees currently in the data store:

```
NSManagedObjectContext *context = // Defined and configured elsewhere
NSFetchRequest *request = [NSFetchRequest fetchRequestWithEntityName:@"Employee"];
NSError *fetchError = nil;
NSArray *allEmployees = [context executeFetchRequest:request error:&fetchError];
```

When you need to create a new managed object, you'll normally do so by way of the managed object context. The following line of code finds an entity named `Employee` in the managed object context, creates a new managed object based on that entity, inserts it in the managed object context, and returns it as `newEmployee`:

```
Employee *newEmployee = [NSEntityDescription
    insertNewObjectForEntityForName:@"Employee"
    inManagedObjectContext:context];
```

It is common for entities to have the same name as the `NSManagedObject` subclass that uses them, but this is not required.

After the user has worked with the app for a while, there will probably be changes that need to be saved. Saving goes through the `NSManagedObjectContext`, which will save any outstanding changes on any objects loaded from or added to the context:

```
NSError *saveError = nil;
[context save:&saveError];
```

Persistent Stores and Persistent Store Coordinators

The managed object context doesn't actually save objects itself, but rather makes use of another object that handles the necessary file-level interaction. Core Data saves objects to a persistent data store. The data store itself is managed by a persistent store coordinator, which is an instance of `NSPersistentStoreCoordinator`. This is where managed objects finally become SQLite records, or part of a binary file, or are converted to some other format suitable for saving to a file. You rarely work directly with the persistent store coordinator except when you create it. After that, all interaction goes through the managed object context.

Why does the persistent store remain separate? It is possible to use more than one persistent store simultaneously. The `NSPersistentStoreCoordinator`, as its name suggests, is responsible for coordinating the persistent stores. You might use only one data store in an app, but the Core Data stack doesn't restrict you to just one. It's possible to use multiple data stores simultaneously, via the same managed object context, putting objects into specific stores based on your own app's requirements. That's a fairly advanced topic, so it's not covered here.

The persistent store coordinator uses two other classes to manage data: `NSPersistentStore` and `NSManagedObjectModel`. `NSPersistentStore` represents the actual data store. One instance of this class is allowed per data store file. `NSManagedObjectModel` contains all of the app's entity descriptions. When your app loads a data store, it's important that the data in the `NSPersistentStore` match the entities declared in the `NSManagedObjectModel`. If they don't, it won't be possible to load the data store.

Adding Core Data to PhotoWheelPrototype

When you create a new project in Xcode, one of the options available to you is to have Xcode automatically add code and files related to Core Data. That is convenient, but Xcode's template Core Data code is not always what you want. Also, sometimes you may need to add Core Data to a project that didn't previously use it. PhotoWheelPrototype doesn't have Core Data yet, so in this section we'll go through adding Core Data to the project.

This section builds on code from the previous chapter.

Adding the Core Data Framework

Before you can write any code using Core Data classes, you need to add the Core Data framework to the project. This framework contains the header files and implementations for Core Data classes. Until the framework is added, the compiler and linker won't know about Core Data.

To see the frameworks used in PhotoWheelPrototype, click on the project entry in the file navigator and then click on the app target in the editor pane (Figure 13.1). In

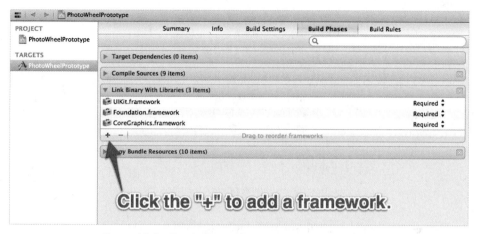

Figure 13.1   Xcode view of frameworks used in an app

Figure 13.2   Adding the Core Data framework

the Editor area, the Build Phases tab has a section named Link Binary With Libraries that lists the currently used frameworks. Don't worry if you see a slightly different list of frameworks—as long as your project is compiling successfully, you've got all the frameworks you need.

To add a framework, click the **+** button at the bottom of the framework list. Xcode will present a list of known frameworks available for the project (Figure 13.2). Select CoreData.framework from the list and click the **Add** button. Xcode will then add Core Data to the project.

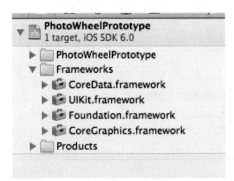

Figure 13.3   Keeping project files organized

When you add the framework, Xcode puts it at the top of the list in the Project navigator, as the first item in the project. This approach works, but it makes more sense to put Core Data with the rest of the frameworks used by the app. Expand the Frameworks folder and drag CoreData.framework into it (Figure 13.3).

Adding the framework allows the linker to use Core Data classes. Next, you need to make sure that the compiler knows about the class declarations so that it can compile the code. You'll be using Core Data in a variety of places in the app, so the best place to do this is in the prefix header file *PhotoWheelPrototype-Prefix.pch*. This file already imports headers for UIKit and Foundation. Edit the file and add *CoreData.h* (Listing 13.1).

Listing 13.1   **Adding Core Data to the Prefix Header File**

```
#ifdef __OBJC__
    #import <UIKit/UIKit.h>
    #import <Foundation/Foundation.h>
    #import <CoreData/CoreData.h>
#endif
```

Setting up the Core Data Stack

The set of objects necessary to use Core Data is often referred to as a *stack*. The managed object context depends on the persistent store coordinator, which in turn depends on the managed object model. The model is at the bottom of the stack, so you'll start there and build upward.

First, you need to create the file that will contain the managed object model. Create a new file in Xcode. Within the category list on the left of the new file window is a section labeled Core Data, and within that section is a file type called Data Model (Figure 13.4). Use this file type and create a file named *PhotoWheelPrototype.xcdatamodeld* (Xcode will add the *.xcdatamodeld* extension). You'll create Core Data entities in this file.

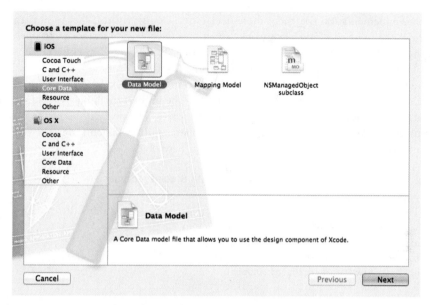

Figure 13.4   Adding a Core Data model file

The extension *.xcdatamodeld* is used for an uncompiled model file. When you build the app, it will be compiled into a *.momd* file.

Next, you need to add code to load the data model file and configure the Core Data stack. In this case, you'll add the setup methods to the application delegate. That's convenient when you have one data store that you use throughout the app, but it is not always ideal. In many cases, it makes sense to set up Core Data in a dedicated model manager class or in one of the view controllers. In this case, though, you'll put it in the app delegate.

Edit *AppDelegate.h* and add the code shown in Listing 13.2. This code creates a property for the NSManagedObjectContext, which will be used in other parts of the app. It also declares a utility method called saveContext that will save any outstanding changes in the managed object context.

Listing 13.2   **Core Data Code for** *AppDelegate.h*

```
@property (readonly, strong, nonatomic)
   NSManagedObjectContext *managedObjectContext;

- (void) saveContext;
```

In *AppDelegate.m*, add a class extension above the @implementation that declares properties for the Core Data stack (Listing 13.3). A class extension is an anonymous protocol that can be used to declare new methods and properties for a class. Putting it in the implementation file keeps these declarations semi-private. They're not really private in the sense that other languages sometimes have private instance variables, but keeping the declaration out of the header file avoids "advertising" its existence and makes it not quite so convenient to use from other objects.

The `NSManagedObjectContext` appears again in the class extension, but this time with `readonly` changed to `readwrite`. This way the property will be writable within `AppDelegate` but read-only when used by other classes. The declarations of the managed object model and the persistent store coordinator will be hidden from other classes, which makes sense because they have no need for these objects.

Listing 13.3 Class Extension Declaring Core Data Stack Properties

```
@interface AppDelegate ()
@property (readwrite, strong, nonatomic)
   NSManagedObjectContext *managedObjectContext;
@property (readwrite, strong, nonatomic)
   NSManagedObjectModel *managedObjectModel;
@property (readwrite, strong, nonatomic)
   NSPersistentStoreCoordinator *persistentStoreCoordinator;
@end
```

Next, add the method to create the managed object model file (Listing 13.4). This method loads the compiled *.momd* file that corresponds to the uncompiled *.xcdatamodeld* file you created earlier. The code looks for the model file in the app's bundle and allocates an `NSManagedObjectModel` object with its contents.

Listing 13.4 Creating the Managed Object Model Instance

```
- (NSManagedObjectModel *)managedObjectModel
{
   if (_managedObjectModel != nil) {
      return _managedObjectModel;
   }

   NSURL *modelURL = [[NSBundle mainBundle]
                  URLForResource:@"PhotoWheelPrototype"
                  withExtension:@"momd"];
   _managedObjectModel = [[NSManagedObjectModel alloc]
                  initWithContentsOfURL:modelURL];
   return _managedObjectModel;
}
```

Now add code for the persistent store coordinator (Listing 13.5). This method creates the persistent store coordinator using the managed object model created previously. It then adds a data store to the coordinator. If the data store exists, it must contain only entities defined in the data model, and the definitions must match. If the data store doesn't exist yet, the method creates an empty one. This version creates a SQLite-backed data store, indicated by `NSSQLiteStoreType`.

Listing 13.5   **Creating the Persistent Store Coordinator**

```
- (NSPersistentStoreCoordinator *)persistentStoreCoordinator
{
    if (_persistentStoreCoordinator != nil) {
        return _persistentStoreCoordinator;
    }

    NSURL *applicationDocumentsDirectory = [[[NSFileManager defaultManager]
                                    URLsForDirectory:NSDocumentDirectory
                                    inDomains:NSUserDomainMask]
                                    lastObject];
    NSURL *dataStoreURL = [applicationDocumentsDirectory
            URLByAppendingPathComponent:@"PhotoWheelPrototype.sqlite"];

    NSError *error = nil;
    _persistentStoreCoordinator = [[NSPersistentStoreCoordinator alloc]
                    initWithManagedObjectModel:[self managedObjectModel]];

    if (![_persistentStoreCoordinator
            addPersistentStoreWithType:NSSQLiteStoreType
            configuration:nil
            URL:dataStoreURL
            options:nil
            error:&error]) {
        NSLog(@"Unresolved error loading data store: %@, %@",
            error, [error userInfo]);
        abort();
    }

    return _persistentStoreCoordinator;
}
```

The last part of the Core Data stack is the managed object context (Listing 13.6). The code that creates the context makes use of the persistent store coordinator method in Listing 13.5, which in turn uses the managed object model created in Listing 13.4. Collectively, these three objects form the Core Data "stack."

Listing 13.6   **Creating the Managed Object Context**

```
- (NSManagedObjectContext *)managedObjectContext
{
    if (_managedObjectContext != nil) {
        return _managedObjectContext;
```

```
    }

    NSPersistentStoreCoordinator *coordinator =
                    [self persistentStoreCoordinator];
    if (coordinator != nil) {
      _managedObjectContext = [[NSManagedObjectContext alloc]
                    initWithConcurrencyType:NSMainQueueConcurrencyType];
      [_managedObjectContext setPersistentStoreCoordinator:coordinator];
    }

    return _managedObjectContext;
}
```

Finally, you need to pass a reference to this managed object context to the `Master VieweController` so that it can make use of the data store when reading and writing photos and albums. First, of course, `MasterViewController` needs to be able to hold a reference to the managed object context. Add a new managed object property to *MasterViewController.h*:

```
@property (strong, nonatomic)
    NSManagedObjectContext *managedObjectContext;
```

Once that step is complete, add a line to set a value for the new property in *AppDelegate.m*, in the `application:didFinishLaunchingWithOptions:` method. Add this code just after the line that sets `DetailViewController:`.

```
[masterViewController setManagedObjectContext:
    [self managedObjectContext]];
```

Now `MasterViewController` has access to the managed object context.

Using Core Data in PhotoWheel

Now it's time to use Core Data to implement the model classes described earlier in the chapter.

The Core Data Model Editor

In Xcode, find the file named *PhotoWheelPrototype.xcdatamodeld* that you created earlier. Click on it to bring up the model editor, shown in Figure 13.5. The model editor lists the entities in the model along with their attributes, relationships, and fetched properties. The toggle at the lower-right corner of the editor switches between a table-style view and a graph style similar to an entity-relationship diagram. As with other Xcode editors, you can click the Editor toggle at the top of the window to show or hide the utility section of the window on the right. Make sure it is showing, because you'll need it to configure the entities.

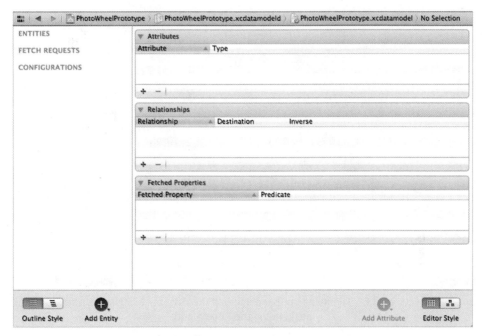

Figure 13.5   The Xcode Core Data model editor

There is not much to see, because you haven't created any entities yet.

Adding the Entities

To create the Photo entity:

1. Click the **Add Entity** button at the bottom of the window. You'll see a new entity appear in the editor. Set its name to Photo.

2. In the Inspector, set the Class to be Photo as well. This tells Core Data that instances of the Photo entity should be instances of a subclass of NSManaged Object that is also named Photo. The entity and the class aren't required to have the same name, but it is convenient to make them the same. So far you don't have a Photo class, but you can still configure the class name here.

3. In the Attributes section of the editor, click the **+** button to create a new attribute. Set its name to dateAdded, and use the popup menu under Type to set the attribute type to Date.

4. Create another new attribute and name it originalImageData. This will save the original image data received from the camera. Set the attribute type to Binary Data.

5. Select the originalImageData attribute. In the Inspector pane on the right, find and select a check box labeled Allows External Storage (Figure 13.6). This

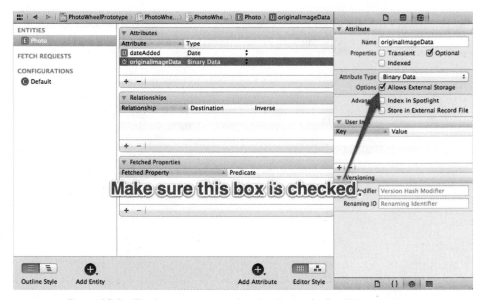

Figure 13.6   The Inspector pane showing the `originalImageData` attribute on the Photo entity

setting tells Core Data that the image data should not be kept directly in the data store, but rather should be automatically saved in an external file. This will prevent excessive memory use when loading Photo entities.

6. Repeat the previous two steps for properties named `thumbnailImageData` and `largeImageData`.

To create the `PhotoAlbum` entity:

1. Click the **Add Entity** button at the bottom of the window. Name the new entity `PhotoAlbum`.

2. Set the Class for the `PhotoAlbum` entity to be a class named `PhotoAlbum`.

3. Add an attribute named `name` and set its type to String.

4. Add an attribute named `dateAdded` and set its type to Date.

Now that the entities exist, click the Editor style toggle at the bottom of the window to switch to the graph view. You'll see both entities with their attributes listed below them. You can drag them around in the graph view and arrange them as you like. You can work in either the model editor's table view or the graph view. The following steps describe using the graph view.

You need to add the relationship between the `Photo` entity and the `PhotoAlbum` entity. This will be a one-to-many relationship from `PhotoAlbum` to `Photo`, because each album can contain multiple photos but each photo can belong to only one album.

1. Click once on the `PhotoAlbum` entity to select it.

2. Click and hold the **Add Attribute** button. A menu of options appears. Click **Add Relationship** to add a relationship from the `PhotoAlbum` entity. Notice that the button's label changes to read *Add Relationship*. The button's label changes to reflect the most recently used choice from the popup menu.

3. Double-click on the new relationship to make its name editable, and set its name to `photos`.

4. In the Inspector, click on the popup menu labeled Destination and select `Photo` as the destination entity.

5. Check the box in the Inspector labeled To-Many Relationship. Also check the box labeled Ordered, so that the order will be maintained on the relationship. Without this the relationship would be unordered, and you'll be adding code soon that needs to know the order.

6. Click on the popup menu labeled Delete Rule and select the Cascade option. This setting means that deletion of a `PhotoAlbum` will cascade to related `Photos` and delete them as well. At this point the model should look like Figure 13.7. You may notice at this point that Xcode is showing a warning about the photos

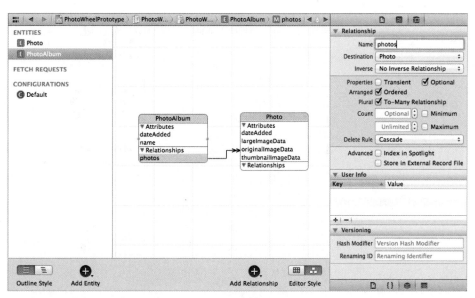

Figure 13.7   Model editor after adding the `photos` relationship to the
`PhotoAlbum` entity

relationship not having an inverse relationship. Don't worry about that, you'll fix it in the following steps.

7. Click once on the Photo entity to select it.

8. Click the **Add Relationship** button (the one that earlier read **Add Attribute**).

9. Double-click on the new relationship to make its name editable, and set its name to photoAlbum.

10. In the Inspector, click on the popup menu labeled Destination and select PhotoAlbum as the destination entity.

11. In the Inspector, click on the popup menu labeled Inverse and select photos as the inverse relationship. This tells Core Data that PhotoAlbum's photos relationship and Photo's photoAlbum relationship are opposite ends of the same relationship.

12. In the Inspector, uncheck the box marked Optional. Because photos must belong to an album, this relationship is mandatory. Contrast that with PhotoAlbum's photos relationship. It was left as optional, because a photo album may be empty.

13. Leave the Delete Rule for this relationship set to Nullify. This tells Core Data that when a Photo is deleted, incoming relationships should be set to nil. In this case, it means that deleting a Photo doesn't mean that the corresponding PhotoAlbum should be deleted.

At this point the model should look like Figure 13.8.

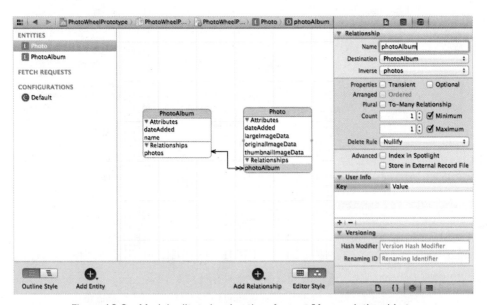

Figure 13.8   Model editor showing the photoAlbum relationship to
the Photo entity

Creating `NSManagedObject` Subclasses

Now that you have created the model entities, you can have Xcode create custom `NSManagedObject` subclasses that match the entities. When Xcode creates the class files, it looks at the existing entities and the class names configured for each one. If any entity has a class other than `NSManagedObject`, it offers to create a custom subclass for that entity. The subclasses Xcode creates include properties that correspond to the attributes and relationships of the entity.

Before you do that, let's continue the discussion from earlier about thinking ahead when designing a data model. Suppose that you want to add new attributes to one or both of the entities in version 1.1 of PhotoWheel. Perhaps you would like to add location information so that you could show photos on a map. Recall also from the earlier discussion the idea that you might want to add custom methods to your model classes to implement model-specific behavior.

These two requirements conflict if you have Xcode generate your subclasses. On the one hand, when Xcode generates managed object classes, it overwrites the existing file and replaces it with one matching the current state of the entities in the data model. If you have previously added custom methods, they will be wiped away. On the other hand, creating and managing your subclasses by hand is tedious and error prone. You would need to update the subclass code anytime you update the entity, making the same change in two different places.

How can you resolve this conflict? With a little bit of trickery, you can use generated subclasses without overwriting your custom code. To do so, you create two classes for each entity: one that will be generated by Xcode and the other that will be a subclass of the first. Xcode can then generate your model classes, and you can add methods without conflict. You'll do this by temporarily renaming the entity subclasses.

1. In the model editor, change the name of the `PhotoAlbum` entity's class to `_PhotoAlbum`.

2. In the model editor, change the name of the `Photo` entity's class to `_Photo`.

3. Click one of the entities, and then **Shift-click** on the other so that both entities are selected.

4. On Xcode's **File** menu, select **New > File**.

5. In the new file window, select Core Data from the list on the left and `NSManaged Object` subclass from the options on the right (Figure 13.9). Click **Next**.

6. Save the new files. There are four new files, consisting of both header and implementation files for each of the `_Photo` and `_PhotoAlbum` classes. These define two subclasses of `NSManagedObject`.

7. On Xcode's **File** menu, select **New > File**. Create an Objective-C class named `Photo`. Set the superclass to be `_Photo` (Figure 13.10). This creates a subclass of `_Photo` called `Photo`.

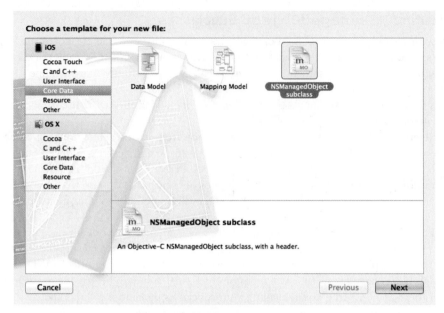

Figure 13.9   Creating custom `NSManagedObject` subclasses in Xcode

Figure 13.10   Creating the `Photo` class with a custom superclass

8. Repeat the previous step, creating a class named `PhotoAlbum` whose superclass is `_PhotoAlbum`.

9. Go back to the model editor and change the `Photo` entity's class name back to `Photo` and the `PhotoAlbum` entity's class name back to `PhotoAlbum`.

What did you just do? You used Xcode to automatically create two classes, `_Photo` and `_PhotoAlbum`, that match the entities you created earlier. You also created two subclasses, `Photo` and `PhotoAlbum`. Xcode generated the superclasses, and your custom code will go in the subclasses. This keeps your code separate from code generated by Xcode. Keep in mind that you'll have to repeat the temporary renaming process if you change the entities later.

Why not skip the last step and leave the class names as the underscored names? The class names saved in the model are the classes Core Data will return when creating managed objects. If the `PhotoAlbum` entity's class were named `_PhotoAlbum`, Core Data would create instances of `_PhotoAlbum` that would not contain any custom behaviors added in the `PhotoAlbum` subclass. When the name is changed back, Core Data provides `PhotoAlbum` instances that contain the custom code.

Take a look at the generated code. Xcode creates properties for each of the entity's attributes and relationships. For to-many relationships, it also creates custom accessor methods for adding and removing objects. Listing 13.7 shows the generated code for _PhotoAlbum.h. The `photos` property contains all of the album's photos and can be used to look up the album contents. To add and remove individual photos, you would use the accessor methods `addPhotosObject:` and `removePhotosObject:`.

Listing 13.7 **Automatically Generated Code in _PhotoAlbum.h**

```
#import <Foundation/Foundation.h>
#import <CoreData/CoreData.h>

@class _Photo;

@interface _PhotoAlbum : NSManagedObject

@property (nonatomic, retain) NSString * name;
@property (nonatomic, retain) NSDate * dateAdded;
@property (nonatomic, retain) NSOrderedSet *photos;
@end

@interface _PhotoAlbum (CoreDataGeneratedAccessors)

- (void)insertObject:(_Photo *)value inPhotosAtIndex:(NSUInteger)idx;
- (void)removeObjectFromPhotosAtIndex:(NSUInteger)idx;
- (void)insertPhotos:(NSArray *)value atIndexes:(NSIndexSet *)indexes;
- (void)removePhotosAtIndexes:(NSIndexSet *)indexes;
- (void)replaceObjectInPhotosAtIndex:(NSUInteger)idx
```

```
                            withObject:(_Photo *)value;
- (void)replacePhotosAtIndexes:(NSIndexSet *)indexes
                        withPhotos:(NSArray *)values;
- (void)addPhotosObject:(_Photo *)value;
- (void)removePhotosObject:(_Photo *)value;
- (void)addPhotos:(NSOrderedSet *)values;
- (void)removePhotos:(NSOrderedSet *)values;
@end
```

If you look at the implementation file _PhotoAlbum.m_ (Listing 13.8), you'll see that there is not much there. All of the properties are listed as @dynamic declarations, and that's it. Declaring properties as @dynamic implies that the necessary method declarations will be created at run time, or that dynamic method resolution will be used to handle calls to the method. NSManagedObject takes care of those tasks. These are a couple of the interesting features of Objective-C—namely, that new methods can be created while an app is running, and that calls to nonexistent methods can be handled dynamically.

Listing 13.8   **Automatically Generated Code in _PhotoAlbum.m_**

```
#import "_PhotoAlbum.h"
#import "_Photo.h"


@implementation _PhotoAlbum

@dynamic name;
@dynamic dateAdded;
@dynamic photos;


@end
```

Alternative Subclassing Techniques

The multistep process for keeping generated code separate from custom code described in this chapter is effective but can be vulnerable to errors. If you regenerate the class files without first changing the class names, you could accidentally wipe out custom code. Good version control software is a must when using this approach, so that code can be recovered if necessary. A few alternative approaches to generating subclasses can also be useful in projects with more entity types.

One approach is to use Objective-C categories instead of the two-level inheritance scheme you used in this chapter. In this approach, custom code goes not in your NSManaged Object subclass, but rather in a category defined on that subclass. The managed object subclass can be regenerated by Xcode and overwritten whenever necessary, and your custom code remains safe because it resides in a different file. For PhotoWheel, you would then have managed object subclasses called `Photo` and `PhotoAlbum` but with no corresponding `_Photo` or `_PhotoAlbum` classes. For the `Photo` entity, the custom category files might be named *Photo+custom.h* and *Photo+custom.m*. The header file would look something like this:

```
#import "Photo.h"

@interface Photo (custom)

- (void)saveImage:(UIImage *)newImage;

- (UIImage *)originalImage;
- (UIImage *)largeImage;
- (UIImage *)thumbnailImage;

@end
```

This is almost identical to the content of *Photo.h* except for the `@interface` line. The implementation file *Photo+custom.m* would also be nearly the same as the current *Photo.m*. When you wanted to use `Photo` and get access to the custom code, you would import *Photo+custom.h* instead of *Photo.h*.

Another approach, which is commonly used with larger projects, is to generate subclasses using an open source command-line tool called *mogenerator*,[2] written by Jonathan "Wolf" Rentzsch. It follows the same general two-level class system used earlier in this chapter, where one class contains generated class files based on entities and the other class subclasses the first. Unlike the approach described in this chapter, however, mogenerator doesn't require any subclass renaming process. Also, unlike Xcode's subclass generation, it offers numerous options to configure how the source code will be generated and which templates will be used for the source files. Mogenerator is easy to use, but if a team of people is working on an app, everyone who edits the Core Data model must install this tool.

Adding Custom Code to Model Objects

Now that we have a place to safely add custom code, which code do we need? You may have noticed earlier that all of the image-related attributes on the `Photo` entity used the binary data type. This data type corresponds to an instance of `NSData`. To draw images on the screen, however, we'll need `UIImage` instances. Adding custom code to translate between the `NSData` in the data store and the `UIImage` needed for the user interface is an obvious choice.

---

2. mogenerator: http://rentzsch.github.com/mogenerator/

Start with code to handle a new picture from the camera. You'll have a `UIImage`, and you need to create several images of differing sizes and save all of them. Add a method declaration in *Photo.h*:

```
- (void)saveImage:(UIImage *)newImage;
```

The method definition goes in *Photo.m* and is shown in Listing 13.9. The listing also includes related methods that resize images, because we plan to use multiple image sizes. We won't discuss these methods in detail here. If you would like to investigate them in greater depth, consult Xcode's built-in documentation for the methods and functions they use.

Listing 13.9   Saving a New Photo in Multiple Sizes in an `NSManagedObject` Subclass

```
- (UIImage *)image:(UIImage *)image scaleAspectToMaxSize:(CGFloat)newSize
{
    CGSize size = [image size];
    CGFloat ratio;
    if (size.width > size.height) {
        ratio = newSize / size.width;
    } else {
        ratio = newSize / size.height;
    }

    CGRect rect =
        CGRectMake(0.0, 0.0, ratio * size.width, ratio * size.height);
    UIGraphicsBeginImageContext(rect.size);
    [image drawInRect:rect];
    UIImage *scaledImage = UIGraphicsGetImageFromCurrentImageContext();
    return scaledImage;
}


- (UIImage *)image:(UIImage *)image scaleAndCropToMaxSize:(CGSize)size
{
    // Adjust for retina display.
    CGFloat scale = [[UIScreen mainScreen] scale];
    CGSize newSize = CGSizeMake(size.width * scale, size.height * scale);

    CGFloat largestSize =
        (newSize.width > newSize.height) ? newSize.width : newSize.height;
    CGSize imageSize = [image size];

    // Scale the image while maintaining the aspect and making sure the
    // the scaled image is not smaller than the given new size. In
    // other words, we calculate the aspect ratio using the largest
    // dimension from the new size and the smaller dimension from the
    // actual size.
    CGFloat ratio;
```

```objc
   if (imageSize.width > imageSize.height) {
      ratio = largestSize / imageSize.height;
   } else {
      ratio = largestSize / imageSize.width;
   }

   CGRect rect =
      CGRectMake(0.0, 0.0,
                  ratio * imageSize.width, ratio * imageSize.height);
   UIGraphicsBeginImageContext(rect.size);
   [image drawInRect:rect];
   UIImage *scaledImage = UIGraphicsGetImageFromCurrentImageContext();

   // Crop the image to the requested new size while maintaining
   // the inner most parts of the image.
   CGFloat offsetX = 0;
   CGFloat offsetY = 0;
   imageSize = [scaledImage size];
   if (imageSize.width < imageSize.height) {
      offsetY = (imageSize.height / 2) - (imageSize.width / 2);
   } else {
      offsetX = (imageSize.width / 2) - (imageSize.height / 2);
   }

   CGRect cropRect = CGRectMake(offsetX, offsetY,
                                 imageSize.width - (offsetX * 2),
                                 imageSize.height - (offsetY * 2));

   CGImageRef croppedImageRef =
      CGImageCreateWithImageInRect([scaledImage CGImage], cropRect);
   UIImage *newImage = [UIImage imageWithCGImage:croppedImageRef];
   CGImageRelease(croppedImageRef);

   return newImage;
}

- (void)createScaledImagesForImage:(UIImage *)originalImage
{
   // Save thumbnail
   CGSize thumbnailSize = CGSizeMake(75.0, 75.0);
   UIImage *thumbnailImage = [self image:originalImage
                  scaleAndCropToMaxSize:thumbnailSize];
   NSData *thumbnailImageData = UIImageJPEGRepresentation(thumbnailImage,
                                                    0.8);
   [self setThumbnailImageData:thumbnailImageData];

   // Save large (screen-size) image
```

```
    CGRect screenBounds = [[UIScreen mainScreen] bounds];
    // Calculate size for retina displays
    CGFloat scale = [[UIScreen mainScreen] scale];
    CGFloat maxScreenSize = MAX(screenBounds.size.width,
                            screenBounds.size.height) * scale;

    CGSize imageSize = [originalImage size];
    CGFloat maxImageSize = MAX(imageSize.width,
                            imageSize.height) * scale;

    CGFloat maxSize = MIN(maxScreenSize, maxImageSize);
    UIImage *largeImage = [self image:originalImage
                scaleAspectToMaxSize:maxSize];
    NSData *largeImageData = UIImageJPEGRepresentation(largeImage, 0.8);
    [self setLargeImageData:largeImageData];
}


- (void)saveImage:(UIImage *)newImage
{
    NSData *originalImageData = UIImageJPEGRepresentation(newImage, 0.8);
    [self setOriginalImageData:originalImageData];
    [self createScaledImagesForImage:newImage];
}
```

The saveImage: method starts off by converting the UIImage to an NSData object using JPEG compression and saving that as the original image data. Next, the method calls the createScaledImagesForImage: method to scale the image to other sizes using the image-scaling methods. In each case, the code scales the incoming UIImage to a smaller size, converts it to NSData, and calls one of the generated accessor methods.

Going in the other direction, it would be convenient to be able to ask a Photo for a UIImage even though the image is saved in the data store as binary data. To make it so, add the following convenience method declarations to *Photo.h*:

```
- (UIImage *)originalImage;
- (UIImage *)largeImage;
- (UIImage *)thumbnailImage;
```

The method definitions in *Photo.m* are straightforward and are shown in Listing 13.10.

Listing 13.10   **Convenience Methods to Get UIImage Objects from Binary Data in the Data Store**

```
- (UIImage *)originalImage
{
    return [UIImage imageWithData:[self originalImageData]];
```

```
}

- (UIImage *)largeImage
{
    return [UIImage imageWithData:[self largeImageData]];
}

- (UIImage *)thumbnailImage
{
    return [UIImage imageWithData:[self thumbnailImageData]];
}
```

The PhotoAlbum class has a few custom methods of its own. First, you'll override NSManagedObject's awakeFromInsert method (Listing 13.11). This method is called when a managed object is first inserted into a managed object context and is guaranteed to be called only once on any object. You'll use this method to set the photo album's add date.

Listing 13.11 Setting the Add Date on Insertion into the Managed Object Context

```
- (void)awakeFromInsert
{
    [super awakeFromInsert];
    [self setDateAdded:[NSDate date]];
}
```

Next, you'll add a convenience method for creating a new photo album (Listing 13.12). This method takes two arguments: the desired album name and the managed object context into which the new album should be inserted. The second argument is used because this is a class method rather than an instance method. Instances of PhotoAlbum have a reference to their managed object context, which can be looked up using the managedObjectContext property. The PhotoAlbum class does not belong to a managed object context, so the context needs to be passed in by the caller of this method.

Listing 13.12 Adding a New Photo Album to a Managed Object Context

```
+ (PhotoAlbum *)newPhotoAlbumWithName:(NSString *)albumName
                          inContext:(NSManagedObjectContext *)context
{
    PhotoAlbum *newAlbum = [NSEntityDescription
                      insertNewObjectForEntityForName:@"PhotoAlbum"
                      inManagedObjectContext:context];
    [newAlbum setName:albumName];

    NSMutableOrderedSet *photos =
        [newAlbum mutableOrderedSetValueForKey:@"photos"];
```

```
for (int index=0; index<10; index++) {
    Photo *placeholderPhoto = [NSEntityDescription
                               insertNewObjectForEntityForName:@"Photo"
                               inManagedObjectContext:context];
    [photos addObject:placeholderPhoto];
}
return newAlbum;
}
```

The code starts off by creating a new `PhotoAlbum` and setting its name. The add date will be set automatically in `awakeFromInsert`. Next, the code fills out the album with placeholder objects. This step ensures that photos can be added to the album at any index instead of only at the end of the current photo list. The new `Photo` instances won't have any of their properties set and will use minimal memory.

Because this code makes use of the `Photo` class, make sure to import the header file for that class at the top of the file:

```
#import "Photo.h"
```

`PhotoAlbum` also has a custom method to look up all albums in a managed object context (Listing 13.13). This method will be called when `MasterViewController` first loads, so that it can display the full album list.

Listing 13.13 Looking Up All Photo Albums in a Managed Object Context

```
+ (NSMutableOrderedSet *)allPhotoAlbumsInContext:
   (NSManagedObjectContext *)context
{
   NSFetchRequest *fetchRequest = [NSFetchRequest
                             fetchRequestWithEntityName:@"PhotoAlbum"];

   NSSortDescriptor *sortDescriptor = [NSSortDescriptor
                                sortDescriptorWithKey:@"name"
                                ascending:YES];
   NSArray *sortDescriptors = @[sortDescriptor];
   [fetchRequest setSortDescriptors:sortDescriptors];

   NSError *error = nil;
   NSArray *photoAlbums = [context executeFetchRequest:fetchRequest
                                    error:&error];

   if (photoAlbums != nil) {
      return [NSMutableOrderedSet orderedSetWithArray:photoAlbums];
   } else {
      return [NSMutableOrderedSet orderedSet];
   }
}
```

The first thing this code does is create a fetch request for the entity named Photo Album. The entity name used here is just an NSString, but an entity with that name must be present in the managed object context when the fetch request executes. The sort descriptor requests that the results of the request be ordered by name. Sorting is handled internally by Core Data; all that's necessary is to provide the key or keys by which you want to sort.

The method then executes the fetch. If any albums are found, the code creates a mutable ordered set containing the same elements as the array and returns it. This method returns a mutable ordered set so that the caller can add new albums, and because that's what MainViewController expects. If the managed object context doesn't contain any albums yet, the result will be nil, and in that case the method returns an empty mutable ordered set.

Make sure to add declarations in *PhotoAlbum.h* that correspond to the methods defined in Listings 13.12 and 13.13.

Reading and Saving Photo Albums with Core Data

Now you'll update MasterViewController to work with photo albums. Add the code highlighted in Listing 13.14 to the class extension at the top of the *MasterView Controller.m* file.

Listing 13.14   **Class Extension Additions for MasterViewController**

```
@interface MasterViewController ()
@property (readwrite, assign) NSUInteger currentAlbumIndex;
@end
```

This code declares the property currentAlbumIndex, which will be used to keep track of the album being displayed in the detail view, so that MasterViewController can show the user which one is currently selected.

The list of albums can be set up in viewDidLoad. Listing 13.15 shows an updated version of *MasterViewController.m*'s viewDidLoad that handles this task.

Listing 13.15   **Setting Up the List of Photo Albums**

```
- (void)viewDidLoad
{
  [super viewDidLoad];
  // Do any additional setup after loading the view, typically from a
  // NIB file.
  self.navigationItem.leftBarButtonItem = self.editButtonItem;

  UIBarButtonItem *addButton =
  [[UIBarButtonItem alloc]
   initWithBarButtonSystemItem:UIBarButtonSystemItemAdd
   target:self
```

```
        action:@selector(insertNewObject:)];
    self.navigationItem.rightBarButtonItem = addButton;


    self.title = NSLocalizedString(@"Albums", @"Albums");

    [self setData:[PhotoAlbum allPhotoAlbumsInContext:
                      [self managedObjectContext]]];

    if ([[self data] count] == 0) {
        PhotoAlbum *newAlbum = [PhotoAlbum
                              newPhotoAlbumWithName:@"First album"
                              inContext:[self managedObjectContext]];
        [self setData:[NSMutableArray arrayWithObject:newAlbum]];
        [[self managedObjectContext] save:nil];
    }

    [self.tableView selectRowAtIndexPath:[NSIndexPath indexPathForRow:0
                                                           inSection:0]
                        animated:NO
                        scrollPosition:UITableViewScrollPositionMiddle];
}
```

The first highlighted line loads all existing photo albums into `MasterViewCon`
`troller`'s `data` array, using the convenience method defined earlier. The following
code handles the first-run scenario when no albums exist yet. If there are no albums, the
code creates an initial album and saves it in the data set. It then tells the managed object
context to save changes so that this new album will be recorded in the data store.

It's also a good idea to show the user which album is currently selected, so change
the cell configuration section of `tableView:cellForRowAtIndexPath:` to match
the code in Listing 13.16.

Listing 13.16 Configuring Table Cells to Show Photo Album Information

```
// Configure the cell.
PhotoAlbum *album = [[self data] objectAtIndex:[indexPath row]];
[[cell textLabel] setText:[album name]];

if ([indexPath row] == [self currentAlbumIndex]) {
    [cell setAccessoryType:UITableViewCellAccessoryCheckmark];
} else {
    [cell setAccessoryType:UITableViewCellAccessoryNone];
}
```

This code looks up a photo album corresponding to the current table index path
and sets the cell's `text` to that album's name. Next, it shows a check mark if the album
is the currently selected album.

It's possible for the user to delete photo albums in `MasterViewController`. The current implementation of the deletion handling code just deletes an entry in the `data` collection. Because photo albums are now being saved by Core Data, however, we also need to tell Core Data to delete the album. Change the deletion code so that it looks like Listing 13.17.

Listing 13.17   **Deleting Photo Albums**

```
- (void)tableView:(UITableView *)tableView
  commitEditingStyle:(UITableViewCellEditingStyle)editingStyle
  forRowAtIndexPath:(NSIndexPath *)indexPath
{
  if (editingStyle == UITableViewCellEditingStyleDelete) {
    // Delete the photo album
    PhotoAlbum *currentAlbum = [[self data] objectAtIndex:
                                    [indexPath row]];
    [[self managedObjectContext] deleteObject:currentAlbum];

    [[self data] removeObjectAtIndex:[indexPath row]];

    [tableView deleteRowsAtIndexPaths:@[indexPath]
                  withRowAnimation:UITableViewRowAnimationFade];

    // Handle deleting the currently selected album
    if ([indexPath row] == [self currentAlbumIndex]) {
      [self setCurrentAlbumIndex:0];
      NSIndexPath *firstRowIndexPath = [NSIndexPath indexPathForRow:0
                                                      inSection:0];

      if ([[self data] count] == 0) {
        // Handle deleting the last photo album
        PhotoAlbum *newAlbum = [PhotoAlbum
                            newPhotoAlbumWithName:@"First album"
                            inContext:[self managedObjectContext]];
        [self setData:[NSMutableArray arrayWithObject:newAlbum]];
        [tableView insertRowsAtIndexPaths:@[firstRowIndexPath]
                    withRowAnimation:UITableViewRowAnimationNone];
      } else {
        [tableView reloadRowsAtIndexPaths:@[firstRowIndexPath]
                    withRowAnimation:UITableViewRowAnimationNone];
      }
      [tableView selectRowAtIndexPath:firstRowIndexPath
                          animated:NO
                    scrollPosition:UITableViewScrollPositionMiddle];
      [[self detailViewController] setPhotoAlbum:
          [[self data] objectAtIndex:0]];
    }
```

```
    NSError *error = nil;
    if (![[self managedObjectContext] save:&error]) {
        NSLog(@"Error deleting album: %@, %@", error, [error userInfo]);
    }
  }
}
}
```

Listing 13.17 adds a lot of code, but the main purpose is covered in the first few lines. The code looks up the `PhotoAlbum` that corresponds to the row being deleted. It then tells the managed object context to delete the album, and also removes the same album from `MasterViewController`'s collection of albums. Next, the code updates the table view by telling it to delete the row. Core Data changes aren't saved yet, because more changes might happen later on in the method.

The rest of the method covers a couple of special cases. What if the user deleted the currently selected album? You'll need to update the currently selected album and tell the detail view about the new selection. But wait! What if the user deleted the last album that exists? If there are no more albums, the code creates a new empty album, using the same steps performed previously in `viewDidLoad`. Because at least one album exists, the code then selects the first album in the list (which might be the only album) as the current album.

Now that the method is finished with any possible Core Data updates, it saves changes via the managed object context.

You also need to change the code that handles editing photo album names to handle Core Data entities properly. First, change the code in *MasterViewController.m* that loads the `NameEditorViewController` to look like Listing 13.18.

Listing 13.18   Loading the Name Editor for a Core Data Photo Album Entity

```
- (void)tableView:(UITableView *)tableView
  accessoryButtonTappedForRowWithIndexPath:(NSIndexPath *)indexPath
{
    NameEditorViewController *newController =
    [[NameEditorViewController alloc] initWithDefaultNib];
    [newController setDelegate:self];
    [newController setEditing:YES];
    [newController setIndexPath:indexPath];
    PhotoAlbum *currentAlbum = [[self data] objectAtIndex:[indexPath row]];
    NSString *name = [currentAlbum name];
    [newController setDefaultNameText:name];
    [newController setModalPresentationStyle:UIModalPresentationFormSheet];
    [self presentViewController:newController animated:YES completion:nil];
}
```

The only change in Listing 13.18 is that the code now looks up the name property of the selected photo album, which is defined on the `PhotoAlbum` entity.

You also need to update the callback from `NameEditorViewController` to handle new album names and new albums. Make the method look like Listing 13.19.

Listing 13.19   Handling Photo Album Name Editor Callbacks with Core Data

```
- (void)nameEditorViewControllerDidFinish:
    (NameEditorViewController *)controller
{
    NSString *newName = [[controller nameTextField] text];
    if (newName && [newName length] > 0) {
        if ([controller isEditing]) {
            PhotoAlbum *album = [[self data]
                                    objectAtIndex:[[controller indexPath] row]];
            [album setName:newName];
        } else {
            PhotoAlbum *newAlbum = [PhotoAlbum
                                    newPhotoAlbumWithName:newName
                                    inContext:[self managedObjectContext]];
            [[self data] addObject:newAlbum];
        }
        [[self managedObjectContext] save:nil];
        [[self tableView] reloadData];
    }
}
```

If the controller was editing an album name, this code finds the `PhotoAlbum` being edited and updates its name. If the controller was not editing an album name, the code creates a new `PhotoAlbum` with the requested name and adds it to the data array. In either case, the code tells the `managedObjectContext` to save the change that was just made.

Adding New Photos to an Album with Core Data

Now let's see how to place pictures into photo albums while using Core Data. Our first step is to give `DetailViewController` a reference to the currently selected photo album. Add a new property to *DetailViewController.h* to hold this reference, but this time make it an instance of `PhotoAlbum`:

```
@property (strong, nonatomic) PhotoAlbum *photoAlbum;
```

You also need to declare the `PhotoAlbum` class so that the preceding code will compile. Add this declaration at the top of *DetailViewController.h*, above the `@interface` line:

```
@class PhotoAlbum;
```

In *DetailViewController.m*, be sure to import *PhotoAlbum.h* so that the compiler will know where the class is defined. This step is necessary to compile code that uses `PhotoAlbum` instances:

```
#import "PhotoAlbum.h"
```

Now you need to tell `DetailViewController` which album is selected. You'll do this back in `MasterViewController`, where the album selection is managed. First, add a line to `MasterViewController`'s `viewDidLoad`, telling the detail view controller to use the first album in the list. Make it the last line in the method, so that this action happens after the data property has been initialized.

```
[[self detailViewController] setPhotoAlbum:[[self data] objectAtIndex:0]];
```

Next, fill in `MasterViewController`'s implementation of `tableView:didSelectRowAtIndexPath:` so that both the detail and master views will be updated appropriately when the user taps on a photo album (Listing 13.20).

Listing 13.20 **Changing the Selected Album**

```
- (void)tableView:(UITableView *)tableView
   didSelectRowAtIndexPath:(NSIndexPath *)indexPath
{
   if ([indexPath row] != [self currentAlbumIndex]) {
      NSIndexPath *oldCurrentAlbumIndexPath = [NSIndexPath
                           indexPathForRow:[self currentAlbumIndex]
                           inSection:0];
      [self setCurrentAlbumIndex:[indexPath row]];
      [tableView reloadRowsAtIndexPaths:
                     @[indexPath, oldCurrentAlbumIndexPath]
               withRowAnimation:UITableViewRowAnimationNone];

      PhotoAlbum *selectedAlbum = [[self data]
                           objectAtIndex:[indexPath row]];
      [[self detailViewController] setPhotoAlbum:selectedAlbum];
   }
}
```

This code initially checks whether the row that is currently selected is the same as the row that was already selected. This situation would arise when the user taps on the currently selected album. The table view would call this method, but you don't need to do anything in such a case.

If the user taps on a different row, the code needs to update the table view, the current album index, and the detail view. First, it gets an `NSIndexPath` for the previously selected row and updates the current index to store the newly selected row. Then it tells the table view to reload the rows at the indexes of both the old and new selections. This step generates calls to `tableView:cellForRowAtIndexPath:` for both of those index paths, and removes the check mark at the old selected row and adds a check mark at the new selection. It's important to update the current album index *before* updating the table, because `tableView:cellForRowAtIndexPath:` makes use of the current index.

The rest of the method looks up the `PhotoAlbum` for the selected row in the data array and tells `detailViewController` that the selection has changed.

Getting new photos from the camera or photo library happens in *DetailViewController.m* in the `UIImagePickerControllerDelegate` callback (Listing 13.21).

Listing 13.21   Adding New Photos to a Photo Album Using Core Data

```
- (void)imagePickerController:(UIImagePickerController *)picker
didFinishPickingMediaWithInfo:(NSDictionary *)info
{
    // If the popover controller is available,
    // assume the photo is selected from the library
    // and not from the camera.
    BOOL takenWithCamera = ([self imagePickerPopoverController] == nil);

    // Dismiss the popover controller if available;
    // otherwise, dismiss the camera view.
    if ([self imagePickerPopoverController]) {
        [[self imagePickerPopoverController] dismissPopoverAnimated:YES];
        [self setImagePickerPopoverController:nil];
    } else {
        [self dismissViewControllerAnimated:YES completion:nil];
    }

    // Retrieve and display the image.
    UIImage *image = [info objectForKey:UIImagePickerControllerOriginalImage];
    [[self selectedPhotoWheelViewCell] setImage:image];

    Photo *targetPhoto = [[[self photoAlbum] photos] objectAtIndex:
                        [self selectedWheelViewCellIndex]];
    [targetPhoto saveImage:image];
    [targetPhoto setDateAdded:[NSDate date]];

    NSError *error = nil;
    [[[self photoAlbum] managedObjectContext] save:&error];

    if (takenWithCamera) {
        UIImageWriteToSavedPhotosAlbum(image, nil, nil, nil);
    }
}
```

The new code looks up the "target" photo in the album using the index of the selected cell view. The new image is saved using `Photo`'s `saveImage:` method, which was discussed earlier. This method creates multiple photo sizes as JPEG data and saves that data in the target photo. The code then sets the photo's add date to the current date and time. The code then asks the managed object context to save the new changes.

Listing 13.21 requires a couple of other minor updates to `DetailViewController` before it will compile. You need to add a property in `DetailViewController` called `selectedWheelViewCellIndex`. It is an integer that saves the index of the thumbnail view the user tapped on. Add the declaration to the class extension at the top of *DetailViewController.m*:

```
@property (assign) NSUInteger selectedWheelViewCellIndex;
```

You also need to make sure that `selectedWheelViewCellIndex` has the right value when saving a photo. Update the `cellTapped:` method to save this value when the user begins the process of adding a photo, by adding the highlighted line shown in Listing 13.22.

Listing 13.22   Saving the Cell Index When Adding a New Photo

```
- (void)cellTapped:(UIGestureRecognizer *)recognizer
{
    [self setSelectedPhotoWheelViewCell:
        (PhotoWheelViewCell *)[recognizer view]];
    [self setSelectedWheelViewCellIndex:[[self data] indexOfObject:
                                    [self selectedPhotoWheelViewCell]]];

    BOOL hasCamera = [UIImagePickerController isSourceTypeAvailable:
                        UIImagePickerControllerSourceTypeCamera];
    if (hasCamera) {
        [self presentPhotoPickerMenu];
    } else {
        [self presentPhotoLibrary];
    }
}
```

The code in Listing 13.21 uses the `Photo` class, so be sure to import the header for that class at the top of *DetailViewController.m*:

```
#import "Photo.h"
```

Displaying Photos in an Album with Core Data

When the user selects a new album, `DetailViewController` needs to update its view to show photos from that album. Because `MasterViewController` is already setting `DetailViewController`'s photoAlbum property when that happens, the best way to handle this task is by creating a custom setter method for that property (Listing 13.23).

Listing 13.23   Updating the Wheel View When a New Photo Album Is Selected

```
- (void)setPhotoAlbum:(PhotoAlbum *)photoAlbum
{
    _photoAlbum = photoAlbum;
```

```
    UIImage *defaultPhoto = [UIImage imageNamed:@"defaultPhoto.png"];
    for (NSUInteger index=0; index<10; index++) {
        PhotoWheelViewCell *cell = [[self data] objectAtIndex:index];
        Photo *photo = [[[self photoAlbum] photos] objectAtIndex:index];
        UIImage *thumbnail = [photo thumbnailImage];
        if (thumbnail != nil) {
            [cell setImage:thumbnail];
        } else {
            [cell setImage:defaultPhoto];
        }
    }
}
```

The first line in this method actually sets the new value of the photo album property. The rest of the code updates the user interface by running through the album, updating the wheel view as it goes. In each pass through the loop, the code finds both the cell view and the photo corresponding to the loop counter. If the photo has a thumbnail version, the code displays that image in the cell. Otherwise, it displays a default image, indicating that no photo exists at that index.

With these changes, the app is ready for use as a prototype, now using Core Data to store photos. The app uses Core Data to automatically sort photo albums based on album properties. We have not added undo management, but if you wanted to do so, Core Data would work directly with NSUndoManager to simplify the process.

Using SQLite Directly

Core Data is extremely useful as an app's model layer, but it's not ideal in all cases. In some situations, your needs might be a better match for a database than for an object store. For example, if you routinely need to update a flag on a large collection of records, it is difficult to do so efficiently in Core Data. In that case, you might prefer to work with SQLite directly. In most cases Core Data will be easier, but in cases where it is not a good match, you can create and use your own SQLite files.

SQLite offers a powerful API but it can be intimidating at first. It is written in C, so you'll have to do some work to convert between database records and your own model objects. You can simplify this process somewhat by using an Objective-C wrapper for SQLite. Two open source projects, FMDB[3] and PLDatabase,[4] can greatly simplify using SQLite in Objective-C code but otherwise don't come between your code and the database. You'll still have to put some effort into converting between your model objects and database records, but if the advantage of more direct database access is important enough, this approach may be worth the extra work.

---

3. FMDB: https://github.com/ccgus/fmdb
4. PLDatabase: http://code.google.com/p/pldatabase/

Summary

This chapter presented different approaches to implementing the model layer of an iPad app, and two alternatives were implemented. Core Data is frequently—though not always—the better choice. At this point the PhotoWheelPrototype project can get new photos, display them, and manage the albums that contain them. Now let's move on to implementing the rest of the user interface and other useful app features.

Exercises

1. Update the method `-tableView:moveRowAtIndexPath:toIndexPath:` found in *MasterViewController.m* to make it possible for users to rearrange photo albums and update the status in the data store. Because photo albums are currently sorted by name, you'll need to add a numeric property to store the user sort order. You'll also need to update this sort order when the user moves an album to a new index.

Storyboarding in Xcode

Up to this point, you have been working on building the prototype app for PhotoWheel. Certain design concepts were proven and development techniques explored, and you learned more about building apps for the iPad. Now it's time to use what you learned by starting to build the "real" PhotoWheel app. To start things off, let's talk about a new way of designing the user interface using a feature called a storyboard.

What Is a Storyboard?

In the previous chapters, you learned how to create the user interface using IB and NIB files. Mac and iOS developers have been creating user interfaces for years using this approach, but the approach could be better. Imagine, for example, how helpful it would be to see the entire user interface of your application on one screen, or to view related screens at once.

And how cool would it be if you didn't have to write the code to transition from one screen to another? Imagine creating a user interface that displays a button, and when that button is tapped it transitions the screen to a new view. Now imagine doing this without writing any code. That is exactly what Apple has done with the storyboard feature, which was introduced with Xcode 4.2 and iOS 5.

Apple engineers have improved the way iOS developers can create user interfaces. They have made it possible for developers to see the entire makeup of an app's user interface, and they have eliminated the need for the trivial code used to transition from one screen to another. This is all done within a storyboard—but what is a storyboard?

Storyboarding streamlines the process of creating user interfaces and defines the transitions between view controllers. Under the hood, a storyboard still uses NIB files, but instead of having multiple NIBs within your project, you now have a single storyboard file that contains all the information that would otherwise be found in multiple NIBs. With a storyboard, you continue to use Interface Builder to design the UI because, after all, it's all based on NIB files.

Everything you already know about using IB applies to a storyboard. The same inspectors are available. The same Object library is available. You still have view controllers, and you still define outlets and actions. You connect objects to outlets and actions the same way you always have (e.g., **Control-click** and drag, Assistant editor). With a storyboard, you create a user interface exactly the same way you did with individual NIB files; the only difference is that you can now see all of the screens at one time.

> **Note**
>
> You are not limited to a single storyboard within a project. A project can contain as many storyboards as needed. Larger projects, for example, may have multiple storyboards, each representing a collection of related screens or specific areas of the application. Think of a storyboard as a collection of related NIBs (or screens) stored in a single file.

Using a Storyboard

You use a storyboard in much the same way you would use a NIB file. The only difference is that instead of your project including multiple NIB files, you now have a single storyboard containing a collection of NIBs. You can, however, intermix storyboards and NIBs within your project. Using a storyboard does not lock you into a single approach for UI design.

When you are creating a new project, most of the project templates give you the option of using a storyboard. The template code generated for the project will differ based on whether you select this option. Suppose, for example, you create a new project called MyAwesomeApp. This will generate the plist file *MyAwesomeApp-Info.plist*. This plist file contains settings about the app used by the operating system and the runtime environment. The file includes settings such as the name of the app, which is displayed on the iPad's Home screen. The app name is determined by a setting named Bundle Display Name (or CFBundleDisplayName, if you look at the raw key).

> **Note**
>
> When viewing the *Info.plist* for a project, you have the option to view the key name in plain English (e.g., Bundle Display Name) or as the raw key name (e.g., CFBundleDisplayName). To switch between the two view options, **Control-click** (or right-click) the plist editor and select **Show Raw Keys/Values** from the popup menu (Figure 14.1).

A project that uses a NIB file as the starting UI for the app (i.e., a project created from a template with the Use Storyboard option turned off) will have the raw key NSMainNibFile setting in its *Info.plist*. The key's value is the NIB file name that is used when the app is launched. A project using a storyboard as the starting UI will have the UIMainStoryboardFile setting defined in the *Info.plist* with the storyboard file name as the key's value.

Another notable difference between an app that launches with a NIB file and one that launches with a storyboard is the main window. All iOS applications have a main window, which contains the root view controller that manages the initial screen of the

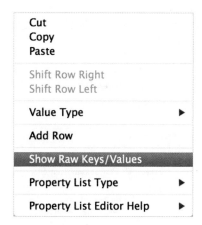

Figure 14.1   Use the popup menu to show and hide raw key values.

app. The generated project template for a NIB-based project will include a NIB and an outlet for the main window. This is not the case with a storyboard project, however. When the app launches with a storyboard, the main window is not defined in the project. Instead, it is automatically created when the storyboard loads.

Note

To better understand this difference in the NIB and storyboard approaches, create two new single-view application projects. In one, turn on the Use Storyboard option; in the other, turn off this option. Take a look at the generated project files. The storyboard-based project doesn't have any NIB files, only a single *MainStoryboard.storyboard* file. The code in the app delegate is also different. In the `-application:didFinishLaunchingWithOptions:` method for the NIB-based project, the `rootViewController` is set for the window. This code is not present in storyboard-based projects, as this task is handled behind the scenes.

Scenes

Storyboarding introduces two new concepts to UI design: a scene and a segue.

A scene is a view controller representing a particular aspect of the screen. For iPhone applications, a scene typically represents the full screen of the device. The same can be true for iPad apps. Alternatively, however, a scene for the iPad might represent only a portion of the screen, with a collection of scenes being used to form the entire screen at run time. In other words, multiple scenes are displayed simultaneously to form the whole screen. (You will learn how to break up the screen into multiple scenes in Chapter 15, "Doing More with View Controllers.")

Each scene is managed by a view controller, and every storyboard file has one and only one view controller flagged as the initial view controller (Figure 14.2). The initial view controller is the first scene displayed by the storyboard when it loads.

Figure 14.2   The Is Initial View Controller flag available in
the Attributes inspector

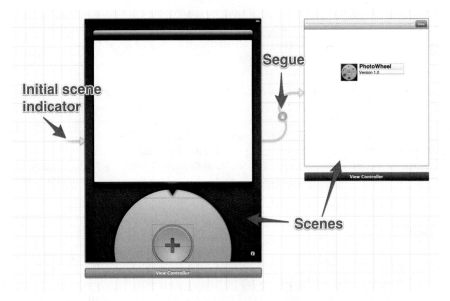

Figure 14.3   Sample storyboard with two scenes and one segue

Segues

The other new concept introduced with storyboards is that of a segue. A segue represents the transition between two scenes (Figure 14.3). It provides the magic needed to produce an animated transition from one scene to another without writing code.

A segue performs a transition from one scene to another when some event or action occurs within the first scene. For example, when a button is tapped in one scene, a segue performs the necessary work to display the next scene. The transition is often animated, with the new scene sliding up from the bottom or sliding in from right to left, similar to what you might see in a Keynote presentation. Other animated transitions are available as well, and you can even create your own custom animation sequence for a segue (which you will do later in this chapter).

What makes a segue cool—at least from the developer's perspective—is that the relationship between the two scenes and the transition is defined visually using Interface Builder. In other words, you don't have to write the code for it.

Granted, we as developers know that at some point code is needed, and this is also true with segues. While a segue manages the transition between two scenes, it doesn't have the smarts to pass data between the scenes. Also, in many cases a new scene must be told by the previous scene which content to display. Thankfully there is an event, `prepareForSegue:sender:`, that you override should you need to pass data between scenes. (You'll learn more about this method and using segues in the next chapter.)

Storyboarding PhotoWheel

So now you know what a storyboard is: a visual design canvas for creating user interfaces consisting of scenes (view controllers) and segues (transitions between scenes). To really understand a storyboard, however, you have to give it a go. Fortunately for you, it's time to create the real PhotoWheel application, so using a storyboard for the UI design seems appropriate. While we're at it, now is also a good time to introduce another feature in Xcode called workspace.

Workspace

An Xcode workspace is a container for one or more related projects. It provides the following benefits:

- The Project navigator provides quick access to related projects.
- Xcode automatically detects dependencies between projects and builds them in the correct sequence.
- Project files are visible to other projects, so there is no need to copy shared libraries into project folders.
- The scope of Xcode's content-aware features, such as code completion, extends across all projects within the workspace.

A workspace can also contain related projects that don't necessarily share code and are not dependent on one another. You can, for example, create a workspace containing the PhotoWheel prototype and the new PhotoWheel project. These two projects are related but not dependent on each other. With the workspace, you can switch quickly between the projects, make changes to either project, and build and run the projects, all from a single workspace window.

To create a new workspace, select **File > New > Workspace** (or **Control-Command-N**). Name the workspace "LearningiPadProgramming" and save it to the same directory containing the PhotoWheelPrototype Xcode project. You should now have an empty workspace window.

> **Note**
>
> Feel free to rename the directory containing the workspace file to "LearningiPadProgramming." This will help avoid confusion later when you use Finder to look for the workspace file. Be sure to close the workspace window before you rename the directory or Xcode will have a fit.

Select **File > Add Files to "LearningiPadProgramming"** (or **Option-Command-A**). Select the PhotoWheelPrototype Xcode project file and click the **Add** button (Figure 14.4). You now have one project contained in the LearningiPad-Programming workspace.

Now add a new project to the workspace. To do this, select **File > New > Project** (or **Shift-Command-N**). Alternatively, you can **Control-click** the Project navigator and select **New Project** from the popup menu. Select the **Empty Application** template under **iOS > Application**. Click the **Next** button to continue.

For the project options, enter "PhotoWheel" as the Product Name, select iPad for the Device Family, and select the Use Core Data option. Also, select the Use Automatic Reference Counting option. Click the **Next** button.

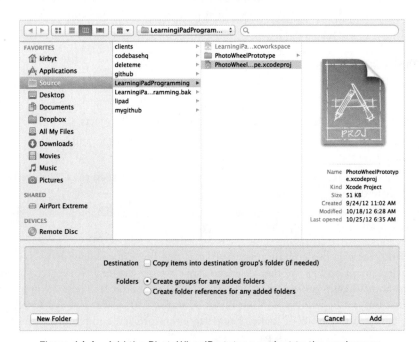

Figure 14.4   Add the PhotoWheelPrototype project to the workspace.

Set the Add to field to the LearningiPadProgramming workspace. This will auto-select the directory containing the workspace file as the default location for the new project. Also make sure LearningiPadProgramming is selected as the group, as seen in Figure 14.5.

Click the **Create** button to create the new project; this also adds the project to the workspace. You should now have a LearningiPadProgramming workspace containing two projects, PhotoWheel and PhotoWheelPrototype, as seen in Figure 14.6.

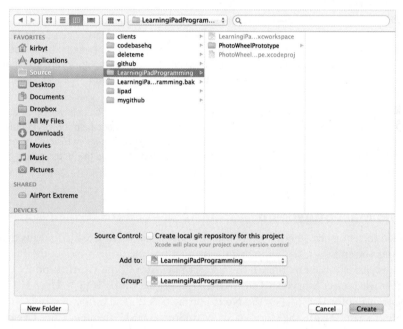

Figure 14.5   Create a new project in the LearningiPadProgramming workspace.

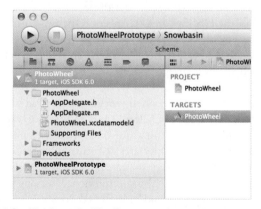

Figure 14.6   The LearningiPadProgramming workspace contains two projects, PhotoWheel and PhotoWheelPrototype.

Did you notice that there was no option for a storyboard? The Empty Application template creates a bare-bones project. At the moment, the project does not support a main storyboard or a NIB file. You can change this condition manually with a few simple steps. While we're at it, let's do a couple of other things to the project so that you can concentrate on development.

Why Are We Using the Empty Application Template?

Xcode's application templates are a great way to quickly get started on a new project. The same is true for file templates. The template generates the necessary code so that you can quickly get started, but over time you may find yourself deleting generated project files, renaming files, and deleting template code you won't ever use. Templates may also change with each release of Xcode, which means you must continually relearn what each template will and will not do for you.

Sometimes it's just easier to work with empty templates. With this approach, you do all the work, but with experience you'll find that it actually saves you time because you do not have to clean up the files and code generated by the template. Many developers choose to use empty templates instead of the existing application templates simply to avoid this housekeeping.

Add the Main Storyboard

You need to set up the PhotoWheel project to use a storyboard, which means that the first thing you must do is add the main storyboard to the project. Select the Photo-Wheel project or any of its files in the Project navigator. Type **Command-N** to create a new file. Select Storyboard as the file type (found under **iOS > User Interface**, as shown in Figure 14.7). Click the **Next** button. Select iPad as the device family, and click **Next** again. Name the storyboard "MainStoryboard," then click the **Create** button. The new storyboard file is added to the PhotoWheel project.

Before the storyboard can be used, it needs an initial view controller representing the initial scene. Select MainStoryboard in the Project navigator to open it. Open the Object library found in the Utilities area (**Control-Option-Command-3**). Drop a view controller object onto the storyboard's designer canvas. Next, drop a label onto the view managed by the view controller. This will give you something visual when you test that the storyboard is loading properly. Your storyboard should look similar to the one in Figure 14.8.

One thing you will quickly realize when working with iPad scenes is that they tend to take up a lot of screen real estate. A helpful tip is to hide parts of the workspace that you are not using while working on a storyboard. For instance, hide the Navigator area (**Command-0**) and the Utilities area (**Option-Command-0**). You can also double-click the design canvas to zoom in and out. This is helpful when you want to view multiple scenes at once. You can also use the hover buttons at the bottom left and right corners of the designer to show and hide the IB dock and to zoom in and out.

Just be aware that when you zoom out on a storyboard, edits cannot be performed. You must zoom in on a scene to make edits, add and remove objects, and so on.

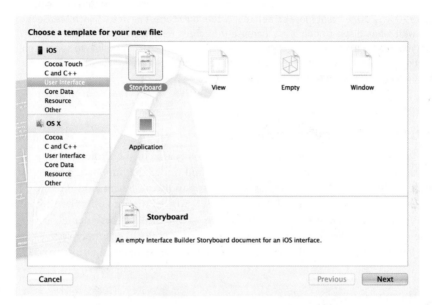

Figure 14.7   Add a new storyboard to the project.

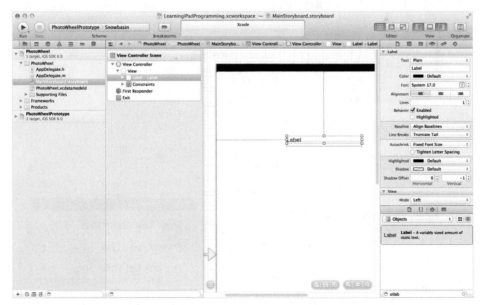

Figure 14.8   Screen shot of the PhotoWheel workspace with the main storyboard open in the IB editor

MacBook Pro with Retina Display Users

If you have a MacBook Pro with retina display, then you can change the screen resolution to 1920 × 1200 to claim more screen real estate for Xcode. I have a 15-inch MacBook Pro with retina display, and I often increase the screen resolution when I'm working on storyboards for iPad apps. The higher screen resolution makes it possible to see the entire scene and edit at the same time. Just remember to increase the font size for text within Xcode so that the source code is readable as well.

Set `UIMainStoryboardFile`

Next, you need to tell the project to use the storyboard. In the Project navigator, select the file *PhotoWheel-Info.plist*. It can be found under the Supporting Files group. **Control-click** the Editor area to display the popup menu. Select Add Row from the menu, as shown in Figure 14.9, to add a new row to the info.plist file. If you are viewing the keys in plain English, type "Main Storyboard file base name" as the key for the new row. (The editor should find the key for you if you simply type "Main story.") If you are viewing the raw keys, the key name is `UIMainStoryboardFile`.

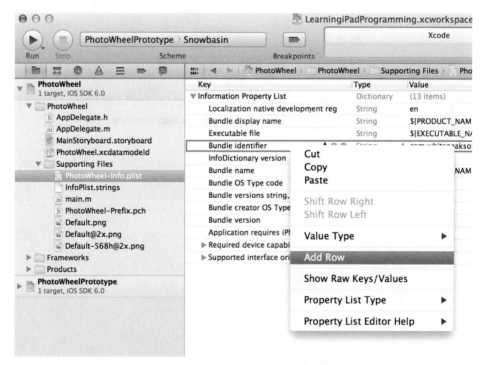

Figure 14.9   Add a row to the plist by Control-clicking the editor and selecting Add Row from the popup menu.

Next, enter "MainStoryboard" for the value. This is the name of the storyboard file you just created. However, do not include the file extension; it will be added automatically at run time. The setting is shown in Figure 14.10. Be sure to save (**Command-S**) your changes to the file.

Main storyboard file base name ⇕ ⊕ ⊖	String	⇕	MainStoryboard

Figure 14.10   Set the "Main storyboard file base name" to "MainStoryboard."

Update AppDelegate

The final step of the process is to change the -application:didFinishLaunching WithOptions: method in *AppDelegate.m* so that it will not create the main window. This may seem odd given that all iOS applications must have a main window, but the window is created automatically when the main storyboard is loaded. If the code in the app delegate were to remain, the main storyboard would not be attached to the correct window.

Open the file *AppDelegate.m* found in the Project navigator. Delete the first few lines of code in the -application:didFinishLaunchingWithOptions: method so that it matches the code in Listing 14.1.

Listing 14.1 Changes to *AppDelegate.m*

```
- (BOOL)application:(UIApplication *)application
didFinishLaunchingWithOptions:(NSDictionary *)launchOptions
{
    [self.window makeKeyAndVisible];
    return YES;
}
```

Save your changes and run the app. Make sure you have set the active scheme to PhotoWheel and the run destination to iPad 6.0 Simulator, as shown in Figure 14.11. You'll see PhotoWheel running in the simulator with its one scene containing the label. This outcome tells you that the project has been properly set up to use the main storyboard.

> **Note**
>
> This work is done automatically when you select a project template that has the Use Storyboard option turned on. Because this option is not available with the Empty Application template, you must handle the setup yourself.

Figure 14.11   Select PhotoWheel as the active scheme, and select iPad 6.0 Simulator as the run destination.

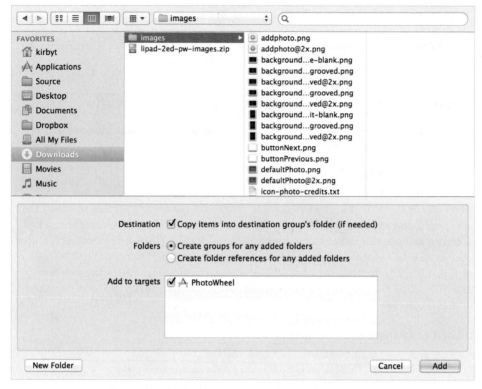

Figure 14.12   Add images to the PhotoWheel project.

Add Images

One more thing must happen before you start work on the PhotoWheel app. A number of images are used in the app—everything from the app icon to background images for views. Instead of adding the images piecemeal as you read the rest of the book, let's add those images now. This will save you steps later, and it will save trees (as in printed pages) because we won't have to tell you to add an image here and there.

Download the Images

The images used to create PhotoWheel can be downloaded from this book's Web site.[1] Download the .zip file containing the images, and unzip the archive on your system.

Now that you have downloaded the images used in PhotoWheel (you just did that, right?), it's time to add them to the PhotoWheel project. With the PhotoWheel project selected, select **File > Add Files to "PhotoWheel"** (or **Option-Command-A**).

---

1. Download source code and images: http://www.learningipadprogramming.com/
   source-code/

Navigate to and select the *images* folder that was created when you unpacked the *.zip* file. Be sure to select the Destination option of "Copy items into destination group's folder (if needed)" as shown in Figure 14.12; this copies the images into the Photo-Wheel project directory. Click the **Add** button to add the images to the project.

The images needed to complete PhotoWheel are now part of the project, and they will be available when you need them. There's no need to worry about adding images to the project in later parts of the book.

Retina Images

Take a moment to look through the list of images added to the PhotoWheel project. You'll notice two versions of each image: a normal-size version and a retina version. A retina version image is double the size of the normal-size image. For example, if a normal image is sized at 25 × 25 pixels, then the retina version is sized at 50 × 50 pixels.

You can easily identify the retina images by the @2x in the file name. iOS uses this file naming convention to determine which image to display at run time, freeing your app from the burden of checking the device's display type and loading the correct image. When your app references an image by name—say, *addphoto.png*—the runtime environment will look for and load *addphoto@2x.png* on devices supporting a retina display. On non-retina devices, *addphoto.png* is loaded.

If the @2x image is missing from the app and the app is running on a retina device, then the normal image is stretched to twice its size. However, a stretched image looks pixelated, so you should always include both the normal and retina images in your applications.

App Icon

With the images in place, there's no better time than the present to add the app icon to the project. When looking through the images, you probably noticed the multiple icon files (*Icon*.png*). Each of these represents the app icon; they are just at different resolutions. iPhone app icons are 57 × 57 pixels in size. iPad app icons are 72 × 72 pixels. Other sizes are used for things such as Spotlight's search icon, the Settings icon, and retina display. The different sizes enable the icon designer to add and remove detail as needed to make the best-looking app icon for the particular size.

iOS knows which icon to use for display purposes. If, for example, the app icon is displayed in the Settings app, iOS looks for an icon of size 29 × 29 pixels. If that image isn't found, iOS will use the main app icon (72 × 72 pixels for iPad and 57 × 57 pixels for iPhone) and scale it down to the appropriate size. If you have the app icon stored at different sizes, you can tell iOS about them by adding icon references in the project's *Info.plist*.

To accomplish this with the PhotoWheel app, open *PhotoWheel-Info.plist* and add the entries shown in Figure 14.13 to the plist. This tells iOS about the different-size app icons for PhotoWheel.

▼ Icon files	Array	(7 items)
Item 0	String	Icon.png
Item 1	String	Icon@2x.png
Item 2	String	Icon72x72.png
Item 3	String	Icon144x144.png
Item 4	String	IconSmall–50x50.png
Item 5	String	IconSmall.png
Item 6	String	IconSmall@2x.png

Figure 14.13   Add the list of icon file names to the *PhotoWheel-Info.plist*.

Initial View Controller

As previously mentioned, each storyboard will have an initial view controller, which consists of the first scene displayed when the storyboard is loaded. MainStoryboard has only one scene at the moment, so it is the initial view controller. If the storyboard contains multiple scenes, you can change the initial view controller by selecting the view controller and then choosing the Initial Scene setting in the Attributes inspector, as shown in Figure 14.14. Because MainStoryboard has only one scene for the moment, you do not need to worry about changing this setting right now. Instead, let's focus on setting up the storyboard.

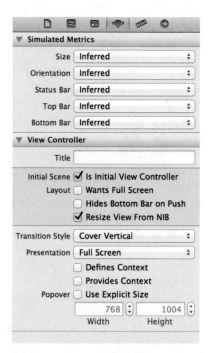

Figure 14.14   A storyboard with one scene flagged
as the initial view controller

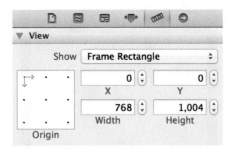

Figure 14.15   Size inspector values for the image view

Open MainStoryboard and select the one and only scene. Delete the label object added earlier, as it is no longer needed. You now have a clean slate to work with.

Drop an image view (UIImageView) onto the view managed by the scene's view controller. Set the image view to fill the entire view. A quick way to accomplish this is to open the Size inspector (**Option-Command-5**) and set the X, Y, Width, and Height values, as shown in Figure 14.15.

Next, open the Attributes inspector (**Option-Command-4**) and set the Image name to *background-portrait-grooved.png*. You can open the drop-down list to see the available images—that is, the images added to the project earlier.

Now add two more image views. The settings you want to use are listed in Table 14.1.

Next, add a button to the view. The button is listed in the Object library as Round Rect Button, or you can filter on "Button" or "UIButton." In the Attributes inspector, set the Type to Custom and set the Image to *stack-add.png*; this image is used when the button is in a normal state. To add the image representing the button in a down state, change the State Config from Default to Highlighted. Now set the Image to *stack-add-down.png*. The button, which is displayed as an image, now has visible normal and down states.

Switch to the Size inspector and set the following values for the button: X = 295, Y = 846, and Height and Width = 178. You should now see a round **+** button at the bottom of the scene.

One more visual addition to the scene is needed. Drop another Round Rect Button (UIButton) onto the view. Change its Type to Info Light. Set X = 722 and Y = 959; you cannot change its Width and Height because those are controlled by the system.

Table 14.1   **UIImageView Settings**

Image Name	X	Y	Width	Height
stack-viewer-bg-portrait.png	26	18	716	717
stack-bg.png	109	680	551	550

Figure 14.16   The PhotoWheel app running with the main scene
displayed in the simulator

The main scene is now complete. Run the app and take a look at your work. The
scene should look like Figure 14.16.

> **Note**
>
> If the arrow pointing to the wheel is not visible, you may need to reorder the images. You
> can accomplish this by selecting the image view for *stack-viewer-bg-portrait.png* and then
> selecting **Editor > Arrange > Send to Front** from the menu bar.

Another Scene

Another scene is needed, one that is displayed when the info button (the **i** button
at the lower right of the UI) is tapped. Create the new scene in MainStoryboard by
dropping in a new view controller from the Object library. You may want to zoom
out so that you can see the two views side by side, as shown in Figure 14.17.

This new scene displays the About screen for the app when the user taps the info
button found on the main scene. The first thing to add is a toolbar that is displayed
across the top of the scene. Find the toolbar in the Object library, drop it onto the
view of the new scene, and place it at the top of the view.

The toolbar comes with a default button labeled "Item." Let's move this button to
the right side of the toolbar. Next, filter the Object library with the word "Flexible" to
locate the flexible space bar button item in the object list. Drop this object just to the left
of the Item button in the toolbar, which moves the **Item** button to the far right.

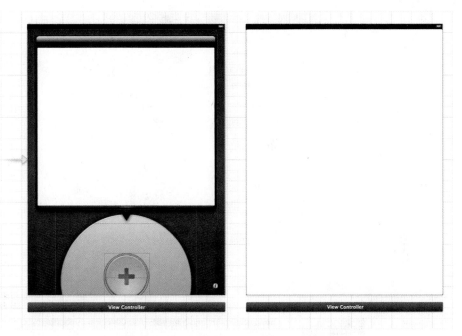

Figure 14.17   Storyboard with two scenes, zoomed out to see
both at the same time

Note

Another fixed space bar button item is available that you can use to separate toolbar items by a specific set of pixels.

The **Item** button is now positioned correctly, but we need to change it to read "Done." One way to do this is by changing the title of the button, but an even better way is to change the button's identifier. Select the **Item** button, and then open the Attributes inspector. Open the Identifier drop-down list to see the list of available system buttons. This list includes the buttons most commonly used in iOS apps, including the **Done** button. Change the Identifier from Custom to Done. This changes the display style of the button and sets its label to "Done."

Why Is This Approach Better?

Setting a button's identifier in the Attributes inspector is better because your app will use system-provided buttons whenever possible. One benefit here is that the buttons have already been localized and internationalized by Apple. Also, using system-provided buttons helps ensure consistency between apps, reducing the learning curve for the user.

Figure 14.18   Font settings popover

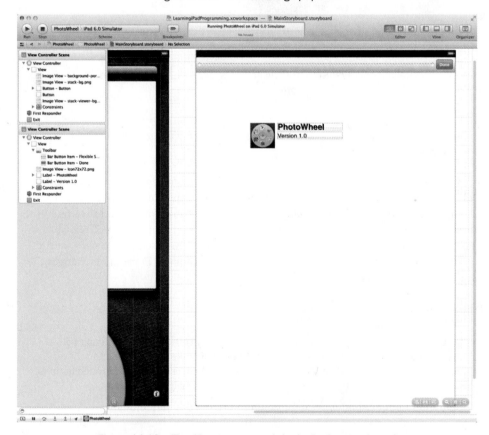

Figure 14.19   The About scene as it looks in the storyboard

Let's display the information about the app on the About scene. This scene will include the app icon in an image view, along with the name of the app and its version number. To accomplish this, drop an image view onto the view. Set the image name to *Icon72x72.png*. From the Size inspector, set X = 160, Y = 190, and Width and Height = 72.

Now add a label (`UILabel`) to the view, and set its Text to "PhotoWheel." In the Attributes inspector, set the Font to System Bold 24.0. (You can click the T icon in the Font field to display the popover with font settings, as shown in Figure 14.18.) Lastly, resize the label's width so that the text, "PhotoWheel," is not truncated. You can eyeball the position of the label or set the size manually (X = 240, Y = 190, Width = 193, and Height = 21).

Place another label below the PhotoWheel label. Set its Text to "Version 1.0" and its Font to System 18. Use the alignment guides (covered in Chapter 3, "Getting Started with Interface Builder") to position and size the label based on the PhotoWheel label, or set the size manually (X = 240, Y to= 215, Width = 193, and Height = 21). The scene should look similar to the one in Figure 14.19.

Creating a Segue

The storyboard now has two scenes, but there is no segue (also known as a transition) between them. What we want is to have the About scene display when the user taps the info button on the main scene. This can be accomplished without writing a single line of code.

Adjust the designer display so that you can see both scenes. You do not need to zoom completely out, but you do need to see portions of both scenes at the same time. Next, **Control-click** on the info button (**i**) in the main scene and drag it anywhere on the About scene. This displays the Storyboard Segues HUD, showing the various action segues that are available. Select modal to create a segue between the info button and the About scene. A line with an arrow at the end is drawn between the two scenes; the arrow represents the segue and shows the relationship between the two scenes.

Note

If your segue is not working when you run the app, it's possible that the segue was not created from the info button. The easiest way to fix this problem is to delete the segue and create it again, making sure you **Control-click** and drag from the info button to the About scene.

You can fine-tune the transition managed by the segue by clicking the segue arrow and then opening the Attributes inspector. Set the Identifier to AboutSceneSegue. The Identifier can be used to perform segues programmatically. Next, set the style, presentation, and transition for the segue.

We want the segue Style to be Modal, which should already be set for you. This style displays the About scene on top of the main scene. Set the Presentation to Form Sheet; this choice resizes the About scene to the smaller form size. Finally, leave the

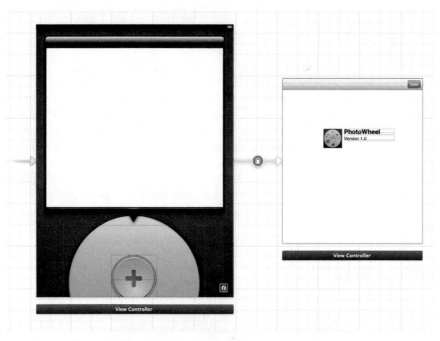

Figure 14.20 The storyboard with two scenes and a segue

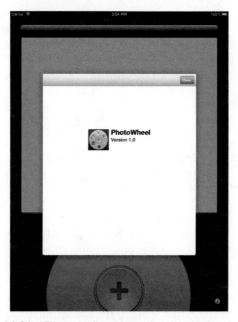

Figure 14.21 The completed app when run in the simulator

Transition set to Default (although you should play with other transition styles so that you can see how they differ). The storyboard should now look like Figure 14.20.

Run the app and take a look at your handiwork. The app displays the main scene when launched, and the About scene appears when the user taps the info button, as shown in Figure 14.21. All of this was accomplished without writing a single line of code. Of course, you'll quickly see that code is needed to dismiss the About scene when the **Done** button is tapped. You'll learn how to add code behind a scene in the next chapter, so for now you must quit the app to dismiss the About scene.

Summary

This chapter introduced a new way of creating user interfaces called storyboarding. A storyboard is built on top of Interface Builder, so everything you already know about building a UI in IB still applies. You also learned how to set up an empty application project to support storyboarding, and you were introduced to workspaces, a way to quickly access related projects from the same workspace window.

Exercises

1. Open *PhotoWheel-Info.plist*. Switch between the plain English and raw key values views.

2. Create a single-view application project. Select the Use Storyboard option. Now create a second project, but this time do not select the Use Storyboard option. Compare the two projects.

3. Create a workspace and add the two projects created in the previous exercise to the workspace.

4. Open MainStoryboard and change the style, presentation, and transitions for the AboutSceneSegue.

15

View Controllers and Segues

In Chapter 14, "Storyboarding in Xcode," you learned how to use a storyboard to build the initial user interface for PhotoWheel. You created the main storyboard, added two scenes to it, and used a segue to display the About scene from the main scene. All of this was accomplished without writing a single line of code—but we developers know an app cannot really be useful unless there is code.

This chapter shows you how to do more with your scenes by writing custom view controller classes, with each view controller managing a storyboard scene. You will also learn how to create and use custom segues to give your app that special somethin'-somethin'.

Implementing a View Controller

You learned early on in the book that when using a NIB file for a screen, a view controller class is implemented to coordinate the interactions between the view and model classes. You do the same with a storyboard. Each scene in the storyboard has its own view controller. In fact, to create a scene in a storyboard, you drop a view controller object from the Object library onto the design canvas. As a consequence, each scene, at a minimum, has a view controller, which is of type `UIViewController`. To do more, however, you will need to create your own `UIViewController` subclass.

Let's take a look at the About scene created in the last chapter. A segue connects the About scene to the main scene by way of the info button found in the lower-right corner of the main scene. When the user taps the button, the About scene is displayed. To close the About scene, the user taps the **Done** button, but it doesn't work. That's because you have not told the **Done** button what to do when the button is tapped.

How do you tell the **Done** button to dismiss the About scene? If you are thinking, "Use another segue," then you're partly right. iOS 6 introduced a new concept called an unwind segue. A segue guides the user forward through the app's UI. Conversely, an unwind segue takes the user backward—back to a previous scene within the storyboard.

Creating an unwind segue is different from creating a normal segue. First, you need to define a special action method, called an unwind action, in the view controller for the scene that you want to unwind to (i.e., the destination view controller). Then you must connect the action on an object, such as a button, to the unwind action method. Let's walk through the steps.

A custom view controller class must be defined before you can define the unwind segue action method. Your first instinct might be to create a custom view controller class for the About scene. After all, the **Done** button exists on the About scene, and the About scene is the scene you want to dismiss. However, for an unwind segue to work correctly, you must define the unwind action method on the destination scene. This means you need to create a custom view controller class for the main scene.

Start by selecting the PhotoWheel project in the workspace. Press **Command- N** to create a new file. Select the Objective-C class template and click the **Next** button. Name the class `MainViewController` and make it a subclass of `UIViewController` (Figure 15.1). Click the **Next** button, and save the class file in the project directory by clicking the **Create** button. The `MainViewController` has been added to the PhotoWheel project.

An unwind segue is needed for the **Done** button, so open the file *MainView Controller.m* and add the declaration for the unwind action method `-dismissAbout:` in the class extension section.

The class extension is the `@interface` section found toward the top of the file. It is used to extend the public interface of the class. Because the class extension is contained in the *.m* file, items such as ivars, properties, and methods remain private to the class. In other words, these items can be referenced only within the implementation of the class. However, Interface Builder is still able to detect outlets and actions defined

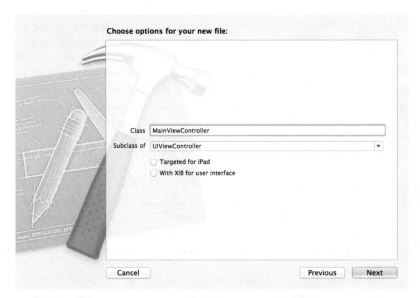

Figure 15.1   Create a new class named `MainViewController`, a subclass of `UIViewController`.

in the class extension, so you can make the appropriate connections in your NIB and storyboard files.

The changes you need to make to *MainViewController.m* are shown in Listing 15.1.

Listing 15.1 *MainViewController.h* **with the New Action Method -`dismissAbout`:**

```
#import "MainViewController.h"

@interface MainViewController ()
- (IBAction)dismissAbout:(UIStoryboardSegue *)segue;
@end

@implementation MainViewController

// Other code left out for brevity's sake.

- (IBAction)dismissAbout:(UIStoryboardSegue *)segue
{

}

@end
```

Notice that the unwind action method differs slightly from a standard action method. A standard action method has a parameter named `sender` that is of type `id`. The unwind action method also has a single parameter, but its type is `UIStoryboardSegue`. This slight difference is important. The parameter type is used by IB to detect that the action method is intended for an unwind segue.

The implementation for -`dismissAbout`: is blank. You do not need to do anything in this method. The segue handles the transition from the source scene to the destination scene for you. However, you can include code in this method should you need to retrieve information from the source or destination scenes prior to the actual transition. Suppose the source scene has a return value property that is needed by the destination scene. You can include code in the unwind segue action method that retrieves this property value and store it in the destination view controller.

For dismissing the About scene, no additional code is needed—hence the blank implementation.

Before the unwind segue can be used, you must change the class type of the main storyboard scene from `UIViewController` to `MainViewController`, and you must connect the **Done** button to the unwind segue action.

To accomplish this, open the *MainStoryboard.storyboard* file. Select the view controller for the main scene. If the document outline is visible (**Editor > Show Document Outline**), you can click the View Controller object in the IB dock. Otherwise, click the View Controller object in the object bar below the scene (Figure 15.2).

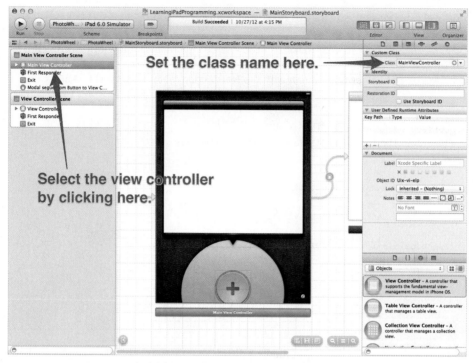

Figure 15.2   The Main View Controller Scene in the main storyboard

Open the Identity inspector (**Option–Command–3**). The Class defaults to UI ViewController. Change this value to MainViewController. Now the scene is aware of the MainViewController you created.

Next, connect the **Done** button to the -dismissAbout: unwind segue action declared in MainViewController. To accomplish this, **Control-drag** from the **Done** button to the Exit icon in the About scene. This will display a HUD showing the available unwind segue actions. Select dismissAbout: to connect the **Done** button to this action (Figure 15.3).

> **Note**
>
> Because the **Done** button is inside the toolbar, you might need to click the **Done** button twice to select it if the designer is zoomed in on the About scene.

Note that you connected the **Done** to the Exit icon in the About scene, not the Main View Controller scene. Yet the action -dismissAbout: is defined in the MainViewController class. How does this work?

When the **Done** button is tapped, the unwind segue executes. This unwind segue sends its assigned action message, which in this case is -dismissAbout:. The

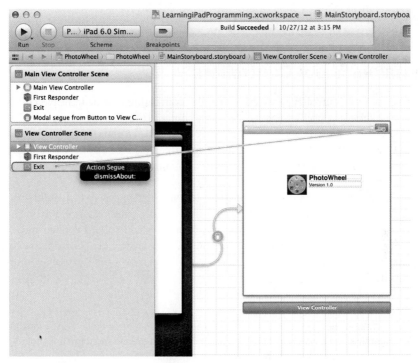

Figure 15.3   Connect the Done button to the `-dismissAbout:`
unwind segue action.

application framework checks the current view to see if it responds to this message. If it does not, the message is passed to the superview. If the view is managed by a view controller, the message is passed to the view controller before going to the superview. This gives the view controller a chance to respond to messages not handled by its views. The message is passed on to the superview if the view controller does not handle it. The message continues up the chain of potential responders (i.e., views and view controllers) until one is found that responds to the message.

Collectively, this string of views and view controllers is called the responder chain. The responder chain makes it possible for other objects in the view hierarchy to respond to a particular message. In the case of the **Done** button, the responder for the `-dismissAbout:` action is the `MainViewController`, but the unwind segue in the About scene does not know this, nor does it care. All it cares about is that some object in the responder chain will handle the event. This mechanism is how an unwind segue in one scene is associated to a destination view controller.

That's it. The **Done** button is now connected to the `-dismissAbout:` action method via an unwind segue, and when the user taps the button the About scene is closed. Save your changes and run the app. Everything should work smoothly now.

Now that the About scene is complete, let's take a look at how to break out a larger scene into a series of smaller scenes, each managed by its own view controller.

Container View Controllers

A container view controller is a view controller containing one or multiple child view controllers. It is used as a way to present content from a combination of different view controllers. `UINavigationController`, `UITabBarController`, and `UISplitViewController` are examples of container view controllers. A container view controller is the parent of the controllers it contains, forwarding messages and events to its children.

Using a custom container view controller in your iPad app is really useful, as it enables you to break down the entire screen into smaller parts, each of which is managed by its own view controller. In this way, each view controller becomes more focused in its role within the application. The code for each view controller becomes smaller and easier to maintain, and a view controller can become a reusable component within the application.

> **Note**
>
> Using a container view controller to separate pieces of the UI into smaller parts managed independently is not a new concept. The pattern has been around for some time now, especially in the Web world, where it is known as a composite view.

To make your own container view controller, you create a new class that subclasses `UIViewController`. Within your view controller class, you make use of the various containment view methods provided by `UIViewController`:

- `-addChildViewController:`
- `-removeFromParentViewController`
- `-transitionFromViewController:toViewController:duration: options:animations:completion:`
- `-willMoveToParentViewController:`
- `-didMoveToParentViewController:`

`UIViewController` also includes the property `childViewControllers`, which is a read-only `NSArray` containing the child view controllers for the container view controller.

A key feature of the container view controller is message forwarding. Prior to iOS 5's enhancements to `UIViewController` for container view controllers, it was up to the developer to create her own containment model, and building in reliable message forwarding was difficult to achieve. This is no longer the case. Important messages and events are forwarded to each child view controller, including rotation messages and view events such as -viewWillAppear:, -viewDidAppear:, -viewWillDisappear:, and -viewDidDisappear:.

Message forwarding can be turned off by overriding the methods -shouldAuto maticallyForwardRotationMethods and -shouldAutomaticallyForward AppearanceMethods in the container view controller. If the return value for these methods is NO, messages will not be forwarded to the child view controllers. The default implementations for these methods return YES, which means message forwarding is turned on by default.

Warning

If you do turn off forwarding, it is up to you to forward the appropriate messages to the child view controllers.

Using a container view controller is as simple as calling -addChildViewControl ler: and adding an instance of another view controller. When the view controller is added as a child, it receives the message -willMoveToParentViewController:, which includes the parent view controller as a parameter. You override this method in the child view controller to perform any necessary logic prior to the view controller becoming a child of the parent controller. It is then up to your code to perform any transitions needed for the presentation of the child view controller.

Once the transition is complete, your code must call -didMoveToParentView Controller: on the child view controller. This method is not called automatically because the parent view controller does not know about the transition, if any, for the child view controller. You can override this method in your child view controller to perform any necessary logic after the view controller has become a child of the parent controller.

Removing a child view controller from the parent follows a reverse workflow. You must first call -willMoveToParentViewController:, passing nil for the new parent view controller. You then call -removeFromParentViewController on the child view controller, which automatically calls -didMoveToParentViewController:.

Create a Container View Controller

Let's take advantage of containment views in our PhotoWheel app. The main screen has two distinct areas: the photo viewer at the top and the photo album wheel at the bottom. Managing both of these areas within the same view controller will result in a very lengthy view controller class that will be difficult to maintain. To get around this problem, let's make the main view controller a container view controller and separate the other two areas into child view controllers of the main controller.

You already created a custom view controller class named MainViewController for the main scene. Now do the same for the two child view controllers.

By now, the steps to create a new class should be familiar to you—but as a quick reminder, you want to press **Command-N** and select the Objective-C class template.

Name the first class `PhotosViewController` and make it a subclass of `UIView Controller`. Because you are using a storyboard, leave the "Target for iPad" and "With XIB for user interface" options turned off. Then save the new class to the PhotoWheel project directory. It will be the view controller for the scene displayed at the top of the main screen.

Do this again, but name the second class `AlbumsViewController`. This view controller will manage the scene displayed at the bottom of the main screen.

Add the Child Scenes

`PhotosViewController` and `AlbumsViewController` are the view controller classes for two new scenes you will create in the storyboard. Prior to iOS 6 and Xcode 4.5, there was no way within the storyboard to indicate that a scene was a child of another scene. This meant you were required to write code in the container view controller to add the child view controllers. This situation changed with iOS 6 and Xcode 4.5. Now it's possible to accomplish the same thing without writing a single line of code. Let's see how. . . .

iOS 5 Support

If you require iOS 5 support in your app, then you must programmatically add the child view controllers to the container view controller. The steps presented in this section only work with iOS 6 and later. Chapter 15, "Doing More with View Controllers," from the first edition of this book shows you how to accomplish the same view controller containment for the main screen but using code instead of IB.

The main scene in your storyboard already has the visual elements defined for the photos and albums display. The fastest way to split this scene into multiple scenes is to copy the visual elements from the main scene and paste them into new child scenes. If you were starting from scratch, you wouldn't need the copy–paste approach. That said, the steps are basically the same whether you are starting from scratch or cutting up an existing scene.

Here are the steps to follow:

1. Open the *MainStoryboard.storyboard* file.

2. Select and drag a *Container View* from the Objects library, and drop it on the main scene. You can filter the Objects library by typing "contain" in the filter bar.

3. Size and position the container view on top of the image view displaying the image *stack-viewer-bg-portrait.png*. This is the top screen area that will display the photos from an album. If you like, you can use the Size inspector to size and position the container view. Just set X = 26, Y = 20, Width = 716, and Height = 715.

4. Notice that a new scene with an attached segue is created for you when you drop the container view on the main scene. Move the new scene so that it sits next to the main scene in the design canvas.

5. Using the Document Outline, select the image view containing the image *stack-viewer-bg-portrait.png*, and cut it to the clipboard (**Command-X**).

6. Select the new child scene created when you dropped the container view onto the main scene, and paste the image view into the scene (**Command-V**).

7. Position the image view to fill the entire scene. A quick way to do this is to set X and Y equal to 0 in the Size inspector. Notice that the scene is automatically sized to the width and height defined by the container view in the main scene, so you do not need to set those values.

8. Select the view for the child scene, open the Attributes inspector (**Option-Command-4**), and set the background color to Clear Color.

9. Select the view controller object for the new child scene, open the Identity inspector, and set the Class to `PhotosViewController`. Make sure you are changing the class for the view controller, and not for the image view.

You storyboard should now look similar to Figure 15.4.

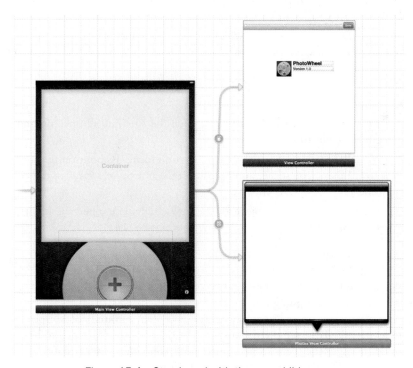

Figure 15.4   Storyboard with the new child scene

When you dropped the container view onto the main scene, a new scene with an attached segue was created for you. This segue is called an *embedded segue*. It connects the child scene with the container view found in another scene.

If you were trying to use an existing scene as a child scene, you would still drag and drop a container view onto the main scene, but this time you would delete the scene and embedded segue created for you. Next, you would **Control-drag** from the container view to the existing child scene to create the embedded segue.

Because you do not have an existing child scene for albums display area, you'll continue using the copy-paste approach. Follow these steps to move the bottom portion of the main scene to a child scene.

1. Drag a container view onto the main scene.

2. Size and position the container view to cover the image view displaying the image *stack-bg.png*. If you like, use the Size inspector (**Option-Command-5**) to set X = 109, Y = 680, Width = 551, and Height = 550.

3. Make sure the newest container view appears in front of the other container view. If you do not, then the pointer from the top image view will be hidden by the disc image. You can change the order by dragging and dropping the container view object in the Document Outline, or you can select the container view and choose **Editor > Arrange > Send Forward** or **Send Backward** as needed.

4. Using the Document Outline, select the image view containing the image *stack-bg.png* and the button displaying the *stack-add.png* image, and cut them to the clipboard (**Command-X**).

5. Move the new child scene so that it sits to the right of the main scene on the design canvas.

6. Select the view in the new child scene, open the Attributes inspector, and set its background color to Clear Color.

7. Paste the clipboard contents into the new child scene. Reposition the image view to fill the entire scene, and reposition the button to appear in the center of the scene.

8. Select the view controller object for the new child scene, open the Identity inspector, and set the Class to `AlbumsViewController`.

Your storyboard should now look similar to Figure 15.5.

Take a look at your handiwork by building and running the project. How does it look? Not so good, eh? The background color for the views in the child scenes was set to Clear Color, so what's going on?

The container views in the main scene also have a background color. Both are set to white by default. To make them transparent—a characteristic needed to see the background image of the main scene—select both container views and change the background color from White Color to Clear Color in the Attributes inspector.

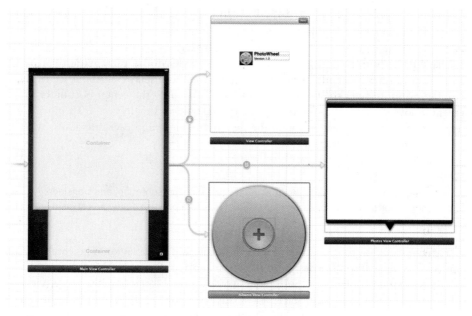

Figure 15.5   Storyboard with two child scenes

Now run the app again. The app looks like it did before you split the main scene into child scenes. At this point, you may be asking yourself, "Why bother? After all, the app looks the same as it did before."

The benefit of using view controller containment is to separate responsibilities into individual view controllers. This makes your code much more manageable compared to having a single, monolithic view controller for the main screen of the app. The benefits of containment will become clearer in the next chapter, Chapter 16, "Building the Main Screen."

Containment also makes reuse of views and view controllers much easier. Photo Wheel is too small of an app to warrant much reuse, but in larger apps, it's not uncommon for the same view to be presented within multiple screens. By using containment and child view controllers, you can easily reuse the child scene in other areas of your app.

Segue

Before we move on to building out the PhotoWheel app, let's talk a bit more about segues. A segue, as you already know, manages the transition between two scenes. You have already seen examples of segues in action. You used a modal segue to display the About scene, and you used an unwind segue to dismiss the About scene.

You also know that a segue is defined visually within the storyboard, and you use the Attributes inspector to fine-tune it. You fine-tune the segue by combining its style, presentation, and transition. For instance, the segue for the About scene created in Chapter 14, "Storyboarding in Xcode," uses the style Modal, presentation Form Sheet, and transition Default. When this segue is used to display the About scene, the scene animates up from the bottom (transition). It fills only the center portion of the screen; it does not take over the full screen (presentation). In addition, it's a modal view (style), meaning it sits on top of the underlying view, and user interaction with the underlying view is disabled.

> **Note**
>
> Not all segue types have the same three properties: style, presentation, and transition. A push segue, for example, has style and destination, and a popover segue has style, direction, anchor, and pass-through.

This combination of properties defines the segue and its behavior. The combination you use depends on the design of the scene and app. For example, if the app was using a navigation controller, a push segue would be used to push a new scene (view controller) onto the navigation stack. Alternatively, a popover segue might be used to display a view within a popover. There's even a replace-style segue that replaces one scene with another.

But what if you cannot find the ideal segue for your app's needs? For such a case, you can create a custom segue.

Creating a Custom Segue

A custom segue is a segue that you implement to suit the needs of your app. Creating a custom segue gives you complete control over the segue's behavior. Suppose you want to have an explosion-style animation that starts from the center of the screen when transitioning from one scene to another. (Not that you would, but let's use that as an example.) The iOS SDK doesn't provide a segue for this type of effect, so you will need to create one.

To create a custom segue, you create a new class that subclasses `UIStoryboardSegue`. In the class implementation, you override the `-(void)perform` method to perform the custom transition. The segue provides access to both the source and destination view controllers, so you can change the transition based on these two controllers.

Let's take a closer look at a custom segue by creating one.

Setting the Scene

PhotoWheel needs a way to display a photo browser when a photo is tapped, and the photo browser needs a way to return to the main scene with a tap of a finger. But unlike the About scene, the photo browser should not be modal; it should fill the entire screen.

iOS provides a controller class named `UINavigationController` that manages a stack of view controllers. The top view controller in the stack is the visible controller. A new controller is added to the stack with a push (the `-pushViewController:animated:` method). This makes the new controller the top controller, which in turn makes it the visible controller. To return to a previous controller in the stack, a pop is performed. The navigation controller enables an app to pop the top controller (`-popViewControllerAnimated:`) or pop to a specific controller within the stack (`-popToViewController:animated:`), including the root view controller (`-popToRootViewControllerAnimated:`), which is at the bottom of the stack.

The navigation controller is perfect for PhotoWheel! The main view controller is the root controller on the navigation stack because it's the first controller displayed. When the user taps a photo, the photo browser view controller is pushed onto the navigation stack. This displays the photo browser.

To get back to the main scene, the user needs to tap a **Back** button, which is provided by the navigation controller. The navigation controller displays a navigation bar at the top of the screen. A **Back** button is displayed on the left that enables the user to navigate back to the previous view controller in the stack.

Before you implement the custom segue, let's add the photo browser scene to the storyboard. Also, let's use the standard push segue to transition between the main scene and the photo browser scene.

Open the *MainStoryboard.storyboard* file and create a new scene by dropping a view controller object onto the design canvas. This new scene will be the photo browser that you implement later.

Next, drop a Round Rect Button somewhere onto the Photos View Controller scene. This button will be used on a temporary basis to test the transition from the main scene to the photo browser scene. Wait? The transition from the *main* scene to the photo browser scene? Yes, this is correct.

If the button you placed in the Photos View Controller scene were placed in the main scene, you would **Control-drag** from the button to the new photo browser scene to create a new segue. However, you're using child scenes now. If you were to connect the button in the child scene to the photo browser scene, then the segue would transition the child scene to the photo browser scene. In other words, the segue would attempt to display the photo browser scene within the child scene, but because the child scene was not contained in the navigation controller, nothing would happen.

We want to replace the main scene with the photo browser scene when the button is tapped; we don't want to replace just the child scene. Therefore you will not connect the button to the photo browser scene. Instead, you will create a new segue that connects the main scene to the photo browser scene, and you will programmatically call that segue when the user taps the button.

Let's start by adding the action method that is called when the button is tapped. The segue should be performed in the main scene, not the child scene, so you will add the action to `MainViewController`. Open the file *MainViewController.m* and add the code shown in Listing 15.2.

Listing 15.2 **New Action to Perform Segue**

```
#import "MainViewController.h"

@interface MainViewController ()
- (IBAction)dismissAbout:(UIStoryboardSegue *)segue;
- (IBAction)pushPhotoBrowser:(id)sender;
@end

@implementation MainViewController

- (IBAction)dismissAbout:(UIStoryboardSegue *)segue
{

}

- (IBAction)pushPhotoBrowser:(id)sender
{
    [self performSegueWithIdentifier:@"PushPhotoBrowser" sender:sender];
}

@end
```

The method -performSegueWithIdentifier:sender: is used to programmatically start the segue. This method can be used to perform any segue defined in the current storyboard for the view controller.

Next, open the file *MainStoryboard.storyboard* and make the following changes:

1. Create a push segue between the main scene and the photo browser scene. You can accomplish this by **Control-dragging** from the main scene to the photo browser scene, as shown in Figure 15.6.

2. Select *Push* as the segue type.

3. Click the segue, open the Attributes inspector, and set the Identifier to "Push-PhotoBrowser." Note that the identifier value must match the identifier specified in Listing 15.2.

It's now time to connect the button to the –pushPhotoBrowser: action. The action is defined in MainViewController. Thus, instead of making the connection via the File's Owner, you will connect the button to the action by way of the First Responder. This uses the responder chain, discussed earlier, to find and invoke the method defined in the MainViewController. To make the connection, click-drag from the button to the First Responder object in the Photos View Controller Scene, and select the pushPhotoBrowser event (Figure 15.7).

If you run the app, you might be surprised to learn that the new scene does not appear when the button is tapped. This is because the new scene is pushed onto the

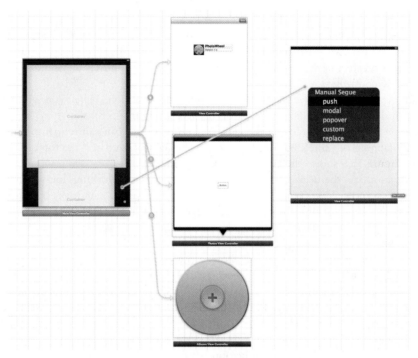

Figure 15.6   Creating a segue between the main and photo browser scenes

Figure 15.7   Connecting the button to the action method

navigation stack, but the storyboard does not have a scene with a navigation controller. You can quickly remedy this problem by selecting the main scene in the storyboard and choosing **Editor > Embed In > Navigation Controller** from the menu bar. These steps create a new scene for the navigation controller and set the scene as the initial view controller.

Run the app again to see the navigation controller in action. When you tap the button in the child scene (at the center on the left of Figure 15.8), the photo browser scene is pushed onto the stack (at the right in Figure 15.8). You can return to the main scene by tapping the **Back** button displayed in the navigation bar at the top of the screen. Figure 15.8 shows the two scenes side by side.

Navigation and the transition between the two scenes are working, but some things are not quite right. The navigation bar at the top of the main scene looks out of place. Not only that, but it causes the rest of the screen to shift downward. You can fix this problem by hiding the navigation bar—but if you hide it, the navigation bar won't be visible in the second scene. If it's not visible there, the user won't have any way of returning to the main scene from the photo browser scene.

The other issue is the transition from the main scene to the photo browser scene. While the default transition of sliding the next view from right to left is fine for many apps, it won't look so great once PhotoWheel displays pictures. The effect we want is to have the transition explode from the touch point, so that when you touch a photo, the image expands out in a view. This is the perfect job for a custom segue.

First things first: Let's fix the navigation bar display before we move on to the custom segue.

The navigation bar should have a black style. This makes it blend in better with the PhotoWheel app's look and feel. To change the style, you need to open the Document

Figure 15.8   Side-by-side view of the main and photo browser scenes

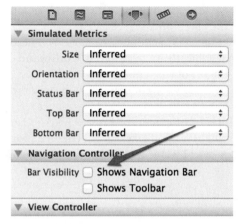

Figure 15.9   Deselect the Shows Navigation Bar option.

Outline, select the Navigation Controller Scene, and click on the disclosure icon for the Navigation Controller object. Click on the navigation bar object to select it, then open the Attributes inspector (**Option-Command-4**). In the Inspector, change the Style from Default to Black Translucent.

Next, you want to hide the navigation bar so that it does not appear on the main screen. To hide the navigation bar, open the *MainStoryboard.storyboard* file and select the Navigation Controller Scene. Open the Attributes inspector (**Option-Command-4**) and deselect the Shows Navigation Bar attribute (shown in Figure 15.9). You can see that the navigation bar is hidden in the storyboard scenes when you deselect this option.

Now that the navigation bar is hidden, the user will not have a way to return to the main scene from the photo browser scene. There are two possible ways to solve this problem:

- Show the navigation bar in `-viewWillAppear:` for the photo browser view controller.
- Include the showing of the navigation bar in the custom segue.

In PhotoWheel, we have chosen the second option because it enables you to control the animation sequence for presenting the navigation bar. Let's implement that custom segue.

Implementing a Custom Segue

A custom segue is needed to override the default visual transition provided by the push segue. To use a custom segue, you change the segue attributes using the Attributes inspector. Open the main storyboard if it isn't already open. Select the segue that is performed when the button is tapped, and open the Attributes inspector. Change the Style from Push to Custom, and set the segue Class to `CustomPushSegue`. Now when the button is tapped, the custom push segue is used, and it handles the transition from the main scene to the photo browser scene.

But where is the class CustomPushSegue? Answer: You need to create it.

Start by creating a new Objective-C class. Press **Command-N** and select Objective-C class from the list of file templates. Name the class CustomPushSegue and set it as a subclass of UIStoryboardSegue. Finally, save the new class to the PhotoWheel project.

A UIStoryboardSegue subclass must override the -perform method. This is where the animation for the transition takes place. The -perform implementation for CustomPushSegue is given in Listing 15.3. Open *CustomPushSegue.m* and make the changes to your code.

Listing 15.3 *CustomPushSegue.m*

```
#import "CustomPushSegue.h"
#import "UIView+PWCategory.h"                                          // 1

@implementation CustomPushSegue

- (void)perform
{
    UIView *sourceView = [[self sourceViewController] view];          // 2
    UIView *destinationView = [[self destinationViewController] view]; // 3

    UIImageView *sourceImageView;
    sourceImageView = [[UIImageView alloc]
                        initWithImage:[sourceView pw_imageSnapshot]]; // 4

    UIImageView *destinationImageView;
    destinationImageView = [[UIImageView alloc]
                            initWithImage:[destinationView pw_imageSnapshot]];
    CGRect originalFrame = [destinationImageView frame];
    [destinationImageView setFrame:CGRectMake(originalFrame.size.width/2,
                                              originalFrame.size.height/2,
                                              0,
                                              0)];
    [destinationImageView setAlpha:0.3];                             // 5


    UINavigationController *navController;
    navController = [[self sourceViewController] navigationController]; // 6
    [navController pushViewController:[self destinationViewController]
                             animated:NO];                            // 7

    UINavigationBar *navBar = [navController navigationBar];          // 8
    [navController setNavigationBarHidden:NO];
```

```
[navBar setFrame:CGRectOffset(navBar.frame,
                             0,
                             -navBar.frame.size.height)];            // 9

[destinationView addSubview:sourceImageView];                        // 10
[destinationView addSubview:destinationImageView];                   // 11

void (^animations)(void) = ^ {                                       // 12
    [destinationImageView setFrame:originalFrame];                   // 13
    [destinationImageView setAlpha:1.0];                             // 14

    [navBar setFrame:CGRectOffset(navBar.frame,
                                 0,
                                 navBar.frame.size.height)];         // 15
};

void (^completion)(BOOL) = ^(BOOL finished) {                        // 16
    if (finished) {
        [sourceImageView removeFromSuperview];
        [destinationImageView removeFromSuperview];
    }
};

[UIView animateWithDuration:0.6
              animations:animations
              completion:completion];                                // 17
}

@end
```

Let's walk through the code and see what is happening:

1. On the second line, you see `#import "UIView+PWCategory.h"`. This is a category on `UIView` that you will implement momentarily. (It will have a method named `pw_imageSnapshot`.) This method takes a screen shot of the view and returns that screen shot as a `UIImage`. Screen shot images of the source and destination views are used to simplify the animation sequence for this segue and improve performance for the sequence.

2–3. At the top of `-perform`, two local variables are set, one for the source view and another for the destination view. The local variables make referencing the views easier later in the code.

4. Local variables are now set for image views that contain the source and destination screen shot images. These image views—not the actual images—are what will be animated.

5. The original frame for the destination image view is saved to a local variable. The destination image view frame is then set with a Width and Height of 0 and is placed in the center of the screen. The alpha for the destination image view is set to 0.3. This value gives the view a transparent look. Setting the alpha to 0.0 will hide the view, and setting it to 1.0 will make it fully visible. As part of the animation sequence, this view will go from a transparent look (alpha = 0.3) to fully visible (alpha = 1.0).

Note

The ultimate goal is to perform the segue animation sequence from the photo that has been touched, but no photos are displayed in PhotoWheel yet. Therefore, the animation sequence starts from the center of the screen. The code for the segue will evolve over time as you build the app, and eventually the animation sequence will start from the appropriate location.

6–7. The next line of code saves a reference to the navigation controller to a local variable. The navigation controller is then used to push the destination view controller onto the navigation controller stack. Note that the animated flag is set to NO. This means that the default animation used during a push is turned off. The default animation sequence is not needed because the segue is performing the animation sequence.

8. Following the push of the destination view controller, a reference to the navigation bar is saved. The navigation bar is then unhidden. Remember, we need the navigation bar to be displayed on the destination view controller (i.e., the photo browser scene). Without it, the user will have no way to return to the main scene.

9. Simply showing the navigation bar during the animation sequence is okay, but having it slide down from the top would look even better. After the navigation bar is unhidden, it is moved off the top of the screen. CGRectOffset() is used to adjust the frame for the navigation bar. It returns a rectangle that is offset from the source rectangle. In this case, the offset is the negative of the navigation bar's height, which moves it off the top of the screen by the same number of points as the height.

Note

CGRectOffset is but one of the many helper functions found in CGGeometry, which makes working with and manipulating CGRect, CGSize, and CGPoint variables easier. For a complete list of functions, take a look at the CGGeometry Reference document.[1]

1. CGGeometry Reference: http://developer.apple.com/library/ios/#documentation/ GraphicsImaging/Reference/CGGeometry/Reference/reference.html

10–11. The source image view (containing the screen shot of the source view) and the destination image view (containing the screen shot of the destination view) are now added to the view hierarchy of the destination view controller. Why do this?

The destination view controller has been pushed onto the navigation stack. That makes the destination view controller the topmost controller, which means its view is the visible view. Adding the screen shot images from the source and destination views to the destination view controller's view hierarchy makes these image views the visible elements on the screen. Moreover, because the destination image view starts out as an alpha of 0.3, the source image view shows through the transparency of the destination image view.

12. With the destination view controller having been set up, it's now time to define the animation sequence. An animation block is defined for the animation sequence, which performs three primary steps.

13. The code resizes the destination image view to its original size. The resize operation is animated, so the visual effect is that the view grows in size.

14. The destination image view goes from a transparent visual state to a fully visible state by setting the alpha to 1.0. This, too, is animated, so the transition from transparent to fully visible occurs gradually during the animation sequence. The source image view is hidden once the destination image view is fully visible.

15. The navigation bar slides down from the top of the screen. Here CGRectOffset is used again, this time to move the navigation bar to the top of the screen. Because the move is animated, the user sees a slide-down effect. That's it for the animation sequence.

16. Following the animation sequence is the completion block declaration. The completion block is called once the animation sequence is complete. The completion block removes the source and destination image views from the destination view controller's view hierarchy. These static images of the screens are no longer needed, which is why they are removed. Because it is the destination image view that is the visible element on the screen, and because this element consists of an exact screen shot of the destination view, removing the image views is not noticeable to the user.

17. The final line of code in -perform executes the animation sequence. The duration for the sequence is set to 0.6 second, and the animation and completion blocks are passed in.

Slow Motion

To see the animation sequence in slow motion, change the duration to some number of seconds longer than 0.6 second, such as 20 or 30 seconds.

Before You Compile

Before you compile and run the app, you still need to add the `UIView+PWCategory` to the PhotoWheel project. Press **Command-N** to create a new file. This time select the Objective-C category template instead of the class template. Name the category "PWCategory" and set the "Category on" field to `UIView`, as seen in Figure 15.10.

Open *UIView+PWCategory.h* and add the code in Listing 15.4.

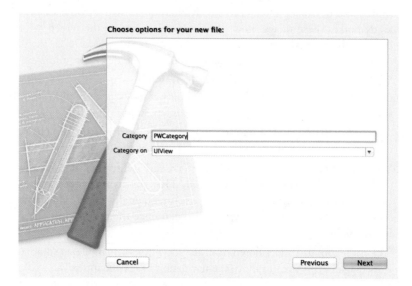

Figure 15.10   Select the Objective-C category template

Listing 15.4   *UIView+PWCategory.h*

```
#import <UIKit/UIKit.h>

@interface UIView (PWCategory)

- (UIImage *)pw_imageSnapshot;

@end
```

Now open *UIView+PWCategory.m* and add the code in Listing 15.5.

Listing 15.5   *UIView+PWCategory.m*

```
#import "UIView+PWCategory.h"
#import <QuartzCore/QuartzCore.h>

@implementation UIView (PWCategory)
```

```
- (UIImage *)pw_imageSnapshot
{
    UIGraphicsBeginImageContext([self bounds].size);
    [[self layer] renderInContext:UIGraphicsGetCurrentContext()];
    UIImage *image = UIGraphicsGetImageFromCurrentImageContext();
    UIGraphicsEndImageContext();

    return image;
}

@end
```

> **Note**
>
> A category extends a class. Because you are not the owner of the class, it is always a good idea to prefix category method names. This reduces the chances of a conflict should the class owner, which in this case is Apple, decide to add a method name `imageSnapshot`.

You should now be able to compile and run the app. When you do, tap the button that invokes `CustomPushSegue` and watch your handiwork in action.

Customizing the Pop Transitions

A segue is a great way to visually represent a transition between two scenes. However, in the case of a navigation-based app (meaning an app, such as PhotoWheel, that uses a navigation controller), a segue defines the transition for pushing only. There is no way to define a segue for popping a view controller from the navigation controller stack. Even an unwind segue will not help out here.

If you can't use a segue for the pop transition, which other options are available? You could create your own navigation controller model, but that would be time-consuming. After all, who really wants to reinvent that wheel? (No pun intended.) The easier approach is to subclass `UINavigationController`.

Subclassing the navigation controller is an easy way to override the default behavior provided by the class. But keep in mind that `UINavigationController` does a lot for you, and it can be easy to mess something up by subclassing it. In fact, the documentation for `UINavigationController` says, "This class is not intended for subclassing." This statement doesn't mean you can't subclass it, but it is a warning to deter you from doing so.

That said, there is no other way, other than subclassing, to override the default transition from a pop on the navigation controller. To have a pop transition that is consistent with the push segue, you must subclass `UINavigationController`. There is no getting around it.

To subclass `UINavigationController`, create a new class (**Command-N**) using the Objective-C class template. Name the class `CustomNavigationController` and make it a subclass of `UINavigationController`. Leave the options "Targeted for iPad" and "With XIB for user interface" turned off.

To change the pop transition, you must override the -popViewControllerAnimated: method. The new implementation is shown in Listing 15.6. Open *Custom NavigationController.m* and add the code from the listing to your class implementation.

Listing 15.6   *CustomNavigationController.m*

```objc
#import "CustomNavigationController.h"
#import "UIView+PWCategory.h"


@implementation CustomNavigationController


- (UIViewController *)popViewControllerAnimated:(BOOL)animated
{
    UIViewController *sourceViewController = [self topViewController];

    // Animate image snapshot of the view
    UIView *sourceView = [sourceViewController view];
    UIImage *sourceViewImage = [sourceView pw_imageSnapshot];
    UIImageView *sourceImageView = [[UIImageView alloc]
                                    initWithImage:sourceViewImage];

    NSArray *viewControllers = [self viewControllers];
    NSInteger count = [viewControllers count];
    NSInteger index = count - 2;

    UIViewController *destinationViewController;
    destinationViewController = [viewControllers objectAtIndex:index];
    UIView *destinationView = [destinationViewController view];
    UIImage *destinationViewImage = [destinationView pw_imageSnapshot];
    UIImageView *destinationImageView = [[UIImageView alloc]
                                         initWithImage:destinationViewImage];

    [super popViewControllerAnimated:NO];

    [destinationView addSubview:destinationImageView];
    [destinationView addSubview:sourceImageView];

    CGRect frame = [destinationView frame];
    CGPoint shrinkToPoint = CGPointMake(frame.size.width / 2,
                                        frame.size.height / 2);
```

```
void (^animations)(void) = ^ {
    [sourceImageView setFrame:CGRectMake(shrinkToPoint.x,
                                         shrinkToPoint.y,
                                         0,
                                         0)];
    [sourceImageView setAlpha:0.0];

    // Animate the nav bar, too
    UINavigationBar *navBar = [self navigationBar];
    [navBar setFrame:CGRectOffset(navBar.frame, 0, -navBar.frame.size.height)];
};

void (^completion)(BOOL) = ^(BOOL finished) {
    [self setNavigationBarHidden:YES];
    // Reset the nav bar position
    UINavigationBar *navBar = [self navigationBar];
    [navBar setFrame:CGRectOffset(navBar.frame, 0, navBar.frame.size.height)];

    [sourceImageView removeFromSuperview];
    [destinationImageView removeFromSuperview];
};

[UIView transitionWithView:destinationView
                  duration:0.3
                   options:UIViewAnimationOptionTransitionNone
                animations:animations
                completion:completion];

    return sourceViewController;
}

@end
```

The code in Listing 15.6 is similar to the code for CustomPushSegue, so a thorough walk-through is not necessary. The primary difference is that the code for -popView ControllerAnimated: reverses the animation sequence found in CustomPushSegue. Also, -popViewControllerAnimated: returns a reference to the view controller that is popped from the navigation stack. The rest of the code should look familiar to you.

To use the new CustomNavigationController class, we need to change the class name for the navigation controller created in the initial view controller defined in the storyboard. Open the file *MainStoryboard.storyboard*. Select the navigation controller in the Navigation Controller Scene, and then open the Identity inspector. Change the class from UINavigationController to CustomNavigationController, as shown in Figure 15.11.

Run the app again and check out the new pop transition. That looks much better.

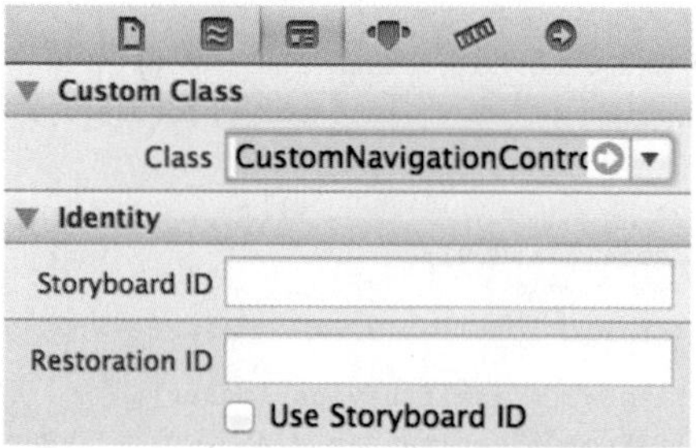

Figure 15.11   Set the class name for the navigation view controller

Fixing the Done Bug

Unwind segues are new in iOS 6 and, as with any new software feature, the chances for bugs are greater because the feature is new. This true for the code you write, and it's true for the code Apple engineers write. We're all human, after all, and bugs (unfortunately) happen in software development.

You may have noticed that the **Done** button on the About scene no longer dismisses the scene. This bug was introduced into the app after the main scene was embedded into the navigation controller. Although the bug is realized in the PhotoWheel app, it's not caused by the code in PhotoWheel. Instead, there is a bug in the unwind segue feature. This bug only appears on the iPad; it does not happen on the iPhone.

When an unwind segue is used to dismiss a modal view and the destination view is contained in a navigation controller, the unwind action is called, but the transition from the source view controller to the destination view controller never happens. In other words, the source scene is not dismissed.

This is only true for the iPad—the unwind segue correctly performs the dismiss transition on the iPhone. I verified this in a sample project that recreates the problem on both iOS 6.0 and the first beta version of iOS 6.1, and I submitted a bug report to Apple (often called a radar).

It's fine and dandy that the bug has been identified and a radar has been filed,[2] but what do you do when this bug crops up in your app? You find a workaround, of course, and the workaround for PhotoWheel is a simple one to implement.

Open the file *MainViewController.m* and replace the unwind action - (IBAction) dismissAbout:(UIStoryboardSegue *) segue with a standard action. The implementation for the new -dismissAbout: action is:

```
- (IBAction)dismissAbout:(id)sender

{

    [self dismissViewControllerAnimated:YES completion:nil];

}
```

_____

2. Unwind segue bug: rdar://12693349

Note that incoming parameter type has been changed from `UIStoryboardSegue` to `id`. You need to make the same parameter type change to the forward declaration in the class extension found at the top of the *.m* file.

Next, open the *MainStoryboard.storyboard* file and connect the **Done** button to the new `-dismissAbout:` action. To do this, **Control-drag** from the button to the First Responder object in the About scene and select `dismissAbout:` in the list of received actions.

Finally, **Control-click** the Exit icon in the About scene and disconnect the unwind segue by clicking the small **x** next to "Bar Button Item – Done Action."

Test the workaround by running the app, tapping the **i** button to present the About scene, and tapping the **Done** button to dismiss it. The About scene should now dismiss.

Summary

In this chapter, you learned how to implement view controllers for scenes defined in the main storyboard. Storyboarding is a powerful feature, and it helps reduce the amount of source code required. Nevertheless, it does not completely eliminate the need for source code, as you now know.

You also learned how to use view controller containment to separate a screen into multiple scenes that are pieced together to form the full screen. With containment, you end up with view controllers that are focused on a particular purpose. This makes the code easier to maintain, and it makes it possible to reuse the view controller, if needed, in other parts of the application.

In addition to learning about view controllers, you learned how to use segues and unwind segues to transition between views. Finally, you wrote your own custom segue that performs its own animation sequence during the view transition.

At this point, you are ready to put together the rest of the main screen and have a functional app.

Exercises

1. Slow down the animation sequence in `CustomPushSegue` and observe how the animation sequence works. You can slow down the animation sequence in one of two ways: change the duration in code or select **Debug > Toggle Slow Animations** from the menu bar in the iOS Simulator.

2. Change the background color for the photo browser scene to black or some other color to see the `CustomPushSegue` animation sequence better. Set the background color using the Attributes inspector, and then set it to a different color in code.

3. Update the About view controller scene to programmatically display the version number. (Hint: You want to create a custom view controller class named `AboutViewController` and add an outlet to it that is connected to the version label defined in the scene. Then, in the `-viewDidLoad` event for the view controller, retrieve the version number from the application bundle and set the label. The code to retrieve the version number is `[[[NSBundle mainBundle] infoDictionary] objectForKey:@"CFBundleVersion"]`.)

16

Building the Main Screen

Welcome to the longest chapter in the book. This chapter is long because it walks you through the process of building the core piece of PhotoWheel. It is not broken into multiple chapters because this core piece focuses on one area: the main screen of the application. This chapter also provides the foundation needed for the remaining chapters. As a reward for completing it, you'll have a functioning photo app that you can show off to others. If you thought you could work through this chapter over your morning coffee, you might find that it's time for lunch by the time you have completed it.

To better understand why this chapter is so long—and why it isn't broken into multiple chapters—here is a list of the things you will learn and accomplish:

- ***Reusing the prototype code***

  A good amount of code presented in this chapter originated in the prototype app. However, tweaks to the code are needed in places.

- ***Setting up the PhotoWheel Core Data model***

  Like the reusable code, the Core Data model is copied from the prototype. However, tweaks are needed to support PhotoWheel.

- ***Making changes to the WheelView class***

  The original implementation of this class suited the needs of the prototype app, but Photo-Wheel is no prototype app. The WheelView class will be beefed up to become more powerful and flexible.

- ***Completing the photos scene***

  The photos scene is the child scene displayed at the top of the screen. You will complete the UI design and implementation for this scene. In other words, you will finally be able to view photos stored within a photo album.

- ***Building a functional photo album manager***

  This task includes adding and removing photo albums, and adding photos to albums.

The extra time spent on this chapter is worthwhile. By the end, you will have a functioning photo app that you can show off to family and friends. Not only that, but you will also have built the foundation needed for the remainder of the book. After completing this chapter, you can focus on adding cool new features to PhotoWheel, such as importing photos from Flickr, syncing with iCloud, and displaying a slideshow of your photos using AirPlay.

Now top off your coffee mug, get settled in your favorite comfy chair, and prepare to build the main screen of PhotoWheel.

Reusing Prototype Code

Starting with Chapter 8, "Creating a Master-Detail App," you implemented various concepts that ultimately will roll into the PhotoWheel app. While the prototype app itself is a throwaway, that doesn't mean that all of the code has to be tossed. On the contrary, the prototype app contains some real gems that can and will be used in PhotoWheel.

To reuse the code, you must copy the files from the PhotoWheelPrototype project into the PhotoWheel project. One way to do so is to drag and drop the file references from the PhotoWheelPrototype project into the PhotoWheel project within the LearningiPadProgramming workspace. However, this action copies only file references, not the actual files. While this might be fine when you want to share files between projects, it's not what you need to do here, because you need to make additional changes to files common to the two projects. You don't want a change needed for PhotoWheel to break your PhotoWheelPrototype app (and vice versa), so the best solution is to copy the files, not just the file references. Unfortunately, this cannot be done in Xcode, so you will need to use Finder instead.

Copy Files

Open Finder and navigate to the *PhotoWheelPrototype* project directory. A quick way to do this is to **Control-click** (or right-click) any file in the PhotoWheelPrototype project, then select **Show in Finder** from the popup menu. Next, select the following files in Finder and drop them into the PhotoWheel project in Xcode (Figure 16.1):

- *_Photo.h* and *_Photo.m*
- *_PhotoAlbum.h* and *_PhotoAlbum.m*
- *Photo.h* and *Photo.m*
- *PhotoAlbum.h* and *PhotoAlbum.m*
- *PhotoWheelViewCell.h* and *PhotoWheelViewCell.m*
- *SpinGestureRecognizer.h* and *SpinGestureRecognizer.m*
- *WheelView.h* and *WheelView.m*

Xcode prompts you for options when copying files into a new project. Make sure you check "Copy items into destination group's folder (if needed)" and the Add to PhotoWheel target (Figure 16.2).

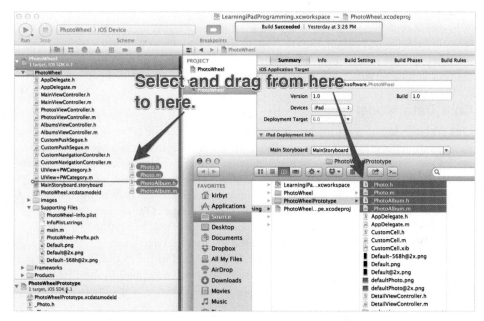

Figure 16.1   Dropping files into the PhotoWheel Xcode project

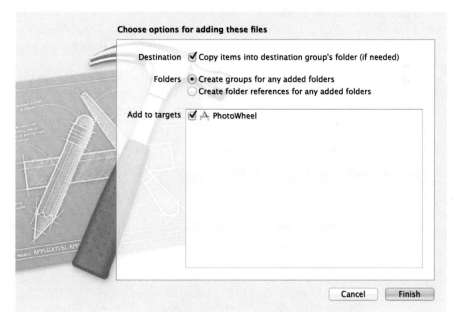

Figure 16.2   Copy file options

With the "Copy items into destination" option selected, the files from the Photo-WheelPrototype project directory are copied into the PhotoWheel project directory. If you do not select this option, the files will remain in the PhotoWheelPrototype project directory and file references will be added to the PhotoWheel project. Future changes to the files will be reflected in both projects, which is not what is wanted here.

Core Data Model

One file you do not want to copy is the Core Data model file (*PhotoWheelPrototype.xc datamodeld*). This is an inappropriate file name for the PhotoWheel project, and renaming a Core Data model is not the easiest task to accomplish. Besides, the PhotoWheel project already has a data model file named *PhotoWheel.xcdatamodeld*.

While the original Core Data model file isn't needed, you do want to use the same data model in PhotoWheel as was used in the prototype app. One option is to re-create the entries in the PhotoWheel data model, but an easier way is to copy and paste the entries from the prototype data model into the PhotoWheel data model.

Open the *PhotoWheelPrototype.xcdatamodeld* data model in the PhotoWheelPrototype project. Select the entities `Photo` and `PhotoAlbum` and copy them to the clipboard (**Command-C**). Next, open the *PhotoWheel.xcdatamodeld* file in the PhotoWheel project and paste (**Command-V**) the entities.

The Core Data model for PhotoWheel now includes the entities needed by the app. However, the copy–paste trick doesn't copy all the settings. Inverse relationships and Delete Rules must be set up again.

Select the `Photo` entity in the PhotoWheel Core Data model. Set the `photoAlbum` inverse relationship to `photos` (Figure 16.3). Next, set the Delete Rule for the relationships.

Select the `Photo` entity, and then select the `photoAlbum` relationship within the entity. In the Data Model inspector (**Option-Command-3**), set the Delete Rule to Nullify. Next, select the `PhotoAlbum` entity, select the `photos` relationship, and set its Delete Rule to Cascade.

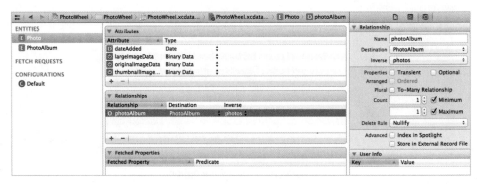

Figure 16.3   Set the inverse relationship.

> **Note**
>
> Refer to Chapter 13, "Data Persistence," if you need a refresher on setting the inverse relationship and Delete Rule.

You are already working on the Core Data model for PhotoWheel, so now is as good a time as any to make one additional change.

When PhotoWheel displays a photo from an album, the photo thumbnail will be sized at 100 × 100 pixels. This size does not yet exist in the `Photo` model, so you will need to add it. With the PhotoWheel Core Data model open, select the `Photo` entity. Add a new attribute to `Photo` named `smallImageData`, set its Type to Binary Data, and turn on the "Allows External Storage" option. Save the Core Data model file.

At this point, you can regenerate the _Photo model class, but because it is only one field, it's faster to make the class change by hand. Open _Photo.h and add a new declared property named `smallImageData`. Next, open _Photo.m and add the `@dynamic` statement for `smallImageData`. The updated _Photo.h and .m files are shown in Listing 16.1.

Listing 16.1 **Updated `_Photo` Class**

```
///////
// _Photo.h
///////
#import <Foundation/Foundation.h>
#import <CoreData/CoreData.h>

@class _PhotoAlbum;

@interface _Photo : NSManagedObject

@property (nonatomic, retain) NSDate * dateAdded;
@property (nonatomic, retain) NSData * originalImageData;
@property (nonatomic, retain) NSData * thumbnailImageData;
@property (nonatomic, retain) NSData * largeImageData;
@property (nonatomic, retain) NSData * smallImageData;
@property (nonatomic, retain) _PhotoAlbum *photoAlbum;

@end


///////
// _Photo.m
///////
#import "_Photo.h"
#import "_PhotoAlbum.h"
```

```
@implementation _Photo
@dynamic dateAdded;
@dynamic originalImageData;
@dynamic thumbnailImageData;
@dynamic largeImageData;
@dynamic smallImageData;
@dynamic photoAlbum;

@end
```

Now open the *Photo.h* model class and add a method named -smallImage that returns a pointer to a UIImage. Open *Photo.m*, add the implementation for -smallImage, and update the -saveImage: method to save the small image as a 100 × 100-pixel image. The updated source code is given in Listing 16.2.

Listing 16.2 **Updated Photo Class**

```
///////
//  Photo.h
///////
#import "_Photo.h"

@interface Photo : _Photo

- (void)saveImage:(UIImage *)newImage;

- (UIImage *)originalImage;
- (UIImage *)largeImage;
- (UIImage *)thumbnailImage;
- (UIImage *)smallImage;

@end


///////
//  Photo.m
///////
#import "Photo.h"

@implementation Photo

// Other code left out for brevity's sake.

- (void)createScaledImagesForImage:(UIImage *)originalImage
{
```

```
    // Save thumbnail
    CGSize thumbnailSize = CGSizeMake(75.0, 75.0);
    UIImage *thumbnailImage = [self image:originalImage
                    scaleAndCropToMaxSize:thumbnailSize];
    NSData *thumbnailImageData = UIImageJPEGRepresentation(thumbnailImage,
                                                            0.8);
    [self setThumbnailImageData:thumbnailImageData];

    // Save small image
    CGSize smallSize = CGSizeMake(100.0, 100.0);
    UIImage *smallImage = [self image:originalImage scaleAndCropToMaxSize:smallSize];
    NSData *smallImageData = UIImageJPEGRepresentation(smallImage, 0.8);
    [self setSmallImageData:smallImageData];

    // Save large (screen-size) image
    CGRect screenBounds = [[UIScreen mainScreen] bounds];
    // Calculate size for retina displays
    CGFloat scale = [[UIScreen mainScreen] scale];
    CGFloat maxScreenSize = MAX(screenBounds.size.width,
                                screenBounds.size.height) * scale;

    CGSize imageSize = [originalImage size];
    CGFloat maxImageSize = MAX(imageSize.width,
                                imageSize.height) * scale;

    CGFloat maxSize = MIN(maxScreenSize, maxImageSize);
    UIImage *largeImage = [self image:originalImage
                    scaleAspectToMaxSize:maxSize];
    NSData *largeImageData = UIImageJPEGRepresentation(largeImage, 0.8);
    [self setLargeImageData:largeImageData];
}

// Other code left out for brevity's sake.

- (UIImage *)smallImage
{
    return [UIImage imageWithData:[self smallImageData]];
}

@end
```

The Core Data model is now ready for use. Next up: updating the `WheelView` class to make it more useful.

Changes to WheelView

PhotoWheel is different from the prototype app in that the spinning wheel of photos contains thumbnails of each photo album, whereas in the prototype app the spinning wheel displayed photos from within the selected photo album.

To support the needs of PhotoWheel, a few changes are needed to the WheelView class. The current implementation limits the number of cells displayed in the wheel. Sure, an app can tell WheelView to display 200 photos, but the result would be unusable. The cells would be crammed together, making it impossible to find and view the desired photo album's thumbnail.

PhotoWheel will not limit the number of photo albums; the user can create as many photo albums as he desires. As a consequence, the WheelView class must be updated to support a finite number of visible cells (photo album thumbnails). While this change is easy to implement, it leads to a bigger issue. If the wheel view has been configured with seven visible cells and the data source has more than seven cells, how should all the cells be displayed? A wrapping feature is needed.

The wrapping feature displays the first cell when the end has been reached. Even more important, it continuously displays cells in sequential order within the bounds of the visible cells. As the user spins the wheel, the last of the visible cells is replaced with the next cell to display. Because only the top two-thirds of the wheel is displayed in PhotoWheel, the user never sees this replacement. Instead, the user sees a continuous flow of photo album thumbnails moving in a circular fashion.

The WheelView class also needs another change related to the display of an unknown number of cells. In the prototype app, the DetailViewController class managed a cache of WheelViewCell instances. The cache loads all the needed cells into memory during the -viewDidLoad event. While this is fine for the prototype app, such a mechanism will not fly for PhotoWheel. The user may have 200 photo albums. Loading 200 wheel view cells is wasteful, especially considering that only seven will be displayed at any given time.

The WheelView class needs updating to manage the cell cache. This step will help conserve valuable system resources and simplify the code in the view controller class. Managing the cache, however, is only one part of the update needed. The WheelView class must support dequeuing of unused cells to improve performance, and it must notify a delegate when a cell has been selected. In other words, it needs to behave like the UITableView class.

Make the changes to WheelView by opening the file *WheelView.h* and applying the changes shown in Listing 16.3.

> **Note**
>
> The complete source code for the WheelView class is shown in Listings 16.3 and 16.4. This makes it easier to follow the code while reading instead of looking at just the changes.

Listing 16.3   **Updated *WheelView.h***

```objc
#import <UIKit/UIKit.h>

@protocol WheelViewDataSource;
@protocol WheelViewDelegate;
@class WheelViewCell;

typedef enum  {
    WheelViewStyleWheel,
    WheelViewStyleCarousel,
} WheelViewStyle;


@interface WheelView : UIView

@property (nonatomic, strong) IBOutlet id<WheelViewDataSource> dataSource;
@property (nonatomic, strong) IBOutlet id<WheelViewDelegate> delegate;
@property (nonatomic, assign) WheelViewStyle style;
@property (nonatomic, assign) NSInteger selectedIndex;              // 1

- (id)dequeueReusableCell;                                         // 2
- (void)reloadData;                                               // 3
- (WheelViewCell *)cellAtIndex:(NSInteger)index;                  // 4

@end



@protocol WheelViewDataSource <NSObject>
@required
- (NSInteger)wheelViewNumberOfCells:(WheelView *)wheelView;
- (WheelViewCell *)wheelView:(WheelView *)wheelView cellAtIndex:(NSInteger)index;
@optional
- (void)wheelView:(WheelView *)wheelView
didSelectCellAtIndex:(NSInteger)index;                            // 5
@end

@protocol WheelViewDelegate <NSObject>                            // 6
@optional
- (NSInteger)wheelViewNumberOfVisibleCells:(WheelView *)wheelView;
@end

@interface WheelViewCell : UIView
@end
```

Let's run through this code:

1–4. The updated class interface isn't much different from the original. A new
selectedIndex property has been added along with three methods. The
method -dequeueReusableCell returns a reusable WheelViewCell to the
caller. The method -reloadData reinitializes and loads data into the wheel
view. Finally, the method -cellAtIndex: returns the WheelViewCell
instance for the specific index.

5. The WheelViewDataSource protocol has been updated with the new
optional message -wheelView:didSelectCellAtIndex:. This message is
received by the data source when the user selects a cell in the wheel view.

6. A new protocol has been added, WheelViewDelegate. It has one optional
method, -wheelViewNumberOfVisibleCells:. If this method is not implemented in the delegate, WheelView will display all cells. This default behavior
is overridden by implementing the new method in the delegate and returning
the number of cells to display. This behavior is used in conjunction with the
wrapping feature mentioned earlier.

Changes to the WheelView class interface are minor compared to those in the
implementation. While the original logic for the display of each cell and style setting
is still in place, a number of other changes have been made. The complete source code
listing is shown in Listing 16.4. Update your code to match it.

Listing 16.4   **Updated *WheelView.m***

```
#import "WheelView.h"
#import <QuartzCore/QuartzCore.h>
#import "SpinGestureRecognizer.h"


#pragma mark - WheelViewCell

@interface WheelViewCell ()                                          // 1
@property (nonatomic, assign) NSInteger indexInWheelView;            // 2
@end

@implementation WheelViewCell                                        // 3
@end



#pragma mark - WheelView

@interface WheelView ()
@property (nonatomic, assign) CGFloat currentAngle;
@property (nonatomic, strong) NSMutableSet *reusableCells;           // 4

// The visible cell indexes are stored in a mutable dictionary
// instead of a mutable array because the number of visible cells
```

```objc
// can change. Using an array requires additional logic to maintain
// the dimensions of the array. This is avoided by using the
// dictionary where the key represents the element index number.
@property (nonatomic, strong) NSMutableDictionary *visibleCellIndexes;   // 5
@end

@implementation WheelView

- (void)commonInit                                                       // 6
{
    [self setSelectedIndex:-1];
    [self setCurrentAngle:0.0];

    [self setVisibleCellIndexes:[NSMutableDictionary dictionary]];

    SpinGestureRecognizer *spin = [[SpinGestureRecognizer alloc]
                                initWithTarget:self action:@selector(spin:)];
    [self addGestureRecognizer:spin];

    [self setReusableCells:[NSMutableSet set]];
}

- (id)init                                                               // 7
{
    self = [super init];
    if (self) {
        [self commonInit];
    }
    return self;
}

- (id)initWithCoder:(NSCoder *)aDecoder
{
    self = [super initWithCoder:aDecoder];
    if (self) {
        [self commonInit];
    }
    return self;
}

- (id)initWithFrame:(CGRect)frame
{
    self = [super initWithFrame:frame];
    if (self) {
        [self commonInit];
    }
    return self;
```

```objc
}

- (NSInteger)numberOfCells                                          // 8
{
    NSInteger cellCount = 0;
    id<WheelViewDataSource> dataSource = [self dataSource];
    if ([dataSource respondsToSelector:@selector(wheelViewNumberOfCells:)]) {
        cellCount = [dataSource wheelViewNumberOfCells:self];
    }
    return cellCount;
}


- (NSInteger)numberOfVisibleCells                                   // 9
{
    NSInteger cellCount = [self numberOfCells];
    NSInteger numberOfVisibleCells = cellCount;
    id<WheelViewDelegate> delegate = [self delegate];
    if (delegate &&
        [delegate respondsToSelector:@selector(wheelViewNumberOfVisibleCells:)])
    {
        numberOfVisibleCells = [delegate wheelViewNumberOfVisibleCells:self];
    }
    return numberOfVisibleCells;
}


- (BOOL)isSelectedItemForAngle:(CGFloat)angle                       // 10
{
    // The selected item is one whose angle is
    // at or near 0 degrees.
    //
    // To calculate the selected item based on the
    // angle, we must convert the angle to the
    // relative angle between 0 and 360 degrees.

    CGFloat relativeAngle = fabsf(fmodf(angle, 360.0));

    // Pad the selection point so it does not
    // have to be exact.
    CGFloat padding = 20.0;    // Allow 20 degrees on either side.

    BOOL isSelectedItem =
        relativeAngle >= (360.0 - padding) || relativeAngle <= padding;
    return isSelectedItem;
}


- (BOOL)isIndexVisible:(NSInteger)index                             // 11
{
```

```objc
        NSNumber *cellIndex = [NSNumber numberWithInteger:index];
        __block BOOL visible = NO;
        void (^enumerateBlock) (id, id, BOOL *) = ^(id key, id obj, BOOL *stop) {
            if ([obj isEqual:cellIndex]) {
                visible = YES;
                *stop = YES;
            }
        };
        [[self visibleCellIndexes] enumerateKeysAndObjectsUsingBlock:enumerateBlock];
        return visible;
}


- (void)queueNonVisibleCells                                          // 12
{
    NSArray *subviews = [self subviews];
    for (id view in subviews) {
        if ([view isKindOfClass:[WheelViewCell class]]) {
            NSInteger index = [(WheelViewCell *)view indexInWheelView];
            BOOL visible = [self isIndexVisible:index];
            if (!visible) {
                [[self reusableCells] addObject:view];
                [view removeFromSuperview];
            }
        }
    }
}


- (NSInteger)cellIndexForIndex:(NSInteger)index                      // 13
{
    NSInteger numberOfCells = [self numberOfCells];
    NSInteger numberOfVisibleCells = [self numberOfVisibleCells];
    NSInteger offset = MAX([self selectedIndex], 0);

    NSInteger cellIndex;
    if (index < (numberOfVisibleCells/2)) {
        cellIndex = index + offset;
        if (cellIndex > numberOfCells - 1) cellIndex = cellIndex - numberOfCells;
    } else {
        cellIndex = offset - (numberOfVisibleCells - index);
        if (cellIndex < 0) cellIndex = numberOfCells + cellIndex;
    }

    return cellIndex;
}


- (NSSet*)cellIndexesToDisplay                                       // 14
{
```

```
    NSInteger numberOfVisibleCells = [self numberOfVisibleCells];
    NSMutableSet *cellIndexes =
        [[NSMutableSet alloc] initWithCapacity:numberOfVisibleCells];
    for (NSInteger index = 0; index < numberOfVisibleCells; index++)
    {
        NSInteger cellIndex = [self cellIndexForIndex:index];
        [cellIndexes addObject:[NSNumber numberWithInteger:cellIndex]];
    }
    return cellIndexes;
}


- (void)setAngle:(CGFloat)angle                                    // 15
{
    [self queueNonVisibleCells];                                   // 16
    NSSet *cellIndexesToDisplay = [self cellIndexesToDisplay];     // 17

    // The following code is inspired by the carousel example at
    // http://stackoverflow.com/questions/5243614/3d-carousel-effect-on-the-ipad

    CGPoint center = CGPointMake(CGRectGetMidX([self bounds]),
                                 CGRectGetMidY([self bounds]));
    CGFloat radiusX = MIN([self bounds].size.width,
                          [self bounds].size.height) * 0.35;
    CGFloat radiusY = radiusX;
    if ([self style] == WheelViewStyleCarousel) {
        radiusY = radiusX * 0.30;
    }


    NSInteger numberOfVisibleCells = [self numberOfVisibleCells];
    float angleToAdd = 360.0f / numberOfVisibleCells;


    // If there are more cells than the number of visible cells,
    // we wrap the cells. Wrapping allows all cells to display
    // within a finite number of visible cells. Cells are displayed in
    // sequential order. When the end is reached, the display wraps
    // to the beginning.
    //
    // Because there is a finite number of visible cells, one cell
    // is replaced with a wrapping cell as the user scrolls through
    // (spins) the wheel. At any given time there is one and only one
    // cell that requires replacing. The cell to replace is determined
    // by comparing the contents of visibleCellIndexes to
    // cellIndexesToDisplay.
    // visibleCellIndexes can contain one index not found in
    // cellIndexesToDisplay.
    // This is the index that is replaced. It is replaced with the one
    // index in cellIndexesToDisplay not found in visibleCellIndexes.
```

```objc
BOOL wrap = [self numberOfCells] > numberOfVisibleCells;              // 18

// Lay out visible cells.
for (NSInteger index = 0; index < numberOfVisibleCells; index++)
{
    NSNumber *cellIndexNumber;
    if (wrap) {
        cellIndexNumber = [[self visibleCellIndexes]
                        objectForKey:[NSNumber numberWithInteger:index]];
        if (cellIndexNumber == nil) {
            // First time through, visibleCellIndexes is empty--hence the nil
            // cellIndexNumber. Initialize it with the appropriate cell
            // index.
            cellIndexNumber =
                [NSNumber numberWithInteger:[self cellIndexForIndex:index]];
        }
    } else {
        // Cell indexes are sequential when wrapping is turned off.
        cellIndexNumber = [NSNumber numberWithInteger:index];
    }


    if (wrap && ![cellIndexesToDisplay containsObject:cellIndexNumber]) {
        // Replace the wrapping cell index.
        __block NSNumber *replacementNumber = nil;
        NSArray *array = [[self visibleCellIndexes] allValues];
        void (^enumerateBlock) (id, BOOL *) = ^(id obj, BOOL *stop) {
            if (![array containsObject:obj]) {
                replacementNumber = obj;
                *stop = YES;
            }
        };
        [cellIndexesToDisplay enumerateObjectsUsingBlock:enumerateBlock];

        cellIndexNumber = replacementNumber;
    }


    NSInteger cellIndex = [cellIndexNumber integerValue];
    WheelViewCell *cell = [self cellAtIndex:cellIndex];

    if (cell == nil) {
        cellIndex = -1;    // No cell, no cell index.
    }

    // If index is not within the visible indexes, the
    // cell is missing from the view and must be added.
```

```objc
BOOL visible = [self isIndexVisible:cellIndex];
if (!visible) {
  [[self visibleCellIndexes] setObject:cellIndexNumber
                              forKey:[NSNumber numberWithInteger:index]];
  [cell setIndexInWheelView:cellIndex];
  [self addSubview:cell];
}

// Set the selected index if it has changed.
if (cellIndex != [self selectedIndex] &&
    [self isSelectedItemForAngle:angle])                        // 19
{
  [self setSelectedIndex:cellIndex];
  if ([[self dataSource]
      respondsToSelector:@selector(wheelView:didSelectCellAtIndex:)])
  {
    [[self dataSource] wheelView:self didSelectCellAtIndex:cellIndex];
  }
}

float angleInRadians = (angle + 180.0) * M_PI / 180.0f;         // 20

// Get a position based on the angle
float xPosition = center.x + (radiusX * sinf(angleInRadians))
               - (CGRectGetWidth([cell frame]) / 2);
float yPosition = center.y + (radiusY * cosf(angleInRadians))
               - (CGRectGetHeight([cell frame]) / 2);

float scale = 0.75f + 0.25f * (cosf(angleInRadians) + 1.0);

// Apply location and scale
if ([self style] == WheelViewStyleCarousel) {
  [cell setTransform:CGAffineTransformScale(
              CGAffineTransformMakeTranslation(xPosition, yPosition),
              scale, scale)];
  // Tweak alpha using the same system as applied for scale, this
  // time with 0.3 as the minimum and a semicircle range of 0.5
  [cell setAlpha:(0.3f + 0.5f * (cosf(angleInRadians) + 1.0))];

} else {
  [cell setTransform:CGAffineTransformMakeTranslation(xPosition,
                                                      yPosition)];
  [cell setAlpha:1.0];
}

[[cell layer] setZPosition:scale];

// Work out what the next angle will be
angle += angleToAdd;
```

```
    }
}

- (void)layoutSubviews                                            // 21
{
    [self setAngle:[self currentAngle]];
}

- (void)setStyle:(WheelViewStyle)newStyle                         // 22
{
    if (_style != newStyle) {
        _style = newStyle;

        [UIView animateWithDuration:0.3 animations:^{
            [self setAngle:[self currentAngle]];
        }];
    }
}

- (void)spin:(SpinGestureRecognizer *)recognizer                  // 23
{
    CGFloat angleInRadians = -[recognizer rotation];
    CGFloat degrees = 180.0 * angleInRadians / M_PI;   // Radians to degrees
    [self setCurrentAngle:[self currentAngle] + degrees];
    [self setAngle:[self currentAngle]];
}

- (id)dequeueReusableCell                                         // 24
{
    id view = [[self reusableCells] anyObject];
    if (view != nil) {
        [[self reusableCells] removeObject:view];
    }
    return view;
}

- (void)queueReusableCells                                        // 25
{
    for (UIView *view in [self subviews]) {
        if ([view isKindOfClass:[WheelViewCell class]]) {
            [[self reusableCells] addObject:view];
            [view removeFromSuperview];
        }
    }

    [[self visibleCellIndexes] removeAllObjects];
    [self setSelectedIndex:-1];
}
```

```
- (void) reloadData                                                    // 26
{
  [self queueReusableCells];
  [self layoutSubviews];
}

- (WheelViewCell *) cellAtIndex: (NSInteger) index                     // 27
{
  if (index < 0 || index > [self numberOfCells] - 1) {
    return nil;
  }

  WheelViewCell *cell = nil;
  BOOL visible = [self isIndexVisible:index];
  if (visible) {
    for (id view in [self subviews]) {
      if ([view isKindOfClass:[WheelViewCell class]]) {
        if ([view indexInWheelView] == index) {
          cell = view;
          break;
        }
      }
    }
  }

  if (cell == nil) {
    cell = [[self dataSource] wheelView:self cellAtIndex:index];
  }

  return cell;
}

@end
```

Let's walk through the code together, highlighting the changes:

1–3. The implementation for WheelViewCell has been moved to the top of the
source code file. Also, a new private declared property named indexInWheel
View has been added. This private property is used by WheelView to track the
index for the cell, which may be different from the display index. Remember,
the new WheelView can have fewer visible cells than the total number of cells.

> **Note**
>
> The WheelViewCell class extension and implementation were moved to the top to make
> the compiler aware of the class within the WheelView implementation. If the code remained
> at the bottom, the WheelView class would not compile.

4–5. Two new declared properties have been added to the `WheelView` class extension: `reusableCells` and `visibleCellIndexes`. `reusableCells` is a mutable set used to manage the cache of reusable `WheelViewCell` instances. `visibleCellIndexes` is a mutable dictionary of indexes representing the visible cells.

5. You might be wondering why `visibleCellIndexes` is declared as `NSMutableDictionary` instead of `NSMutableArray`. Admittedly, it does seem strange, but there's a good reason for this approach.

    The number of visible cells can change. If an array were used, a change in the number of visible cells would require a change in the array's dimension. Also, the indexes for cells to display are not necessarily calculated in sequential order. They are displayed sequentially, but that doesn't mean each cell to display is determined sequentially. Therefore, if an array were used, additional code would be needed to ensure that elements were added to the array to fill holes that might exist as each cell is processed.

    The dictionary eliminates the need for additional array management code. Also, because a dictionary's contents are not order dependent, `WheelView` doesn't need to worry about checking the bounds of an array and filling holes in it. Instead, the class stores the index value as an `NSNumber`, which is used as the key to the dictionary. Note that this index is an index within the range of visible cell indexes. In other words, it is a value between 0 and the number of visible cells.

    The object stored in the dictionary for the visible cell index key is the actual cell index. It is also stored as an `NSNumber`, because `NSDictionary` can store only object references. The actual cell index value is some number between 0 and the total number of cells.

6–7. The method `-commonInit` is updated to initialize the selected index, `visibleCellIndexes`, and `reusableCells` properties. The remaining `init*` methods remain the same as before.

8–9. The init methods are followed by two helper methods, `-numberOfCells` and `-numberOfVisibleCells`. Each returns a value retrieved from the data source. These values are used throughout the `WheelView` class. The helper methods were created to eliminate the duplication of code in `WheelView`.

10. The method `-isSelectedItemForAngle:` is responsible for determining whether a wheel view cell is "selected" based on the specified angle. A cell is considered selected when it is displayed at the top of the wheel, at degree 0.0 plus or minus 20.0 degrees.

11. Another helper method named `-isIndexVisible:` has been added. This method enumerates the `visibleCellIndexes` to see if it contains the specific cell index. A block is used to perform the enumeration. If a number is found in the `visibleCellIndexes` that matches the cell index number, the cell is visible and `YES` is returned to the caller; otherwise, `NO` is returned.

12. The next method, -queueNonVisibleCells, removes any nonvisible wheel view cells from the view and places them into the local cache reusable Cells.

13–14. The next two methods are -cellIndexForIndex: and -cellIndexesTo Display. The method -cellIndexForIndex: converts a visible cell index (a number between 0 and the number of visible cells) to a cell index (a number between 0 and the total number of cells). This method is used by -cellIn dexesToDisplay, which returns an NSSet of cell indexes to display. As you will see in a moment, this set is compared to visibleCellIndexes to find the cell that is replaced during wrapping.

15–20. The method -setAngle: has been updated to queue nonvisible cells, retrieve the set of cell indexes to display, support cell wrapping, and set the selected index. The code to transform a cell to a particular position as the wheel spins remains the same as before.

21–23. The methods -layoutSubviews, -setStyle:, and -spin: remain unchanged from the earlier implementation. The remaining methods, however, are new to this implementation.

24. The method -dequeueReusableCell returns a reusable cell from the cache. It grabs any object from the cache. It doesn't matter which object is grabbed, because all of them are available for reuse. The object is then removed from the cache and returned to the caller. If there are no available objects in the cache, nil is returned to the caller, and the caller is expected to create a new instance of the cell.

25. The method -queueReusableCells is called when data is reloaded in the wheel view. This method takes all the visible cells currently in the view and moves them to the reusable cell cache.

26. The method -reloadData queues any reusable cells and calls -layoutSub views, which in turn starts the process of displaying cells within the view.

27. Finally, there's -cellAtIndex:. This method returns a reference to the cell at the specified index. It is used internally by the WheelView class and can be used externally by other classes, such as a view controller.

Now that the new WheelView class is in place, it's time to put it to good use displaying photo albums.

Displaying Photo Albums

The next thing you want to tackle is the display of photo albums. In PhotoWheel, photo albums are displayed as thumbnails in the disc at the bottom of the screen. This arrangement differs from the prototype app, where the albums were displayed in a table view. Luckily, the `WheelView` class has been implemented as a generic view class, which means that you can use it to display the photo album thumbnails.

Open the main storyboard and select the Albums View Controller Scene. This is the scene with the image of the disc. Drag a `UIView` into this scene. Set its position and size: X = 31, Y = 33, Width = 488, and Height = 484.

The new view should appear on top of the disc image view but under the round **+** button. To accomplish this, you need to rearrange the views in the view hierarchy. Open the Document Outline (**Editor > Show Document Outline**) and expand the view hierarchy for the scene. Drag and drop the views to rearrange the view order within the hierarchy. The order should match that shown in Figure 16.4.

After the view hierarchy has been set, the new view will partially hide the disc image view, so set the Background color to Clear (found in the Attributes inspector) for the new view.

The new view is of type `UIView`. You need to change this type to the `WheelView` class. Open the Identity inspector and change the class from `UIView` to `WheelView`. Now that the view is of type `WheelView`, its `dataSource` and `delegate` outlets can be set. Connect the `WheelView`'s `dataSource` to the Albums View Controller Scene. Remember, you can accomplish this by **Control-clicking** (right-clicking) the view and dragging the `dataSource` connector to the view controller, or you can **Control-drag** from the view to the view controller to make the connection. Both approaches work correctly.

Do the same for the `WheelView`'s `delegate`, connecting it to the `AlbumsView Controller`.

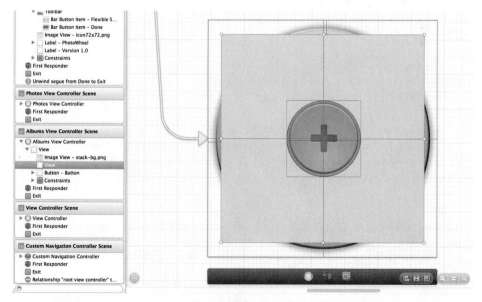

Figure 16.4   Set the view hierarchy.

Implementing the Photo Albums View Controller

With the wheel view in place, it's time to implement the `AlbumsViewController`. This controller serves as the data source and delegate for the `WheelView` instance, which means it must implement code conforming to the `WheelViewDataSource` and `WheelViewDelegate` protocols.

Start with the interface file, *AlbumsViewController.h*. Let the compiler know that the class conforms to these two protocols. Also add `NSFetchedResultsController Delegate` to the list of protocols, as a fetched-results controller will be used to retrieve the photo albums. Next, add an outlet for the `WheelView` object; it will be used in the implementation of the view controller. Finally, add a new property for the managed object context, and an action for the **+** button that adds a new photo album. The source code is shown in Listing 16.5.

Listing 16.5 Updated *AlbumsViewController.h*

```
#import <UIKit/UIKit.h>
#import "WheelView.h"

@interface AlbumsViewController : UIViewController
<NSFetchedResultsControllerDelegate, WheelViewDataSource, WheelViewDelegate>

@property (nonatomic, strong) NSManagedObjectContext *managedObjectContext;
@property (nonatomic, weak) IBOutlet WheelView *wheelView;

- (IBAction)addPhotoAlbum:(id)sender;

@end
```

While you are making changes, make sure you return to the Albums View Controller Scene in the main storyboard and connect the `WheelView` object to the `wheel View` outlet and the **+** button to the `-addPhotoAlbum:` action. Otherwise, the app will not display and add photo albums properly.

Also make sure to connect the `-addPhotoAlbum:` action to the *Touch Up Inside* event of the button. This is done for you automatically when you **Control-click** and drag to make the connection. In contrast, you must manually select the event if you use the popup HUD to make the connection.

> **Note**
>
> You may be wondering how and when the `managedObjectContext` property is set. It will be set in the `MainViewController` when the `AlbumsViewController` instance is created from the storyboard. You'll implement this code once the implementation for `AlbumsViewController` is complete.

With the interface complete, it's time to shift your attention to the implementation. Open *AlbumsViewController.m* and update it with the code in Listing 16.6.

Listing 16.6   **Updated *AlbumsViewController.m***

```objectivec
#import "AlbumsViewController.h"
#import "PhotoWheelViewCell.h"                                          // 1
#import "PhotoAlbum.h"
#import "Photo.h"

@interface AlbumsViewController ()                                     // 2
@property (nonatomic, strong)
NSFetchedResultsController *fetchedResultsController;                  // 3
@end

@implementation AlbumsViewController

#pragma mark - Actions

- (IBAction)addPhotoAlbum:(id)sender                                   // 4
{

}

#pragma mark - NSFetchedResultsController and NSFetchedResultsControllerDelegate

- (NSFetchedResultsController *)fetchedResultsController               // 5
{
    if (_fetchedResultsController) {                                  // 6
        return _fetchedResultsController;
    }

    NSString *cacheName = NSStringFromClass([self class]);            // 7
    NSFetchRequest *fetchRequest =
    [NSFetchRequest fetchRequestWithEntityName:@"PhotoAlbum"];        // 8

    NSSortDescriptor *sortDescriptor =
        [NSSortDescriptor sortDescriptorWithKey:@"dateAdded"
                                      ascending:YES];                 // 9
    [fetchRequest setSortDescriptors:@[sortDescriptor]];

    NSFetchedResultsController *newFetchedResultsController;
    newFetchedResultsController = [[NSFetchedResultsController alloc]
        initWithFetchRequest:fetchRequest
        managedObjectContext:[self managedObjectContext]
        sectionNameKeyPath:nil
        cacheName:cacheName];                                         // 10
    [newFetchedResultsController setDelegate:self];                   // 11

    NSError *error = nil;
    if (![newFetchedResultsController performFetch:&error])           // 12
```

```
    {
      // Replace this implementation with code to handle the
      // error appropriately.
      NSLog(@"Unresolved error %@, %@", error, [error userInfo]);
      abort();
    }

    [self setFetchedResultsController:newFetchedResultsController];    // 13
    return _fetchedResultsController;                                  // 14
}


- (void)controller:(NSFetchedResultsController *)controller
  didChangeObject:(id)anObject
      atIndexPath:(NSIndexPath *)indexPath
    forChangeType:(NSFetchedResultsChangeType)type
     newIndexPath:(NSIndexPath *)newIndexPath                         // 15
{
    [[self wheelView] reloadData];
}



#pragma mark - WheelViewDataSource and WheelViewDelegate methods     // 16

- (NSInteger)wheelViewNumberOfVisibleCells:(WheelView *)wheelView    // 17
{
    return 7;
}


- (NSInteger)wheelViewNumberOfCells:(WheelView *)wheelView           // 18
{
    NSArray *sections = [[self fetchedResultsController] sections];
    NSInteger count = [[sections objectAtIndex:0] numberOfObjects];
    return count;
}


- (WheelViewCell *)wheelView:(WheelView *)wheelView
                cellAtIndex:(NSInteger)index                         // 19
{
    PhotoWheelViewCell *cell = [wheelView dequeueReusableCell];      // 20
    if (!cell) {
      cell = [[PhotoWheelViewCell alloc]
            initWithFrame:CGRectMake(0, 0, 75, 75)];                 // 21
    }

    NSIndexPath *indexPath;
    indexPath = [NSIndexPath indexPathForRow:index inSection:0];
    NSFetchedResultsController *frc = [self fetchedResultsController];
```

```
    PhotoAlbum *photoAlbum = [frc objectAtIndexPath:indexPath];        // 22
    Photo *photo = [[photoAlbum photos] lastObject];                   // 23
    UIImage *image = [photo thumbnailImage];
    if (image == nil) {
        image = [UIImage imageNamed:@"defaultPhoto.png"];              // 24
    }
    [cell setImage:image];                                             // 25

    return cell;                                                       // 26
}


- (void)wheelView:(WheelView *)wheelView
didSelectCellAtIndex:(NSInteger)index                                  // 27
{

}
```

@end

Now let's walk through the code to see what is happening:

1–3. The first things you notice are the additional #import statements. They are
followed by the class extension for AlbumsViewController. The class extension adds a private declared property named fetchedResultsController.
The fetched-results controller is used to populate the wheel view with photo
albums.

4. The next method in Listing 16.6 is -addPhotoAlbum:. This action is connected to the + button in the Albums View Controller Scene. The implementation is empty for the moment. You'll add the code that adds a new photo
album momentarily.

5. The action is followed by the custom fetched-results controller getter method,
-fetchedResultsController. NSFetchedResultsController manages
the results of a Core Data fetched request. It is optimized for the mobile platform
and designed for use with UITableView. However, because WheelView is modeled after UITableView, the fetched-results controller can be used with it as
well.

6. The first thing the getter method does is check whether the ivar for the
fetched-results controller has already been set. If it has, the reference to the
ivar is returned. If the ivar has not been set (its value is nil), the getter
method initializes it.

7. NSFetchedResultsController can optionally use a cache. This cache
reduces the overhead of figuring out section and index information managed by the controller. The cache name used in this getter method is the
view controller class name. The class name is returned by the C function
NSStringFromClass().

8. A new fetch request object is created next using the class method +fetch RequestWithEntityName:. This method provides a convenient way to create an NSFetchRequest object that is configured for a particular entity without having to use an NSEntityDescription object. Here the fetch request is configured for the PhotoAlbum entity. Note that this name must match the entity name defined in the PhotoWheel Core Data model.

9. A sort descriptor is created and added to the fetch request. The sort descriptor tells Core Data how to sort the fetched results. In this particular case, the fetched results are sorted by the dateAdded field in ascending order.

10–11. The fetch request is then added to the fetched-results controller, and the view controller is made the delegate of the fetched-results controller. As a consequence, AlbumsViewController will receive messages from the fetched-results controller as needed (such as when new data is added to the fetched results).

12–14. The fetched results controller is finally told to perform the fetch. This action retrieves the data from Core Data so that it can be used within the view controller. Also, the declared property fetchedResultsController is set to the new fetched-results controller. This, in turn, sets the ivar _fetchedRe sultsController, which is returned at the end of the method.

15. Following the fetched-results controller getter method is the -controller: didChangeObject:atIndexPath:forChangeType:newIndexPath: method. This NSFetchedResultsControllerDelegate method is called by the fetched-results controller whenever data changes in the fetched results. Its implementation is simple. The method reloads the data in wheelView. As a result, the display is automatically updated to show the changes the moment they happen. For example, when the user taps the + button, the new photo album displays immediately. No additional coding is needed, just the call to -reloadData.

Note

Had you used a UITableView instead of a WheelView, you could do a number of things other than -reloadData to show the data change. UITableView has methods to insert and remove individual rows, and to update particular rows. These enhanced behaviors are not implemented in the WheelView class, however, so -reloadData will have to suffice.

16. The last code changes to the AlbumsViewController class involve the WheelViewDataSource and WheelViewDelegate protocol methods. These methods are called by WheelView to display cells within the view, and to report back to the view controller which cell has been selected by the user.

17. The first of these methods is -wheelViewNumberOfVisibleCells:. It returns the value 7, which means that no more than seven photo album thumbnails will be displayed at once in the wheel view. More than seven cells can exist, but a maximum of seven cells will be displayed at any given time.

18. The next method is -wheelViewNumberOfCells:. This method returns the total number of cells or, in the case of PhotoWheel, the total number of photo albums. The count is retrieved from the fetched-results controller. The sections array contains the data for each section. Remember, the fetched-results controller is designed for UITableView, which can have one or more sections. There is always only one section when using the WheelView, so the section at index zero contains the list of photo albums.

19–26. The method -wheelView:cellAtIndex: is responsible for constructing WheelViewCell, setting its properties, and returning it to the caller, which happens to be the wheelView. This method first retrieves a reusable cell, if any are available. If no reusable cells are available, a new cell is created. Next, the photo album model object is retrieved from the fetched results by way of the fetched-results controller. The last photo of the photo album is used as the thumbnail of the photo album. If there is no photo or thumbnail for the photo, the *defaultPhoto.png* image is used as the thumbnail. The image is added to the cell for display, and the cell is returned to the caller.

27. Finally, there is the -wheelView:didSelectCellAtIndex: method. This method is called when the user selects a new photo album in the wheel view. A photo album is selected when the arrow from the photos popover image points to a cell (Figure 16.5). For now, we'll leave the implementation of this method empty.

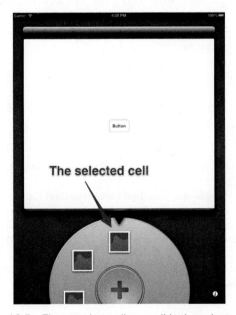

Figure 16.5   The top photo album cell is the selected cell.

Setting the Managed Object Context

Before the app will run, one other change is needed. The `AlbumsViewController` needs a reference to the managed object context set up by the app delegate. This view controller is decoupled from the app delegate, so it expects that its `managedObject Context` property will be set by the user of the object.

> **Note**
>
> When possible, it's always a good thing to decouple view controllers, and classes in general, from one another. This will make the design of your application more flexible. One way to decouple a view controller from other dependencies is to pass references into the controller, as is done with the managed object context.

The appropriate place to set the `managedObjectContext` property of `AlbumsView Controller` is at the time the controller instance is created. However, the instance of the view controller is created by the storyboard during the transition of an embedded segue. Therefore, you need to implement `-prepareForSegue:sender:` in the `MainViewController` class. This method gives the receiver the opportunity to prepare the source and destination view controllers prior to the segue transition.

For your particular case, this means passing a managed object context reference to the `AlbumsViewController` instance, which is the destination view controller for the embedded segue you defined earlier in the storyboard.

Open *MainViewController.m* and update the code to set the `managedObjectCon text` property for the `AlbumsViewController` instance, as shown in Listing 16.7.

Listing 16.7   Updated *MainViewController.m*

```
#import "MainViewController.h"
#import "AlbumsViewController.h"
#import "AppDelegate.h"


@implementation MainViewController

// Other code left out for brevity's sake.

- (void)prepareForSegue:(UIStoryboardSegue *)segue sender:(id)sender
{
    id destinationVC = [segue destinationViewController];           // 1
    if ([destinationVC isKindOfClass:[AlbumsViewController class]]) {  // 2
        UIApplication *app = [UIApplication sharedApplication];
        AppDelegate *appDelegate = (AppDelegate *)[app delegate];   // 3

        NSManagedObjectContext *context;
        context = [appDelegate managedObjectContext];               // 4
```

```
        [destinationVC setManagedObjectContext:context];                    // 5
    }
}

@end
```

Now let's walk through the code in Listing 16.7:

1. A local variable is set to the `destinationViewController` reference provided by the incoming segue reference.

2. An `if` statement is used to check the class type of the destination view controller. We're only interested in setting the managed object context for an instance of the `AlbumsViewController` class.

3. For the managed object context property to be set, it must first be retrieved from the app delegate. The `AppDelegate` class contains the code that initializes the managed object context. To retrieve the app delegate, you use the `UIApplication` class. It has a class method named `+sharedApplication`, which returns a reference to the current application object. You call the delegate property on the current application object to get the reference to the `AppDelegate` instance.

4. Once you have a reference to the `AppDelegate`, a reference to the managed object context provided by the `AppDelegate` is stored in the local variable `context`.

5. The local variable `context` is then used to set the `-managedObjectContext` property on the destination view controller, which is an instance of `AlbumsViewController`.

> **Note**
>
> Decoupling the app delegate from the main view controller is often the preferred approach. However, the two are coupled in Listing 16.7 to show you how to retrieve a reference to the app delegate should you ever need it.

At this point, the PhotoWheel app will compile and run. You will not see any photo albums, however, because there are no photo albums in the Core Data persistent store. You need to implement the action for adding a photo album first before you can see photo albums in the wheel view.

> **Note**
>
> The Core Data model has been changed in this chapter. Therefore, the first time the app is run and it references the managed object context, an exception is thrown, indicating that the data model has changed. To fix this, delete previous versions of PhotoWheel from the simulator and iPad before running the app. You need to do this only once, as the data model will not change again.

Adding Photo Albums

Before the user can see a photo album in the wheel view, he needs to add one to the data store. But before that can happen, you must implement the -addPhotoAlbum: action method in *AlbumsViewController.m*. Open *AlbumsViewController.m* and scroll to the -addPhotoAlbum: method. Add the implementation shown in Listing 16.8.

Listing 16.8 **Updated -addPhotoAlbum:**

```
- (IBAction)addPhotoAlbum:(id)sender
{
   NSManagedObjectContext *context = [self managedObjectContext];     // 1
   PhotoAlbum *photoAlbum;
   photoAlbum = [NSEntityDescription
     insertNewObjectForEntityForName:@"PhotoAlbum"
     inManagedObjectContext:context];                                 // 2
   [photoAlbum setDateAdded:[NSDate date]];                           // 3

   // Save the context.
   NSError *error = nil;
   if (![context save:&error])                                        // 4
   {
      // Replace this implementation with code to handle
      // the error appropriately.
      NSLog(@"Unresolved error %@, %@", error, [error userInfo]);
      abort();
   }
}
```

Now when the user taps the **+** button at the bottom of the PhotoWheel screen, a new photo album is added. The code to accomplish this is straightforward:

1. A local variable stores a reference to the managed object context.
2. A new entity description is inserted for the entity name PhotoAlbum.
3. The dateAdded property for the entity is set to the current date.
4. The context is saved.

Because a fetched-results controller is used to manage the data, AlbumsViewController automatically receives a message from this controller telling it to update the wheel view display.

Run the app and test that photo albums can be added. Check your work if you cannot add new photo albums. Remember, if nothing is happening, check the outlet and action connections defined in the Photo Albums View Controller Scene. Nothing will happen if these connections are missing.

Managing Photo Albums

So far, you have updated PhotoWheel to add and display photo albums, but more work is needed. The user should be able to select a photo album to view its photos. The user may also want to give the photo album a name. In addition, the user will certainly want to remove any photo albums accidentally created.

Now is as good a time as any to implement these features, starting with the selection of a photo album.

Selecting the Photo Album

Most of the work of selecting a photo album has already been done. The `WheelView` class knows how to detect the selected cell, and it knows when the selected cell changes. It also sends a message to its delegate when the selected cell changes. All that is needed to complete this feature is to implement the `WheelViewDelegate` method `-wheelView:didSelectCellAtIndex:` found in *AlbumsViewController.m.*

What should this implementation do? It should notify the `PhotosViewController`—the other child view controller displayed at the top of the screen—that a different photo album has been selected. The `PhotosViewController` is responsible for displaying the details of the photo album, including the title and the photos contained within the album. It is also responsible for deleting a photo album, adding photos to the album, and setting the album title. But first things first.

The `AlbumsViewController` needs to know about the `PhotosViewController`. Without a reference to the photos view controller, the albums view controller will not be able to tell it when a photo album has been selected.

The best place to tell `AlbumsViewController` about the existence of `PhotosViewController` is in the `MainViewController` at the time the view controllers are created. As before, you can change the `-prepareForSegue:sender:`, but there is a problem with this approach: there is no way of knowing which view controller is created first. To solve this problem, additional logic must be included to handle the creation of the view controllers in any order. Once both are created, the `AlbumsViewController` can be told about the `PhotosViewController`.

This approach introduces an even bigger problem, however: it couples `PhotosViewController` to `AlbumsViewController`. For a small app like PhotoWheel, this coupling is perfectly fine, but for larger apps, this type of coupling will limit the flexibility of the app's design. What's needed here is a decoupling of the two view controllers.

A few different approaches to decoupling view controllers may be implemented in Cocoa. One approach you have already used is delegation. With delegation, an object can handle a task for another object without either object knowing about the other. All that is known is the protocol—that is, the interface for the communication from one object to the other.

Notifications are another approach to decoupling in Cocoa. Notifications allow an object to broadcast an event (i.e., a notification) to zero, one, or more listeners. An object that wishes to act on a particular notification will register itself as an observer of the notification. The observer/listener object receives the notification sent out from the sender object.

Unlike in delegation, where only one delegate can be connected to an object at a time, notifications can have multiple receivers. In turn, you can have multiple view controllers handle the same notification, which can be very handy at times. Also, with notifications, the sender and receiver objects know nothing about each other; there is no coupling between the two objects at all.

A notification is a string value. Any string value can be used for this purpose. To eliminate the possibility of typos in the string value, you should define the string value as a constant. Not only will this eliminate typos, but it also provides a compile-time check for the notification string.

To broadcast a notification, you use the notification center. In Cocoa, the notification center is defined by the `NSNotificationCenter` class. This class provides the mechanism needed for broadcasting the notification within the application. You do not need to create an instance of this class. Instead, you use the `+defaultCenter` class property to retrieve a reference to the default notification center used by the application.

Let's set up a notification that tells the `PhotosViewController` that a new album has been selected. The first thing you should do is define a constant for the notification string value. Where you define the constant is up to you and will depend on the application. For larger apps, constants might be stored either in a common *constants.h* file or in more specific source files. You can define the constant using the `#define` statement, which is a C preprocessor statement for defining constants. You can also define the string constant as an external reference to an `NSString`, but let's keep matters simple for now.

Take a look at the file *PhotoWheel-Prefix.pch*. It is the precompiled header file for the project. The precompiled header is used to speed up compile times for your project. Also, items referenced in the *.pch* file are available to all other areas of the application. For example, *PhotoWheel-Prefix.pch* includes common `#import` statements, which eliminates the need for including these `#import` statements in your custom classes.

> **Note**
>
> For the purpose of the PhotoWheel project, the *.pch* file is a good place for defining the notification string constant. The same may not be true for other projects. I tend to prefer defining constants in other, more appropriate areas of the project, such as in related class files or in a common header file.

To define the notification string constant, add the following line of code to the bottom of the *PhotoWheel-Prefix.pch* file:

```
#define kPhotoWheelDidSelectAlbum @"didSelectAlbum"
```

Note that the string value can be any value you like, though it should be unique enough to not match the string value of another notification string used in your app.

With the notification string constant defined, let's move on to sending the notification. Open the file *AlbumsViewController.m* and scroll to the `-wheelView:didSelect`

CellAtIndex: method. This delegate method is called by the WheelView object when the selected photo album changes. The selected album changes as the user spins the wheel of albums. The implementation for this method will send the kPhotoWheelDidSelectAlbum notification. The code for sending the notification is shown in Listing 16.9.

Listing 16.9   Send the kPhotoWheelDidSelectAlbum Notification

```
- (void)wheelView:(WheelView *)wheelView
didSelectCellAtIndex:(NSInteger)index
{
    NSDictionary *userInfo = nil;

    // index = -1 means no selected cell and nothing to retrieve
    // from the fetched results.
    if (index >= 0) {                                          // 1
        NSIndexPath *indexPath = nil;
        indexPath = [NSIndexPath indexPathForRow:index inSection:0];    // 2

        NSFetchedResultsController *frc = [self fetchedResultsController];
        PhotoAlbum *photoAlbum = [frc objectAtIndexPath:indexPath];    // 3
        userInfo = @{ @"PhotoAlbum":photoAlbum };              // 4
    }

    NSNotificationCenter *nc = [NSNotificationCenter defaultCenter];
    [nc postNotificationName:kPhotoWheelDidSelectAlbum         // 5
                      object:nil
                    userInfo:userInfo];
}
```

Let's take a closer look at what this code is doing.

1. A check is done to ensure the index value is greater than −1. A −1 value indicates that there is no selected album.

2. An NSIndexPath object is created using the index value. The index path is needed to retrieve the photo album object from the fetched-results controller.

3. A reference to the selected PhotoAlbum object is retrieved from the fetched-results controller.

4. There may be times, when posting a notification, that you need to send additional data with the notification. The userInfo parameter makes this possible. The parameter is an instance of NSDictionary, and it can contain any additional data you see fit for the notification. For the kPhotoWheelDidSelectAlbum notification, the userInfo dictionary is used to pass a reference to the selected PhotoAlbum object.

5. The notification is posted via the notification center. This last step will broadcast the notification throughout the app.

The notification sender is complete. Now it's time to implement the receiver. To do this, open the file *PhotosViewController.m* and add the code changes in Listing 16.10.

Listing 16.10   **Receive the kPhotoWheelDidSelectAlbum Notification**

```
#import "PhotosViewController.h"
#import "PhotoAlbum.h"                                             // 1

@interface PhotosViewController ()
@property (nonatomic, strong) PhotoAlbum *photoAlbum;             // 2
@end

@implementation PhotosViewController

- (void)dealloc                                                   // 3
{
   NSNotificationCenter *nc = [NSNotificationCenter defaultCenter];
   [nc removeObserver:self name:kPhotoWheelDidSelectAlbum object:nil];
}

- (void)viewDidLoad
{
   [super viewDidLoad];
   NSNotificationCenter *nc = [NSNotificationCenter defaultCenter];
   [nc addObserver:self                                          // 4
         selector:@selector(didSelectAlbum:)
             name:kPhotoWheelDidSelectAlbum
           object:nil];
}

- (void)didSelectAlbum:(NSNotification *)notification             // 5
{
   PhotoAlbum *photoAlbum = nil;
   NSDictionary *userInfo = [notification userInfo];
   if (userInfo) {
      photoAlbum = userInfo[@"PhotoAlbum"];
   }
   [self setPhotoAlbum:photoAlbum];
   [self reloadData];
}

- (void)reloadData                                                // 6
{
   NSLog(@"%s", __PRETTY_FUNCTION__);
}

@end
```

Let's walk through the code.

1. The file *PhotoAlbum.h* is imported into the class.

2. A declared property of type `PhotoAlbum` is defined in the class extension. This will store the reference to the selected photo album.

3. Each notification observer must be removed. The instance of `PhotosView Controller` removes itself as the observer to the `kPhotoWheelDidSelect Album` notification in the `dealloc` method. The `dealloc` method is called as the object instance is being released.

4. In the `viewDidLoad` method, the `PhotosViewController` instance registers itself as an observer of the `kPhotoWheelDidSelectAlbum` notification, and it specifies the selector `didSelectAlbum:` as the receiving method for the notification. Thus, when the notification is received, the method `-didSelectAlbum:` is called.

5. The method `-didSelectAlbum:` checks whether a `userInfo` dictionary is provided with the notification. If there is no `userInfo` dictionary, then the `photoAlbum` property is set to `nil`. If the dictionary is available, the `PhotoAlbum` instance is retrieved and the `photoAlbum` property is set to the selected photo album instance. Finally, the `reloadData` method is called.

6. The method `reloadData` is used to update the UI with the selected photo album data. You'll complete the implementation for this method later. For now, an `NSLog` statement is used to output the photo album object to the debug window. This approach makes it easier to debug the application and ensure the notification is being sent and received properly.

At this point, you should save your changes and run the app. You should see that `-reloadData` is being called as you spin the photo album wheel.

More Information

For more information on sending and receiving notifications, read the Notification Programming Topics[1] in the iOS developer documentation.

Naming the Photo Album

A nice feature to give the user is the ability to name a photo album. This name can be then displayed in the toolbar at the top of the photo album view. The same area can also be used to edit the album name—simply tap the name and it becomes editable.

---

1. Notification Programming Topics: https://developer.apple.com/library/ios/#documentation/Cocoa/Conceptual/Notifications/Introduction/introNotifications.html%23//apple_ref/doc/uid/10000043i

Of course, the toolbar does not yet exist; you must add it. You also need to add a text field to the toolbar for the photo album name as well as two bar button items to the toolbar. One bar button item is displayed on the left side of the toolbar and the other on the right. The left button is an action button that will display a menu of action items. The right button is the add button that's used to add a photo to the album.

Let's implement these requirements in your app. First open *MainStoryboard.storyboard*. Select the Photos View Controller Scene, and delete the Round Rect Button that was used to test the custom push segue—it's no longer needed.

Next, drop a `UIToolbar` onto the scene. Position it at the top of the popover image view in the area that looks like a toolbar area (set the position and size: X = 9, Y = 6, Width = 698, and Height = 44). Set the Style for the toolbar to Black Opaque, and set its Background color to Clear.

Now add two buttons (`UIBarButtonItem`) and a text field (`UITextField`) to the toolbar. Use the flexible spacing object to position the buttons and text field. There should be buttons on the left and right sides of the text field; the text field should be in the middle of the toolbar. Set the text field Width to 533. Set the Placeholder property to "Tap to edit." Set the Alignment to Center and the Border Style to nothing. Finally, set the Text Color to White and the Background to Clear.

Change the Identifier for the left button to Action, and change the Identifier for the right-side button to Add. The finished scene should look like Figure 16.6.

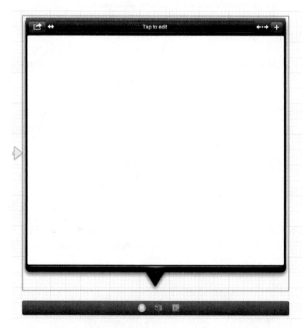

Figure 16.6 The finished photos view controller scene

Now open *PhotosViewController.m* and add the following outlets and actions to the class extension:

- Outlet named `toolbar` of type `UIToolbar`
- Outlet named `textField` of type `UITextField`
- Outlet named `addButton` of type `UIBarButtonItem`
- Action named `showActionMenu`
- Action named `addPhoto`

Alternatively, if you prefer, these can be added to the *PhotosViewController.h* file. You can either do this work by hand or use the Assistant editor. Be sure to connect the outlets and actions. The code changes are shown in Listing 16.11.

Listing 16.11 **Updated `PhotosViewController` Class**

```
#import "PhotosViewController.h"
#import "PhotoAlbum.h"

@interface PhotosViewController ()
@property (nonatomic, strong) PhotoAlbum *photoAlbum;
@property (nonatomic, weak) IBOutlet UIToolbar *toolbar;
@property (nonatomic, weak) IBOutlet UITextField *textField;
@property (nonatomic, weak) IBOutlet UIBarButtonItem *addButton;

- (IBAction)showActionMenu:(id)sender;
- (IBAction)addPhoto:(id)sender;
@end

@implementation PhotosViewController

// Other code left out for brevity's sake.

#pragma mark - Actions

- (IBAction)showActionMenu:(id)sender
{

}

- (IBAction)addPhoto:(id)sender
{

}

@end
```

> **Note**
>
> You can declare outlets and actions either in the class header or in the class extension. This hasn't always been the case. At one time, outlets and actions had to be defined in the class header, which is why you will see lots of sample code defining them in the header file.
>
> Where should you define outlets and actions? It's really a matter of personal preference, but recently more Objective-C programmers have started defining them in the class extension. This makes sense, too, because outlets and actions are typically used by the class implementation only, and defining them private to the class keeps the public header focused on what is truly public.

One last connection is needed in the photos controller scene. **Control-drag** the text field to the photos view controller object, and make the view controller the delegate of the text field.

With the scene in place, turn your attention back to the implementation of `Photos ViewController`. A number of things must happen to prepare this class to manage a photo album. First, the `-reloadData` method must be implemented. It should present the photo album data to the user. If there is no photo album, the toolbar should be hidden. This prevents the user from manipulating a `nil` photo album.

`PhotosViewController` must also respond to `UITextFieldDelegate` methods. These responses control the user experience while editing the photo album name, and they tell the controller when to save the updated album name. The updated version of *PhotosViewController.m* is given in Listing 16.12. Apply these changes to your code.

Listing 16.12   Updated *PhotosViewController.m*

```
#import "PhotosViewController.h"
#import "PhotoAlbum.h"

@interface PhotosViewController ()
@property (nonatomic, strong) PhotoAlbum *photoAlbum;
@property (nonatomic, weak) IBOutlet UIToolbar *toolbar;           // 1
@property (nonatomic, weak) IBOutlet UITextField *textField;
@property (nonatomic, weak) IBOutlet UIBarButtonItem *addButton;

- (IBAction)showActionMenu:(id)sender;                             // 2
- (IBAction)addPhoto:(id)sender;
@end

@implementation PhotosViewController

// Other code left out for brevity's sake.

- (void)reloadData                                                 // 3
{
    PhotoAlbum *album = [self photoAlbum];
    if (album) {
        [[self toolbar] setHidden:NO];
```

```objc
      [[self textField] setText:[album name]];
   } else {
      [[self toolbar] setHidden:YES];
      [[self textField] setText:@""];
   }
}

- (void)saveChanges                                                      // 4
{
   PhotoAlbum *album = [self photoAlbum];
   NSManagedObjectContext *context = [album managedObjectContext];
   NSError *error = nil;
   if (![context save:&error])
   {
      // Replace this implementation with code to handle the
      // error appropriately.
      NSLog(@"Unresolved error %@, %@", error, [error userInfo]);
      abort();
   }
}

#pragma mark - UITextFieldDelegate methods                               // 5

- (BOOL)textFieldShouldBeginEditing:(UITextField *)textField             // 6
{
   [textField setBorderStyle:UITextBorderStyleRoundedRect];
   [textField setTextColor:[UIColor blackColor]];
   [textField setBackgroundColor:[UIColor whiteColor]];
   return YES;
}

- (void)textFieldDidEndEditing:(UITextField *)textField                  // 7
{
   [textField setBackgroundColor:[UIColor clearColor]];
   [textField setTextColor:[UIColor whiteColor]];
   [textField setBorderStyle:UITextBorderStyleNone];

   [[self photoAlbum] setName:[textField text]];
   [self saveChanges];
}

- (BOOL)textFieldShouldReturn:(UITextField *)textField                   // 8
{
   [textField resignFirstResponder];
   return NO;
}

@end
```

Let's run through the code in Listing 16.12:

1–2. The outlets and actions are defined privately in the `PhotosViewController` class extension.

3. The implementation for `-reloadData` has changed. It checks whether the view controller has a reference to a `PhotoAlbum` instance. If it does, the toolbar is made visible and the text field's `text` property is set to the photo album's name. When the photo album is `nil`, the toolbar is hidden.

4. The method `-saveChanges` is a helper method. Saving the context is needed throughout the controller, so having a common save changes method is helpful.

    This method retrieves the managed object context from the `photoAlbum` property. `photoAlbum` is an instance of `PhotoAlbum`, which is a subclass of `NSManagedObject`. A managed object knows its context, so we're able to use that context instead of passing in a reference to the managed object context as part of the `kPhotoWheelDidSelectAlbum` notification.

5–6. The save helper method is followed by the `UITextFieldDelegate` methods. These methods represent the meat of what you are trying to accomplish at the moment. The first delegate method, `-textFieldShouldBeginEditing:`, is called just before editing in the text field begins. Here the code changes the text field border style, text color, and background to give the appearance of being in an edit mode.

7. The edit mode appearance is reset in the `-textFieldDidEndEditing:` method. This method is called after editing in the text field has ended. In addition to the visual appearance of the text field being reset, the edited text is saved as the photo album's name.

8. The last of the `UITextFieldDelegate` methods used in this controller is `-textFieldShouldReturn:`. This method is called when the user taps the **Return** button on the virtual keyboard. The implementation of this method dismisses the keyboard. The method `-resignFirstResponder` on the text field is called to dismiss the keyboard.

Congratulations! The app now supports editing of the photo album name. Build and run the app, and test the new feature. Note that as you spin the photo album wheel, the album name in the toolbar will change, and the toolbar will show and hide itself based on whether a photo album has been selected.

Fixing the Toolbar Display

When you ran the app, you may have noticed that the toolbar looks a little odd. The background for the toolbar has been set to Clear, but it's not clear. Instead, the toolbar sits on top of the image and hides the rounded corners of the background image. To fix this problem, a little hackery is needed.

Setting the background color to Clear for the toolbar does not actually make it clear. However, setting the background *image* for the toolbar to a clear, transparent image does work. All you need is a 1 × 1-pixel transparent image; you can then set the background image on the toolbar to the transparent image.

The code change, shown in Listing 16.13, to *PhotosViewController.m* is needed to make the toolbar background transparent.

Listing 16.13   **Make the Toolbar Background Transparent**

```
- (void)viewDidLoad
{
    [super viewDidLoad];
    NSNotificationCenter *nc = [NSNotificationCenter defaultCenter];
    [nc addObserver:self
           selector:@selector(didSelectAlbum:)
               name:kPhotoWheelDidSelectAlbum
             object:nil];

    UIImage *image = [UIImage imageNamed:@"1x1-transparent"];
    [[self toolbar] setBackgroundImage:image
                    forToolbarPosition:UIToolbarPositionAny
                            barMetrics:UIBarMetricsDefault];
}
```

Save your changes, and then build and run the app again. The toolbar should look much better, as shown in Figure 16.7.

Figure 16.7   The cleaned-up version of the toolbar

Removing the Photo Album

If the user can add a photo album, then surely he will want to remove one. Photo-
Wheel needs a way for the user to delete a photo album. The action button on the left
side of the toolbar is a good place to display a menu of actions, including Delete Photo
Album. When the user taps this action item, the app should prompt for confirmation;
otherwise, the user may end up deleting his favorite set of photos accidentally.

To make all of this happen, open *PhotosViewController.m* and scroll to the `-show`
`ActionMenu:` action method. Create a `UIActionSheet` and add a button with the
title "Delete Photo Album." Then show the action sheet from the action button. You
must also set the view controller as the delegate for the action sheet, which means
you must add `UIActionSheetDelegate` to the list of conforming protocols on the
`PhotosViewController` class extension.

Finally, display the `UIAlertView` to confirm the delete with the user. This is the
user's last chance to back out of the action before the photo album is gone forever.

The code changes to accomplish all of this are shown in Listing 16.14.

Listing 16.14   **Add Photo Album Deletion Support**

```
#import "PhotosViewController.h"
#import "PhotoAlbum.h"

@interface PhotosViewController () <UIActionSheetDelegate>
// Other code left out for brevity's sake.
@end

@implementation PhotosViewController

// Other code left out for brevity's sake.

- (IBAction)showActionMenu:(id)sender
{
    UIActionSheet *actionSheet = [[UIActionSheet alloc] init];
    [actionSheet setDelegate:self];
    [actionSheet addButtonWithTitle:@"Delete Photo Album"];
    [actionSheet showFromBarButtonItem:sender animated:YES];
}

#pragma mark - Confirm and delete photo album

- (void)confirmDeletePhotoAlbum
{
    NSString *message;
    NSString *name = [[self photoAlbum] name];
    if ([name length] > 0) {
        message = [NSString stringWithFormat:
                    @"Delete the photo album \"%@\". This action cannot be undone.",
                    name];
```

```
   } else {
      message = @"Delete this photo album? This action cannot be undone.";
   }
   UIAlertView *alertView = [[UIAlertView alloc]
                              initWithTitle:@"Delete Photo Album"
                              message:message
                              delegate:self
                              cancelButtonTitle:@"Cancel"
                              otherButtonTitles:@"OK", nil];
   [alertView show];
}


#pragma mark - UIAlertViewDelegate methods

- (void)alertView:(UIAlertView *)alertView
clickedButtonAtIndex:(NSInteger)buttonIndex
{
   if (buttonIndex == 1) {
      PhotoAlbum *album = [self photoAlbum];
      NSManagedObjectContext *context = [album managedObjectContext];
      [context deleteObject:album];
      [self saveChanges];
      [self setPhotoAlbum:nil];
      [self reloadData];
   }
}


#pragma mark - UIActionSheetDelegate methods

- (void)actionSheet:(UIActionSheet *)actionSheet
clickedButtonAtIndex:(NSInteger)buttonIndex
{
   // Do nothing if the user taps outside the action
   // sheet (thus closing the popover containing the
   // action sheet).
   if (buttonIndex < 0) {
      return;
   }

   [self confirmDeletePhotoAlbum];
}

@end
```

That's it. Photo albums can now be deleted.

A Better Photo Album Thumbnail

The photo album thumbnails look okay, but there's room for improvement. For instance, the thumbnail icons don't exactly convey a collection of photos to the user. Also, the photo album name is not even displayed. It's time to change this element's appearance. `

Open *PhotoWheelViewCell.h* and replace the interface code with the code in Listing 16.15.

Listing 16.15   Updated *PhotoWheelViewCell.h*

```
#import "WheelView.h"

@interface PhotoWheelViewCell : WheelViewCell

@property (nonatomic, weak) IBOutlet UIImageView *imageView;
@property (nonatomic, weak) IBOutlet UILabel *label;

+ (PhotoWheelViewCell *)photoWheelViewCell;

@end
```

By now, this code change shouldn't look too foreign to you. Two outlets are added as declared properties. The image view is used to display the thumbnail, and the label is used to display the photo album name.

What might look a little different to you is the class method +photoWheelView Cell. The + at the beginning of the method name indicates that this is a class method, not an instance method. The method is used to return a photo wheel view cell.

> **Note**
>
> Methods like +photoWheelViewCell are sometimes called convenience methods, reflecting the fact that they are provided as a matter of convenience. In this particular case, the method makes it more convenient to create a new PhotoWheelViewCell instance.

Now open *PhotoWheelViewCell.m* and update the implementation with the code given in Listing 16.16. This new code replaces all of the old code.

Listing 16.16   Updated *PhotoWheelViewCell.m*

```
#import "PhotoWheelViewCell.h"

@implementation PhotoWheelViewCell

+ (PhotoWheelViewCell *)photoWheelViewCell
{
    NSString *nibName = NSStringFromClass([self class]);
```

```
    UINib *nib = [UINib nibWithNibName:nibName bundle:nil];
    NSArray *nibObjects = [nib instantiateWithOwner:nil options:nil];
    // Verify that the top-level object is of the correct type.
    NSAssert2([nibObjects count] > 0 &&
              [[nibObjects objectAtIndex:0] isKindOfClass:[self class]],
              @"Nib '%@' does not contain top-level view of type %@.",
              nibName, nibName);
    return [nibObjects objectAtIndex:0];
}

@end
```

The previous implementation of PhotoWheelViewCell used a CALayer to draw an image onto the view. The new PhotoWheelViewCell uses a NIB file to define the view layout. The code in +photoWheelViewCell returns an instance of the cell created in the NIB *PhotoWheelViewCell.xib*, which you have not created yet.

The first line of code retrieves the name of the class. The class name will be the name of the NIB. The next line of code sets a local variable to the NIB instance. The class method -nibWithNibName:bundle: found on UINib is used to retrieve the NIB instance. The NIB is then instantiated, and an array of objects found in the NIB is returned. A quick verification check is performed to ensure that the array has at least one object and the top-level object is of the expected class type, which is PhotoWheelViewCell. Finally, the top-level object is returned to the caller.

Once you complete the code changes, create a new NIB file and add it to the PhotoWheel project. Creating a NIB file is similar to creating other project files. Press **Command-N** to create a new file. Select **iOS > User Interface**, and then select the Empty file template, as shown in Figure 16.8. Click the **Next** button, and then select iPhone as the Device Family. Click the **Next** button, and save the NIB file as PhotoWheelViewCell.

Why Select iPhone as the Device Family?

The photo wheel view cell is a small view. When you select iPhone as the device family, IB creates a smaller view than it would have if you had selected iPad.

Open the NIB file *PhotoWheelViewCell.xib*. Drag a view onto the design canvas. Change the class name for the view to PhotoWheelViewCell. Set the Background color to Clear, and give the view a Width of 97 and a Height of 117.

Depending on the version of Xcode you are using, you may need to change the simulated size metric before you can resize the view. With the view selected, go to the Attributes inspector (**Option-Command-4**) and change the Size to Freeform. With this change, you will be able to resize the view to any dimension you like.

Drop a UIImageView into the view. Set the image name to *defaultPhoto.png* and set the frame position and size: X = 12, Y = 10, Width = 75, and Height = 75. **Control-drag**

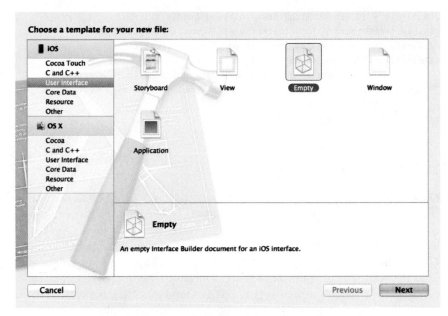

Figure 16.8   Create a new NIB using the Empty file template.

the photo wheel view cell view object to the image view, and connect it to the `image`
`View` outlet. This is the image view that displays the photo album thumbnail image.

Now add a new auto layout constraint to the image view to pin the width of the
image view to 75. Auto layout is covered in Chapter 18, "Supporting Device Rotation," so for now follow these steps and worry about understanding them later.

1. Select the image view.

2. Select **Editor > Pin > Width** from the menu bar.

This creates a new auto layout constraint that restricts the width of the image view
to 75 points. If you didn't do this, the width of the image view would be resized to
match the image's width. Because retina images are twice the size of normal images,
displaying a retina version of the thumbnail image here will cause the image view
width to increase from 75 to 150, which is not the effect we want in the app.

You don't need to add a height constraint because it was added for you automatically when the image view was dropped into the container view.

Moving on . . . drag another `UIImageView` onto the view. Set the image name to
stack-overlay.png, and set the frame position and size: X = 0, Y = 0, Width = 97, and
Height = 97.

Finally, drag a `UILabel` onto the view. In the Attributes inspector, set Line Breaks to
Truncate Middle and Alignment to Center. Set the Text Color to Default (or Black) and
the Font size to 14. In the Size inspector, set the frame: X = 0, Y = 90, Width = 97, and

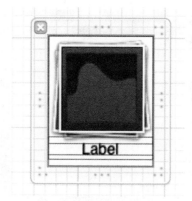

Figure 16.9   UI for the `PhotoWheelViewCell` NIB file

Height = 21. Now **Control-drag** the photo wheel view cell view object to the label, connecting it to the label outlet.

The final results should look like Figure 16.9.

To use the new and improved `PhotoWheelViewCell`, open *AlbumsViewController.m* and scroll to the method `-wheelView:cellAtIndex:`. Update the implementation with the code changes in Listing 16.17.

Listing 16.17   **Updated `-wheelView:cellAtIndex:` Method**

```
- (WheelViewCell *)wheelView:(WheelView *)wheelView cellAtIndex:(NSInteger)index
{
    PhotoWheelViewCell *cell = [wheelView dequeueReusableCell];
    if (!cell) {
        cell = [PhotoWheelViewCell photoWheelViewCell];                      // 1
    }

    NSIndexPath *indexPath;
    indexPath = [NSIndexPath indexPathForRow:index inSection:0];
    NSFetchedResultsController *frc = [self fetchedResultsController];
    PhotoAlbum *photoAlbum = [frc objectAtIndexPath:indexPath];
    Photo *photo = [[photoAlbum photos] lastObject];
    UIImage *image = [photo thumbnailImage];
    if (image == nil) {
        image = [UIImage imageNamed:@"defaultPhoto.png"];
    }

    [[cell imageView] setImage:image];                                      // 2
    [[cell label] setText:[photoAlbum name]];                               // 3

    return cell;
}
```

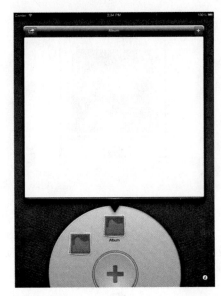

Figure 16.10   PhotoWheel with the new thumbnail display style

Three lines of code were changed in this update, so let's take a look at them:

1. If a reusable cell is not returned, a new cell is created using the convenience method +photoWheelViewCell on PhotoWheelViewCell.

2. The second change replaces [cell setImage:image] with [[cell image View] setImage:image]. The previous implementation of the photo wheel view cell handled drawing the image on the layer, but the new implementation uses an image view instead.

3. The third and final change is the addition of the line [[cell label] set Text:[photoAlbum name]]. This change displays the photo album name in the wheel.

Run the app to see how the new thumbnail looks—a definite improvement, as you can see in Figure 16.10.

Adding Photos

You have accomplished a lot in this chapter so far, but a bit more must be done. The last major component missing from PhotoWheel is the display of photos. Of course, before the app can display photos, the user must have a way to add them.

You already added the + button (also known as the add button) to the toolbar, and in the prototype app you wrote code to pick an image from the Photos app library or the camera. It's time to pull those pieces together and give the user a way to add photos to the photo album.

Start by opening *PhotosViewController.m* and adding `UIImagePickerController`
`Delegate` and `UINavigationControllerDelegate` to the list of conforming protocols to the class extension. Yes, it seems strange to include `UINavigationControl`
`lerDelegate` in the list of protocols, but it's required to be a delegate of `UIImage`
`PickerController`. It's not a big deal, though. All of the methods of `UINavigation`
`ControllerDelegate` are optional, so there are no required `UINavigationControl`
`lerDelegate` methods to implement.

Next, add the code that makes it possible for a user to add a photo to the photo
album. You have already written this code. It's in the prototype app, but for the sake
of completeness, the updated *PhotosViewController.m* is shown in Listing 16.18. You
need to apply the same changes to your code.

Listing 16.18   **Updated** *PhotosViewController.m*

```
#import "PhotosViewController.h"
#import "PhotoAlbum.h"
#import "Photo.h"                                            // 1

@interface PhotosViewController () <UIActionSheetDelegate,
UIImagePickerControllerDelegate, UINavigationControllerDelegate>    // 2

// Other code left out for brevity's sake.

@property (nonatomic, strong) UIImagePickerController
*imagePickerController;                                      // 3
@property (nonatomic, strong) UIPopoverController
*imagePickerPopoverController;                               // 4
@end

@implementation PhotosViewController

// Other code left out for brevity's sake.

- (UIImagePickerController *)imagePickerController            // 5
{
   if (_imagePickerController) {
      return _imagePickerController;
   }

   UIImagePickerController *imagePickerController = nil;
   imagePickerController = [[UIImagePickerController alloc] init];
   [imagePickerController setDelegate:self];
   [self setImagePickerController:imagePickerController];

   return _imagePickerController;
}
```

```objc
- (IBAction)addPhoto:(id)sender                                    // 6
{
    if ([self imagePickerPopoverController]) {
        [[self imagePickerPopoverController] dismissPopoverAnimated:YES];
    }

    [self presentPhotoPickerMenu];
}

- (void)actionSheet:(UIActionSheet *)actionSheet
clickedButtonAtIndex:(NSInteger)buttonIndex                        // 7
{
    // Do nothing if the user taps outside the action
    // sheet (thus closing the popover containing the
    // action sheet).
    if (buttonIndex < 0) {
        return;
    }

    NSMutableArray *names = [[NSMutableArray alloc] init];          // 8

    if ([actionSheet tag] == 0) {
        [names addObject:@"confirmDeletePhotoAlbum"];

    } else {
        BOOL hasCamera = [UIImagePickerController
                    isSourceTypeAvailable:UIImagePickerControllerSourceTypeCamera];
        if (hasCamera) [names addObject:@"presentCamera"];
        [names addObject:@"presentPhotoLibrary"];
    }

    SEL selector = NSSelectorFromString([names objectAtIndex:buttonIndex]);
#pragma clang diagnostic push
#pragma clang diagnostic ignored "-Warc-performSelector-leaks"
    [self performSelector:selector];
#pragma clang diagnostic pop
}

#pragma mark - Image picker helper methods

- (void)presentCamera
{
    // Display the camera.
    UIImagePickerController *imagePicker = [self imagePickerController];
    [imagePicker setSourceType:UIImagePickerControllerSourceTypeCamera];
    [self presentViewController:imagePicker animated:YES completion:nil];
}
```

```objc
- (void)presentPhotoLibrary
{
    // Display assets from the photo library only.
    UIImagePickerController *imagePicker = [self imagePickerController];
    [imagePicker setSourceType:UIImagePickerControllerSourceTypePhotoLibrary];

    UIPopoverController *newPopoverController =
    [[UIPopoverController alloc] initWithContentViewController:imagePicker];
    [newPopoverController presentPopoverFromBarButtonItem:[self addButton]
                                 permittedArrowDirections:UIPopoverArrowDirectionAny
                                                 animated:YES];
    [self setImagePickerPopoverController:newPopoverController];
}

- (void)presentPhotoPickerMenu
{
    UIActionSheet *actionSheet = [[UIActionSheet alloc] init];
    [actionSheet setDelegate:self];
    BOOL hasCamera = [UIImagePickerController
                        isSourceTypeAvailable:UIImagePickerControllerSourceTypeCamera];
    if (hasCamera) {
        [actionSheet addButtonWithTitle:@"Take Photo"];
    }
    [actionSheet addButtonWithTitle:@"Choose from Library"];
    [actionSheet setTag:1];
    [actionSheet showFromBarButtonItem:[self addButton] animated:YES];
}

#pragma mark - UIImagePickerControllerDelegate methods

- (void)imagePickerController:(UIImagePickerController *)picker
didFinishPickingMediaWithInfo:(NSDictionary *)info
{
    // If the popover controller is available,
    // assume the photo is selected from the library
    // and not from the camera.
    BOOL takenWithCamera = ([self imagePickerPopoverController] == nil);

    if (takenWithCamera) {
        [self dismissViewControllerAnimated:YES completion:nil];
    } else {
        [[self imagePickerPopoverController] dismissPopoverAnimated:YES];
        [self setImagePickerPopoverController:nil];
    }

    // Retrieve and display the image.
    UIImage *image = [info objectForKey:UIImagePickerControllerOriginalImage];
```

```
    PhotoAlbum *album = [self photoAlbum];
    NSManagedObjectContext *context = [album managedObjectContext];
    Photo *newPhoto =
    [NSEntityDescription insertNewObjectForEntityForName:@"Photo"
                                    inManagedObjectContext:context];
    [newPhoto setDateAdded:[NSDate date]];
    [newPhoto saveImage:image];
    [newPhoto setPhotoAlbum:[self photoAlbum]];

    [self saveChanges];
}

@end
```

Now for the walk-through, highlighting the changes:

1–4. *Photo.h* is added to the list of imports. The protocols `UIImagePickerCon` `trollerDelegate` and `UINavigationControllerDelegate` have been added to the list of confirming protocols. Two declared properties have also been added to the class extension; the first is a reference to the image picker, and the second is a reference to the popover controller used to present the image picker.

5. A custom getter method has been created for `imagePickerController`. It lazy loads the `UIImagePickerController` instance used by the view controller.

6. The getter is followed by `-addPhoto:`. Previously its implementation was empty, but now it starts the process for picking an image. It also dismisses the popover controller if it is open.

7. The method `-actionSheet:clickedButtonAtIndex:`, which is a callback for the `UIActionSheetDelegate` protocol, has been modified to support more than one action sheet. The action button displays one action sheet, and the add button displays the other. Both use the `PhotosViewController` instance as their delegates, so the same callback method is called regardless of the sending action sheet. The tag property on the action sheet is used to distinguish between the two action sheets. A tag value of 0 indicates that the action sheet is used by the action button. A tag value of 1 indicates that the action sheet is used by the add button.

8. To make the code in `-actionSheet:clickedButtonAtIndex:` more maintainable, a mutable array is used to list the selector names for each menu item within the action sheet. The `buttonIndex` is then used to retrieve the selector name from the array, and `-performSelector:` is called to invoke the selector. This dynamic approach to calling selectors is a powerful feature of Objective-C not found in many other compiled programming languages.

> **Note**
>
> The PhotoWheel project uses ARC to transfer responsibility for memory management of objects to the compiler. Because the selector is unknown in the `-performSelector:` call, a "possible memory leak" warning message is reported by the compiler. This warning is legitimate given that ARC does not know the selector—the selector is determined at runtime. In fact, the code in question does not cause a leak. Therefore, it is safe to ignore the warning message, and that's exactly what the `#pragma clang` statements do. They tell the compiler to ignore the warning, so you can have a clean build.

The remaining code in Listing 16.18 is similar to the code you wrote for the prototype app for picking an image. Refer to Chapter 12, "Adding Photos," if you need a refresher on what the code is doing.

Displaying Photos

The final piece missing from PhotoWheel is the display of photos. A nice way to present the photos is to lay them out in a grid, and the collection view, which you learned about in Chapter 10, "Using Collection and Custom Views," is the perfect object for this task.

Open the storyboard file *MainStoryboard.storyboard*, and then select and zoom in on the Photos View Controller Scene. Drag and drop a `UICollectionView` from the Objects library to the Photos View Controller Scene. Size the collection view to fill the white space area of the background image. If you like, you can use the Size inspector to manually set the frame: X = 16, Y = 51, Width = 684, and Height = 597.

Next, you need to create the cell that is displayed in the collection view. In Chapter 10, you did this by creating a new NIB file for the collection view cell. Now, however, you will create a prototype collection view cell directly in the collection view.

When you added the collection view to the scene, a prototype collection view cell was created for you in the upper-left corner of the collection view. You can click in the upper-left corner to select this cell, or you can select it from the Document Outline, as shown in Figure 16.11. The prototype cell allows you to design the cell's look directly within the storyboard. There's no need to create a separate NIB file for the cell.

A collection view can have one or more prototype cells in it. To add another prototype cell, simply drag and drop a "collection view cell" from the Objects library onto the collection view. Each cell has its own unique reuse identifier, which you set in the Attributes inspector. This identifier is used to dequeue the appropriate cell for display at run time.

Only one prototype cell is needed for the PhotoWheel app, so do not add a second one. Select the cell that was created for you, and set the reuse identifier to "Thumbnail-Cell" in the Attributes inspector.

The cell's default size is 50 × 50 points, but we want to display the thumbnail image at a size of 100 × 100 pixels. You can set a custom cell size on the prototype cell, but changing the default size of the cell is more appropriate here. Select the

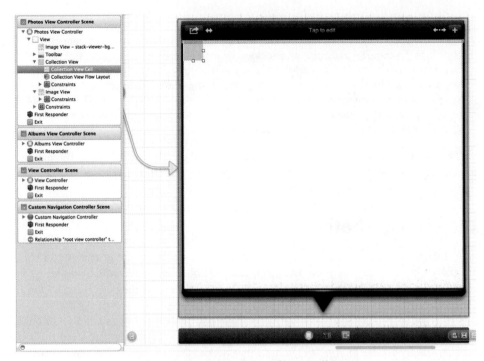

Figure 16.11   A prototype collection view cell

collection view, and open the Size inspector. Here you will find the default size for all cells displayed in the collection view. Change the cell size from a width and height of 50 to 100.

Let's not have the cell flushed up against the edges of the collection view; let's have a bit of spacing instead. While you still have the Size inspector open for the collection view, set the Section Insets for top, bottom, left, and right to 10 (Figure 16.12). This will move the cell off the edges by 10 points.

Now you need to add an image view to the prototype collection view cell. The image view is used to display the thumbnail of the photo. Drag an image view from the Objects library and drop it onto the prototype cell. The image view should be sized to fill the entire space of the cell.

A custom class is needed for the cell to set the image on the image view, so create a new Objective-C class. Name the call "ThumbnailCell" and make it a subclass of UICollectionViewCell. Next, open the file *ThumbnailCell.h* and add an outlet of type UIImageView. Name the outlet imageView. The code change is shown in Listing 16.19.

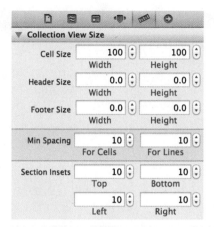

Figure 16.12   Collection view size settings

Listing 16.19   **Add an Outlet for the Image View**

```
#import <UIKit/UIKit.h>

@interface ThumbnailCell : UICollectionViewCell

@property (nonatomic, weak) IBOutlet UIImageView *imageView;

@end
```

Return to the storyboard and assign `ThumbnailCell` as the class type for the prototype collection view cell. To do this, select the prototype cell in the storyboard scene, open the Identity inspector, and change the class from `UICollectionViewCell` to `ThumbnailCell`. Finally, **Control-drag** from the thumbnail cell in the Document Outline to the image view to connect the outlet (Figure 16.13)

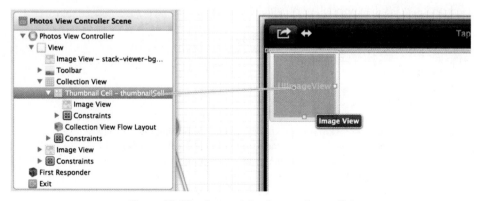

Figure 16.13   Connect the image view outlet

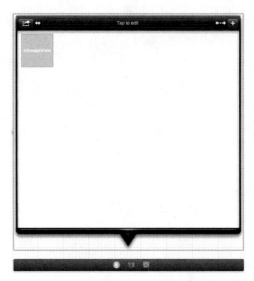

Figure 16.14   Completed scene with collection view,
prototype cell, and drop shadow

There's one last visual change to make. To soften the look as a user scrolls the grid up, place a drop shadow under the toolbar. The easiest way to accomplish this is to drag a UIImageView into the scene. Set the image name to *stack-viewer-shadow.png*, and set its frame position and size: X = 9, Y = 51, Width = 698, and Height = 8.

The completed scene should look like Figure 16.14.

Using the Collection View

Next, you need to add the code that works with the collection view and prototype cell to display the photos within the photo album. The code should be familiar to you now because it's similar to other code you have written up to this point.

Open the file *PhotosViewController.m* and apply the changes shown in Listing 16.20.

Listing 16.20   **Code Changes to Display Photos**

```
#import "PhotosViewController.h"
#import "PhotoAlbum.h"
#import "Photo.h"
#import "ThumbnailCell.h"

@interface PhotosViewController () <UIActionSheetDelegate,
UIImagePickerControllerDelegate, UINavigationControllerDelegate,
UICollectionViewDataSource, UICollectionViewDelegate,
NSFetchedResultsControllerDelegate>

// Other code left out for brevity's sake.
```

```objc
@property (nonatomic, weak) IBOutlet UICollectionView *collectionView;
@property (nonatomic, strong) NSFetchedResultsController *fetchedResultsController;
@end

@implementation PhotosViewController

// Other code left out for brevity's sake.

#pragma mark - NSFetchedResultsController and NSFetchedResultsControllerDelegate

- (NSFetchedResultsController *)fetchedResultsController
{
    if (_fetchedResultsController) {
        return _fetchedResultsController;
    }

    PhotoAlbum *album = [self photoAlbum];
    NSManagedObjectContext *context = [album managedObjectContext];
    if (!context) {
        return nil;
    }

    NSString *cacheName = [NSString stringWithFormat:@"%@-%@",
                              [self.photoAlbum name], [self.photoAlbum dateAdded]]];
    NSFetchRequest *fetchRequest = [[NSFetchRequest alloc] init];
    NSEntityDescription *entityDescription =
    [NSEntityDescription entityForName:@"Photo"
                inManagedObjectContext:context];
    [fetchRequest setEntity:entityDescription];

    NSSortDescriptor *sortDescriptor =
    [NSSortDescriptor sortDescriptorWithKey:@"dateAdded" ascending:YES];
    [fetchRequest setSortDescriptors:[NSArray arrayWithObject:sortDescriptor]];

    NSPredicate *predicate = nil;
    predicate = [NSPredicate predicateWithFormat:@"photoAlbum = %@", [self
photoAlbum]];
    [fetchRequest setPredicate:predicate];

    NSFetchedResultsController *newFetchedResultsController =
    [[NSFetchedResultsController alloc] initWithFetchRequest:fetchRequest
                                        managedObjectContext:context
                                          sectionNameKeyPath:nil
                                                   cacheName:cacheName];
    [newFetchedResultsController setDelegate:self];
    [self setFetchedResultsController:newFetchedResultsController];

    NSError *error = nil;
```

```objc
    if (![[self fetchedResultsController] performFetch:&error])
    {
       // Replace this implementation with code to handle the
       // error appropriately.

       NSLog(@"Unresolved error %@, %@", error, [error userInfo]);
       abort();
    }


    return _fetchedResultsController;
}

- (void)controllerDidChangeContent:(NSFetchedResultsController *)controller
{
    [[self collectionView] reloadData];
}

#pragma mark - UICollectionViewDataSource and UICollectionViewDelegate

- (NSInteger)collectionView:(UICollectionView *)collectionView
     numberOfItemsInSection:(NSInteger)section
{
    NSFetchedResultsController *frc = [self fetchedResultsController];
    NSInteger count = [[[frc sections] objectAtIndex:section] numberOfObjects];
    return count;
}

- (UICollectionViewCell *)collectionView:(UICollectionView *)collectionView
                cellForItemAtIndexPath:(NSIndexPath *)indexPath
{
    ThumbnailCell *cell =
    [collectionView dequeueReusableCellWithReuseIdentifier:@"ThumbnailCell"
                                              forIndexPath:indexPath];

    NSFetchedResultsController *frc = [self fetchedResultsController];
    Photo *photo = [frc objectAtIndexPath:indexPath];
    [[cell imageView] setImage:[photo smallImage]];

    return cell;
}

- (void)collectionView:(UICollectionView *)collectionView
didSelectItemAtIndexPath:(NSIndexPath *)indexPath
{

}

@end
```

The code changes start by importing *ThumbnailCell.h*. Next, the protocols `UICol lectionViewDataSource`, `UICollectionViewDelegate`, and `NSFetchedRe sultsControllerDelegate` are added to the list of conforming protocols for the class. Finally, code for setting up the fetched-results controller and managing the collection view is added to the class.

At this point, it's time to test the changes. Run the app and see what happens.

The collection view has a black background, but even worse, the collection view does not display any photos. So what's going on here?

The fix for the background is easy. Just open the scene in the storyboard, select the collection view, and change its background color from default to white.

The second fix is easy as well. The collection view must be connected to the `col lectionView` outlet, and its delegate and data source must be connected to `Photos ViewController`. You can connect the outlet by **Control-dragging** from the Photos View Controller in the Document Outline to the collection view, and you can connect the delegate and data source by doing just the opposite—**Control-dragging** from the collection view in the Document Outline to the Photos View Controller.

Once the connections have been made, build and run the app. You should now see photos in the collection view, assuming you have added photos to a photo album (Figure 16.15).

Let's make one other change that will make the collection view come to life. Go back to the Photos View Controller scene in the storyboard, and select the collection view. Open the Attributes inspector and turn on the "Bounce Vertically" option. With this option turned on, the user can interact with the collection and receive visual

Figure 16.15   PhotoWheel with photos

feedback even when the number of photos displayed is less than what is needed to cause scrolling within the collection view.

And that is it.

Summary

Congratulations! You made it through the book's longest chapter. Go on, pat yourself on the back; you deserve it. You have accomplished quite a bit in this chapter.

You took advantage of existing code from the prototype to help speed up development. You made the `WheelView` class more robust, and you used a collection view to display a grid of photos. You now have, for the first time, a functional photo app that is worth showing off.

Award yourself for a job well done by taking a break. When you're feeling refreshed and ready, we'll tackle adding new features to PhotoWheel in Chapter 17, "Creating a Photo Browser."

Exercises

1. Modify the add photo logic in `PhotosViewController` to save new photos to the camera roll (refer to Chapter 12, "Adding Photos," for pointers on how to do this).

17

Creating a Photo Browser

In this chapter, you will add a full-screen photo browser to PhotoWheel. You will also learn more ways to use the `UIScrollView` *class.*

The `UIScrollView` *class provides a way to present a view that is larger than the visible area on the screen. Swiping touch gestures are used to scroll the content area horizontally and vertically, and the pinch gesture is used to zoom in and out. As you build the photo browser, you will learn how to use the scroll view to scroll content and zoom in and out of the view.*

It's time to get started.

Using the Scroll View

You will use the scroll view for two different purposes as you build the photo browser. First, you will use the class to build a full-screen photo browser. This browser enables users to flick through an album of photos by swiping left and right with a finger. Later, you will use the `UIScrollView` class to enable the user to zoom in and out on a photo.

To begin, you need a view controller for the photo browser. Create a new Objective-C class named `PhotoBrowserViewController` that is a subclass of `UIViewController`. This class will respond to scroll events, so add `UIScrollViewDelegate` to the list of protocols supported by the class. Your new class will also need an outlet for the scroll view itself, so add an outlet named `scrollView` and make it a pointer to the `UIScroll View` type.

The photo browser will be launched from the main screen when a photo is tapped. The photo browser will display the tapped photo, and the user can scroll left and right through the other photos. To support this feature, the view controller must be told the index to the starting photo. For this purpose, add a declared property of type `NSInteger` with the name `startAtIndex` to the public interface.

The photo browser must also know which photos to display. One approach to solve this problem is to pass in the photo album model object to the view controller. Another approach is to pass in the managed object context and object ID for the model object, and then fetch the photos from the Core Data store. Let's go with yet another approach, and simply tell the photo browser view controller which photos to display by passing in an array of photo objects. This means adding a declared property of type NSArray with the name photos.

The interface code for these requirements is shown in Listing 17.1.

Listing 17.1   *PhotoBrowserViewController.h*

```
#import <UIKit/UIKit.h>

@interface PhotoBrowserViewController : UIViewController <UIScrollViewDelegate>

@property (nonatomic, weak) IBOutlet UIScrollView *scrollView;
@property (nonatomic, assign) NSInteger startAtIndex;
@property (nonatomic, strong) NSArray *photos;

@end
```

With the easy part out of the way, it's time to add the implementation, shown in Listing 17.2. You must copy this code into your controller class. An explanation of the code is provided after the listing.

Listing 17.2   *PhotoBrowserViewController.m*

```
#import "PhotoBrowserViewController.h"
#import "Photo.h"                                          // 1

@interface PhotoBrowserViewController ()
@property (nonatomic, assign) NSInteger currentIndex;      // 2
@property (nonatomic, strong) NSMutableArray *photoViewCache;  // 3
@end

@implementation PhotoBrowserViewController

- (void)viewDidLoad                                        // 4
{
    [super viewDidLoad];

    // Make sure to set wantsFullScreenLayout or the photo
    // will not display behind the status bar.
    [self setWantsFullScreenLayout:YES];                   // 5

    // Set the view's frame size. This ensures that the scroll view
    // autoresizes correctly and avoids surprises when retrieving
    // the scroll view's bounds later.
    CGRect frame = [[UIScreen mainScreen] bounds];         // 6
    [[self view] setFrame:frame];

    UIScrollView *scrollView = [self scrollView];          // 7
```

```
    // Set the initial size.
    [scrollView setFrame:[self frameForPagingScrollView]];
    [scrollView setDelegate:self];
    [scrollView setBackgroundColor:[UIColor blackColor]];
    [scrollView setTranslatesAutoresizingMaskIntoConstraints:YES];
    [scrollView setAutoresizingMask:UIViewAutoresizingFlexibleWidth |
     UIViewAutoresizingFlexibleHeight];
    [scrollView setAutoresizesSubviews:YES];
    [scrollView setPagingEnabled:YES];
    [scrollView setShowsVerticalScrollIndicator:NO];
    [scrollView setShowsHorizontalScrollIndicator:NO];

    [self initPhotoViewCache];                                      // 8
}

- (void)viewWillAppear:(BOOL)animated                               // 9
{
    [super viewWillAppear:animated];
    [self setScrollViewContentSize];
    [self setCurrentIndex:[self startAtIndex]];
    [self scrollToIndex:[self startAtIndex]];
    [self setTitleWithCurrentIndex];
}

#pragma mark - Helpers

- (NSInteger)numberOfPhotos                                         // 10
{
    NSInteger numberOfPhotos = [[self photos] count];
    return numberOfPhotos;
}

- (UIImage*)imageAtIndex:(NSInteger)index                           // 11
{
    Photo *photo = [[self photos] objectAtIndex:index];
    UIImage *image = [photo largeImage];
    return image;
}

#pragma mark - Helper methods

- (void)initPhotoViewCache                                          // 12
{
    // Set up the photo's view cache. We keep only three views in
    // memory. NSNull is used as a placeholder for the other
    // elements in the view cache array.
```

```
   NSInteger numberOfPhotos = [self numberOfPhotos];
   NSMutableArray *cache = nil;
   cache = [[NSMutableArray alloc] initWithCapacity:numberOfPhotos];
   for (int i=0; i < numberOfPhotos; i++) {
      [cache addObject:[NSNull null]];
   }
   [self setPhotoViewCache:cache];
}


- (void)setScrollViewContentSize                              // 13
{
   NSInteger pageCount = [self numberOfPhotos];
   if (pageCount == 0) {
      pageCount = 1;
   }

   CGRect bounds = [[self scrollView] bounds];
   CGSize size = CGSizeMake(bounds.size.width * pageCount,
                            // Divide in half to prevent horizontal
                            // scrolling.
                            bounds.size.height / 2);
   [[self scrollView] setContentSize:size];
}


- (void)scrollToIndex:(NSInteger)index                        // 14
{
   CGRect bounds = [[self scrollView] bounds];
   bounds.origin.x = bounds.size.width * index;
   bounds.origin.y = 0;
   [[self scrollView] scrollRectToVisible:bounds animated:NO];
}


- (void)setTitleWithCurrentIndex                              // 15
{
   NSInteger index = [self currentIndex] + 1;
   if (index < 1) {
      // Prevents the title from showing 0 of n when the user
      // attempts to scroll the first page to the right.
      index = 1;
   }
   NSInteger count = [self numberOfPhotos];
   NSString *title = nil;
   title = [NSString stringWithFormat:@"%1$i of %2$i", index, count, nil];
   [self setTitle:title];
}


#pragma mark - Frame calculations
```

```
#define PADDING  20

- (CGRect)frameForPagingScrollView                                    // 16
{
   CGRect frame = [[UIScreen mainScreen] bounds];
   frame.origin.x -= PADDING;
   frame.size.width += (2 * PADDING);
   return frame;
}


- (CGRect)frameForPageAtIndex:(NSUInteger)index                       // 17
{
   CGRect bounds = [[self scrollView] bounds];
   CGRect pageFrame = bounds;
   pageFrame.size.width -= (2 * PADDING);
   pageFrame.origin.x = (bounds.size.width * index) + PADDING;
   return pageFrame;
}


#pragma mark - Page management

- (void)loadPage:(NSInteger)index                                     // 18
{
   if (index < 0 || index >= [self numberOfPhotos]) {
      return;
   }

   NSMutableArray *photoViewCache = [self photoViewCache];
   id currentView = [photoViewCache objectAtIndex:index];
   if ([currentView isKindOfClass:[UIImageView class]] == NO) {
      // Load the photo view.
      CGRect frame = [self frameForPageAtIndex:index];
      UIImageView *newView = [[UIImageView alloc] initWithFrame:frame];
      [newView setContentMode:UIViewContentModeScaleAspectFit];
      [newView setBackgroundColor:[UIColor clearColor]];
      [newView setImage:[self imageAtIndex:index]];

      [[self scrollView] addSubview:newView];
      [photoViewCache replaceObjectAtIndex:index withObject:newView];
   }
}

- (void)unloadPage:(NSInteger)index                                   // 19
{
   if (index < 0 || index >= [self numberOfPhotos]) {
      return;
   }
```

```
    NSMutableArray *photoViewCache = [self photoViewCache];
    id currentView = [photoViewCache objectAtIndex:index];
    if ([currentView isKindOfClass:[UIImageView class]]) {
        [currentView removeFromSuperview];
        [photoViewCache replaceObjectAtIndex:index withObject:[NSNull null]];
    }
}


- (void)setCurrentIndex:(NSInteger)newIndex                         // 20
{
    _currentIndex = newIndex;

    [self loadPage:_currentIndex];
    [self loadPage:_currentIndex + 1];
    [self loadPage:_currentIndex - 1];
    [self unloadPage:_currentIndex + 2];
    [self unloadPage:_currentIndex - 2];

    [self setTitleWithCurrentIndex];
}

#pragma mark - UIScrollViewDelegate

- (void)scrollViewDidScroll:(UIScrollView *)scrollView              // 21
{
    if ([scrollView isScrollEnabled]) {
        CGFloat pageWidth = scrollView.bounds.size.width;
        float fractionalPage = scrollView.contentOffset.x / pageWidth;
        NSInteger page = floor(fractionalPage);
        if (page != [self currentIndex]) {
            [self setCurrentIndex:page];
        }
    }
}

@end
```

Let's take a closer look at the implementation:

1. *Photo.h* is imported, so the browser can use Photo objects.

2. Two declared properties are added to the class extension: currentIndex and photoViewCache. The first property, currentIndex, is the index value for the photo currently displayed.

3. The second property, photoViewCache, is a mutable array of photo views. Each photo view is an instance of UIImageView. A photo album can contain a large number of photos. Therefore, loading each photo into memory

increases the chance of out-of-memory crashes for PhotoWheel. To conserve memory and help avoid memory-related crashes, the photo browser will store up to three photo views in memory at any given time. The `photoViewCache` property contains the reference to the array containing the three photo views.

4. The `-viewDidLoad` method is added so that additional setup for the view can be performed.

5. The photo browser will display photos in full-screen screen. This means that the photo will display behind the status bar. To make this happen, you must set the `wantsFullScreenLayout` flag to `YES`. This gives the photo browser a full 768 × 1024 set of points to work with.

6. The view controller's top view is sized and positioned to use the entire screen, including the points behind the status bar. Explicitly setting the frame for the view helps ensure that autoresizing views like the scroll view will be sized correctly. This issue becomes much more important in Chapter 18, "Supporting Device Rotation," when you modify PhotoWheel to support all device orientations.

7. Properties for an outlet can be set in a storyboard or NIB file, but they can also be set in code. Sometimes setting outlet properties in code is preferred because it clarifies which property values have been changed. It is not always easy to see this when looking at the inspectors for an outlet object in a storyboard or NIB file.

    This consideration is why property values for the scroll view are set in the `-viewDidLoad` method. It makes it clear which values have changed to accommodate the needs of the photo browser.

8. The photo view cache is initialized. The details of what happens in the method are discussed momentarily.

9. The method `-viewWillAppear` is added to set the scroll view content size and current index. It also scrolls the view to the starting index, which is the index of the photo thumbnail tapped on the main screen. The title, which is displayed at the center of the navigation bar, is updated to display the current index.

10–11. A couple of helper methods are provided to retrieve the number of photos and the image at a particular index.

12. The method `-initPhotoViewCache` creates the instance of the mutable array and initializes it with `NSNull` objects. `NSNull` is a singleton class that represents null objects. It is used in places where `nil` is not allowed, such as in the contents for `NSArray`, `NSDictionary`, and `NSSet`.

13. The method `-setScrollViewContentSize` determines the content size (i.e., the scrollable area) based on the number of photos. Each photo represents a page—hence the local variable name `pageCount`.

14. The method -scrollToIndex: does as its name implies: it scrolls the scroll view to a specific index, where the index is the index value for a photo.

15. The method -setTitleWithCurrentIndex updates the display for the title in the navigation bar.

16. The method -frameForPagingScrollView is called in -viewDidLoad, and it sets the frame (position and size) for the scroll view. This is not the content size, but rather the actual size of the viewable area of the scroll view. However, there is a little sleight of hand going on here. The viewable area of the scroll view (that is, the frame) is actually 40 points wider than the iPad's screen. There are exactly 20 points to the left and right of the scroll view.

    Why do this? We want to have a bit of space between the photos when scrolling—20 points of space, to be precise. The 20 points are specified in the C macro PADDING. By setting the scroll view's frame to be 40 points (2 × PADDING) wider, and taking into account the padding when calculating the frame for each photo, we can produce a visual effect whereby the scroll view and photo appear in full-screen mode but, in fact, are wider than the physical screen. This effect is achieved by allowing the visible area of the scroll view to be clipped by the physical dimensions of the iPad's screen (Figure 17.1), thus making the 20-point spacing visible only when scrolling.

17. The method -frameForPageAtIndex: calculates the frame (position and size within the content area of the scroll view) for the page (i.e., the photo) at a specified index. The calculation takes into account the padding used to space out the photos when scrolling.

18. The method -loadPage: loads the page (i.e., the photo) into memory and adds it to the scroll view. It starts by verifying that the index is within the range of available photo indexes. It then retrieves a reference to the view from the photoViewCache. If the reference points to an instance of UIImageView, nothing happens. The image view already contains the photo to display. However, if the reference is an NSNull object and not UIImageView, a new image view is created, configured to display the photo at the specified index, and added to the scroll view. The photoViewCache is also updated, replacing the NSNull object with the UIImageView object.

19. The method -unloadPage: does the opposite of -loadPage:. It removes UIImageView from memory and from the scroll view, and it updates the photoViewCache, replacing the image view with an NSNull object.

20. The method -setCurrentIndex: is the final piece of the sleight-of-hand magic trick. It is here, in this custom setter method for currentIndex, that pages are loaded and unloaded. The current, previous, and next pages are always loaded. The previous set of pages is unloaded, leaving only three photos loaded into memory at any given time.

Figure 17.1   Illustration of the scroll view frame

21. The implementation for PhotoBrowserViewController wraps up with the
    implementation of the UIScrollViewDelegate callback method -scroll
    ViewDidScroll:. This method determines the index for the current photo
    and sets the currentIndex property accordingly. This fires the custom
    -setCurrentIndex setter method, which in turns loads and unloads the
    appropriate pages.

Setting Up the Photo Browser UI

Now that the PhotoBrowserViewController class is completed, it's time to update
the user interface for the photo browser. Open the *MainStoryboard.storyboard* file and
select the View Controller scene that you used earlier to test the custom segue. Highlight the view controller, open the Identity inspector, and change the class from
UIViewController to PhotoBrowserViewController.

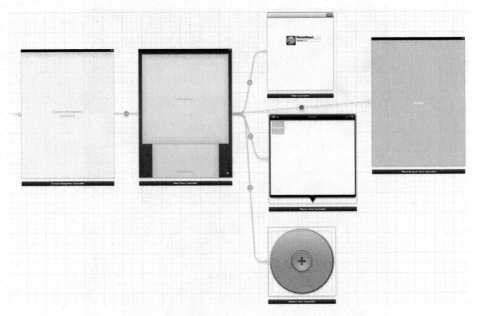

Figure 17.2   Updated storyboard with new segue

Next, add a scroll view to the scene. Size it to fill the entire container view, and then connect it to the `scrollView` outlet defined in the `PhotoBrowserViewController` class.

Take a look at Figure 17.2 for an example of what the updated storyboard looks like.

Launching the Photo Browser

To launch the photo browser, the user taps a photo thumbnail displayed on the main screen. To make this possible for the user, your code must perform the segue programmatically. The `PhotosViewController` is told when the thumbnail image is tapped, but it cannot perform the `PushPhotoBrowser` segue because that segue is defined in the Main View Controller scene. This gives you two options for performing the segue from the `PhotosViewController` instance.

The first option is to reference the `parentViewController` object for the `PhotosViewController` and then call `-performSegueWithIdentifier:sender:` on the parent view controller. The code would look like this:

```
UIViewController *parent = [self parentViewController];
[parent performSegueWithIdentifier:@"PushPhotoBrowser" sender:self];
```

This code makes the assumption that the `PushPhotoBrowser` segue is available to the parent view controller. If the segue is not available, then a runtime exception is thrown.

The second option is to send an action and let the responder chain find an object that can respond to it. This was the approach used earlier, albeit in IB, when the button was used to test the push to the photo browser. The same approach can be performed in code, which looks like this:

```
UIApplication *app = [UIApplication sharedApplication];
[app sendAction:@selector(pushPhotoBrowser:) to:nil from:self forEvent:nil];
```

> **Note**
>
> The -sendAction:to:from:forEvent: method returns a BOOL value indicating whether a responder object was able to handle the action. YES is returned if a responder handled the action message; otherwise, NO is returned. A runtime exception is *not* thrown if the action is not handled by a responder.

The -sendAction:to:from:forEvent: method sends the action defined by the @selector up the responder chain. You can limit the send action to a specific target by setting the to parameter. The from parameter is the sender of the action, and the forEvent allows you to send additional information about the event that originated the action.

The -sendAction:to:from:forEvent: decouples the PhotosViewController from its parent, so let's use it to push the photo browser screen into place. Open the file *PhotosViewController.m*, and scroll to the -collectionView:didSelectItemAtIndexPath: method added to the class in an earlier chapter. Change the implementation to send the action, as shown in Listing 17.3.

Listing 17.3 **Sending an Action Programmatically**

```
- (void)collectionView:(UICollectionView *)collectionView
didSelectItemAtIndexPath:(NSIndexPath *)indexPath
{
    UIApplication *app = [UIApplication sharedApplication];
    [app sendAction:@selector(pushPhotoBrowser:) to:nil from:self forEvent:nil];
}
```

This code sends the message pushPhotoBrowser:, which in turn performs the segue PushPhotoBrowser from the MainViewController. However, if you run the app, you'll see that no photos are displayed. This outcome occurs because PhotoBrowserViewController, which is the destination view controller for the segue, has not been told about the photos, nor has it been told the starting index value.

To provide this information, you override the -prepareForSegue:sender: method in the MainViewController class. This method returns a reference to the segue, which, as you may remember from building the CustomPushSegue class, has references to the source and destination view controllers. This is your one opportunity to provide additional information to the source and destination view controllers prior to the execution of the segue.

In the particular case of the `MainViewController` class, the segue needs to update the destination controller with the `photos` and `startAtIndex` values. Previously, you used this method to pass the managed object context to the `AlbumsViewController`. Now, an additional check is needed before passing the array of photos and the starting photo index. The code listing to accomplish this task is shown in Listing 17.4.

Listing 17.4 Preparing the Destination Controller

```
- (void)prepareForSegue:(UIStoryboardSegue *)segue sender:(id)sender
{
    id destinationVC = [segue destinationViewController];
    if ([destinationVC isKindOfClass:[AlbumsViewController class]]) {
        UIApplication *app = [UIApplication sharedApplication];
        AppDelegate *appDelegate = (AppDelegate *)[app delegate];

        NSManagedObjectContext *context;
        context = [appDelegate managedObjectContext];

        [destinationVC setManagedObjectContext:context];

    } else if ([[segue identifier] isEqualToString:@"PushPhotoBrowser"]) {
        [destinationVC setPhotos:[sender photos]];
        [destinationVC setStartAtIndex:[sender selectedPhotoIndex]];
    }
}
```

Before You Compile

You need to add the following `#import` statements to *MainViewController.m* before the code in Listing 17.4 will compile:

```
#import "PhotosViewController.h"
#import "PhotoBrowserViewController.h"
```

A new `if` statement is added that checks the segue identifier string value to determine whether it equals "PushPhotoBrowser." The code could have checked the class type of the destination view controller, as it did for the embedded segue, but this time around we want the app to make sure it is performing the "PushPhotoBrowser" segue. Because the app knows which segue is being performed, some assumptions can be made. For instance, it can be assumed that the destination view controller is an instance of `PhotoBrowserViewController`. Additional safeguards could be added, such as checking the class type for the destination view controller, but these security measures are not necessary for our app.

The other assumptions made are that the source view controller is an instance of `MainViewController` and that the sender is an instance of `PhotosViewControl` ler. Again, checks could be added to implement more defensive programming, but they aren't necessary for this particular app.

If the segue being performed is, in fact, the "PushPhotoBrowser" segue, then the destination view controller's photos and startAtIndex properties are set to the values returned by the sender, which just happens to be the instance of PhotosView Controller. Thus, for this code to work, the PhotosViewController class must be updated to return these values.

The code changes needed for PhotosViewController are shown in Listing 17.5.

Listing 17.5   **Changes to `PhotosViewController`**

```
///////
//  PhotosViewController.h
///////
#import <UIKit/UIKit.h>

@interface PhotosViewController : UIViewController

@property (nonatomic, assign, readonly) NSInteger selectedPhotoIndex;    // 1

- (NSArray *)photos;                                                     // 2

@end


///////
//  PhotosViewController.m
///////

@interface PhotosViewController () <UIActionSheetDelegate,
UIImagePickerControllerDelegate, UINavigationControllerDelegate,
UICollectionViewDataSource, UICollectionViewDelegate,
NSFetchedResultsControllerDelegate>

// Other code left out for brevity's sake.

@property (nonatomic, assign, readwrite) NSInteger selectedPhotoIndex;   // 3

@end

@implementation PhotosViewController

// Other code left out for brevity's sake.

- (void)collectionView:(UICollectionView *)collectionView
didSelectItemAtIndexPath:(NSIndexPath *)indexPath
{
```

```
    [self setSelectedPhotoIndex:[indexPath item]];                    // 4
    UIApplication *app = [UIApplication sharedApplication];
    [app sendAction:@selector(pushPhotoBrowser:) to:nil from:self forEvent:nil];
}


#pragma mark - Public Methods

- (NSArray *)photos                                                   // 5
{
    NSArray *photos = [[self fetchedResultsController] fetchedObjects];
    return photos;
}


@end
```

Let's take a look at what is happening with this code change.

1. The declared property `selectedPhotoIndex` is added to the public interface for the `PhotosViewController` class. Note that the property is set as
   `readonly`. As a consequence, users of this class cannot change the value of this
   property.

2. The method `-photos` is declared. A read-only property could have been used,
   but using the method is cleaner, and it does not require storing the `photos` array
   in memory for the `PhotosViewController` class.

3. The declared property `selectedPhotoIndex` is defined as read-only in its public interface, but the code within the `PhotosViewController` needs to set the
   property value. Therefore, the declared property is redefined as a `readwrite`
   property in the class extension. This means the property value can be changed
   privately—that is, within the class's implementation.

4. The `selectedPhotoIndex` is set when the view controller is told which photo
   has been tapped by the user.

5. The array of `Photo` objects is fetched from the fetched-results controller and
   returned to the caller.

At this point, you now have a basic full-screen photo browser included in the app.
Build and run the app to see the photo browser in action.

Improving the Push and Pop

The push and pop of the photo browser are nice, but there is room for improvement. For a better user experience, the push should start where the photo thumbnail is tapped, and the pop should return to the same location. To accomplish this,
the push location must be stored somewhere so that it can be used by both the
`CustomPushSegue` and `CustomNavigationController` classes. Each of these
classes knows about the `MainViewController`. It is the `sourceViewController`

in the custom segue, and it is the destination view controller in the custom navigation controller. Clearly, then, the `MainViewController` is a good place to store the tap-from location.

The problem, however, is that `MainViewController` does not know the tap-from location. It must be told the location by its child view controller `PhotosViewController`. This means adding and setting a `selectedPhotoFrame` property in the `PhotosViewController` class, and storing the same property value in the `MainViewController`.

Also, we want the app to expand the photo that was tapped as it transitions from the main scene to the photo browser scene. To do this, the image for the selected photo must also be provided by the `MainViewController`.

Start by adding and setting the `selectedPhotoFrame` and `selectedPhotoImage` in the `PhotosViewController` class. The code changes are showing in Listing 17.6.

Listing 17.6 Add and set `selectedPhotoFrame` to `PhotosViewController`

```
///////
//  PhotosViewController.h
///////
#import <UIKit/UIKit.h>

@interface PhotosViewController : UIViewController

@property (nonatomic, assign, readonly) NSInteger selectedPhotoIndex;
@property (nonatomic, assign, readonly) CGRect selectedPhotoFrame;

- (NSArray *)photos;
- (UIImage *)selectedPhotoImage;

@end


///////
//  PhotosViewController.m
///////

// Other code left out for brevity's sake.
@interface PhotosViewController () <UIActionSheetDelegate,
UIImagePickerControllerDelegate, UINavigationControllerDelegate,
UICollectionViewDataSource, UICollectionViewDelegate,
NSFetchedResultsControllerDelegate>

// Other code left out for brevity's sake.

@property (nonatomic, assign, readwrite) CGRect selectedPhotoFrame;

@end
```

```
@implementation PhotosViewController

// Other code left out for brevity's sake.

- (void)collectionView:(UICollectionView *)collectionView
didSelectItemAtIndexPath:(NSIndexPath *)indexPath
{
    [self setSelectedPhotoIndex:[indexPath item]];

    UICollectionViewCell *cell = [collectionView cellForItemAtIndexPath:indexPath];
    CGRect cellFrame = [cell frame];
    cellFrame = [[self view] convertRect:cellFrame fromView:collectionView];
    [self setSelectedPhotoFrame:cellFrame];

    UIApplication *app = [UIApplication sharedApplication];
    [app sendAction:@selector(pushPhotoBrowser:) to:nil from:self forEvent:nil];
}

- (UIImage *)selectedPhotoImage
{
    NSInteger index = [self selectedPhotoIndex];
    NSIndexPath *indexPath = [NSIndexPath indexPathForItem:index inSection:0];
    NSFetchedResultsController *frc = [self fetchedResultsController];
    Photo *photo = [frc objectAtIndexPath:indexPath];
    return [photo largeImage];
}

@end
```

The changed code retrieves the frame from the collection view cell that was tapped by the user. The frame is then converted to the coordinate system of the Photos ViewController's container view. This conversion is needed so the correct location is used during the transition.

Next, the MainViewController needs to be told the selected photo's frame and then needs to expose this frame as a public read-only property. The code to accomplish this is shown in Listing 17.7.

Listing 17.7   **Storing the Selected Photo's Frame in MainViewController**

```
///////
//  MainViewController.h
///////
#import <UIKit/UIKit.h>

@interface MainViewController : UIViewController

@property (nonatomic, assign, readonly) CGRect selectedPhotoFrame;
```

```
@property (nonatomic, strong, readonly) UIImage *selectedPhotoImage;

@end

///////
//  MainViewController.m
///////
@interface MainViewController ()
@property (nonatomic, assign, readwrite) CGRect selectedPhotoFrame;
@property (nonatomic, strong, readwrite) UIImage *selectedPhotoImage;
// Other code left out for brevity's sake.
@end

@implementation MainViewController

// Other code left out for brevity's sake.

- (void)prepareForSegue:(UIStoryboardSegue *)segue sender:(id)sender
{
    id destinationVC = [segue destinationViewController];
    if ([destinationVC isKindOfClass:[AlbumsViewController class]]) {
        UIApplication *app = [UIApplication sharedApplication];
        AppDelegate *appDelegate = (AppDelegate *)[app delegate];

        NSManagedObjectContext *context;
        context = [appDelegate managedObjectContext];

        [destinationVC setManagedObjectContext:context];

    } else if ([[segue identifier] isEqualToString:@"PushPhotoBrowser"]) {
        [destinationVC setPhotos:[sender photos]];
        [destinationVC setStartAtIndex:[sender selectedPhotoIndex]];

        id sourceVC = [segue sourceViewController];
        CGRect frame = [sender selectedPhotoFrame];
        frame = [[self view] convertRect:frame fromView:[sender view]];
        [sourceVC setSelectedPhotoFrame:frame];
        [sourceVC setSelectedPhotoImage:[sender selectedPhotoImage]];
    }
}

@end
```

Here the MainViewController is told the frame and image for the selected photo.
It stores these data so they can be referenced later by the custom push segue and custom navigation controller.

Also, the frame is converted to the coordinate system for `MainViewController`'s container view. The conversion makes it possible for the custom segue to use the correct screen location when placing the images used to animate the view transition.

Next, the custom push segue must be updated to use the new properties on the main view controller. The new implementation is similar to the previous one, except that instead of using a snapshot of the destination view controller's view, the selected image returned from the main view controller is used. This will make the animation sequence smoother for the view transition.

Open *CustomPushSegue.m* and replace the implementation with the one provided in Listing 17.8.

Listing 17.8   Updated `CustomPushSegue` Implementation

```
#import "CustomPushSegue.h"
#import "UIView+PWCategory.h"
#import "MainViewController.h"                                    // 1

@implementation CustomPushSegue

- (void)perform
{
    id sourceViewController = [self sourceViewController];        // 2
    id destinationViewController = [self destinationViewController];

    UIView *sourceView = [sourceViewController view];
    UIImage *sourceViewImage = [sourceView pw_imageSnapshot];
    UIImageView *sourceImageView = nil;
    sourceImageView = [[UIImageView alloc] initWithImage:sourceViewImage];

    UIInterfaceOrientation orientation;
    orientation = [sourceViewController interfaceOrientation];
    BOOL isLandscape = UIInterfaceOrientationIsLandscape(orientation);   // 3

    UIApplication *app = [UIApplication sharedApplication];
    CGRect statusBarFrame = [app statusBarFrame];                // 4

    CGFloat statusBarHeight;
    if (isLandscape) {                                           // 5
        statusBarHeight = statusBarFrame.size.width;
    } else {
        statusBarHeight = statusBarFrame.size.height;
    }
    CGRect imageViewFrame = [sourceImageView frame];
    CGRect newFrame = CGRectOffset(imageViewFrame, 0, statusBarHeight);
    [sourceImageView setFrame:newFrame];                         // 6
```

```objc
    CGRect destinationFrame = [[UIScreen mainScreen] bounds];
    if (isLandscape) {                                              // 7
        destinationFrame.size = CGSizeMake(destinationFrame.size.height,
                                           destinationFrame.size.width);
    }

    UIImage *destinationImage = [sourceViewController selectedPhotoImage];
    UIImageView *destinationImageView = nil;
    destinationImageView = [[UIImageView alloc] initWithImage:destinationImage];
    [destinationImageView setContentMode:UIViewContentModeScaleAspectFit];
    [destinationImageView setBackgroundColor:[UIColor blackColor]];

    CGRect frame = [sourceViewController selectedPhotoFrame];
    frame = CGRectOffset(frame, 0, statusBarHeight);
    [destinationImageView setFrame:frame];
    [destinationImageView setAlpha:0.3];

    UINavigationController *navController = nil;
    navController = [sourceViewController navigationController];
    [navController pushViewController:destinationViewController animated:NO];

    UINavigationBar *navBar = [navController navigationBar];
    [navController setNavigationBarHidden:NO];
    [navBar setFrame:CGRectOffset(navBar.frame, 0, -navBar.frame.size.height)];

    UIView *destinationView = [destinationViewController view];
    [destinationView addSubview:sourceImageView];
    [destinationView addSubview:destinationImageView];

    void (^animations)(void) = ^ {
        [destinationImageView setFrame:destinationFrame];
        [destinationImageView setAlpha:1.0];

        [navBar setFrame:CGRectOffset(navBar.frame, 0, navBar.frame.size.height)];
    };

    void (^completion)(BOOL) = ^(BOOL finished) {
        if (finished) {
            [sourceImageView removeFromSuperview];
            [destinationImageView removeFromSuperview];
        }
    };

    [UIView animateWithDuration:0.6 animations:animations completion:completion];
}

@end
```

Let's walk through the key changes to the custom push segue.

1. The *MainViewController.h* header file is imported.

2. Local variables are used to store references to the `sourceViewController` and `destinationViewController`. This makes later code more readable.

3–5. The photo browser uses the entire screen, which means that the frame used to display the `sourceImageView` must be offset by the height of the status bar. If the offset does not happen, the image will jump during the animation sequence.

You retrieve the status bar frame from the application, which is retrieved from `UIApplication`. Although device orientation and rotation have not been covered yet, the code here takes orientation into consideration. The current orientation mode is checked. If the device orientation is landscape, the status bar height is actually the width value from the frame. Otherwise, it is the height value from the frame. Why? The frame size does not change when the device is rotated. Therefore, you must make the necessary adjustment based on the current orientation.

6. The `sourceImageView`'s `frame` is set to include the offset from the status bar height.

7. The last change to consider is the adjustment made to the destination frame. It, too, must be adjusted to support the landscape orientation. (Chapter 18, "Supporting Device Rotation," provides full coverage of rotation and orientation support.)

A similar change is needed for the `CustomNavigationController` class. Open *CustomNavigationController.m* and update it so that it uses the `-selectedPhotoFrame` method on the destination view controller. The needed code changes are shown in Listing 17.9.

Listing 17.9 Updated `CustomNavigationController` Class

```
#import "CustomNavigationController.h"
#import "UIView+PWCategory.h"
#import "MainViewController.h"                                    // 1


@implementation CustomNavigationController

- (UIViewController *)popViewControllerAnimated:(BOOL)animated
{
    UIViewController *sourceViewController = [self topViewController];

    // Animate image snapshot of the view.
    UIView *sourceView = [sourceViewController view];
    UIImage *sourceViewImage = [sourceView pw_imageSnapshot];
```

```
UIImageView *sourceImageView = nil;
sourceImageView = [[UIImageView alloc] initWithImage:sourceViewImage];

// Offset the sourceImageView frame by the height of the status bar.
// This prevents the image from dropping down after the view controller
// is popped from the stack.
UIInterfaceOrientation orientation;
orientation = [sourceViewController interfaceOrientation];
BOOL isLandscape = UIInterfaceOrientationIsLandscape(orientation);    // 2

UIApplication *app = [UIApplication sharedApplication];
CGRect statusBarFrame = [app statusBarFrame];
CGFloat statusBarHeight;
if (isLandscape) {
   statusBarHeight = statusBarFrame.size.width;
} else {
   statusBarHeight = statusBarFrame.size.height;
}
CGRect newFrame;
newFrame = CGRectOffset([sourceImageView frame], 0, -statusBarHeight);
[sourceImageView setFrame:newFrame];


NSArray *viewControllers = [self viewControllers];
NSInteger count = [viewControllers count];
NSInteger index = count - 2;

id destinationViewController = nil;
destinationViewController = [viewControllers objectAtIndex:index];
UIView *destinationView = [destinationViewController view];
UIImage *destinationViewImage = [destinationView pw_imageSnapshot];
UIImageView *destinationImageView = nil;
destinationImageView = [[UIImageView alloc] initWithImage:destinationViewImage];

[super popViewControllerAnimated:NO];

[destinationView addSubview:destinationImageView];
[destinationView addSubview:sourceImageView];

CGRect selectedPhotoFrame = [destinationViewController selectedPhotoFrame];
CGPoint shrinkToPoint = CGPointMake(CGRectGetMidX(selectedPhotoFrame),
                                    CGRectGetMidY(selectedPhotoFrame));

void (^animations)(void) = ^ {
   [sourceImageView setFrame:CGRectMake(shrinkToPoint.x, shrinkToPoint.y,
                                 0, 0)];
```

```
    [sourceImageView setAlpha:0.0];

    // Animate the nav bar, too.
    UINavigationBar *navBar = [self navigationBar];
    [navBar setFrame:CGRectOffset(navBar.frame, 0, -navBar.frame.size.height)];
  };

  void (^completion)(BOOL) = ^(BOOL finished) {
    [self setNavigationBarHidden:YES];
    // Reset the nav bar's position.
    UINavigationBar *navBar = [self navigationBar];
    [navBar setFrame:CGRectOffset(navBar.frame, 0, navBar.frame.size.height)];

    [sourceImageView removeFromSuperview];
    [destinationImageView removeFromSuperview];
  };

  [UIView transitionWithView:destinationView
                    duration:0.3
                     options:UIViewAnimationOptionTransitionNone
                  animations:animations
                  completion:completion];

  return sourceViewController;
}

@end
```

The changes include the following:

1. Import the *MainViewController.h* header file.

2. The sourceImageView's frame is offset by the height of the status bar. This prevents the image from jumping during the animation.

Build and run the app to test the changes. Tap a photo thumbnail to animate the push from the tapped photo cell. When the user closes the photo browser (by tapping the **Back** button), the animation ends at the same tapped photo cell. This bit of extra polish really enhances the user experience.

Adding Chrome Effects

If you have played with the iPad's Photos app, you have likely noticed that it is a full-screen photo browser that auto-hides the chrome. In the case of PhotoWheel's photo browser, the chrome is the combination of the status and navigation bars at the top of the screen. You'll need to add this auto-hide feature to the PhotoWheel photo browser as well, so that the UI looks smooth and elegant without the user even noticing the various types of bars.

An NSTimer is used to determine when it's time to hide the chrome. The NSTimer class creates a timer that waits for a certain interval to elapse and then fires, sending a message (action) to an object (target).

The code changes made to *PhotoBrowserViewController.m* to manage the display of the chrome are shown in Listing 17.10. Apply these changes to your code. And, of course, an explanation of the changes is provided after the listing.

Listing 17.10   **Auto-hiding the Chrome**

```
#import "PhotoBrowserViewController.h"

@interface PhotoBrowserViewController ()

// Other code left out for brevity's sake.

@property (nonatomic, assign, getter=isChromeHidden) BOOL chromeHidden; // 1
@property (nonatomic, strong) NSTimer *chromeHideTimer;                 // 2
@property (nonatomic, assign) CGFloat statusBarHeight;                  // 3
@end

@implementation PhotoBrowserViewController

// Other code left out for brevity's sake.

- (void)viewDidLoad
{
    // Other code left out for brevity's sake.

    // Must store the status bar size while it is still visible.
    UIApplication *app = [UIApplication sharedApplication];
    CGRect statusBarFrame = [app statusBarFrame];                       // 4
    if (UIInterfaceOrientationIsLandscape([self interfaceOrientation])) {
        [self setStatusBarHeight:statusBarFrame.size.width];
    } else {
        [self setStatusBarHeight:statusBarFrame.size.height];
    }
}

// Other code left out for brevity's sake.

- (void)viewWillAppear:(BOOL)animated
{
    // Other code left out for brevity's sake.

    [self startChromeDisplayTimer];                                     // 5
```

```
    }

- (void)viewWillDisappear:(BOOL)animated                          // 6
{
    [self cancelChromeDisplayTimer];
    [super viewWillDisappear:animated];
}

// Other code left out for brevity's sake.

#pragma mark - Page management

- (void)loadPage:(NSInteger)index
{
    if (index < 0 || index >= [self numberOfPhotos]) {
        return;
    }

    id currentView = [[self photoViewCache] objectAtIndex:index];
    if ([currentView isKindOfClass:[UIImageView class]] == NO) {
        // Load the photo view.
        CGRect frame = [self frameForPageAtIndex:index];
        UIImageView *newView = [[UIImageView alloc] initWithFrame:frame];
        [newView setContentMode:UIViewContentModeScaleAspectFit];
        [newView setBackgroundColor:[UIColor clearColor]];
        [newView setImage:[self imageAtIndex:index]];

        UITapGestureRecognizer *tap = [[UITapGestureRecognizer alloc]
                                initWithTarget:self
                                action:@selector(imageTapped:)];  // 7
        [newView addGestureRecognizer:tap];                       // 8
        [newView setUserInteractionEnabled:YES];                  // 9

        [[self scrollView] addSubview:newView];
        [[self photoViewCache] replaceObjectAtIndex:index withObject:newView];
    }
}

// Other code left out for brevity's sake.

#pragma mark - UIScrollViewDelegate

// Other code left out for brevity's sake.

- (void)scrollViewWillBeginDragging:(UIScrollView *)scrollView    // 10
{
    [self hideChrome];
```

```
}

#pragma mark - Chrome helpers

- (void)toggleChromeDisplay                                    // 11
{
   [self toggleChrome:![self isChromeHidden]];
}


- (void)toggleChrome:(BOOL)hide                                // 12
{
   [self setChromeHidden:hide];
   if (hide) {
      [UIView beginAnimations:nil context:nil];
      [UIView setAnimationDuration:0.4];
   }

   CGFloat alpha = hide ? 0.0 : 1.0;

   UINavigationBar *navbar = [[self navigationController] navigationBar];
   [navbar setAlpha:alpha];

   [[UIApplication sharedApplication] setStatusBarHidden:hide];

   if (hide) {
      [UIView commitAnimations];
   }

   if ( ! [self isChromeHidden] ) {
      [self startChromeDisplayTimer];
   }
}

- (void)hideChrome                                             // 13
{
   NSTimer *timer = [self chromeHideTimer];
   if (timer && [timer isValid]) {
      [timer invalidate];
      [self setChromeHideTimer:nil];
   }
   [self toggleChrome:YES];
}

- (void)startChromeDisplayTimer                                // 14
{
   [self cancelChromeDisplayTimer];
   NSTimer *timer = nil;
```

```
    timer = [NSTimer scheduledTimerWithTimeInterval:5.0
                                             target:self
                                           selector:@selector(hideChrome)
                                           userInfo:nil
                                            repeats:NO];
    [self setChromeHideTimer:timer];
}


- (void)cancelChromeDisplayTimer                              // 15
{
    if ([self chromeHideTimer]) {
        [[self chromeHideTimer] invalidate];
        [self setChromeHideTimer:nil];
    }
}


#pragma mark - Gesture handlers

- (void)imageTapped:(UITapGestureRecognizer *)recognizer      // 16
{
    [self toggleChromeDisplay];
}

@end
```

Walking through the changes, you'll note the following:

1–2. The class extension for PhotoBrowserViewController has been updated
   with two new declared properties: chromeHidden and chromeHideTimer.
   The chromeHidden property is a Boolean flag indicating the current status
   for the chrome—that is, either hidden or visible. The chromeHideTimer
   property is a reference to the current NSTimer used to auto-hide the chrome.

3. A third property, statusBarHeight, has been added to the class extension.
   The status bar height is stored during the -viewDidLoad method while the
   status bar is still visible. Once it is hidden, the status bar frame will no longer
   be available, which is why the height is saved to this property.

4. The status bar height is saved for later use. A check for the interface orientation is made. If the orientation is landscape, the width value in the status bar
   frame is the actual height; otherwise, the status bar frame height is the height.

5. An override for the method -viewWillAppear: is updated with a call to
   -startChromeDisplayTimer. This, of course, starts the timer used to auto-
   hide the chrome.

6. Another override method, this time on `-viewWillDisappear:`, is added. Here the method `-cancelChromeDisplayTimer` is called to cancel the timer prior to the view disappearing.

7–8. The user should be able to show and hide the chrome with a tap of the finger. For this reason, a tap gesture recognizer is added to the `UIImageView` that displays the photo. The recognizer calls the `-imageTapped:` method defined at the end of the listing.

9. Even though the tap gesture recognizer has been added to the image view, the tap won't work until the `userInteractionEnabled` flag on the image view is set to `YES`. This flag is set to `NO` by default, which means the view does not receive any touch events.

10. Another `UIScrollViewDelegate` callback method is added, `-scrollView WillBeginDragging:`. Here the chrome is told to hide when the user begins to scroll through the photos.

11. The first of the chrome-related helper methods is `-toggleChromeDisplay`. This method does as its name implies: it toggles the chrome display. If the chrome is hidden, calling this method will show it. If the chrome is visible, calling this method will hide it.

12. The method `-toggleChrome:` will toggle the chrome based on the hide flag. Pass in `YES` and the chrome is hidden. Pass in `NO` and the chrome is made visible. This is also where the animation for showing and hiding the chrome is performed.

13. The method `-hideChrome` forces the chrome to hide. It also invalidates the timer, which means it will stop firing. The chrome is hidden so the timer is no longer needed. The timer calls this method when it fires.

14. The `-startChromeDisplayTimer` method creates a timer that runs for 5 seconds (`5.0`). The timer calls `-hideChrome` when it fires.

15. The last chrome-related helper method is `-cancelChromeDisplayTimer`. This method invalidates the timer, causing it to stop firing.

16. The last change to the `PhotoBrowserViewController` class is the addition of the `-imageTapped:` method. This method is called when the user taps the photo.

After you have added the changes to your code, build and run the app. Display the photo browser, and see how the chrome display works. When the chrome is displayed, it auto-hides after 5 seconds. Tap the photo to toggle between showing and hiding the chrome. Scrolling while the chrome is visible will also hide it. Check your work if you do not see these behaviors.

Zooming

Your photo browser is coming along nicely, and it is already pretty useful. But let's not stop here. Let's add another feature that users will expect. Let's make it possible for users to zoom in and out on the photo by double tapping and pinching.

To accomplish this, you will use another `UIScrollView`. You can implement your own zoom using tap and pinch gestures, but why do that when the `UIScrollView` provides most of the functionality for you?

Currently, the `UIImageView` class is used to display the photo within the browser. You will replace this with a new custom class derived from `UIScrollView`. But before you can replace the `UIImageView` used in the `PhotoBrowserViewController` class, you need to create the new scroll view subclass.

Create a new Objective-C class. Name the class `PhotoBrowserPhotoView`, and make it a subclass of `UIScrollView`. Next, add the source code for the interface and implementation files as shown in Listing 17.11.

Listing 17.11 **`PhotoBrowserPhotoView` Class**

```
///////
//   PhotoBrowserPhotoView.h
///////
#import <UIKit/UIKit.h>

@class PhotoBrowserViewController;                          // 1

@interface PhotoBrowserPhotoView : UIScrollView <UIScrollViewDelegate>  // 2


@property (nonatomic, assign) NSInteger index;             // 3
@property (nonatomic, weak) PhotoBrowserViewController
*photoBrowserViewController;                                // 4

- (void)setImage:(UIImage *)newImage;                      // 5
- (void)turnOffZoom;                                       // 6


@end


///////
//   PhotoBrowserPhotoView.m
///////
#import "PhotoBrowserPhotoView.h"
#import "PhotoBrowserViewController.h"                      // 7

@interface PhotoBrowserPhotoView ()                        // 8
@property (nonatomic, strong) UIImageView *imageView;      // 9
```

```objc
@end

@implementation PhotoBrowserPhotoView

- (id)initWithFrame:(CGRect)frame                                       // 10
{
    self = [super initWithFrame:frame];
    if (self) {
        [self setDelegate:self];
        [self setMaximumZoomScale:5.0];
        [self setShowsHorizontalScrollIndicator:NO];
        [self setShowsVerticalScrollIndicator:NO];
        [self loadSubviewsWithFrame:frame];
        [self setBackgroundColor:[UIColor clearColor]];
        [self setAutoresizingMask:UIViewAutoresizingFlexibleWidth|
         UIViewAutoresizingFlexibleHeight];

        UITapGestureRecognizer *doubleTap = [[UITapGestureRecognizer alloc]
                                            initWithTarget:self
                                            action:@selector(doubleTapped:)];
        [doubleTap setNumberOfTapsRequired:2];
        [self addGestureRecognizer:doubleTap];

        UITapGestureRecognizer *tap = [[UITapGestureRecognizer alloc]
                                            initWithTarget:self
                                            action:@selector(tapped:)];
        [tap requireGestureRecognizerToFail:doubleTap];
        [self addGestureRecognizer:tap];
    }
    return self;
}


- (void)loadSubviewsWithFrame:(CGRect)frame                             // 11
{
    frame.origin = CGPointMake(0, 0);
    UIImageView *newImageView = [[UIImageView alloc] initWithFrame:frame];
    [newImageView setAutoresizingMask:UIViewAutoresizingFlexibleWidth|
     UIViewAutoresizingFlexibleHeight];
    [newImageView setContentMode:UIViewContentModeScaleAspectFit];
    [self addSubview:newImageView];

    [self setImageView:newImageView];
}

- (void)setImage:(UIImage *)newImage                                    // 12
{
    [[self imageView] setImage:newImage];
}
```

```objc
- (BOOL)isZoomed                                               // 13
{
    return !([self zoomScale] == [self minimumZoomScale]);
}


- (CGRect)zoomRectForScale:(float)scale withCenter:(CGPoint)center    // 14
{
    // The following is derived from the ScrollViewSuite sample project
    // provided by Apple:
    // http://bit.ly/pYoPat

    CGRect zoomRect;

    // The zoom rect is in the content view's coordinates.
    // At a zoom scale of 1.0, it would be the size of the
    // imageScrollView's bounds.
    // As the zoom scale decreases, so that more content is visible,
    // the size of the rect grows.
    zoomRect.size.height = [self frame].size.height / scale;
    zoomRect.size.width = [self frame].size.width  / scale;

    // Choose an origin so as to get the right center.
    zoomRect.origin.x = center.x - (zoomRect.size.width  / 2.0);
    zoomRect.origin.y = center.y - (zoomRect.size.height / 2.0);

    return zoomRect;
}

- (void)zoomToLocation:(CGPoint)location                       // 15
{
    float newScale;
    CGRect zoomRect;
    if ([self isZoomed]) {
        zoomRect = [self bounds];
    } else {
        newScale = [self maximumZoomScale];
        zoomRect = [self zoomRectForScale:newScale withCenter:location];
    }

    [self zoomToRect:zoomRect animated:YES];
}

- (void)turnOffZoom                                            // 16
{
    if ([self isZoomed]) {
        [self zoomToLocation:CGPointZero];
    }
```

```
}

#pragma mark - Touch gestures

- (void)doubleTapped:(UITapGestureRecognizer *)recognizer           // 17
{
    [self zoomToLocation:[recognizer locationInView:self]];
}


- (void)tapped:(UITapGestureRecognizer *)recognizer                 // 18
{
    [[self photoBrowserViewController] toggleChromeDisplay];
}

#pragma mark - UIScrollViewDelegate methods

- (UIView *)viewForZoomingInScrollView:(UIScrollView *)scrollView   // 19
{
    return [self imageView];
}

@end
```

Let's walk through the code and see what is happening, starting with the header file *PhotoBrowserPhotoView.h*.

1. The forward declaration for the class PhotoBrowserViewController is made.

2. The PhotoBrowserPhotoView class is the delegate to itself, the scroll view. Therefore, UIScrollViewDelegate is added to the list of protocols.

3. The class also has a property named index. This is the index to the photo displayed in the scroll view.

4. The property photoBrowserViewController is added. This weak reference to the photo browser enables the photo view to talk back to the browser.

5. The method -setImage: is called by the photo browser. It passes an image reference for the photo that is displayed.

6. The method -turnOffZoom is provided so that the photo browser can turn off zooming when the user begins to scroll through the collection of photos.

The interface in Listing 17.11 is followed by the implementation. The changes to the implementation include the following:

7. The *PhotoBrowserViewController.h* header file is imported.

8. A class extension for PhotoBrowserPhotoView is declared.

9. An image view is added. This is the image view responsible for displaying the photo.

10. The -initWithFrame: override method initializes the view, setting properties on the scroll view, and adds tap and double-tap gestures.

11. The method -loadSubviewsWithFrame: is responsible for creating the image view used to display the photo.

12. The method -setImage: sets the image for the image view. The photo browser calls this method.

13. The method -isZoomed returns YES when the user has zoomed in on the photo; otherwise, it returns NO.

14. The method -zoomRectForScale:withCenter: is responsible for calculating the zoom rect based on a center point.

15. The method -zoomToLocation: does as the name implies: it zooms to a location within the photo.

16. The method -turnOffZoom is provided so that the photo browser can request that the zoom be turned off during scrolling.

17–18. Two touch gestures are assigned to the view: a double tap and a tap. The double tap will zoom to the tapped location within the photo. The tap toggles the chrome display. The tap gesture is managed in the PhotoBrowserPhotoView class instead of the photo browser because it relies on the double-tap gesture failing first.

19. The last method of the class is -viewForZoomingInScrollView:. This is a UIScrollViewDelegate method, and it returns a reference to the view that is used for zooming within the scroll view. For this particular case, that view is the image view.

With the new class in place, it's time to replace UIImageView used in the photo browser with PhotoBrowserPhotoView. In addition to replacing the image view with the new photo view, the -toggleChromeDisplay method must be made public so that it can be used in the PhotoBrowserPhotoView class.

Open the PhotoBrowserViewController class and apply the changes in Listing 17.12.

Listing 17.12 Changes to the PhotoBrowserViewController Class

```
///////
//  PhotoBrowserViewController.h
///////

@interface PhotoBrowserViewController : UIViewController <UIScrollViewDelegate>

// Other code left out for brevity's sake.

- (void) toggleChromeDisplay;                                    // 1

@end
```

```
///////
//  PhotoBrowserViewController.m
///////
#import "PhotoBrowserViewController.h"
#import "Photo.h"
#import "PhotoBrowserPhotoView.h"                              // 2

// Other code left out for brevity's sake.

@implementation PhotoBrowserViewController

// Other code left out for brevity's sake.

#pragma mark - Page management

- (void)loadPage:(NSInteger)index
{
    if (index < 0 || index >= [self numberOfPhotos]) {
        return;
    }

    id currentView = [[self photoViewCache] objectAtIndex:index];
    if ([currentView isKindOfClass:[PhotoBrowserPhotoView class]]==NO) { // 3
        // Load the photo view.
        CGRect frame = [self frameForPageAtIndex:index];
        PhotoBrowserPhotoView *newView = [[PhotoBrowserPhotoView alloc]
                                      initWithFrame:frame];         // 4
        [newView setBackgroundColor:[UIColor clearColor]];          // 5
        [newView setImage:[self imageAtIndex:index]];               // 6
        [newView setPhotoBrowserViewController:self];               // 7
        [newView setIndex:index];                                   // 8

        [[self scrollView] addSubview:newView];
        [[self photoViewCache] replaceObjectAtIndex:index withObject:newView];
    } else {
        [currentView turnOffZoom];
    }
}

- (void)unloadPage:(NSInteger)index
{
    if (index < 0 || index >= [self numberOfPhotos]) {
        return;
    }

    id currentView = [[self photoViewCache] objectAtIndex:index];
    if ([currentView isKindOfClass:[PhotoBrowserPhotoView class]]) {    // 9
        [currentView removeFromSuperview];
```

```
        [[self photoViewCache] replaceObjectAtIndex:index withObject:[NSNull null]];
    }
}

// Other code left out for brevity's sake.

@end
```

Here is a quick rundown of the changes to the `PhotoBrowserViewController` class:

1. The `-toggleChromeDisplay` method declaration has been added to the public interface.

2. The *PhotoBrowserPhotoView.h* header file is imported in the *PhotoBrowserView Controller.m* implementation file.

3. The check for the `UIImageView` class in the `-loadPage:` method has been changed to check for the `PhotoBrowserPhotoView` class.

4–8. The `UIImageView` code has been replaced with `PhotoBrowserPhotoView` code. The background color is set to clear; the image is set to the current photo; and the photo browser reference is set to enable callbacks to the view controller.

9. The `UIImageView` class check found in the `-unloadPage:` has been replaced with a check for the `PhotoBrowserPhotoView` class.

And with that, your photo browser now supports zooming on a photo. As always, build and run the app to test the changes. Check your work if zooming isn't working properly.

> **Note**
>
> Hold down the **Option** key and use your mouse to simulate a pinch gesture when using the iPad Simulator.

Deleting a Photo

Before moving on, you need to add one more feature to the photo browser—the ability to delete a photo. In addition to adding the new delete feature, you will be laying the foundation for future enhancements to the photo browser. The "Delete Photo" action asks the user to confirm the deletion of the photo; it is made available to the user as a button on the navigation bar displayed at the top of the screen.

More actions will be added in later chapters, so an action button will be displayed in the navigation bar. This means PhotoWheel needs to display three buttons in the navigation bar: the **Back** button on the left and two buttons on the right, one for delete and the other for the action menu. But to make the app more fun, let's not stop with two buttons on the right. Let's make it three buttons—one each for delete, action, and slideshow.

> **Note**
>
> This chapter walks you through the steps to delete a photo. Chapter 19, "Printing with AirPrint," and Chapter 20, "Sending Email," show how to implement additional actions. Chapter 23, "Producing a Slideshow with AirPlay," shows you how to implement the slideshow feature.

First, the new buttons must be added to the navigation bar. Open the file *Photo BrowserViewController.m* and add the new method `-addButtonsToNavigationBar`. Next, update the `-viewDidLoad` method to call the `-addButtonsToNavigation Bar` method. The complete set of code changes is shown in Listing 17.13, with a full explanation of the changes to follow.

Listing 17.13   **Updates to *PhotoBrowserViewController.m***

```
#import "PhotoBrowserViewController.h"
#import "Photo.h"
#import "PhotoBrowserPhotoView.h"

#define ACTIONSHEET_TAG_DELETE 1                              // 1
#define ACTIONSHEET_TAG_ACTIONS 2                             // 2

@interface PhotoBrowserViewController () <UIActionSheetDelegate>   // 3

// Other code left out for brevity's sake.

@property (nonatomic, strong) UIBarButtonItem *actionButton;   // 4

@end

@implementation PhotoBrowserViewController

- (void)viewDidLoad
{
    [super viewDidLoad];

    // Make sure to set wantsFullScreenLayout or the photo
    // will not display behind the status bar.
    [self setWantsFullScreenLayout:YES];

    // Set the view's frame size. This ensures that the scroll view
    // autoresizes correctly and avoids surprises when retrieving
    // the scroll view's bounds later.
```

```
    CGRect frame = [[UIScreen mainScreen] bounds];
    [[self view] setFrame:frame];

    UIScrollView *scrollView = [self scrollView];
    // Set the initial size.
    [scrollView setFrame:[self frameForPagingScrollView]];
    [scrollView setDelegate:self];
    [scrollView setBackgroundColor:[UIColor blackColor]];
    [scrollView setTranslatesAutoresizingMaskIntoConstraints:YES];
    [scrollView setAutoresizingMask:UIViewAutoresizingFlexibleWidth |
     UIViewAutoresizingFlexibleHeight];
    [scrollView setAutoresizesSubviews:YES];
    [scrollView setPagingEnabled:YES];
    [scrollView setShowsVerticalScrollIndicator:NO];
    [scrollView setShowsHorizontalScrollIndicator:NO];

    [self addButtonsToNavigationBar];                                // 5
    [self initPhotoViewCache];

    // Must store the status bar size while it is still visible.
    UIApplication *app = [UIApplication sharedApplication];
    CGRect statusBarFrame = [app statusBarFrame];
    if (UIInterfaceOrientationIsLandscape([self interfaceOrientation])) {
        [self setStatusBarHeight:statusBarFrame.size.width];
    } else {
        [self setStatusBarHeight:statusBarFrame.size.height];
    }
}


// Other code left out for brevity's sake.

#pragma mark - Helper methods

- (void)addButtonsToNavigationBar                                    // 6
{
    UIBarButtonItem *trashButton = nil;
    trashButton = [[UIBarButtonItem alloc]
                   initWithBarButtonSystemItem:UIBarButtonSystemItemTrash
                   target:self
                   action:@selector(deletePhoto:)];
    [trashButton setStyle:UIBarButtonItemStyleBordered];

    UIBarButtonItem *actionButton = nil;
    actionButton = [[UIBarButtonItem alloc]
                    initWithBarButtonSystemItem:UIBarButtonSystemItemAction
                    target:self
                    action:@selector(showActionMenu:)];
```

```objc
    [actionButton setStyle:UIBarButtonItemStyleBordered];
    [self setActionButton:actionButton];

    UIBarButtonItem *slideshowButton = nil;
    slideshowButton = [[UIBarButtonItem alloc]
                        initWithTitle:@"Slideshow"
                        style:UIBarButtonItemStyleBordered
                        target:self
                        action:@selector(slideshow:)];

    NSArray *buttons = @[slideshowButton, actionButton, trashButton];
    [[self navigationItem] setRightBarButtonItems:buttons];
}

// Other code left out for brevity's sake.

#pragma mark - Actions

- (void)deletePhotoConfirmed                                     // 7
{
    NSInteger count = [self numberOfPhotos];
    NSInteger indexToDelete = [self currentIndex];
    [self unloadPage:indexToDelete];

    // Delete the photo from photos, and send notification
    // to delete the photo from the Core Data store.
    NSMutableArray *photos = [[self photos] mutableCopy];
    [photos removeObjectAtIndex:indexToDelete];
    [self setPhotos:photos];

    NSDictionary *userInfo = nil;
    userInfo = @{@"index":[NSNumber numberWithInteger:indexToDelete]};
    NSNotificationCenter *nc = [NSNotificationCenter defaultCenter];
    [nc postNotificationName:kPhotoWheelDidDeletePhotoAtIndex
                      object:nil
                    userInfo:userInfo];

    if (count == 1) {
        // The one and only photo was deleted. Pop back to
        // the previous view controller.
        [[self navigationController] popViewControllerAnimated:YES];
    } else {
        NSInteger nextIndex = indexToDelete;
        if (indexToDelete == count) {
            nextIndex -= 1;
        }
        [self setCurrentIndex:nextIndex];
```

```objc
      [self setScrollViewContentSize];
   }
}

- (void)deletePhoto:(id)sender                                       // 8
{
   [self cancelChromeDisplayTimer];
   UIActionSheet *actionSheet = nil;
   actionSheet = [[UIActionSheet alloc] initWithTitle:nil
                                             delegate:self
                                    cancelButtonTitle:nil
                               destructiveButtonTitle:@"Delete Photo"
                                    otherButtonTitles:nil, nil];
   [actionSheet setTag:ACTIONSHEET_TAG_DELETE];
   [actionSheet showFromBarButtonItem:sender animated:YES];
}

- (void)showActionMenu:(id)sender                                    // 9
{
   NSLog(@"%s", __PRETTY_FUNCTION__);
}

- (void)slideshow:(id)sender                                         // 10
{
   NSLog(@"%s", __PRETTY_FUNCTION__);
}

#pragma mark - UIActionSheetDelegate methods

- (void)actionSheet:(UIActionSheet *)actionSheet
clickedButtonAtIndex:(NSInteger)buttonIndex                          // 11
{
   [self startChromeDisplayTimer];

   // Do nothing if the user taps outside the action
   // sheet (thus closing the popover containing the
   // action sheet).
   if (buttonIndex < 0) {
      return;
   }

   if ([actionSheet tag] == ACTIONSHEET_TAG_DELETE) {
      [self deletePhotoConfirmed];
   }
}

@end
```

Let's walk through the code changes together:

1–2. Two #defines are created, representing each action sheet. Each action sheet will have a tag value matching one of these C macros.

3. Two action sheets are used in the photo browser. To respond to the action sheets, the photo browser must implement methods from the UIAction SheetDelegate protocol. The protocol is added to the list of conforming protocols so that the compiler can do the appropriate checks to ensure conformity with the protocols.

4. A new declared property is added to the PhotoBrowserViewController class extension. The property, actionButton, is a reference to the action button displayed in the toolbar embedded in the navigation bar. The reference is stored in a property so it can be used to position the popover control displayed when the user taps the button.

5. The -viewDidLoad method is updated to include a call to the -addButtons ToNavigationBar method.

6. The method -addButtonsToNavigationBar is responsible for creating the bar button items that are displayed on the right side of the navigation bar.

7. The method -deletePhotoConfirmed is called after the user has confirmed the delete request. This method deletes the photo from the local array of photos and then sends a notification message to tell other parts of the app to delete the photo from the Core Data store. A notification is used to decouple the code here from the code that actually deletes the photo from the Core Date store.

   If the photo deleted is the last one in the photo album, the photo browser is popped from the navigation stack and the user returns to the main screen. Otherwise, adjustments are made to the browser's scroll view to accommodate the new number of photos.

8. The method -deletePhoto: is called when the user taps the delete button in the navigation bar. It creates and displays an action sheet. The action sheet has one item, "Delete Photo." The user must tap this item to confirm the delete request. This method also stops the chrome display timer. The chrome must remain visible while the action sheet is displayed.

9–10. Stub methods for the action menu and slideshow have been added. The implementations for these methods will be completed in later chapters.

11. The UIActionSheetDelegate method -actionSheet:clickedButtonAt Index: is next in the class implementation. This method starts the chrome display timer. The action sheet is no longer visible; therefore, the chrome should auto-hide in 5 seconds. Next, it checks whether a button was tapped; if that is the case, it calls the -deletePhotoConfirmed method. The -actionSheet:clickedButtonAtIndex: method will undergo additional enhancements in later chapters, which is why the action sheet tag value is checked within the method's implementation.

One last change is needed before you can compile the code. The notification string value kPhotoWheelDidDeletePhotoAtIndex must be defined. Open the file *Photo Wheel-Prefix.pch* and add the following line to the bottom of the file:

```
#define kPhotoWheelDidDeletePhotoAtIndex @"didDeletePhotoAtIndex"
```

At this point, you should build and run the app to test the changes. Don't worry about deleting a photo. Nothing is deleted right now. Before a photo can be deleted, an observer of the kPhotoWheelDidDeletePhotoAtIndex notification must be implemented.

Test your changes. Ensure that each button calls the appropriate action method, and verify that the delete confirmation action sheet is displayed when the user taps the delete button.

After you verify the changes, update the PhotosViewController class to listen for the kPhotoWheelDidDeletePhotoAtIndex notification, and have it delete the photo from the Core Data store. To do this, open the file *PhotosViewController.m* and add the implementation shown in Listing 17.14.

Listing 17.14 Updated *PhotosViewController.m*

```objectivec
@implementation PhotosViewController

- (void)dealloc
{
    NSNotificationCenter *nc = [NSNotificationCenter defaultCenter];
    [nc removeObserver:self name:kPhotoWheelDidSelectAlbum object:nil];
    [nc removeObserver:self name:kPhotoWheelDidDeletePhotoAtIndex object:nil];
}

- (void)viewDidLoad
{
    [super viewDidLoad];
    NSNotificationCenter *nc = [NSNotificationCenter defaultCenter];
    [nc addObserver:self
           selector:@selector(didSelectAlbum:)
               name:kPhotoWheelDidSelectAlbum
             object:nil];

    [nc addObserver:self
           selector:@selector(didDeletePhotoAtIndex:)
               name:kPhotoWheelDidDeletePhotoAtIndex
             object:nil];

    UIImage *image = [UIImage imageNamed:@"1x1-transparent"];
    [[self toolbar] setBackgroundImage:image
                    forToolbarPosition:UIToolbarPositionAny
                            barMetrics:UIBarMetricsDefault];
}
```

```
- (void)didDeletePhotoAtIndex:(NSNotification *)notification
{
    NSDictionary *userInfo = [notification userInfo];
    NSNumber *indexNumber = userInfo[@"index"];
    NSInteger index = [indexNumber integerValue];

    NSIndexPath *indexPath = [NSIndexPath indexPathForRow:index inSection:0];
    Photo *photo = [[self fetchedResultsController] objectAtIndexPath:indexPath];
    NSManagedObjectContext *context = [photo managedObjectContext];
    [context deleteObject:photo];
    [self saveChanges];
}
```

PhotosViewController now observes the kPhotoWheelDidDeletePhotoAt
Index notification message. When it receives the notification, the photo model object
is first retrieved from the fetched-results controller and then deleted from the managed
object context. Finally, the context is saved, causing the photo to be deleted from the
Core Data store.

Congratulations! Your PhotoWheel app now has a full-screen photo browser complete with zooming and delete functionality, as seen in Figure 17.3.

Figure 17.3   The PhotoWheel photo browser

Summary

In this chapter, you learned two more ways to leverage `UIScrollView`. You learned how to use it to display scrollable content as pages in a memory-efficient manner, and you learned how the scroll view can be used to zoom in on content. You also implemented a few additional enhancements to the app, such as launching the photo browser from the tapped photo thumbnail and deleting a photo. But we won't stop working on PhotoWheel just yet. There are more features just itching to be written by you as you continue reading this book.

But first, there's an important issue to resolve. When the user rotates the iPad, the PhotoWheel UI does not rotate to match the device orientation. This is not good and must be fixed, which is exactly what you will do in the next chapter.

Exercise

1. Modify the pop animation for the photo browser so that the animation ends on the cell for the photo currently displayed in the browser.

18

Supporting Device Rotation

It is important that iPad apps support all device orientations, but what does this actually mean? It means that your application should rotate the user interface to match the orientation of the device. Most iPhone applications can get away with not rotating because of the small form factor of the phone and the way users hold it, but the same is not true for the iPad.

An iPhone user tends to hold the device in a portrait orientation with the **Home** button at the bottom. An iPad user, in contrast, will hold the iPad in different orientations based on how she picks it up. If your app does not rotate based on the current orientation, you force the user to rotate her iPad, which is not an ideal user experience.

This chapter shows you how to support interface rotation within your app. Along the way, you will update PhotoWheel so that it can be used regardless of how the user is holding the iPad—with the **Home** button on the bottom, top, left, or right.

How to Support Rotation

Supporting rotation—or rather *enabling* rotation—for your app is easy. You simply specify the supported interface orientations in your app's *info.plist*. You can also specify the supported orientations at the view controller level by overriding the `-supported InterfaceOrientations` method. This method is called when the user changes the device orientation. Be aware that this method is called only on the root view controller or topmost controller that fills the window. Child view controllers will not receive this message, as they do not participate in the decisions about the supported interface orientations.

Rotation Support Prior to iOS 6

Prior to iOS 6, your view controller subclass would override the `-shouldAutorotate ToInterfaceOrientation:` method and return YES for the supported interface orientations. This method has been deprecated in iOS 6 and should no longer be used.

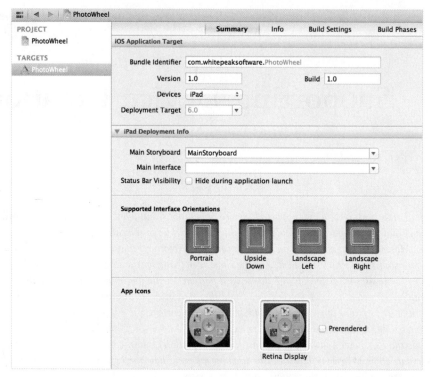

Figure 18.1   Supported Interface Orientation settings on the Summary tab

For most apps, setting the supported interface orientations in the app's *info.plist* is all you need to do. The prototype app you wrote earlier in the book (in Chapters 8 through 13) supports rotation, and it required nothing more than specifying the supported interface orientations, which was handled automatically by the Master-Detail application template.

You can see, and set, the supported interface orientations from the project's Summary tab (Figure 18.1). Changes here to the supported interface orientations are saved to the app's *info.plist*, or you can edit the *info.plist* directly.

While it is a simple matter to specify the supported interface orientation, sometimes additional work is needed. You may wish to disable a feature during rotation, for example, or you may want to perform custom animation during the rotations. Or perhaps the user interface is simply too complex to rely solely on Auto Layout constraints to support rotation. Whatever the situation might be, you can override additional methods to handle the unique needs of your app.

Suppose you wish to disable a feature during a rotation. Override the method `-willRotateToInterfaceOrientation:duration:` and turn off the feature. Override the method `-didRotateFromInterfaceOrientation:` to turn the feature back on.

If you want to perform custom animations during a rotation, your view controller subclass should override the `-willAnimateRotationToInterfaceOrientation:duration:` method. This method is called within the animation block used to rotate the view. You override this method when you need to set additional view properties that can animate. For example, suppose you need to move a button from one location to another during rotation. Set the frame for the button during this method call, and it will animate to its final destination.

Supported Orientations

There are six device orientations:

- Portrait
- Portrait upside down
- Landscape left
- Landscape right
- Face up
- Face down

Upside down, left, and right indicate the position of the **Home** button on the iPad. In portrait upside down orientation, for example, the device is held in portrait mode and the **Home** button is at the top. In landscape left, the device is held in landscape mode and the **Home** button is on the right; landscape right has the Home button on the left.

Did you catch the comment about landscape left and right? The device orientation is landscape left when the **Home** button is on the right, and the device orientation is landscape right when this button is on the left. The device orientation is based on the direction in which the device is rotated. Hold your iPad in your hands with the **Home** button at the bottom. Now rotate it to the left (turning the device counterclockwise). Where is the **Home** button? It's on the right, and the device orientation is landscape left.

Adding to the confusion are the four interface orientations: portrait, portrait upside down, landscape left, and landscape right. The **Home** button positions for the interface orientations portrait and portrait upside down are the same as the device orientations portrait and portrait upside down. Conversely, the **Home** button positions for the two interface orientation landscape modes are the opposite of the landscape device orientations. The interface orientation landscape left means the **Home** button is on the left of the device, and landscape right means the **Home** button is on the right. This is the opposite of the landscape modes for device orientation.

Under most circumstances, an iPad app needs to concern itself only with the interface orientation, not the device orientation. Moreover, most iPad apps do not care if the device is face up or face down. Because of this, the typical iPad app relies on the view controller rotation mechanism described in the last section to support rotation.

You may be wondering how this rotation mechanism is used when your app is launched and the device is in landscape mode. Prior to iOS 6, applications were launched in portrait mode. This happened because the `UIViewController` class displays views in portrait mode only. This characteristic explains why developers tend to design the app's UI in portrait.

After the app delegate's `-application:didFinishLaunchingWithOptions:` method returned, the app's root view controller received the `-shouldAutorotate ToInterfaceOrientation:` method call. If `YES` was returned, the view controller received the other rotation method calls, which in turn caused the user interface to rotate. The UI would be fully rotated by the time the user sees it.

This approach changed starting with iOS 6. Now the app is launched in the current orientation of the device. The additional rotation methods are not called because the view controller does not rotate on launch. The view controller, however, must lay out the subviews based on the current interface orientation, and Cocoa Auto Layout constraints can be used to help with this process.

Using Cocoa Auto Layout

Cocoa Auto Layout, introduced in iOS starting with version 6, manages the layout of user interface elements by using what are called constraints. A constraint is a rule that describes the relationship between UI elements. For example, a constraint can be used to define the exact width of a text field as it appears within its parent view, or it can be used to define the spacing between a label and a text field. The set of constraints defined for the view and its subviews is processed by the constraint satisfaction system, which arranges the elements in a way that best matches the defined constraints.

Typically, you define constraints using Interface Builder. When you drop a new object into the container view, you will see guidelines that help illustrate the constraint. For instance, if you position a label at an appropriate distance from the top and left edges of the container view, you will see solid blue guidelines extending from the label to the top and left edges (Figure 18.2). These gridlines are a visual representation of the constraint defined for the label element and its relationship to its parent view.

IB defines constraints for you as you size and position UI elements. In addition, you can create constraints explicitly. Suppose, for example, you want a text field to maintain its height and width even after its parent view has resized. You can pin the text field's height and width by creating two new constraints. Select the text field and then select **Editor > Pin > Height** and **Editor > Pin > Width** to create two constraints, one each for the current height and width of the text field. Also, you can select the constraint object in the Document Outline and then use the Attributes inspector to change the settings for the constraint.

Constraints do not have to be absolute values, either. A constraint can be defined that says the width of the UI element can be any value up to a certain value, or it can define a rule that says the width can be a minimum size and greater.

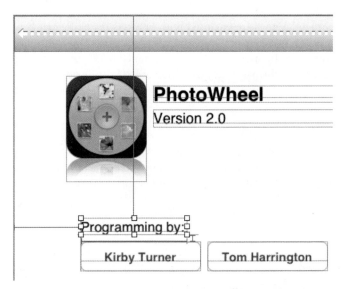

Figure 18.2   Blue guidelines representing the constraints for
the selected object

One benefit when using Cocoa Auto Layout is that you do not have to worry as
much about the layout as views resize and rotate. If, for example, you design your app's
UI in portrait orientation, and you define the constraints to automatically stretch and
shrink each element accordingly, then when the interface orientation changes to landscape orientation, Cocoa Auto Layout will adjust the UI for the landscape layout. This
is exactly what happens in the PhotoWheel prototype app.

Constraints are used in the prototype app to define the relationship between the UI
elements, such as the distance between elements, and the relative sizes of UI elements.
When the device is rotated, the Auto Layout system processes the constraints to determine the best layout for the UI.

However, you can do only so much using IB, which means that sometimes you
must define the Auto Layout constraints in code. The more complex the layout, the
more likely code is needed to define the constraints. The same is true if there are
sufficient differences between the portrait and landscape layouts, which you will see
momentarily in PhotoWheel.

Remember, a constraint can define the relationship between UI elements. This
relationship can be represented in terms of an expression. This factor led Apple engineers to create an ASCII-Art–inspired format string for defining constraints. Called
the Visual Format Language, it is a particular set of grammar used to define Auto Layout constraints programmatically.

To use the Visual Format Language, you call the `-constraintsWithVisualFor
mat:options:metrics:views:` method on a view, passing the visual format string

as the first argument. Views are enclosed with brackets in the format language, and the connections between views are represented with a hyphen. An additional hyphen with a number of points can be used to define the distance between the two views. For example, the following format string says there are 10 points between the label and the text field views:

```
[label]-10-[textFIeld]
```

The name of each view used in the Visual Format Language comes from the `views` dictionary, which is passed as the final argument in the `-constraintsWithVisual Format:options:metrics:views:` call. The dictionary keys represent the view names used in the format string, and the dictionary key values are references to the views themselves. To assist in creating the `views` dictionary, you can use the `NSDic tionaryOfVariableBindings` function. It takes the name of the variable, making it the key, while the object it references is the value. The `views` dictionary for the sample format string is

```
NSDictionary *views = NSDictionaryOfVariableBindings(label, textField);
```

The code to define the constraint looks like this:

```
NSDictionary *viewsDictionary = NSDictionaryOfVariableBindings(label, textField);
NSArray *constraints = [NSLayoutConstraint
    constraintsWithVisualFormat:@"[label]-10-[textField]"
    options:0
    metrics:nil
    views:views];
```

The Visual Format Language provides a visualization of the relationship between UI elements, but there are times when the expression cannot be represented visually. To create a constraint that cannot be expressed using the Visual Format Language, you use the method `-constraintWithItem :attribute:relatedBy:toItem:attribute:multiplier:constant:`.

Now that you have a high-level understanding of Cocoa Auto Layout, let's take a look at how constraints are used in PhotoWheel to display the UI in landscape orientation after the device is rotated.

More Information

For more information on Cocoa Auto Layout and the Visual Format Language, read the Cocoa Auto Layout Guide[1] available in the Developer Documentation.

---

1. Cocoa Auto Layout Guide: https://developer.apple.com/library/ios/#documentation/ UserExperience/Conceptual/AutolayoutPG/Articles/Introduction.html

Customized Rotation

Relying solely on Cocoa Auto Layout constraints defined in IB for rotation support may not be an option for your app. In addition to resizing a screen element, perhaps an element needs to change positions, such as moving from the top of the screen to the far right side of screen. This requires changing the relationship between UI elements. You need to define Auto Layout constraints for both portrait and landscape layouts, which is something you cannot do using only IB.

> **Note**
>
> You should rely on Auto Layout constraints defined in IB as much as possible. Even if your app requires customizing the rotation sequence, try using IB-defined constraints on subviews to help reduce the amount of code you have to write. You'll likely find that using a combination of IB and programmatically defined constraints produces the best user experience.

The UI for PhotoWheel uses background images for visual effects. The UI also has a top-down look and feel to it, with the contents of a photo album being displayed at the top and the "wheel" of albums being displayed at the bottom. Other visual effects are applied as well, such as the arrow pointing to the selected photo album.

If PhotoWheel were to rely solely on Auto Layout constraints defined in IB to support a landscape UI, the UI would look odd. The constraints are defined for a portrait layout. When displayed in landscape orientation, elements may be stretched, shrunken, and placed in the wrong position. To correct these problems, you need to define portrait and landscape layouts using Auto Layout constraints, and you need to change the set of constraints prior to rotation.

Run the app and rotate the device. If you are using the simulator, you can press **Command-Left** and **Command-Right** to rotate a simulated device. As expected, the UI looks a mess and unusable (Figure 18.3).

To get proper portrait and landscape layouts, certain layout constraints defined in IB must be discarded and new constraints created programmatically. To keep things as simple as possible, the Visual Format Language will be used as much as possible. The method call to create a constraint using the Visual Format Language is rather lengthy, so a C macro is defined and used to make the code more readable. This should be especially helpful for those readers using the electronic version of this book.

Open the file *PhotoWheel-Prefix.pch* and add the following code snippet to the bottom of the file:

```
#define ADD_CONSTRAINT(PARENT, FORMAT, VIEWS) [PARENT addConstraints:\
   [NSLayoutConstraint constraintsWithVisualFormat:FORMAT \
   options:0 metrics:nil views:VIEWS]];
```

Next, outlets are needed for the UI elements found in the main scene. Open the file *MainViewController.m* and define outlets for the two container views, the

Figure 18.3   PhotoWheel in landscape mode

background image view, and the info button in the class extension. The code is found
in Listing 18.1.

Listing 18.1   **Define Outlets in the `MainViewController`**

```
@interface MainViewController ()
// Other code left out for brevity's sake.
@property (nonatomic, weak) IBOutlet UIView *albumsView;
@property (nonatomic, weak) IBOutlet UIView *photosView;
@property (nonatomic, weak) IBOutlet UIImageView *backgroundImageView;
@property (nonatomic, weak) IBOutlet UIButton *infoButton;
@end
```

Now open the *MainStoryboard.storyboard* and connect the appropriate UI elements to
the outlets.

With the outlets in place and connected, it's time to write the code that will create the Auto Layout constraints and manage the interface rotation. Open the file
MainViewController.m and make the changes found in Listing 18.2. The code changes
are explained after the listing.

Listing 18.2   **Programmatically Creating Auto Layout Constraints**

```
@implementation MainViewController
// Other code left out for brevity's sake.
```

```objc
- (void)viewWillAppear:(BOOL)animated
{
    [super viewWillAppear:animated];
    [self rotateToInterfaceOrientation:[self interfaceOrientation]];    // 1
}


#pragma mark - Rotation and Auto Layout

- (void)updateViewConstraints                                          // 2
{
    [super updateViewConstraints];
    [self updateViewConstraintsForInterfaceOrientation:
     [self interfaceOrientation]];
}


- (void)updateViewConstraintsForInterfaceOrientation:
(UIInterfaceOrientation)interfaceOrientation                           // 3
{
    UIView *parentView = [self view];
    UIView *albumsView = [self albumsView];
    UIView *photosView = [self photosView];
    UIImageView *backgroundImageView = [self backgroundImageView];
    UIButton *infoButton = [self infoButton];
    NSDictionary *views = NSDictionaryOfVariableBindings(              // 4
      photosView, albumsView, backgroundImageView, infoButton);

    [parentView removeConstraints:[parentView constraints]];          // 5

    ADD_CONSTRAINT(parentView, @"V:|-0-[backgroundImageView]-0-|", views)// 6
    ADD_CONSTRAINT(parentView, @"H:|-0-[backgroundImageView]-0-|", views)

    if (UIInterfaceOrientationIsLandscape(interfaceOrientation)) {    // 7
        ADD_CONSTRAINT(parentView, @"V:[infoButton]-17-|", views)      // 8
        ADD_CONSTRAINT(parentView, @"H:[infoButton]-25-|", views)      // 9

        ADD_CONSTRAINT(parentView, @"V:[photosView(719)]", views)      // 10
        ADD_CONSTRAINT(parentView, @"H:|-18-[photosView(738)]", views) // 11
        [parentView addConstraint:                                     // 12
         [NSLayoutConstraint constraintWithItem:photosView
                                      attribute:NSLayoutAttributeCenterY
                                      relatedBy:NSLayoutRelationEqual
                                         toItem:parentView
                                      attribute:NSLayoutAttributeCenterY
                                     multiplier:1.0f
                                       constant:0.0f]];
```

```objc
      ADD_CONSTRAINT(parentView, @"V:|-100-[albumsView(550)]", views)    // 13
      ADD_CONSTRAINT(parentView, @"H:|-700-[albumsView(551)]", views)

  } else {                                                               // 14
      ADD_CONSTRAINT(parentView, @"H:[infoButton]-26-|", views)
      ADD_CONSTRAINT(parentView, @"V:[infoButton]-28-|", views)

      ADD_CONSTRAINT(parentView, @"V:|-18-[photosView(716)]", views)
      ADD_CONSTRAINT(parentView, @"H:[photosView(717)]", views)
      [parentView addConstraint:
       [NSLayoutConstraint constraintWithItem:photosView
                                    attribute:NSLayoutAttributeCenterX
                                    relatedBy:NSLayoutRelationEqual
                                       toItem:parentView
                                    attribute:NSLayoutAttributeCenterX
                                   multiplier:1.0f constant:0.0f]];

      ADD_CONSTRAINT(parentView, @"V:|-680-[albumsView(550)]", views)
      ADD_CONSTRAINT(parentView, @"H:|-109-[albumsView(551)]", views)
  }
}


- (void)rotateToInterfaceOrientation:
(UIInterfaceOrientation)toInterfaceOrientation                          // 15
{
  [self updateViewConstraintsForInterfaceOrientation:toInterfaceOrientation];

  UIImage *image = nil;
  if (UIInterfaceOrientationIsLandscape(toInterfaceOrientation)) {
      image = [UIImage imageNamed:@"background-landscape-right-grooved"];
  } else {
      image = [UIImage imageNamed:@"background-portrait-grooved"];
  }
  [[self backgroundImageView] setImage:image];
}

- (void)willRotateToInterfaceOrientation:                               // 16
(UIInterfaceOrientation)toInterfaceOrientation
                            duration:(NSTimeInterval)duration
{
  [super willRotateToInterfaceOrientation:toInterfaceOrientation
                                 duration:duration];
  [self rotateToInterfaceOrientation:toInterfaceOrientation];
}

@end
```

Let's walk through these changes.

1. The method -viewWillAppear: is overridden so a call to -rotateToInter faceOrientation: can be made. This will ensure the screen has been properly rotated prior to display. Remember, iOS 6 differs from earlier versions of iOS in which the view controller always displayed in portrait orientation first, then relied on the rotation messages when launched in landscape orientation. With iOS 6, you have to adjust the layout yourself if your portrait and landscape layouts are different enough that Auto Layout cannot make the adjustments for you. PhotoWheel's layouts for the two orientations are indeed different—hence the need to make the call to -rotateToInterfaceOrientation:.

2. The -updateViewConstraints is called when constraints for the view controller's view need updating. You override this method when you want to add, change, or remove constraints. PhotoWheel's implementation for this method calls the helper method -updateViewConstraintsForInterfaceOrienta tion:, passing in the current interface orientation as the argument.

3. The method -updateViewConstraintsForInterfaceOrientation: is created for PhotoWheel, and it is called from multiple places within the view controller class. This method removes all the constraints created by IB from the view controller's view. It then adds two new sets of constraints: one set for the landscape layout and the other set for the portrait layout. For the landscape layout, the photos scene is displayed on the left side of the screen, and the albums scene is displayed on the right. In portrait mode, the photos scene is displayed at the top, and the albums scene is displayed at the bottom. This repositioning of elements—that is, the change in relationships between UI elements—is why the Auto Layout constraints must be redefined for each interface orientation (i.e., landscape and portrait).

4. NSDictionaryOfVariableBindings is used to create the views dictionary. This dictionary is used by the Visual Format Language system to reference the views identified in the visual format string. Note that the dictionary can be created manually as well; you do not have to use NSDictionaryOfVariableBind ings. When creating the dictionary manually, remember the key is the name used in the visual format string and the value is the reference to the view.

5. The -removeConstraints: method removes constraints referenced in the first argument from the receiving view. In PhotoWheel, all the constraints defined in the view controller's view are removed.

6. There is only one constraint common to both interface orientations. This constraint fills the entire view with the background image view. Because there is only one common constraint, it's easier to recreate it than to avoid removing it in the previous call.

7. A check is made to determine the interface orientation that was passed into the method. The app doesn't care if the interface orientation is landscape left,

landscape right, portrait upside down, or portrait. It just wants to know if the orientation is landscape or portrait—and that's what the function `UIInterface OrientationIsLandscape` tells us. If the interface orientation is landscape left or right, this function returns `YES`; otherwise, it returns `NO`, which means the orientation is either portrait or portrait upside down.

8. Constraints for the info button's position are added to the view controller's view. The first constraint sets the vertical position as denoted by the "V:" in the format string. The pipe character is a shortcut symbol for the parent view. In this case, the parent view is the view controller's view. The hyphen indicates that the element will be positioned by some offset from the other element. For instance, "[infoButton]-|" says to position the `infoButton` an appropriate number of points from the right edge of the parent view. "[infoButton]-17-|" does the same except that an exact number of points is specified. In other words, the format string says, "Position the `infoButton` 17 points from the right edge of the parent view."

9. The horizontal position for the info button is set with the next constraint, which is positioned 25 points from the bottom edge of the parent view. The "H:" is used to indicate that the constraint is for the horizontal plane.

10. The format string "V:[photosView(719)]" sets the height of the `photosView` to 719 points. There are no other views mentioned in the format string, so only the height is set. Its relationship to other views has not been defined.

11. The next format string, "H:|-18-[photosView(738)]", sets the width of the `photoViews` to 738 points. It also positions the view 18 points from the left edge of its parent view.

12. As mentioned earlier, sometimes the relationship between views cannot be expressed using the visual format string. In those cases, you create the constraint by calling `+constraintWithItem:attribute:relatedBy:toItem:attri bute:multiplier:constant:` on the `NSLayoutConstraint` class. In PhotoWheel, this method is used to center the `photosView` on the Y-axis within the parent view.

13. Last for the landscape orientation is the `albumsView`. The height of the `albumsView` is set to 550 points, and the view is placed 100 points from the left edge of its parent view. The `albumsView` width is set to 551 points, and it is positioned 700 points from the top edge of the parent view.

14. The `else` block defines the Auto Layout constraints for the portrait layout. Each UI element is sized and positioned for display in the portrait interface orientation.

15. The next method in the code change is `-rotateToInterfaceOrientation:`. This method is specific to PhotoWheel, and it is called from the `-viewWill Appear:` and `-willRotateToInterfaceOrientation:duration:`

methods. The `-rotateToInterfaceOrientation:` method calls `-update`
`ViewConstraintsForInterfaceOrientation:`, which creates the Auto
Layout constraints needed for the current interface orientation. It then changes
the background image to *background-landscape-right-grooved.png* when the current interface orientation is landscape, and to *background-portrait-grooved.png* for
portrait.

16. The last change in Listing 18.1 is the implementation for `-willRotateToInter`
`faceOrientation:duration:`. This method is overridden, giving the view controller the opportunity to make any necessary adjustments prior to iOS rotating the
screen. The method calls `-rotateToInterfaceOrientation:`, which creates the
appropriate Auto Layout constraints and sets the background image based on the new
interface orientation.

Build and run the app to test your changes. Rotate the device. UI elements defined
in the main scene should now be properly displayed in both portrait and landscape
orientations (Figure 18.4). However, the views for the children view controllers have
been not adjusted for landscape. A bit more work is needed.

Figure 18.4   Main scene displayed in landscape

> **More Information**
>
> Read the Visual Format Language[2] guide for a complete list of grammar and syntax used in a visual format string.

Checking the Interface Orientation

When checking the interface orientation, you can use the macros `UIInterfaceOrientationIsLandscape` and `UIInterfaceOrientationIsPortrait`. `UIInterfaceOrientationIsLandscape` checks whether the interface orientation is landscape left or right, and `UIInterfaceOrientationIsPortrait` checks whether the orientation is portrait or portrait upside down. You can use the `UIInterfaceOrientation` enumeration if you need to perform a more specific check—for example, `if (toInterfaceOrientation == UIInterfaceOrientationPortraitUpsideDown)`.

There are four `UIInterfaceOrientation` options:

- `UIInterfaceOrientationPortrait`
- `UIInterfaceOrientationPortraitUpsideDown`
- `UIInterfaceOrientationLandscapeLeft`
- `UIInterfaceOrientationLandscapeRight`

Rotating the Photos Scene

Let's tackle the photos scene first.

To reduce the amount of code needed to support the landscape orientation for the photos scene, we'll use a combination of Auto Layout constraints defined in the IB and some defined in code. For the main scene, all of the IB-created constraints were tossed out and replaced with constraints created programmatically. This was necessary because the layout for landscape is sufficiently different from the portrait layout. This, however, is not the case for the photos scene.

The layout is similar between the portrait and landscape orientations. While the theme here is rotation and supporting two orientations, in reality the two layouts are almost the same. The UI elements remain in basically the same position for both layouts. The only major differences relate to the size of the elements. For instance, the width for the toolbar and shadow bar must change based on the orientation, and the collection view's width and height must change based on the layout. In general, though, the layout is the same for both portrait and landscape orientations.

---

2. Visual Format Language: https://developer.apple.com/library/ios/#documentation/
    UserExperience/Conceptual/AutolayoutPG/Articles/formatLanguage.html

For this reason, you will rely mainly on the Auto Layout constraints defined in IB—but this is where you start to feel the pain. It will seem as if IB has a mind of its own as you try to adjust the constraints. Moving a UI element can, and oftentimes will, change the constraints already defined. This may or may not break what progress you have already made. In some cases, you may have to trick IB into creating the necessary constraint for you by doing things like moving a UI element up and then back down by one point.

Working with IB to define constraints that work for two layouts is definitely more of an art than a science. But with patience, you can achieve the desired effect . . . that is, until you add another UI element to the scene.

Trial and Error

Mastering Auto Layout constraints is not something you learn overnight. It involves lots of trial and error. Even the steps presented in this section of the book may not work perfectly for every reader. But given enough time, you will become more comfortable with Cocoa Auto Layout, and working with it will become easier for you.

Here's what you want to achieve when adding more Auto Layout constraints to the photos scene:

1. Have the background image view completely fill the entire container view.

2. Position the toolbar, shadow bar, and collection view a set number of points from the left edge of the container view.

3. Have the toolbar and shadow bar share the same widths. In other words, their widths are equal.

4. Have the collection view and shadow bar share the same top alignment.

Why are these the constraints needed to support both portrait and landscape layouts? By defining these constraints, you reduce the amount of code needed to adjust the layout based on the interface orientation during rotation. For instance, when you say that the shadow bar will always have the same width as the toolbar, you then simply need to change the toolbar's width in code based on the interface orientation. The Auto Layout system will handle resizing the shadow bar for you based on the width of the toolbar.

Before you start tinkering with the Auto Layout constraints, you might want to make a snapshot of your project. Xcode's snapshot feature stores a backup copy of your current project or workspace. Should something go wrong, you can restore the project back to the previous snapshot. To make a snapshot, select **File > Create Snapshot** from the menu or press **Control-Command-S**. To restore your project to a previously saved snapshot, select **File > Restore Snapshot**.

With your project snapshot saved, let's start adding constraints to the photos scene. Open the file *MainStoryboard.storyboard* and select the photos scene. Next, perform the following steps to fill the container view with the background image view.

Use the Document Outline

You will want to use the Document Outline to select the objects in the steps that follow.

1. Select the Image View object for the background image. Select **Editor > Pin > Leading Space to Superview.**

2. Select the Image View object (again) for the background image. Select **Editor > Pin > Trailing Space to Superview.**

3. Select the Image View object (once more time) for the background image. Select **Editor > Pin > Top Space to Superview.**

4. Select the Image View object (one last time) for the background image. Select **Editor > Pin > Bottom Space to Superview.**

Yes, you must keep reselecting the image view after each pin.

Next up is setting the horizontal spacing for the toolbar, shadow bar, and collection view. Here are the steps:

1. Select the Toolbar, Collection View, and Image View objects. Make sure you select the Image View for the shadow image. You can select more than one object by holding down the **Command** key as you click on the object.

2. Select **Editor > Pin > Leading Space to Superview** from the menu bar. This sets a horizontal spacing constraint for each selected object.

3. Find the constraint named "Center X Alignment – Collection View – Image View – stack-viewer-shadow.png" and delete it. To delete it, select the constraint and then press the **Delete** key.

4. Find the constraint named "Center X Alignment – Image View – stack-viewer-bg-portrait.png – Image View – stack-viewer-shadow.png" and delete it.

The reason you must delete the "Center X Alignment" constraints is that they conflict with the horizontal constraints you just created. If you were to run the app before deleting the "Center X Alignment" constraints, you would see a message in the Debug window informing you of this conflict.

Note

A constraint with the purple color icon is a default constraint created by IB, and it cannot be deleted. A blue color icon constraint is a nondefault constraint created by you or by IB, and it can be deleted.

Now set the width for the toolbar and shadow bar with the following steps:

1. Select the Toolbar and Image View objects. Make sure you select the Image View for the shadow image.

2. Select **Editor > Pin > Widths Equally** from the menu bar.

Lastly, you want to define a constraint that sets the top alignment for the collection view and shadow bar. Chances are good that IB has already created this constraint for you. The constraint has been created for you if you see "Top Alignment – Collection View – Image View – stack-viewer-shadow.png" and "Vertical Space (51) – Collection View – View" in the list of constraints for the container view. If by chance the constraint is missing, perform these steps to create it:

1. Select the Collection View and Image View objects. Make sure you select the Image View for the shadow image.

2. Select **Editor > Pin > Top Space to Superview** from the menu bar.

Two constraints are listed, even though the intention is to create a single "top alignment" constraint. The "vertical space" constraint works with the "top alignment" constraint to define the placement of the related UI elements—in this case, the collection view and shadow bar.

You have defined the constraints needed to support both layouts, but the landscape layout still wouldn't display properly if you were to run the app. That's because a bit of code is needed. Open *PhotosViewController.m* and make the code changes in Listing 18.3.

Listing 18.3   **Code Change to `PhotosViewController` to Support Landscape Orientation**

```
@interface PhotosViewController ()
// Other code left out for brevity's sake.

@property (nonatomic, weak) IBOutlet UIImageView *backgroundImageView;  // 1
@property (nonatomic, weak) IBOutlet NSLayoutConstraint
*toolbarWidthConstraint;                                                // 2
@property (nonatomic, weak) IBOutlet NSLayoutConstraint
*collectionViewVerticalSpacingConstraint;                               // 3

@end

@implementation PhotosViewController
// Other code left out for brevity's sake.

- (void)viewWillAppear:(BOOL)animated                                   // 4
{
    [super viewWillAppear:animated];
    [self rotateToInterfaceOrientation:[self interfaceOrientation]];
}

#pragma mark - Rotation and Auto Layout                                 // 5

- (void)updateViewConstraints
{
```

```objectivec
    [super updateViewConstraints];
    [self updateViewConstraintsForInterfaceOrientation:[self interfaceOrientation]];
}


- (void)updateViewConstraintsForInterfaceOrientation:
(UIInterfaceOrientation)interfaceOrientation
{
    UICollectionView *collectionView = [self collectionView];
    [collectionView removeConstraints:[collectionView constraints]];
    NSDictionary *views = @{ @"collectionView" : collectionView };          // 6

    if (UIInterfaceOrientationIsLandscape(interfaceOrientation)) {
        ADD_CONSTRAINT(collectionView, @"V:[collectionView(632)]", views);// 7
        ADD_CONSTRAINT(collectionView, @"H:[collectionView(664)]", views);
        [[self collectionViewVerticalSpacingConstraint] setConstant:52];  // 8
        [[self toolbarWidthConstraint] setConstant:678];                  // 9

    } else {
        ADD_CONSTRAINT(collectionView, @"V:[collectionView(596)]", views);
        ADD_CONSTRAINT(collectionView, @"H:[collectionView(684)]", views);
        [[self collectionViewVerticalSpacingConstraint] setConstant:51];
        [[self toolbarWidthConstraint] setConstant:698];
    }
}


- (void)willRotateToInterfaceOrientation:
(UIInterfaceOrientation)toInterfaceOrientation
                                duration:(NSTimeInterval)duration
{
    [self rotateToInterfaceOrientation:toInterfaceOrientation];
}

- (void)rotateToInterfaceOrientation:
(UIInterfaceOrientation)toInterfaceOrientation
{
    [self updateViewConstraintsForInterfaceOrientation:toInterfaceOrientation];

    UIImage *image = nil;
    if (UIInterfaceOrientationIsLandscape(toInterfaceOrientation)) {
        image = [UIImage imageNamed:@"stack-viewer-bg-landscape-right"];
    } else {
        image = [UIImage imageNamed:@"stack-viewer-bg-portrait"];
    }
    [[self backgroundImageView] setImage:image];
}

@end
```

The code changes are similar to those made to `MainViewController`, but there are some noticeable differences.

1. An outlet is defined for the background image view. This is needed to change the image based on the interface orientation.

2–3. An Auto Layout constraint is an object, and because it's an object, a reference to the constraint can be stored. Generally, a constraint is immutable, but the `constant` property can be set on an existing constraint. This allows your app to change the constraint at runtime. The `toolbarWidthConstraint` and the `collectionViewVerticalSpacingConstraint` are defined as outlets, so they can be connected in the photos scene and accessed in code.

4. The `-viewWillAppear:` method is overridden so that the layout can be set up for the current interface orientation.

5. The rest of the code changes follow the same pattern found in *MainViewCon troller.m*. The `-updateViewConstraints` is overridden so that the constraints can be updated; `-willRotateToInterfaceOrientation:duration:` is overridden so that the background image can be changed based on the current interface orientation.

6. The `views` dictionary is created, but this time the dictionary is created manually instead of by calling `NSDictionaryOfVariableBindings`. This is done just to show you an alternative way of creating the `views` dictionary.

7. Constraints are added to the collection view to set its width and height. As an alternative, outlets could have been used.

8. The vertical spacing for the collection view is set to `52`. This means the collection view is 52 points from the top edge of its superview. In portrait orientation, the vertical spacing is set to `51`. The 1-point difference is needed because the inside edge of the background image is different by 1 pixel. Note that setting this constraint's `constant` value affects the shadow bar, too. You do not see this in code, but the relationship between the collection view and the shadow bar's top alignment is defined in the storyboard.

9. The toolbar width constraint is set to `698`. This not only changes the width of the toolbar, but also changes the width of the shadow bar due to the "widths equal" constraint you set up earlier.

All that remains now is to connect the outlets. Open the file *MainStoryboard.story board* and select the photos scene. Connect the `backgroundImageView` outlet defined in the File's Owner to the image view that displays the background image.

Next, connect the `toolbarWidthConstraint` outlet to the toolbar's width constraint. You can find this constraint by first clicking the disclosure button for the toolbar, then clicking the disclosure button for the constraints under the toolbar object in the Document Outline.

Lastly, connect the `collectionViewVerticalSpacingConstraint` outlet to the "Vertical Space (51) – Collection View – View" constraint found under the container

Figure 18.5   The main screen displayed in landscape orientation

view. Once the outlets have been connected, run the app and test the layouts by rotating the device. Assuming all went well, you should see the photos scene nicely laid out in landscape mode (Figure 18.5).

Rotating the Albums Scene

Changing the albums scene to support the landscape layout is a snap because the work is already done for you. Cocoa Auto Layout and the work done in `MainViewControl ler` handle the repositioning of the scene. However, there is one slight problem: the wheel view does not make appropriate adjustments for landscape orientation.

In portrait mode, the selected album is displayed at the top of the wheel (0.0 degrees). In landscape mode, the selected photo album should be displayed at the left of the wheel (−90.0 or 270.0 degrees). A tweak is needed to the `WheelView` class to offset the wheel by a certain number of degrees.

Open the *WheelView.h* file. Add a new declared property named `angleOffset` of type `CGFloat`. The property declaration should look like this:

```
@property (nonatomic, assign) CGFloat angleOffset;
```

Next, open the file *WheelView.m*. At the bottom of the implementation section, add the following custom setter method:

```
- (void)setAngleOffset:(CGFloat)angleOffset
{
    if (_angleOffset != -angleOffset) {
        _angleOffset = -angleOffset;
        [self layoutSubviews];
    }
}
```

This method adjusts the given angle offset. This adjustment is needed because, internally, 0.0 degrees of the wheel view is actually at the bottom of the view, not the top. However, we tend to think of a circle's 0-degree point as the top of the circle. The setter method also calls -layoutSubviews, which forces the wheel view to redraw the contents each time the angle offset is set.

Finally, scroll to the middle of the method -(void)setAngle:(CGFloat)angle and replace the line of code that reads

```
float angleInRadians = (angle + 180.0) * M_PI / 180.0f;
```

with the following line of code:

```
float angleInRadians = ((angle + [self angleOffset]) + 180.0) * M_PI / 180.0f;
```

The WheelView class now supports an angle offset that can be used to control the "virtual top" of the wheel. You want to set this property in the -willRotateTo InterfaceOrientation:duration: method in the AlbumsViewController class. The angle offset should be set to 0.0 for portrait mode and 270.0 (or −90.00) for landscape mode. Make the change to your code; Listing 18.4 shows the modified code.

Listing 18.4   **Update to the *AlbumsViewController.m* File**

```
- (void)viewWillAppear:(BOOL)animated
{
    [super viewWillAppear:animated];
    [self rotateToInterfaceOrientation:[self interfaceOrientation]];
}


#pragma mark - Rotation


- (void)rotateToInterfaceOrientation:
(UIInterfaceOrientation)toInterfaceOrientation
{
    CGFloat angleOffset;
    if (UIInterfaceOrientationIsLandscape(toInterfaceOrientation)) {
        angleOffset = 270.0;
    } else {
        angleOffset = 0.0;
```

```
    }
    [[self wheelView] setAngleOffset:angleOffset];
}

- (void)willRotateToInterfaceOrientation:
(UIInterfaceOrientation)toInterfaceOrientation
duration:(NSTimeInterval)duration
{
    [self rotateToInterfaceOrientation:toInterfaceOrientation];
}
```

Rotating the About View

The main screen is not the only screen that must support rotation. The About screen must also handle rotation, but there's nothing to do for the About screen—it rotates nicely without any additional work.

Rotating the Photo Browser

The photo browser must rotate as well. As is true for the About screen, no action is needed by you to make it rotate. However, some trouble spots do crop up when the photo browser is rotated. The vertical spacing for navigation bar is off by 20 points when rotating, while the chrome is hidden and the contents of the scroll view do not resize properly.

The photo browser is not your standard iOS screen. It displays a scroll view, which contains one or more scroll views. Each sub-scroll view displays a photo that the user may or may not have zoomed in on. In addition, the photo browser shows and hides chrome. Collectively, these factors make the photo browser a bit more challenging to rotate.

The best way to describe what needs to happen is to show you the updated source code, then walk you through it. You will need to update your source code with the same set of changes. Start with the `PhotoBrowserPhotoView` class. It needs a new method to reposition the photo, when zoomed, after the content size for the scroll view changes, which happens when the device is rotated.

Open the header file for the `PhotoBrowserPhotoView` class and add the new method declaration shown in Listing 18.5.

Listing 18.5 **New Method Declarations for the `PhotoBrowserPhotoView` Class**

```
#import <UIKit/UIKit.h>

@class PhotoBrowserViewController;

@interface PhotoBrowserPhotoView : UIScrollView <UIScrollViewDelegate>
```

```
@property (nonatomic, assign) NSInteger index;
@property (nonatomic, weak) PhotoBrowserViewController
*photoBrowserViewController;

- (void)setImage:(UIImage *)newImage;
- (void)turnOffZoom;

- (void)restoreAfterRotation;

@end
```

Now open the implementation file for the `PhotoBrowserPhotoView` class and add the new method; the code is shown in Listing 18.6.

Listing 18.6   **New Method Implementations for `PhotoBrowserPhotoView`**

```
#pragma mark - Rotation

- (void)restoreAfterRotation
{
    [self turnOffZoom];
    [self setContentSize:[self bounds].size];
    [[self imageView] setFrame:[self bounds]];
}
```

This method is called by `PhotoBrowserViewController` during the rotation animation. It restores the size and position of the image view within the scroll view. It starts by turning off the zoom if the user has zoomed in on the photo. Next, this method sets the context size for the scroll view equal to the size of the scroll view. The scroll view has been rotated, so the bounds have changed, which is why the content size must be reset. Lastly, the image view is resized to fill the content area.

Next, you must make the necessary changes to the `PhotoBrowserViewController` class so that rotation is handled properly. The code changes are in Listing 18.7, and an explanation of the changes follows the listing.

Listing 18.7   **Changes to `PhotoBrowserViewController`**

```
#pragma mark - Rotation

- (void)willRotateToInterfaceOrientation:(UIInterfaceOrientation)
toInterfaceOrientation duration:(NSTimeInterval)duration
{
    [[self scrollView] setScrollEnabled:NO];
}

- (void)willAnimateRotationToInterfaceOrientation:(UIInterfaceOrientation)
toInterfaceOrientation duration:(NSTimeInterval)duration
```

```
{
    [self setScrollViewContentSize];
    [self alignScrollViewSubviews];
    [self scrollToIndex:[self currentIndex]];
    [self repositionNavigationBar];
}


- (void)didRotateFromInterfaceOrientation:(UIInterfaceOrientation)
fromInterfaceOrientation
{
    [[self scrollView] setScrollEnabled:YES];
}


- (void)alignScrollViewSubviews
{
    NSMutableArray *cache = [self photoViewCache];
    NSArray *subviews = [[self scrollView] subviews];
    [subviews enumerateObjectsUsingBlock:^(id obj, NSUInteger idx, BOOL *stop) {
        NSInteger indexInCache = [cache indexOfObject:obj];
        [obj setFrame:[self frameForPageAtIndex:indexInCache]];
        [obj restoreAfterRotation];
    }];
}


- (void)repositionNavigationBar
{
    if ([self isChromeHidden]) {
        UINavigationBar *navbar = [[self navigationController] navigationBar];
        CGRect frame = [navbar frame];
        frame.origin.y = [self statusBarHeight];
        [navbar setFrame:frame];
    }
}
```

The first new method in Listing 18.7 is -willRotateToInterfaceOrientation :duration:. You override this UIViewController method when you wish to perform some work prior to the rotation. The current interface orientation is unchanged at the time this method is called, so this method is not a good place for repositioning UI elements during rotation. However, it is an ideal place to do something like, say, turn off scrolling on a scroll view. And that's exactly what happens in this particular implementation of -willRotateToInterfaceOrientation:duration:.

The scroll view can potentially fire off scrolling-related delegate method calls during rotation. If this happens, PhotoWheel might scroll to another image, making it the current photo displayed. This is not the behavior the user expects, which explains why scrolling of the scroll view is temporarily turned off.

Scrolling is turned back on for the scroll view in the -didRotateFromInterface Orientation method. You override this UIViewController method when you need to perform tasks after a rotation, such as turning on scrolling for a scroll view.

The method -willAnimateRotationToInterfaceOrientation:duration: is responsible for laying out the scroll view and its contents during the rotation. When this UIViewController method is called, the interface orientation for the view controller has been updated with the new orientation, and the bounds of the view have been updated. As a consequence, this method is an ideal spot for laying out the subviews based on the new interface orientation.

The implementation for -willAnimateRotationToInterfaceOrientation :duration:, in Listing 18.7, sets the content size for the scroll view. It then sizes and positions the scroll view subviews, which are the photos currently contained in the scroll view. After the subviews have been laid out, the scroll view content offset is reset to show the photo for the current index. Lastly, the navigation bar is repositioned. This step is needed because a hidden navigation bar will not receive rotation messages, causing its position to be wrong when the chrome is displayed again.

Listing 18.7 wraps up with the two helper methods called during the rotation animation. The first method, -alignScrollViewSubviews, loops through the subviews found in the scroll view, setting the new frame for each and calling the -restoreAfter Rotation. The second method, -repositionNavigationBar, repositions the navigation bar if it is hidden during rotation.

And with that, the photo browser now supports all possible interface orientations. Build the app, run it, and test the latest set of changes.

Launch Images

One last topic related to orientation is the use of launch images. A launch image is an image that is displayed the moment the user taps the app icon on the **Home** screen. iOS is responsible for displaying the launch image and hiding it when your app is ready to run. Using a launch image gives the user the impression that the app has launched quickly, even though it may still be loading.

Note

You might be tempted to use the launch image as a splash screen for your app. *Don't!* Users don't want to see your splash screen. They want to use your app. Need some convincing? Listen to Mike Lee's talk on *Making Apps That Don't Suck.*[3]

---

3. *Making Apps That Don't Suck*: http://www.infoq.com/presentations/Making-Apps-That-Dont-Suck

A launch image is not a splash screen. Instead, it is an image representing the initial launch state of your app. It typically looks like the first screen of your app with no content.

An easy way to make a screen shot of your app is to use Organizer. With your device connected to your computer, open Organizer and select Devices, then select Screenshots under the section for your device. With your app running, click the **New Screenshot** button in Organizer. This takes a screen shot of your app's current screen, as shown in Figure 18.6. You can also click Save as Launch Image to add the image to your project.

When you create the launch image for your iPad app, you actually need to create four images: one image each for portrait and landscape modes for retina and non-retina displays. iOS will use the appropriate image based on the device orientation and display type when the app is launched. The recommended size for the portrait launch images is 768 × 1004 pixels for normal displays and 1536 × 2008 pixels for retina displays. The recommended size for the landscape image is 1024 × 748 pixels (2048 × 1496 pixels for retina). This leaves 20 points (20 pixels for normal displays and 40 pixels for retina displays) at the top to display the status bar.

Figure 18.6   Screen shots available in Organizer

Key	Type	Value
▼ Information Property List	Dictionary	(16 items)
Localization native development reg	String	en
Bundle display name	String	${PRODUCT_NAME}
Executable file	String	${EXECUTABLE_NAME}
Bundle identifier	String	com.whitepeaksoftware.${PRODUCT_NAME:rfc1034identifier}
InfoDictionary version	String	6.0
Bundle name	String	${PRODUCT_NAME}
Bundle OS Type code	String	APPL
Bundle versions string, short	String	1.0
Bundle creator OS Type code	String	????
Bundle version	String	1.0
Application requires iPhone environ	Boolean	YES
▶ Required device capabilities	Array	(1 item)
▶ Supported interface orientations (iPa	Array	(4 items)
Main storyboard file base name	String	MainStoryboard
▶ Icon files	Array	(7 items)
Launch image (iPad)	String	Default.jpg

Figure 18.7   Specify the launch image in the project's *info.plist*.

Once you have the launch images, you need to tell your app about them. Add the launch images to your Xcode project and then open the *info.plist* file for the project. Add a new row with the key Launch Image [or Launch Image (iPad)] and set the value to the file name of the portrait version of your launch image, as shown in Figure 18.7.

You can skip the *info.plist* step by naming the portrait image *Default.png* and the landscape image *Default-Landscape.png*. The iPad will look for these images when the launch image is not defined in the *info.plist*. If, however, you wish to use a different name for the launch images, you must update the project's *info.plist* file.

The launch images for PhotoWheel are included in the set of images you added to the project back in Chapter 14, "Storyboarding in Xcode." These images are named *PW-Default.jpg*, *PW-Default@2x.jpg*, *PWDefault-Landscape.jpg,* and *PWDefault-Landscape @2x.jpg*. Find these files under the Images group in the Project navigator. Click each file name and rename it by removing the *PW* at the beginning of each name (Figure 18.8). Be sure to set the Launch Image key in the *info.plist* file to *Default.jpg* because the file name differs from the default *Default.png*. PhotoWheel will now use these *.jpg* images as the launch images.

Summary

So there you have it—rotation and orientation in a nutshell. As you have seen, adding rotation support is never easy unless the app relies solely on Auto Layout. But armed with the knowledge from this chapter, you have no excuse for not supporting each interface orientation in your iPad apps.

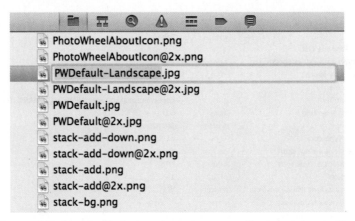

Figure 18.8   Use the Project navigator to rename the launch image files.

When adding rotation to your apps, remember to use Auto Layout as much as possible. It will save you time and code. Nevertheless, you shouldn't restrict your app to portrait mode just because Auto Layout alone doesn't work for you. Take the time needed to support both portrait and landscape orientations in your UI. Your reward for the extra time and effort will be satisfied users of your app.

Exercises

1. Change the landscape UI layout so that the photo album wheel is displayed on the left side instead of the right. Use the images *background-landscape-left-grooved. png* and *stack-viewer-bg-landscape-left.png* for the left-handed landscape layout.

2. Take screen shots of PhotoWheel and other apps using Organizer.

Printing with AirPrint

AirPrint is a feature that makes it possible to print wireless from the iPad. This is a welcome feature for many iPad users who prefer having a hard copy of content such as receipts from online purchases, documents, and images.

In this chapter, you will learn about the printing subsystem provided by iOS and explore how to incorporate printing into your own apps.

How Printing Works

Printing is a feature you build into your app—it is not something that is automatically provided to users of each and every app on the device. Your app must provide a way for the user to request content to be printed. This usually takes the form of a tap on a button displayed in a navigation bar or toolbar. When a user wants to print from your app, he taps the button (or whatever mechanism is provided by your app), which then presents the printer options. The user selects the desired printer and number of copies to print (Figure 19.1). And with a tap on the **Print** button, the content is sent to the printer.

Figure 19.1 The Printer Options view displayed in a popover on the iPad

> **Note**
>
> On the iPad, the Printer Options view is displayed in a popover, which you present from the button or view tapped by the user. The Printer Options view slides up from the bottom to fill the entire screen when presented on an iPhone or iPod touch.

Each print request issued by the user creates a print job. A print job consists of the combination of the content to print and the information needed to print, such as the printer name, name of the print job, and number of copies to print.

A print job is sent to the printing subsystem where the data is saved to storage (i.e., the data is spooled). The print job is then placed in the print queue, where it waits for its turn to be printed. The print queue operates on a first-in, first-out basis, and multiple applications on the same device can submit multiple print jobs to the printing subsystem. Thus a user can print from your app and, while waiting for that print job to complete, print again from another app.

Print Center

The user can check the status of a print job that is printing or waiting to print by double tapping the **Home** button and selecting the Print Center app in the multitasking UI (Figure 19.2). Print Center is a background system application that is available only when a print job is processing. Print Center makes it possible for the user to view detailed information about each print job and cancel jobs that are printing or waiting.

Figure 19.2   Print Center showing the details of a print job

Requirements for Printing

Printing is available on any iOS device that supports multitasking and is running iOS version 4.2 or greater. If the device does not meet these minimum requirements, printing won't be available. In your app, it is up to you to check whether the device supports printing. If printing isn't supported, your app should not give the user an option to print. The option to print should be made available only when the device actually supports printing. You will learn how to do this in a moment.

Printing API

The programmatic interface for printing is provided by UIKit. The UIKit Printing API provides classes and a protocol giving you complete control of printing content from your application. Printing is managed through the shared instance of `UIPrint InteractionController`. The controller contains information about the print job (`UIPrintInfo`) and the paper (`UIPrintPaper`). It also contains the content to be printed. The content can consist of a single image or PDF document, an array of images or PDF documents, a print formatter (`UIPrintFormatter`), or a page renderer (`UIPrintPageRenderer`). The controller can also have a delegate object that conforms to the `UIPrintInteractionControllerDelegate` protocol.

The content types that are easiest to print are images and PDF documents. The content comprises an object reference to a `UIImage`, `NSData`, `NSURL`, or `ALAsset`. An `NSURL` object referring to the location of an image or PDF document must use the `file:` or `asset-library:` scheme or any scheme capable of returning an `NSData` object. To print an image or PDF document, set the `printingItem` property on the shared `UIPrintInteractionController` instance. To print a collection of images or PDF documents, store the object references in an `NSArray` and set the `printingItems` property.

To print slightly complex content that does not require headers and footers and can span multiple pages, you use one of the `UIPrintFormatter` concrete subclasses. These subclasses include `UISimpleTextPrintFormatter`, `UIMarkupTextPrint Formatter`, and `UIViewPrintFormatter`. Create an instance of the appropriate formatter object and then set the `printFormatter` property on the shared `UIPrint InteractionController` instance.

For complex content that can include headers and footers, use a custom class derived from `UIPrintPageRenderer`. A print renderer object draws pages of content to be printed, with or without using formatter objects. This approach is definitely the hardest way to print content, but it also gives you the maximum level of control over the printed output.

Adding Printing to PhotoWheel

PhotoWheel displays photos, and printing images is a task that is made easy with the `UIPrintInteractionController` class. So let's give the PhotoWheel user the option to print a photo from the photo browser.

The navigation bar in the photo browser already has an action button. This is the perfect place to display an action menu with a print option. Here is how it should work from the point of view of the user. First, the user taps the action button to display the action menu. Next, the user taps the Print menu item. The Printer Options view is displayed. The user selects the printer and then taps the **Print** button. The current photo is sent to the printer, and the printer produces a copy of the photo.

The code to make this happen is simple. The `-showActionMenu:` method in the `PhotoBrowserViewController` class is changed to display the action sheet. The action sheet delegate callback `-actionSheet:clickedButtonAtIndex:` checks which menu item is tapped. If it is the Print action menu item, `-printCurrentPhoto` is called. This new method prepares the shared `UIPrintInteractionController` instance and then displays it so that the user can print the photo.

That's all it takes to print a photo.

The code to accomplish the steps just described is shown in Listing 19.1. Apply the same code changes to your version of the *PhotoBrowserViewController.m* file.

Listing 19.1 **Add Print Support to the `PhotoBrowserViewController` Class**

```
- (void)showActionMenu:(id)sender                                    // 1
{
    [self cancelChromeDisplayTimer];
    UIActionSheet *actionSheet = [[UIActionSheet alloc] init];
    [actionSheet setDelegate:self];
    [actionSheet setTag:ACTIONSHEET_TAG_ACTIONS];
    if ([UIPrintInteractionController isPrintingAvailable]) {
        [actionSheet addButtonWithTitle:@"Print"];
    }

    [actionSheet showFromBarButtonItem:sender animated:YES];
}


#pragma mark - Printing

- (void)printCurrentPhoto
{
    [self cancelChromeDisplayTimer];                                 // 2
    UIImage *currentPhoto = [self imageAtIndex:[self currentIndex]]; // 3

    UIPrintInteractionController *controller =
        [UIPrintInteractionController sharedPrintController];        // 4
    if(!controller){
        NSLog(@"Couldn't get shared UIPrintInteractionController!");
        return;
    }
```

```
    UIPrintInteractionCompletionHandler completionHandler =
      ^(UIPrintInteractionController *printController, BOOL completed,
        NSError *error)
    {
      [self startChromeDisplayTimer];
      if(completed && error)
        NSLog(@"FAILED! due to error in domain %@ with error code %u",
             error.domain, error.code);
    };                                                         // 5

    UIPrintInfo *printInfo = [UIPrintInfo printInfo];          // 6
    [printInfo setOutputType:UIPrintInfoOutputPhoto];          // 7
    [printInfo setJobName:[NSString stringWithFormat:@"photo-%i",
                           [self currentIndex]]];              // 8

    [controller setPrintInfo:printInfo];                       // 9
    [controller setPrintingItem:currentPhoto];                 // 10

    [controller presentFromBarButtonItem:[self actionButton]
                               animated:YES
                      completionHandler:completionHandler];    // 11
}


#pragma mark - UIActionSheetDelegate methods

- (void)actionSheet:(UIActionSheet *)actionSheet
clickedButtonAtIndex:(NSInteger)buttonIndex
{
   [self startChromeDisplayTimer];

   // Do nothing if the user taps outside the action
   // sheet (thus closing the popover containing the
   // action sheet).
   if (buttonIndex < 0) {
      return;
   }

   if ([actionSheet tag] == ACTIONSHEET_TAG_DELETE) {
      [self deletePhotoConfirmed];
   } else if ([actionSheet tag] == ACTIONSHEET_TAG_ACTIONS) {  // 12
      [self printCurrentPhoto];
   }
}
```

Let's take a closer look at the code in Listing 19.1.

1. The NSLog() statement originally in -showActionMenu: is replaced with code that creates and shows an action sheet. A check is performed to confirm that the device supports printing. If the device does not have this capability, the Print menu item is not added to the action sheet.

   The chrome display timer is also turned off. The chrome should remain visible while the action sheet is displayed.

2. The method -printCurrentPhoto is the workhorse of the print feature for the photo browser. It starts by canceling the chrome display timer. The chrome should remain visible while the Printer Options view is displayed.

3. A reference to the current photo is retrieved; this is the content to be printed.

4. A reference to the shared UIPrintInteractionController is retrieved. This step is followed by a check to ensure that a valid reference is returned. If it is not, an error message is logged to the console.

5. A completion block is created. This block is called when the print request completes. Within the block, the chrome display timer is started again, and if an error occurred, it is logged to the console.

6–8. A new instance of UIPrintInfo is created. The output type is set to UIPrintInfoOutputPhoto, which produces the best-quality output for images, and the print job is named. Naming the print job is optional, but you should give the job a name that the user will recognize should the user need to cancel something he has queued up to print.

9. The printInfo object is assigned to the printInfo property found on the shared UIPrintInteractionController object.

10. The printingItem property for the shared UIPrintInteractionController is set to the photo reference, which is a pointer to UIImage. This tells the controller which content to print.

11. The Printer Option view is presented to the user.

The code change is ready to test, but how do you test printing? One option that saves paper and doesn't require a physical printer is to use the Printer Simulator.

The Printer Simulator

Included with Xcode is the Printer Simulator (Figure 19.3). The Printer Simulator registers different simulated printer types that can be used from your app to test printing, as shown in Figure 19.4.

The Printer Simulator is launched from the iOS Simulator by selecting the **File > Open Printer Simulator** menu item. The simulated printers are available to your app running in the iOS Simulator and on your iPad (as long as your iPad and the

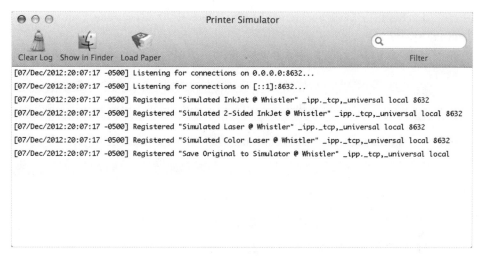

Figure 19.3   The Printer Simulator running on a development Mac computer

Figure 19.4   A list of simulated printers made available
courtesy of the Printer Simulator

Printer Simulator are on the same network), and they remain available as long as the Printer Simulator continues running. When you quit the simulator, the simulated printers are unregistered and no longer available to your app.

Summary

This chapter gave you a basic understanding of how printing works in iOS. You also got to see printing in action by adding a print feature to PhotoWheel. This discussion merely scratches the surface of printing in iOS, however. To learn more, read the Printing section of the Drawing and Printing Guide for iOS.[1]

Exercises

1. Add a print option to the main screen that allows the user to print all photos.

2. Enable multiple selection on the photos collection view, and change the print option on the main screen to print only the selected photos.

---

1. *Drawing and Printing Guide for iOS*: http://developer.apple.com/library/ios/ #documentation/2DDrawing/Conceptual/DrawingPrintingiOS/Introduction/ Introduction.html

20

Sharing with Others

We live in a connected society where sharing tidbits of your life is as easy as tapping a button. Email, texting, Facebook, and Twitter have all become common aspects of modern life, and for this reason many iPad apps offer some sort of sharing feature to its users. There are two main reasons for this:

1. *Users want to share your app's content with family and friends.*

2. *Sharing is easy to implement in iOS apps.*

PhotoWheel is no different. Users will want to share their favorite photos with others, and because adding sharing support is so simple, it would be a disservice to PhotoWheel users if we didn't include the feature. That is the focus of this chapter: to show you how to share content from your iPad app.

Sending Email

Several different frameworks provided by iOS make sharing content possible. For example, the Social framework lets your app interact with social networking services such as Facebook and Twitter. The Message UI framework makes it easy to send email and SMS text messages. You can also use the `UIActivityViewController` class found in the UIKit framework to easily offer various services to your app users, from sending email to printing to posting an update to Facebook.

Let's start with sending email using the Message UI framework.

How It Works

iOS includes the Message UI Framework, which provides specialized view controllers for composing email and SMS messages. Once the user finishes composing an email, the message is sent to the appropriate subsystem; from there, it is then sent out for delivery to the recipients.

The subsystem for sending an email message is the Mail app within each iOS device. To send email from your app, the user must configure the device with a

default email account. If the device is not set up with email, your app won't be able
to send mail messages and, therefore, your app should not give the user the option to
send mail.

To send an email from your app (on a properly configured device), the app first
displays the mail composition view (Figure 20.1). The `MFMailComposeViewCon`
`troller` class found in the Message UI Framework provides this view. The app can
provide initial information for the email message such as a subject, recipients, message
body, and attachments. The user can add to, change, and even delete the app-provided
information in the mail composition view.

To send the message, the user simply taps the **Send** button and off it goes. This
action sends the email message to the Mail app, where it is placed into the Outbox.
The Mail app is then responsible for sending the email message when there is an available network connection.

If the user decides not to send the email while in the message composition view,
she needs to tap the **Cancel** button. The **Cancel** button gives her two choices: to
delete the draft or to save it as a draft message where it can later be edited and sent
(or deleted). Deleting the draft means that the mail message is gone forever. A deleted
message is never sent to the Mail app. A saved draft, in contrast, is sent to the Mail
app. The user can decide later to edit and send the email from within the Mail app.

The Message UI Framework is designed in such a way that it leverages iOS's Mail
app to handle the complexities of composing, queuing, and sending messages. From

Figure 20.1   The mail composition view

a developer's perspective, the Message UI Framework enables you to focus on what is important—building your app—without getting bogged down by having to write an entire messaging interface for your app. The best part is that all of this simplicity is transparent to the user. The Message UI Framework allows users to compose and send messages from your app, regardless of whether they are connected to a network. When a user isn't connected to a network (for example, when her iPad is in Airplane mode), messages are stored in Mail's Outbox until the user connects to a cellular or Wi-Fi network. The next time the user connects to a network and launches Mail, any messages in the queue from your app and others will be sent.

The `MFMailComposeViewController` Class

The `MFMailComposeViewController` class provides a standard email composition view that is displayed within your app. Because this view is provided by the system, the user sees the same view regardless of which app she is using. This consistency across third-party apps makes it easier for users to send email because the email experience remains the same.

To send an email from your app, your app creates an instance of the `MFMailComposeViewController` class. Initial message information, such as the list of recipients, subject, and message body, are set using this class. The view controller is then presented to the user as a modal view controller. The user edits the message (if any) and sends it on its way.

To make all of this work properly, your app must provide a delegate object that conforms to the `MFMailComposeViewControllerDelegate` protocol. The delegate object is responsible for dismissing the view presented by the `MFMailComposeViewController` at the appropriate time.

Let's take a look at some code to better understand how sending email from your app works.

The `SendEmailController` Class

As part of learning how to send email, you will update the PhotoWheel app to allow users to email their photos. Users can send email from two different places within PhotoWheel:

- From the photo browser, the user will be able to send an email containing the current photo.
- From the photo album child view (displayed within the main screen), the user will be able to send an email containing all photos in a photo album.

To implement this, you add the code that uses the `MFMailComposeViewController` class to both the `PhotoBrowserViewController` and the `PhotosViewController`. The code needed in the two view controllers is the same; thus, rather than implementing this twice, a better design is to consolidate redundant code by creating a new controller class to handle message sending.

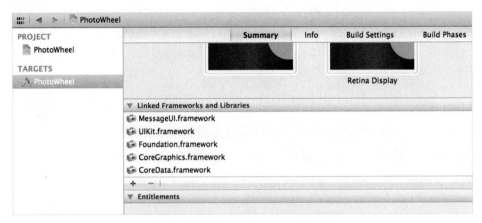

Figure 20.2   The project summary editor

But before you can create a new controller class, you need to add the Message UI Framework to the project. In the Project navigator, click the PhotoWheel project. In the Editor area, select the PhotoWheel target and then the Summary tab. Scroll down to view the list of Linked Frameworks and Libraries (shown in Figure 20.2). Click the **+** button under the Linked Frameworks and Libraries section, and add MessageUI.framework to the project.

Now you are ready to create the new controller class for sending emails.

Introducing the `SendEmailController` Class

The new controller, `SendEmailController`, has a simple interface with two proper-ties (`viewController` and `photos`), as shown in Listing 20.1. The `viewController` property is a reference to the view controller using the `SendEmailController` class. This view controller must conform to the `SendEmailControllerDelegate` proto-col. The `photos` property is a reference to the set of photos to send.

> **Note**
>
> This new controller class is not a view controller, but it is still called a controller class because it controls the setup, display, and dismissal of the `MFMailComposeViewController` class.

Listing 20.1   *SendEmailController.h*

```
#import <Foundation/Foundation.h>
#import <MessageUI/MessageUI.h>
#import <MessageUI/MFMailComposeViewController.h>


@protocol SendEmailControllerDelegate;
```

```
@interface SendEmailController : NSObject <MFMailComposeViewControllerDelegate>

@property (nonatomic, weak) UIViewController<SendEmailControllerDelegate>
*viewController;
@property (nonatomic, strong) NSSet *photos;


- (id)initWithViewController:(UIViewController<SendEmailControllerDelegate> *)
viewController;
- (void)sendEmail;

+ (BOOL)canSendMail;

@end


@protocol SendEmailControllerDelegate <NSObject>
@required
- (void)sendEmailControllerDidFinish:(SendEmailController *)controller;
@end
```

The `SendEmailController` class also has two instance methods: `-initWithViewController:` and `-sendEmail`. The first method is used to initialize the class instance. The second method displays the mail composition view managed by the `MFMailComposeViewController` class instance.

The class method `+canSendMail` wraps the `[MFMailComposeViewController canSendMail]` call. It is provided so that the photo browser and photos view controller classes do not have to include the Message UI Framework header files.

The class interface is followed by the `SendEmailControllerDelegate` protocol definition. The protocol has one required method that the delegate view controller must implement, `-sendEmailControllerDidFinish:`. This method informs the view controller that the send email request has completed.

Now that you know what the interface to the class looks like, it's time to create it. Start by adding a new Objective-C class to the project. Name the class `SendEmailController` and make it a subclass of `NSObject`. After the class files are added to the project, update the *SendEmailController.h* file with the code in the Listing 20.1. Be sure to include the header files from the Message UI Framework.

Next, open the file *SendEmailController.m* and add the implementation code shown in Listing 20.2.

Listing 20.2   *SendEmailController.m*

```
#import "SendEmailController.h"
#import "Photo.h"

@implementation SendEmailController
```

```objc
- (id)initWithViewController:(UIViewController<SendEmailControllerDelegate> *)
viewController
{
    self = [super init];
    if (self) {
        [self setViewController:viewController];
    }
    return self;
}

- (void)sendEmail
{
    MFMailComposeViewController *mailer = [[MFMailComposeViewController alloc]
                                            init];
    [mailer setMailComposeDelegate:self];
    [mailer setSubject:@"Pictures from PhotoWheel"];

    __block NSInteger index = 0;
    [[self photos] enumerateObjectsUsingBlock:^(id photo, BOOL *stop) {
        index++;
        UIImage *image;
        if ([photo isKindOfClass:[UIImage class]]) {
            image = photo;
        } else if ([photo isKindOfClass:[Photo class]]) {
            image = [photo originalImage];
        }

        if (image) {
            NSData *imageData = UIImageJPEGRepresentation(image, 1.0);
            NSString *fileName = [NSString stringWithFormat:@"photo-%i", index];
            [mailer addAttachmentData:imageData
                             mimeType:@"image/jpeg"
                             fileName:fileName];
        }
    }];

    [[self viewController] presentViewController:mailer animated:YES completion:nil];
}


- (void)mailComposeController:(MFMailComposeViewController*)controller
          didFinishWithResult:(MFMailComposeResult)result
                        error:(NSError*)error
{
    UIViewController<SendEmailControllerDelegate> *viewController =
        [self viewController];
    [viewController dismissViewControllerAnimated:YES completion:nil];
```

```
    if (viewController && [viewController respondsToSelector:
                            @selector(sendEmailControllerDidFinish:)])
    {
        [viewController sendEmailControllerDidFinish:self];
    }
}


+ (BOOL)canSendMail
{
    return [MFMailComposeViewController canSendMail];
}

@end
```

The implementation file starts by importing *Photo.h*. The Photo class is used to retrieve the photo, as you will see momentarily. This is followed by the -initWith ViewController: method, which is provided as a matter of convenience. All this method does is set the viewController property to the view controller reference passed in on the method call.

The -sendEmail method is the juicy goodness that uses the Message UI Framework. This method begins by creating a local instance of the MFMailComposeView Controller class. The SendEmailController class instance is set as the delegate to the view controller, and the subject is set to a string literal.

Next, the method enumerates the set of photos using a block. To make this class more flexible, the photo set can contain either UIImage or Photo object references. A check is performed on the object class type, and a local variable for the image is set based on the outcome of the class check. The image is then added as an attachment to the email message.

Once the enumeration block completes, the mail compose view controller is presented to the user. It is presented from the view controller provided at the time the SendEmailController class is initialized.

Why Support UIImage and Photo Objects?

The photo browser does not know about Photo objects; it only knows about UIImage objects. Thus, when it wants to send an email, it needs to pass a UIImage object in the photo set.

The PhotosViewController can do the same. It can build the photo set using UIImage object references instead of Photo model objects, but this would require the allocation of a UIImage object for each photo. Such an approach could cause a memory problem, so references to the managed model object are passed instead. The assumption here, be it good or bad, is that MFMailComposeViewController will manage the memory for attaching a potentially large number of images to an email message.

The next method in the listing is -mailComposeController:didFinishWith
Result:error:. It is a delegate method of the MFMailComposeViewController
Delegate protocol. The implementation dismisses the mail composition view and
then informs the SendEmailControllerDelegate view controller that the send
email request has finished.

The last method of the SendEmailController class is the class method +canSend
Mail. It is a wrapper for the class method of the same name on the MFMailCompose
ViewController class. This method returns YES if the device has been properly con-
figured to send email and NO otherwise.

Using SendEmailController

Now it's time to update the PhotoBrowserViewController and PhotosView
Controller classes to use the new SendEmailController class. Start with the
PhotoBrowserViewController class. The class interface must be modified to tell
the compiler that it adopts the SendEmailControllerDelegate protocol. The class
implementation must be modified to display an Email action item on the action button's action sheet, and the action sheet callback must be modified to present the mail
message composition view to the user by way of the SendEmailController.

The code changes are shown in Listing 20.3. Make these same changes to your
copy of the PhotoBrowserViewController class.

Listing 20.3 Updated **PhotoBrowserViewController** Class

```
///////
//   PhotoBrowserViewController.m
///////
#import "PhotoBrowserViewController.h"
#import "Photo.h"
#import "PhotoBrowserPhotoView.h"
#import "SendEmailController.h"                                    // 1

#define ACTIONSHEET_TAG_DELETE 1
#define ACTIONSHEET_TAG_ACTIONS 2

@interface PhotoBrowserViewController () <UIActionSheetDelegate,
SendEmailControllerDelegate>                                      // 2
@property (nonatomic, strong) SendEmailController *sendEmailController; // 3
// Other code left out for brevity's sake.
@end

@implementation PhotoBrowserViewController

// Other code left out for brevity's sake.

- (void)showActionMenu:(id)sender
{
```

```
    [self cancelChromeDisplayTimer];
    UIActionSheet *actionSheet = [[UIActionSheet alloc] init];
    [actionSheet setDelegate:self];
    [actionSheet setTag:ACTIONSHEET_TAG_ACTIONS];

    if ([SendEmailController canSendMail]) {                           // 4
        [actionSheet addButtonWithTitle:@"Email"];
    }

    if ([UIPrintInteractionController isPrintingAvailable]) {
        [actionSheet addButtonWithTitle:@"Print"];
    }

    [actionSheet showFromBarButtonItem:sender animated:YES];
}

// Other code left out for brevity's sake.

#pragma mark - UIActionSheetDelegate methods

- (void)actionSheet:(UIActionSheet *)actionSheet
clickedButtonAtIndex:(NSInteger)buttonIndex
{
    [self startChromeDisplayTimer];

    // Do nothing if the user taps outside the action
    // sheet (thus closing the popover containing the
    // action sheet).
    if (buttonIndex < 0) {
        return;
    }

    if ([actionSheet tag] == ACTIONSHEET_TAG_DELETE) {
        [self deletePhotoConfirmed];

    } else if ([actionSheet tag] == ACTIONSHEET_TAG_ACTIONS) {
        // Button index 0 can be Email or Print. It depends on whether
        // the device supports that feature.
        if (buttonIndex == 0) {                                        // 5
            if ([SendEmailController canSendMail]) {
                [self emailCurrentPhoto];
            } else if ([UIPrintInteractionController isPrintingAvailable]) {
                [self printCurrentPhoto];
            }
        } else {
            // If there is a button index 1, it
            // will also be Print.
```

```
            [self printCurrentPhoto];
        }
    }
}

// Other code left out for brevity's sake.

- (void)emailCurrentPhoto                                          // 6
{
    UIImage *currentPhoto = [self imageAtIndex:[self currentIndex]];
    NSSet *photos = [NSSet setWithObject:currentPhoto];

    SendEmailController *controller = [[SendEmailController alloc]
                                    initWithViewController:self];
    [controller setPhotos:photos];
    [controller sendEmail];

    [self setSendEmailController:controller];
}

- (void)sendEmailControllerDidFinish:(SendEmailController *)controller  // 7
{
    if ([controller isEqual:[self sendEmailController]]) {
        [self setSendEmailController:nil];
    }
}

@end
```

Reviewing the code, you will notice the following:

1–2. The *SendEmailController.h* header file is imported, and the SendEmailCon
trollerDelegate protocol is listed as one of the protocols supported by the
PhotoBrowserViewController class.

3. The sendEmailController declared property is added to the class extension. A reference to the SendEmailController class instance is kept while it
is being used.

4. The action sheet displaying the list of action items is updated to include Email
if the device is able to send email messages.

5. The action sheet callback is updated to check for the Email action item. This
item is at button index 0 if the device supports sending email; otherwise, it is
not available. The method -emailCurrentPhoto is called when it is determined that the user has indeed tapped the Email action item.

6. The method -emailCurrentPhoto grabs a reference to the current photo and adds it to an NSSet object. Then it creates a new instance of the class SendEmailController, passes the photo set, and tells the controller to send email. This action, in turn, presents the mail composition view to the user. Last, -emailCurrentPhoto sets the private declared property sendEmailController to the instance just created.

7. The method -sendEmailControllerDidFinish: is called by the Send EmailController instance, informing the photo browser that the send email request has finished. At this point, the property reference to the SendEmailController instance is set to nil, releasing it from memory.

A similar set of changes is made to the PhotosViewController class. The only difference is that instead of sending a UIImage object reference in the photo set, the photo set contains the collection of Photo model object references from the photo album. The code changes for the PhotosViewController class are shown in Listing 20.4. Make the same changes to your project.

Listing 20.4   **Updated `PhotosViewController` Class**

```
///////
//  PhotosViewController.m
///////
#import "PhotosViewController.h"
#import "PhotoAlbum.h"
#import "Photo.h"
#import "ThumbnailCell.h"
#import "SendEmailController.h"

@interface PhotosViewController () <UIActionSheetDelegate,
UIImagePickerControllerDelegate, UINavigationControllerDelegate,
UICollectionViewDataSource, UICollectionViewDelegate,
NSFetchedResultsControllerDelegate, SendEmailControllerDelegate>
@property (nonatomic, strong) SendEmailController *sendEmailController;
// Other code left out for brevity's sake.
@end

@implementation PhotosViewController

// Other code left out for brevity's sake.

- (IBAction)showActionMenu:(id)sender
{
    UIActionSheet *actionSheet = [[UIActionSheet alloc] init];
    [actionSheet setDelegate:self];

    if ([SendEmailController canSendMail]) {
```

```
        [actionSheet addButtonWithTitle:@"Email Photo Album"];
    }

    [actionSheet addButtonWithTitle:@"Delete Photo Album"];
    [actionSheet showFromBarButtonItem:sender animated:YES];
}

// Other code left out for brevity's sake.

- (void)actionSheet:(UIActionSheet *)actionSheet
clickedButtonAtIndex:(NSInteger)buttonIndex
{
    // Do nothing if the user taps outside the action
    // sheet (thus closing the popover containing the
    // action sheet).
    if (buttonIndex < 0) {
        return;
    }

    NSMutableArray *names = [[NSMutableArray alloc] init];

    if ([actionSheet tag] == 0) {
        if ([SendEmailController canSendMail]) [names addObject:@"emailPhotos"];
        [names addObject:@"confirmDeletePhotoAlbum"];

    } else {
        BOOL hasCamera = [UIImagePickerController
                    isSourceTypeAvailable:UIImagePickerControllerSourceTypeCamera];
        if (hasCamera) [names addObject:@"presentCamera"];
        [names addObject:@"presentPhotoLibrary"];
    }

    SEL selector = NSSelectorFromString([names objectAtIndex:buttonIndex]);
#pragma clang diagnostic push
#pragma clang diagnostic ignored "-Warc-performSelector-leaks"
    [self performSelector:selector];
#pragma clang diagnostic pop
}

// Other code left out for brevity's sake.

#pragma mark - Email and SendEmailControllerDelegate methods

- (void)emailPhotos
{
    PhotoAlbum *album = [self photoAlbum];
    NSSet *photos = [[album photos] set];
```

```
    SendEmailController *controller = [[SendEmailController alloc]
                                  initWithViewController:self];
    [controller setPhotos:photos];
    [controller sendEmail];

    [self setSendEmailController:controller];
}

- (void)sendEmailControllerDidFinish:(SendEmailController *)controller
{
    if ([controller isEqual:[self sendEmailController]]) {
        [self setSendEmailController:nil];
    }
}

@end
```

Congratulations! Your version of PhotoWheel now supports email. This will surely delight your app's users.

Activity View Controller

You just learned how to send email using the Message UI framework. Earlier, in Chapter 19, "Printing with AirPrint," you learned how to print a photo. These types of services have become so common in iOS apps that Apple decided to provide the `UIActivityViewController` class to accommodate them.

You can use the `UIActivityViewController` class to provide access to a variety of services from within your application. It takes very little code to use the activity view controller, yet doing so makes sharing content from your app much more robust.

The activity view controller presents the user with a set of services that can be used based on the content provided by your application. Best of all, the activity view controller knows which services are available to the user. As a consequence, your app does not have to worry if mail has been configured or if the user has set up a Facebook account on the device. The activity view controller performs the checks for your app.

Let's take a look at how to use the `UIActivityViewController`.

Using the Activity View Controller

The `UIActivityViewController` is a great way to share content from your application. To see how easy it is to use, let's replace the action menu in the photo browser with the activity view controller. Open the file *PhotoBrowserViewController.m* and apply the changes in Listing 20.5.

Listing 20.5   **Add the Activity View Controller**

```objc
@interface PhotoBrowserViewController () <UIActionSheetDelegate,
SendEmailControllerDelegate, UIPopoverControllerDelegate>
@property (nonatomic, strong) UIPopoverController *activityPopover;
// Other code left out for brevity's sake.
@end

@implementation PhotoBrowserViewController
// Other code left out for brevity's sake.

- (void)showActionMenu:(id)sender
{
    [self cancelChromeDisplayTimer];

    if ([self activityPopover]) {
        [[self activityPopover] dismissPopoverAnimated:YES];
        [self setActivityPopover:nil];

    } else {
        UIImage *currentPhoto = [self imageAtIndex:[self currentIndex]];
        NSArray *activityItems = @[currentPhoto];
        UIActivityViewController *activityVC = nil;
        activityVC = [[UIActivityViewController alloc]
                        initWithActivityItems:activityItems
                        applicationActivities:nil];

        UIPopoverController *popover = nil;
        popover = [[UIPopoverController alloc]
                    initWithContentViewController:activityVC];
        [popover setDelegate:self];
        [popover presentPopoverFromBarButtonItem:sender
                        permittedArrowDirections:UIPopoverArrowDirectionAny
                                        animated:YES];
        [self setActivityPopover:popover];
    }
}

#pragma mark - UIPopoverControllerDelegate Methods

- (void)popoverControllerDidDismissPopover:(UIPopoverController *)popoverController
{
    if (popoverController == [self activityPopover]) {
        [self setActivityPopover:nil];
    }
}

@end
```

Let's take a walk through the code . . .

Your app is responsible for presenting the activity view controller. iPad apps are expected to display the activity view controller in a popover while iPhone apps display the controller modally. The code in Listing 20.5 starts by adding a popover controller, named `activityPopover`, to the class extension. This popover is used to display the activity view controller.

The next change in the listing is a completely new implementation for the `-show ActionMenu:` method. Previously, this method set up and presented an action sheet to the user. This has been replaced with the setup and presentation of the activity view controller.

An instance of `UIActivityViewController` is created with an array of activity items. An activity item is an object that represents the content you wish to share or be used by the services offered in the activity view controller. Here a `UIImage` representing the current photo is passed in as the activity item.

One or more objects can be passed in as activity items, and the object types for each item do not have to match. For instance, you might want to pass in a string followed by a photo. For example:

```
NSArray *activityItems = @[@"Share me", currentPhoto];
```

This will add both the string literal "Share me" with the `currentPhoto` as content to be used by the service. If the user selects the Mail service, for example, then an email is composed containing the string "Share me" followed by the photo. If the user selects Twitter, then a tweet is composed, again containing the string literal and the photo as an attachment.

After the activity view controller instance is created, it is used to create a new popover controller instance. Finally, the popover is presented to the user (Figure 20.3), and that's it. The activity view controller does all the hard work for you, from determining which services are available to invoking the service and passing in the supplied activity items to the selected service.

This discussion merely scratches the surface of what the activity view controller can do. You can specify which services to make available while hiding others from the user. You can even override how the content is generated based on the activity type. This capability can be handy when you want to send more detailed content in an email message while keeping the content shorter for a tweet or Facebook posting. To learn more about how to do this, read the `UIActivityItemSource` Protocol Reference[1] in the Developer Documentation.

---

1. `UIActivityItemSource` Protocol Reference: http://developer.apple.com/library/ios/#documentation/UIKit/Reference/UIActivityItemSource_protocol/Reference/Reference.html

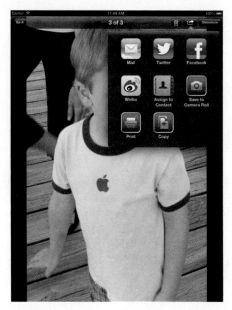

Figure 20.3   The activity view controller in action

Summary

As you just learned, it is not especially difficult to configure your iPad apps to share content. The Message UI Framework and iOS's Mail app handle most of the work for you when you want to send an email, and the `UIActivityViewController` gives your app users access to different services available on their devices. Your app simply needs to prepare the content and then present the activity view controller; the rest of the work is done for you.

Now that you know how to share content from your app, let's look at adding new content via web services.

Exercises

1. Modify the code to send the large image instead of the original image.
2. Enable multi-selection on the photos collection view, and change the send email feature on the main screen to send only the selected photos.
3. Change the main screen to use the activity view controller to share selected photos.

Web Services

Many of today's apps have some level of integration with Web servers and services hosted on the Internet. There are many reasons why an iPad app might need to talk with a Web server. For instance, the app might need to download an image or a movie file, or perhaps it needs to upload a file to a server. Other examples include calling a Web service to perform calculations, to update leaderboards, or to request data that gets displayed in your app. Whatever the reason may be, chances are good that one day you will need to incorporate Web services into your app.

This chapter provides a basic introduction to using Web services. The focus is on the most common type of Web services in use today: RESTful Web services. This chapter does not attempt to cover every aspect of communicating with a Web server, but it does provide a jump start to using Web services within your app.

In this introduction to Web services, you will learn how to communicate with a Web server using the Cocoa classes, and you will learn how to parse JSON data. You will also learn how to use blocks to simplify your code for asynchronous processing and concurrent programming.

Let's get started.

The Basics

The term *Web service* means different things to different people. Say "Web service" to a C# programmer, and SOAP-based services will likely come to mind. Say "Web service" to a Ruby programmer, and REST-based services will likely be the first thing to come to mind. To some, a Web site is a Web service; to others, a Web service is an API.

Why does this happen? Why does "Web service" mean different things to different people?

Technology people tend to think differently when hearing the term "Web service" because they typically think in terms of the technology with which they are most familiar. The technologies we are most comfortable with tend to influence our technical decisions and our way of thinking. A C# programmer who is writing a client-server solution where .NET is used on both ends will most likely use SOAP-based Web services, because this is the preferred approach of .NET. To this programmer, a

Web service is a SOAP-based service. But ask that same programmer to build a version of the same client app on the Mac desktop and iOS device, and his eyes will be opened to a new approach to Web services, because SOAP-based services are not the preferred approach in the Cocoa world.

So, what is a Web service?

From a generic point of view, a Web service is a method for communicating between two systems over a network, typically using HTTP. The rest of the techno-mumbo-jumbo surrounding Web services consists of approaches, protocols, and techniques built on top of this generic definition. This is not to belittle the mumbo-jumbo. On the contrary, it plays a very important role in deciding how communication between the two systems is achieved.

This being said, it is important to clarify the focus of this chapter with regard to Web services. This chapter teaches you how to use REST-compliant Web services, often called RESTful Web services. REST—that is, representational state transfer—is the style of architecture used by the Web and HTTP. Roy Fielding introduced the term REST in his doctoral dissertation released in 2000. A RESTful Web service has four basic design principles:

- It uses HTTP methods explicitly (GET, POST, PUT, and DELETE).
- It is stateless.
- It uses directory-structure-like URLs.
- It transfers data in XML or JSON (JavaScript Object Notation).

These design principles are not always strictly followed. For instance, a RESTful Web service is not limited to transferring data using XML or JSON. Data coming back from the server can be plaintext, CSV formatted, or another format other than XML and JSON.

The adoption of RESTful Web services was slow, but REST has now become the choice for the majority of Web services hosted on the Internet today. Its popularity reflects its ease of use. Whereas other Web service methods such as SOAP require a toolkit or framework (typically provided by the programming environment's vendor), RESTful Web services can be used without any toolkit. That is not to say there are no RESTful frameworks. In fact, many such frameworks exist for many different programming languages. Even so, the power of REST derives from the reality that a framework is not needed. Any programming environment that can make an HTTP call can make use of RESTful Web services. Even a Web browser can be used to call a RESTful Web service.

RESTful Web Services Using Cocoa

Cocoa does not provide a RESTful framework, but it does provide the classes that make it possible to call and consume RESTful Web services from your iOS app. There are five of these classes:

- NSURL
- NSURLRequest
- NSURLConnection
- NSXMLParser
- NSJSONSerialization

NSURL is the object containing the URL to the Web service you want to call. The NSURLRequest object is used to build the HTTP request, and an NSURLConnection object is used to submit the request over the network. When using the NSURLConnection object, you assign it a delegate object that conforms to the NSURLConnectionDelegate protocol. This protocol provides optional methods for interacting with the connection object as its state changes (e.g., authentication challenges and blocks of incoming data are received).

Once all the data has been received, you use either the NSXMLParser or NSJSON Serialization class to parse the contents of the data. NSXMLParser is an event-driven XML parser that works in a similar fashion to a SAX parser. It notifies a delegate about the items (e.g., elements, attributes) found as it processes the XML document.

The NSJSONSerialization class converts JSON data to Foundation objects (such as NSDictionary, NSArray, NSString, and NSNumber) and Foundation classes into JSON data. This class was introduced into the iOS SDK with the release of iOS 5. Prior to iOS 5, developers relied on open source libraries such as JSON Framework[1] and TouchJSON.[2]

Armed with these five classes, you should be able to interact with any RESTful Web service available today, including Flickr.

Flickr

Flickr is a Web site for publishing and sharing photos. Flickr also provides an API based on RESTful Web services that developers like you can use in apps like Photo-Wheel. In fact, that is what you will do now: You will update PhotoWheel so that users can search Flickr for photos and add photos to a PhotoWheel photo album.

Before the code presented in this chapter will work, you must set up a Flickr account and request a Flickr API Key, which Flickr uses to identify your app. The key is free for noncommercial use under the following conditions:[3]

- Your app doesn't make money.
- Your app makes money, but you're a family-run, small, or independent business.

---

1. JSON Framework: https://github.com/stig/json-framework
2. TouchJSON: https://github.com/TouchCode/TouchJSON
3. Flickr conditions and application for a noncommercial key: http://www.flickr.com/services/apps/create/apply

- You're developing a product that is not currently commercial but might be in the future.
- You're building a personal Web site or blog where you are using only your own images.

> **Note**
>
> A commercial key is available to organizations working the major brands or looking to make a profit from products and services related to Flickr beyond that of a family-run, small, or independent business.

To request a Flickr API Key, you must first sign up with Flickr. Go to **www. flickr.com**, click Sign Up, and follow the instructions for creating a new account. Once you have a Flickr account, sign in to your account and go to **www.flickr.com/ services/apps/create/apply**. Click the **Apply for Non-Commercial Key** button and tell Flickr about your app (Figure 21.1). You will receive the key within minutes of submitting your application information. You can find the key by opening the You

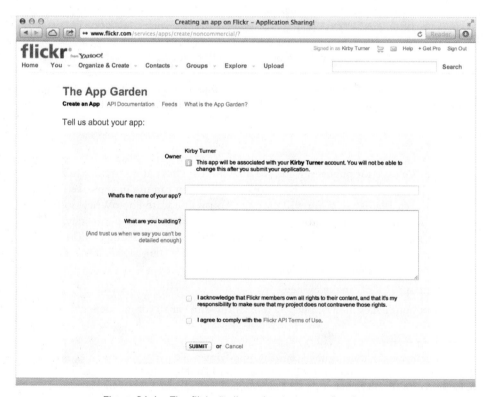

Figure 21.1   The flickr "tell us about your app" web page

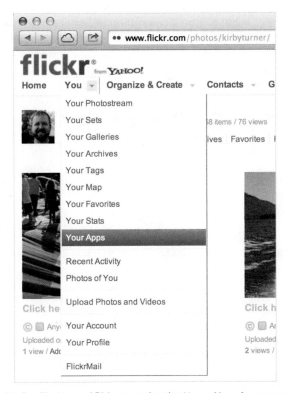

Figure 21.2   Find your API keys under the **You > Your Apps** menu item

drop-down menu and selecting Your Apps (Figure 21.2). The key is used by your app to make calls to the Flickr Web services.

Adding Flickr to PhotoWheel

Once you have your Flickr API Key, you can update PhotoWheel to display and save photos from Flickr. To accomplish this, you need to make a number of changes to PhotoWheel, including the following:

- Add a new scene and view controller for the Flickr photo display.
- Add a search feature to the Flickr scene.
- Add a class wrapper for the Flickr API calls used by PhotoWheel.
- Parse the Flickr JSON response data.
- Download photos from Flickr asynchronously.

Let's start by adding the new view controller. Create a new Objective-C class named `FlickrViewController` and make it a subclass of `UIViewController`. Add the outlets and actions shown in Listing 21.1. Be sure to add `UICollectionViewDataSource`,

UICollectionViewDelegate, and UISearchBarDelegate as protocols to the
FlickrViewController class. Don't worry about completing the implementation for
the class; just get it started so that the UI can be set up in the storyboard (alternatively,
you can use the Assistant editor while piecing together the UI). The stubbed view controller code is shown in Listing 21.1.

Listing 21.1 Stubbed **FlickrViewController** Class

```
///////
//  FlickrViewController.h
///////
#import <UIKit/UIKit.h>

@class PhotoAlbum;

@interface FlickrViewController : UIViewController <
UICollectionViewDataSource, UICollectionViewDelegate,
UISearchBarDelegate>

@property (nonatomic, weak) IBOutlet UICollectionView *collectionView;
@property (nonatomic, weak) IBOutlet UIView *overlayView;
@property (nonatomic, weak) IBOutlet UISearchBar *searchBar;
@property (nonatomic, weak) IBOutlet UIActivityIndicatorView *activityIndicator;
@property (nonatomic, strong) PhotoAlbum *photoAlbum;

- (IBAction)save:(id)sender;
- (IBAction)cancel:(id)sender;

@end


///////
//  FlickrViewController.m
///////
#import "FlickrViewController.h"

@interface FlickrViewController ()

@end

@implementation FlickrViewController

- (IBAction)save:(id)sender
{

}
```

```
- (IBAction)cancel:(id)sender
{

}
```

@end

A new class is added to the view controller that you have not used before: the `UISearchBar` class. This class provides a text field that can be used for text-based searches. It is used in the Flickr scene to capture search terms from the user.

The declared property `overlayView` might have you scratching your head, too. It is a dark, transparent view that is displayed on top of the collection view to prevent the user from interacting with the collection view during searches.

Another new class included in the `FlickrViewController` class interface is `UIActivityIndicatorView`. It displays a spinning wheel to indicate to the user that something is happening in the app and to please wait.

Updating the Flickr View Controller Scene

With the Flickr view controller class started, it's time to update the storyboard to include the new Flickr scene. Open the file *MainStoryboard.storyboard*. Drag a new view controller object into the storyboard to create a new scene. Select the view controller in the Document Outline, open the Identity inspector, and change the class name to `FlickrViewController`.

Add a toolbar to the top of the Flickr scene. Next, add a **Cancel** button to the left side of the toolbar and a **Save** button to the right side. Use the Attributes inspector for each button to set the Identifier field to Cancel and Save, respectively. Use a flexible spacing bar button item to set the spacing between the two buttons.

Connect the **Save** button to the `-save:` action defined in the `FlickrViewController` class. Connect the **Cancel** button to the `-cancel:` action.

Add a search bar under the toolbar, and then connect it to the `searchBar` outlet defined in the `FlickrViewController` class. Also set `FlickrViewController` as the `delegate` to the search bar object. If the `delegate` is not set, the search bar will not function properly.

Add a `UICollectionView` object to the Flickr scene. This view should fill the remaining space of the container view. If you like, you can change the background color to green to make the view easier to see while you resize it—just be sure to change it to white when you are done. This view is used to display the photos retrieved from Flickr. Be sure to set the Flickr View Controller as the `dataSource` and `delegate` for the collection view, and connect the collection view to the `collectionView` outlet.

With the collection view selected, open the Size inspector and set the cell size width and height to 75.

Select the collection view prototype cell found in the collection view, and open the Attributes inspector. Set the Identifier field to "PhotoCell." This name will be used as the reuse identifier for the cell at run time.

Next, add a `UIImageView` object to the collection view prototype cell. Make sure the image view fills the entire cell. Open the Attributes inspector and set the Tag field for the image view to 1.

Add a second `UIImageView` object to the same prototype cell. Give the second image a width and height of 29, and set the Tag field in the Attributes inspector to 2. Then set the Image field, also while working in the Attributes inspector, to *addphoto. png*. This will display a small plus sign inside of a circle. Now move the image view to the lower-right corner of the cell.

> **Note**
>
> This time the collection view cell is not given a custom class name. The collection view in the Photos View Controller scene uses a custom class for its collection view cell, but using a custom class is not a requirement. Later in this chapter, you will see how you can use the `tag` property to get a reference to subviews within the cell. This approach of using the `tag` property is a quick and handy way to configure the presentation of a cell without defining a custom cell class.

Add another `UIView` object that sits on top of the collection view. Make sure the new view also fills the area, and set its background color to black. Then connect the view to the `overlayView` outlet.

Next, drag an activity indicator object to the Flickr scene and position it in the center of the screen. In the Attributes inspector for the activity indicator, turn on the Hides When Stopped option. When you have finished, connect the activity indicator to the `activityIndicator` outlet defined in the `FlickrViewController` class.

Last, create a new segue between the Photos View Controller scene and the Flickr View Controller scene. It should be a modal segue. Set its Identifier to `Present FlickrScene` and the Presentation to Form Sheet. Leave the Transition as Default.

The updated storyboard should look like the one in Figure 21.3.

> **Note**
>
> Make sure the view hierarchy has the collection view, the overlay view, and the activity indicator at the levels shown in Figure 21.3. If a different view hierarchy is used, the scene may not display properly.

Displaying the Flickr Scene

To make sure the Flickr scene displays properly, add a new action item to the add button displayed in the photos view controller scene. In case you do not remember, this button calls the `-addPhoto:` action method, which in turn calls the `-presentPhotoPickerMenu` method.

Open the file *PhotosViewController.m* and apply the changes shown in Listing 21.2.

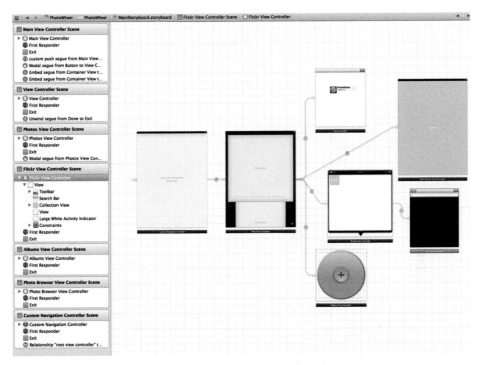

Figure 21.3   Updated storyboard

Listing 21.2   *PhotosViewController.m* Changes

```
#import "PhotosViewController.h"
#import "PhotoAlbum.h"
#import "Photo.h"
#import "ThumbnailCell.h"
#import "SendEmailController.h"
#import "FlickrViewController.h"                        // 1

// Other code left out for brevity's sake.

@implementation PhotosViewController

// Other code left out for brevity's sake.

- (void)actionSheet:(UIActionSheet *)actionSheet
clickedButtonAtIndex:(NSInteger)buttonIndex
{
    // Do nothing if the user taps outside the action
    // sheet (thus closing the popover containing the
    // action sheet).
```

```
    if (buttonIndex < 0) {
        return;
    }

    NSMutableArray *names = [[NSMutableArray alloc] init];

    if ([actionSheet tag] == 0) {
        if ([SendEmailController canSendMail]) [names addObject:@"emailPhotos"];
        [names addObject:@"confirmDeletePhotoAlbum"];

    } else {
        BOOL hasCamera = [UIImagePickerController
                        isSourceTypeAvailable:UIImagePickerControllerSourceTypeCam
era];
        if (hasCamera) [names addObject:@"presentCamera"];
        [names addObject:@"presentPhotoLibrary"];
        [names addObject:@"presentFlickr"];                             // 2
    }

    SEL selector = NSSelectorFromString([names objectAtIndex:buttonIndex]);
#pragma clang diagnostic push
#pragma clang diagnostic ignored "-Warc-performSelector-leaks"
    [self performSelector:selector];
#pragma clang diagnostic pop
}

// Other code left out for brevity's sake.

- (void)presentFlickr                                                   // 3
{
    [self performSegueWithIdentifier:@"PresentFlickrScene" sender:self];
}

- (void)presentPhotoPickerMenu
{
    UIActionSheet *actionSheet = [[UIActionSheet alloc] init];
    [actionSheet setDelegate:self];
    BOOL hasCamera = [UIImagePickerController
                    isSourceTypeAvailable:UIImagePickerControllerSourceTypeCam
era];
    if (hasCamera) {
        [actionSheet addButtonWithTitle:@"Take Photo"];
    }
    [actionSheet addButtonWithTitle:@"Choose from Library"];
    [actionSheet addButtonWithTitle:@"Choose from Flickr"];             // 4
    [actionSheet setTag:1];
    [actionSheet showFromBarButtonItem:[self addButton] animated:YES];
```

```
}

// Other code left out for brevity's sake.

- (void)prepareForSegue:(UIStoryboardSegue *)segue sender:(id)sender      // 5
{
    if ([[segue destinationViewController]
        isKindOfClass:[FlickrViewController class]])
    {
        [[segue destinationViewController] setPhotoAlbum:[self photoAlbum]];
    }
}
```

@end

Let's take a look at the changes:

1. The *FlickrViewController.h* header is imported.

2. The presentFlickr selector name is added to the array of selectors available for the add action sheet.

3. The -presentFlickr method is added. It is responsible for performing the segue PresentFlickrScene.

4. The "Choose from Flickr" action item is added to the action sheet.

5. The -prepareForSegue:sender: method is added to the view controller. It performs a check to ensure that the FlickrViewController is the destination view controller. It's always a good idea to check the type of the source and destination view controllers when preparing for a segue, as the app may crash if it encounters an unexpected controller type.

   If the destination view controller is the FlickrViewController class, the current photoAlbum managed object is passed to the destination view controller.

You can build and run the app if you like, but note that it will crash when you tap the "Choose from Flickr" action item. This failure occurs because the FlickrView Controller class has not been properly implemented yet. But before this class can be implemented, a couple of other new classes must be created and implemented.

Wrapping the Flickr API

Before the FlickrViewController can display photos from Flickr, the app must know how to communicate with Flickr. PhotoWheel will use the Flickr RESTful Web service API to communicate with Flickr. Because the Web service is RESTful, PhotoWheel relies on standard Cocoa classes for communicating with the Flickr Web server.

> **Note**
>
> The Flickr API class presented here is a basic wrapper for some Flickr API calls. If you need to add full Flickr support to your app, consider using a Flickr API framework such as ObjectiveFlickr.[4]

PhotoWheel uses only one Flickr API: the search API. For illustration purposes, however, the simple Flickr API wrapper class you are about to create supports four API calls. The extra calls are implemented to show you how you would update the class should you need to support additional API calls.

> **Note**
>
> Read the Flickr API documentation[5] if you want a better understanding of how each API works.

The Flickr API wrapper will be an Objective-C class, so add a new Objective-C class to the PhotoWheel project. Name this class `SimpleFlickrAPI` and make it a subclass of `NSObject`. The class will wrap four API calls, as shown in Listing 21.3.

Listing 21.3 *SimpleFlickrAPI.h*

```
#import <Foundation/Foundation.h>

@interface SimpleFlickrAPI : NSObject

// Returns a set of photos matching the search string.
- (NSArray *)photosWithSearchString:(NSString *)string;

// Returns the Flickr NSID for the given user name.
- (NSString *)userIdForUsername:(NSString *)username;

// Returns a Flickr photo set for the user. userId is the Flickr NSID
// of the user.
- (NSArray *)photoSetListWithUserId:(NSString *)userId;

// Returns the photos for a Flickr photo set.
- (NSArray *)photosWithPhotoSetId:(NSString *)photoSetId;

@end
```

Naturally, the implementation for the `SimpleFlickrAPI` class is more involved. The implementation code is provided in Listing 21.4. Add the code to your version of *SimpleFlickrAPI.m*, and then review the walk-through of the code.

---

4. ObjectiveFlickr: https://github.com/lukhnos/objectiveflickr
5. Flickr API documentation: http://www.flickr.com/services/api/

Listing 21.4   *SimpleFlickrAPI.m*

```objc
#import "SimpleFlickrAPI.h"
#import <Foundation/NSJSONSerialization.h>                          // 1

// Changes this value to your own application key. More info
// at http://www.flickr.com/services/api/misc.api_keys.html.
#define flickrAPIKey @"YOUR_FLICKR_APP_KEY"                         // 2

#define flickrBaseURL \
@"http://api.flickr.com/services/rest/?format=json&"               // 3

#define flickrParamMethod @"method"                                // 4
#define flickrParamAppKey @"api_key"
#define flickrParamUsername @"username"
#define flickrParamUserid @"user_id"
#define flickrParamPhotoSetId @"photoset_id"
#define flickrParamExtras @"extras"
#define flickrParamText @"text"

#define flickrMethodFindByUsername @"flickr.people.findByUsername"  // 5
#define flickrMethodGetPhotoSetList @"flickr.photosets.getList"
#define flickrMethodGetPhotosWithPhotoSetId @"flickr.photosets.getPhotos"
#define flickrMethodSearchPhotos @"flickr.photos.search"


@implementation SimpleFlickrAPI

- (NSArray *)photosWithSearchString:(NSString *)string            // 6
{
    NSDictionary *parameters = @{
        flickrParamMethod : flickrMethodSearchPhotos,
        flickrParamAppKey : flickrAPIKey,
        flickrParamText : string,
        flickrParamExtras : @"url_t, url_s, url_m, url_sq",
    };                                                             // 7
    NSDictionary *json = [self flickrJSONSWithParameters:parameters];  // 8
    NSDictionary *photoset = [json objectForKey:@"photos"];        // 9
    NSArray *photos = [photoset objectForKey:@"photo"];            // 10
    return photos;                                                 // 11
}

- (NSString *)userIdForUsername:(NSString *)username              // 12
{
    NSDictionary *parameters = @{
        flickrParamMethod : flickrMethodFindByUsername,
        flickrParamAppKey : flickrAPIKey,
```

```
            flickrParamUsername : username,
        };
        NSDictionary *json = [self flickrJSONSWithParameters:parameters];
        NSDictionary *userDict = [json objectForKey:@"user"];
        NSString *nsid = [userDict objectForKey:@"nsid"];

        return nsid;
}


- (NSArray *)photoSetListWithUserId:(NSString *)userId           // 13
{
        NSDictionary *parameters = @{
            flickrParamMethod : flickrMethodGetPhotoSetList,
            flickrParamAppKey : flickrAPIKey,
            flickrParamUserid : userId,
        };
        NSDictionary *json = [self flickrJSONSWithParameters:parameters];
        NSDictionary *photosets = [json objectForKey:@"photosets"];
        NSArray *photoSet = [photosets objectForKey:@"photoset"];
        return photoSet;
}


- (NSArray *)photosWithPhotoSetId:(NSString *)photoSetId         // 14
{
        NSDictionary *parameters = @{
            flickrParamMethod : flickrMethodGetPhotosWithPhotoSetId,
            flickrParamAppKey : flickrAPIKey,
            flickrParamPhotoSetId : photoSetId,
            flickrParamExtras : @"url_t, url_s, url_m, url_sq",
        };
        NSDictionary *json = [self flickrJSONSWithParameters:parameters];
        NSDictionary *photoset = [json objectForKey:@"photoset"];
        NSArray *photos = [photoset objectForKey:@"photo"];
        return photos;
}


#pragma mark - Helper methods

- (NSData *)fetchResponseWithURL:(NSURL *)URL                    // 15
{
        NSURLRequest *request = [NSURLRequest requestWithURL:URL];     // 16
        NSURLResponse *response = nil;                                 // 17
        NSError *error = nil;                                          // 18
        NSData *data = [NSURLConnection sendSynchronousRequest:request
                                             returningResponse:&response
                                                         error:&error];  // 19
        if (data == nil) {                                             // 20
```

```
      NSLog(@"%s: Error: %@", __PRETTY_FUNCTION__,
            [error localizedDescription]);
   }
   return data;                                              // 21
}


- (NSURL *)buildFlickrURLWithParameters:(NSDictionary *)parameters     // 22
{
   NSMutableString *URLString = [[NSMutableString alloc]
                                  initWithString:flickrBaseURL];
   for (id key in parameters) {
      NSString *value = [parameters objectForKey:key];
      [URLString appendFormat:@"%@=%@&", key,
       [value stringByAddingPercentEscapesUsingEncoding:NSUTF8StringEncoding]];
   }
   NSURL *URL = [NSURL URLWithString:URLString];
   return URL;
}


- (NSString *)stringWithData:(NSData *)data                   // 23
{
   NSString *result = [[NSString alloc] initWithBytes:[data bytes]
                                               length:[data length]
                                             encoding:NSUTF8StringEncoding];
   return result;
}


- (NSString *)stringByRemovingFlickrJavaScript:(NSData *)data     // 24
{
   // Flickr returns a JavaScript function containing the JSON data.
   // We need to strip out the JavaScript part before we can parse
   // the JSON data. Ex: jsonFlickrApi(JSON-DATA-HERE).

   NSMutableString *string = [[self stringWithData:data] mutableCopy];
   NSRange range = NSMakeRange(0, [@"jsonFlickrApi(" length]);
   [string deleteCharactersInRange:range];
   range = NSMakeRange([string length] - 1, 1);
   [string deleteCharactersInRange:range];

   return string;
}


- (id)flickrJSONSWithParameters:(NSDictionary *)parameters     // 25
{
   NSURL *URL = [self buildFlickrURLWithParameters:parameters];
   NSData *data = [self fetchResponseWithURL:URL];
   NSString *string = [self stringByRemovingFlickrJavaScript:data];
```

```
    NSData *jsonData = [string dataUsingEncoding:NSUTF8StringEncoding];

    NSLog(@"%s: json: %@", __PRETTY_FUNCTION__, string);

    NSError *error = nil;
    id json = [NSJSONSerialization
               JSONObjectWithData:jsonData
               options:NSJSONReadingAllowFragments
               error:&error];
    if (json == nil) {
        NSLog(@"%s: Error: %@", __PRETTY_FUNCTION__,
              [error localizedDescription]);
    }

    return json;
}

@end
```

Let's walk through the code so that you understand what is happening:

1. The NSJSONSerialization header file is imported. The Flickr API supports both XML and JSON. JSON is used by the SimpleFlickrAPI class because it is easier to parse and use than XML.

2. This #define is where your Flickr API Key is stored. This must match the key provided by Flickr.

3. Each RESTful API uses the same base URL. The base URL is stored as a macro, making it easy to change should Flickr ever change the URL. Also note the query string parameter format. It is set to JSON, which tells the Flickr API to return data formatted with JSON. You can change the parameter value to xml if you want XML returned by Flickr.

4. The Flickr API uses different parameter names. Instead of the Flickr API parameter names being hard-coded throughout, they are defined here as macros. The Flickr API parameters are defined as query string parameters on the HTTP GET request.

5. The Flickr API includes a parameter named method. This parameter defines which API method is called. The API methods supported by this simple wrapper are defined here as macros.

6. The first Flickr API wrapped by the class is flickr.photos.search. It is wrapped in the method -photosWithSearchString:. This method takes a search string, asks Flickr to find any matching photos, and then returns an array of photos to the caller.

7. The first thing this method does is create a dictionary of Flickr parameters. This key-value pairing is used to construct the query string that is used when calling the Flickr Web server. The API method and key are the first two parameters in the dictionary; they are followed by the search string provided by the caller. The Flickr parameter extras provides a way for calling apps to request additional data to be included in the response data. The value `url_t` tells the Flickr API to include the thumbnail of the photo. `url_s` is a small version of the photo, `_m` is the medium-size version, and `_sq` returns a square (75 × 75-pixel) version of the photo.

   Note that the API does not actually return the photo image file. Instead, the response data includes the URL to the photo image. By telling the API to include the `url_t`, `url_s`, `url_m`, and `url_sq` photos in the extras parameter, you are telling the Flickr API to return the URLs to these photos.

8. The parameters are passed to the method `-flickrJSONWithParameters:`. As you will see in a moment, this method is responsible for making the call to the Flickr Web server. It also gathers the response data from the Web server and parses it into Foundation objects (e.g., `NSDictionary`, `NSArray`, `NSString`) using the `NSJSONSerialization` object.

9–10. The JSON data from Flickr for this API is converted into an `NSDictionary` object by the `NSJSONSerialization` class. The dictionary contains a key named photos, which represents the Flickr photo set for the search results. The `photoset` is another dictionary containing the key photo, and `photo` is an `NSArray` of photos. Each photo in the array is a dictionary containing data about the photo, including the URLs requested in the extras parameter.

11. The photos array is returned to the caller.

12–14. Examples of calling other Flickr API methods are provided. These methods are not used by PhotoWheel but are provided here as examples of how to make other API calls. You can see from these examples that a specific design pattern is followed: A dictionary of parameters is created; the parameters are passed to the method that communicates with Flickr; the response data is returned and parsed; and the requested data is returned to the caller.

15. The method `-fetchResponseWithURL:` is responsible for making the actual Web service call to the Flickr Web server. The URL passed in consists of the Flickr API URL with parameters.

16. This method first creates an `NSURLRequest` object for the given URL.

17. A `nil` `NSURLResponse` object is created. This response object is used to retrieve additional information, such as headers, from the HTTP response.

18. A `nil` pointer to an `NSError` is created. This pointer is set to a valid object reference if an error occurs during the request.

19. The NSURLConnection is used to call the Flickr Web server synchronously for the given request. The response and error pointers are set to valid object references if any are created during the request process. The synchronous call returns the data as an NSData object. This is a stream of the response data coming from the Flickr Web server, which is formatted as JSON.

20. If nil is returned for the response data, an error occurred during the request. The error is logged to the console. A more robust Flickr framework would return the error to the caller so that the caller can log it or report the error to the user.

21. Finally, the data is returned.

22. The method -buildFlickrURLWithParameters: takes the dictionary of parameters and creates the URL to the API call. This is done by appending each key-value pair in the dictionary as a query string parameter to the base Flickr API URL.

23. The method -stringWithData: converts the contents of an NSData object to a string. As you will see momentarily, the response data from Flickr requires a bit of tweaking before NSJSONSerialization can parse it.

24. The method -stringByRemovingFlickrJavaScript: returns a cleaned-up version of the Flickr API response data. The Flickr API wraps the response data in a JavaScript function, but the SimpleFlickrAPI wants only the JSON data. Consequently, the response data is converted from an NSData object to an NSString object. The JavaScript function is then stripped from the string, resulting in the string containing only the JSON-formatted data.

25. The method -flickrJSONWithParameters: is called by the wrapper methods defined at the top of the class. This method pulls all the pieces together to make the API call. It uses the parameters to create the API URL; it then uses this URL to fetch the response data from Flickr. It removes the JavaScript function provided by Flickr. It then uses the NSJSONSerialization class to convert the JSON data into Foundation objects, which are returned to the caller. The method also logs the JSON data to the console so that you can see what the data looks like coming from Flickr.

That's it for making the Flickr API Web service call. As you can see, the majority of the code in the class deals with preparing the request and parsing the response. The actual Web service call takes only a few lines of code, as seen in the method -fetchResponseWithURL:. No additional toolkit or framework (beyond what is provided by the iOS SDK) is needed to make the API call. There is no need to convert the data into a SOAP message or any of that mess. Instead, a standard HTTP GET request with query string parameters is made and the response data is returned. Easy-peasy.

Downloading Photos Asynchronously

The Flickr API wrapper class `SimpleFlickrAPI` makes a synchronous call to the Flickr Web server. However, more times than not, you will need to make asynchronous calls to a Web server. PhotoWheel can get away with making a synchronous call to the Flickr API because the app waits for the Flickr call to return a list of photos. Sometimes, however, you don't want your users waiting. One such time is when PhotoWheel is displaying the photos from Flickr.

Once the search completes and the list of photos is returned, the Flickr scene must display the photos in the collection view. It is here that the photos should be downloaded asynchronously, for two primary reasons:

- You want the app to remain responsive to the user. It should not appear frozen. The user should be allowed to do things such as tap the **Cancel** button to close the Flickr scene without having to wait until all the photos have downloaded.

- The search results can include more than one photo, and often there will be many more. Downloading and displaying 100 photos synchronously would take a long time, which in turn would annoy the user. However, the user will perceive downloading the same number of photos asynchronously as fast because, well, it is faster.

One way to download the photos asynchronously is to create a separate thread for each download request, which downloads an image synchronously within the secondary thread. While this approach works, it is not necessary.

`NSURLConnection` uses the CFNetwork framework, which is extremely efficient at handling hundreds, if not thousands, of download requests without blocking the main thread of the app. This is due, in part, to the combination of the run loop and threads created as needed by the CFNetwork framework.

What Is the Runtime Loop?

When an iOS application is launched, a main thread is created for the app. The main thread is the primary thread running the app. The app is able to respond to events that are detected by the default run loop created on the main thread. The run loop is always running, performing various tasks ranging from updating the UI to checking for hardware input to processing `NSTimer` object events. One of the tasks performed by the run loop is to check for incoming network data requested by `NSURLConnection` objects.

To learn more about this, read the Main Event Loop section[6] of the Cocoa Application Competencies for iOS guide in the Apple documentation.

---

6. Main Event Loop: http://developer.apple.com/library/ios/#DOCUMENTATION/General/Conceptual/Devpedia-CocoaApp/MainEventLoop.html

The efficiencies of the CFNetwork framework combined with the run loop on the main thread make it possible to have simultaneous downloads without your explicitly creating and managing threads in your app.

> **Note**
>
> For more information on simultaneous downloads without creating your own threads, read the blog post *Downloading Images for a Table without Threads*[7] by Jeff LaMarche. This blog post is also the inspiration for the `ImageDownloader` class you create in this chapter.

Theory aside, how do you download multiple images (or any data, for that matter) from a Web server simultaneously without creating your own thread? For starters, you use `NSURLConnection`, but instead of making the call synchronously as you did in the `SimpleFlickrAPI` class, you make the call asynchronously. The asynchronous call still runs on the main thread, but it does not block the app thanks to the run loop and the secret sauce in CFNetwork.

As the `NSURLConnection` object receives data from the network, it calls its delegate object. The delegate object implements the optional methods from the `NSURLConnectionDelegate` protocol.

How would this scheme work in the Flickr scene, which displays the downloaded photos in the collection view? One approach is to define an array of `NSURLConnection` objects in the `FlickrViewController`. This array contains the same number of `NSURLConnection` objects as there are photos in the search results. The problem, however, is that the code becomes very messy, very fast.

Each `NSURLConnection` object calls the same set of delegate methods, and each delegate method needs to know that the downloaded data belongs to a particular photo. In addition, each downloaded photo must be displayed in the appropriate collection view cell, which further complicates the code.

A much cleaner approach is to create a new class that is responsible for downloading an image. Instead of the `FlickrViewController` class managing an array of `NSURLConnection` objects, it can manage an array of this new image downloader object. One problem still exists, however: The image download is asynchronous. The new image download class needs to notify the `FlickrViewController` that the image has downloaded and is ready for display. The view controller must then display the image in the correct collection view cell. The image downloader class could use a delegate object, but it would introduce the same unnecessary mess in the view controller as did the `NSURLConnection` delegate.

It would be great if the view controller could tell the image downloader class to execute a particular snippet of code upon completion of the download. With blocks,

---

7. Downloading Images for a Table without Threads: http://iphonedevelopment.blogspot.com/2010/05/downloading-images-for-table-without.html

you can do exactly that. You can define a block of code that is executed by the image downloader object after the download has completed.

Let's take a look at the code in Listing 21.5.

Listing 21.5 **ImageDownloaderClass**

```
///////
//  ImageDownloader.h
///////
#import <Foundation/Foundation.h>

typedef void(^ImageDownloaderCompletionBlock)(UIImage *image,
NSError *);                                                  // 1

@interface ImageDownloader : NSObject

@property (nonatomic, strong, readonly) UIImage *image;      // 2

- (void)downloadImageAtURL:(NSURL *)URL
            completion:(ImageDownloaderCompletionBlock)completion;  // 3

@end



///////
//  ImageDownloader.m
///////
#import "ImageDownloader.h"

@interface ImageDownloader ()
@property (nonatomic, strong, readwrite) UIImage *image;        // 4
@property (nonatomic, strong) NSMutableData *receivedData;      // 5
@property (nonatomic, copy) ImageDownloaderCompletionBlock completion;  // 6
@end

@implementation ImageDownloader

- (void)downloadImageAtURL:(NSURL *)URL
            completion:(void(^)(UIImage *image, NSError*))completion// 7
{
    if (URL) {
        [self setCompletion:completion];
        [self setReceivedData:[[NSMutableData alloc] init]];
        NSURLRequest *request = [NSURLRequest requestWithURL:URL];
        NSURLConnection *connection = [[NSURLConnection alloc]
                                    initWithRequest:request
```

```
                                    delegate:self
                                    startImmediately:NO];
        [connection scheduleInRunLoop:[NSRunLoop currentRunLoop]
                            forMode:NSRunLoopCommonModes];            // 8
        [connection start];                                          // 9
    }
}

#pragma mark - NSURLConnection delegate methods                      // 10

- (void)connection:(NSURLConnection *)connection
didReceiveResponse:(NSURLResponse *)response                         // 11
{
    [[self receivedData] setLength:0];
}

- (void)connection:(NSURLConnection *)connection
    didReceiveData:(NSData *)data                                    // 12
{
    [[self receivedData] appendData:data];
}

- (void)connectionDidFinishLoading:(NSURLConnection *)connection     // 13
{
    [self setImage:[UIImage imageWithData:[self receivedData]]];
    [self setReceivedData:nil];

    ImageDownloaderCompletionBlock completion = [self completion];
    if (completion) {
        completion([self image], nil);
    }
}

- (void)connection:(NSURLConnection *)connection
  didFailWithError:(NSError *)error                                  // 14
{
    [self setReceivedData:nil];

    ImageDownloaderCompletionBlock completion = [self completion];
    if (completion) {
        completion(nil, error);
    }
}

@end
```

You need to add the `ImageDownloader` class to your PhotoWheel project. To do so, create a new Objective-C class. Name this class `ImageDownloader`, make it a subclass of `NSObject`, and then copy in the code from Listing 21.5. Here is an explanation of the code you are copying:

1. The `ImageDownloader` class stores a completion block that is called once the image has been downloaded. To make the code more readable, the `ImageDownloaderCompletionBlock` typedef is defined. This approach means that you do not have to redeclare the block definition everywhere it is used.

2. The declared property image is a read-only property that returns the reference to the `UIImage` object containing the downloaded image. Its value is `nil` if the image has not been downloaded.

3. The `ImageDownloader` class has one public method, `-downloadImageAtURL:completion:`. It takes two parameters: the URL to the image and the completion block.

4. A class extension is defined for internal use. The first declared property of the class extension is `image`, which is redeclared as a writable property to allow updates internal to the class.

5. The declared property `receivedData` contains the data downloaded by the `NSURLConnection` object. The data can be received over the network in blocks (or batches), which explains why `receivedData` is mutable. This characteristic allows the class to append data to the property as data is received from the network.

6. The declared property completion stores a reference to the code block provided by the caller. This block is called once the download has completed.

7. The first method found in the implementation is `-downloadImageAtURL:completion:`. A public method, it is called by the `FlickrViewController`. This method checks that a URL is provided, and if so, it stores the reference to the completion block. It also starts the download request.

   The download request is similar to what you saw when implementing the `SimpleFlickrAPI` class. The difference here is that the `NSURLConnection` object is set up for asynchronous instead of synchronous use. The `receivedData` property is allocated with a new `NSMutableData` object. The `NSURLRequest` object is created with the given URL, and the `NSURLConnection` object is created and initialized with the request object and the `ImageDownloader` class instance as the `delegate`. The `startImmediately` flag is set to `NO` to give the class time to do more setup before starting the download.

8. Because you told the `NSURLConnection` object not to start immediately, the run loop for the object can be changed. The default run loop for an `NSURLConnection` object is the run loop for the current thread. The call `[NSRunLoop currentRunLoop]` returns the same run loop, the one for the

current thread. Thus the run loop for this NSURLConnection object does not actually change. What does change, however, is the mode.

There are two modes for a run loop: NSDefaultRunLoopMode and NSRunLoop CommonModes. NSDefaultRunLoopMode, the most commonly used run loop mode, is intended to deal with objects other than NSURLConnection. In contrast, NSRunLoopCommonModes is used to register objects with all run loop modes in a common mode set. In essence, an object added to the common run loop mode is monitored by all run loops in the common mode set. Therefore, you should always use NSRunLoopCommonModes when using NSURLConnection asynchronously. Without it, the responsiveness of NSURLConnection will not be as good and your Web service calls will seem slower to respond.

9. Once the run loop mode for the connection object has been set, the connection object starts the request process to download the image.

10. The remaining methods in the ImageDownloader class are callback methods from the NSURLConnect object.

11. The method -connection:didReceiveResponse: is called when the Web server responds to the request. The method might be called multiple times, as is the case when the original request results in one or more redirects. When the method is called, the receivedData property is reset with a length of zero, clearing any previously stored data. This ensures that only the data received from the final request is captured.

12. The method -connection:didReceiveData: is called as data is received from the network. This method can be called multiple times during a single request. The data is appended to the data already stored in the receivedData property.

13. The method -connectionDidFinishLoading: is called after the request has completed and all data has been received. This method converts the data stored in receivedData to a UIImage object. It then calls the completion block, passing a reference to the UIImage object.

14. The last method of the class, -connection:didFailWithError:, is called if an error is detected at any time during the download process. When this method is called, the error message is forwarded to the completion block.

And that, my friends, is how you make an asynchronous call to a Web server. First, you create an NSURLRequest object for an NSURL. Next, you create an NSURLConnec tion object and initialize it with a request and delegate object. You set the run loop mode to common modes, and then start the request process. Finally, you implement methods from the NSURLConnectionDelegate protocol that responds to events from the NSURLConnection object.

Although the ImageDownloader class is designed to download an image, the same pattern can be used to download other types of data.

Image Caching

One concept not discussed here is caching downloaded images. In the real world, you don't want to keep downloading the same image over and over. Instead, you want to store the downloaded image (or whatever the asset might be) to the file system. As you will see momentarily, the `FlickrViewController` class uses a poor man's approach to caching the image. If the `ImageDownloader` object already has an image, that image is used instead of downloading it again.

If image caching is important to your app, you should roll your own cache manager or use an open source framework such as SDWebImage,[8] which provides image caching for you.

Implementing `FlickrViewController`

With the `SimpleFlickrAPI` and `ImageDownloader` classes complete, you can once again turn your attention to the `FlickrViewController` class and complete its implementation.

The `FlickrViewController` class is responsible for performing a number of tasks. It searches Flickr for photos matching the search criteria provided by the user. It displays the matching photos in the collection view. It allows the user to select and deselect photos. Finally, it saves selected photos to the current photo album.

The code to accomplish all of this work is shown in Listing 21.6. Open the file *FlickrViewController.m* in your PhotoWheel project and add the code from this listing.

As you add the code, you might notice that a good amount of it looks familiar. Many of the patterns you saw in earlier chapters are implemented here as well, such as the data source and delegate methods for the collection view.

Listing 21.6   Updated *FlickrViewController.m* File

```
#import "FlickrViewController.h"                              // 1
#import "SimpleFlickrAPI.h"
#import "ImageDownloader.h"
#import "Photo.h"
#import "PhotoAlbum.h"

@interface FlickrViewController ()
@property (nonatomic, strong) NSArray *flickrPhotos;         // 2
@property (nonatomic, strong) NSMutableArray *downloaders;   // 3
@property (nonatomic, assign) NSInteger showOverlayCount;    // 4
@end
```

---

8. SDWebImage: https://github.com/rs/SDWebImage

```objectivec
@implementation FlickrViewController

- (void)viewDidLoad
{
    [super viewDidLoad];

    [self setFlickrPhotos:[NSArray array]];
    [[self overlayView] setAlpha:0.0];                                  // 5

    UITapGestureRecognizer *tap = [[UITapGestureRecognizer alloc]
                                    initWithTarget:self
                                    action:@selector(overlayViewTapped:)];// 6
    [[self overlayView] addGestureRecognizer:tap];

    [[self collectionView] setAlwaysBounceVertical:YES];
    [[self collectionView] setAllowsMultipleSelection:YES];             // 7
}

- (BOOL)disablesAutomaticKeyboardDismissal                              // 8
{
    return NO;
}

#pragma mark - Save photos

- (void)saveContextAndExit
{
    PhotoAlbum *photoAlbum = [self photoAlbum];
    NSManagedObjectContext *context = [photoAlbum managedObjectContext];
    NSError *error = nil;
    if (![context save:&error])
    {
        // Replace this implementation with code to handle
        // the error appropriately.
        NSLog(@"Unresolved error %@, %@", error, [error userInfo]);
        abort();
    }

    [self dismissViewControllerAnimated:YES completion:nil];
}

- (void)saveSelectedPhotos
{
    PhotoAlbum *photoAlbum = [self photoAlbum];
    NSManagedObjectContext *context = [photoAlbum managedObjectContext];

    NSArray *indexes = [[self collectionView] indexPathsForSelectedItems];
```

```
    __block NSInteger count = [indexes count];                      // 9

   if (count == 0) {                                                // 10
      [self dismissViewControllerAnimated:YES completion:nil];
      return;
   }

   ImageDownloaderCompletionBlock completion =
   ^(UIImage *image, NSError *error) {                              // 11
      NSLog(@"block: count: %i", count);
      if (image) {
         Photo *newPhoto = [NSEntityDescription
                          insertNewObjectForEntityForName:@"Photo"
                          inManagedObjectContext:context];
         [newPhoto setDateAdded:[NSDate date]];
         [newPhoto saveImage:image];
         [newPhoto setPhotoAlbum:photoAlbum];
      } else {
         NSLog(@"%s: Error: %@", __PRETTY_FUNCTION__,
               [error localizedDescription]);
      }

      count--;                                                      // 12
      if (count == 0) {
         [self saveContextAndExit];
      }
   };

   for (NSIndexPath *indexPath in indexes) {                        // 13
      NSInteger index = [indexPath item];
      NSDictionary *flickrPhoto = [[self flickrPhotos] objectAtIndex:index];
      NSURL *URL = [NSURL URLWithString:[flickrPhoto objectForKey:@"url_m"]];
      NSLog(@"URL: %@", URL);
      ImageDownloader *downloader = [[ImageDownloader alloc] init];
      [downloader downloadImageAtURL:URL completion:completion];

      [[self downloaders] addObject:downloader];
   }
}

#pragma mark - Actions

- (IBAction)save:(id)sender                                         // 14
{
   [[self overlayView] setUserInteractionEnabled:NO];

   void (^animations)(void) = ^ {
```

```objc
      [[self overlayView] setAlpha:0.4];
      [[self activityIndicator] startAnimating];
   };

   [UIView animateWithDuration:0.2 animations:animations];

   [self saveSelectedPhotos];
}

- (IBAction)cancel:(id)sender
{
   [self dismissViewControllerAnimated:YES completion:nil];
}


#pragma mark - Overlay methods

- (void)showOverlay:(BOOL)showOverlay                                  // 15
{
   BOOL isVisible = ([[self overlayView] alpha] > 0.0);
   if (isVisible != showOverlay) {
      CGFloat alpha = showOverlay ? 0.4 : 0.0;
      void (^animations)(void) = ^ {
         [[self overlayView] setAlpha:alpha];
         [[self searchBar] setShowsCancelButton:showOverlay animated:YES];
      };

      void (^completion)(BOOL) = ^(BOOL finished) {
         if (finished) {
            // Do other cleanup if needed.
         }
      };

      [UIView animateWithDuration:0.2 animations:animations
                       completion:completion];
   }
}

- (void)showOverlay                                                    // 16
{
   self.showOverlayCount += 1;
   BOOL showOverlay = (self.showOverlayCount > 0);
   [self showOverlay:showOverlay];
}

- (void)hideOverlay                                                    // 17
{
```

```
   self.showOverlayCount -= 1;
   BOOL showOverlay = (self.showOverlayCount > 0);
   [self showOverlay:showOverlay];
   if (self.showOverlayCount < 0) {
      self.showOverlayCount = 0;
   }
}

- (void)overlayViewTapped:(UITapGestureRecognizer *)recognizer        // 18
{
   [self hideOverlay];
   [[self searchBar] resignFirstResponder];
}

#pragma mark - Flickr

- (void)fetchFlickrPhotoWithSearchString:(NSString *)searchString
{
   [[self activityIndicator] startAnimating];                         // 19
   [self showOverlay];
   [[self overlayView] setUserInteractionEnabled:NO];

   SimpleFlickrAPI *flickr = [[SimpleFlickrAPI alloc] init];
   NSArray *photos = [flickr photosWithSearchString:searchString];    // 20

   NSMutableArray *downloaders = [[NSMutableArray alloc]
                              initWithCapacity:[photos count]];
   for (NSInteger index = 0; index < [photos count]; index++) {
      ImageDownloader *downloader = [[ImageDownloader alloc] init];    // 21
      [downloaders addObject:downloader];
   }

   [self setDownloaders:downloaders];                                 // 22
   [self setFlickrPhotos:photos];                                     // 23

   [[self collectionView] reloadData];                                // 24
   [self hideOverlay];
   [[self overlayView] setUserInteractionEnabled:YES];
   [[self searchBar] resignFirstResponder];
   [[self activityIndicator] stopAnimating];
}

#pragma mark - UISearchBarDelegate methods                            // 25

- (BOOL)searchBarShouldBeginEditing:(UISearchBar *)searchBar
{
   [self showOverlay];
```

```
    return YES;
}

- (void)searchBarTextDidEndEditing:(UISearchBar *)searchBar
{
    [searchBar resignFirstResponder];
    [self hideOverlay];
}

- (void)searchBarSearchButtonClicked:(UISearchBar *)searchBar          // 26
{
    [self fetchFlickrPhotoWithSearchString:[searchBar text]];
}

- (void)searchBarCancelButtonClicked:(UISearchBar *)searchBar
{
    [searchBar resignFirstResponder];
    [self hideOverlay];
}

#pragma mark - UICollectionViewDataSource and UICollectionViewDelegate  // 27

- (NSInteger)collectionView:(UICollectionView *)collectionView
numberOfItemsInSection:(NSInteger)section
{
    NSInteger count = [[self flickrPhotos] count];
    return count;
}

- (UICollectionViewCell *)collectionView:(UICollectionView *)collectionView
cellForItemAtIndexPath:(NSIndexPath *)indexPath
{
    UICollectionViewCell *cell = [collectionView
        dequeueReusableCellWithReuseIdentifier:@"PhotoCell"
        forIndexPath:indexPath];

    UIImageView *photoImageView = (UIImageView *)[cell viewWithTag:1];    // 28
    UIImageView *selectedImageView = (UIImageView *)[cell viewWithTag:2];

    NSArray *selectedIndexPaths = [collectionView indexPathsForSelectedItems];
    BOOL isSelected = [selectedIndexPaths containsObject:indexPath];
    [selectedImageView setHidden:!isSelected];

    ImageDownloaderCompletionBlock completion =
    ^(UIImage *image, NSError *error) {                                   // 29
        if (image) {
```

```
            [photoImageView setImage:image];
      } else {
            NSLog(@"%s: Error: %@", __PRETTY_FUNCTION__,
                  [error localizedDescription]);
      }
   };

   NSInteger index = [indexPath item];
   NSArray *downloaders = [self downloaders];
   ImageDownloader *downloader = [downloaders objectAtIndex:index];
   UIImage *image = [downloader image];                              // 30
   if (image) {
      [photoImageView setImage:image];
   } else {
      NSDictionary *flickrPhoto = [[self flickrPhotos] objectAtIndex:index];
      NSURL *URL = [NSURL URLWithString:[flickrPhoto objectForKey:@"url_sq"]];
      [downloader downloadImageAtURL:URL completion:completion];
   }

   return cell;
}

- (void)collectionView:(UICollectionView *)collectionView
didSelectItemAtIndexPath:(NSIndexPath *)indexPath
{
   UICollectionViewCell *cell = nil;
   cell = [collectionView cellForItemAtIndexPath:indexPath];
   UIImageView *selectedImageView = (UIImageView *)[cell viewWithTag:2];
   [selectedImageView setHidden:NO];
}

- (void)collectionView:(UICollectionView *)collectionView
didDeselectItemAtIndexPath:(NSIndexPath *)indexPath
{
   UICollectionViewCell *cell = nil;
   cell = [collectionView cellForItemAtIndexPath:indexPath];
   UIImageView *selectedImageView = (UIImageView *)[cell viewWithTag:2];
   [selectedImageView setHidden:YES];
}

@end
```

Even though a lot of the code looks familiar, let's still walk through it, just to make sure you understand everything that's going on.

1. The various header files for classes used by the view controller are imported. They include the two new classes you created, SimpleFlickrAPI and Image Downloader.

2. The property flickrPhotos stores a local copy of the photo data returned from Flickr.

3. The property downloaders stores an ImageDownloader object for each photo in the flickrPhotos array. This is a quick-and-dirty attempt at caching the downloaded images. Each image is downloaded once for each photo for the life of the view controller. The images are cached to memory, which could lead to out-of-memory errors. Given that the Flickr API returns a maximum of only 100 photos per request, however, the potential for memory errors is low for this particular app.

4. The property showOverlayCount stores a stack count of the show and hide requests for the overlay. It is used to ensure that the overlay is not prematurely hidden.

5. The alpha for the overlay view is set to 0.0, which makes the view invisible.

6. A tap gesture is added to the overlay view, albeit for usability's sake only. When the view controller is in search mode, the user can tap the overlay view to exit the mode.

7. The collection view is configured for multiple selections. Multi-select is used to save more than one photo at a time to the photo album.

8. The method -disablesAutomaticKeyboardDismissal is an override method for UIViewController. This method is used to determine whether the input view (i.e., the virtual keyboard) is automatically dismissed when changing controls. By default, the method returns NO except when the presentation style is UIModalPresentationFormSheet, for which the default return value is YES.

   The problem with the default behavior in the FlickrViewController class is that the keyboard does not dismiss when [[self searchBar] re signFirstResponder] is called. This happens because the presentation style for the view controller is UIModalPresentationFormSheet. This is not the desired behavior for this view controller, so the method is overridden to return NO.

9. The number of selected cells is stored in the local variable count. The __block directive is used to make the variable mutable within the completion block defined a few lines down.

10. If the number of selected cells is zero, the view controller is dismissed and program control exits the method. Nothing else needs to be done.

11. The completion block for the `ImageDownloader` object is defined. If the block receives an image, a new `Photo` model object is created and its properties are set.

12. The local variable `count` is decremented by one. Because the variable was declared with the `__block` directive, it is mutable within the block. When the count reaches zero, all images have been downloaded and added to the photo album. Now the managed object context is saved and the view controller is dismissed.

13. Outside of the block is a `for` loop that downloads the medium-size image for each photo found in the Flickr search results. The downloaders are added to the `downloaders` array to ensure that they stay alive until the view controller is dismissed.

14. The method `-save:` is called when the user taps the **Save** button. Its primary role is to call the `-saveSelectedPhotos` method (described in code lines 9–13). It also turns off user interaction on the overlay view. This prevents the user from tapping the view—an action that normally hides the overlay. The `-save:` method displays the overlay view to prevent the user from interacting with the collection view, as well as the activity indicator informing the user that work is in progress.

15. The method `-showOverlay:` is called to show and hide the overlay when the search bar is in use. Pass in `YES` to show the overlay view, and `NO` to hide it.

16–17. The methods `-showOverlay` and `-hideOverlay` manage the display of the overlay view. Each call to `-showOverlay` increments the `showOverlayCount` property, and each call to `-hideOverlay` decrements the `count`. When the count is greater than zero, the overlay view is visible; otherwise, it is hidden.

18. When the overlay view is tapped, the gesture recognizer calls the `-overlay ViewTapped:` method. This method hides the overlay view and the keyboard if displayed.

19–24. The method `-fetchFlickrPhotoWithSearchString:` is called to search Flickr. It displays the activity indicator telling the user that something is happening. It creates an instance of the `SimpleFlickrAPI` and then performs the search. When the search is complete, the property `downloaders` is populated with instances of the `ImageDownloader` objects. The download process has not started, however. The photos returned from the Flickr API call are stored in the `flickrPhotos` property. Last, the collection view data is reloaded with the photos returned from Flickr.

25. Callback methods for the `UISearchBarDelegate` control the user experience when using the search bar.

26. The callback method -searchBarSearchButtonClicked: is called when it is time to perform the search. It calls the -fetchFlickrPhotoWithSearch String: method.

27. The UICollectionViewDataSource and UICollectionViewDelegate callback methods are implemented.

28. The collection view is set up to support multi-selection. When a cell is allocated, the selected indicator image must be displayed. A custom collection view cell class is not used, so the -viewWithTag: method is called on the cell to retrieve a reference to the UIImageView instance used to display the image *addphoto.png*. If the cell is selected, the image view is displayed; otherwise, it is hidden from the display.

29. Each cell displays an image of the photo from Flickr. However, the image must be downloaded first. The completion block for the ImageDownloader object is defined. The completion block sets the image property for cell's photoImageView to the image passed in to the block.

30. If the image was previously downloaded, the cell's image is set right away. There is no reason to download it again.

Those are the highlights from Listing 21.6. Build and run the app to test your changes.

> **Note**
>
> If the Flickr search is not working, make sure that the outlet and delegate connections for the search bar have been made. Also verify the outlet and data source connections for the collection view. Finally, check your Flickr API Key. If it is missing or invalid, the search will fail with an "Invalid API Key (Key has invalid format)" message from Flickr. You can see this message in the debug console window shown in Figure 21.4.

Figure 21.4   Invalid API key error message displayed in the Debug Console window

One More Thing

When you ran PhotoWheel to test the Flickr changes, did you notice how the app freezes while searching Flickr? Even the activity indicator does not appear.

The problem is the synchronous call to Flickr made by the `SimpleFlickrAPI` object. Unlike the asynchronous call to the Flickr Web server in the `ImageDownloader` class, the synchronous call in `SimpleFlickrAPI` blocks the main thread from performing additional steps in the run loop. This explains why, for example, the activity indicator never appears. A quick solution to this problem is to use the `SimpleFlickrAPI` object on a background thread, but there's a better way to resolve this issue.

Grand Central Dispatch (GCD) is a C-level API for concurrent programming. GCD offers three benefits over traditional multithreaded programming: It is easy to use, it is efficient, and its performance is better. The GCD API makes heavy use of blocks—a technique that makes it easier to define a unit of work in code as compared to creating a thread. Blocks also make your code more readable because the unit of work is coded in one place. When using threads, the unit of work is usually spread across multiple functions or even relegated to a separate class file.

GCD uses dispatch queues to process units of work. Three types of dispatch queues are found in GCD: the main queue, global queues, and custom queues. The main queue executes on the main thread, and it is the same as performing a task on the main thread such as updating the UI. Global queues are concurrent queues shared throughout the lifetime of the app. Custom queues are queues you create.

> **Note**
>
> For a more complete introduction to Grand Central Dispatch, read Mike Ash's blog post *Intro to Grand Central Dispatch, Part I: Basics and Dispatch Queues.*[9]

To prevent blocking on the main thread during the Flickr fetch process, you can dispatch the fetch process to a global asynchronous queue. Once the process completes, you dispatch another unit of work to the main queue to update the UI. The code to accomplish this task is shown in Listing 21.7.

Listing 21.7   **Updated Save Process to Use GCD**

```
- (void)fetchFlickrPhotoWithSearchString:(NSString *)searchString
{
    [[self activityIndicator] startAnimating];
    [self showOverlay];
    [[self overlayView] setUserInteractionEnabled:NO];

    dispatch_async(dispatch_get_global_queue(DISPATCH_QUEUE_PRIORITY_DEFAULT, 0), ^{
```

9. Intro to Grand Central Dispatch: http://www.mikeash.com/pyblog/friday-qa-2009-08-28
   -intro-to-grand-central-dispatch-part-i-basics-and-dispatch-queues.html

```
SimpleFlickrAPI *flickr = [[SimpleFlickrAPI alloc] init];
NSArray *photos = [flickr photosWithSearchString:searchString];

NSMutableArray *downloaders = [[NSMutableArray alloc]
                                   initWithCapacity:[photos count]];
for (NSInteger index = 0; index < [photos count]; index++) {
    ImageDownloader *downloader = [[ImageDownloader alloc] init];
    [downloaders addObject:downloader];
}

[self setDownloaders:downloaders];
[self setFlickrPhotos:photos];

dispatch_async(dispatch_get_main_queue(), ^{
    [[self collectionView] reloadData];
    [self hideOverlay];
    [[self overlayView] setUserInteractionEnabled:YES];
    [[self searchBar] resignFirstResponder];
    [[self activityIndicator] stopAnimating];
});
});
}
```

This code is almost identical to the original code, with the exception of the two dispatch calls. The first dispatch call, `dispatch_async`, queues the unit of work in a global asynchronous queue. The global queue is retrieved by the function `dispatch_get_global_queue`.

Inside the block defining the first unit of work is another `dispatch_async` call. This time the main queue is used. As a consequence, the unit of work defined in the second block is performed on the main thread, which is required because the unit of work is updating the user interface.

Apply this change to your version of the `FlickrViewController` class, and then build and run the app to see the difference made by using GCD.

What's Missing

Because this chapter is a basic overview, it has left out a number of topics. Authentication and security are two topics that come to mind; reachability is another.

Reachability is a term often used by iOS programmers to refer to a network's accessibility. This word comes from the name of a class found in a networking sample[10] provided by Apple. The `Reachability` class is used to determine the current state of the

_____

10. Reachability sample project: http://developer.apple.com/library/ios/#samplecode/Reachability/Introduction/Intro.html

network and to monitor changes in the network state. Apple recommends that any app using the network check the status of the network and gracefully handle situations where the network is not available.

Summary

This chapter provided a basic overview of making RESTful Web service calls using the classes provided by Cocoa. It simply dipped a toe into the waters with its introduction to Web services; by no means does this chapter constitute a complete guide to using Web services in iOS apps. Full coverage of Web services would fill an entire book, but the topics covered in this chapter should point you in the right direction for building more robust support for Web services within your apps.

Exercises

1. It is possible for the Flickr search to return no photos. Included in the JSON data is the photo count. Update the app to check the photo count, and if the count is zero, display a "No photos found" message to the user.

2. The Flickr thumbnail images displayed in the collection view in `FlickrViewController` are 75 × 75 pixels. Ideally for retina displays you want to display a 150 × 150-pixel image in the 75 × 75-point `UIImageView`. Modify the code to download a larger image size, and then scale it down to 150 × 150 pixels for display in the 75 × 75-point image view.

3. Set your iPad to Airplane mode and run PhotoWheel. Try searching Flickr and see what happens. Which changes can be made to improve the user experience?

Syncing with iCloud

At this point PhotoWheel is pretty useful—users can work with their photos in a variety of ways. But the app is limited to a single device. It is increasingly common for people to have more than one iOS device and often a Mac as well. Wouldn't it be great if PhotoWheel could sync its data across multiple devices so that users could have their app data available on any of their devices? In this chapter we'll expand PhotoWheel to use Apple's iCloud service to sync photos and albums to different devices via the Internet. The technique we'll cover makes Core Data into a cloud-enabled data storage system.

Syncing Made Simple

In earlier releases of iOS, syncing data from one device to another was difficult. There were no standard, drop-in frameworks that would easily manage syncing data across multiple devices. App developers came up with various schemes to handle these issues, but they were mostly created for single apps. The bottom line was: *Syncing is hard.* It often seems simple enough at first, but in practice it is very tricky to get it right. Resolving conflicts without losing user data is a challenge that has defeated many developers.

Syncing also requires some means of transmitting an app's data from one device to another. This requirement has been satisfied by means such as building a Web server into an app so that data could be requested from other devices or by running an online service of some kind to handle syncing. Some apps used online services such as Dropbox to make data available across different devices. While quite useful, these services didn't really provide sync mechanisms.

Beginning with iOS 5.0, Apple introduced an online service called iCloud. With iCloud, users get access to a variety of cloud-based services such as automatic device backup and syncing of music, contacts, and other data across devices. The feature we're most interested in for PhotoWheel is built-in support for third-party apps that want to sync their own app data across iOS devices. With iCloud, Apple has solved part of the syncing problem for you, providing both API support for your apps and the online server support necessary to make syncing happen. Apple provides a free iCloud account to any user with an iOS 5 device, so your users can easily access this service at no extra charge.

However, keep in mind it often happens that *syncing is still hard*. This chapter will cover the Core Data iCloud API, including some of the complications that can arise.

iCloud Concepts

The key concept when working with iCloud is *ubiquitous content*. Data is said to be ubiquitous if the iCloud service monitors it and ensures that it is kept in sync among multiple devices that use the same iCloud account. In contrast, local content exists only in the app and is not synced via iCloud. Up to now PhotoWheel has used only local content, but in this chapter we'll make it ubiquitous.

Ubiquitous content is managed by the ubiquity daemon, a service that runs on iOS devices as a separate process from your app that manages interaction with iCloud. Apps don't talk to iCloud servers directly, but instead create content locally and tell the ubiquity daemon that it should be synced. Transfers to and from the iCloud servers happen asynchronously under the control of the ubiquity daemon.

When creating ubiquitous content, the general flow is to create a local file or other local data and then notify iOS that it should be ubiquitous. The ubiquity daemon uploads the content to the iCloud servers. As your app updates its data, the daemon updates the server data as well. This may not happen immediately, but it usually happens fairly quickly.

If the user has the app installed on more than one device, the ubiquity daemon will also download new changes created on other devices. Your app will be notified that this has happened and can update its state appropriately.

File Coordinators and Presenters

Ubiquitous content can be read and written both by the app that created the content and by the iCloud daemon. To coordinate access to the data, iOS 5 introduced the concepts of a *file coordinator* and a *file presenter*.

A file coordinator is just an instance of `NSFileCoordinator`. It acts as a read/write lock for file access. Multiple read requests can proceed simultaneously, but writing to a file requires an exclusive lock. When using a file coordinator, an app requests either read or write access to the data before accessing it, and the framework uses a read/write lock to keep the data intact.

A file presenter is any object that implements the `NSFilePresenter` protocol. If data is changed in a write action managed by an `NSFileCoordinator`, the file presenter for that data is notified of the change. It can then make whatever updates are necessary to present the new data to the user. You might implement this protocol on your model objects, your view controllers, or both, depending on how your app needs to respond to changes to its data.

The file presenter protocol also declares methods that notify your app of any sync conflicts. Although iCloud resolves most conflicts internally, it is not always possible to handle conflicts automatically. In such a case, your app will be notified of a new version of the data via the file presenter. The app must then resolve the conflicts, asking the user for help if it can't handle the conflict silently.

Combining these two, then, if an app using iCloud needs to update its data, it requests a write lock from an `NSFileCoordinator` and makes its changes. Another copy of the app, on a different device, receives a notification of this change via objects that implement `NSFilePresenter`.

UIDocument and UIManagedDocument

You don't necessarily need to use file coordinators and presenters in your own code. As a convenience, iOS 5 also introduced the `UIDocument` class for managing document-based data. Document-based data comprises any data that can be considered as individual, independent documents rather than as a single data store for an entire application. Word processors and spreadsheets are examples of apps that have document-based data, whereas calendars and to-do list applications usually are not document based.

`UIDocument` implements the `NSFilePresenter` protocol and uses file coordinators to handle data access. To use `UIDocument`, you create a custom subclass that can manage your app's document data. `UIDocument` will create and use file coordinators as needed. Your subclass will need to implement the file presenter methods, however, because `UIDocument`'s implementations of these methods mostly do nothing.

If you have document-based data and you're using Core Data, you can take advantage of `UIManagedDocument`, which is a subclass of `UIDocument`. It creates and manages its own Core Data stack. By default, the `UIManagedDocument` subclass searches the app bundle for managed object models. It creates a persistent store coordinator and managed object context based on the file URL you provide when instantiating `UIManagedDocument`. This process can be customized if necessary.

Note that neither `UIDocument` nor `UIManagedDocument` is actually tied to iCloud. Each can be used for purely local document-based data that is never synced.

Ubiquitous Persistent Stores

If you're using Core Data but your data doesn't fit the document paradigm, you can still simplify the process of working with iCloud. Rather than create file coordinators and presenters, it is possible to just configure the persistent store coordinator to make its data ubiquitous. Setting up the Core Data stack is more or less the same as when you're not using iCloud. The major change involves adding code to handle incoming changes from iCloud. The iCloud daemon will update the data store automatically, and the app will need to respond to these changes. Using this method is convenient for apps that already have Core Data stores, because existing data stores can be easily moved to iCloud storage.

When a ubiquitous persistent store is used, incoming changes are reconciled with local data on a record-by-record basis, preserving changes to individual attributes of entities. Core Data already incorporates conflict management because handling conflicts is necessary when working with multiple threads. Conflicts are handled either automatically based on a merge policy you choose or by custom code you write to resolve conflicts.

This is the approach Apple recommends for "shoebox" apps—apps that contain a collection of related data but where the data doesn't fit the document paradigm or where the app simply does not expose documents to the user. PhotoWheel matches this description, so we'll use this approach to make PhotoWheel work with iCloud.

Warning

Core Data's iCloud API is a very convenient way to add syncing support to an app. The concepts and API are relatively straightforward, but actual syncing depends on iOS's built-in iCloud support and on the iCloud servers. Even with correct code, it can often be difficult to get iCloud working reliably with Core Data. Confusing error messages and failures to connect to iCloud are unfortunately not rare. For example, one maddeningly common error message reads simply "Unable to initiate item download"; it occurs when your app code is not actually trying to download anything. This message doesn't indicate that the app's code is incorrect, but rather is a sign of internal problems dealing with iCloud. When this error occurs, the Core Data stack will not be available and the only recourse is to try again later. At the same time, when using iCloud it's not unusual to see console messages that look and sound a lot like errors but that do not actually indicate that anything is wrong.

This chapter presents the API as it is intended to work. In practice, you may find that it does not work quite so well as you would hope. If you decide to incorporate iCloud into an app that you hope to release, be sure to *extensively* test every part of the app that relates to iCloud in any way with a variety of users.

Device Provisioning, Revisited

Chapter 6, "Provisioning Your iPad," discussed setting up an App ID and a provisioning profile for use when developing apps. Before you can start working with iCloud, you need to make some changes to the App ID configuration and update your provisioning profile. Apps cannot access iCloud services unless the App ID has been configured for iCloud and the provisioning profile has been generated with this configuration. The steps you need to follow to enable an app to use iCloud are described in the following sections.

Configuring the App ID

Up to now, everything you have done with PhotoWheel could have been done using a wildcard App ID—that is, one with an *, which can be used with multiple applications. That is convenient during development but it won't work with iCloud. If you're using a wildcard App ID, you need to replace it with an explicit App ID. The differences and the process for creating an App ID are discussed in Chapter 6, "Provisioning Your iPad."

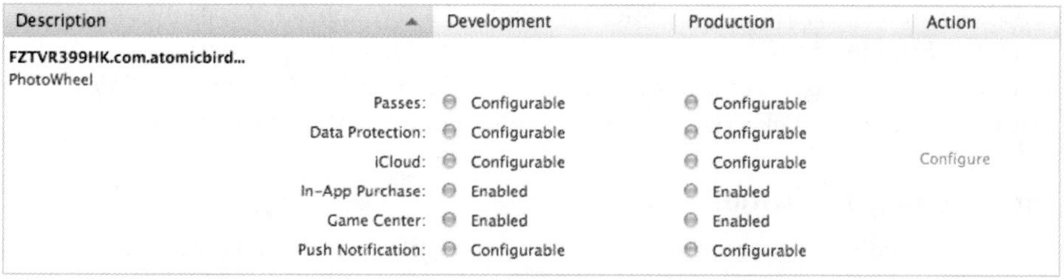

Description		Development	Production	Action
FZTVR399HK.com.atomicbird... PhotoWheel				
	Passes:	⊖ Configurable	⊖ Configurable	
	Data Protection:	⊖ Configurable	⊖ Configurable	
	iCloud:	⊖ Configurable	⊖ Configurable	Configure
	In-App Purchase:	⊖ Enabled	⊖ Enabled	
	Game Center:	⊖ Enabled	⊖ Enabled	
	Push Notification:	⊖ Configurable	⊖ Configurable	

Figure 22.1   Current configuration of the PhotoWheel App ID

Once you have an explicit App ID, you need to configure it for use with iCloud. Start by logging in to the iOS Developer Center and going to the Provisioning Portal. In the portal, click App IDs in the navigation section on the left to see a list of your App IDs. Find the PhotoWheel App ID. The Provisioning Portal shows various capabilities available with this App ID (Figure 22.1). In-App Purchase and Game Center are enabled by default with explicit App IDs. Other features, including iCloud, are disabled but configurable. Click the Configure link in the rightmost column of the table to start configuring iCloud.

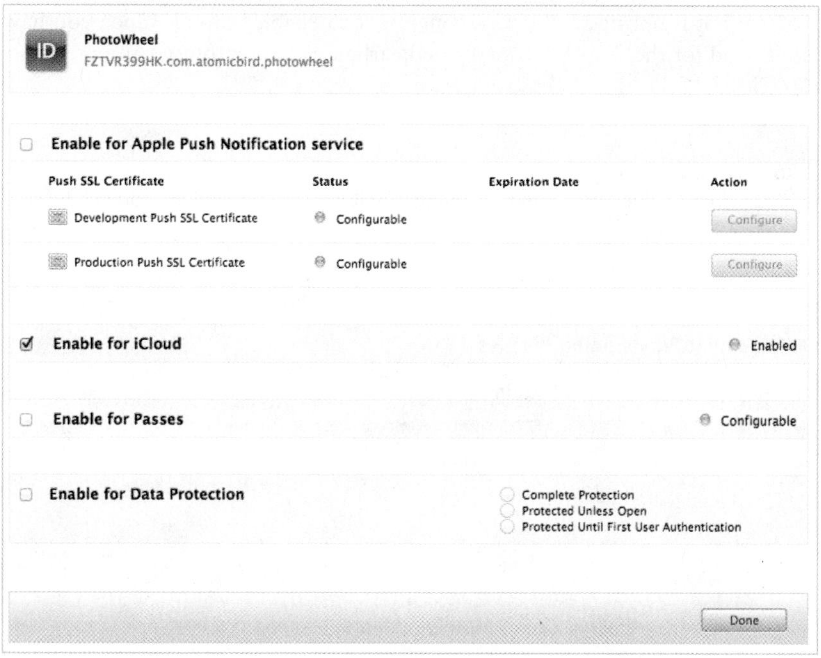

Figure 22.2   Configuration options for the PhotoWheel App ID

Once you do this, you'll see options to configure the App ID in various ways. Click the **Enable for iCloud** check box (Figure 22.2). The provisioning portal will then show a warning about provisioning profiles that use this App ID. You'll deal with that in a minute, so click **OK** in the warning message and then click **Done**.

Provisioning for iCloud

Next, you need to regenerate your provisioning profile so that it includes the correct entitlements for the app to use iCloud. The Provisioning Portal doesn't have an option to simply regenerate an existing provisioning profile. To force it to regenerate the profile, you must edit the profile and make a simple, even meaningless change—adding or removing a device, for example. You can even remove a device and then add it back— even if the result is the same as the starting point, the portal's **Submit** button will then be enabled. Changing the name is a good idea because doing so makes it easy to distinguish the previous profile from the regenerated one.

Find the provisioning profile in the portal and click the **Edit** link, and then click **Modify** in the popup window (Figure 22.3).

Make your change to the provisioning profile and click **Submit**. Download the revised profile. To replace the previous copy, find it in Xcode's Organizer window (see Chapter 6, "Provisioning Your iPad," if you're not sure how). Select the old version, click the **–** button to delete it, and then install the new version.

If you didn't previously generate a provisioning profile, you need to create one now, although it is not necessary to regenerate it to enable iCloud. Once you have enabled iCloud for the App ID as described earlier, all new provisioning profiles will include iCloud.

> **Note**
>
> The iPad Simulator does not support working with iCloud. When testing iCloud code, you must use a real iOS device.

Figure 22.3   Modifying a provisioning profile

Configuring iCloud Entitlements

Finally, the app needs a custom entitlements file. Entitlements files are XML property list files used by iOS that contain metadata about an application. To use iCloud, you need one that contains information about how the app will use iCloud. Specifically, the entitlements file will list container identifiers, which are used to determine where iCloud data is stored.

Xcode makes it easy to add the entitlements file. Select the PhotoWheel project in the navigator, and then the PhotoWheel app target in the editor. If you scroll down in the editor pane, you'll see a section named Entitlements (Figure 22.4).

Check the Entitlements box. When you do, Xcode creates a new file in the project, called *PhotoWheel.entitlements*. Also check the box labeled Enable iCloud.

One of the entitlements sections is labeled Ubiquity Containers. If Xcode hasn't created an entry in this section, click the **+** button at the bottom of this section to add a container entry. Doing so adds a blank line for the container identifier for the app. The container identifier can be any string that makes sense to you, but it is convenient to make it the same as the app's Bundle ID.

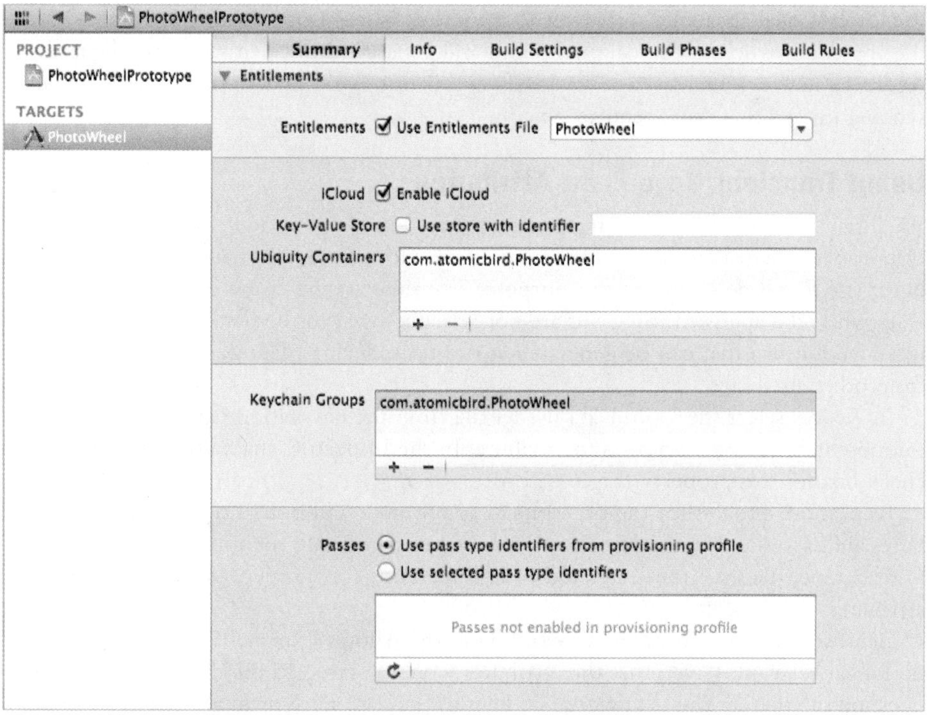

Figure 22.4   Enabling custom entitlements for iCloud

iCloud Considerations for PhotoWheel

Now that PhotoWheel is ready to use iCloud, you can start adding code to sync the app's data between devices. The existing Core Data model could be used as is, with no changes. You'll need to add a couple of extra configuration options when the app starts up and code to handle new incoming changes from the cloud. Before doing that, though, let's give a little thought to whether that is really the best approach.

Don't Sync More Than You Need to Sync

Although iCloud accounts are available for free to any iOS user, the data storage space is not unlimited. A free account is capped at 5GB of data, an amount that includes space taken up by device backups. Also, transfer to and from the cloud does not occur instantly. An iOS device might rely on a slow mobile phone network, yet you still want syncing to happen as fast as possible. Given these possibilities, it's a good idea to consider whether you really want to sync all of the app's data or whether you could sync some of it and generate the rest locally.

Recall that PhotoWheel saves multiple versions of each photo: the original photo as well as scaled versions. If you just add iCloud support to the current model, everything will be synced. Of course, it is not really necessary to sync all of the photos for the PhotoWheel app—the scaled versions can be created from the original photo. Thus the app could sync just the original photo and generate the scaled versions whenever it receives a new original from iCloud. Given this fact, we'll update the model to avoid syncing images that don't require syncing.

Using Transient Core Data Attributes

We'll still be using Core Data to manage the data model, but now we don't want Core Data to save the scaled images in the data store. Core Data has a "transient" attribute type that is designed for this purpose. Transient attributes are managed by Core Data while the app is running but are not actually saved to the data store. They are intended for data that can be generated at run time, such as data that can be derived from other attributes.

In Xcode, select the Core Data model file from the navigation pane. Click on the Photo entity's `largeImageData` attribute. In the Inspector, enable the Transient check box for this property (Figure 22.5).

Repeat this process for the `thumbnailImageData` and `smallImageData` attributes and save the data model. You don't need to regenerate the model class for the Photo entity, because the generated code is the same for transient and permanent attributes.

Because these attributes are now transient, the Allows External Storage setting is no longer relevant. Given that the attributes won't be saved to the data store at all, the question of whether the data would be kept in the data store or in an external file no longer makes sense. It's not necessary to uncheck the setting, and it's not harmful to leave it enabled, but it will have no effect for a transient attribute.

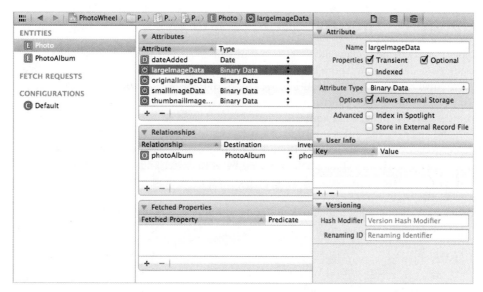

Figure 22.5   Making the `largeImageData` attribute transient

Changing Core Data Models

When creating a Core Data stack, it is crucial that the entities defined in the data model exactly match instances stored in any existing data stores. Any model change can prevent Core Data from initializing the stack without some help. This help takes the form of data model migration, which can be simple or complex depending on how much the model has changed.

If the app has not been released yet, it is common practice to bypass this issue by simply removing the app from the iPad and starting with a fresh copy. The first time the new build of the app runs, there is no data store and therefore no compatibility issues. That's what you'll do here, so after you change the model, make sure to remove the app from your iPad before attempting to compile and run it again. If you don't, the app will raise an exception as soon as it tries to load the data store.

Of course, if the app had already been released, this wouldn't be an acceptable solution. You would need to handle model migration so that your users' data would be preserved when they upgraded to the latest version of your app. Migrating data models to new versions will not be covered here, but Apple provides a detailed guide in the iOS developer documentation, called *Core Data Model Versioning and Data Migration*.[1]

---

1. Core Data Model Versioning and Data Migration: https://developer.apple.com/library/ ios/#documentation/Cocoa/Conceptual/CoreDataVersioning/Articles/Introduction.html

Updating PhotoWheel for iCloud

Now that the scaled image attributes are transient, you need to make some code changes to deal with keeping these images in external files. Until now, Core Data has been putting images in external files because of the Allows External Storage setting. You don't want the scaled images to be sent to iCloud, however, so now you need to handle external image files yourself. The code will need to create scaled images on demand and save the images outside of Core Data.

To do this, the app needs a method that returns the file path to use for one of the scaled image attributes. This method is used by both getter and setter methods to read and write the file, as shown in Listing 22.1. Add this method to *Photo.m*.

Listing 22.1   Generating a Unique Path for an Attribute of a Managed Object

```
- (NSURL *)fileURLForAttributeNamed:(NSString *)attributeName
{
   if ([[self objectID] isTemporaryID]) {
      NSError *error = nil;
      [[self managedObjectContext]
        obtainPermanentIDsForObjects:[NSArray arrayWithObject:self]
        error:&error];
   }
   NSUInteger filenameID = [[[[self objectID] URIRepresentation]
                        absoluteURL] hash];
   NSString *filename = [NSString stringWithFormat:@"%@-%d",
                     attributeName, filenameID];
   NSURL *documentsDirectory = [[[NSFileManager defaultManager]
                       URLsForDirectory:NSDocumentDirectory
                       inDomains:NSUserDomainMask]
                       lastObject];
   return [documentsDirectory URLByAppendingPathComponent:filename];
}
```

This method generates a file name unique to the current photo by looking up the photo's `objectID`. The `objectID` is a unique identifier that is part of every managed object. The first part of the method checks whether the `objectID` is temporary. When a managed object is first created, it has a temporary `objectID`. That ID is replaced with a permanent value when you save changes to the managed object context. If you need a permanent `objectID` before saving, you can ask the managed object context to make an early conversion. You need a permanent ID so that the generated file name won't change when you save changes.

The managed object ID is opaque but can be converted to a URI. The code in Listing 22.1 does this and then asks `NSString` to calculate a hash value for the absolute URI string. This results in an integer unique to the current photo. The method uses this file ID to create a file name by combining it with the attribute name. For example, if the attribute name is `thumbnailImageData` and the file name ID is *1234567890*, the file name would be *thumbnailImageData-1234567890*. The file name doesn't include an extension like *jpg* or *png*, but the app doesn't need one to read and use the file.

The file name is then added to the app's document directory path to produce a full path to a file that can be used for data owned by a specific `Photo` instance and that contains a specific attribute's image data.

Next, you need to add custom accessor methods for the `largeImage`, `smallImage`, and `thumbnailImage` attributes, which handle getting the data to and from files. The first step here is to create the setters. You'll need one setter per scaled image attribute; these methods are called `setLargeImageData:`, `setSmallImageData:`, and `setThumbnailImageData:`. These three methods are identical except for the attribute name, so most of the code can be put in a common method used by all of the new setters. That makes four new methods, shown in Listing 22.2. Add these methods to *Photo.m*.

Listing 22.2   Custom Attribute Setters for Scaled Image Attributes

```
- (void)setImageData:(NSData *)imageData
  forAttributeNamed:(NSString *)attributeName
{
  // Do the set
  [self willChangeValueForKey:attributeName];
  [self setPrimitiveValue:imageData forKey:attributeName];
  [self didChangeValueForKey:attributeName];

  // Now write to a file, because the attribute is transient.
  [imageData writeToURL:[self fileURLForAttributeNamed:attributeName]
          atomically:YES];
}


- (void)setLargeImageData:(NSData *)largeImageData
{
  [self setImageData:largeImageData
     forAttributeNamed:@"largeImageData"];
}


- (void)setSmallImageData:(NSData *)smallImageData
{
  [self setImageData:smallImageData
     forAttributeNamed:@"smallImageData"];
}


- (void)setThumbnailImageData:(NSData *)thumbnailImageData
{
  [self setImageData:thumbnailImageData
     forAttributeNamed:@"thumbnailImageData"];
}
```

The incoming data is saved on the managed object using the `setPrimitiveValue`
`:forKey:` method of `NSManagedObject`. This method is used when overriding setters on managed objects. It sets the value on the managed object directly without
implicitly calling any other setter method. The calls to `willChangeValueForKey:`
and `didChangeValueForKey:` are a necessary detail of writing a custom Core Data
setter method, and they ensure that features such as undo management work. Normally, they would be handled by the dynamically generated setter method.

Along with custom setter methods, we need custom getters. As is true for the setters, the actual work of getting the data is identical for all scaled image attributes; the
only difference is the attribute name. Thus this code will follow the same pattern of
putting the common code in a single method called by the attribute-specific getters.
This code is shown in Listing 22.3. Add this code to *Photo.m*.

Listing 22.3 **Custom Getter Methods for Non-synced Image Data**

```objc
- (NSData *)imageDataForAttributeNamed:(NSString *)attributeName
{
    // Get the existing data for the attribute, if possible.
    [self willAccessValueForKey:attributeName];
    NSData *imageData = [self primitiveValueForKey:attributeName];
    [self didAccessValueForKey:attributeName];

    // If we don't already have image data, get it.
    if (imageData == nil) {
        NSURL *fileURL = [self fileURLForAttributeNamed:attributeName];
        if ([[NSFileManager defaultManager] fileExistsAtPath:
            [fileURL path]]) {
            // Read image data from the appropriate file, if it exists.
            imageData = [NSData dataWithContentsOfURL:fileURL];
            [self willChangeValueForKey:attributeName];
            [self setPrimitiveValue:imageData forKey:attributeName];
            [self didChangeValueForKey:attributeName];
        } else {
            // If the file doesn't exist, create it.
            [self createScaledImagesForImage:[self originalImage]];
            [self willAccessValueForKey:attributeName];
            imageData = [self primitiveValueForKey:attributeName];
            [self didAccessValueForKey:attributeName];
        }
    }

    return imageData;
}
```

```
- (NSData *)largeImageData
{
    return [self imageDataForAttributeNamed:@"largeImageData"];
}


- (NSData *)smallImageData
{
    return [self imageDataForAttributeNamed:@"smallImageData"];
}


- (NSData *)thumbnailImageData
{
    return [self imageDataForAttributeNamed:@"thumbnailImageData"];
}
```

The `imageDataForAttributeNamed:` method handles a variety of cases to get the image data. First, it calls `primitiveValueForKey:` to check whether the image data has already been loaded; if it has been loaded, the method returns the data. If the image data has not already been loaded, the method looks for a file containing image data, using the `fileURLForAttributeNamed:` method discussed earlier. If that file exists, the method loads image data from it. If the file doesn't exist, its absence implies that the external files have not been created yet, which would be the case if the photo had just been received from iCloud. In that case the method calls the `createScaledImagesForImage:` method created in Chapter 13, "Data Persistence." Recall that the `createScaledImagesForImage:` method creates the scaled images and the files and also calls the setter methods for the scaled image attributes.

The `imageDataForAttributeNamed:` includes extra code that is necessary when using a custom getter method on a managed object. In this case it uses `primitiveValueForKey:`, the getter complement to `setPrimitiveValue:forKey:`. It also uses `willAccessValueForKey:` and `didAccessValueForKey:` to notify the superclass that the method is accessing the attribute value directly. Again, this would normally be called by the dynamically generated getter.

The code in listings 22.2 and 22.3 represents one approach to dealing with transient attributes in Core Data. The values of transient attributes are typically generated "lazily"—that is, only when needed instead of all of them being generated in advance. In this case the transient attribute values depend on other attributes of the same managed object, but in general they can depend on any information available while the app is running. The decision whether to cache the transient data by saving it to a file depends on how much work it takes to generate the data. In the PhotoWheel case, scaling images is relatively expensive in terms of CPU time, so caching makes sense. If a transient value were trivial to calculate, it would be better to not cache it but rather to calculate the value on the fly.

Syncing Photos with iCloud

PhotoWheel now has the changes it needs to minimize the amount of data it syncs via iCloud. At this point, you can make the changes needed to actually sync the data. You'll make two types of changes: one to make the app's persistent store coordinator work with ubiquitous data and one to make the app respond to incoming changes from the cloud.

> **Note**
>
> When testing an app with iCloud, you should create a new iCloud account that you use only for testing purposes. You'll need to sync test data and you may need to simply remove all of the app's iCloud data at various times. You probably want to be able to use your own app without constantly adding test data to your personal data or wiping it all out. Apple allows you to create more than one iCloud account. You'll need to log out from iCloud on your iPad and create a new, free account.

Making the Persistent Store Coordinator Ubiquitous

You tell a persistent store coordinator that it should make its data ubiquitous by providing iCloud-related configuration options when creating the coordinator. The only required option is called `NSPersistentStoreUbiquitousContentNameKey`. This option just indicates the name that should be used for the data in iCloud. If you like, you may also set a value for `NSPersistentStoreUbiquitousContentURLKey`, which allows control over the directory where the ubiquitous data is stored. If you don't provide a value for this key, Core Data will generate a directory name.

To enable cloud storage on the persistent store coordinator, replace the existing `persistentStoreCoordinator` method in AppDelegate.m with the version from Listing 22.4.

Listing 22.4 Configuring the Persistent Store Coordinator to Work with iCloud

```
- (NSPersistentStoreCoordinator *)persistentStoreCoordinator
{
    if (_persistentStoreCoordinator != nil)
    {
        return _persistentStoreCoordinator;
    }

    _persistentStoreCoordinator = [[NSPersistentStoreCoordinator alloc]
                    initWithManagedObjectModel:[self managedObjectModel]];

    NSURL *applicationDocumentsDirectory = [[[NSFileManager defaultManager]
                        URLsForDirectory:NSDocumentDirectory
                        inDomains:NSUserDomainMask]
                        lastObject];
    NSURL *storeURL = [applicationDocumentsDirectory
```

```
                    URLByAppendingPathComponent:@"PhotoWheel.sqlite"];

   dispatch_async(
         dispatch_get_global_queue(DISPATCH_QUEUE_PRIORITY_DEFAULT, 0), ^{

      // Build a URL to use as NSPersistentStoreUbiquitousContentURLKey
      NSURL *cloudURL = [[NSFileManager defaultManager]
                     URLForUbiquityContainerIdentifier:nil];

      NSDictionary *options = nil;

      if (cloudURL != nil) {
         NSString* coreDataCloudContent = [[cloudURL path]
                         stringByAppendingPathComponent:@"Photowheel"];
         cloudURL = [NSURL fileURLWithPath:coreDataCloudContent];

         options = @{NSPersistentStoreUbiquitousContentNameKey :
                        @"com.mycompany.photowheel",
                   NSPersistentStoreUbiquitousContentURLKey:
                         cloudURL
         };
      }

      NSError *error = nil;
      [_persistentStoreCoordinator lock];
      if (![_persistentStoreCoordinator
            addPersistentStoreWithType:NSSQLiteStoreType
            configuration:nil
            URL:storeURL
            options:options
            error:&error])
      {
         NSLog(@"Unresolved error %@, %@", error, [error userInfo]);
         abort();
      }
      [_persistentStoreCoordinator unlock];

      dispatch_async(dispatch_get_main_queue(), ^{
         NSLog(@"asynchronously added persistent store!");
         [[NSNotificationCenter defaultCenter]
          postNotificationName:kRefetchAllDataNotification
          object:self
          userInfo:nil];
      });
   });

   return _persistentStoreCoordinator;
}
```

This version of `persistentStoreCoordinator` starts off the same way the old version did, but then it uses `dispatch_async` to finish setting up the coordinator on a background thread. Everything in the block passed to `dispatch_async` will happen asynchronously on a different thread. This tactic avoids blocking the main thread, which controls the user interface. Connecting to iCloud requires Core Data to do extra work that can take a while, especially if there's a lot of preexisting iCloud data. Among other things, this work includes downloading any new changes that might have occurred since the last time the app ran on the current device. These changes are downloaded and integrated with the app's data store. Putting iCloud setup on a background thread lets the user interface stay responsive while the background thread waits. Any fetch requests the app runs to manage the UI will not return any results immediately, however, because the persistent store coordinator doesn't have a data store yet.

The first thing that happens in the background is building `cloudURL`, the URL where iCloud data will go. The code starts off by calling `NSFileManager`'s `URLForUbiquityContainerIdentifier:` method. This method asks iOS for the appropriate iCloud location in which to store iCloud data for your container ID. If you pass `nil` for the container ID, the method uses the first container ID found in the app's entitlements. Usually that's all you need, but in more complex cases you might have more than one container. You can't choose the URL's location—although you can create files and directories below the level of this URL. The code does just that by appending "Photowheel" to the URL and then setting `cloudURL` to the combined path.

Note that the `cloudURL` is not the same location as the actual data store file. That location is in `storeURL` and remains in the app's documents directory. With `cloudURL`, you're configuring how the persistent store coordinator works with iCloud, but the actual data store is in the same place it has always been. The location in `cloudURL` is used by Core Data to manage iCloud data.

The `persistentStoreCoordinator` custom getter method then creates a dictionary to contain the various options that the persistent store coordinator will use. It sets `cloudURL` as the value of `NSPersistentStoreUbiquitousContentURLKey` and *com.mycompany.photowheel* as the value of `NSPersistentStoreUbiquitousContent NameKey`. It is not necessary to use the app's Bundle ID for this key but it's convenient. Actually, the key can be anything that makes sense to you and to other developers on your team.

If `URLForUbiquityContainerIdentifier:` returns `nil`, the app leaves options set to `nil`. This would happen if the user has not configured an iCloud account. It would also happen if the user did configure an account but did not enable *Documents & Data*, which would mean that apps were not permitted to store data in the iCloud account. This might happen, for example, if you haven't configured the app's entitlements correctly. If you think iCloud should be available to the app but get a return value of `nil` here, review the app's provisioning and entitlements. With a `nil` return value here, the app continues as it would without iCloud, using local-only data.

Now that the options are configured, the `persistentStoreCoordinator` method adds the data store to the persistent store coordinator. Because this code is running in a background thread, it locks and unlocks the coordinator before making the change. Persistent store coordinators are not thread safe, but they have their own locking mechanism in case you need to access one from a different thread.

Once that step is complete, the code posts a notification to tell the rest of the app that the data store is now available. View controllers can listen for this notification and update their views. Up until this point, the persistent store coordinator didn't have a data store, so fetch operations would return no data. Now that the data store is available, view controllers need to refetch data to get data from the store. The method does this in another dispatch_async call, which calls back from the background to the main thread. It does this because the user interface should be updated only on the main thread.

The notification name is kRefetchAllDataNotification, which isn't defined yet. This notification will be posted by the app delegate and received in view controllers, so the notification name needs to be defined somewhere available to all of those classes. A convenient place to do so is in *PhotoWheel-Prefix.pch*, which is automatically included in all source files in the project. Add this single line to *PhotoWheel-Prefix.pch*:

```
#define kRefetchAllDataNotification @"RefetchAllDatabaseData"
```

Now you can use this notification name anywhere it is needed. It is a common convention to name constant variables or defined constants with names that start with k, but this nomenclature is not required.

Of course, that notification won't do any good unless the view controllers are actually listening for it. Both PhotosViewController and AlbumsViewController manage views using data from the data store, so both of them need to receive this notification and update their view. Add the code from Listing 22.5 to *AlbumsViewController.m*.

Listing 22.5   Updating AlbumsViewController When the Persistent Store Coordinator Has Loaded the Data Model

```
- (void)viewDidLoad
{
    [super viewDidLoad];

    [[NSNotificationCenter defaultCenter] addObserver:self
                  selector:@selector(handleCloudUpdate:)
                      name:kRefetchAllDataNotification
                    object:[[UIApplication sharedApplication] delegate]];
}

- (void)handleCloudUpdate:(NSNotification *)notification
{
    [self setFetchedResultsController:nil];
    [[self wheelView] reloadData];
}
```

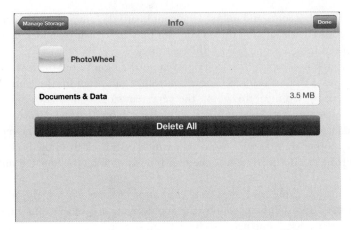

Figure 22.6   Deleting Documents & Data on iOS

When the notification is posted, this code gets rid of the existing fetched-results controller and then tells `wheelView` to reload its data. The fetched-results controller is re-created on demand in the `fetchedResultsController` method, which is called when `wheelView` starts asking for data. This time the fetch returns data found in the data store.

Now you need to make a couple of related changes so that `NSNotificationCenter` won't try to call the method when the view controller doesn't exist. The view controller should unregister for the notification when it is deallocated. Add a `dealloc` method to *AlbumsViewController.m* with the code from Listing 22.6.

Listing 22.6   **Unregistering for Notifications in `AlbumsViewController`**

```
- (void)dealloc
{
    [[NSNotificationCenter defaultCenter] removeObserver:self
                                    name:kRefetchAllDataNotification
                                    object:nil];
}
```

You need to make similar changes in `PhotosViewController`. The changes there are nearly identical to the ones just given, with the following exceptions:

- `PhotosViewController` already has a `-viewDidLoad` method, so add the code that begins observing `kRefetchAllDataNotification` to that method.
- `PhotosViewController` already has a `-dealloc` method, so add the code that stops observing `kRefetchAllDataNotification` to that method.
- Instead of calling `[[self wheelView] reloadData]` when the notification is posted, the `-handleCloudUpdate:` method should call `[self reload]` to reload the photo collection view.

Monitoring iCloud Data

When working with an app that sends data to iCloud, it's helpful to get confirmation that data is actually reaching the cloud server. It's also important to be able to delete the app's iCloud data, effectively resetting the iCloud state for the app.

You have a few options available for checking the cloud state for your app and clearing out iCloud data. The obvious place to do so is in the iOS Settings app (Figure 22.6). In the iCloud section, tap **Storage & Backup** and then **Manage Storage** to see all apps on the device that have uploaded data iCloud. Tap on a specific app to see information about how much space each app uses. Tapping the **Edit** button on this screen lets you delete an app's iCloud data.

It's also possible to perform these operations on your Mac, if you're logged in to the same iCloud account. On Macs, the iCloud daemon downloads all iCloud data for all apps that the iCloud account uses, including iOS apps. Look in the Mac's System Preferences application, in the iCloud section. Clicking the **Manage** button brings up a view with the same information available on the iPad (Figure 22.7). As with the iPad, you can delete an app's iCloud data here.

Note

Checking the iCloud data on a Mac works only if the Mac is using the same iCloud account. If you're using a test iCloud account on your iPad, you'll need to use the same account on the Mac for this approach to work. If you're not using the same account, don't delete data this way.

The methods described here are purely local. In some cases, the command to delete the app's data might not have reached the iCloud server yet. If that happens, you might think you have deleted the data but then discover old data in your app. Fortunately,

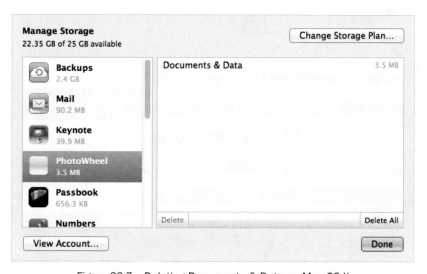

Figure 22.7   Deleting Documents & Data on Mac OS X

Apple provides a way to check in with the server and see what's happening. In your Web browser, go to **https://developer.icloud.com/** and log in with the same account you use for testing your app. You'll be able to browse the current iCloud data as it exists on the iCloud server. If you've deleted data on your iPad or Mac but the server still shows the data as being present, you may need to wait briefly for the deletion to take effect. If you wait and the data still doesn't disappear, try deleting the data from a different device.

Receiving Changes from iCloud

Great! Now the app can send data to iCloud. That's half the battle. Next, you need to make it notice incoming changes from the cloud relating to changes made on other devices.

When new changes are available, the iCloud daemon will download them in the background. These changes are saved to the data store automatically. Once this step is complete, the persistent store coordinator will post a notification with the ungainly name of NSPersistentStoreDidImportUbiquitousContentChangesNotification. At that point the data store is up-to-date with the latest iCloud changes, but they won't automatically show up in your app. Any managed objects in memory are still valid, and their values don't change. The app needs to tell any managed object contexts that it is using to get the incoming changes, and the app can then update its objects and views to reflect the new data.

To listen for this notification, change the managedObjectContext method in *AppDelegate.m* to look like Listing 22.7.

Listing 22.7   **Updated Code to Create the Managed Object Context**

```
- (NSManagedObjectContext *)managedObjectContext
{
    if (_managedObjectContext != nil) {
        return _managedObjectContext;
    }

    NSPersistentStoreCoordinator *coordinator =
                                    [self persistentStoreCoordinator];
    if (coordinator != nil) {
        _managedObjectContext = [[NSManagedObjectContext alloc]
                    initWithConcurrencyType:NSMainQueueConcurrencyType];
        [_managedObjectContext setPersistentStoreCoordinator:coordinator];
        [_managedObjectContext
                setMergePolicy:NSMergeByPropertyObjectTrumpMergePolicy];
        [[NSNotificationCenter defaultCenter]
        addObserver:self
        selector:@selector(mergeChangesFromCloud:)
        name:NSPersistentStoreDidImportUbiquitousContentChangesNotification
        object:coordinator];
```

```
    }
    return _managedObjectContext;
}
```

This code makes a few changes from the previous version. First, it changes the initialization of the context to use `NSMainQueueConcurrencyType`. As a consequence, any code executed by the managed object context will be performed on the main thread. To make that happen, it is necessary first to enclose any code that uses the context in a block, and then to execute that block using either `performBlock:` or `performBlockAndWait:`. Those methods can be called from any thread, and the managed object context will perform the block on the main thread. If you know that your code will run on the main thread, it's not necessary to use those methods.

In the previous version, the code didn't indicate which concurrency type to use, which means that the managed object context used the default concurrency type of `NSConfinementConcurrencyType`. That doesn't add any threading help; it just means that you assume responsibility for making sure that the context is used on only one thread. A third option is `NSPrivateQueueConcurrencyType`, which is similar to `NSMainQueueConcurrencyType` except that code executed by the managed object context is executed on a background queue. Typically `NSMainQueueConcurrencyType` would be used for managed object contexts that work with the user interface, and one of the other options would be used for background tasks such as downloading data from a Web service.

The next change is that this version of the method explicitly sets the context's merge policy. Merge policies are used when you need to tell a managed object context about changes to the data store that were made somewhere else—for example, by a different managed object context—or on a different device, as when changes arrive from iCloud. The merge policy determines how conflicts will be resolved. By default, conflicts cause merging to fail, which means that calling `save:` on the managed object context fails. With the `NSMergeByPropertyObjectTrumpMergePolicy` option enabled, if changes in memory conflict with objects loaded by the context, the in-memory changes should take priority. `NSManagedObjectContext` defines several other automatic merge policies that you can choose from depending on your app's requirements. You can also write custom code to merge changes if none of those options make sense in your app.

Once the context exists, the code adds `self` as an observer for incoming iCloud changes and arranges for notifications to call a method named `-mergeChangesFromCloud:`. That method is shown in Listing 22.8.

Listing 22.8 Callback for `NSPersistentStoreDidImportUbiquitousContentChangesNotification`

```
- (void)mergeChangesFromCloud:(NSNotification *)notification
{
    [[self managedObjectContext] performBlock:^{
```

```
    [[self managedObjectContext]
     mergeChangesFromContextDidSaveNotification:notification];
    [[self managedObjectContext] processPendingChanges];
  }];
}
```

The code in `mergeChangesFromCloud:` begins by merging the incoming changes into the managed object context using the `mergeChangesFromContextDidSave Notification:` method. This is often necessary even without iCloud, in cases where an app needs more than one managed object context. For example, an app might use a background thread to import a lot of data that should not be available to the main thread until all the changes have been saved. In that case it could use a secondary managed object context for the import operation and then merge those changes to the main thread when it finished. The built-in merging system has been designed to make one managed object context notice changes made in a different context, but it works just as well no matter where the changes actually come from. That makes it ideal for use with iCloud. If there are any unsaved changes in memory, they will be automatically merged with the incoming changes according to the merge policy in force for the managed object context.

How do you make the view controllers update their views to show the new changes? Believe it or not, we have already covered that. In PhotoWheel, the view controllers interact with Core Data using `NSFetchedResultsController`. One of the great things about that class is that it notices changes in the managed object context automatically and notifies its delegate. Because both `AlbumsViewController` and `PhotosView Controller` act as delegates to their `NSFetchedResultsController`, they are already configured to automatically receive any changes sent from iCloud.

Going Further with iCloud

This chapter has covered the basics of getting iCloud running in a new application. There are several other concerns that you may need to address, depending on the nature of your app.

Preexisting Data Stores

If you're adding iCloud support to an existing app that uses Core Data, you can't simply add iCloud options when adding the persistent store and expect to get full syncing. Syncing over iCloud depends on transaction logs, which are created whenever you save changes to the data store. Adding iCloud options when data already exists in the store does not automatically generate transactions for the existing data.

How do you get the transaction logs for existing data? By moving the data to a new data store. To do so, follow these steps:

1. Create a new empty data store, and include iCloud options when adding the persistent store.

2. Migrate the existing non-iCloud data store to the new data store file. `NSPersistentStoreCoordinator` provides a method that accomplishes this task in one step, called `migratePersistentStore:toURL:options:withType:error:`. In most cases that's all you need, but if you have very large data stores then you might need to use custom migration code.

3. Use the new iCloud data store. Delete the old local-only store.

This process means that every existing object is added to the new data store. In turn, every object appears in the outgoing transaction logs.

Duplicate Detection

In some situations, your app might receive an incoming iCloud update that creates a new object that duplicates an existing object. The most likely scenario is the preexisting data store situation described previously. In that case, each device upgrading to iCloud will send out object creation transactions for every object in the data store. If different devices already have some of the same data, they'll get new objects that duplicate what they already have. Unfortunately, iCloud does not automatically resolve the duplication, so if the user has more than one device, duplicates are inevitable.

It's also possible for duplicates to occur in other situations—for example, if the user is working offline and creates duplicate objects on more than one device, and then later connects those devices to the Internet.

You can handle this problem by running a de-duplication process whenever your app receives incoming changes that create new objects. The methods used for detecting that two objects are duplicates depend on your data model: Which field or fields would need to be identical before you would consider two objects to be duplicates instead of just being similar items?

Apple provides a good example of duplicate detection in its SharedCoreData sample application. This code was described in detail at WWDC 2012 in session 227, *Using iCloud with Core Data*.

Repeated Calls to `awakeFromInsert`

The `NSManagedObject` class has a method called `awakeFromInsert`, which is called once when a new managed object is inserted into a managed object context for the first time. It's common to override this method in `NSManagedObject` subclasses and use it as a general-purpose initializer.

That's fine when you're not using iCloud, but consider the life cycle of an object with iCloud. An object is created on one device and inserted into a managed object context. When this happens, `awakeFromInsert` is called. The object is then sent to iCloud and received on other devices. But there's the catch: On the receiving device, the object is inserted into a managed object context! In turn, `awakeFromInsert` is called again. Without iCloud, an object would be inserted for the first time into only one managed object context. With iCloud, it may be inserted into different contexts on different devices.

Extra calls to this method might or might not be a problem depending on which kind of initialization you do. In many cases it would result in duplicate but harmless extra work. In other cases it could lead to incorrect data. For example, if your managed objects have an attribute that records the date they were created, you would run the risk of changing that date every time the object synced to a new device. If calling the code more than once is potentially a problem, put the initialization code in a different method and call it yourself, instead of relying on Core Data to call the initialization code automatically.

Deleted Documents and Data

Earlier in this chapter we discussed the need to delete your app's iCloud data at times during testing. That ability is useful for getting back to a known starting point. If your app's users do it, however, it can be a problem—because they might delete the data *while your app is running.*

If that happens, your app is in trouble. Any existing transaction logs will disappear instantly. Your app's persistent store coordinator will still try to write transaction logs for new changes, but will fail because there's no place to write them. The most likely result will be a messy crash. What's worse is that there's no built-in notification that the user has deleted the data.

It's tempting to think that you might deal with this scenario by checking the iCloud status whenever your app enters the foreground on the user's iPad. For example, you could call `URLForPersistentStore:` and check for a `nil` result, or you could use `NSFileManager`'s `ubiquityIdentityToken` method. That approach doesn't go nearly far enough, though—don't forget, the user may have other iOS devices or Macs, and can delete your app's data from any of them.

To deal with this possibility, several developers have devised sentinel file schemes to create notifications. The general approach is to create an iCloud document outside of Core Data and then use an `NSFilePresenter` or `NSMetadataQuery` to provide notification if that file ever disappears. You can then take appropriate action. One example of such a scheme is NSConferenceiPhoneCoreDataRecipes[2] found in Black Pixel's Github repository. Other approaches to this problem are also possible, and solutions are still evolving, so be sure to look for current solutions.

Another challenge in this scenario is deciding how the app should respond. The user might have deleted the data by accident—but then again, maybe not. Perhaps the user decided that he doesn't want your app using iCloud for some reason. It's possible to recover by moving data back to iCloud, but that might not be what the user

---

2. NSConferenceiPhoneCoreDataRecipes: https://github.com/blackpixel/
   NSConferenceiPhoneCoreDataRecipes

wants. Consider what seems appropriate for your app and your users, and ask the user if there's no obvious answer.

Summary

Syncing is hard—not just from a technical standpoint, but also for logistical reasons. Many developers have made the mistake of thinking that this process would be simple, only to end up with code that never quite works right or that is still unfinished even after long development periods. With iCloud, some of the heavy lifting is done for you, at no extra charge. PhotoWheel now syncs its photos via iCloud, so it can be used on multiple devices with the same data. It is these kinds of details that really make an app appealing.

In the next chapter we'll cover displaying photos over a wireless connection to external displays using Apple's AirPlay technology, so that PhotoWheel can present a slideshow of its photos.

Exercises

1. The code in this chapter that monitors incoming iCloud changes updates `Photos` `ViewController` and `AlbumsViewController`. But what if the user is viewing a photo in the photo browser, and the app receives an incoming change that deletes that photo? The best response is probably to return from the photo browser to the album view. Investigate how you could do this and implement the necessary code.

2. Merging changes from iCloud makes use of the managed object context's merge policy. Investigate the merge options defined by the `NSMergePolicy` class and choose one to use in PhotoWheel. Most likely, you would want to use `NSMerge` `ByPropertyObjectTrumpMergePolicyType`, which gives priority to unsaved local changes, but you might prefer one of the other options. You set a merge policy by using the `setMergePolicy:` method on the managed object context.

3. iCloud also has a key-value store that can be used to sync simple data about app state across devices; it is located in the `NSUbiquitousKeyValueStore` class. Investigate the key-value store and use it to save the current photo to iCloud. You'll need to add a new iCloud entitlement to the app.

23

Producing a Slideshow with AirPlay

Browsing through photos on the iPad's built-in screen works pretty well, but wouldn't it be nice to put on a slideshow with fancy transitions? Even better, wouldn't it be great to be able to show this slideshow on a larger external display, such as that big HDTV in your living room? Maybe even using an Apple TV to run the show over a wireless link?

In this chapter, you'll learn how to add a slideshow to PhotoWheel and make it work with external displays, whether connected via a video adapter or via wireless connections to AirPlay destinations.

External Display Options

All iPads support external displays. With the original iPad, video output worked with apps that were specifically coded to detect and use external displays. Displays had to use wired connections via a video adapter plugged into the iPad's 30-pin dock connector. Several adapters were available for digital video out, VGA displays, and other formats.

With more recent iPads, the external display system capabilities are *greatly* enhanced. These iPads can automatically mirror the internal display to a wired external display, so everything that happens on the built-in screen also happens on the external display. Also, newer iPads support AirPlay destinations such as the Apple TV, making it possible to use wireless video connections to external displays.

In all cases, using an external display changes a requirement that is otherwise absolute: the screen size. External displays will have different sizes and aspect ratios from the built-in display. Apps using external displays need to avoid making assumptions about screen size.

App Requirements for External Displays

In the simplest case, then, if your app is running on an iPad 2 or later, you don't actually need to do anything to use an external display. Whatever your app does on its main screen will automatically appear on an external display so long as the user has enabled device mirroring.

But we can do a whole lot better than that. Simply mirroring the internal display often doesn't produce the best user experience. If the external display doesn't have a touch-sensitive screen—and it almost certainly does not—it makes little sense to display user interface controls there. What is necessary and useful on the internal display becomes distracting clutter for someone sitting across the room watching a display that wouldn't handle touch events even if the viewer were close enough to reach it. A better app would make more appropriate use of an external display by leaving out useless content.

For apps that update their user interface based on device orientation, device rotation must also be considered when using an external display. The external display won't rotate when the iPad does, so you should consider whether the external display's content should adjust to match the device orientation. In some cases it will, but in many cases it won't. In PhotoWheel it doesn't, so in this chapter you'll make sure that external display content doesn't follow device rotation.

External Display API

Fortunately, the API to make an app work with a wired external display is almost exactly the same as the API for wireless AirPlay displays. Once the iPad connects to the device, this wireless connection becomes available to apps in exactly the same way as a wired display connection.

The starting point for working with external displays is the UIScreen class. It provides a class method, screens, that returns an array containing UIScreen instances for all currently available screens (Listing 23.1).

Listing 23.1 **Getting a List of All Currently Connected Screens**

```
NSArray *screens = [UIScreen screens];
if ([screens count] > 1) {
    NSLog(@"External display is connected");
}
```

The internal screen is guaranteed to be the first entry in the screens array. If the array contains more than one item, an external display is connected and available for use. It isn't currently possible to have more than one external display; only one AirPlay device can be selected at a given time. Connecting a wired external display terminates an AirPlay session, and it's not possible to initiate an AirPlay session while a wired external display is connected.

`UIScreen` provides methods and properties that provide details about the screen. The bounds property tells you the screen resolution. Some displays support more than one resolution. The `availableModes` property is an array of screen modes, each of which contains a supported screen resolution. By default, the `UIScreen` instance for an external display has its mode set to the one in the `preferredMode` property. That is usually the display's native resolution. Apps can change the mode, and therefore the resolution, if necessary, but only to modes defined in `availableModes`.

`UIScreen` posts notifications to let your app know when displays are connected or removed, in the form of the appropriately named `UIScreenDidConnectNotifica tion` and `UIScreenDidDisconnectNotification`. Both of these pass the newly connected or disconnected screen as the notification's object. It is important to listen for these notifications because displays can come and go at any time.

The typical flow when using an external display would be as follows:

1. When the app is ready to use an external display, it calls `[UIScreen screens]` to find out if one is currently connected. If so, it can start using it.

2. If the app receives `UIScreenDidDisconnectNotification`, it stops trying to use the external display.

3. If the app receives `UIScreenDidConnectNotification`, it gets the new screen and starts using it.

To put content on an external screen, an app creates a new instance of `UIWindow`. Normally just one `UIWindow` fills the iPad's display, but an external display needs its own instance. iPads don't support spanning a single window across multiple displays, so the existing window isn't sufficient. Once you have created the new `UIWindow`, you can move it to the external display by setting its `screen` property to the right `UIScreen` instance.

Attaching an External Display

You have a few options for attaching external displays. For wired connections, this process is straightforward: Get the appropriate video adapter, plug it in, and you're done. The display will be available to your app as the second entry in the `[UIScreen screens]` array.

For wireless connections over AirPlay, the work is only very slightly more involved. The most common approach is to use an Apple TV. Make sure the Apple TV and your iPad are on the same Wi-Fi network. Then, double-tap the iPad's **Home** button to show the application switcher, and drag to show the audio controls. If an AirPlay device is available, an AirPlay menu will appear (Figure 23.1).

You'll need to select the AirPlay device from the popup menu and enable mirroring. At that point, the Apple TV will be available as an external display indistinguishable

Figure 23.1   Enabling device mirroring over AirPlay

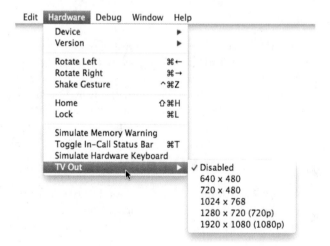

Figure 23.2   External display options in the iOS Simulator

from a wired display. Turning mirroring on and off will trigger `UIScreenDidConnect Notification` and `UIScreenDidConnectNotification` updates in your app.

If you don't have an Apple TV, several commercial applications are available to act as AirPlay destinations on a Mac (or a PC running Windows). In effect, they produce a simulated Apple TV, at least as far as using AirPlay is concerned. Both AirServer[1] and Reflector[2] will do the job. Both offer multiple screen resolutions and will work just like an Apple TV in your app. Neither application is free, but both are considerably cheaper than an Apple TV.

It's also possible to use have the iOS Simulator simulate an external display. The simulator's Hardware menu has an item labeled TV Out, which lists several screen resolutions (Figure 23.2).

If you select one of the TV Out options, the iOS Simulator opens a new window matching the size you selected. This window acts as an external display connected to the simulator. It's not a perfect solution. There is no automatic mirroring, so the simulator acts more like the original iPad than more recent models. Also, you can't simulate connecting and disconnecting displays while the app is running, because changing the TV Out option causes the simulated app to quit. Even so, the iOS Simulator is extremely convenient when you're debugging code that uses an external display.

Adding a Slideshow to PhotoWheel

PhotoWheel's slideshow will make use of two view controllers:

- `ExternalSlideShowViewController`: This class is used for external displays. It handles displaying photos and transitions between them, but doesn't provide any user interface controls and won't respond to device rotation.

- `MainScreenSlideShowViewController`: This class is used for the main screen. The main screen shows the same slideshow as the external display, so `MainScreen SlideShowViewController` will be a subclass of `ExternalSlideShowView Controller`. This relationship means that it inherits the code to display photos and transitions. This subclass adds code to detect and manage external displays and to create and destroy instances of `ExternalSlideShowViewController` as needed. It also adds user interface controls to allow the user to control the slideshow and runs the timer to automatically advance to the next photo. It responds to device rotation in the usual iPad style by rotating the display and controls.

`MainScreenSlideShowViewController` is in charge of the slideshow, because it always exists during slideshows (even if there are no external displays). Instances of `ExternalSlideShowViewController` will update their displays only when instructed to do so by `MainScreenSlideShowViewController`.

Start by creating these two classes. Don't forget to make `MainScreenSlideShow ViewController` a subclass of `ExternalSlideShowViewController`!

---

1. AirServer: http://www.airserverapp.com/
2. Reflector: http://www.reflectorapp.com

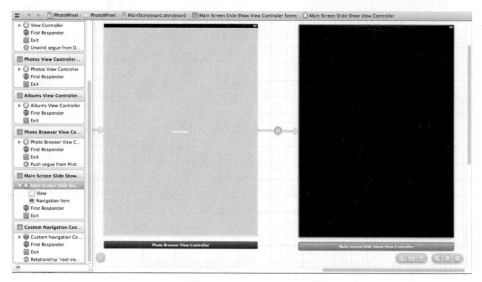

Figure 23.3   Adding the slideshow view controller to the storyboard

Updating the Storyboard

The existing `PhotoBrowserViewController` already has a **Slideshow** button that
was added in Chapter 17, "Creating a Photo Browser." We'll build on that capability to load the slideshow. Edit *MainStoryboard.storyboard* and add a new view controller
with a push segue from `PhotoBrowserViewController` (Figure 23.3).

Make the new view controller an instance of `MainScreenSlideShowViewCon`
`troller`, and name the segue `SlideshowSegue`. Set the background color of the
new view to black.

We'll implement the rest of the slideshow in code.

Adding the Slideshow Display

The first code we'll add implements `ExternalSlideShowViewController`. This
class handles displaying photos and transitions between them, and it is the superclass of
`MainScreenSlideShowViewController`.

To display photos, the class needs some way to find photos in the album. We'll do
this the same way as `PhotoBrowserViewController`—namely, by using an array of
photos. Because `PhotoBrowserViewController` will create the slideshow, the slideshow can use the same array as the photo browser.

Make *ExternalSlideShowViewController.h* look like Listing 23.2.

Listing 23.2   Interface for **`ExternalSlideShowViewController`**

```
#import <UIKit/UIKit.h>

@interface ExternalSlideShowViewController : UIViewController
```

```
@property (nonatomic, assign) NSInteger currentIndex;
@property (nonatomic, strong) NSArray *photos;

@property (nonatomic, strong) UIView *currentPhotoView;

@end
```

The first two instance variables deal with managing the photos. The `photos` array will be the same photo array used in the photo browser, and the `currentIndex` tells us which photo is currently displayed.

The last instance variable is a `UIView`, which displays the current photo. In most cases we would declare `currentPhotoView` in the implementation file instead of in the header. In this case, however, the subclass needs to know about it. Putting this declaration in the header file allows code in `MainScreenSlideShowViewControl ler` to access the view. If it were in the implementation file, the controller would be private, even from subclasses.

The slideshow display is handled in the custom setter method for `currentIndex`. Each time the photo index changes, this method updates the display to show the newly current photo. This method is shown in Listing 23.3. Add it to `ExternalSlideShow ViewController.m`. Also be sure to add an `#import` for `Photo.h` at the top of that file so that the compiler will know about the Photo class.

Listing 23.3   Custom Setter Method for `currentIndex` in `ExternalSlideShow ViewController`

```
- (void) setCurrentIndex: (NSInteger) rawNewCurrentIndex
{
    NSInteger currentIndex = rawNewCurrentIndex;
    if ((currentIndex == [self currentIndex]) &&
        ([[[self view] subviews] count] != 0))
    {
        return;
    }

    if (currentIndex < 0) {
        currentIndex = [[self photos] count] - 1;
    }
    if (currentIndex >= [[self photos] count]) {
        currentIndex = 0;
    }

    // Create a new image view for the current photo.
    Photo *newPhoto = [[self photos] objectAtIndex:currentIndex];
    UIImage *newImage = [newPhoto largeImage];
    UIImageView *newPhotoView = [[UIImageView alloc] initWithImage:newImage];
```

```
[newPhotoView setContentMode:UIViewContentModeScaleAspectFit];
CGRect photoViewFrame = [[self view] bounds];
[newPhotoView setFrame:photoViewFrame];
[newPhotoView setAutoresizingMask:
    (UIViewAutoresizingFlexibleWidth|UIViewAutoresizingFlexibleHeight)];

if ([self currentPhotoView] == nil) {
    // If there's no photo view yet, just add the new one.
    [[self view] addSubview:newPhotoView];
} else {
    // If there's already a photo view, replace it with animation.
    NSInteger transitionOptions;
    // Use the incoming value of the new index to decide if we're
    // moving forward or backward through the photos. Curl up for
    // moving forward, down for moving backward.
    if (rawNewCurrentIndex > [self currentIndex]) {
        transitionOptions = UIViewAnimationOptionTransitionCurlUp;
    } else {
        transitionOptions = UIViewAnimationOptionTransitionCurlDown;
    }

    // Replace the current photo view with the new one.
    [UIView transitionFromView:[self currentPhotoView]
                        toView:newPhotoView
                      duration:1.0
                       options:transitionOptions
                    completion:^(BOOL finished) {
                    }];
}

[self setCurrentPhotoView:newPhotoView];
_currentIndex = currentIndex;
}
```

First, the setter checks the incoming value to see if it matches the current value. If so, it's best to skip the rest of the method with its work of looking up a photo and creating a view for it. The method continues, however, if [self view] doesn't have any subviews yet, because that state indicates that no photo is currently being displayed. This will happen the first time the setter is called.

Next, the setter checks the new value for currentIndex to make sure it is valid. It needs to be a valid index for the photos array. The index can't be less than zero, and the upper limit depends on the number of photos in the album.

Next, this method gets the photo at the requested index and creates first a UIImage containing the photo's largeImage and then a UIImageView to display it. The content mode tells the image view to scale the photo to fit the display subject to the constraint that the aspect ratio (shape) cannot change. The autoresizing mask tells the image view that its size and shape should change when its parent view's size and shape change, so that it always fills the parent view.

If currentPhotoView is nil, this result implies that no photo is being displayed. Such would be the case when the slideshow first loads. In that case the code just adds newPhotoView to the view hierarchy. Otherwise, the code arranges to replace currentPhotoView with newPhotoView using a fancy visual transition. If the new index is greater than the old one or if the index has wrapped around to zero, the transition is a page curl upward. If the new index is less than the old one or if the index has wrapped around to the upper end of the range, the transition is a page curl downward. The code chooses the transition by comparing the original incoming new index value to the current index.

The code replaces the old photo view with the new one using a UIView class method that replaces one view with another in the view hierarchy. One line of code removes currentPhotoView from the view hierarchy and inserts newPhotoView in its place. The options argument specifies how the change should occur. The last argument takes a block that executes when the animation finishes. We don't need to do anything when that happens, so we leave it empty. The code then updates the values of currentPhotoView and currentIndex.

That takes care of most of ExternalSlideShowViewController, but there's one more detail to cover. We want to ignore device rotation in this class, so that the external display won't rotate when the device does. Add the method in Listing 23.4 to ExternalSlideShowViewController to implement this feature.

Listing 23.4   **Disabling Autorotation on External Displays**

```
- (BOOL)shouldAutorotate
{
    return NO;
}
```

Managing External Displays

Now that the app can display slideshow photos, let's add the internal screen component that will handle detecting and managing external displays.

MainScreenSlideShowViewController subclasses ExternalSlideShowViewController but does not add any new public instance variables. It does add several private instance variables in a class extension. Add the declarations in Listing 23.5 to *MainScreenSlideShowViewController.m*.

Listing 23.5   **Private Instance Variables in `MainScreenSlideShowViewController`**

```
@interface MainScreenSlideShowViewController ()
@property (nonatomic, strong) NSTimer *slideAdvanceTimer;
@property (nonatomic, assign, getter = isChromeHidden) BOOL chromeHidden;
@property (nonatomic, strong) NSTimer *chromeHideTimer;
@property (nonatomic, strong) ExternalSlideShowViewController
                                    *externalDisplaySlideshowController;
@property (nonatomic, strong) UIWindow *externalScreenWindow;
@end
```

The new instance variables serve the following purposes:

- `slideAdvanceTimer`: This variable periodically calls a method that automatically advances to the next photo while the slideshow is running.

- `chromeHidden`, `chromeHideTimer`: These variables are used to make the user interface controls show and hide automatically. They work just like the ones in `PhotoBrowserViewController`, so we won't spend any time on them here.

- `externalDisplaySlideshowController`: When an external display is connected, this variable will point to the `ExternalSlideShowViewController` displaying photos on that display.

- `externalScreenWindow`: When an external display is connected, this variable will point to the `UIWindow` instance managing content on that display.

As you might guess from the inclusion `chromeHidden` and `chromeHideTimer`, the slideshow will show and hide user interface controls in the same way as `Photo BrowserViewController`. In fact, the code is exactly the same, so you can just copy all of the methods in the Chrome helpers section of *PhotoBrowserViewController.m* into *MainScreenSlideShowViewController.m*.

To detect and configure external displays, we'll add two methods to `MainScreen SlideShowViewController`. The code in Listing 23.6 looks for any external displays and returns the result. If no external displays are found, it returns nil. `MainScreen SlideShowViewController` calls this method from `viewDidLoad:` to determine whether an external display is already available.

Listing 23.6   **Detecting External Displays**

```
- (UIScreen *)getExternalScreen
{
    NSArray *screens = [UIScreen screens];
    UIScreen *externalScreen = nil;
    if ([screens count] > 1) {
        // The internal screen is guaranteed to be at index 0.
        externalScreen = [screens lastObject];
    }
```

```
    return externalScreen;
}
```

When an external display is connected, `MainScreenSlideShowViewController` will call the `configureExternalScreen:` method in Listing 23.7 to create the display's window and view controller.

Listing 23.7 **Configuring an External Display**

```
- (void)configureExternalScreen:(UIScreen *)externalScreen
{
    // Clear any existing external screen items
    [self setExternalDisplaySlideshowController:nil];
    [self setExternalScreenWindow:nil];

    // Create a new window and move it to the external screen
    [self setExternalScreenWindow:[[UIWindow alloc]
                      initWithFrame:[externalScreen applicationFrame]]];
    [[self externalScreenWindow] setScreen:externalScreen];

    // Create a ExternalSlideShowViewController to handle slides on the
    // external screen
    ExternalSlideShowViewController *externalSlideController =
            [[ExternalSlideShowViewController alloc] init];
    [self setExternalDisplaySlideshowController:externalSlideController];
    [externalSlideController setPhotos:[self photos]];
    [externalSlideController setCurrentIndex:[self currentIndex]];

    // Add the external slideshow view to the external window and
    // resize it to fit
    [[self externalScreenWindow] addSubview:
            [externalSlideController view]];
    [[externalSlideController view]
            setFrame:[[self externalScreenWindow] frame]];

    // Set the external screen view's background color to match the
    // one configured in the storyboard
    [[externalSlideController view]
     setBackgroundColor:[[self view] backgroundColor]];

    // Show the window
    [[self externalScreenWindow] makeKeyAndVisible];
}
```

This method begins by removing any window and view controller that already exist for an external screen. Because the app will be detecting display connect and disconnect events, these objects should already be `nil`. With AirPlay, though, it's sometimes possible to receive multiple connection events with no intervening disconnect event. For this reason, it's best to make sure that the app starts "clean" here.

This method then creates a `UIWindow` for the external display. The window's `frame` is the same as the `applicationFrame` property of the screen—that is, the area available for use by the app. The next step is to move this window to the new screen. You can move a window to a new screen at any time, but if the window already has content, it can be an expensive operation. Consequently, it's best to move the window first and add content to it later.

Next we create an `ExternalSlideShowViewController` to display slides on the external display. Because this is a new instance, we also need to set the `photos` array and the `currentIndex` of the new view controller to match `self`'s values. They need to be the same as their counterparts in `MainScreenSlideShowViewController` so that the internal and external displays will show the same photos.

Once the view controller exists, we add its view to the `UIWindow` we just created and resize the view to match the window's `size`. External displays come in a variety of sizes, so we can't determine the size in advance; thus we need to set the view's `size` here. We then set the view's background color to match `[self view]`'s background color, which is the one configured in the storyboard. Finally, we call `makeKeyAndVisible` to make the new window visible on the external display. At this point, the slideshow actually appears there.

We'll make use of these methods in `viewDidLoad`. We need to check whether an external display is already connected and register for notifications of screens being connected and disconnected. Use the code in Listing 23.8 for `MainScreenSlide ShowViewController`'s `viewDidLoad`.

Listing 23.8 **Setting up External Screen Management in `MainScreenSlideShowViewController`**

```
- (void)viewDidLoad
{
    [super viewDidLoad];

    // Make sure to set wantsFullScreenLayout or the photo
    // will not display behind the status bar.
    [self setWantsFullScreenLayout:YES];

    [self updateNavBarButtonsForPlayingState:YES];

    // Check for an extra screen existing right now
    UIScreen *externalScreen = [self getExternalScreen];
    if (externalScreen != nil) {
        [self configureExternalScreen:externalScreen];
    }
```

```
    // Add observers for screen connect/disconnect
    NSNotificationCenter *nc = [NSNotificationCenter defaultCenter];
    [nc addObserver:self
           selector:@selector(screenDidConnect:)
               name:UIScreenDidConnectNotification
             object:nil];
    [nc addObserver:self
           selector:@selector(screenDidDisconnect:)
               name:UIScreenDidDisconnectNotification
             object:nil];
}

- (void)screenDidConnect:(NSNotification *)notification
{

    UIScreen *newExternalScreen = [notification object];
    [self configureExternalScreen:newExternalScreen];

}

- (void)screenDidDisconnect:(NSNotification *)notification
{

    [self setExternalDisplaySlideshowController:nil];
    [self setExternalScreenWindow:nil];

}
```

The code in viewDidLoad starts by setting wantsFullScreenLayout to YES, as with the photo browser. It then invokes a method called updateNavBarButtonsFor PlayingState:. This method handles the slideshow controls, and we'll discuss it shortly.

Next, viewDidLoad calls the getExternalScreen method to look for external displays. If one is found, it calls configureExternalScreen to set up the display's contents.

Following this, the code registers for UIScreenDidConnectNotification and UIScreenDidDisconnectNotification to track screen events. If a new display is connected, the code calls the screenDidConnect method, which uses configure ExternalScreen to add content to the screen. If a display is disconnected, the code calls screenDidDisconnect. That method disposes of the externalDisplaySlide showController and externalScreenWindow instance variables, as they are no longer needed.

Advancing to the Next Photo

The app can now display slideshow-related view controllers on one or more displays. To actually perform a slideshow, we need to add a timer to automatically advance to the next slide at regular intervals. We also need to arrange for the main screen slideshow controller to tell the external display when to change photos. We'll do this in `MainScreenSlideShowViewController`, as it is always present during slideshows.

Create another custom setter method for `currentIndex` so that setting the current index on the main screen slideshow controller also updates the external display, if there is one. This setter is given in Listing 23.9.

Listing 23.9   **Custom Setter for `currentIndex` in**
              `MainScreenSlideShowViewController`

```
- (void) setCurrentIndex: (NSInteger) currentIndex
{
    [super setCurrentIndex:currentIndex];
    [[self externalDisplaySlideshowController]
            setCurrentIndex:currentIndex];

    [[self currentPhotoView] setUserInteractionEnabled:YES];
    UITapGestureRecognizer *photoTapRecognizer =
    [[UITapGestureRecognizer alloc]
     initWithTarget:self
     action:@selector(photoTapped:)];
    [[self currentPhotoView] addGestureRecognizer:photoTapRecognizer];
}
```

First, of course, the setter calls `super`'s implementation, which we discussed earlier. Next, it calls `setCurrentIndex` on the external display's view controller to update the photo displayed there. If there is no external display, `[self externalDisplay SlideShowController]` will be nil. As you probably recall, sending a message to `nil` in Objective-C is valid and is equivalent to doing nothing, so we don't need to check for `nil` first.

The code does a little more setup for `currentPhotoView`, adding a tap gesture recognizer that calls the `photoTapped:` method. As with `PhotoBrowserViewController`, this is part of the chrome-hiding system. Buttons will automatically hide after a few seconds but will reappear when the user taps on the screen.

Advancing to the next photo is managed by an `NSTimer`, which periodically updates `currentIndex`. Add an implementation of `viewWillAppear:` for this class, using the code in Listing 23.10.

Listing 23.10   **Creating a Timer to Automatically Move to the Next Photo**

```
- (void) viewWillAppear: (BOOL) animated
{
    [super viewWillAppear:animated];
```

```
NSTimer *timer = [NSTimer scheduledTimerWithTimeInterval:5.0
                                          target:self
                                        selector:@selector(advanceSlide:)
                                        userInfo:nil
                                         repeats:YES];
    [self setSlideAdvanceTimer:timer];

    [self startChromeDisplayTimer];
}
```

This code creates an `NSTimer` that calls the `advanceSlide:` method on `self` every 5 seconds. It also creates the chrome display timer, again as in the photo browser.

The `advanceSlide:` method is shown in Listing 23.11.

Listing 23.11 Advancing to the Next Photo

```
- (void)advanceSlide:(NSTimer *)timer
{
    [self setCurrentIndex:[self currentIndex] + 1];
}
```

This method simply increments `currentIndex`. Doing so calls both `self` and super's custom setter methods, which in turn update the photo display on both internal and external displays. This method doesn't bother checking whether the new value is valid, because that task is handled in the setter.

`MainScreenSlideShowViewController` should clean up after itself when it leaves the screen. As part of this clean-up, it needs to remove the slideshow and chrome timers as well as objects that manage the external display. This activity should happen in `viewWillDisappear`, which will be called whenever the user ends a slideshow. Make `MainScreenSlideShowViewController`'s `viewWillDisappear` method look like Listing 23.12.

Listing 23.12 Cleaning up `MainScreenSlideShowViewController` Data When a Slideshow Ends

```
- (void)viewWillDisappear:(BOOL)animated
{
    [self cancelChromeDisplayTimer];
    [[self slideAdvanceTimer] invalidate];
    [self setSlideAdvanceTimer:nil];
    [self setExternalDisplaySlideshowController:nil];
    [self setExternalScreenWindow:nil];
}
```

Adding Slideshow User Interface Controls

The main screen slideshow display will include some basic user interface controls. Users will be able to pause or resume slideshows and to manually advance to the next or previous photo in the album. We'll handle these tasks with buttons on the navigation bar, again using an approach similar to `PhotoBrowserViewController`.

The `-updateNavBarButtonsForPlayingState:` method in Listing 23.13 creates these buttons. It takes one argument, a `BOOL` that indicates whether the navigation bar should include a play button or a pause button.

Listing 23.13 **Adding Slideshow Controls**

```
- (void)updateNavBarButtonsForPlayingState:(BOOL)playing
{
    UIBarButtonItem *rewindButton = [[UIBarButtonItem alloc]
                initWithBarButtonSystemItem:UIBarButtonSystemItemRewind
                target:self
                action:@selector(backOnePhoto:)];
    [rewindButton setStyle:UIBarButtonItemStyleBordered];
    UIBarButtonItem *playPauseButton;
    if (playing) {
        playPauseButton = [[UIBarButtonItem alloc]
                initWithBarButtonSystemItem:UIBarButtonSystemItemPause
                target:self
                action:@selector(pause:)];
    } else {
        playPauseButton = [[UIBarButtonItem alloc]
                initWithBarButtonSystemItem:UIBarButtonSystemItemPlay
                target:self
                action:@selector(resume:)];
    }
    [playPauseButton setStyle:UIBarButtonItemStyleBordered];
    UIBarButtonItem *forwardButton = [[UIBarButtonItem alloc]
            initWithBarButtonSystemItem:UIBarButtonSystemItemFastForward
            target:self
            action:@selector(forwardOnePhoto:)];
    [forwardButton setStyle:UIBarButtonItemStyleBordered];

    NSArray *slideShowControls = @[forwardButton, playPauseButton,
                            rewindButton];

    [[self navigationItem] setRightBarButtonItems:slideShowControls];
}
```

The general idea in this method is the same as in `PhotoBrowserViewController`'s `addButtonsToNavigationBar` method. The code creates several `UIBarButtonItem` instances and adds them to the navigation item. The difference here is that the collection of buttons depends on the `playing` argument. If `playing` is `YES`, the toolbar includes a pause button. If playing is `NO`, the toolbar includes a play button.

The actions triggered by these buttons are shown in Listing 23.14.

Listing 23.14 **Actions for Slideshow Controls**

```
- (void)pause:(id)sender
{
    [[self slideAdvanceTimer] setFireDate:[NSDate distantFuture]];
    [self updateNavBarButtonsForPlayingState:NO];
}


- (void)resume:(id)sender
{
    [[self slideAdvanceTimer] setFireDate:[NSDate date]];
    [self updateNavBarButtonsForPlayingState:YES];
}

- (void)backOnePhoto:(id)sender
{
    [self pause:nil];
    [self setCurrentIndex:[self currentIndex] - 1];
}

- (void)forwardOnePhoto:(id)sender
{
    [self pause:nil];
    [self setCurrentIndex:[self currentIndex] + 1];
}
```

In the `-pause:` method, we want to stop the automatic photo advance timer. We could do this in several different ways. Here, we choose to manually change the timer's fire time. Normally, this event repeats at regular intervals, but it is possible to override this behavior and tell an `NSTimer` when it should fire next. It should sit idle until that time occurs. In the preceding code, we set the time to `[NSDate distantFuture]`. The exact meaning of `distantFuture` is not documented except to say that it is centuries into the future. For our purposes, we can regard this value as meaning "never," which effectively pauses the timer. This method also updates the toolbar buttons so that the pause button will be replaced by a play button.

When `-resume:` is called, we undo the effects of `-pause:`. To resume automatic slide advancement, we again update the timer's fire date, this time telling it to fire immediately. The timer firing will then continue at its scheduled interval. We again update the toolbar buttons, this time putting the pause button back.

The `-backOnePhoto:` and `-forwardOnePhoto:` methods move to the previous and next photos, respectively, by changing `currentIndex`. Again, we don't bother checking whether the new values for `currentIndex` are valid here because the setter method will take care of that task. In both cases we also pause the auto-advance timer, because tapping either of these buttons implies that the user wants to take control of the photo display.

Updating the Photo Browser

Great, we now have a slideshow! Except . . . we don't have any code to load it yet. We need to do something about that.

`PhotoBrowserViewController` already has a placeholder method called `-slideshow:` that is connected to the **Slideshow** button. In addition, we now have a segue named `SlideshowSegue` that loads the slideshow. The obvious thing to do, then, is to connect these two by implementing `slideshow:`, as shown in Listing 23.15.

Listing 23.15   **Loading the Slideshow from `PhotoBrowserViewController`**

```
- (void)slideshow:(id)sender
{
    [self performSegueWithIdentifier:@"SlideshowSegue" sender:self];
}
```

We also need to tell the new slideshow which photo it should start at and provide it with some photos. We'll do this by implementing `prepareForSegue:` in `PhotoBrowserViewController`, as shown in Listing 23.16.

Listing 23.16   **Configuring the Slideshow in `PhotoBrowserViewController`**

```
- (void)prepareForSegue:(UIStoryboardSegue *)segue sender:(id)sender
{
    if ([[segue identifier] isEqualToString:@"SlideshowSegue"]) {
        MainScreenSlideShowViewController *slideShowController =
                                      [segue destinationViewController];
        [slideShowController setPhotos:[self photos]];
        [slideShowController setCurrentIndex:[self currentIndex]];
        [self setSlideShowController:slideShowController];

        [self setTitle:@"Photo Browser"];
    }
}
```

This method is straightforward; all it does is provide the new `MainScreenSlide ShowViewController` with some photos and an index in the list of photos. Make sure to add an `#import` statement for *MainScreenSlideShowViewController.h* so that the compiler will know about that class here. The code also saves a reference to the slide-show controller, which we'll provide by adding the following declaration in the class extension:

```
@property (nonatomic, strong) MainScreenSlideShowViewController *slideShowController;
```

The code in Listing 23.16 also changes self's title to be "Photo Browser." This text will appear in the navigation bar's "back" button while the slideshow is running.

Why do we need to keep a reference to the slideshow controller, you may ask? There's one more thing we really should do, for consistency of user experience. The slideshow will start with whatever photo is being displayed in the photo browser. When the slideshow finishes, the photo browser should show the last photo displayed. Going back to the initial photo would be slightly jarring, as it would unexpectedly change photos when the slideshow finishes. We'll accomplish this goal by changing PhotoBrowserViewController's viewWillAppear:, replacing the lines that set currentIndex and scrolling to that index with the lines shown in Listing 23.17.

Listing 23.17 **Updated Code to Set currentIndex in PhotoBrowserViewController's viewDidAppear:**

```
if ([self slideShowController] == nil) {
    [self setCurrentIndex:[self startAtIndex]];
    [self scrollToIndex:[self startAtIndex]];
} else {
    [self setCurrentIndex:[[self slideShowController] currentIndex]];
    [self scrollToIndex:[[self slideShowController] currentIndex]];
    [self setSlideShowController:nil];
}
```

In this updated code, if the view is appearing for the first time, it proceeds as before—that is, it sets currentIndex to the value of startIndex and updates the scroll view. However, if the view is loading because a slideshow has just finished, the code instead updates currentIndex to the slideshow's index value. This way, the photo browser shows whatever photo was just shown in the slideshow. The code then disposes of the slideShowController reference, as it is no longer needed.

Finishing Up

We need one more change to make the slideshow work. Back in Chapter 15, "View Controllers and Segues," you added CustomNavigationController to produce a nice zooming effect when popping a view controller off of the naviga-tion stack. The effect won't work here without some changes, because the code depends on instance variables that the slideshow controller doesn't have. Given that the zooming effect doesn't make sense in this case, we'll arrange to bypass it and let

`UINavigationController` handle the transition. Add the code in Listing 23.18 to the `-popViewControllerAnimated:` method in `CustomNavigationController`.

Listing 23.18   **Preventing Unwanted Zoom Animations**

```
if (![sourceViewController isKindOfClass:
      [PhotoBrowserViewController class]]) {
    return [super popViewControllerAnimated:animated];
}
```

Also, be sure to add an `#import` of *PhotoBrowserViewController.h* in this class.

The preceding code bypasses all of the work for the animation unless the view controller being popped is an instance of `PhotoBrowserViewController`. As that's the only time when a transition is appropriate, it's the only time the code for the transition will run.

Summary

A slideshow on an external display is a great way to share photos with a group of people—just don't overdo it on the vacation photos. In this chapter, we covered how to run a slideshow and how to make use of both wired and wireless external displays. The code for making use of external displays will work with any kind of content and uses the familiar Cocoa Touch APIs. You can also take AirPlay further and send audio or video over the wireless link. Many apps can benefit from intelligent use of external displays, and now PhotoWheel is among them.

In the next chapter we'll explore the Core Image framework. We'll add fun and entertaining image transformations and see how to make PhotoWheel locate and zoom in on faces in a picture.

Exercises

1. The slideshow transition in `setCurrentIndex:` uses a page-curl effect when changing slides. Experiment with other transition effects, such as the flip-style transitions offered by `UIViewAnimationOptionTransitionFlipFromRight` and `UIViewAnimationOptionTransitionFlipFromLeft`.

2. This chapter's code didn't set the animation timing to use when changing slides, so it used the default setting of `UIViewAnimationOptionCurveEaseInOut`. Look up some other view animation options in the documentation for `UIView` and try different timing options. Try some others, such as `UIViewAnimationOption CurveEaseIn` or `UIViewAnimationOptionCurveLinear`.

Visual Effects with Core Image

Sometimes photos don't come out as well as you hoped. Perhaps the image is too dark, or too light, or maybe the people have red eyes. Most photo management software includes basic editing features to help you deal with these problems as well as visual effects that can be applied to change photos in fun and interesting ways. Wouldn't it be nice if PhotoWheel could do that, too? By the end of this chapter, it will: Enter Core Image.

In this chapter we'll use Core Image to add these features and more. We'll explore creating filters to create visual effects and to automatically enhance photos. We'll also see how Core Image can locate faces in a picture.

Core Image Concepts

Core Image provides visual effects for use with both photos and video. It includes a variety of color alterations and enhancements, image compositing effects for combining multiple images, automatic photo enhancement including red-eye repair, and face detection. It works nondestructively on images, and effects can be chained together to perform more complex transformations.

We'll focus mainly on `CIFilter`, the Core Image Filter class. A `CIFilter` typically takes one or two images and one or more configuration parameters as inputs and produces a single output image. iOS includes numerous built-in filters that perform different image operations. `CIFilter`s work on instances of `CIImage`, which is Core Image's image class. Figure 24.1 shows a simple example.

`CIFilter`s can be chained together by simply connecting the output image of one filter to the input image of another filter. In this way, you can combine multiple effects to create more complex results. Figure 24.2 shows an example of using multiple filters on the same original image.

An important concept when using Core Image is that `CIFilter` does not actually produce images. Instead, it produces image *recipes*—that is, instructions for how to create a particular image. Setting up filters defines the steps from input image to output, but does not actually render the filtered output image. Getting the output image from a `CIFilter` doesn't apply the filter; instead, it creates a recipe for a filtered image.

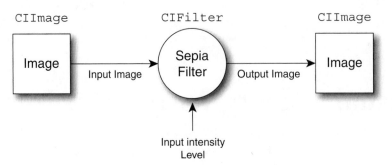

Figure 24.1   Single `CIFilter` example with one input image and one configuration parameter

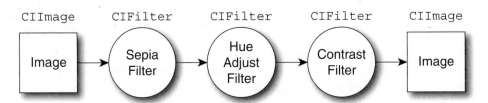

Figure 24.2   Chaining multiple `CIFilters` for more complex effects

Rendering filtered images is the responsibility of a Core Image context, which is an instance of `CIContext`. `CIContexts` do the work of applying the `CIFilter`'s recipe to produce the final image. Once the final image is rendered, a `UIImage` can be used to display the image on the screen or to save it to a file or to the user's photo library.

CPU or GPU?

`CIContexts` can process images on either the CPU or the GPU, giving you a choice between software and hardware image rendering. You can specify which approach to use when you create the context.

It's tempting to think that the GPU would always be the better choice because it's dedicated to graphics processing and leaves the CPU free for other work. That's not always the case, though. Both CPU and GPU `CIContexts` have limits on the size of their input and output images, and the GPU limit is much smaller than the CPU limit. Also, Core Animation uses the GPU, so if your app is doing animations, the GPU may already be busy with other work. Finally, CPU rendering uses higher-precision math and can produce more accurate results.

Introducing `CIFilter`

iOS includes numerous built-in filters. You could read about them in the documentation, but you can also ask the runtime environment what is available. You can get a list of all filter names directly from `CIFilter`:

```
NSArray *filterNames = [CIFilter filterNamesInCategory:kCICategoryBuiltIn];
```

As the method name implies, a variety of filter categories exist. Some filters belong to more than one category. The preceding line of code asks for all built-in filters. For PhotoWheel, we might look up filters in the `kCICategoryStillImage` category instead, as it contains all filters that work on still images.

Filter names are strings. Some examples include `CIHueAdjust`, `CICrop`, and `CIColorInvert`. `CIFilter` can also provide detailed information about how to use each filter via its `attributes` method. Filter attributes describe each of the filter's inputs, including acceptable values. For example, the code in Listing 24.1 looks up information on the `CISepiaTone` filter.

Listing 24.1   **Looking up Attributes of the `CISepiaTone` Filter**

```
CIFilter *sepiaFilter = [CIFilter filterWithName:@"CISepiaTone"];
NSLog(@"CISepiaTone attributes: %@", [sepiaFilter attributes]);
```

The result of running this code is shown in Listing 24.2.

Listing 24.2   **Attributes of `CISepiaTone` Filter**

```
2012-12-04 21:04:57.098 CIDemo[3337:907] CISepiaTone attributes: {
    CIAttributeFilterCategories =     (
        CICategoryColorEffect,
        CICategoryVideo,
        CICategoryInterlaced,
        CICategoryNonSquarePixels,
        CICategoryStillImage,
        CICategoryBuiltIn
    );
    CIAttributeFilterDisplayName = "Sepia Tone";
    CIAttributeFilterName = CISepiaTone;
    inputImage =     {
        CIAttributeClass = CIImage;
        CIAttributeType = CIAttributeTypeImage;
    };
    inputIntensity =     {
        CIAttributeClass = NSNumber;
        CIAttributeDefault = 1;
        CIAttributeIdentity = 0;
        CIAttributeMax = 1;
```

```
        CIAttributeMin = 0;
        CIAttributeSliderMax = 1;
        CIAttributeSliderMin = 0;
        CIAttributeType = CIAttributeTypeScalar;
    };
}
```

From this output, we see that `CISepiaTone` has two inputs. The first, `inputImage`, is an image to filter; the second, `inputIntensity`, is the intensity of the sepia tone effect. The attributes dictionary indicates the expected class for each argument and a Core Image type field. For the intensity input, it also includes a variety of details about acceptable values, including the minimum, the maximum, the default, and suggestions for which values to use on a slider-style UI control. The attributes even include `CIAttributeFilterDisplayName`, a suggested display name suitable for presenting data to users. By inspecting filter attributes it is possible to generate user interface controls for filters dynamically, without hard-coding any of the information about the filter.

Filter Types

Built-in filters are grouped into more than a dozen different categories, but in general they fall into three distinct groups:

- **Filters that alter single images.** These filters take one input image and a variable number of configuration parameters. They include filters that change an image's colors and those that apply an affine transform to an image.

- **Filters that combine images.** These filters take two input images and combine them using one of a variety of image compositing or blending techniques.

- **Filters that generate images.** These filters have no input image but take one or more configuration parameters. They create new images that contain gradients, checkerboards, or other designs whose appearance is determined by the input values.

In this chapter we'll expand PhotoWheel to include some fun image effects that users can apply to pictures in their library.

Using `CIFilter`

Basic `CIFilter` usage is quite simple, although it does involve new classes and concepts. `CIFilter`s work on and produce instances of `CIImage`. Final images are rendered not by the filter or the image, but rather by a `CIContext`. Listing 24.3 shows a simple example of using the `CISepiaTone` filter to apply a sepia tint to an image. This example also illustrates how you can convert between `UIImage` and `CIImage`, which is useful when you're working with UIKit.

Listing 24.3   Using the `CISepiaTone` Filter with a `UIImage`

```
- (UIImage *)sepiaImageFromImage:(UIImage *)myImage
{
    CIImage *myCIImage = [CIImage imageWithCGImage:[myImage CGImage]];

    CIFilter *sepiaFilter = [CIFilter filterWithName:@"CISepiaTone"];
    [sepiaFilter setValue:myCIImage forKey:@"inputImage"];
    [sepiaFilter setValue:@0.9 forKey:@"inputIntensity"];

    CIImage *sepiaImage = [sepiaFilter outputImage];

    CIContext *context = [CIContext contextWithOptions:
                             @{kCIContextUseSoftwareRenderer : @NO}];
    CGImageRef sepiaCGImage = [context createCGImage:sepiaImage
                                          fromRect:[sepiaImage extent]];
    UIImage *sepiaUIImage = [UIImage imageWithCGImage:sepiaCGImage];
    CFRelease(sepiaCGImage);

    return sepiaUIImage;
}
```

The first thing this method does is convert the incoming `UIImage` to a `CIImage` so that `CIFilter` can work with it. This is done using the `CGImage` format defined by Core Graphics. Both `UIImage` and `CIImage` work with `CGImage`, so here it takes on the role of the transfer point from one class to another.

Next, the code creates the `CIFilter`, looking it up by name. As seen earlier, `CISep iaTone` takes two parameters: an input image and an intensity level. The code sets both of these parameters via key-value coding. Key-value coding (KVC) is a technique available in Objective-C that makes it possible to access attributes of an object even if an attribute is not defined as a `@property` and there are no setter or getter methods. KVC is widely used in Core Image and in many other areas. For more information on KVC, see Apple's Key-Value Coding Programming Guide.[1]

The code assigns the result of the filter to `sepiaImage`, which is another `CIImage`. Recall that this step doesn't actually create the image; instead, it creates a recipe for creating an image. At this point the code has defined the path from the original image to the result via the filter but has not actually applied the filter and rendered the output image.

Rendering the result is the `CIContext`'s job. The method in Listing 24.3 creates a `CIContext`, setting the `kCIContextUseSoftwareRenderer` option to `NO`. As a consequence, the `CIContext` will use the GPU to render the image instead of the CPU.

---

1. *Key-Value Coding Programming Guide*: http://developer.apple.com/library/
ios/#documentation/cocoa/conceptual/KeyValueCoding/Articles/Overview.html

Creating a `CIContext` on the fly like this is acceptable if you'll need the context only occasionally, but if you expect to be doing a lot of Core Image work, it's better to make the context an instance variable and reuse it whenever you need it. The final image is rendered as a `CGImage` in the call to `-createCGImage:fromRect:`. The first argument is the `CIImage` just created, and the second is that image's extent, as defined by its size and location.

The code converts the rendered image back to a `UIImage` and returns. Because ARC manages only Objective-C objects, it is necessary to explicitly release the interim `CGImageRef sepiaCGImage`.

Image Analysis

Filters are useful and often fun, but Core Image goes further, offering features that require analyzing the source image instead of merely processing its pixels. One of these capabilities is the auto-enhance feature you have probably noticed in iOS's camera app, which includes red-eye elimination. Another is face detection, which locates any faces found in an image as well as specific facial features like the person's eyes and mouth.

Automatic Enhancement

Image enhancement uses a series of `CIFilters`. Rather than create the filters yourself, though, you can ask `CIImage` to create them for you. A `CIImage` instance analyzes its image to determine which enhancements might be needed and returns an array of `CIFilters`. You then chain these filters together to produce the enhanced image. This chaining of filters resembles the diagram in Figure 24.2, with the output from one filter becoming the input to the next stage. Listing 24.4 shows an example of applying auto-enhance filters to a `UIImage`.

Listing 24.4   **Auto-enhancing a `UIImage`**

```
- (UIImage *)autoEnhancedVersionOfImage:(UIImage *)myImage
{
    CIImage *myCIImage = [CIImage imageWithCGImage:[myImage CGImage]];

    NSArray *autoAdjustmentFilters = [myCIImage autoAdjustmentFilters];
    CIImage *enhancedCIImage = myCIImage;
    for (CIFilter *filter in autoAdjustmentFilters) {
        [filter setValue:enhancedCIImage forKey:kCIInputImageKey];
        enhancedCIImage = [filter outputImage];
    }

    NSLog(@"Auto enhance filters: %@", autoAdjustmentFilters);
    [self setFilteredCIImage:enhancedCIImage];

    CGImageRef enhancedCGImage = [[self ciContext]
```

```
                              createCGImage:enhancedCIImage
                              fromRect:[enhancedCIImage extent]];
    UIImage *enhancedImage = [UIImage imageWithCGImage:enhancedCGImage];
    CFRelease(enhancedCGImage);

    return enhancedImage;
}
```

Like the previous example, the code in Listing 24.4 starts by converting the incoming `UIImage` to a `CIImage`.

Next, it asks the `CIImage` to analyze the image and determine which, if any, filters are needed to enhance it. This step is processor intensive, especially with larger images, so you should consider performing it on a background thread. The result is several `CIFilters` collected in an array. In this case the code asks for all possible auto-adjust filters, which may include red-eye correction. If you don't think you'll need that feature, you can speed up the analysis by turning that enhancement off. In that case you would use `autoAdjustmentFiltersWithOptions:` and set the `kCIImageAuto AdjustRedEye` option to `NO`.

To get the enhanced image, you need to apply each of these filters to the original image. The easiest way to do so is to chain the filters end to end. You can then process the entire filter chain at once when you render the final image. The code in Listing 24.4 does this by using `enhancedCIImage`. Initially the code sets this variable to the original image. At each stage in the `for` loop, the code sets the current filter's input to the current value of `enhancedImageT`, and then updates `enhancedImage` to point to that filter's `outputImage`. When the loop completes, `enhancedImage` points to the output of the final enhancement filter.

In this case the `CIImage` has a more complex image recipe than in the earlier `CISe piaTone` example, but it's still just a recipe and not the final rendered image. The rest of the method in Listing 24.4 renders the result and converts it to `UIImage`. The only rendering difference in this method is that the code uses an instance variable called `ciContext` that contains a `CIContext` instance owned by the class.

Face Detection

Detecting faces also requires analyzing the image, but in this case no `CIFilters` are involved. Instead, you use the `CIDetector` class. `CIDetector` is designed to analyze images and find specific types of features. So far only one detector is available, which locates faces.

`CIDetector` analyzes an image to locate features and returns an array of `CIFea ture` instances corresponding to those features. When detecting faces, the array contains instances of `CIFaceFeature`, which is a subclass of `CIFeature`. Each `CIFace Feature` contains the overall bounds of the detected face. It may also contain eye and mouth locations, when they can be determined. Listing 24.5 shows a code snippet that finds faces in a `CIImage`.

Listing 24.5   **Detecting Faces in an Image**

```
NSDictionary *detectorOptions =
                @{CIDetectorAccuracy : CIDetectorAccuracyLow};
CIDetector *faceDetector = [CIDetector
                            detectorOfType:CIDetectorTypeFace
                            context:nil
                            options:detectorOptions];


NSArray *faces = [faceDetector featuresInImage:[self filteredCIImage]
                                        options:nil];
NSLog(@"Found %d faces", [faces count]);

if ([faces count] > 0) {

    CGRect faceZoomRect = CGRectNull;

    for (CIFaceFeature *face in faces) {
        NSLog(@"Found face at %@", NSStringFromCGRect([face bounds]));
        if ([face hasLeftEyePosition]) {
            NSLog(@"Left eye position: %@",
                NSStringFromCGPoint([face leftEyePosition]));
        }
        if ([face hasRightEyePosition]) {
            NSLog(@"Right eye position: %@",
                NSStringFromCGPoint([face rightEyePosition]));
        }
        if ([face hasMouthPosition]) {
            NSLog(@"Mouth position: %@",
                NSStringFromCGPoint([face mouthPosition]));
        }

        if (CGRectEqualToRect(faceZoomRect, CGRectNull)) {
            faceZoomRect = [face bounds];
        } else {
            faceZoomRect = CGRectUnion(faceZoomRect, [face bounds]);
        }
    }
}
```

This code starts by creating a dictionary to hold options for the face detector. Currently, the only option is the accuracy, which can be high or low. Higher accuracy takes longer to calculate. The code then creates a CIDetector of type CIDetectorTypeFace using these options.

Face detection happens during the call to -featuresInImage:options:. Analyzing the image to find faces may be processor intensive, so you may want to dispatch this process to a background thread.

When this call completes, the code runs through any faces that were found and prints their bounds. For each face, it checks whether the eye and mouth positions were found, and prints those as well.

Adding Core Image Effects to PhotoWheel

Now it's time to add these features to PhotoWheel. We'll be adding the following options to the photo browser:

- A collection of `CIFilter` effects that modify the image in various ways.
- Random configuration of those filters to produce a range of effects. The app will show small preview images demonstrating the effect the filter would have before modifying the image.
- Automatic image enhancement.
- Automatically zoom to crop an image around any faces.

The effects will be cumulative, so that the user can apply multiple effects sequentially. The new code will go in the photo browser, so the user will be able to view and apply filters while browsing photos.

> **Note**
>
> In addition to the code changes presented in this chapter, you must add `CoreImage` `.framework` to the PhotoWheel project, and you must include `#import <CoreImage` `/CoreImage.h>` in the file *PhotoBrowserViewController.m*.

Instance Variables for Filter Management

The photo browser needs a few new instance variables to manage the filtering process. Add the property declarations in Listing 24.8 to the `PhotoBrowserViewController` class extension at the top of *PhotoBrowserViewController.m*.

Listing 24.8 **New Instance Variable Declarations for** **`PhotoBrowserViewController`**

```
@property (readwrite, strong) CIContext *ciContext;
@property (nonatomic, strong) NSMutableArray *imageFilters;
@property (nonatomic, strong) NSMutableArray
                                   *filteredThumbnailPreviewImages;
@property (nonatomic, strong) UIImage *filteredThumbnailImage;
@property (nonatomic, strong) UIImage *filteredLargeImage;

@property (nonatomic, assign) CGFloat filterRadiusFactor;
@property (nonatomic, assign) CGFloat filterCenterFactor;
```

These variables serve the following purposes:

- `ciContext` is a persistent `CIContext` that is used every time a new image is rendered.

- `imageFilters` contains a collection of `CIFilters`. The new code will use the same filter objects for both the small preview images and the full-sized filtered images. This array will hold those filters so they can be reused.

- `filteredThumbnailPreviewImages` contains the small preview images of filter effects, which will be displayed in the UI.

- `filteredThumbnailImage` is the same as the raw, unfiltered thumbnail image at first. As the user applies filters to the image, `filteredThumbnailImage` is updated to contain the results of the most recent filter. Each time the user applies a filter, `filteredThumbnailImage` is updated with a new value selected from `filteredThumbnailPreviewImages`.

- `filteredLargeImage` is initially the same as the raw, unfiltered full-size image. As the user applies filters to the image, `filteredLargeImage` is updated so that it contains the results of the most recent filter.

- `filterRadiusFactor` and `filterCenterFactor` are used to configure filters that depend on the image's size. For example, if a filter has a radius parameter that is equal to half the image's width, `filterRadiusFactor` would be 0.5. That value could be applied to an image of any size by multiplying it by the image width.

User Interface Additions

Now we need to add the various UI elements the app needs to provide to enable the user to control the effects. The effects UI goes in `PhotoBrowserViewController`, as that is where the user views individual images.

The updated UI will have several additional buttons corresponding to instance methods as well as new instance variables that will be used to control the UI's appearance. Start by updating *PhotoBrowserViewController.h* to look like Listing 24.9.

Listing 24.9 New **IBOutlets** and **IBActions** in *PhotoBrowserViewController.h*

```
@interface PhotoBrowserViewController : UIViewController
                                                <UIScrollViewDelegate>

@property (nonatomic, weak) IBOutlet UIScrollView *scrollView;
@property (nonatomic, assign) NSInteger startAtIndex;
@property (nonatomic, strong) NSArray *photos;

- (void)toggleChromeDisplay;

@property (strong, nonatomic) IBOutlet UIView *filterViewContainer;
```

```
@property (strong, nonatomic) IBOutletCollection(UIButton)
                                    NSArray *filterButtons;


// Actions that modify the image
- (IBAction)enhanceImage:(id)sender;
- (IBAction)zoomToFaces:(id)sender;
- (IBAction)applyFilter:(id)sender;


// Actions that save or restore the image
- (IBAction)revertToOriginal:(id)sender;
- (IBAction)saveImage:(id)sender;

- (IBAction)cancel:(id)sender;
```

The `filterViewContainer` property will refer to an overall container view for the Core Image effects view. The `filterButtons` array is something new—an `IBOutlet Collection` instead of an `IBOutlet`. An `IBOutletCollection` is similar to an `IBOutlet` except that it can refer to multiple user interface elements and can be connected to all of them in the storyboard. In this case the `filterButtons` collection will point to several `UIButtons` in the UI that correspond to different `CIFilter` effects. Those buttons will display previews of the filter effects, so we need to have references to them.

The first three `IBActions` apply Core Image effects to the image. The rest of the new `IBActions` provide options to reverse changes, save changes, or simply cancel image editing.

Now we'll add the actual UI elements corresponding to the new `IBOutlets` and `IBActions`. In *MainStoryboard.storyboard*, locate the photo browser view controller. The new UI elements will go at the bottom of the main view and will look like those in Figure 24.3.

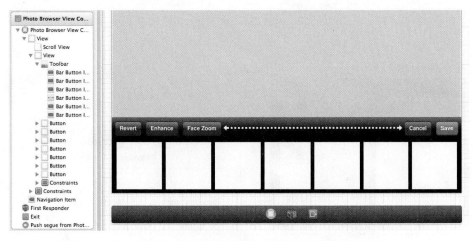

Figure 24.3   New UI elements for Core Image effects

The new elements include a `UIToolbar` and several `UIButtons`, found in an overall container view for filter-related UI. Make sure the container view is at the same level as the scroll view, rather than being a subview of the scroll view. Keep in mind that this "container" view is just a regular UIView that happens to contain a bunch of subviews—it's not the same as the "Container view" item listed in Xcode's object library.

The toolbar contains five `UIBarButtonItems` and a flexible space. Add those items to the toolbar. The buttons on the left should use the Custom identifier in Xcode. The buttons on the right should use the Cancel and Save identifiers, respectively. This choice will make the Save button stand out in blue. Connect these five buttons to the corresponding `IBAction` methods declared in *PhotoBrowserViewController.h*.

The buttons at the bottom should be 100 × 100 points in size, which matches Photo Wheel's small image size. Set the button Type for the buttons to Custom in the Attributes inspector so that they won't automatically be drawn with a rounded border. Set the background color to something that stands out against the background. The buttons will display the images contained in the `filteredThumbnailPreviewImages` array you added earlier. Because the buttons are the same size as the preview images, the button color won't be visible, but it is helpful to set the color to something that makes them visible when editing the user interface.

Go through the buttons and set the tag for each one to values from 0 to 6, starting at 0 on the left and working up to 6 on the right. In UIKit, a *tag* is an arbitrary integer value that you can assign to any `UIView`. Although UIKit doesn't use the tag, you can look up its value by writing code to do so. In this case you'll use the tag to distinguish one filter button from another one. You may need to scroll the Attributes inspector downward to find the Tag option (Figure 24.4). All of these buttons will have the same target, and we'll use the tag values to determine which button was tapped.

Finally, set the target of each of the seven square buttons to be the `-applyFilter:` method added to the header in Listing 24.9.

Connect the new `filterViewContainer` IBOutlet to the container view just as you would connect any other `IBOutlet`. Connecting the `filterButtons` collection

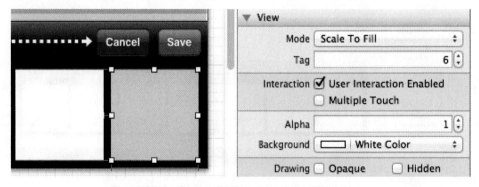

Figure 24.4   Setting the tag value on a `UIButton`

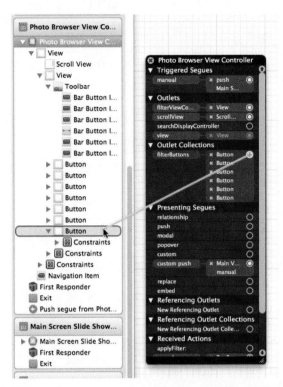

Figure 24.5   Connecting an `IBOutletCollection` to multiple UI elements

works almost the same way, except that because it is a collection, you can now make multiple connections from the same outlet (Figure 24.5).

Next, we need to add code to control when the new filter container view is visible. It shouldn't be visible all the time—just when the user wants to use the filters. At other times it should disappear. The first change, then, is to hide the view when the photo browser first appears. To do so, add the following line of code in `PhotoBrowserViewController`'s `viewWillAppear`, which sets the container's alpha to zero:

```
[[self filterViewContainer] setAlpha:0.0];
```

To make the filter container show and hide, add the methods in Listing 24.10 to *PhotoBrowserViewController.m*.

Listing 24.10   **Showing and Hiding the Filter Overlay View**

```
- (void)showFilters:(id)sender
{
  if ([self imageFilters] == nil) {
    [self setImageFilters:
```

```
        [NSMutableArray arrayWithCapacity:[[self filterButtons] count]]];

    CIContext *context = [CIContext contextWithOptions:
                            @{kCIContextUseSoftwareRenderer : @NO}];
    [self setCiContext:context];

    [self setFilteredThumbnailPreviewImages:[NSMutableArray array]];
  }

  Photo *currentPhoto = [[self photos] objectAtIndex:[self currentIndex]];
  [self setFilteredThumbnailImage:[currentPhoto smallImage]];
  [self setFilteredLargeImage:[currentPhoto originalImage]];

  [self randomizeFilters];

  [[self view] bringSubviewToFront:[self filterViewContainer]];
  [UIView animateWithDuration:0.3 animations:^(void) {
    [[self filterViewContainer] setAlpha:1.0];
  }];
}

- (void)hideFilters
{
  // Hide filter container
  [UIView animateWithDuration:0.3 animations:^(void) {
    [[self filterViewContainer] setAlpha:0.0];
  }];
}
```

The -showFilters: method handles more than just displaying the filter container. If this is the first time the user has asked to use filters, this method initializes some of the instance variables added earlier, creating empty arrays and the CIContext that will render images. It also sets the initial values of filteredThumbnailImage and filteredLargeImage by looking them up in the photos array. It creates a collection of CIFilters using the new randomizeFilters method (which we'll add shortly) and then displays the filter container view. The code fades the filter container gradually into view by animating its alpha value.

The hideFilters method makes the filter container invisible by animating its alpha value back to zero.

Now that we have code to show the filter container, we need some way for the user to trigger that code. For this purpose, we'll add a button to the navigation item that calls the showFilters: method. We already have a method called addButtonsTo NavigationBar that sets up navigation item buttons, and we'll add one more button to the collection. Listing 24.11 shows the updated version of this method, with the new code highlighted.

Listing 24.11 Updated Toolbar Buttons, Including a Button to Show the Filter Container

```
- (void)addButtonsToNavigationBar
{
    UIBarButtonItem *trashButton = nil;
    trashButton = [[UIBarButtonItem alloc]
                    initWithBarButtonSystemItem:UIBarButtonSystemItemTrash
                    target:self
                    action:@selector(deletePhoto:)];
    [trashButton setStyle:UIBarButtonItemStyleBordered];

    UIBarButtonItem *actionButton = nil;
    actionButton = [[UIBarButtonItem alloc]
                    initWithBarButtonSystemItem:UIBarButtonSystemItemAction
                    target:self
                    action:@selector(showActionMenu:)];
    [actionButton setStyle:UIBarButtonItemStyleBordered];
    [self setActionButton:actionButton];

    UIBarButtonItem *slideshowButton = nil;
    slideshowButton = [[UIBarButtonItem alloc]
                    initWithTitle:@"Slideshow"
                    style:UIBarButtonItemStyleBordered
                    target:self
                    action:@selector(slideshow:)];

    UIBarButtonItem *filterButton = [[UIBarButtonItem alloc]
                                initWithTitle:@"Edit"
                                style:UIBarButtonItemStyleBordered
                                target:self
                                action:@selector(showFilters:)];

    NSArray *buttons = @[filterButton, slideshowButton, actionButton,
                        trashButton];
    [[self navigationItem] setRightBarButtonItems:buttons];
}
```

The only change in this code is the addition of the extra button.

One other UI management detail that we need to handle is sorting the buttons in the filterButtons array. Using IBOutletCollection is a convenient way to group the buttons into an array, but unfortunately the order of the array is not guaranteed. To make sure the array is sorted properly so that it corresponds to the tag values, we'll override the setter method for filterButtons and sort the array based on the button tag. The setter will be called when the buttons are first loaded from the story-board. Listing 24.12 provides this method.

Listing 24.12   **Sorting the `filterButtons` Array by Button Tag Values**

```
- (void)setFilterButtons:(NSArray *)filterButtonsFromIB
{
    _filterButtons = [filterButtonsFromIB sortedArrayUsingComparator:
             ^NSComparisonResult(UIButton *button1, UIButton *button2)
                  {
                      return [button1 tag] > [button2 tag];
                  }];
}
```

This method takes the incoming array `filterButtonsFromIB`, which contains the buttons in some unknown order, and sorts it using an `NSComparator` block. The block looks at the tag values for a pair of buttons and returns the result of comparing them. `NSArray` calls the block repeatedly with different pairs of buttons and produces a new, sorted array. The result is an array where the contents are sorted by `tag` value. The code assigns this result to `filterButtons`.

Creating the `CIFilter` Effects

PhotoWheel will use several different filters to produce different visual effects. To provide some variety in these effects, we'll use random values for input parameters. First, we need to be able to get random numbers. Add the `RAND_IN_RANGE` macro to the top of *PhotoBrowserViewController.m*:

```
#define RAND_IN_RANGE(low,high) (low + (high - low) * \
     (arc4random_uniform(RAND_MAX) / (double)RAND_MAX))
```

This macro produces a random number in the range from `low` to `high`, which can be either integer or floating-point values. With `arc4random_uniform`, it isn't necessary to seed the random-number generation process, so we won't add code for that task.

Now we'll create the actual `CIFilters`. The user interface has seven buttons for different filters, and there will be one method per filter. These items are shown in Listing 24.13.

Listing 24.13   **Creating Randomly Configured `CIFilters`**

```
- (CIFilter *)hueAdjustFilter
{
    CIFilter *filter = [CIFilter filterWithName:@"CIHueAdjust"];
    CGFloat inputAngle = RAND_IN_RANGE(-M_PI, M_PI);
    [filter setValue:@(inputAngle) forKey:@"inputAngle"];
    return filter;
}

- (CIFilter *)invertColorFilter
{
```

```objc
    CIFilter *filter = [CIFilter filterWithName:@"CIColorInvert"];
    return filter;
}


- (CIFilter *)affineTileFilter
{
    CGFloat scaleFactor = RAND_IN_RANGE(0.2, 0.8);
    CGAffineTransform transform = CGAffineTransformMakeScale(scaleFactor,
                                                             scaleFactor);
    transform = CGAffineTransformRotate(transform,
                                        RAND_IN_RANGE(0.2, M_PI/2));

    CIFilter *filter = [CIFilter filterWithName:@"CIAffineTile"];
    [filter setValue:[NSValue valueWithBytes:&transform
                                    objCType:@encode(CGAffineTransform)]
              forKey:@"inputTransform"];
    return filter;
}


- (CIFilter *)posterizeFilter
{
    CIFilter *filter = [CIFilter filterWithName:@"CIColorPosterize"];
    CGFloat posterizeLevel = RAND_IN_RANGE(2.0, 30.0);
    [filter setValue:@(posterizeLevel) forKey:@"inputLevels"];

    return filter;
}


- (CIFilter *)bumpDistortionFilter
{
    CIFilter *filter = [CIFilter filterWithName:@"CIBumpDistortion"];
    [filter setValue:@(RAND_IN_RANGE(-1.0, 1.0)) forKey:@"inputScale"];
    return filter;
}


- (CIFilter *)twirlFilter
{
    CIFilter *filter = [CIFilter filterWithName:@"CITwirlDistortion"];
    [filter setValue:@(RAND_IN_RANGE(-M_PI, M_PI)) forKey:@"inputAngle"];
    return filter;
}


- (CIFilter *)circleSplashDistortionFilter
{
    CIFilter *filter = [CIFilter
                        filterWithName:@"CICircleSplashDistortion"];
    return filter;
}
```

The methods in Listing 24.13 create the following types of filters:

- **CIHueAdjust**: Rotates the color cube used in the image by an angle measured in radians. The effect is that all the colors in the image shift their hue by a fixed amount.
- **CIColorInvert**: Inverts image colors. Note that this filter is not actually random because it does not include any numeric parameters.
- **CIAffineTile**: Applies an affine transform to the image and then tiles the result. Affine transforms can change an image's shape or size via matrix math. They can also rotate images or flip or skew them depending on the affine transform. In this case the transform scales the image by a factor ranging from 0.2 to 0.8 and then rotates it by an angle ranging from 0.2 to $\pi/2$ radians.
- **CIColorPosterize**: Adjusts the image's colors to produce a poster-like result.
- **CIBumpDistortion**: Distorts the image by creating a "bump" effect that can appear to project into or out of the screen.
- **CITwirlDistortion**: Rotates pixels around a center point to produce a twirled or swirled effect.
- **CICircleSplashDistortion**: Distorts an image around a center point by producing an effect of colors radiating outward.

We now have everything we need to create the filters and set up the thumbnail preview images in the user interface. This happens in the `randomizeFilters` method mentioned earlier, which was called from `showFilters:`. This method is shown in Listing 24.14.

> **Note**
>
> We'll use the same `CIFilter` instances for both the thumbnail images and the full-size images, but some of the filter effects depend on the image size. The code in Listing 24.13 doesn't initialize all of the parameters of some filters, because the value of those parameters will depend on the image size. These will be configured later, when the filters are applied.

Listing 24.14 Creating New Randomized Filters

```
- (void)randomizeFilters
{
  [[self imageFilters] removeAllObjects];
  [[self filteredThumbnailPreviewImages] removeAllObjects];

  // Hue adjust filter
  CIFilter *hueAdjustFilter = [self hueAdjustFilter];
  [[self imageFilters] addObject:hueAdjustFilter];

  // Invert color filter
```

```objc
CIFilter *invertFilter = [self invertColorFilter];
[[self imageFilters] addObject:invertFilter];

// Affine tile filter
CIFilter *affineTileFilter = [self affineTileFilter];
[[self imageFilters] addObject:affineTileFilter];

// Posterize filter
CIFilter *posterizeFilter = [self posterizeFilter];
[[self imageFilters] addObject:posterizeFilter];

// Bump distort filter
CIFilter *bumpDistortFilter = [self bumpDistortionFilter];
[[self imageFilters] addObject:bumpDistortFilter];

// Twirl distort filter
CIFilter *twirlDistortFilter = [self twirlFilter];
[[self imageFilters] addObject:twirlDistortFilter];

// Circle splash filter
CIFilter *circleSplashDistortionFilter =
                        [self circleSplashDistortionFilter];
[[self imageFilters] addObject:circleSplashDistortionFilter];

CIImage *thumbnailCIImage = [CIImage imageWithCGImage:
                    [[self filteredThumbnailImage] CGImage]];
CGRect extents = [thumbnailCIImage extent];

[self setFilterCenterFactor:RAND_IN_RANGE(0.1, 0.9)];
[self setFilterRadiusFactor:RAND_IN_RANGE(0.1, 0.9)];

for (int i=0; i<[[self imageFilters] count]; i++) {
   CIFilter *filter = [[self imageFilters] objectAtIndex:i];
   [filter setValue:thumbnailCIImage forKey:@"inputImage"];

   if ([[filter attributes] objectForKey:@"inputRadius"] != nil) {
     NSNumber *radius;
     radius = @(extents.size.width * [self filterRadiusFactor]);
     [filter setValue:radius forKey:@"inputRadius"];
   }
   if ([[filter attributes] objectForKey:@"inputCenter"] != nil) {
     CGPoint fCenter;
     fCenter.x = (extents.size.width * [self filterCenterFactor]);
     fCenter.y = (extents.size.height * [self filterCenterFactor]);

     CIVector *inputCenter = [CIVector vectorWithX:fCenter.x
                                                 Y:fCenter.y];
```

```
        [filter setValue:inputCenter forKey:@"inputCenter"];
    }
    CIImage *filterResult = [filter outputImage];

    CGImageRef filteredCGImage = [[self ciContext]
                                  createCGImage:filterResult
                                  fromRect:[thumbnailCIImage extent]];
    UIImage *filteredImage = [UIImage imageWithCGImage:filteredCGImage];
    CFRelease(filteredCGImage);

    [[self filteredThumbnailPreviewImages] addObject:filteredImage];

    UIButton *filterButton = [[self filterButtons] objectAtIndex:i];
    [filterButton setImage:filteredImage
                forState:UIControlStateNormal];
    }
}
```

A lot happens in this method, but it is not as complex as it might seem at first. To begin, the method removes any previously existing filters and filter preview images by clearing the arrays that hold them. It then runs through the CIFilter methods described earlier, creating several filters and collecting them in the imageFilters array.

Next, the method converts the current image in filteredThumbnailImage to a CIImage so that it can be used with CIFilters. It also initializes filterCenter Factor and filterRadiusFactor to random values ranging from 0.1 to 0.9. We use these instance variables so that filters that depend on the image's size will have the same effect on both the small thumbnail image and the full-size image. The code in Listing 24.14 uses a random value for the center. If you wanted to let the user select a center point, you could use touch detection to let the user tap on a point. That point could then become the center point for the filter. You'd also need to scale the point to work on the thumbnail view.

With that work done, the code loops through the filters. In each pass through the loop, the block first looks up a CIFilter in the imageFilters array and sets its input image to the current thumbnail. The code then configures the inputRadius and inputCenter parameters for filters that use them. In PhotoWheel, this will include CIBumpDistortion, CITwirlDistortion, and CICircleSplashDistortion. The values for those parameters depend on the filterCenterFactor and filterRadius Factor values initialized earlier. In the case of inputCenter, the code uses Core Image's CIVector type to represent the center point.

Next, the code gets the filter's output image. It renders that image as a CGImage Ref and converts the rendered image to a UIImage. This UIImage goes into the filteredThumbnailPreviewImages array. Finally, the code updates the user interface with the new thumbnail image.

Applying the Filters

Now that we're creating filters and preview images, we're ready to apply filters to the original large image. Recall that all seven of the new filter buttons at the bottom of the photo browser are connected to the `applyFilter:` method. The implementation of this method is shown in Listing 24.15.

Listing 24.15 **Applying Filters from the Seven Filter Preview Buttons**

```
- (void)applySpecifiedFilter:(CIFilter *)filter
{
   CIImage *inputCIImage = [filter valueForKey:@"inputImage"];;

   // Set input radius or center, where needed.
   CGRect inputExtents = [inputCIImage extent];
   if ([[filter attributes] objectForKey:@"inputRadius"] != nil) {
      NSNumber *radius;
      radius = @(inputExtents.size.width * [self filterRadiusFactor]);
      [filter setValue:radius forKey:@"inputRadius"];
   }
   if ([[filter attributes] objectForKey:@"inputCenter"] != nil) {
      CGPoint fCenter;
      fCenter.x = (inputExtents.size.width * [self filterCenterFactor]);
      fCenter.y = (inputExtents.size.height * [self filterCenterFactor]);

      CIVector *inputCenter = [CIVector vectorWithX:fCenter.x
                                                  Y:fCenter.y];
      [filter setValue:inputCenter forKey:@"inputCenter"];
   }

   CIImage *filteredLargeImage = [filter outputImage];

   // Make sure we're not trying to use infinite extent to create an image
   CGRect cgImageRect;
   if (!CGRectIsInfinite([filteredLargeImage extent])) {
      cgImageRect = [filteredLargeImage extent];
   } else {
      cgImageRect = inputExtents;
   }
   CGImageRef filteredLargeCGImage = [[self ciContext]
                                       createCGImage:filteredLargeImage
                                       fromRect:cgImageRect];

   // Convert the result to a UIImage, display it, and save it for later
   UIImage *filteredImage = [UIImage imageWithCGImage:filteredLargeCGImage];
   [[[self photoViewCache] objectAtIndex:[self currentIndex]]
    setImage:filteredImage];
```

```
    [self setFilteredLargeImage:filteredImage];
    CFRelease(filteredLargeCGImage);
}


- (IBAction)applyFilter:(id)sender
{
    CIFilter *filter = [[self imageFilters] objectAtIndex:[sender tag]];
    CIImage *inputCIImage = [CIImage imageWithCGImage:
                            [[self filteredLargeImage] CGImage]];
    [filter setValue:inputCIImage forKey:@"inputImage"];

    [self applySpecifiedFilter:filter];
    [self setFilteredThumbnailImage:
     [[self filteredThumbnailPreviewImages] objectAtIndex:[sender tag]]];
    [self randomizeFilters];
}
```

The -applyFilter: method looks up the selected filter based on the tag value of the button tapped by the user. Recall that the tag values on the preview buttons range from 0 to 6. These values correspond to the index values used to look up entries in imageFilters. The code sets the filter's input image to the current filtered image and calls -applySpecifiedFilter:.

The -applySpecifiedFilter: method does the work of applying the selected filter to the large image, following the pattern described earlier. It recalculates the inputRadius and inputCenter parameters for filters that need them, because the image size is different here than it was for the thumbnail images.

The code checks the extent of the filter output before converting the result to a CGImageRef. This step deals with differing values for the output extent depending on the filter used. For most of the filters in PhotoWheel, the output is the same size as the input image, but not always. The output of the CIAffineTile filter, for example, has *infinite* extent. That might seem weird or even impossible, but recall that the filter output doesn't contain an image, only an image recipe. This recipe can produce an image as big as you want it to be. Why not just use the input image's size when creating the output image? In some cases we don't want that result. A little later on we'll use the CICrop filter in code that automatically zooms in on faces in a picture. A cropped picture is smaller than the original, so the filter output extent is also smaller. If we used the input size, we wouldn't crop the image; instead, we'd get an image that was the same size as the input. The extent checking here ensures that we specify the appropriate output image size for all of the filters in the app.

The code in Listing 24.15 displays the resulting image in the user interface and saves it in filteredLargeImage. Saving the filtered image in an instance variable makes the filter effects cumulative, because this saved image always contains the result of the most recently applied filter.

Back in `applyFilter:`, the code sets the current value of `filteredThumbnail Image` to one of the previously rendered images in `filteredThumbnailPreview Images`. Again, this step ensures that the filter effects will be cumulative. Finally, the code calls `randomizeFilters` to create new filter options and update the preview thumbnails.

Implementing Auto-Enhance

Using the auto-enhance capability is comparatively simple because we can reuse `-apply SpecifiedFilter:`. What's left is not that different from the sample auto-enhance code presented earlier. The implementation of `-enhanceImage:` is shown in Listing 24.16.

Listing 24.16   PhotoWheel's Image Auto-Enhance Method

```
- (IBAction)enhanceImage:(id)sender {
    CIImage *largeCIImage = [CIImage imageWithCGImage:
                                    [[self filteredLargeImage] CGImage]];
    NSArray *autoAdjustmentFilters = [largeCIImage autoAdjustmentFilters];
    CIImage *enhancedImage = largeCIImage;
    for (CIFilter *filter in autoAdjustmentFilters) {
        [filter setValue:enhancedImage forKey:@"inputImage"];
        enhancedImage = [filter outputImage];
    }
    [self applySpecifiedFilter:[autoAdjustmentFilters lastObject]];
}
```

As discussed earlier in the section on auto-enhancement, this method asks the large `CIImage` for a full set of enhancement filters, chains those filters together, and gets the final resulting `CIImage`. It passes the final filter in the chain to `-applySpecified Filter:`, which handles updating the UI and saving the new image so that further filters can be applied.

Implementing Face Zoom

Earlier we discussed how to locate faces in a photo, but in PhotoWheel we'll take that capability a little further. Once we find faces, we'll automatically zoom the photo in on the faces, based on the face locations found during image analysis. Listing 24.17 shows the method that implements this feature.

Listing 24.17   Finding Faces and Zooming in on Them

```
- (IBAction)zoomToFaces:(id)sender {
    NSDictionary *detectorOptions =
                    @{CIDetectorAccuracy : CIDetectorAccuracyLow};
    CIDetector *faceDetector = [CIDetector
                    detectorOfType:CIDetectorTypeFace
```

```
                                context:nil
                                options:detectorOptions];

    CIImage *largeCIImage = [CIImage imageWithCGImage:
                                 [[self filteredLargeImage] CGImage]];
    NSArray *faces = [faceDetector featuresInImage:largeCIImage
                                          options:nil];

    if ([faces count] > 0) {
       CGRect faceZoomRect = CGRectNull;

       for (CIFaceFeature *face in faces) {
           if (CGRectEqualToRect(faceZoomRect, CGRectNull)) {
              faceZoomRect = [face bounds];
           } else {
              faceZoomRect = CGRectUnion(faceZoomRect, [face bounds]);
           }
       }

       faceZoomRect = CGRectIntersection([largeCIImage extent],
                             CGRectInset(faceZoomRect, -50.0, -50.0));

       CIFilter *cropFilter = [CIFilter filterWithName:@"CICrop"];
       [cropFilter setValue:largeCIImage forKey:@"inputImage"];
       [cropFilter setValue:[CIVector
                            vectorWithCGRect:faceZoomRect]
                    forKey:@"inputRectangle"];

       [self applySpecifiedFilter:cropFilter];
    } else {
       UIAlertView *noFacesAlert = [[UIAlertView alloc]
              initWithTitle:@"No Faces"
              message:@"Sorry, I couldn't find any faces in this picture."
              delegate:nil
              cancelButtonTitle:@"OK"
              otherButtonTitles:nil];
       [noFacesAlert show];
    }
}
```

Detecting faces in `zoomToFaces:` uses the same process that we discussed earlier. What is new here is what we do with the resulting face information.

We can obtain the bounds of each face in the image. To zoom in on the faces, we need to calculate a rectangle that encompasses all of them. The code in Listing 24.17 uses the `faceZoomRect` variable for this purpose. Initially the code sets this variable's value to `CGRectNull`, which is a constant defining a rectangle with no valid location or size.

For each face, the code checks whether `faceZoomRect` is still equal to `CGRectNull`. If so, it saves the current face location in `faceZoomRect`. If `faceZoomRect` has changed, the code calculates the union of the `faceZoomRect` and the new face location. In this way `faceZoomRect` grows to encompass all faces in the photo.

Next, the code adjusts `faceZoomRect` a little. It uses `CGRectInset` to expand `faceZoomRect` by 50 pixels on all sides, thereby widening the zoom slightly. This step isn't strictly needed, but the unmodified `faceZoomRect` can lead to a zoom that feels somewhat cramped. If some faces are close to the edge of the picture, however, widening the zoom like this might result in a rectangle whose bounds go beyond the edge of the picture. The code uses `CGRectIntersection` to ensure that the final value of `faceZoomRect` doesn't exceed the large image's extent.

Now that we have a rectangle containing the faces, we need to crop the image. The code accomplishes this task with the `CICrop` filter, using `faceZoomRect` as the crop area. It then calls `-applySpecifiedFilter` to apply the crop effect.

If no faces were found, the faces array will be empty. In such a case, the code skips the zooming code and displays an appropriate message to the user. A different approach you might want to try is to detect faces in advance and, if none are found, either disable or hide the **Face Zoom** button.

Other Necessary Methods

We need a few utility methods to make the filter view fully useful. Users need to be able to save filtered images or discard them, or revert from the filtered image to the original image and start over. These methods are shown in Listing 24.18.

Listing 24.18 **Filter Utility Methods**

```
- (IBAction)revertToOriginal:(id)sender {
    // Reload the original image for filtering and regenerate the filters
    [self setFilteredThumbnailImage:
        [[[self photos] objectAtIndex:[self currentIndex]] smallImage]];
    [self randomizeFilters];

    // Restore the original large image to the browser
    UIImage *originalImage =
        [[[self photos] objectAtIndex:[self currentIndex]] largeImage];
    [[[self photoViewCache] objectAtIndex:[self currentIndex]]
     setImage:originalImage];
    [self setFilteredLargeImage:originalImage];
}


- (IBAction)saveImage:(id)sender {
    // Save the filtered large image
    if ([self filteredLargeImage] != nil) {
        Photo *currentPhoto = [[self photos] objectAtIndex:
                                         [self currentIndex]];
```

```
      [currentPhoto saveImage:[self filteredLargeImage]];
    }
    // Hide the filter UI
    [self hideFilters];
}

- (IBAction)cancel:(id)sender {
    // Restore original large image
    UIImage *originalImage =
          [[[self photos] objectAtIndex:[self currentIndex]] largeImage];
    [[[self photoViewCache] objectAtIndex:[self currentIndex]]
     setImage:originalImage];
    // Hide the filter UI
    [self hideFilters];
}
```

The -revertToOriginal: method reloads the original images, displays them, and generates new filters using randomizeFilters. It leaves the filter buttons visible so that the user can continue exploring the filter effects.

The -saveImage: method replaces the current original image with the filtered large image, saving changes to the photos array. It hides the filter view, as this step completes filtering for a particular photo.

The -cancel: method restores the original image but, unlike -revertToOriginal:, it doesn't restore the thumbnail or generate new filters. Instead, it simply hides the filter container.

The last necessary detail is making the filter code respond to scroll events in the photo browser. The filter buttons display thumbnail preview images based on the current image. If the user scrolls to a new image, what then? The current preview images aren't useful for the new image. To keep things simple, we'll just hide the filter UI when this happens. Update the setCurrentIndex: method to look like Listing 24.19.

Listing 24.19   **Hiding Filter Controls When the Current Photo Changes**

```
- (void)setCurrentIndex:(NSInteger)newIndex
{
    _currentIndex = newIndex;

    [self loadPage:_currentIndex];
    [self loadPage:_currentIndex + 1];
    [self loadPage:_currentIndex - 1];
    [self unloadPage:_currentIndex + 2];
    [self unloadPage:_currentIndex - 2];

    [self setTitleWithCurrentIndex];
```

```
    if ([[self filterViewContainer] alpha] > 0) {
        [self cancel:self];
    }
}
```

This version of the method adds code at the end to dispose of the filter UI. If `filter ViewContainer` is visible, the code calls `cancel:`. Now whenever the user scrolls to a new photo, it's as if she also tapped the filter UI's **Cancel** button.

Summary

Core Image frequently inspires more than a little trepidation at first. Basic Core Image filtering is surprisingly easy, however, and it can improve images or be used to create fun and interesting visual effects. As often happens with iOS development, the really hard work is already complete and built into a framework. In this chapter, we leveraged the framework to enhance PhotoWheel with features that might appear complex but are surprisingly straightforward.

PhotoWheel is designed for the iPad, but many users will also have iPhones or iPod Touches. To provide the best experience for as many people as possible, it's often a good idea to design an app that can run on both iPad- and iPhone-style screens. In the next chapter we'll discuss how to structure an app so that this is possible.

Exercises

1. Add a new effect using the `CIExposureAdjust` filter. To create the filter, add a new method called `exposureAdjustFilter`, similar to the other filter creation methods described in this chapter. `CIExposureAdjust` takes two arguments: (a) the same input image argument described for other filters in this chapter and (b) `inputEV`, which adjusts exposure and takes values in a range from −10 to 10. To show this filter on the screen, you can either replace one of the existing filters or add another thumbnail view to the user interface. If you choose to add a new thumbnail, you will need to make the existing thumbnails smaller so that there's room for a new one. Don't forget to set the tag on the new thumbnail button!

2. Try to create a more complex multistage effect. For example, use the `CIChecker boardGenerator` filter to create a semitransparent image that you then overlay on the original image. As with the previous exercise, you'll need to either replace one of the existing effects or make room for a new one, and you should add a new method that generates a randomly configured version of the effect. To add this effect, you'll need three filters chained together:

    - A `CICheckerboardGenerator` filter to create the checkerboard. This filter has two color arguments, `inputColor0` and `inputColor1`. Both parameters are `CIColor` instances. Use the `RAND_IN_RANGE` macro to create random instances via `CIColor`'s `+colorWithRed:green:blue:alpha:` method. The filter also has an `inputWidth` argument that should be somewhere in the range of 50 to 100 pixels, and an `inputSharpness` argument that should be a random number from 0 to 1.

- A `CICrop` filter to make the generated checkerboard image the same size as the original image. The generated checkerboard has infinite extent (just like the `CIAffineTile` filter discussed in this chapter), and this step converts it to be the same size as the original image. The input image should be the output from the `CICheckerboardGenerator` in the previous step, and the `inputRectangle` argument should be the original image's size (recall that this is called the `extent` for `CIImage`).

- A `CISourceOverCompositing` filter to combine the original image and the checkerboard into a new image. Make the input image the cropped checkerboard from the previous filter, and make the `inputBackgroundImage` argument the original image.

Going Universal

There are three types of iOS apps: iPad-only, iPhone-only, and universal. Much of what you have learned about creating iPad apps in this book applies to creating iPhone apps as well. Thus, if you are armed with the skills needed to create an iPad app, then you surely have the skills to create an iPhone app. So why limit your app to one device or the other? Why not make your app available to both iPad and iPhone devices?

There are two ways to accomplish this. You can create two separate apps, one for each device type, or you can create a universal app. A universal app is a single application optimized for the iPad, iPhone, and iPod touch devices.

This chapter discusses the pros and cons of creating a universal app, and it explains the steps needed to convert an iPad app to a universal app.

Why Go Universal?

A universal app is a single app that runs like an iPad app on the iPad, yet runs like an iPhone app on the iPhone. The user buys the app once and can run it on any of her iOS devices. This approach provides the best experience for your users, but it does mean more work for you.

Suppose Jane, who owns an iPad, decides to buy your app. She loves your app, and she uses it daily. Jane also loves her iPad, so much so that when her 2-year contract with her cell phone carrier expired, she decided to buy an iPhone.

The first thing Jane does after getting her new iPhone is to download and install your app. After all, she has come to depend on your app daily. She goes to the App Store and searches for your app. One of three scenarios is possible:

1. You have no iPhone version of your app. Jane is disappointed, and a little bit of that love she had for your app dwindles away. She may even stop recommending your app to family and friends because it isn't available on the iPhone.

2. You have an iPhone version of your app, but it will cost Jane another 99 cents to download and install it to her new iPhone. Jane is disappointed. She feels as if you are trying to nickel-and-dime her by charging her a second time for an app that she already purchased.

Ignore the fact that paying 99 cents again for an app used daily is still a great value. This may be what a developer thinks, but it's not what a user like Jane thinks. Jane thinks she is being charged a second time for an app she already bought, and this perception changes her opinion of the app. She loses a bit of love for your app, and she stops recommending it to family and friends because "the developer is a cheapskate for charging twice for the same app."

3. Your app is distributed as a universal app. Jane finds your app in the iPhone App Store, and taps the Install button. She is excited that one of her favorite apps is available for her new iPhone. She tells everyone, from family to her friends on Facebook, how excited she is to finally have an iPhone and how she plans to use your app even more.

Which of these three experiences would you like your users—nay, your customers—to have?

Going universal with your iOS app has two key benefits. First, it extends the number of potential users you have for your application. Second, it delights those users who have both an iPhone and an iPad. These two key benefits are reason enough to make your next iOS app a universal app.

That said, there are also reasons *not* to go universal with your app.

Reason Not to Go Universal

The only good reason not to go universal is if your app differs greatly between the two devices. If your app offers the same core features and experience on both the iPad and the iPhone, and you decide to create two separate applications, one for each device type, then you will likely have a number of negative reviews in the App Store calling you a cheapskate for charging twice for the same app. If, however, your app differs greatly between the two device types, then it only makes sense to sell two different versions of your application.

You might also have business reasons to sell your application as two separate apps. For example, perhaps you need to sell your work as two separate apps to cover the cost of development for both device types. There are plenty of developers who sell iPad and iPhone versions of their app as separate applications even though the functionality is identical. But before you blindly decide to sell your app as two separate versions, consider your app's target audience. Does your target customer understand the value gained in having to pay twice for the same app? If so, then by all means sell your application as two separate apps. If selling the same app twice will anger your users and potentially hurt the reputation of your app and company, however, then you should sell your app as a single universal app.

Users of productivity apps may be more understanding, at least compared to a mainstream consumer. Make sure you understand your target audience before deciding to sell your app twice, and know that you can never go wrong in the customer's mind with a universal app.

Putting aside the debate about whether your app should be a universal app, let's talk about what it takes to transform your app into a universal app.

Making a Universal App

A universal app is nothing more than a single app binary that targets both the iPad and the iPhone. When you create a new project in Xcode, you specify the device target, which can be iPad, iPhone, or Universal. If you have an existing project, you can change the target device type in the Project Summary. Open the project in Xcode, select the project in the Project navigator, and then open the Summary tab. Here you will see a Device field, which is the target device type for the project. Set it to Universal for create a universal app (Figure 25.1).

Alternatively, you can set the Targeted Device Family to iPhone/iPad in the Build Settings. Changing the Device field in the Project Summary changes the Build Settings for you.

Two Storyboards

Changing the device type to Universal gets you a universal app, but it doesn't mean that your app looks great on the two device types. You still face the challenge of implementing the user interface on both the iPad and the iPhone. Depending on the design of your application, you might be able to share some of the scenes between the two devices, but chances are greater that you will need to design iPad-specific and iPhone-specific scenes. In turn, you need two storyboard files in your project, one for iPad scenes and the other for iPhone scenes.

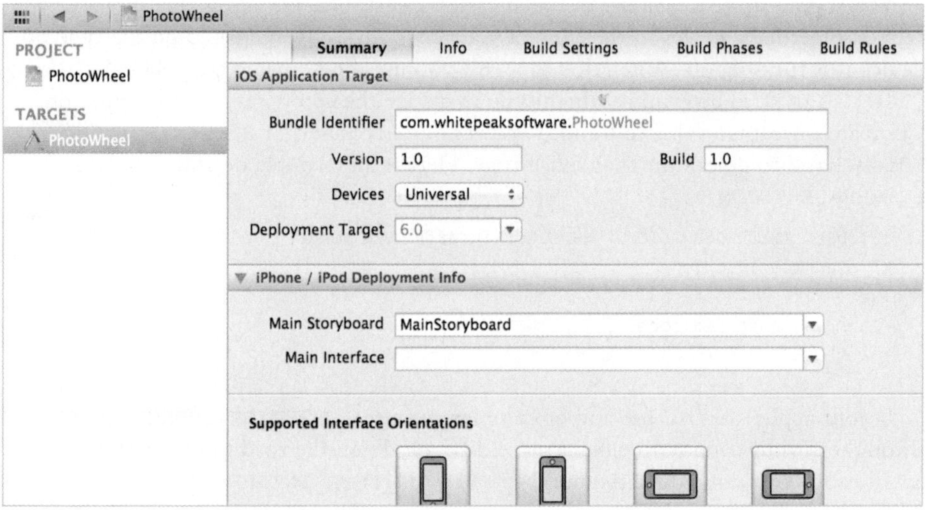

Figure 25.1   Set the target device type in the Project Summary.

It's a good idea to identify the device type for a file or resource in your Xcode project when creating a universal app. PhotoWheel, for example, names its main storyboard file *MainStoryboard.storyboard*. If PhotoWheel were a universal app, there would be two storyboard files, *MainStoryboard_ipad.storyboard* and *MainStoryboard_iphone.storyboard*. How you identify the device type in the file name is up to you, but *_ipad* and *_iphone* suffixes are a common convention used in the iOS developer community.

Creating a storyboard for each device type is not enough for iOS to know which is which, however. Instead, you need to specify explicitly which storyboard is used on iPads and which is used on iPhones. You specify the main storyboard for the particular device in the Project Summary.

The Project Summary displays two sections when the device is set to Universal: iPhone/iPod Deployment Info and iPad Deployment Info. These sections allow you to set device-specific deployment options for your app, including the main storyboard file. If you are using NIB files instead of storyboard files, then you can specify the main interface file.

These sections also let you specify the supported orientations, app icons, and default launch images for each device type. The changes you make here update the project's *info.plist*. This means you can make the changes directly to the *info.plist* file, although the Project Summary provides a cleaner user interface for making the changes.

Separating Code by Device Type

At this point, you have set up your Xcode project to generate a universal app by setting the target device type to Universal. You have also provided device-specific scenes by creating two storyboard files, one for each device type. Now you need to separate your codebase based on device type.

You should strive to achieve as much code reuse as possible across the two device types. Sometimes, however, the flow of your code must diverge based on the type of device it is running on. When this happens, you use the C macro `UI_USER_INTER FACE_IDIOM()` to determine which type of device the app is currently running on. Compare the return value to `UIUserInterfaceIdiomPad` or `UIUserInterface IdiomPhone` to determine the device type. Here is an example of using `UI_USER_ INTERFACE_IDIOM()`:

```
if (UI_USER_INTERFACE_IDIOM() == UIUserInterfaceIdiomPad) {
   // iPad-specific code
} else {
   // iPhone-specific code
}
```

If your application is large and or complex, using `UI_USER_INTERFACE_IDIOM()` throughout your code will make it more difficult down the road to maintain the application. You can reduce the number of `if UI_USER_INTERFACE_IDIOM()` checks in your code by defining device-specific subclasses. This approach can be especially helpful for view controllers, where much of the logic is the same across iPad and iPhone, but some subtle differences arise in the code due to differences in the user interface.

Ideally, you want to put code shared between the iPad and iPhone into the base class, and then derive subclasses from the base class for each device type. As with storyboards, a common naming convention is to use the _ipad and _iphone suffixes. If PhotoWheel were a universal app, then you would see view controllers like this one:

- `PhotosViewController`: Base class containing the share code.
- `PhotosViewController_ipad`: iPad-specific subclass of `PhotosView Controller` containing iPad-specific code.
- `PhotosViewController_iphone`: iPhone-specific subclass of `PhotosView Controller` containing iPhone-specific code.

Relying on inheritance in Objective-C instead of performing `if UI_USER_INTERFACE_IDIOM()` checks throughout your application can make the code much more manageable.

The Tilde

The _ipad and _iphone file name suffixes have been mentioned several times so far. Their use is a naming convention only, and neither Xcode nor iOS does anything differently based on this convention. However, there is another naming convention that iOS *does* use for loading device-specific resources at run time—that is, ~ipad and ~iphone.

Adding the tilde character followed by the device type as a suffix to a resource name tells iOS which device the resource is intended for. For example, suppose you have an image file named *DefaultPhoto.png*. This image may be sized perfectly for the iPad, yet be too large for the iPhone. As a consequence, you need two images, one for each device. You can use the _devicetype approach, which results in two images: *DefaultPhoto_ipad.png* and *DefaultPhoto_iphone.png*. In turn, your code must now perform the `UI_USER_INTERFACE_IDIOM()` check, assuming you're not using a device-specific subclass, to know which image file name to use. Your code will look something like this:

```
UIImage *image = nil;
if (UI_USER_INTERFACE_IDIOM() == UIUserInterfaceIdiomPad) {
    image = [UIImage imageNamed:@"DefaultPhoto_ipad.png"];
} else {
    image = [UIImage imageNamed:@"DefaultPhoto_iphone.png"];
}
```

This strategy works, but it leads to more lines of code to maintain. If, however, you use ~ipad and ~iphone as the file name suffixes, iOS performs the check for you and loads the correct image file based on the device type. Now the code to load the image looks like this:

```
UIImage *image = [UIImage imageNamed:@"DefaultPhoto.png"];
```

This single line of code is much easier to maintain than the multiple-line `if else` check.

Note that you do not include the ~*ipad* or ~*iphone* suffix when specifying the resource file name in the code. If you do, then iOS will not load the image based on the device type. In other words, if you write `[UIImage imageNamed:@"DefaultPhoto~ipad .png"]`, then the iPad version of the image is always loaded regardless of the device type.

> **Note**
>
> In a real universal app, you will have four images, not two. The other two images are for retina display support. Thus, using the same example of *DefaultPhoto*, you will end up with the following images in your project:
>
> - *DefaultPhoto~ipad.png*
> - *DefaultPhoto@2x~ipad.png*
> - *DefaultPhoto~iphone.png*
> - *DefaultPhoto@2x~iphone.png*

The tilde naming convention works with settings found in the *info.plist* file as well. Many of the key names have a normal name, an iPad-specific name, and an iPhone-specific name. The device-specific names use the same ~*ipad* and ~*iphone* naming convention, as you can see in Figure 25.2.

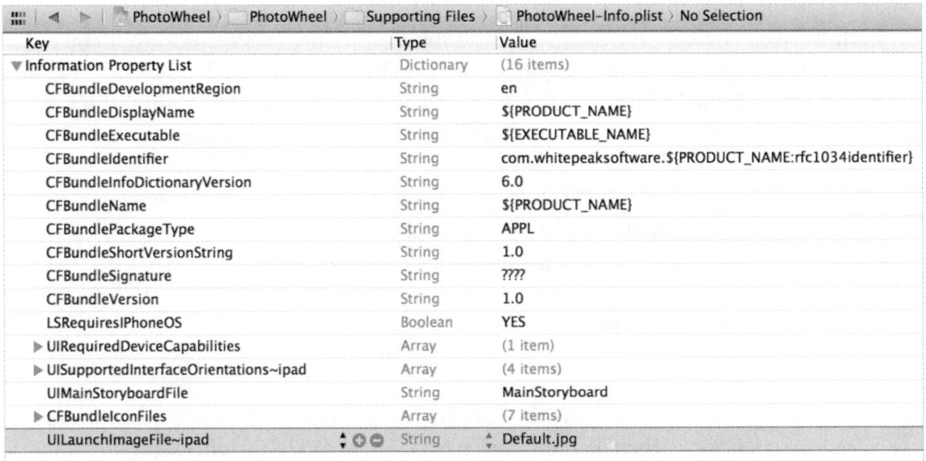

Key	Type	Value
▼ Information Property List	Dictionary	(16 items)
CFBundleDevelopmentRegion	String	en
CFBundleDisplayName	String	${PRODUCT_NAME}
CFBundleExecutable	String	${EXECUTABLE_NAME}
CFBundleIdentifier	String	com.whitepeaksoftware.${PRODUCT_NAME:rfc1034identifier}
CFBundleInfoDictionaryVersion	String	6.0
CFBundleName	String	${PRODUCT_NAME}
CFBundlePackageType	String	APPL
CFBundleShortVersionString	String	1.0
CFBundleSignature	String	????
CFBundleVersion	String	1.0
LSRequiresIPhoneOS	Boolean	YES
▶ UIRequiredDeviceCapabilities	Array	(1 item)
▶ UISupportedInterfaceOrientations~ipad	Array	(4 items)
UIMainStoryboardFile	String	MainStoryboard
▶ CFBundleIconFiles	Array	(7 items)
UILaunchImageFile~ipad	String	Default.jpg

Figure 25.2   Using the ~*devicetype* naming convention in the *info.plist* file

Pitfalls

Making your app universal benefits users (i.e., the customers paying for your app), but it comes at a cost to you, the developer. At the end of the day, you are creating two separate apps packaged as one for sale in the App Store. Even if the functionality is identical between the iPad and iPhone, the outcome is still two separate apps packaged as one. Clearly, creating a universal app requires more development time and more testing time than creating an iPad-only app. Throw in support for older versions of iOS, and you could end up with a fairly time-consuming development effort.

A Simple App That Was Not So Simple

I recently wrapped up development work on a client app. The app started out as an iPhone app, but then the decision was made to make it a universal app. The client also asked that the app support both iOS 5 and iOS 6, the two most widely used versions of iOS at the time the app was being developed.

Functionality was identical between the iPad and iPhone versions of the app, but the UI was different. For instance, where table views were used on the iPhone, collection views were used on the iPad.

The development effort for the app increased as the result of going universal, but the testing effort increased even more. The app had to be tested on every device type that could potentially run the app. This meant testing the app on iPhone 3G, iPhone 4, iPhone 4S, and iPhone 5 devices as well as iPads in the first, second, and third generations. And that was just for testing the app on those devices running iOS 5. The same testing had to occur on all but one of the same set of device types, but this time running iOS 6. The one exception was the first-generation iPad, which cannot run iOS 6.

Imagine testing each new build of your app, going through all the different scenarios supported by the app on all of those different devices running different versions of iOS. All of a sudden, a simple app becomes not so simple.

Avoid Hard-Coding

Development and testing time and effort aside, there are some pitfalls you must avoid when creating a universal app. The first is to avoid hard-coding the sizes and positions of UI elements in your app. Your universal app will run on a number of form factors, and hard-coding size and position means you must perform more checks to determine the device type and screen size. Instead of hard-coding size and position for UI elements, reply on Cocoa Auto Layout constraints.

Even if your app is not universal, you should try to avoid hard-coding the sizes and positions of UI elements in your code because you never know when Apple will introduce a new screen size. Many iOS developers learned this lesson the hard way when Apple announced the iPhone 5 and its new 4-inch screen. When the dimensions of the screen changed, it broke the look of many apps that used hard-coded values for size and position.

Be Defensive

Writing a universal app extends the potential target audience for your app, but it also extends the potential number of devices that your app can run on. This issue requires you to be more defensive in your programming.

Suppose you wrote an app for the iPhone that targets iOS 5 and later. Now you decide to make the app a universal app, but you want to keep support for iOS 5. Let's say this app is a photo app like PhotoWheel.

The original app assumes the device will always have a back-facing camera, and this assumption holds true for iPhone and iPod Touch devices running iOS 5 and greater. The app has been converted to a universal app, and the assumption that all devices have a back-facing camera remains. Your app is approved by Apple and a user with a first-generation iPad buys and installs your app. The user taps the feature that assumes the device has a back-facing camera, and *CRASH*! Your app crashes. The user tries again, and the app crashes again. The user jumps to the conclusion that the app is crap and uninstalls it.

The mistake made here is assuming a back-facing camera is available on all devices running your app. First-generation iPads, however, do not include a camera. This crash could have been prevented with a bit of defensive programming.

What is defensive programming? It is nothing more than preparing your app for the unknown. Hard-coding sizes and positions of UI elements is not defensive programming, whereas not hard-coding those values *is* defensive. Even better, having your code adapt sizing and positioning of UI elements based on the screen dimensions is an example of defensive programming. Checking whether the device supports a back-facing camera is another example.

You want to avoid unforeseen problems by performing checks in your code. Making assumptions in your code is not defensive—and it's a surefire way to crash your app once it is released into the wild.

What are some ways to be more defensive in your programming? For starters, check which capabilities the device supports. You saw an example of this practice in Chapter 12, "Adding Photos." With the PhotoWheel, a check is made to determine whether the device has a camera. If it does not, then the option to take a photo is not presented to the user.

If you are supporting multiple versions of iOS, then you should confirm that a particular feature exists before trying to use it. For example, if you want to use a new C function available in the latest version of iOS but you must also support older iOS versions, then check whether the function is NULL. If the C function is NULL, then it is not available.

When working with objects, query the object to see if it supports the new method that you want to use before calling said method. You can determine whether an object supports the method by calling -respondsToSelector: on the object. If YES is returned, then the method is available and can be called. Otherwise, do not call the method.

You can check that a new class is available by calling NSClassFromString(). If the class exists, then a reference to the class is returned; otherwise, a nil is returned.

And, as you have already seen, you can use UI_USER_INTERFACE_IDIOM() to determine which type of device the app is running on. Don't let your code assume it knows.

Sometimes, a combination of checks is required to be truly defensive. Take, for example. the UIPopoverController class. UIPopoverController is available in iOS but can be used only on the iPad. So what is returned when NSClassFromString(@"UIPopoverController") is run on an iPhone? Nope, nil is not returned. Instead, a reference to the UIPopoverController class is returned. Why? The same version of iOS runs on both the iPad and the iPhone, which means the class is available on iPad *and* iPhone devices. But you cannot use UIPopoverController on an iPhone—doing so will caused an exception to be thrown, potentially crashing your app.

In this case, you want to not only check that the class is available, but also make sure the app is running on an iPad before using the class. For example:

```
Class popoverControllerClass = NSClassFromString(@"UIPopoverController");
if (popoverControllerClass && UI_USER_INTERFACE_IDIOM() ==
UIUserInterfaceIdiomPad) {
    // ...
} else {
    // ...
}
```

You cannot check for the availability of the UIPopoverController class and assume your app is running on an iPad. This class is available on the iPhone, and it will throw an exception if you try using it on iPhone devices.

For more on defensive programming in Objective-C and iOS, watch the Session 130 video from WWDC 2010 titled *Future Proofing Your Applications*.[1]

Summary

Creating a universal app is a great way to extend the potential reach of your app. Moreover, users expect apps they have purchased to run on all the iOS devices they own. By developing a universal app, you give the user the best possible experience. But be smart about making your app universal—make sure doing so makes sense for

---

1. *Future Proofing Your Applications*: https://devcloper.apple.com/videos/wwdc/2010/?id=130

business reasons, as it will be more costly to develop a universal app than an app that targets only the iPad or iPhone.

If you decide to go universal, check the device type in code where appropriate. If your app is large or complex, consider partitioning device-specific code into subclasses. Finally, be defensive in your programming. Don't assume certain device capabilities or iOS features exist. Perform the appropriate checks in code to avoid crashes and to future proof your app.

Exercises

1. Create a new universal app in Xcode. Take a look at the generated code to see how the application template separates iPad-specific resources from iPhone-specific resources.

2. Create a new iPad app in Xcode. Manually convert it to a universal app by following the steps covered in this chapter. Use the sample project in Exercise 1 as a guide.

3. Make PhotoWheel a universal app. Don't worry about making the iPhone version look nice with new artwork. Instead, display a table view of photo albums. When an album is tapped, display the photos available in the album in a collection view. When a photo is tapped, display the photo in a full-screen photo browser.

Part III

The Finishing Touches

26

Debugging

As you develop an app, you'll find at times that the app isn't behaving quite as you expected. Maybe the screen layout seems off, or maybe the app is just crashing. Xcode provides a number of useful tools for finding and fixing bugs. In this chapter we'll discuss these tools as well as the more general question of narrowing down and finding the source of problems.

Understand the Problem

The first thing you need to do when confronted with a bug is to get the most detailed, accurate picture of the problem that you can. Getting a clear picture of the bug from the outside is a crucial first step in understanding what is wrong on the inside. Diving right into the code is rarely the best approach.

What Went Wrong?

Begin by making sure you understand exactly what happened that was unexpected and which steps the user had taken when this happened. If you're testing the app yourself, you may have a pretty good idea already. If someone else was testing the app, try to get as much detail as possible. Without a good description of what seemed to be wrong with the app, it can be almost impossible to track down the cause. A bug description needs to be very specific. Veteran developers have all seen at one time or another a bug report that reads something like "I was using the app and it crashed." Unfortunately, that statement is entirely useless when it comes to fixing the problem. Unless the app is crashing constantly, you don't have anything to go on to find the problem. And if the app *is* crashing constantly, you're probably painfully aware of that fact already.

Reproducing Bugs

Once you have that clear picture, it's time to reproduce the problem. Occasionally there will be situations where you're familiar with the code to the point that the bug description makes it obvious where the code is going wrong. More commonly, though, the cause of the problem is not immediately obvious. In those cases, sit down with the app and make the bug happen. Explore different ways of using the app to see if other circumstances could generate the problem. Maybe taking a slightly different set of steps prevents the bug from appearing or makes it worse. Try to find the minimal test case that gets directly to the bug quickly with as little extra work as possible.

If you find that you can't reproduce the bug, you have a new problem. It is extremely difficult to fix a problem that you can't see. If nothing else, you may not be able to tell if you have fixed the problem even if you change the code. Subtle or intermittent problems may require considerable detective work to uncover where things are going awry. You might need to make your test data resemble the user's test data. In extreme cases you might need to get the user's data onto your own device. Bugs can also depend on timing or, in unusual cases, even the time of day.

Debugging Concepts

Xcode includes a built-in debugger. New developers often underestimate or misunderstand the use of debuggers and avoid them, but they don't know what they are missing. In this section we'll cover some of the tools and techniques offered by debuggers. If you have used debuggers on other platforms, you can skip ahead to the following section, which discusses how Xcode's debugger works.

Without a doubt, **the debugger is the second-most important tool in your arsenal as a developer**. The only tool that is more important is the compiler itself. If you're not using the debugger to investigate your code, you're missing out on an incredibly useful tool. If you haven't used one before, debuggers can seem daunting at first. But whatever time you take to learn to use a good debugger will be repaid many times over in the time saved while finding and fixing bugs.

What Is a "Debugger" Anyway?

A debugger is a specialized tool that can run another application and control and monitor that application's progress. It's like opening the hood on a car engine to inspect and make adjustments while the motor is running. You'll use a debugger to investigate what is actually happening in your code while that code is running. You can understand a lot by reading and thinking about the code, but you'll almost always learn even more when you can see every step of the code as it really happens.

Breakpoints

Probably the most common use of a debugger is to set breakpoints in code. A breakpoint is just a line in the code where you want to see what is happening. You'll set breakpoints on lines you suspect of buggy behavior. Once you have added a breakpoint for a line, you run the code in the debugger and interact with the app normally.

When the code reaches the line with the breakpoint, it stops. It's as though time has suddenly stood still for the app, but not for you. At this point you can use the debugger to inspect the state of the program and see if it is operating the way it should. You can see the values of variables and change them, and even call functions while paused at the breakpoint.

When you're finished with your examination of the program, you can tell the debugger to continue running the program—and it picks up smoothly where it left off. You can also have the debugger step through the code one line at a time, breaking after each one. Doing this can give you a very clear picture of what is happening in the code.

Another kind of breakpoint affects specific conditions instead of specific lines of code. The effect is the same as a breakpoint, but the program stops because an event or situation occurs rather than because it reaches the right line. A good example is an exception breakpoint. Certain kinds of bugs in code cause exceptions to be thrown, and if the exceptions aren't handled properly, the app will crash. An exception breakpoint stops the app whenever an exception is thrown, regardless of where it happened. You can also create what's called a watchpoint to track changes to a variable. With a watchpoint, the debugger will break any time the value of a variable changes. If you're not sure when or why a value changed, watching the variable will help uncover the problem.

Debugging in Xcode

Now let's investigate how you can use these techniques in Xcode.

Setting and Managing Breakpoints

Xcode's options for setting breakpoints are shown in Figure 26.1.

The quickest way to set a breakpoint on a line is in the editor's gutter, which is the vertical band on the left side of the source code pane. To set a breakpoint on a line, click in the gutter next to the line. A blue pointer appears next to the line. You can disable and re-enable a breakpoint by clicking this blue indicator. Figure 26.1 shows two breakpoints in *AppDelegate.m*. The first, in -managedObjectModel, is enabled. The second, in -persistentStoreCoordinator, is disabled.

To remove a breakpoint in the editor gutter, drag the blue pointer out of the gutter.

On the left side of the window is the Breakpoint navigator. It lists all breakpoints, including those that are disabled or that affect other files. Breakpoints are organized by source file. Clicking on one of them opens the corresponding source file at the line where the breakpoint is set. You can also disable and re-enable breakpoints here, by clicking on the blue pointer icon. To delete a breakpoint in the Breakpoint navigator, either drag it out of the navigator or select it and press the **Delete** key.

At the top of the window is the master breakpoint toggle button (**Command-Y**). This button controls whether the app will run with breakpoints or without them.

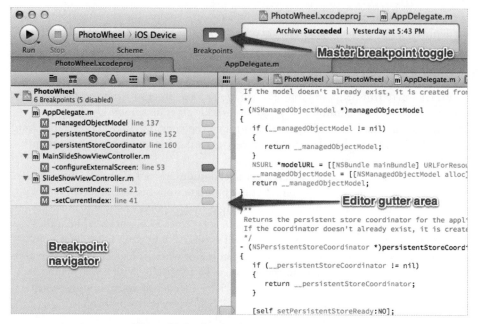

Figure 26.1   Setting breakpoints in Xcode

Clicking this button affects the overall run environment when the app is running. It does not affect whether individual breakpoints are enabled; instead, it determines whether any breakpoints will be used while the app is running. You can change this state while the app is running.

Customizing Breakpoints

If you right-click (or **Control-click**) on a breakpoint in the Breakpoint navigator and select Edit Breakpoint from the popup menu, a popover appears that you can use to customize the breakpoint's behavior (Figure 26.2).

This popover offers the following options:

- Specify a condition that must be true for the breakpoint to stop the app. If you want to stop the app only when a variable has a specific value, you can enter a test for this condition here. This condition might be something like x == 21, which causes the program to stop only when x equals 21.

- Tell Xcode that it should ignore the breakpoint some number of times before stopping. This can be useful for breakpoints in loops, if you want to stop in the loop but only after, say, 50 passes through it. Without this option, you would have to hit the breakpoint 50 times and continue after each one.

- Configure a variety of automatic actions to take when the breakpoint is hit (more on this later).

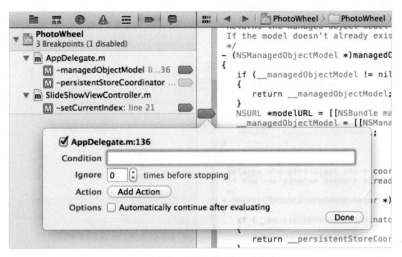

Figure 26.2   Editing a breakpoint

- Tell Xcode that it should automatically continue after executing any custom actions the breakpoint has.

Why would you want to have Xcode automatically continue when it hits a breakpoint? It turns out that breakpoints can do a number of useful things even if the app keeps running. You configure these options in the Action section of the popover.

One good use for breakpoint actions is to replace the NSLog statements that are so common when code is in development. Often you want to know that a method has been called or find out the value of a variable at a particular line, but you don't necessarily want to stop the app to find this out—it's enough just to get the information. Or you might be investigating a bug that depends on getting just the right timing, and stopping the app prevents the bug from happening. Developers frequently add an NSLog statement that prints out the information of interest, which is simple and effective. Unfortunately, it's also messy and can get confusing. NSLog statements have a way of sticking around long after their usefulness has expired, leading to extremely verbose output that can make it hard to find the one line you're interested in. They also really need to be cleaned out before the app is released so as not to fill up the system console on users' iPads.

One of the breakpoint actions is the Log Message action, which simply prints a message to the device console. It has more or less the same effect as using NSLog except that it doesn't clutter up the source code. This action can also speak the text aloud using speech synthesis instead of printing the message, so you can listen for it instead of watching the console. Figure 26.3 shows an example of this behavior. In this case the breakpoint is in the -managedObjectModel method. When the code reaches the line with the breakpoint, it says, "Starting managedObjectModel," and then continues without stopping the app.

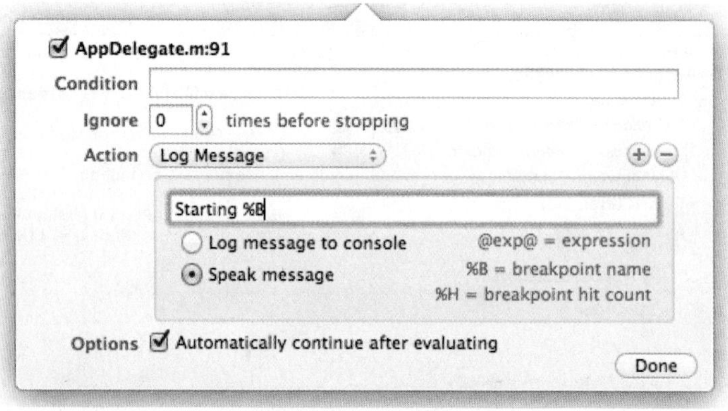

Figure 26.3   Adding a Log Message action to a breakpoint

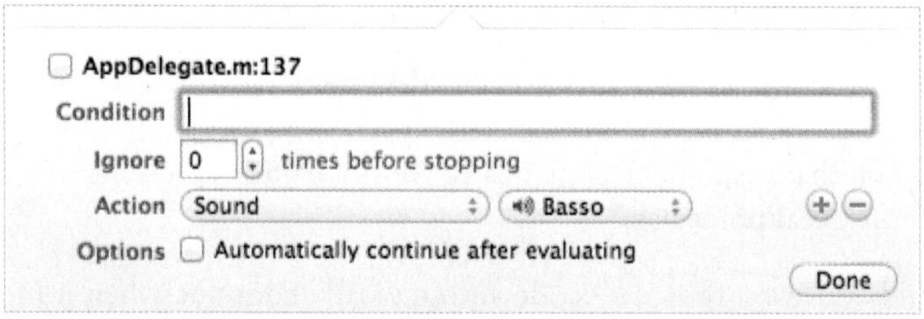

Figure 26.4   Configuring a breakpoint to play a sound and continue

A related option is to have Xcode play a sound when the code hits the breakpoint (Figure 26.4). This approach can be used similarly to having Xcode speak a message. It is useful for monitoring code when you expect to hit a breakpoint frequently. As you use the app, the sounds will often form a rhythm, and if the rhythm breaks, it's a clue that something isn't happening the way it should.

You can add multiple actions to a breakpoint by clicking the **+** button on the right side of the popover.

Hitting a Breakpoint

When the app hits a breakpoint and stops, Xcode will look like Figure 26.5.

There are a number of things of interest in this window:

- **Current line.** The current line in the app is highlighted in the editor, so that you always know where you are in the app. The highlighted line has not been executed yet—the highlighting indicates the next line that would run if the app were to continue.

- **Debug navigator.** This shows the current state of all threads in the app. In Figure 26.5, we see that the app is stopped at a breakpoint in

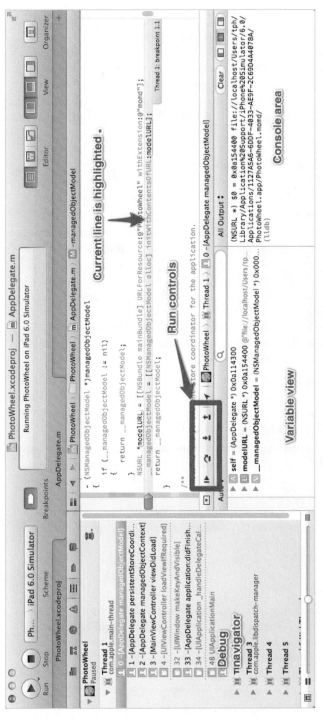

Figure 26.5   Xcode window when stopped at a breakpoint

[AppDelegate managedObjectModel], which is in thread 1. The information displayed under the thread 1 heading is a call stack, showing the method that called -managedObjectModel, the method that called *that* method, and so on. Methods that are part of iOS frameworks rather than the app are grayed out.

You can explore the call stack by clicking on different methods. When you do, the code editor will update to show the current line in that method. In this case we could immediately jump to the line that called -managedObjectModel, for example.

The slider at the bottom of the Debug navigator controls how much detail is included in the call stack. Xcode normally tries to limit the information to methods that are likely to be of interest (i.e., those that are part of your app). You can adjust the level of detail to show more or less information.

- **Run controls.** These four buttons allow you to control what happens next in the program's flow. The first button tells Xcode to continue running the app normally from the current line. The app continues until it reaches another breakpoint, if there are others. Next to this is the "step over" button, which steps forward one line and *does not* step into functions or methods that might be called. After that, the "step into" button also steps forward one line but *will* step into any functions or methods that are called, if the source code is available (it won't step into system framework methods since you don't have the source for them). Finally, the "step out" button tells Xcode that the app should continue running but only until the current function or method ends.

- **Variable view.** This pane normally displays the value of any local variables. In Figure 26.5, you see that modelURL is included here, because it is local to the current method. A popup menu at the top of the variable view selects different modes, such as displaying global variables as well as local variables.

- **Console.** The console displays messages from the debugger about the app's state, as well as the output from any NSLog or other printing statements. The console also has a command-line interface to the debugger, which can be used to control the debug session and to inspect and change variable values. We'll talk about some debugger commands a little later. In Figure 26.5, the breakpoint was configured to print the value of modelURL when the app hit the breakpoint, so you can see the full value in the console.

Checking on Variables

Often the variable view is all you need to check on variables. In Figure 26.5, you can see the URL stored in modelURL—some of it, anyway—and you could get more by dragging the split between the variable view and the console area to the right. You could also hover the mouse pointer over modelURL in the code editor and look at a popup window that has a little more space (Figure 26.6).

The variable view doesn't always have enough information, though. In Figure 26.7, for example, the variable view tells us that `options` is a dictionary and that it has four key-value pairs. That's nice, and sometimes that's all you need to know.

At other times, however, you might want to know which data is actually saved in those key-value pairs. Fortunately, there are a couple of other options. One way is to select the variable in the variable view and right-click (or **Control-click**). The contextual popup menu includes an option to print a description of the variable (Figure 26.8). It also includes some other useful things, like the ability to set a watchpoint on the selected variable.

If you select this menu item, the description is printed in the console area. You can also get detail about an object using the debugger command line. The `po` command in the console is shorthand for "print object." It calls the object's `-description` method and prints the result. You get the same results either way (Figure 26.9).

Figure 26.6   Displaying a variable's value by hovering the mouse pointer over it

Figure 26.7   Variable view information about an `NSDictionary`

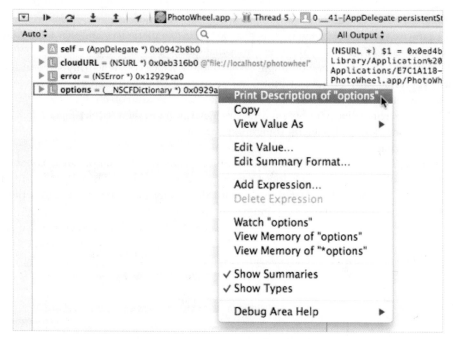

Figure 26.8   The variable view contextual menu

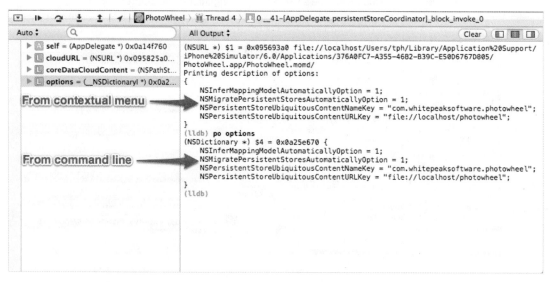

Figure 26.9   `NSDictionary` details in the debugger console

Debugging Example: External Display Code

While I was writing Chapter 23's sample code for using external displays, a puzzling bug cropped up at one point. Although the app was running a slideshow on an external display, the images were off-center. They were too low and off to the left, leaving a large black L-shaped space along the top and right side of the display.

Experimenting with different ways to reproduce the bug didn't turn up a lot of information. The problem occurred anytime a slideshow started, and always in the same way. Well, almost always.

The bug first showed up when using a 720-pixel television as an external display via AirPlay. This meant that the external display resolution was 1280 × 720. At that size, the L-shaped black area was approximately half the width of the screen and half the height. It might have been exactly half but it was difficult to be sure it wasn't off by a few pixels. That might suggest a math error, or that the code might somehow be accidentally using the center point of the window someplace where it should have been using the origin. But on iOS the origin is at the upper-left corner—so using the center instead of the origin would move the photo down and to the right, not down and to the left as was happening.

Further investigation showed that the bug varied depending on the size of the screen. By running the app in the iOS Simulator, I simulated several different external display sizes. With a simulated 1024 × 768 display, the L-shaped area was thinner, occupying maybe one-fourth of the display width and one-third of the height. With a 720 × 480 or 640 × 480 simulated display, the photos disappeared completely, although the page-curl animation still occurred.

It seemed possible that the code in `SlideShowViewController` that displays the photos might be at fault. The code looked okay, but plainly something was not right. Maybe the photo view was off-center for some reason. I set a breakpoint in `-set CurrentIndex:`, just after setting the photo view's frame. When the app reached the breakpoint, I checked the frame in the debug console (Figure 26.10).

Look at the debug command in Figure 26.10. The p command is shorthand for "print." Here I'm printing the value of `newPhotoView`'s frame. When using p, you usually need to typecast the result so that the debugger knows how to format its output. A `UIView`'s frame is a `CGRect`, so that's what I used here. Another detail to notice is that the command calls a method on `newPhotoView` to get the frame. I'm making Objective-C method calls right from the console, which interprets and executes them and then prints the result.

In Figure 26.10, the frame's size is 768 × 1004. That indicates that the view is on the internal display, given that the simulated external display was 1280 × 720. There will be a second `SlideShowViewController` instance for the external display, which means this method will be called more than once on different instances. So I clicked the continue button and the code hit the breakpoint again. This time the frame matched the external display size, so I knew it was the right view (Figure 26.11).

Figure 26.10   Checking a view's frame in the debug console: first pass

Figure 26.11   Checking a view's frame in the debug console: second pass

Figure 26.12   Investigating the external display bug

The photo view's frame looks okay. But something must be wrong, because the photo is in the wrong place. But a view's frame doesn't reflect its absolute position on the screen—it gives the position relative to its enclosing view. In this case newPhoto View is a subview of the SlideShowViewController view, so I checked that next.

As Figure 26.11 shows, the size of the SlideShowViewController view is correct, but its origin is way off. The origin should be at (0,0). Instead, it's shifted—as I had seen on the external display—downward and to the left.

Now I needed to check where the view's origin was set. This happens over in MainSlideShowViewController, in the -configureExternalScreen: method. That method creates a new UIWindow and a new view controller and adjusts the view controller's view to fit the screen. I wasn't sure which step might be wrong, so I decided to set a breakpoint at the beginning of the method and step through it line by line, checking on each part of the process.

As I stepped through the method, I found that the window was the right size. I found this in the console, as shown in Figure 26.12.

The view controller's view was off-center, though, just as I had seen earlier. What could have caused that? Looking through the code, I decided that this line was suspect:

```
[[externalSlideController view] setBounds:externalViewFrame];
```

The problem with that line is that it mixes up a view's bounds with its frame. These are closely related but not the same. A view's frame uses its parent view's coordinate system, while its bounds use the frame's own coordinate system. The frame's origin gives the view's location in its parent view, and the bounds origin is usually

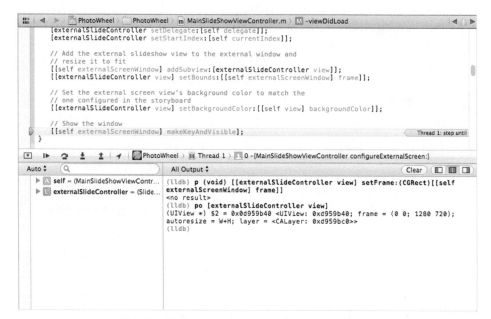

Figure 26.13   Fixing the view's frame in the debugger console

(though not always) at (0, 0). Mixing up bounds and frames is a bad idea and can lead to weirdly misplaced views. Sound familiar? Sometimes this happens because although the bounds origin is usually (0, 0), the frame origin usually is not. When this is the case, setting the bounds origin to the frame origin usually won't do what you want. Here, though, we already know that the frame origin is at (0, 0) because externalScreenWindow is at (0, 0) and that's what we used for the bounds. The other factor is that changing a view's bounds will change its size relative to its *center point*, not relative to its origin. That seemed more likely to be the cause of this bug.

Based on this, I suspected that I would fix the bug if I changed the suspect line to read

```
[[externalSlideController view] setFrame:externalViewFrame];
```

I could use the debugger to verify this hypothesis, without restarting the app and without editing code until I was sure of what I needed (Figure 26.13).

The first command in the console executes the new line of code, as if it were in the app. I'm using p again, albeit with a few differences. First, the argument to p is an Objective-C statement that will change the frame of the view. I'm not simply looking up a value and displaying it; instead, I'm changing values by calling object methods. Second, the method I'm calling returns void, so there's no actual result to display. That's okay, though, because I can check the results in a separate command.

On the second line, I checked the view to make sure the frame was what it should be. It was! I clicked the continue button and the slideshow started. This time the external display images were in the right place, so I changed the code.

Before declaring the problem to be fixed, I went through the tests I had done earlier. In the simulator, I tried the app on multiple external display sizes. Then I tried it using an iPad and a real external display. It still looked good, so I decided the bug was now fixed.

When You Really Need NSLog

Despite all the power the debugger offers, sometimes you just really need to use NSLog. Even the most experienced developers do, at least some of the time. The problems mentioned earlier still exist, though. NSLog statements have a way of outliving their usefulness and cluttering up code. They also fill up the device console with needless messages if you leave them in place when you release the app. What's more, if you have a lot of NSLog statements, writing the messages can affect your app's performance, causing pointless slowdowns.

The second problem, at least, is easy to address. Using a compiler macro and a definition, you can arrange for NSLog statements to appear automatically only in debug builds. Here the basic macro is called DLog, for "debug log," and is shown in Listing 25.1. You can call it whatever you like.

Listing 25.1   **Defining a Macro for Debug-Only NSLog**

```
#ifdef DEBUG
#define DLog(...) NSLog(__VA_ARGS__)
#else
#define DLog(...)
#endif
```

This creates a macro called DLog. A compiler macro tells the compiler that some defined text should be replaced by some other text. The replacement happens before the code is compiled, as part of the preprocessing stage.

In this case, if DEBUG is defined in the app, any use of DLog will be replaced by a call to NSLog. It is not simply equivalent to calling NSLog; it literally is a call to NSLog once preprocessing is complete. Any arguments to DLog will become NSLog arguments. If DEBUG is not defined, any call to NSLog is replaced by an empty string—so when the code compiles, the NSLog statement is already gone. Numerous variations on this macro are available online that modify or add to the NSLog arguments. In this case what you get is exactly what you would get if you used NSLog, but only when DEBUG is defined.

If you put this code in your project's precompiled header file (the *.pch* file), it will be available throughout the app without requiring any extra #import statements.

To use DLog, you need to arrange for DEBUG to be defined for debug builds but not for any other builds. You do this in the app's Build Settings, by adding a new compiler flag that will be used only in debug builds. The easiest way to find the flags section is to type "cflags" in the Build Settings search field (Figure 26.14).

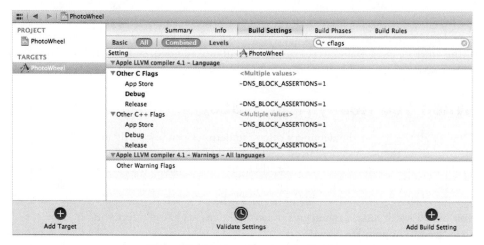

Figure 26.14   Compiler flags in Xcode

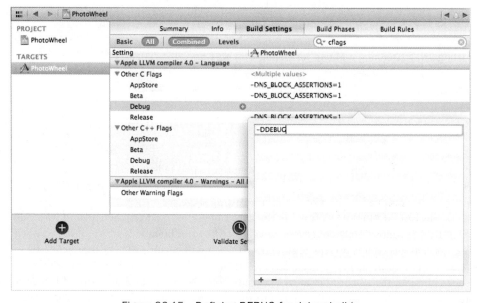

Figure 26.15   Defining DEBUG for debug builds

Xcode automatically creates multiple release configurations. If you double-click next to Debug in the Other C Flags section, a popover view appears where you can add custom flags (Figure 26.15).

The compiler option to create a #define is –D, and we want to define DEBUG, so adding –DDEBUG as shown in Figure 26.15 will make the DLog macro work. With this bit of setup, turning NSLog on for debug builds only is completely automatic.

Profiling Code with Instruments

Some code bugs don't show up as incorrect data or screen layouts. Instead, perhaps the app uses more memory than you think it should. Or maybe it is just too slow in places. The debugger won't help much with this kind of issue.

Xcode includes a separate tool called Instruments, designed for situations just like this. *Instruments* is a graphical profiling tool that helps you understand what is really happening when an app runs. A profiler, like the debugger, is a tool that can run another application and monitor its activities. It is unlike the debugger in that it doesn't work with breakpoints or do anything that would stop the app. Instead, it sits back and lets you interact with the app while it collects data, such as how much memory is in use or how much time the app spends in each method. Instruments provides graphs and detailed statistics about the app's behavior, which can give deep insights into where performance issues are occurring and how to fix them.

It is common to think that you can prevent performance issues by writing better code in the first place. Some code seems obviously inefficient and in need of speed improvements. This is often a mistake and can lead to what is known as premature optimization. The code that looks as if it should be slow is often not a bottleneck, but it's easy to spend a lot of time optimizing it based on incorrect assumptions. There are a variety of reasons for this. Modern compilers are capable of quite a bit of optimization, so inefficiencies in source code may be eliminated once the app is compiled. Other times, the code that actually takes more time to run is not obviously any less efficient than other code. For this reason, profiling code should be an integral part of any attempts at optimization. It's better to see what is actually slow instead of spending lots of time modifying your code only to find out that your guess was wrong.

Even before you undertake profiling, though, consider whether you actually have a problem. It is almost always possible to find a way to make code run a little faster, but it doesn't always make sense to do so. If the app has no appreciable performance problems, it is often not worth the time to try to make it even more efficient. You want to have a great app, of course, but you also want to release it someday, and optimization can be a never-ending challenge. Better code is, well, better, but it's important to keep things in perspective.

Instruments works with both simulator and device builds. You should work with a device whenever possible, because performance on simulator builds is very different from that of device builds. Even relative performance, such as finding that one method takes longer than another without considering absolute time, can be different on simulators and devices. Memory issues will usually be more similar, but they probably won't be identical.

To start Instruments, select **Product > Profile** in Xcode (or press **Command-I**). Xcode builds the app, if needed, and launches Instruments. Instruments starts by showing a scrollable window with various profiling options (Figure 26.16).

Instruments offers numerous profiling tools. The Allocations and Leaks tools monitor memory usage over time. The Time Profiler tool monitors the time spent in each function or method in the app, to help find performance bottlenecks. Other tools monitor

Figure 26.16   Startup options for Instruments

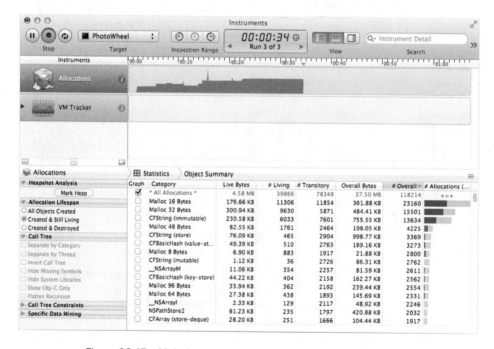

Figure 26.17   Main Instruments window, with the Allocations tool

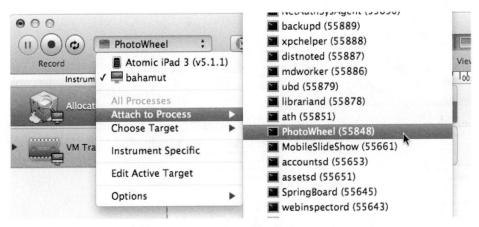

Figure 26.18   Attaching Instruments to a running process

overall system usage, network activity, and graphics performance. You can use more than one tool during the same run if you need data in multiple areas. The startup window lets you select only one, but once Instruments is running you can add others.

Once you select a tool, Instruments starts the app and shows its main window (Figure 26.17). The current tools are shown on the left, next to graphs showing activity over time. The bottom part of the window is the data display, which shows statistics related to the currently selected tool and options for configuring and filtering those numbers.

It's also possible to attach Instruments to an app that is already running. This is handy because often you want to monitor only a specific action in an app. Collecting data from the time the app starts until you reach the area of interest can fill up Instruments with data that is not relevant to the problem you're investigating. To narrow the focus of Instruments in an already-running app, you first start the app and then click the Target popup menu. In the Attach to Process section of the menu, locate your app. Instruments starts recording data for the app. Figure 26.18 shows how you might do this for a simulator build.

Profiling Example: Slideshow UI Control Updates

One area that looks ripe for performance improvement in the PhotoWheel app is the code that handles the play/pause buttons in the slideshow. As you may recall, when the user presses "play" or "pause" in the slideshow, the app rebuilds the entire set of buttons. The buttons aren't cached or reused; instead, the entire panel is thrown out and replaced. Even the forward and back buttons are replaced, and they never change. It doesn't seem as if the app is running slowly here, but at the same time the code is clearly doing more work than it needs to do. Which changes might make it better?

The code of interest executes whenever the user presses "play" or "pause." To make Instruments collect data that focuses on this task, let's use Instruments as follows:

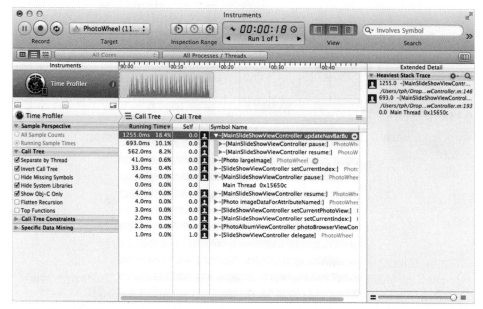

Figure 26.19   Instruments showing time profile results for PhotoWheel's slideshow

1. Start up the app and navigate to the slideshow.
2. Start Instruments using the Time Profiler tool and attach it to the running process.
3. Press "play" and "pause" over and over very quickly for a while.
4. Click the **Stop** button in Instruments to make it stop recording data.

The effect is that while Instruments is running, the app is spending most of its time in the code under investigation. After doing this, Instruments looks like Figure 26.19.

The graph next to the Time Profiler tool shows CPU activity over time. Below the graph is a list of call trees found while Instruments was recording data. This list shows the deepest method call and can be expanded to show more detail. In Figure 26.19, you can see that the call to `-updateNavBarButtonsForPlayingState:` consumed the most CPU at 1255 ms. Instruments also shows that this method was called from two other methods, `-pause:` and `-play:`, and that the 1255 ms was close to evenly distributed between calls from those methods. Several other call trees are listed below these entries, but they didn't use anywhere near as much time.

The box on the lower left has several check boxes that control how call tree information is displayed. Two of these check boxes are often especially useful when finding slow points in your code:

- **Hide System Libraries.** This option limits the display so that it includes only methods and functions in your code. When it is unchecked, the call tree area

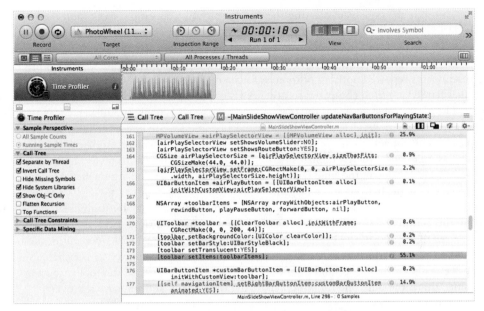

Figure 26.20   Source code display in Instruments

includes entries that relate to code used by iOS and frameworks but that your code did not directly call. This information can be interesting to see, but it can also mean you have a lot of detail that is not directly relevant to the problem you're trying to solve.

- **Show Obj-C Only.** When this option is checked, the call tree display filters out detail that is not directly related to Objective-C method calls. Again, this can be useful information, but it often includes unnecessary detail.

The section on the right shows the stack trace with the greatest impact on the selected call tree. In Figure 26.19 this would show the call from –pause: to -update NavBarButtonsForPlayingState:. The call from -play: is almost as important, but since it took slightly less CPU time overall it is not the "heaviest" stack trace.

None of this is really surprising yet. The steps taken previously pretty much guaranteed that -updateNavBarButtonsForPlayingState: would take the most time, since that is the method that updates the slideshow control buttons. The goal was to find out which parts of that method are consuming most of the time when that method executes.

To get this information, double-click on that method in the Heaviest Stack Trace display. Instruments then replaces the call tree area with the source code for the method. Every line that took a significant portion of the method's run time is highlighted. A number by these lines shows the percentage of time taken by that line. Figure 26.20 shows the results for this method.

The code shown covers creating the AirPlay button, adjusting it to fit, and then updating the toolbar with a new set of buttons. One surprising finding is that the code to re-create the back, play, pause, and forward buttons takes so little time that none of the lines were highlighted. They are not shown in Figure 26.20, but that's because Instruments reported nothing of interest for them. Re-creating them is redundant but takes hardly any time compared to other parts of the method.

The most expensive line is the one updating the toolbar items, at 55.1 percent of the total in this method. That is probably unavoidable unless we redesign the buttons completely. This time wouldn't be reduced by caching copies of buttons or other tricks—as long as we're updating the toolbar's buttons, we need this line. If this method created a significant slowdown, the time taken by this line would be a good argument for reconsidering how the buttons are managed.

One area that *could* be optimized is the creation of the AirPlay button. Creating the button accounts for 25.9 percent of the total method time. Add in other lines that resize the button and create a `UIBarButtonItem` for it, and 29.1 percent of the method is spent creating and configuring this button. But this button never changes—so we could create it once and then reuse the existing copy. Of all the toolbar button items, this is the only one for which changing the code would improve the overall speed of the method.

A possible extra optimization involves the last line shown, where the code updates the navigation item with the new buttons. As it stands, the code creates a new `UIBar ButtonItem` each time it runs, with a custom view containing the toolbar. Then it sets this item as the right bar button item on the navigation item. But the `customView` property of `UIBarButtonItem` is writable. It might be faster to keep a reference to `customBarButtonItem` around and just update its `customView` in this method. The benefit here is not as obvious as with the AirPlay button, because we would be replacing relatively slow code with different code. That new code might be just as slow or even slower. It's not obvious how much time it takes to update `customView`. If we made this change, we would need to do some more profiling to check whether it improved our app's performance.

Summary

Bugs are an unfortunate fact of any software developer's life. You'll never avoid them completely, but with experience you can become very effective at finding and fixing those problems. With Xcode's debugger and Instruments, you are well equipped to deal with unexpected problems in code. Logic errors, incorrect data and settings, and a variety of performance issues can be diagnosed by examining and manipulating code while it is running. When you see a problem, put on your debugging tool belt and fix it!

Effective debugging is crucial for more than a good user experience; it is also a fundamental part of launching an app. An app crashing during Apple's review testing is grounds for immediate rejection. Except in extreme cases, poor performance usually doesn't stop an app from being approved. But it is one of the easiest ways to rack up one-star reviews in the App Store, and that in turn is one of the easiest ways to make an app flop. Take debugging seriously and deal with performance problems in advance. Fixing bugs and improving performance can be a challenge, but it's far, far better to deal with problems privately instead of publicly.

Speaking of the App Store, the next chapter discusses how to get your app ready for submission to Apple so that you can sell it through the App Store.

27

Distributing Your App

Finally, PhotoWheel is complete! Or at least it's ready for a good round of beta testing.

So far you have learned how to build and install PhotoWheel on your own iPad, but eventually you'll want to make it available to other people. During development you'll want to have other people test the app, both while you're working on finishing it and as a final test stage before releasing your app to the world. When your app is ready, you'll want to upload it to the App Store for approval.

This chapter covers how you can prepare and distribute your app for testing and approval.

Distribution Methods

Until now you have deployed apps from Xcode to your own devices. Preparing your app to run on other people's devices requires some extra steps. You can distribute apps using one of two methods:

- **Ad Hoc distribution.** You use this method to distribute your app to testers. Ad Hoc distribution does not go through the App Store. Instead, you build the app and provide copies to testers by whatever means you find convenient. Ad Hoc builds can go to only those devices listed in your iOS Provisioning Portal account, which limits the number of testers. Testers install the app on their devices using iTunes. People who install Ad Hoc builds of apps don't need to belong to the iOS Developer Program; anyone with a device that supports the app can be a tester.

- **App Store distribution.** You use this method when the app is ready to be released to the App Store. An App Store build of the app can't be installed directly on any devices. Instead, you upload the build to Apple. Apple reviews the app and, if it is accepted, the app becomes available through the App Store.

This chapter covers both methods.

The first thing you need to do, for either distribution method, is set up a new signing certificate for distribution builds. The steps to do this are nearly the same as those discussed in Chapter 6, "Provisioning Your iPad," for development certificates. There are two differences. One is that in the Certificates section of the Provisioning Portal, you click the Distribution tab instead of Development; otherwise, the process of creating and downloading a certificate is the same. The second difference is that distribution certificates can be created only by the Team Agent, who is normally the person who created the iPhone Developer Program account. If you're working independently, this is you. If you're part of a team, it might be someone else.

Building for Ad Hoc Distribution

Now let's tackle the process for Ad Hoc distribution. You'll need to set up provisioning and prepare an Ad Hoc build of the app before you can send it out for testing.

Provisioning for Ad Hoc Distribution

Provisioning for Ad Hoc builds is very similar to provisioning for development. There are only a couple of minor differences. To create an Ad Hoc provisioning profile, use the Provisioning section of the Provisioning Portal site, and the Distribution tab within that section (Figure 27.1).

When you click the **New Profile** button, the screen that appears is similar to the one used for development profiles, but not quite identical. Next to Distribution Method, select the Ad Hoc option (Figure 27.2). From this point forward, the provisioning process is the same as for development builds. Name the profile and select an App ID and whichever devices should be included, and then create the profile as described in Chapter 6, "Provisioning Your iPad." If you're planning to send the build to other people for testing, you'll need to have their device IDs in your account and include them in the profile.

Figure 27.1. Distribution Provisioning profile section of the Provisioning Portal

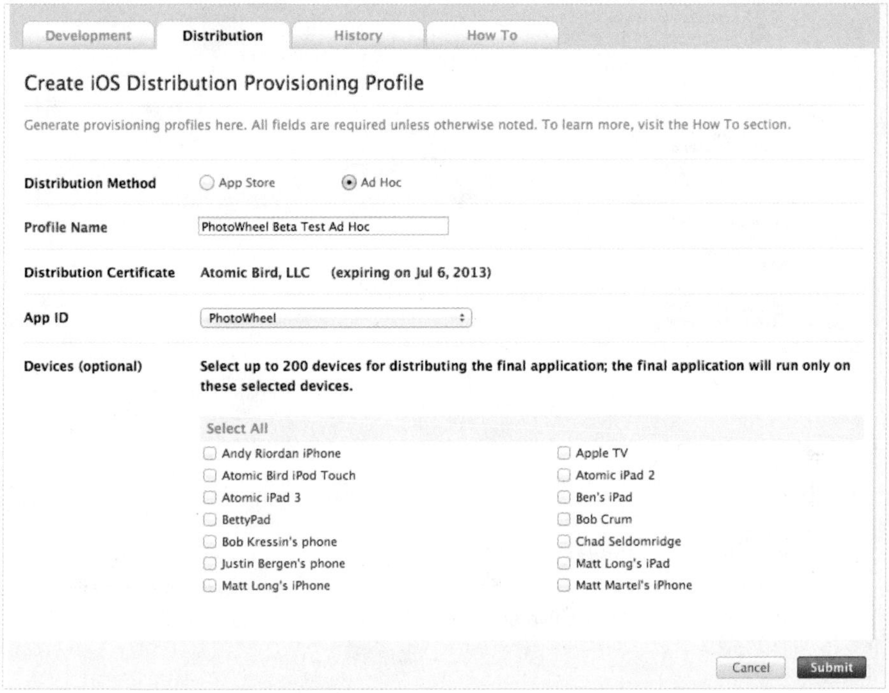

Figure 27.2   Creating an Ad Hoc distribution profile

Prepare the (Ad Hoc) Build

To build an app for Ad Hoc distribution, you need to use the new Ad Hoc provisioning profile. You could just switch between Development and Ad Hoc distribution profiles in Xcode's project settings, but that will become awkward pretty fast. You can't just use one profile, either. While it is possible to build and run an app with an Ad Hoc profile, Xcode can't debug an app built this way. Conversely, it's not possible to distribute an app built with a development profile. You need to have both profiles available for different build requirements. Fortunately, Xcode provides a way to use both in the project and have the right one selected automatically when you build the app.

When building for Ad Hoc distribution, what you'll actually create is an archive file. The archive contains the compiled app and the provisioning profile and can be used by testers to install the app on their iOS devices. Archive settings are found in the default scheme for the project (Figure 27.3). You can display the scheme editor by selecting **Product > Edit Scheme (Command-<)** in Xcode's menu bar.

By default, the archive section of the scheme uses the Release build configuration. Since you'll build an archive for Ad Hoc distribution, the Release configuration will determine which provisioning profile is used. If you take a look at the Test section of the scheme editor, you'll see that it uses the Debug build configuration instead. Xcode automatically creates these configurations when you create a new project.

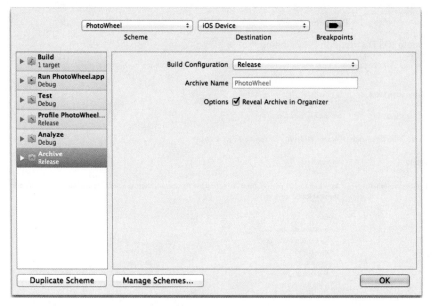

Figure 27.3   Archive settings in the default build scheme

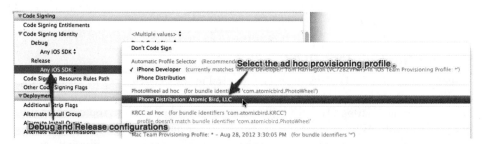

Figure 27.4   Selecting the Ad Hoc provisioning profile for release builds

Code signing settings for the Debug and Release configurations are found in the Build Settings for the app. To use the Ad Hoc provisioning profile for archive builds, you need to tell Xcode to use that profile for the Release configuration.

Figure 27.4 shows the configurations for PhotoWheel app target. These settings are part of the project settings for the PhotoWheel project. They appear in more than one place in Xcode for different purposes. To ensure you've got the right settings, make sure you selected the PhotoWheel project in the Project Navigator pane, and then the PhotoWheel target in the Editor.

To build the Ad Hoc archive, select **Product > Archive** in Xcode. Xcode builds the app, creates the archive file, and opens the Organizer window to show the archive (Figure 27.5). The window also lists both current and previous archives.

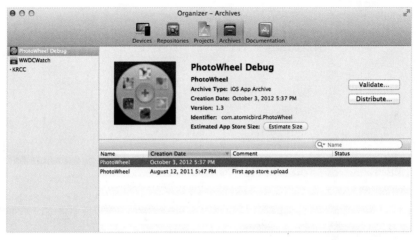

Figure 27.5   Xcode's Organizer window showing an archived build

Figure 27.6   Exporting an app archive from Xcode

The archive is what you will send to testers. To do so, you must save the archive as a file. Click the **Distribute...** button, shown in Figure 27.5. Select "Save for Enterprise or Ad-Hoc Deployment" in the window that appears, and then click the **Next** button (Figure 27.6).

In the next window, select your Ad Hoc provisioning profile from the popup list (Figure 27.7). When you click **Next**, Xcode prompts you to save the file somewhere. Xcode automatically adds the *.ipa* extension to the file name.

When you're ready to send a build to testers, all you need to do is send them this file. They can install it on their devices by dragging it into iTunes and then syncing their device.

Figure 27.7   Select your Ad Hoc provisioning profile to save the Ad Hoc archive.

Simplifying the Ad Hoc Process

Distributing Ad Hoc builds can be inconvenient, especially when the testers are not technically inclined. You need the UDID for each device, and finding this identifier can be confusing for people who are not experts. Likewise, the process of installing an Ad Hoc build in iTunes might seem easy to you, but it won't be for everyone.

Because these problems are so common for iOS developers, commercial services have emerged that can greatly simplify these steps. Device UDIDs can be submitted through convenient GUIs right on the device, and Ad Hoc builds sent directly to devices via "over the air" distribution. Commercial services also include numerous other useful features that can simplify this stage of development. As of this writing the two leading services are Test Flight[1] and Hockey.[2]

Building for App Store Distribution

The build process for the App Store is very similar to the Ad Hoc build process. You'll need to complete a slightly different provisioning process. You'll also need to update the project settings for the new build type.

---

1. Test Flight https://testflightapp.com/
2. http://www.hockeyapp.net/

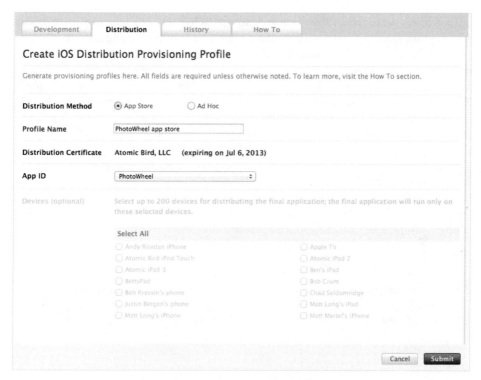

Figure 27.8   Creating an App Store distribution profile

Provisioning for the App Store

Getting an app ready for the App Store requires yet another provisioning profile. Start off as for the Ad Hoc profile. This time, select App Store as the distribution method (Figure 27.8).

This time the devices are grayed out. App Store profiles aren't tied to specific devices, so there is no need to select them. Create and download the profile, and drag it into Xcode.

Prepare the (App Store) Build

Building for the App Store, as with Ad Hoc builds, involves creating an archive. Of course, we have already used the archive setting in the current "Release" build scheme for Ad Hoc builds. Again, you could switch back and forth between provisioning profiles, choosing either the Ad Hoc or the App Store profile as needed. A much better solution would be to create a new build scheme and make its archive setting use the new App Store profile. Switching between schemes is much more convenient than changing provisioning profiles within a scheme.

In Xcode's menu, select **Product > Manage Schemes**. The scheme manager window appears, showing the original build scheme you have been using (Figure 27.9).

Select the existing profile, and then click on the gear menu at the bottom of the window and select Duplicate. The scheme editor appears. Name the scheme something obvious, such as "PhotoWheel App Store," and then click **OK** to save the new scheme. The Shared check box controls whether the new scheme is visible only to you or to others using the same Xcode project file. If you're working on your own, it doesn't matter whether this box is checked. If you're working in a team, you can create either private schemes that are visible only to you or shared schemes that are visible to the entire team.

Now you'll be able to choose which scheme to use from the popup menu at the top of Xcode's main window (Figure 27.10). Choose the original PhotoWheel scheme for development and Ad Hoc builds, and choose the new PhotoWheel App Store scheme for App Store builds. Now whenever you build the app, the settings for the currently selected build scheme will be applied automatically.

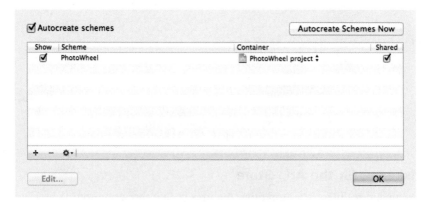

Figure 27.9   Managing build schemes

Figure 27.10   Selecting a build scheme

To go with the new build scheme, you'll also need a new build configuration. In the project settings, select the Info tab. In the Configurations section, click the **+** button at the bottom of the list, and then select Duplicate "Release" Configuration from the popup (Figure 27.11).

Name the configuration so that it is obvious that it will be used for App Store builds. Next, switch over to the Build Settings and locate the Code Signing settings. You'll see a new entry there for the new build configuration. Select the App Store provisioning profile from the list so it will be used with the new build configuration (Figure 27.12).

Finally, you need to configure the App Store build scheme to use the App Store build configuration for archive builds. This works the same as with the Ad Hoc changes, discussed earlier. Make sure you're editing the new App Store build scheme, and set the archive options to use the new App Store build configuration.

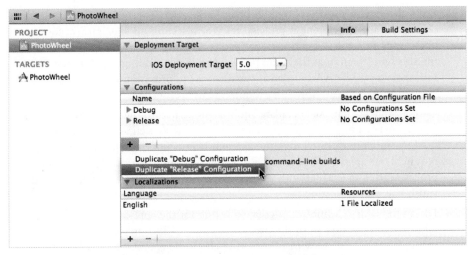

Figure 27.11   Adding a new build configuration

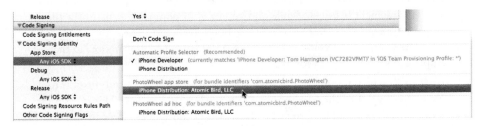

Figure 27.12   Changing Code Signing settings for the App Store build configuration

Next Steps

Submitting apps to the App Store involves a lot more than just building the app, of course—launching software always does. For iPad apps, you need to prepare all of the other information that will appear in the App Store listing. If the app isn't free, you need to set up banking information with Apple so that you can get paid. You also need to be ready to provide support for your app's users. And all of that work is needed just to get the app into the App Store—you still need to consider how to market the app and find your audience. The next sections will cover the various requirements before you can submit your app to Apple.

The App Store Process

If you have never submitted an app to the App Store, the process can seem opaque and confusing at first. Several steps need to be done in the right order to complete the process. These steps are as follows:

1. Build the app for the App Store, as described earlier. You can do this at any time during the app development process. It's worth setting up your project for this phase early to avoid last-minute confusion. You might want to deal with creating this build version at the same time as you begin sending out Ad Hoc builds to testers. You'll be working with certificates and provisioning profiles at that point already, and the App Store requirements are similar.

2. Gather or create various metadata and images related to the app. You'll need to provide everything that will be visible in the store as well as other information used by the store to categorize the app and help people search for apps. These requirements are described in the following sections. It's a good idea to get this process started in parallel with app development, if possible, to avoid rushing to finish it at the last second.

3. Log in to iTunes Connect and create a listing for the application. You'll need all of the information from the previous step here. This work creates an entry in Apple's app database with information about the app but doesn't begin the approval process yet.

4. If your app is not free, go to the Contracts, Tax, and Banking section of iTunes Connect. You'll need to approve the iOS Paid Applications contract, which is a legal agreement between Apple and you or your company. It basically allows Apple to sell your app in the App Store, but you should review the contract before agreeing to it. You'll also need to enter banking information so that Apple can send payments for app sales.

5. Back in Xcode, build an app archive and use the built-in app submission tool. Xcode will validate the app and upload it to iTunes Connect. *This is when the app review process begins.* (This process is described in more detail later in this section.)

6. Wait. Apple will review your app to decide whether to allow it into the App Store. Apple doesn't guarantee that the review will be done in any specific time frame. Typically, it takes about a week. In some cases this process can be much shorter or, unfortunately, much longer. Apple sends automatic emails as your app moves through the approval process, notifying you of events such as when the review process has started and when it has finished.

If Apple approves your app, the final status is Ready for Sale. Congratulations! Your app is public!

What if Apple Rejects the App?

Apple has the final say over whether an app is allowed into the App Store. The vast majority of apps are accepted, but not all. If your app is rejected, Apple will notify you and describe the reasons for the rejection. Apple provides a detailed list of restrictions in the iOS Developer Program Agreement. You should review these restrictions carefully. Be aware, though, that this is not a complete list. Apple can reject an app for any reason it feels is appropriate, and has been known to reject apps for unexpected reasons.

The most common reasons for rejection are purely technical. Usually this means that the app crashed while being reviewed. Crashing is grounds for automatic rejection. Another common technical issue is nonfunctional user interface items—buttons that are visible and appear enabled but that don't work, for example. With technical issues you generally have a clear picture of what is wrong. Fix the issues and resubmit the app.

If you have used undocumented APIs in your app, then the rejection involves more than just a technical issue. Apple provides detailed documentation of frameworks and other APIs available to applications. iOS has many more methods that are not documented, which are intended for internal use by Apple. It's possible to write software that uses these APIs, but doing so is specifically against App Store rules. If you have used undocumented APIs, you need to rewrite code so that you don't use them anymore. The difficulty of this endeavor depends on what specifically the API does and how hard it is to write replacement code.

Apps can also be rejected because of content included with the app. For example, Apple specifically forbids inclusion of pornographic material. Again, the rejection notice will be clear about the reasons, and you can take steps to address those issues.

If your app has been rejected for what you believe to be invalid reasons, you can appeal the rejection. Ultimately, though, Apple is not obligated to accept your app. As noted earlier, most apps are accepted, and it's unlikely yours will be rejected unless you have violated an established rule.

App Information for the App Store

When you submit your app to Apple, you'll need to provide a variety of information related to the app. This section summarizes the information needed. Except where noted, all of these data are required.

- **App name.** You probably already know this information. If you haven't yet selected a name for your masterpiece from the many possibilities, however, it's time to do so. Make sure you are not infringing any copyrights or trademarks with your app's name, as this is grounds to reject the app. The app name can't be one that someone else is already using.

- **SKU number.** The SKU number is any unique code you want to use to identify your app. It is your own product ID for the app, and it will appear in sales reports. You can use any text that makes sense to you, but think ahead to when you might have multiple apps. You might choose to number apps sequentially, or use a date string or any other string that will help you keep track of your apps. SKU numbers are not displayed in the App Store.

- **Bundle ID.** You will need to know the Bundle ID of the app. You will be able to select only App IDs that you have previously created in the Provisioning Portal for your account.

- **Availability date.** You can indicate the date when your app should appear in the store. This is the earliest possible date when this launch can happen, but the actual date could be later. This date does not affect how long it will take for your app to be reviewed. If Apple has not approved your app by this date, the app won't automatically go into the App Store. Instead, it will appear as soon as it has been approved.

- **Price.** If your app isn't free, this is where you set the price. You don't get to specify the actual price; instead, you decide which price tier should be used. Each tier corresponds to a specific price in a variety of world currencies. For example, tier 2 corresponds to $1.99 in the United States and Canada, $2.49 in Australia, €1.59 in most of Europe, £1.19 in the United Kingdom, and so on. The exact values may change from time to time at Apple's discretion based on exchange rates. Current values can be found in Apple's paid applications contract.

- **Educational discount.** If your app is likely to be of interest to educational institutions, you can choose to give them a 50% discount when they purchase multiple copies.

- **Availability by country.** Apple operates the App Store in most countries in the world. Not all apps are available in all countries, however. You decide in which countries your app should be available. Most apps are available in all stores. If your app contains content that you have licensed for use, you may need to restrict availability based on that license.

- **Version number.** The version number for your app is up to you, but it's best to follow typical versioning schemes to avoid confusing users. This information will be displayed in the App Store.

- **Copyright.** This information describes the ownership of the app and will appear in the App Store. Don't include the copyright symbol (©), which is added automatically.

- **Primary and secondary category.** The category determines where the app will appear in the App Store. Every app must have a primary category and may also have a secondary category. To get an idea of which apps go in which categories, visit the App Store in iTunes and tap the Categories tab. If you're not sure which category to use, browse the categories and see which ones seem most appropriate. For PhotoWheel, the primary category would be "Photography" and the secondary category might be "Lifestyle."

- **Contact information.** Provide the name, email address, and phone number of someone whom the app review team can contact if necessary during the review process.

- **Review notes.** Use this area for any information Apple's app review team might need when evaluating your app that is not covered by other fields. This field is optional.

- **Demo account information.** If your app requires login information of some kind, include information on a testing account here. This information is optional.

- **Rating.** You'll need to rate your app in a variety of categories so that Apple can determine an age rating for it. Age ratings go from 4+ for apps that are available to anyone, to 17+ for apps that contain more mature content. The categories include things like violent or sexual content. In each area you can rate your app as having the content never, infrequently, or frequently.

- **App description.** This is where you tell potential customers about your app. The text you provide will appear in the App Store and will be one of the factors people use to decide whether to buy your app. The app description can include a maximum of 4,000 characters. Proofread the text carefully, because spelling or grammar errors will make the app seem amateurish.

- **Keywords.** Identify one or more keywords that describe the app. Keywords are used when people search for apps in the store, so choose yours carefully. Keep in mind that Apple forbids using the names of other apps in the keyword list, so don't list competing apps in the hope of getting more notice in search results. The keyword list is limited to 100 characters. Keywords can be single words or short phrases and are separated by commas.

- **Support email address.** Apple will use this address to get in touch with you about the app if necessary. This address will not be displayed in the store.

- **Support URL.** Supply the URL that users can visit for support issues related to your app. This will be a clickable link in the App Store.

- **Marketing URL.** This is the app's home page, with information about the app. It will be a clickable link in the App Store and is optional.

- **Privacy policy URL.** The URL of your company's privacy policy. You may not need such a policy if you aren't collecting information about users. If you are collecting information, you should be clear about how it will be used. This URL will be a clickable link in the App Store and is optional.

- **EULA (End User License Agreement).** You can provide your own license agreement for your app if Apple's standard EULA doesn't meet your needs. If you do, the agreement will be visible in the App Store. This is optional.

App Store Assets

In addition to metadata about the app, several related files can be uploaded at this stage. These are listed here:

- **Large app icon.** You already have an icon that is used by the app, but you need a much larger version for the App Store. The App Store will use this icon for fancy screen layouts if your app is chosen as one of the featured apps. The large icon must be 1024 × 1024 pixels and can be saved as a JPEG, TIFF, or PNG file. *This is required.*

- **Screen shots.** Screen shots of your app give users a "sneak peek" into its functionality. If your app runs on more than one device type, you can provide device-specific screen shots—for example, both iPhone and iPad screen shots. When users browse the App Store, they'll want to see what your app looks like. Since the App Store doesn't allow users to try apps before buying them, this is one of the main factors people will use when deciding whether to buy your app. Your screen shots should highlight your app's features. Ideally, they should cover all of the most interesting ones. Try to make the screen shots illustrate how users might actually use the app. For PhotoWheel, that would mean giving photo albums names that people might actually use instead of fake names that you might have used in testing. The app will seem more appealing with album names such as "Vacation in Hawaii" or "First Day of School," rather than "Test Album 1," "Test Album 2," and so on.

    You must provide at least one screen shot of your app. You can provide up to five, and if it's possible without being repetitive, you should. Screen shots should be full-screen images.

- **Routing app coverage file.** If your app provides directional routing information, you can upload a GeoJSON file that defines the areas your app covers. This is optional and only useful if your app provides directions.

Using iTunes Connect

You submit and manage apps through iTunes Connect.[3] You can also get to iTunes Connect after logging in to the iOS Dev Center.[4] Figure 27.13 shows the main iTunes Connect page (as of February 2013).

User Roles

Multiple users can have access to the same iTunes Connect account. Different users can be assigned to different roles, depending on which operations they need to perform. You create and manage user accounts in the Manage Users section of the site (Figure 27.13).

Five roles exist:

- **Admin** users can manage the iTunes Connect account, including creating and deleting users.

- **Legal** users can enter into legal agreements such as the iOS Paid Applications contract and can request promotional codes for paid apps.

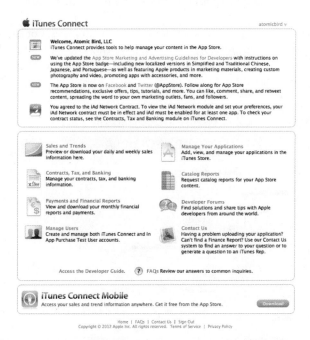

Figure 27.13   iTunes Connect home page

---

3. iTunes Connect: http://itunesconnect.apple.com
4. iOS Dev Center: http://developer.apple.com/ios

- **Finance** users can manage financial details, including sales and banking information as well as contracts.
- **Technical** users can upload and manage apps.
- **Sales** users can access sales reports.

Users can be assigned to multiple roles, if it makes sense to do so.

Managing Applications

The Manage Your Applications section is where you'll set up new applications and make changes for new versions of apps. It is where you'll use the app information and assets you gathered for the app. When you're ready to submit the first version of an app, you need to create an entry for the app in iTunes Connect before you can upload the app archive. Likewise, when updating to a new version of an app, you'll need to create the new version in iTunes Connect before you can upload it. Start the process by clicking the **Manage Your Applications** link, and then click the **Add New App** button in the window that appears.

iTunes Connect will walk you through the process of entering the app metadata and uploading screen shots, beginning with the app name, SKU number, and bundle ID (Figure 27.14).

The rest of the information and assets will come in later stages of the submission process, which progress wizard-style until you have finished with all of the steps. At that point you will have created the app in the iTunes Connect database, and the status will be Waiting for Upload.

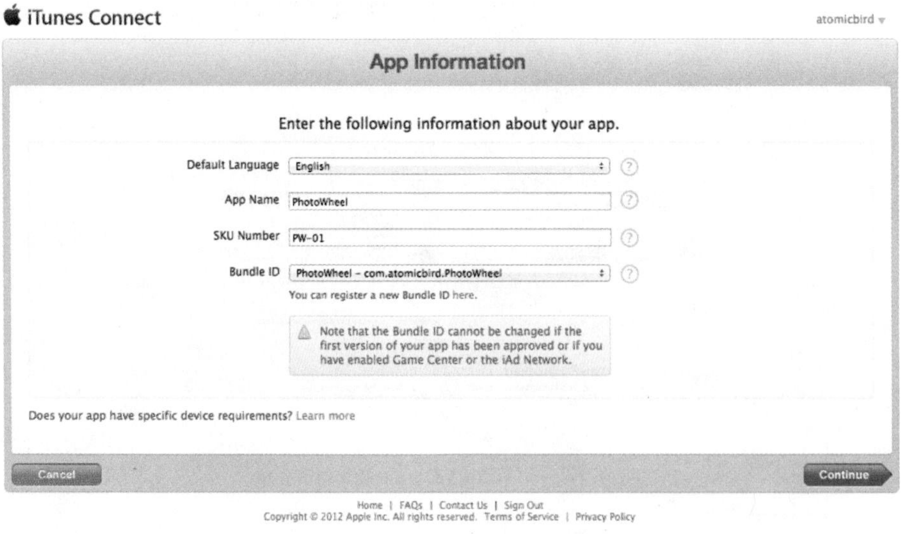

Figure 27.14   Beginning the app submission process in iTunes Connect

Submitting the App

It's time! All the preliminaries are complete, and it's time to upload your app. You can upload apps to iTunes Connect directly from Xcode. To start this process, build an App Store archive as described earlier in this chapter. The Organizer window (shown earlier in Figure 27.5) will open, showing the new archive and any previous archives. It's useful to double-click in the Comment column to add a brief descriptive note to the archive, so that later on you'll know why each archive was created.

When you upload the app, iTunes Connect will perform several automatic checks on the app to verify details such as proper code signing and valid icon files. You can run these checks without submitting the app by clicking the **Validate...** button, shown in Figure 27.5. You can use this button at any time after the app's entry has been created in iTunes Connect, even if you're not ready to submit the app yet.

If the app passes validation, you're ready to go! Click **Distribute...** to begin the upload process. Xcode will ask how you want to distribute the app, as we saw previously in Figure 27.6. This time, choose "Submit to the iOS App Store" and click the **Next** button. Xcode will then prompt you to log in to your iTunes Connect account (Figure 27.15).

When you log in to iTunes Connect, Xcode will check whether you have any apps in the Waiting for Upload stage. If you don't have any, you won't be able to proceed and Xcode will display an error message. If this is the case, make sure you have completed the process described earlier for creating an app entry in iTunes Connect.

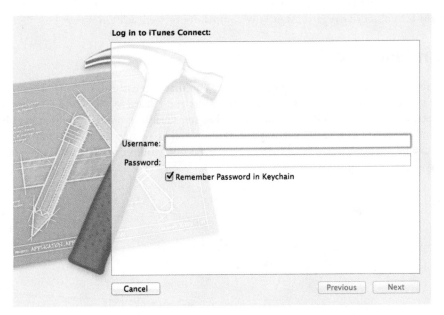

Figure 27.15   Logging in to iTunes Connect from Xcode

Once you have successfully logged in to iTunes Connect, Xcode prompts you for your application name and code signing information. The Application popup menu is populated based on the apps in your account that are in the Waiting for Upload stage. The window is identical to the one shown in Figure 27.7 except that it has an extra pop-up menu that you use to select the application.

As with the iTunes Connect Web site, Xcode walks you through the rest of the upload process.

Next: Take a well-earned break. Writing apps is hard work, and you deserve a rest.

Going Further

Or perhaps not.

One common misconception is that all you need to do to sell an app is get it into the App Store. However, in case you haven't been keeping score, the App Store includes many hundreds of thousands of apps. Even a great app will get lost in the crowd if you don't take some extra steps to get your app noticed.

Marketing and promotion are a major part of what makes some apps more successful than others. Technical aspects are vitally important but are not sufficient to turn a great app idea into a successful app. An app needs a good Web site that provides more information than the App Store, including demo videos when possible. That's just the minimum, though. If you're not experienced in promoting apps, a good place to start learning about this topic is Dave Wooldridge and Michael Schneider's book *The Business of iPhone App Development* (Apress, 2010). Don't neglect this step, or your app may languish in obscurity regardless of how compelling or well written it may be.

Summary

In this chapter you have gone from having an app that you can run on your own iPad to having one that you can share with testers and release to the world. The steps sometimes seem convoluted, but they're the last steps leading to a real app that people around the world can download and use. Building and releasing an app is a big deal and can be a lot of work. But if it were easy, everyone would do it.

You did it! Congratulations!

28

The Final Word

*Whew! You made it to the end of the book. You can confidently say you are an iPad program-
mer—but more important, you can say you are an iOS programmer. See, without your knowing
it, we have surreptitiously taught you all the key things you'll need to launch your career as an
iOS developer. While you have been building the PhotoWheel app, you may not have noticed
that we have shown you how to do the following:*

- *Effectively use Xcode and Interface Builder (Chapters 2 and 3)*
- *Master Objective-C (Chapter 4)*
- *Program with Cocoa Touch (Chapter 5)*
- *Build user interfaces with a storyboard (Chapter 14)*
- *Leverage Core Data (Chapter 13) and iCloud syncing (Chapter 22)*
- *Create multi-touch gestures (Chapter 11)*
- *Build custom views (Chapters 10 and 16)*
- *Use view controllers (Chapter 15) and perform custom view transitions (Chapters 15
  and 17)*
- *Make use of scroll views in different ways (Chapters 16 and 17)*
- *Add print (Chapter 19) and email (Chapter 20) capabilities to your apps*
- *Incorporate AirPlay into your apps (Chapter 23)*
- *Apply image filters and effects using Core Image (Chapter 24)*
- *Diagnose and fix bugs in your apps (Chapter 26)*
- *Hook into Web services from your apps (Chapter 21)*
- *Prepare your apps for submission to the App Store (Chapter 27)*

You can use this list as a guide when you're working on projects in the future.
For example, if you need to work with Core Data, you can flip to Chapter 13 for a
refresher. Need to add multi-touch gesture support for your app? There's a chapter for
that—Chapter 11. The best part of all is that you have built an app from start to finish,
from concept to App Store submission. Congratulations!

What's Next

This book serves as a jumpstart for your becoming an iOS programmer, but there is so much more to learn, especially if being an iOS programmer is a career choice for you. Here are some things you can do to become an even better iOS programmer:

- Continue reading books. A list of recommended books is available at the Learning iPad Programming web site.[1]
- Search and participate in online forums such as the Apple Developer Forums[2] and StackOverflow.[3]
- Read blog sites such as Cocoa Is My Girlfriend,[4] iPhone Development,[5] and Ray Wenderlich's Tutorials for iOS Developers.[6]
- Attend conferences such as Apple's WWDC,[7] 360|iDev,[8] CocoaConf,[9] and NSConference.[10]
- Attend local meet-ups and developer gatherings such as CocoaHeads[11] and NSCoder Night.[12]

And, most important, **always keep learning**.

We wish you all the best, and we can't wait to hear about and see the many cool and exciting apps you will build. You can send your questions, comments, and anything else you would like to share with us to kirby@whitepeaksoftware.com and tph@atomicbird.com.

---

1. Recommended books: http://www.learningipadprogramming.com/recommended-books/
2. Apple Developer Forums: http://devforums.apple.com
3. StackOverflow: http://stackoverflow.com
4. Cocoa Is My Girlfriend: http://www.cimgf.com
5. iPhone Development: http://iphonedevelopment.blogspot.com
6. Tutorials for iOS Developers: http://raywenderlich.com
7. WWDC: http://developer.apple.com/wwdc/
8. 360|iDev: http://360idev.com
9. CocoaConf: http://cocoaconf.com
10. NSConference: http://nsconference.com
11. CocoaHeads: http://cocoaheads.org
12. NSCoder Night: http://nscodernight.com

Installing the Developer Tools

Before you can write your first iPad application, you need the developer's tools. The developer tools consist of everything you need to write iOS and Mac OS X applications, including the integrated development environment (IDE) called Xcode; the user interface designer called Interface Builder; the compiler capable of compiling C, C++, and Objective-C code; the debugger for debugging your code; and Instruments, a tool for tracking memory leaks and profiling your application. A handful of other really useful tools are also included. Collectively, the developer tools are called Xcode, with the Xcode IDE being the primary tool in the arsenal.

Xcode is available for free from the Mac App Store. Members of the iOS Developer Program, which costs $99 per year, also have access to beta versions of Xcode as Apple works on improving its developer tools.

Which is the better option for you? If you are curious about iPad and iPhone programming and do not wish to spend any money upfront, download Xcode from the Mac App Store. After all, it is free. But if you are serious about writing apps for iOS, you need to join the iOS Developer Program. Membership provides benefits that you do not get by simply downloading Xcode from the Mac App Store.

Membership Has Its Privileges

As a member of the iOS Developer Program, not only do you have access to the latest beta version of the development tools (Xcode), but you also have access to a slew of resources that are invaluable to iOS developers. These resources include access to sample code, how-to videos, recent WWDC session videos, and Apple's own Developer Forums.[1] Members also have access to the latest beta build of iOS. Even more important, only members of the iOS Developer Program can have their apps installed on a real device. This means that you must be a member of the Developer Program if you wish to run and test your app on an iPad or iPhone. You must also be a member if you wish to distribute your app. This includes Ad Hoc distribution and distribution through the App Store (see Chapter 27, "Distributing Your App," for more

---

1. Developer Forums: https://devforums.apple.com

information). Without a membership to the iOS Developer Program, you will be limited to running and testing your app through the simulator.

> **Note**
>
> Apple frequently posts beta versions of Xcode, making them available to members. Thankfully, developers can have multiple versions of Xcode installed at the same time on the same machine. In fact, it's not uncommon for iOS developers to have at least two different versions of Xcode installed at any given time—that is, the latest release version and the latest beta version. This practice gives the developer a chance to explore the new features coming in a future release while still being able to work on and submit production apps to Apple.

Joining the iOS Developer Program

When you join the iOS Developer Program, you choose from three program types: Standard Individual, Standard Company, or Enterprise. A fourth program type, University, is available only to higher educational institutions looking to include iOS development in their curriculum. (The University program type is not covered in this book.)

Which program type you choose depends on your needs and purpose. The differences are highlighted in Table A.1.

Table A.1   **iOS Developer Program Benefits**

	Standard Individual	Standard Company	Enterprise Program	University Program
Price	$99 per year	$99 per year	$299 per year	Free
Dev Center Resources	Yes	Yes	Yes	Yes
IOS SDK	Yes	Yes	Yes	Yes
Prerelease Software and Tools	Yes	Yes	Yes	
Ability to Create Development Teams		Yes	Yes	Yes
Access to the Apple Developer Forums	Yes	Yes	Yes	Yes
Technical Support Incidents (per membership year)	2	2	2	2
Test on Devices (iPod touch, iPhone, and iPad)	Yes	Yes	Yes	Yes
Ad Hoc Distribution	Yes	Yes	Yes	
In-House Distribution			Yes	
App Store Distribution	Yes	Yes		

Which Program Type Is Right for You?

Choosing the right program type is important because changing program types in the future can be a bit troublesome. Companies wishing to deploy proprietary in-house apps to employees can join the Enterprise Program. A Dun & Bradstreet number is required for this program type. Individuals and companies wishing to sell their applications through the App Store should select either the Standard Individual or Standard Company option. Standard Individual and Standard Company are the two most commonly selected program types, so let's look at them in more detail.

There is one primary difference between the Standard Individual and Standard Company designations: Standard Company allows you to create development teams. When you do so, you can add team programmers to the account at no additional cost. A team programmer has access to all the same resources that a Standard Individual does. You can add and remove team members at any time, which is handy when you are hiring new iOS programmers or rolling off contract programmers after finishing a project.

Note

An individual can be a team programmer for one or more Standard Company accounts while still having her own account. For instance, I sell my own iPhone and iPad apps, so I enrolled my company under the Standard Company program type. I also do contract programming, which means I am a Team Member for other companies. When I log in to the iOS Development Center Web site, I am asked to select which team I wish to use for the current session, as seen in Figure A.1.

Figure A.1   The Select Your Team prompt is displayed during the login process when you are a member of multiple teams.

The general rule of thumb to follow when deciding which program type is right for you is this: If you are an individual with no plans to set up a company, sign up as an individual. If you are planning to set up, or have already set up, a company (even if you are a one-person company), sign up as a company. If you sign up as an individual and decide later to set up a company presence, you can change your program type. This revision of your status will involve talking with Apple and it may take time to make the transition between program types, but it is possible. If you represent a company that needs to distribute apps in-house only, sign up for the Enterprise Program.

What You Need to Register

Collecting the required registration information before beginning the process will help speed up registration. Table A.2 lists the basic information you need. Free feel to make a copy of this table and use it as a worksheet.

> **Note**
>
> The information needed to enroll in the Apple Developer Program is based on registration within the United States. Information required may differ in other countries.

If you plan to enroll in the Apple Developer Program as a company or organization, then you will need a D-U-N-S Number. D-U-N-S Numbers are assigned and maintained by Dun & Bradstreet, and they are used to identify business entities. Getting a D-U-N-S Number can take a few weeks, so you should start the process for getting a number as soon as possible. More information about D-U-N-S Numbers is available at the Apple Developer Support site.[2]

Create or Use an Existing Apple ID

Apple recommends that you create a new Apple ID if you are enrolling in the iOS Developer Program for business purposes. This is particularly good advice if you are an employee setting up an account for the company you work for. In fact, if you are an employee setting up an account for your employer, then you should consider using a general company email address, such as apple.devacct@company.com, as the new Apple ID instead of your own company email address. This will prevent headaches down the road should you leave your employer for greener pastures.

Apple also recommends setting up a different Apple ID if you currently have an iTunes account to avoid potential accounting and reporting issues. As an indie developer, I use my iTunes account as my Apple ID for the iOS Developer Program, and I have not experienced any issues. However, your mileage may vary.

---

2. D-U-N-S Numbers: https://developer.apple.com/support/D-U-N-S/

Table A.2 **Information Needed to Complete the Apple Developer and iOS Developer Program Registration**

Personal Profile	
Apple ID (Create a new one or use an existing ID.)	
Password	
Birth date	
Security question and answer (for password recovery, etc.)	
Name (account holder's name)	
Email address	
Company or organization name	
Mailing address (street, city, state, ZIP code)	
Telephone number	
If you plan to sell your app and/or use iAds	
Taxpayer identification number (SSN or EIN in the United States)	
Legal entity name (e.g., your name, company name, DBA)	
Address (street, city, state, ZIP code)	
Company contacts (name and contact information for senior management, finance, technical, legal, and promotions; can be the same person)	
Banking Information	
Bank country	
ABA routing number	
Bank name	
Bank account number	
Account holder name	
Bank account type	
Bank account currency	

Installing Xcode

You download and install Xcode through the Mac App Store. The fastest way to find it is to search the Mac App Store using the phrase "Xcode." You can then download Xcode as you would any other app available in the store (Figure A.2).

If you want to install the latest beta version of Xcode, you need to sign in to the iOS Dev Center.[3] If you are a paid member in good standing, you will see a link to the beta area. Within this area, you will find the latest Xcode beta build. Click the download link to download the *.dmg* file. Once it has downloaded, open the *.dmg* file and copy the Xcode app to your *Applications* directory. Because it is a beta build, the app name will be different from the name used by the Mac App Store version. As a consequence, you do not need to worry about overwriting the release version of Xcode.

Once Xcode is installed, you can launch it by clicking the icon found in Launchpad (Figure A.3).

Figure A.2   Xcode's download page in the Mac App Store

---

3. iOS Dev Center: http://developer.apple.com/ios/

Figure A.3   Launch Xcode from Launchpad

First Launch Experience

When you launch a new version of Xcode for the first time, you may be prompted to install additional items such as the command-line tools and developer documentation. Follow the on-screen instructions to install the additional items.

You may also be asked about enabling Developer Mode. You definitely want to enable Developer Mode, if prompted, as it is needed for debugging your apps. Note that you need administration credentials for your machine to enable Developer Mode.

Index

A

Developer's Library

informit.com/devlibrary

ESSENTIAL REFERENCES FOR PROGRAMMING PROFESSIONALS

The Core iOS 6 Developer's Cookbook, Fourth Edition

Erica Sadun

ISBN-13: 978-0-321-88421-3

The Advanced iOS 6 Developer's Cookbook

Erica Sadun

ISBN-13: 978-0-321-88422-0

Programming in Objective-C, Fifth Edition

Stephen G. Kochan

ISBN-13: 978-0-321-88728-3

Other Developer's Library Titles

TITLE	AUTHOR	ISBN-13
Objective-C Phrasebook, Second Edition	David Chisnall	978-0-321-81375-6
Test-Driven iOS Development	Graham Lee	978-0-321-77418-7
Cocoa® Programming Developer's Handbook	David Chisnall	978-0-321-63963-9
Cocoa Design Patterns Applications for the iPhone	Erik M. Buck / Donald A. Yacktman	978-0-321-53502-3

Developer's Library books are available at most retail and online bookstores. For more information or to order direct, visit our online bookstore at **informit.com/store**.

Online editions of all Developer's Library titles are available by subscription from Safari Books Online at **safari.informit.com**.

Addison
Wesley

Developer's Library
informit.com/devlibrary

FREE
Online Edition

Safari
Books Online

Your purchase of *Learning iPad Programming, Second Edition,* includes access to a free online edition for 45 days through the **Safari Books Online** subscription service. Nearly every Addison-Wesley Professional book is available online through **Safari Books Online**, along with over thousands of books and videos from publishers such as Cisco Press, Exam Cram, IBM Press, O'Reilly Media, Prentice Hall, Que, Sams, and VMware Press.

Safari Books Online is a digital library providing searchable, on-demand access to thousands of technology, digital media, and professional development books and videos from leading publishers. With one monthly or yearly subscription price, you get unlimited access to learning tools and information on topics including mobile app and software development, tips and tricks on using your favorite gadgets, networking, project management, graphic design, and much more.

Activate your FREE Online Edition at
informit.com/safarifree

STEP 1:   Enter the coupon code: RUKKQZG.

STEP 2:   New Safari users, complete the brief registration form.
Safari subscribers, just log in.

If you have difficulty registering on Safari or accessing the online edition,
please e-mail customer-service@safaribooksonline.com

 Addison Wesley   Adobe Press   ALPHA   Cisco Press   FT Press FINANCIAL TIMES   IBM Press   Microsoft Press   New Riders   O'REILLY

 Peachpit Press   PRENTICE HALL   que   Redbooks   SAMS   SAS Publishing   vmware PRESS   WILEY   WROX